TWENTIETH
CENTURY
AMERICA

Twentieth Century America

THE UNITED STATES SINCE THE 1890's

by David A. Shannon

UNIVERSITY OF WISCONSIN

RAND McNALLY & COMPANY · CHICAGO

RAND M^cNALLY HISTORY SERIES

FRED HARVEY HARRINGTON, *Consulting Editor*

BORDEN, ed., *America's Ten Greatest Presidents*
FREIDEL AND POLLACK, eds., *Builders of American Institutions*
GATZKE, *The Present in Perspective, 2nd edition*
JONES, *Ancient Civilization*
MOSSE, *The Culture of Western Europe:*
    The Nineteenth and Twentieth Centuries
PALMER, ed., *Atlas of World History*
PALMER, ed., *Historical Atlas of the World*
SELLERS, ed., *The Berkeley Readings in American History*
SELLERS AND MAY, *Synopsis of American History*
SHANNON, *Twentieth Century America*
STARR, NOWELL, LYON, STEARNS, AND HAMEROW,
    A History of the World (2 vols.)
TREADGOLD, *Twentieth Century Russia*
WILLIAMS, ed., *The Shaping of American Diplomacy*
WRIGHT, *France in Modern Times: 1760 to the Present*

To Molly and Sarah

Preface

TEXTBOOK PREFACES ARE AN ODD LITERARY GENRE. Many of them spin an elaborate intellectual justification for the study of their subject. This one shall not do that. I take it as self-evident and accepted that the recent history of the United States well merits serious study. Some textbook prefaces describe in detail what is in the book and the author's philosophical assumptions. For what is in this book, I refer the reader to the Table of Contents and to the chapters themselves. My philosophic assumptions will become apparent to the discerning reader.

But I do want to make clear that the historian, perhaps in recent history especially, necessarily makes judgments. What the historian brings to his subject from his background and values affects his product, even if only in what he decides should receive emphasis and what should be rejected. I am no exception. Some parts of this work have a strong point of view, but I have endeavored to be fair and judicious. Yet students should approach this book—indeed, all books—with an appraising and critical attitude as well as an open mind.

Prefaces frequently tell the story behind the volume. This textbook has no unusual background. It is intended primarily for students in college courses in recent American history. I have taught such courses for the past several years, and this book grew from that experience. Aimed primarily at the college classroom, it developed in a college classroom. Explanations, examples, emphases, and methods that I have found successful in my own teaching are employed here.

Finally, prefaces usually acknowledge the help that the author received. I shall be orthodox and do likewise because I want publicly to express my gratitude. Professors Arthur Dudden of Bryn Mawr College and Warren Susman of Rutgers University read the manuscript for the publisher, saved me from several errors of omission and commission, and offered many useful suggestions. Dr. Willis Heath of the University of Washington applied his fertile mind and skill to the maps. Mr. Paul Vanderbilt, curator of the Iconography Collection of the Wisconsin State Historical Society, was of great help to me in the selection of the illustrations. My wife Jane shared in the book's development from first to last. Lastly, my students in their responses sharpened and modified many of my ideas.

DAVID A. SHANNON

October, 1962

Table of Contents

TABLE OF CONTENTS

PART IV. *WAR AND BOOM AGAIN, 1941–1963*

Part I

THE PROGRESSIVE ERA
1900–1917

CHAPTER ONE

A Look Backward

ON SEPTEMBER 6, 1901, AN ANARCHIST NAMED LEON CZOLGOSZ SHOT the President of the United States, the conservative William McKinley. The President, from Canton, Ohio, was in Buffalo, New York, to attend the Pan-American Exposition. McKinley lingered for eight days before he died. On September 14, Vice-President Theodore Roosevelt of New York, not quite forty-three years old but well known to the American people since 1898, took the presidential oath of office. Roosevelt's moving to the White House signified the beginning of a new era in American politics.

Before we begin to examine this new period we must take a look backward to get our historical bearings. Historical eras do not spring suddenly and full blown from the past; mankind does not break clean from his earlier experience. Just as we must know something of an individual's earlier life to understand him and know the nation's past to understand its present, we must look at least briefly at the late nineteenth-century United States to comprehend the early 1900's.

An Industrial Society

The central fact of late nineteenth-century American history was that the country, within slightly more than a generation's time, changed from a predominantly agricultural society to an industrial power. Most of the other developments of the period—an increase in national wealth, the rise of great cities and all of the consequences of their growth, the creation of a large class of wage earners, the huge increase in the human stream arriving in the New

World from Europe, the change in the nature of politics, the beginnings of an organized labor movement, the heightened class antagonisms, the changed views about society and government, to name only a few—flowed from the central fact of industrialization.

In 1849, the total value of American manufactured products was about $1 billion; by 1899 manufacturing had become so important that the figure was about $13 billion. In 1860 about 1,300,000 wage earners worked in manufacturing; in 1890 there were about 4,250,000. In 1860 the United States ranked fourth among the nations of the world in industrial production; in 1900 it ranked first. In an age when railroads were the only practical means of hauling freight great distances, railroad track mileage was significant. A national transportation system was vital to a national market, and a large market was a prerequisite of mass production. In 1850, there were about nine thousand miles of railroad track in America; in 1900, there were about two hundred thousand miles, not counting siding and yard track. In sum, industry supplanted agriculture as the primary way of creating wealth.

Some of the places that had been small towns in 1860 were cities by 1900, their bleak factories belching black smoke over the tenements or cottages of the families who worked in the factories. About 40 per cent of the population was urban by 1900. Fourteen American cities had populations of over a hundred thousand, and fourteen million people lived in them. Chicago and Philadelphia had over a million inhabitants. New York City, which in 1898 consolidated Manhattan, Brooklyn, the Bronx, Queens, and Staten Island into one municipality, had over three million people.

This industrialization had come about through a combination of many economic forces. Of natural resources the United States had plenty, more and richer than any other country in the western world. Although the labor supply was less than desirable for rapid industrialization, more labor could always be obtained from the displaced peasants of Europe. Capital was adequate, and, besides, English capitalists were eager to invest in American industries that promised good profits. And, very important, the federal and state governments adopted policies designed to advance and protect industrial investment.

Much of the government policy favorable to industry had started during the Civil War and Reconstruction. During the war the federal government had established a monetary and banking scheme that created a standard national currency which was necessary to conduct business on a national scale. The national banking system, while containing serious flaws from any point of view, stimulated the accumulation of capital. Through more than generous grants of public land and other subsidies, the federal and state governments had largely financed a national railroad system owned by private capital and almost without regulation or control from government. Labor and immigration law and executive decisions prevented industrialists from having serious labor problems. Judicial constructions of the Constitution provided business a formidable shield against labor and the occasional effort of a nonconformist government to regulate industry and commerce. Protective tariffs, so high as sometimes to be prohibitive tariffs, assured American industry of the domestic market, and the boundaries of the United States surrounded the largest and most populous free trade area in the world. Given the basic economic prerequisites of resources, capital, and labor, the extremely favorable industrial climate created by government made the growth of the United States from an "underdeveloped area" into an industrial power almost a foregone conclusion.

As industry mushroomed in size, control of it contracted into fewer and fewer hands. Industrial giants, popularly called "trusts," exercised control over American industry by 1900. An oligarchy dominated the American economy. Monopoly or what economists call "oligopoly" (control of a given industry by a handful of huge companies) was a tendency of the impelling economic advantages of size in manufacturing, but businessmen also used ruthless tactics and various legal and illegal devices to reduce competition to a minimum. Sometimes a firm achieved dominance of an industry through a series of mergers, sometimes through control of the important patent rights. A few erstwhile competitors turned to the pool as a device to eliminate competition, but it was illegal in common law and pool partners did not trust one another. John D. Rockefeller's Standard Oil Company invented the trust device by which control of an industry was achieved by exchanging corporation stock certificates with voting rights for trust certificates without voting rights. The new holders of the voting rights, the "trustees," were then free to direct the industry's destinies as they saw fit. Toward the end of the century, the holding company became a favorite method of minimizing competition, a holding company being a company which owns the stock of other companies. Still another device was the interlocking directorate, in which officers of supposedly competitive firms sat on one another's boards of directors. All in all, the record of American business verified Adam Smith's 1776 observation that businessmen could not meet, even for social occasions, without discussing ways to reduce competition.

The late nineteenth-century industrialists who effected this growth and concentration of power were a strong breed. Most of them were still young men when the Civil War ended. A few of them had been in the war. Tough, calculating, ambitious, industrious, and farsighted, they were leonine monarchs of the economic jungle. Lesser beasts existed from their sufferance. Some have compared this generation of businessmen to the robber barons of the Middle Ages and some to pirates of the Spanish Main. But others have looked upon these businessmen favorably and called them a generation of "industrial statesmen." Historians taking this position argue that these men built the industrial plant that created American wealth and strength. A few of these businessmen, however, such as Daniel Drew and Jim Fisk, who used their control of the Erie Railroad to advantage in their stock market manipulations, never produced anything but watered stock; indeed, the Erie deteriorated badly while Drew and Fisk controlled it. Actually, most of these industrialists were both builders and violators of the social code, certainly the code of today and that of most people in their own day. They contributed to American material wealth, but they did not improve the nation's social ethics. Brief sketches of two basic industries, oil and steel, indicate the nature of industrial development.

In 1855, the Yale scientist, Benjamin Silliman, reported that kerosene could be refined from petroleum at little cost, that it was an excellent fuel and illuminant, and that such useful by-products as paraffin and naphtha could be obtained from petroleum when refining it for kerosene. In 1859, oil was struck in Pennsylvania. In 1863, when others were thinking of Vicksburg and Gettysburg, John D. Rockefeller, a twenty-four-year-old partner in a produce com-

5

mission house of Cleveland, went into the oil business. He invested in a refinery that had a superior technology, and it soon became the biggest oil company in Cleveland. He chose to remain in the Cleveland area rather than move to Pittsburgh, then a larger oil center, because Cleveland had better water transportation and competing railroads, while Pittsburgh was dependent upon the Pennsylvania Railroad. In 1867, Rockefeller began one of the sharp commercial practices that were soon to make him dominant in the industry as well as hated and feared by those around him. His shipping was so important to railroads that he was able to persuade them to give him secretly a deduction of fifteen cents on every barrel of oil that he shipped, plus a rebate on oil his competitors consigned. In 1870, he reorganized and recapitalized and called the new firm the Standard Oil Company of Ohio. With the leverage that rebates gave him, he forced competitors to sell out to him or be driven to the wall. Within a few years, Standard Oil controlled about 90 per cent of the oil business. Rockefeller invested part of the enormous profits in completely different fields. His grip on the oil business always remained strong, but his monopoly position disappeared when western oil fields and the great increase in petroleum refining that came with the automobile made the industry too large for even the colossal Standard Oil to control alone.

In 1873, the Carnegie Steel Company opened its J. Edgar Thompson mill near Pittsburgh. Andrew Carnegie owned well over half of the stock of the company. Carnegie, a poor boy when he immigrated from Scotland with his parents, had learned business and made important contacts as the private telegrapher and secretary to a top official of the Pennsylvania Railroad, Thomas A. Scott. He made money on the stock market and invested in all kinds of businesses, notably steel bridge companies. After linking up with Henry Clay Frick, who had built an empire in coal and coke in southern Pennsylvania, Carnegie was in a position to drive his company ahead in what economists call "vertical integration." The company acquired its own ore mines, its own transportation facilities, and its own limestone quarries. It had everything it needed to make steel in one integrated enterprise, and it reinvested most of its rich profits into more capital plant. Carnegie had wider interests than most of his industrial contemporaries, and, in 1900, when he was sixty-five years old, he was ready to sell out and enjoy the rest of his life as a philanthropist. He began negotiations with the banker J. P. Morgan, and, in 1901, a deal was closed. Morgan bought the Carnegie Steel Company for $400 million. He created a holding company, the United States Steel Company, to own and control the Carnegie interests and nine other large corporations in steel or allied fields. The par value of United States Steel stocks and bonds was over a billion dollars, the first American billion-dollar corporation. Actually, almost half of the stock represented "water," but with its roughly 60 per cent control of the steel industry, United States Steel could pay handsome dividends even on watered stock.

This kind of an industrial economy enabled a few people to live in a splendor that had been beyond the means of even most of history's kings. Andrew Carnegie acquired a castle in Scotland with an estate of thirty-two thousand acres. The railroad king, George W. Vanderbilt, built Biltmore near Asheville, North Carolina, a palace with forty master bedrooms and a library of two hundred and fifty thousand volumes, surrounded by an estate of over two hundred square miles. Henry Frick sat on a Renaissance throne in his Fifth Avenue mansion to read the *Saturday Evening Post*. J. P. Morgan owned a series of yachts all, perhaps appropriately, named *Corsair*, the last of which was longer than a football field.

Life for most of the people who earned wages in these millionaires' firms was, to say the least, difficult. Wages were low, in sweat shop industries pitifully low, and employment was not regular. Hours of work were long—an average of almost sixty hours a week in 1900—although in the steel industry a twelve-hour day and seventy-two-hour week was the general rule. Low incomes forced wage earners to seek the cheapest rents they could find, and housing conditions for vast numbers of families in every industrial city were deplorably crowded, dark, and poorly ventilated. Not until 1901 did New York City change its tenement law and prohibit the further construction of "old-law" buildings. A typical block of "old-law" tenements presented buildings with walls flush against one another with a court of twenty feet separating the buildings at the rear. The usual four-room apartment in an "old-law" building had in the front a living room eleven by ten feet with two windows on the street, behind that a somewhat smaller kitchen with a window on a twenty-eight-inch-wide air shaft, and behind that two bedrooms, eight by seven feet, with windows on the air shaft. Two families shared a bathroom in the public hall. As late as 1958, 60 per cent of all the "old-law" apartments ever built, or 389,000 apartment units, were still occupied, although by that time central heating was required. Because wages were low, children frequently had to work to supplement the family income. In 1900, approximately 1,175,000 children between ten and fifteen years of age worked in American industry. Another factor in the low living standard besides low wages was industry's emphasis upon production of capital goods, such as steel rails and machinery, rather than upon consumer goods. Had more consumer goods been manufactured, their price would have declined and thereby raised real wages (*i.e.,* wages in terms of what they would buy).

But for all the poor conditions that prevailed among industrial wage earners, it is difficult to say whether these workers lived a worse life than they did when they or their forefathers were tillers of the soil, either in the United States or Europe. As urban workers, they had less light and air and less of a feeling of identity with the community and were subjected to an artificial and externally imposed work discipline. But, on the other hand, as peasants or farmers they had had less cash, perhaps less comfort, less contact with people different from themselves, and usually less educational opportunity. Certainly, millions of people, both in Europe and America, were willing to forsake their rural homes to try life in an American city.

It was common to say that in this newly industrialized economy "the rich get richer and the poor get poorer," but the statement was not accurate. The economic gap between the rich and the poor certainly became greater. In 1900, Andrew Carnegie's personal income, as opposed to his personal fortune or estate, was over $23 million, and there was no income tax whatsoever. The average wage of workers in his steel mill was between $400 and $500 for the year. That figure being the average, many workers received somewhat less. In general, real wages gradually improved. There were numerous short-term fluctuations, but over a generation's time real wages were better. A more ac-

7

curate version of the saying would be, "the rich get richer and the poor get slightly less poor."

Changes in Politics

With such changes in the nation's economy, it followed that there should be accompanying changes in the nation's politics. Business received from government almost all that it wanted. What it wanted was aid from government, which it received in land grants from the public domain, a high protective tariff, favorable tax policies, and advantageous labor and monetary legislation. What business did not want was government regulation of business or aid to other interests in the economy. On the one hand, business wanted a "hand-out" state, and on the other it wanted a "hands-off" state, or laissez faire economy. The business community did not suffer a single major defeat in the arena of national politics from either party. Congress enacted no laws that business was unitedly determined to defeat. Such measures as the Interstate Commerce Act of 1887 and the Sherman Antitrust Act of 1890 were no more than minor concessions and were administered as business wished until the twentieth century.

Neither party had national leaders of distinction between the death of Lincoln and the very end of the century. The Republicans had only Grants, Garfields, and McKinleys to fill the conservative shoes of Hamilton, Webster, and Clay. The Democrats had only Seymours, Tildens, and Clevelands to take the place of Jefferson, Jackson, and Benton. Outstanding men avoided politics to pursue business careers. Voters came not to expect men of vision and vigorous leadership in politics. Honest men were about all that was anticipated, and they were rare enough.

The Republican party dominated national politics throughout the period. Only twice, in 1884 and in 1892, when Grover Cleveland was elected, was the Democratic party successful in electing a president, although several times it came close. Democratic candidates for Congress fared better. After the first years of Reconstruction, party majorities in Congress were small, and the Democrats organized Congress several times. But so far as basic economic policy was concerned (except for some halfway silver measures enacted at rural insistence and some mild Democratic tariff reforms) it made little actual difference which party was in control.

From Andrew Johnson's hectic four years until Theodore Roosevelt moved up to the presidency, Capitol Hill rather than the White House was the center of Washington's power. Presidents seldom tried to exercise strong leadership, and the men who dominated Congress saw no need to abdicate. Congressmen and Senators had no desire to yield to an executive power that might be used against the special economic interests they represented in their districts or states, and dominant southern conservative Democrats understood that, so long as Dixie remained solidly Democratic ("the solid South"), they were in a better position to preserve their region's several peculiar institutions with a strong Congress than they would be with a strong executive.

Political machines dominated both parties at the state and local level. Political machines were nothing new in the American experience, but the post-Civil War generation developed them to a new efficiency. The power of a political machine at the bottom lay in its ability to deliver votes, and machines could deliver the vote by clever exploitation of the poverty and ignorance of most of the urban population. In a day when there was almost no governmental aid to the down-and-out, a politician could gain voter loyalty by gifts of a bag of coal or a basket of food. A job with the city or a "fix" for a brush with the law could gain a machine wardheeler a whole clan's vote. It took money, sometimes a great deal of it, to lubricate a machine and to finance the circus of a campaign. Money in relatively small amounts came from officeholders indebted to the machine for their jobs and in larger amounts from men with business interests who thought it wise to have friends in one or both of the parties. The cynic who said that "politics is the art of getting votes from the poor and money from the rich, on the pretext of protecting each from the other" must have been thinking primarily of state and municipal machines. The secret of getting and keeping power within a machine was discriminating use of patronage. A successful "boss" ran his "invisible government" by keeping the "boys" in government jobs. Patronage was the link between local and state organizations, and from state leaders to the White House and Congress in the case of federal appointments.

Machine politicians, particularly at the municipal level, were frequently rather low and crude characters, strangers to the more polite society of upper-middle-class America. An urban political clubroom was no place for sensitive people who disliked cigar smoke, cuspidors, and uncouth language. The story about the mischievous boy who broke up a meeting of the city council and sent the councilmen running for the exits by putting his head in the door and yelling, "Hey, mister, your saloon's on fire," was told in several cities, and it could have been true in many. Machine tactics frequently were a denial of representative government. Until the secret ballot, which came into general use in the late 1880's and early 1890's, buying votes was common. In the old system, the parties rather than election boards provided the ballots. The voter took the ballot of the party of his choice and publicly put it in the box. To guarantee that a bought vote stayed bought, politicians had their party's ballots printed on brightly colored paper. The counting of votes was often a sham, and party workers voted under assumed names in several precincts.

The more disreputable machines outraged upper-middle-class reformers who tried, usually in vain, to clean up politics. One cannot but wonder how much the good government people, commonly called "goo-goos," were motivated by a desire for honesty in politics and how much by a patrician disdain for the low types, frequently of Irish background, who manned the machines. In any case, "goo-goos" seldom had lasting influence because they failed to get at the roots of machine power: the machines' support from favor-seeking businessmen and the existence of a large poverty-stricken and ignorant population. Civil service and ballot reforms, while useful, merely changed the rules of the game a little. The Pendleton Act of 1883 creating the civil service system applied only to the federal government, and as late as 1917 only 60 per cent of federal employees were civil service appointments. When those who cried, "Throw the rascals out," were successful, it was not long before there was another set of rascals in power. Improvement was never better than gradual.

Two well-known cases of two kinds of corruption typify the extent of corruption and the failure to clean it up. Both took place in New York in the late 1860's and early 1870's. The "boss" of Tammany Hall, the Democratic organization in New York City, was one William M. Tweed, whose main fault as a corruptionist was that he worked too fast and too obviously. He and his close associates milked the city for an estimated $100 million in about three years. The courthouse built while he ruled actually cost about $3 million; the Tweed Ring doctored the books to make the cost $11 million. This was an example of corruption beginning with a politician. At about the same time there was a battle between Daniel Drew, Jim Fisk, and Jay Gould on one side and Cornelius Vanderbilt on the other for control of the Erie Railroad. The Gould team issued literally bales of new stock in order to maintain control but had no legal permission to do so. After the fact, they went to the state legislature for authority. Vanderbilt was determined to defeat them there. Agents actually went onto the floor of the legislature with suitcases of money and bought votes. The price of an ordinary assemblyman was $20,000. One key legislator first accepted Vanderbilt's bribe of $75,000 and then sold out to Gould for $100,000. The Tweed Ring was thrown out of office by a reform group of Democrats led by Samuel J. Tilden, who became the Democratic presidential candidate in 1876. Tweed died in prison. But Tammany Hall lived. The kind of corruption from businessmen of which the Gould-Vanderbilt disgrace was an example—in this case with Republican politicians primarily—received less attention than did the Tweed type. Well into the twentieth century, reformers in New England, for example, complained with good cause about the corrupting influence of the New York, New Haven, and Hartford Railroad in their state legislatures.

Agriculture and the Agrarian Revolt, 1865-1890

The most important political battles of the late nineteenth century revolved around agriculture. There were more people dependent upon farming than any other kind of economic activity despite the tremendous growth of industry. Farmers were in deep economic trouble from about 1870 until the very last years of the century, especially farmers in the South and West who produced cash crops for the national and world markets. But so firmly had industry assumed power in Washington that not until 1896 were they successful in even bringing national politics to focus on the farm issue.

The agriculturist's economic trials were many, including the weather, but most of his troubles were attributable to monetary deflation and to the railroads. During the Civil War, the Union issued millions of dollars in greenbacks, and western farmers, made optimistic by good farm prices, went into debt to a greater extent than usual to buy new machinery for improving their efficiency and to buy more and new land. After the war, however, the federal government pursued vigorously deflationary policies. In 1865, there was about $1 billion in circulation; by 1870, the government had withdrawn about one-fourth of this money. The national per capita money in circulation dropped from $31.18 to $20.10 in these five years, and in the West and South there was far less circulating medium per person than in the commercial Northeast. Farm prices dropped precipitously immediately after the war and continued generally downward until they reached their low point in 1896, the more serious declines coming during the depressions that began in 1873 and 1893. The decline of prices benefited creditors and harmed debtors. If a wheat farmer in 1864 borrowed $1,000 and his note was due when wheat prices had dropped 40 per cent, he, in effect, had to pay his principal with 40 per cent more wheat than he would have if prices had remained constant. Related to deflationary government policy was the farmer's difficulty in getting further credit. Interest rates were sometimes usurious, running as high as 15 and 20 per cent per year. The usury problem was most serious in the South, where outside creditors' interest took the profits of staple crops before they were even harvested and where the sharecropper victim of the crop-lien system bore the lion's share of the burden.

The farmer was "damned without the railroad and damned with it." For most farmers of cash crops, the railroad was the only means of getting his product to a market. This being the situation, farm land within reasonable distance of a railroad was the most desirable, and many farmers had voted taxes upon themselves so that local government could subsidize the railway companies to build through their area. But if the railroad had no competition, either from water transportation or from other railroads (and this was usually the case west of Chicago) it could charge the farmer whatever freight rates it thought it could squeeze. Railroads had high overhead costs in bonded indebtedness and depreciation on expensive equipment, and when an important shipper such as Rockefeller demanded a rebate, they were hardly in a position to refuse. But farmers were not Rockefellers. A farmer could not afford to boycott a railroad, and even if he could he could not hurt the railroad much. Railroad rates were grossly inequitable. Some farmers who shipped from a noncompetitive point had to pay as much for a hundred miles of transportation as more favorably situated shippers paid for five hundred miles. Sometimes freight charges took as much as half of a farmer's gross.

There was a time-honored way to deal with such troubles through representative political institutions. Farmers entered politics with considerable fervor, and in the states of the upper Mississippi valley, where agricultural distress was perhaps the most intense and political institutions the most democratic, farmers enjoyed local success. Their first political vehicle was the Grange, or the Patrons of Husbandry, which had been started in 1867 as a social uplift organization. The Grange did not participate directly in politics, but Grangers certainly did. In the 1870's, they won control of the legislatures of Illinois, Wisconsin, Iowa, and Minnesota and used their power in an attempt to bring the railroads under control. The railroads resisted with every means possible, including bribes to legislators, but all four states passed some kind of regulation of rates. In 1876, the United States Supreme Court upheld the constitutionality of the Illinois statute in Munn v. Illinois, and, subsequently, in Peik v. Chicago and Northwestern Railroad, it went so far as to uphold a Wisconsin law which fixed rates for freight in interstate commerce that originated in Wisconsin. In 1886, however, the Court reversed the Wisconsin decision in the Wabash case. The following year Congress went through the motions of stepping into the interstate commerce breach when it created the Interstate

Commerce Commission, the first federal regulatory body in American history. The ICC, however, had insufficient powers to be effective with the railroads, whose position the courts upheld in almost every test. As the new century began, the railroads were practically without regulation in interstate commerce, and only a handful of states exercised any effective regulation of intrastate traffic.

A detailed account of the agrarian effort to solve the problem of deflation would be unnecessarily complicated in this present look backward into the late nineteenth century. Suffice it to say that agrarians first turned to the Greenback party in an effort to rectify deflation through paper money. The Greenbackers ran presidential candidates in 1876, 1880, and 1884, reaching the peak of their strength in 1878. In that year they succeeded in preventing the further retirement of Civil War greenbacks, or, in other words, stopping further deflation. Before monetary reform through greenbackism was played out, considerable sentiment for inflation through making silver legal tender as well as gold began. Until the 1870's, very little silver was mined in the United States, and the official price of silver at the mint was too low for people who owned silver to profit by turning it in for minting. At the end of Grant's first term a new mint act repealed all previous mint provisions and failed to list the silver dollar as an authorized coin. No one paid much attention to the action at the time because no one turned in silver to the mints anyway. Soon thereafter, however, American production of silver increased tremendously as deposits of the metal were found in the Far West. At the same time, several European countries dumped their silver coins on the market as they adopted gold as a single standard. The world price of silver fell rapidly, declining to a point that would have made the old official price profitable for silver miners. Silver, however, had already been "demonetized."

Silver miners began to agitate for silver money, and debtor farmers took up the cry. They demanded "free and unlimited coinage of silver at the ratio of 16 to 1." In other words, they demanded that all silver brought to federal mints be purchased and minted, the price to be paid for the silver to be one sixteenth the current price of gold. Considering the large amounts of silver then being produced, their program would have brought inflation, but not the kind of "run-away" inflation possible with printing press money. In 1878, agrarians and their allies in Congress managed to enact the Bland-Allison Act over Hayes's veto. The act enjoined the Treasury to buy from $2 million to $4 million worth of silver each month, to coin silver dollars, and to issue silver certificates in larger denominations. Each administration in control during the law's twelve years of life opposed silver, and the Treasury bought only the minimum amount required by the law. The amount of money per capita in circulation increased only slightly.

The 1880's were hard years for farmers. Prices were low and weather was bad. Agrarians turned again to demands for "free and unlimited" silver coinage. In order to head them off, the Republicans enacted in 1890 the Sherman Silver Purchase Act, which was much less than the agrarians wanted. No Democrat voted for the measure and no Republican opposed it. The law provided that each month the Treasury would buy 4,500,000 ounces of silver at the market price (not dollars' worth of the metal as with the Bland-Allison Act), that it then be stored as bullion, and that Treasury certificates be issued equal to the cost of the silver. Temporarily, but only temporarily, the law provided for the purchase of more silver than did the act it replaced. Again the silver law fell far short of the agrarian cry of "free and unlimited coinage of silver at the ratio of 16 to 1." The measure did not dispel the agrarian specter that haunted creditor conservatives. Indeed, agrarianism soon reached a new pitch of intensity and became the central issue of national politics.

Populism and Bryanism

In the early 1880's, the Granger movement all but disappeared but was replaced by regional farmers' alliances. The three most important were the Northern Alliance, the Southern Alliance, and the Colored Alliance. At first, alliance men tried to solve agriculture's problems through co-ops, but when these proved inadequate they, too, moved into politics. In the congressional elections of 1890, alliance representatives won the balance of power in Kansas, Nebraska, South Dakota, and Minnesota, and in the South, working within the Democratic party, they won the governorships of North Carolina, South Carolina, and Georgia and legislative control in other states. In the Senate there were two Northern Alliance men, and in the House there were eight who declared themselves independent of either major party. Several alliance southerners called themselves Democrats. Encouraged by their success, representatives of the alliances met with leaders from the Knights of Labor in the spring of 1891 in an attempt to organize a third national party. Not until the following year were arrangements complete and the People's party, generally called the Populists, finally launched.

The Populist platform called for monetary inflation through free and unlimited coinage of silver at a ratio to gold of sixteen to one until the amount of money in circulation rose to a minimum of $50 per capita, but the Populists were not merely monetary reformers. They advocated government ownership and operation of the railroads and the telephone and telegraph industries, a system that most of the capitalist nations of western Europe either had already adopted or would soon. They stated their support of the sub-Treasury plan, an idea of Dr. C. W. Macune, a Southern Alliance leader, which called for the federal government to build warehouses for nonperishable crops, accept such crops from farmers, and lend up to 80 per cent of the crop's value in an especially issued paper money. Except for the paper money aspect of the plan, it had many similarities to the scheme actually adopted in the 1930's. The Populists also demanded a graduated income tax, postal savings banks, the Australian secret ballot, direct election of United States senators, the initiative and referendum, and a single term for the president. Most of these demands later came to be enacted in some form or another. In 1892, their presidential candidate, James B. Weaver of Iowa, who had been the Greenback candidate in 1880, received about 9 per cent of the popular vote and twenty-two electoral votes, carrying Nevada, Idaho, Colorado, Kansas, and North Dakota. Ex-President Grover Cleveland, the Democratic candidate, won the election.

Some of the Populist leaders were extremely colorful rural types who became objects of ridicule from their more conservative opponents and from

13

some historians of a later day. Mary Ellen Lease of Kansas, for example, who was in most ways not an unusual Great Plains kind of woman, is remembered almost altogether for her advice to farmers to "raise less corn and more hell." Senator William A. Peffer of Kansas, many historians point out, had an unusually luxuriant beard, but beards were not unusual in Peffer's generation. Southern agrarians, such as Tom Watson of Georgia and Ben Tillman of South Carolina, were sometimes rabidly anti-Negro, but that was not unusual among politicians whose base was southern poor white. Earlier in his career Watson had cooperated with Negroes in politics. Many of the Populist leaders were intellectually unsophisticated, prone to be extreme in their language, and parochial in their social points of view. But it is by no means clear that they had these characteristics to a greater extent than political and economic conservatives from the same strata of society in the same regions. And some Populists, such as the Chicago journalist Henry Demerest Lloyd, were urban intellectuals.

Grover Cleveland's return to the White House in March, 1893, came at an unfortunate time, for six weeks later the economy went into a slump such as there had never been. The panic began with the failure of the Philadelphia and Reading Railroad, and the stock market soon collapsed. Before the end of the year, 573 banks and loan companies, most of them in the West and South, had closed their doors. Great railroads went into bankruptcy. Unemployment and irregular employment created desperate conditions in the working class. Farm prices skidded to new lows. For about half of the decade, the times were anything but the "Gay Nineties" that Hollywood has nostalgically misinterpreted.

Cleveland acted as earlier presidents had during depressions. To him the depression was not a government matter. The federal government should do nothing to disturb the business community upon whose confidence, as Cleveland and other conservatives saw it, would ultimately be built the foundation of economic recovery. Business did not like silver money, even the limited amount of it permitted under the Sherman Silver Purchase Act, and Cleveland used his power to bring about the law's repeal. The President had to use his patronage powers as a carrot and stick to get the congressional votes for his silver law repeal despite his civil service principles. His position split his party into "silverites" and "gold bugs." His next step, to increase the government's gold reserves, was no more popular with agrarians. The Treasury twice issued bonds totaling $50 million in exchange for gold, but this borrowing had little effect on the reserve because most of the gold used to buy the bonds had been obtained by presenting legal-tender currency in exchange for gold. The gold merely went from the Treasury to the bond buyer and then back again, while the government paid 5 per cent interest. Cleveland then made a deal with J. P. Morgan and August Belmont in which the bankers, in exchange for an immediate profit of $7 million bought with gold a bond issue of $62 million and agreed to use their influence to prevent further raids on the federal gold reserve. The immediate cry was that Cleveland had "sold out to Wall Street." The Democratic tariff law of 1894, the Wilson-Gorman Act, was nearly as unpopular. The Wilson bill, when it went through the House, was the kind of downward revision that the Democrats had promised in the 1892 campaign, but the Democratic Senate tacked on over six hundred amendments that made it almost as high as the McKinley Tariff of 1890 it replaced. The new law did contain an income tax provision, but the Supreme Court declared the tax un-

14

constitutional the following year. Two further actions of the administration widened the split in the Democratic party. An odd lumber dealer from Massillon, Ohio, Jacob S. Coxey, led a march of unemployed on Washington—"a petition in boots" he called it—to demand a federal public works program. The administration had Coxey arrested for walking on the grass. Then in 1894 Cleveland sent army units to Chicago to break a railroad strike led by Eugene V. Debs, then a Populistic Democrat, over the objections of the Democratic governor of Illinois, John Peter Altgeld.

It was not surprising that the Populists increased their vote about 40 per cent in the 1894 congressional elections. In some states the Populists ran as a third ticket; in some, where the Republicans were silver minded, they fused with the Republicans; in still others they captured the Democratic party. Because the depression was identified with Cleveland, the Republicans did well, capturing control of the House of Representatives and gaining strength in the Senate. Still, silver sentiment cut across party lines and silverites in Congress could have passed free silver legislation. They knew, however, that such a bill would run into a presidential veto, and they waited for the 1896 presidential election with confidence.

The 1896 Republican national convention adopted a platform that stated its opposition to free silver and thereby caused a small split within the party. Senator Henry M. Teller of Colorado, a leading silver state, proposed an amendment to the platform approving of free silver and received the support of over one hundred delegates. When the measure lost, he and thirty-three other delegates bolted the convention. At the direction of Marcus Alonzo Hanna, Republican boss of Ohio, the convention went ahead to nominate William McKinley, then an Ohio senator, and a corporation executive, Garret A. Hobart, as his running mate.

The outcome of the inevitable struggle between "gold bugs" and "silverites" at the Democratic convention was indicated by the passage of free silver resolutions at thirty preceding state conventions. During the debate on the platform, a thirty-six-year-old former Congressman from Nebraska, William Jennings Bryan, delivered perhaps the most famous speech in American political history. A magnificent orator, Bryan aroused tumultuous enthusiasm with his address and its famous last sentence: "You shall not press down upon the brow of labor this crown of thorns, you shall not crucify mankind upon a cross of gold." The convention then went on to adopt a strong free silver plank by a two to one vote and to nominate the young orator as its presidential candidate. The Democratic second position went to Arthur Sewall, a rich banker and shipbuilder from Maine. "Gold bug" Democrats would not support Bryan. They met later in a convention of their own and nominated an independent ticket, but they actually hoped for McKinley's victory. President Cleveland was among them.

The Populists had scheduled their convention to meet last, thinking that "gold bugs" would dominate both the major parties and leave the silver field to them. Now they faced the problem of submerging their own identity by endorsing Bryan or running their own ticket and splitting the silver vote. They also were troubled by the fact that the Democrats had by no means adopted a Populist platform; the Democrats had taken over only the silver issue. Had the Populists been able to nominate either Governor Altgeld or Debs they might have run an independent ticket. But Altgeld was ineligible for the presi-

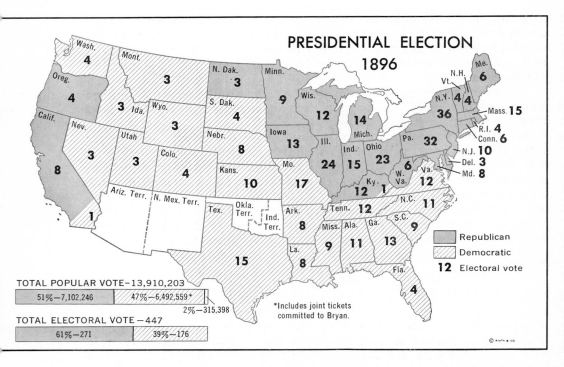

PRESIDENTIAL ELECTION
1896

Republican
Democratic
12 Electoral vote

TOTAL POPULAR VOTE—13,910,203

| 51%—7,102,246 | 47%—6,492,559* |
| | 2%—315,398 |

*Includes joint tickets committed to Bryan.

TOTAL ELECTORAL VOTE—447

| 61%—271 | 39%—176 |

dency since he had not been born in the United States, and Debs refused to allow his name to be placed in nomination. The Populists then nominated Bryan as their presidential candidate upon their own more radical platform. They could not swallow Arthur Sewall and ran Tom Watson for the vice-presidency.

The campaign was the most passionately contested political battle since the election of 1860. Realizing that his candidate was no oratorical match for Bryan, Hanna kept McKinley at home in Canton, where he received small delegations and issued calm platitudes. Hanna collected unprecedented sums of money from businessmen and spent it on antisilver pamphlets, speeches, and the usual carnival type of campaigning. McKinley was also helped by employers who told their workers that if Bryan were elected they need not come back to work. Bryan fought a vigorous campaign and thoroughly frightened the economically orthodox. More than a few people believed the Republican chant:

If you vote for Billy Bryan on Election Day
The Devil's sure to get you on the Judgment Day.

When Bryan invaded rock-ribbed New England, Yale students forgot their customary good manners and pelted him with rotten vegetables.

McKinley won by about a half-million popular votes. The Republican candidate received 271 electoral votes to Bryan's 176. Bryan did not carry one state north of Dixie and east of the Mississippi, and he lost Kentucky, West Virginia, Iowa, Minnesota, North Dakota, California, and Oregon, too. He failed to carry any counties in New England or New Jersey and led in only one in New York. The campaign and its results were significant. By endorsing the Democratic candidate, the Populists committed suicide. They lingered on after 1896 but were a dying organization. More important, the election results indicated that in a showdown political battle between agriculture and industry, agriculture could not win. The day Thomas Jefferson had dreaded had arrived.

The Republican party interpreted its victory as an endorsement of economic conservatism. Within only months after inauguration, it enacted the Dingley Tariff, which made earlier tariffs seem circumspectly low. Under McKinley, who had been advertised during the campaign as "the advance agent of prosperity," the depression did indeed lift, but under circumstances that seemed at least partially to validate the economic thought of the agrarian inflationists. New discoveries of gold deposits in South Africa, Australia, and Alaska along with the new cyanide process of extracting gold from low-grade ores steadily increased the quantity of gold against which new currency could be issued. An increase in the quantity of monetary metal by another method had been the demand of the silverites.

The War with Spain and Colonial Imperialism

The late 1890's saw the American people undergo the most explosive burst of colonial imperialism in their history. Within a matter of only months in 1898, the United States acquired a large overseas colonial empire. If one does not count the acquisition of Alaska in 1867, which did not much interest Americans until the discovery of gold there in the late 1890's, these overseas imperialist adventures of 1898 were a new departure in the nation's policies.

The imperialist outburst was a result of an intricate interplay of many factors (economic, political, and cultural) which had been building for a long time. The economic factor—a desire for overseas markets and profitable investments—played no small influence. The depression of 1893 and thereafter crystallized the economic imperialist impulse. Depression America certainly was not a likely place for profitable investment. Factories were closed because the domestic market was inadequate. People did not have the money to buy the factories' products. Albert Beveridge, an ardently imperialist Republican from Indiana, put this economic factor quite clearly in 1898 while running for the Senate: "American factories are making more than the American people can use; American soil is producing more than they can consume. Fate has written our policy for us; the trade of the world must and shall be ours."

Beveridge's use of the word "fate" indicated another stream of imperialist thought. From the early seventeenth until the late nineteenth centuries, the American people had expanded across a vast continent, conquering all that lay before them—a wilderness, harsh elements, the Indians, and, to an extent, the Spanish, the Mexicans, and the Canadians. "Manifest Destiny" had been the rationale of much of this expansion; it was somehow or other written in the stars, people argued, that the United States should control the continent. Now, in the 1890's, the continent's challenge was over, and, the imperialists said, fate had destined America for expansion into the Pacific and elsewhere.

The thinking of Alfred Thayer Mahan, a captain in the United States

17

Navy, influenced many key people although he did not have a wide popular following. Mahan maintained that in the history of the world great national power, prosperity, and prestige had come to countries with great naval strength. Therefore, the United States should have a huge navy and merchant fleet. In that day before the development of oil-burning vessels, bulky and heavy coal seriously limited a ship's range. In order to sail over all the seas, or even one ocean as vast as the Pacific, a navy had to have a network of bases and coaling stations. "Big navy" people, therefore, supported the drive for expansion. Incidentally, other nations of the world thought similarly and scrambled to establish or extend their colonial empires.

Several aspects of the imperialistic rationale may conveniently be grouped together as the "burden arguments," the idea that Americans as Caucasians, as founders of a distinctive form of government, or as Christians had a special obligation or burden to be assumed toward people who were not Caucasians, did not have the American system of government, or were not Christian. Many Americans shared with the British the idea of the "white man's burden." It was an English writer, Rudyard Kipling, who gave this notion its most permanent expression in his poem "The White Man's Burden."

> Take up the White Man's burden—
> Send forth the best ye breed—
> Go, bind your sons to exile
> To serve your captives' need;
>
> To wait in heavy harness
> On fluttered folk and wild—
> Your new-caught sullen peoples,
> Half devil and half child.

Many people of all races today resent the assumption in Kipling's lines of Anglo-Saxon superiority, but millions of people then genuinely believed their racial heritage imposed upon them a special duty to govern people who were not white, to extend to the rest of humanity the advantages they assumed God had granted them. The "American burden" argument was only a variant of Anglo-Saxonism. The articulate Beveridge put it this way:

> God has made us master organizers of the world to establish system where chaos reigns. He has given us the spirit of progress to overwhelm the forces of reaction throughout the earth. He has made us adept in government that we may administer government among savage and senile peoples. . . . And of all our race He has marked the American people as His chosen nation to finally lead in the regeneration of the world.[1]

That ideas such as these were sincerely held only made them the more formidable. The "Christian burden" was a reassertion of the ancient missionary idea dressed up in nationalistic language. Some American Protestants were as concerned with converting Roman Catholic non-Caucasians such as the Filipinos as they were with bringing non-Christians into the fold.

---

[1] *Congressional Record*, 56th Cong., 1st sess. (Washington, 1900), p. 711.

The war with Spain brought the country territorial empire. The war arose from tensions in Cuba, then part of the decrepit Spanish empire. Due partly to American tariff policy on sugar, economic conditions among the Cubans were extremely poor, and Cuban nationalists began an insurrection. The Spanish commander, Valeriano Weyler, tried to suppress the insurrection with brutal methods, including concentration camps. At that time, William Randolph Hearst was trying to break into the New York City newspaper field with the *Journal*, and he discovered that lurid accounts of Spanish oppression in Cuba sold newspapers. The public became highly aroused against the Spanish when in January, 1898, Cuban nationalists stole a letter from the mails that had been written by the Spanish minister in Washington to a friend in Havana and gave it to the American press. In the letter the minister had written a most undiplomatic but not entirely inaccurate appraisal of President McKinley. The Department of State demanded the minister's recall. Then on February 15, 1898, the American battleship *Maine* exploded and sank in Havana harbor with the loss of 266 lives. Chauvinists called for war, crying "Remember the *Maine*," although neither then nor since has there been conclusive evidence as to how and in what circumstances the ship exploded. McKinley wanted to keep the peace, but he yielded to the sword-rattlers. Although the Spanish government on April 9 agreed to stop all hostilities in Cuba, McKinley asked Congress for a declaration of war on April 11. Congress complied on April 17, demanding that Spain withdraw from Cuba and declaring the island's independence. In an amendment to the war resolution sponsored by Senator Teller, Congress pledged that the nation would not annex Cuba.

Never before was there such a war. The armistice was signed just four months and twenty-five days after the declaration. Only 379 American servicemen died in battle or from battle wounds. About five thousand died from disease, many of them victims of the "embalmed beef" that meat packers sold the army. Secretary of State John Hay called it "a splendid little war." One of its heroes, Theodore Roosevelt, said years later, "It wasn't much of a war, but it was the best war we had."

There were two main theaters of fighting, the Philippines and the Caribbean. Almost two months before the declaration of war, Assistant Secretary of the Navy Roosevelt, on an afternoon when the Secretary was out of the office, cabled Commodore George Dewey, commander of the Asiatic Fleet at Hong Kong, to prepare to sail on Manila in the event of war. Early in the morning of May 1, Dewey steamed into Manila Bay and easily destroyed the Spanish fleet, which its commander recognized was helpless and moved to shallow water so his men could escape more easily. Though few Americans had more than a vague idea where the Philippines were, they cheered Dewey without restraint. As quickly as possible, Congress elevated Dewey to Admiral, the third American officer ever to achieve that rank. Dewey, however, had not captured the islands nor even the city of Manila. A Filipino revolt for independence had begun before Dewey arrived, and both the Spanish and the Americans feared the insurrectionists more than they did one another. Not until August, after the armistice, did an American armed force gain control of Manila.

After farcical naval ineptitude in Cuban waters, the administration decided that an expeditionary force to the island would be necessary. American troops

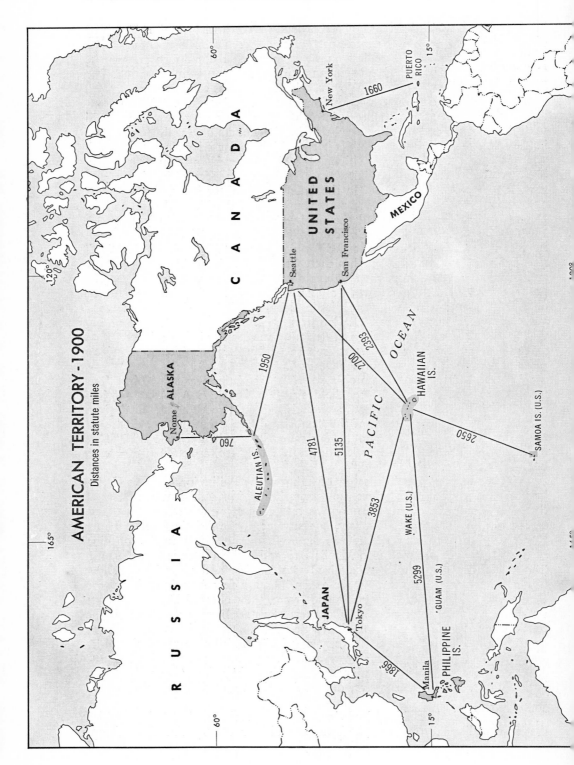

AMERICAN TERRITORY-1900

Distances in statute miles

did not land in force in Cuba until June 22, and the fighting, which was on a few occasions sharp but terribly confused, was over less than a month later. In the very last days of the war, indeed after Spain had already begun armistice negotiations, the War Department finally made a landing on Puerto Rico and took it with only three killed and forty wounded.

The whole conduct of the war, in military intelligence, planning, and health and in logistics, was scandalously bad. The confusion in Washington, in army camps in the States, and in the fields of operations was beyond belief. The United States won because the Spanish were even more poorly organized. The Spanish fleet, for example, was in such bad condition that its commander declared he would not be responsible when he was ordered to sail from Spain to the Caribbean. Had the enemy been as organized and efficient as the British, French, Germans, or Japanese, the results probably would have been disastrous.

The treaty negotiators met at Paris on October 1, 1898. The status of the Philippine Islands was their main point of difference, the Spanish asserting that inasmuch as the United States had not taken control of Manila until after the armistice it had no valid claim. At first the American demand was only for Manila, but later in the month McKinley instructed his negotiators to demand the entirety of the islands. The President later told a delegation of visiting Methodists on November 21, 1898, how he had made his decision.

> I am not ashamed to tell you, gentlemen, that I went down on my knees and prayed . . . for light and guidance. . . . And one night late it came to me this way— . . . (1) That we could not give them back to Spain—that would be cowardly and dishonorable; (2) that we could not turn them over to France or Germany—our commercial rivals in the Orient—that would be bad business and discreditable; (3) that we could not leave them to themselves—they were unfit for self-government—and they would soon have anarchy and misrule over there worse than Spain's was; and (4) that there was nothing left for us to do but to take them all, and to educate the Filipinos, and uplift and civilize and Christianize them. . . .

Considering that America at the time controlled only Manila, a tiny corner of an archipelago greater in area than Great Britain, and that most Filipinos were already Christians, the President's reasoning was remarkable. After long dickering, the Spanish agreed to cede all the Philippines, and the United States compensated Spain with $20 million. The United States also acquired Guam in the Marianas as a naval base, as well as Puerto Rico in the Caribbean. Spain abandoned all claims to Cuba, which would be independent but temporarily under American control.

McKinley submitted the treaty to the Senate in January, 1899. After long debate between imperialists and anti-imperialists, to be described in Chapter 7, the Senate ratified the treaty by a two-vote margin. Congress had already annexed the Hawaiian Islands. In 1893, American citizens in Hawaii had overthrown the native government, established a republic, and asked for American annexation. Cleveland would not oblige. In 1897, after McKinley had taken office, a treaty of annexation was arranged, but since opponents of the idea numbered more than one-third of the Senate, McKinley did not submit the treaty for ratification. In July, 1898, during the war with Spain, Congress annexed Hawaii by a joint resolution, which required only a simple majority

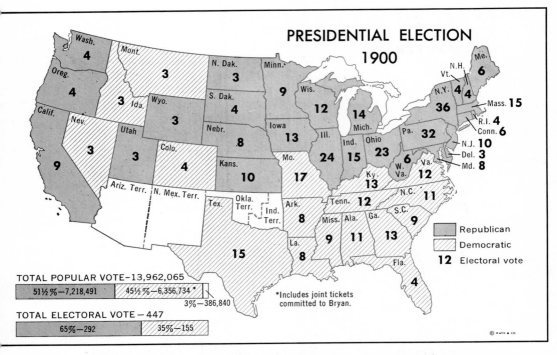

PRESIDENTIAL ELECTION
1900

Wash. 4
Oreg. 4
Calif. 9
Nev. 3
Mont. 3
Ida. 3
Wyo. 3
Utah 3
Colo. 4
Ariz. Terr.
N. Mex. Terr.
N. Dak. 3
S. Dak. 4
Nebr. 8
Kans. 10
Okla. Terr.
Ind. Terr.
Tex. 15
Minn. 9
Iowa 13
Mo. 17
Ark. 8
La. 8
Wis. 12
Ill. 24
Ind. 15
Ky. 13
Tenn. 12
Miss. 9
Ala. 11
Ga. 13
Mich. 14
Ohio 23
W. Va. 6
Va. 12
N.C. 11
S.C. 9
Fla. 4
Pa. 32
N.Y. 36
Vt.
N.H. 4
Me. 6
Mass. 15
R.I. 4
Conn. 6
N.J. 10
Del. 3
Md. 8

Republican
Democratic
12 Electoral vote

TOTAL POPULAR VOTE—13,962,065
51½%—7,218,491 | 45½%—6,356,734 * | 3%—386,840

*Includes joint tickets
committed to Bryan.

TOTAL ELECTORAL VOTE — 447
65%—292 | 35%—155

rather than the two-thirds majority necessary to ratify a treaty. In 1899, the United States acquired two other Pacific possessions, part of the Samoan Island group and Wake Island. Disputes between Germany, Great Britain, and America over Samoa had been going on for over a decade when, by a treaty in December, 1899, Germany and the United States divided the islands between themselves with Great Britain's acquiescence. The United States received the island of Tutuila, the harbor of Pago Pago, and a series of smaller isles. Wake, a tiny dot on the map roughly half way between the Philippines and Hawaii and at the time unclaimed and uninhabited, was taken by the Navy for a cable base in January, 1899.

Americans were far from unanimous in their approval of the new empire. In the presidential campaign of 1900, in which the two major candidates of 1896 faced one another again, Bryan opposed imperialism. There were other issues, and one can never know for sure what a majority thought about empire, but the imperialist McKinley was re-elected, and his running mate was the swashbuckling expansionist, Theodore Roosevelt.

Thus, by the beginning of the twentieth century, the United States owned a colonial empire, and the people at least seemed to assent to the imperial decision. The empire spread from the Caribbean almost to the Asian mainland. When it was 6:00 A.M. in Puerto Rico, it was 7:00 P.M. the next day in the Philippines. Within the empire were most of the races of mankind, speaking a wide variety of languages and having a considerable range of cultures. In less than 125 years the Americans had come full circle. They had evolved from revolutionists against one colonial empire to become guardians of another.

CHAPTER TWO

Progressive Republicanism

THE PERIOD FROM ABOUT THE BEGINNING OF THE TWENTIETH CENTURY until the United States entered the war in the spring of 1917 has come to be known generally as the Progressive Era. America had not had such a wave of reform sentiment since the 1840's. Voters read in their newspapers and magazines exposures of injustice, became indignant about the inequities that arose, for the most part, from the new industrial economy and its accompanying politics. Aroused voters supported candidates who promised reform. Laboring men organized themselves into trade unions to a greater degree than they had previously. Intellectuals and artists broke from tradition, and the excitement of their innovation lent their work a vitality that was new and welcome.

The new president, Theodore Roosevelt, fitted the general mood of America remarkably well. He too was a reformer, an innovator, and a vital person. The White House had become about the last place in the United States where one would look for liveliness, but "Teddy," as he was popularly called by people who did not know him personally, transformed even that institution from its post-Lincoln doldrums.

The New Chief Executive

Roosevelt was born October 27, 1858, to a wealthy New York family of long-standing high social position. As a boy his health was poor, but, as he was fond of recalling in adulthood, a regimen of exercise developed him into an unusually vigorous physical specimen. His triumph over his physical inadequacies, however, is not so important in understanding the man as realizing the implications of his family background. The family gave him a personal and economic security denied to all but a few. It afforded him the best formal education that the United States at the time had to offer: qualified private tutors, extended travel and stays in Europe, Groton, and Harvard. The boy learned from his father the tradition that a person of such comfortable position has a certain responsibility to society, a kind of American version of *noblesse oblige*. His father was certainly not a reformer nor sympathetic to laboring people, but he did assume a nonpolitical role in New York civic affairs.

In the fall of 1880, a few months after his graduation from Harvard as Phi Beta Kappa, Roosevelt joined his neighborhood Republican club in New York. The next year he ran for the state assembly and won. Two things are important here: first, it was highly unusual for a young man of Roosevelt's position to enter politics, especially at such a low and local level, and his action indicated an intense interest in political matters; second, from the very beginning he was a Republican. He was to prove a loyal party man. To him, any Republican was, by the fact that he was a Republican, better than any Democrat. In 1884, he held his nose and supported James G. Blaine, his party's presidential candidate, against Grover Cleveland, who, while no prize, was the better of the candidates when measured by Roosevelt's scheme of personal values. He did not become a Mugwump during the 1884 campaign as did many of his upper-middle-class educated friends; he went out and took the stump for a man who, he privately admitted, was not a "fit nominee." Only once in his whole career did TR depart from the path of the party regularity—in 1912 —and he returned to the fold then as quickly as was decently possible. After his wife died in early 1884 (he later remarried) he went to Dakota Territory and became a cattle rancher, but he kept his hand in politics back home. In 1886, he accepted the thankless task of running for mayor of New York on the Republican ticket. He ran a strong third in a race with Abram S. Hewitt, a reform Democrat, and Henry George, the Single Tax philosopher who ran as an independent. He later served on the federal Civil Service Commission and the New York Police Commission, two other thankless assignments. After McKinley's first defeat of Bryan, he asked Republican leaders to be named Assistant Secretary of the Navy. They rewarded his regularity.

Then came the war with Spain. Almost immediately, the belligerent Roosevelt accepted a lieutenant-colonel's commission and assignment as second in command of the Rough Riders, a special cavalry outfit of cowboys, and wired Brooks Brothers to tailor his uniform. He declined command of a regiment on the grounds it would take him a month to master the science of war and the conflict with Spain might be over by then. In the rampant confusion to get aboard a troop transport in Tampa Bay before other regiments could fill it up, the Rough Riders had to leave their horses. Only the officers had mounts in this particular cavalry regiment in Cuba. The cowboys walked. Roosevelt fought courageously in the battle of San Juan Hill. It is true that in a war of normal scale San Juan Hill would be only a minor skirmish, but Roosevelt did demonstrate leadership and did become a war hero.

As a hero and a politician, TR was destined for higher office. The Republican boss of New York, Senator Thomas C. Platt, picked him to run for governor. Chauncey Depew of the New York Central Railroad, the favorite after-dinner speaker of his generation among conservative businessmen and politicians, placed the young hero's name before the state convention. Roosevelt won in a close race. As governor in 1899 and 1900, he showed himself to be an able administrator and neither the tool nor the implacable opponent of Boss Platt. Nevertheless, Platt wanted him out of New York, and the death of Vice-President Hobart created a vacancy for an easterner as McKinley's 1900 running mate. He was nominated and elected despite his personal wishes. He recognized the vice-presidency as the political dead end it usually was in those days, but he would not displease his party and even a poor office was better than no office. Being the Vice-President was not enough for TR's energies. Thinking his political career was over, he arranged to study law with Chief Justice Edward D. White. He thought of becoming a professor of history. Then an assassin elevated him to the presidency.

It is easy to ridicule Theodore Roosevelt, but he must be taken seriously. It is true that he conducted newspaper interviews while running through Washington's Rock Creek Park, led queer crusades for simplified spelling, took boxing lessons while he was President, and wrote articles against what he called "Nature Fakers." He furnished his home at Oyster Bay, Long Island, with trophies of his big-game hunting. Huge elephant tusks formed an arch into the library. But to dismiss him as a blustering, energetic case of arrested development is to make a basic mistake. He was much, much more than that.

To try to label TR as a progressive or a conservative, a radical or a reactionary is difficult and of not much value. The problem too easily becomes a semantic exercise. Measured against the economic thought of a later generation, he clearly was conservative. He frequently asserted he was a true conservative because he was progressive enough to welcome changes that would in the long run conserve the American economic and political order. Certainly, he was a staunch advocate of capitalism. Among friends who considered themselves progressive, TR said he was a progressive. Undoubtedly, many mossbacks in both parties regarded him as a radical. Especially in his foreign policies and, sometimes, in his stand on civil liberties, he would be regarded as a reactionary by today's standards. He hated extremes—to him a rough-shod business buccaneer and a Socialist were equally dangerous—yet he could be extreme in his methods.

Roosevelt placed a high value upon social order, upon social efficiency, and upon power. He recognized that in the new industrial order, power could be dangerous to the public's welfare, but he thought the new industrialism was more promising than it was threatening. Roosevelt held that government should be powerful in order to regulate private strength, and within powerful government there should be a powerful executive.

A simple and poor society [he said] can exist as a democracy on a basis of sheer individualism. But a rich and complex industrial society cannot so exist; for some individuals, and especially those artificial individuals called corporations, become so very big that the ordinary individual . . . cannot deal with them on terms of equality. It therefore becomes necessary for these individuals to combine in their turn, first in order to act in their collective capacity through that biggest of all combinations called government, and second, to act, also in their own self-defense, through private combinations, such as farmers' associations and trade-unions.

In sum, Roosevelt welcomed a corporate society. Yet, the quotation does not explain everything. TR's words and deeds did not always coincide perfectly. Some of his actions were inconsistent with this statement of his, although as a general guide the quotation illuminates his administrations.

President and Congress, Progressive and Old Guard

Roosevelt was a regular Republican, but it must be remembered that no political party of significant size represents a unity of interest. During TR's presidency, three main groups may be discerned within the GOP. Roosevelt himself epitomized one Republican tendency: a loosely held-together group of reformers, some of them quite mild and some more thoroughgoing, many from the middle class, frequently from the professions, and most of them living in urban communities. Their main concern was efficiency and political morality —the "cleaning up" of politics and government. During Roosevelt's years in national politics, this group grew in size and influence. The Old Guard, by far the strongest group in the party when TR moved to the White House, was economically conservative, performed the political chores of powerful economic interests, and, frequently, was corrupt or at least soiled in its political arrangements. Its power lay in the state machines. Here belonged Tom Platt's New York state organization, Pennsylvania's machine led by Senator Matthew Quay, Connecticut's Orville H. Platt, and Rhode Island's Nelson Aldrich. Finally, there was a small group that represented agrarian interests. Small at the time TR became President, this wing of the party grew steadily although it never achieved control nationally. In this group were Robert Marion LaFollette of Wisconsin, whose organization became powerful in the state during the Roosevelt years, and one wing of the Iowa party, led by Albert B. Cummins. The agrarian progressives had similarities to the Roosevelt reformer, but they were usually farther to the left economically, seldom an ally of the Roosevelt progressives in foreign policy, and a world apart socially. The Republicans were not the only group with factions. The Democratic party, too, was composed of many elements: southern Bourbons, agrarians from South and West, and northern city machines such as Tammany.

In Roosevelt's first days in office, the Old Guard controlled the party and Congress, and Congress since the death of Lincoln had controlled the federal government. In order to enact any program of his own and be elected president in his own right in 1904, Roosevelt had to make an accommodation with his powerful opponents within the party and undermine their strength. He did both remarkably well. Cautiously but efficiently TR whittled into the powerful Senator Hanna's base in the Midwest and South and fenced with him in Washington. Hanna's power was considerably reduced well before his death in 1904. TR also succeeded in easing Tom Platt aside in his own state. With skill, the former Civil Service commissioner discovered, one could appoint qualified men and still build one's political strength.

All this politicking would ease the problem of getting the nomination in 1904, but meanwhile something had to be done to get some program of his

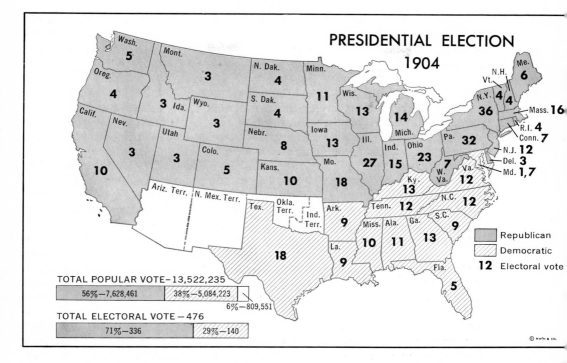

PRESIDENTIAL ELECTION 1904

Republican
Democratic
12 Electoral vote

TOTAL POPULAR VOTE—13,522,235

56%—7,628,461	38%—5,084,223

6%—809,551

TOTAL ELECTORAL VOTE — 476

71%—336	29%—140

own through Congress. Nelson Aldrich, together with Platt of Connecticut, John C. Spooner of Wisconsin, and William B. Allison of Iowa, effectively controlled the Senate. Aldrich had been born poor, had acquired modest fortune as a wholesale grocer, and had become rich after he became a senator in 1881. The biggest wedding of 1901 had been the one for his only daughter when she married John D. Rockefeller, Jr. In 1902, Joseph G. Cannon of Illinois, Uncle Joe as he was more generally called, became Speaker of the House and ruled it with an iron hand, using as leverage his power to assign all House committee appointments and his chairmanship of the all-important Rules Committee. An incredible vulgarian personally, Uncle Joe was a thorough reactionary economically. Roosevelt appears to have arranged a tacit understanding with the Old Guard congressional leadership that he would keep hands off monetary, banking, and tariff matters. In exchange, the Old Guard would not throw hopelessly unsurmountable obstacles in his congressional path on other matters.

By 1904, Roosevelt had won sufficient control of his party to make his nomination routine and had gotten into the statutes enough of his "Square Deal" program to show his record to the voters. The Democrats, discouraged with their twice-defeated Bryan, nominated an obscure, colorless, and conservative judge from New York, Alton B. Parker. The Democratic strategy proved defective. Parker ran a dull campaign and went down to overwhelming defeat in November. Roosevelt's popular plurality was over 2,500,000; the electoral count was 336 to 140. Parker did not carry one state outside the Solid South, and Roosevelt won about as many southern counties as he lost in the North and West.

27

The Square Deal and Business

President Roosevelt acquired a reputation as a "trust-buster," and he did invigorate the Sherman Antitrust Act, but his purpose was neither to eliminate trusts nor halt the concentration of industrial power. Indeed, he regarded big business combinations as inevitable and approved of them if they rationalized the industrial process and did not gouge the public with their power. Rather, his purpose was to extend the powers of the federal government so that it could police business and require it to operate in a manner he conceived as consistent with the public interest. It is true that he had the disdain of a patrician for many businessmen and deeply resented the imperious attitude of J. P. Morgan, who regarded the government as only a force, and probably an inferior force, to be bargained with as he would bargain with a business combination. Yet TR never attacked bigness in business as such. Upon several occasions he instituted proceedings under the Sherman Antitrust Act of 1890 when political expediency dictated or when some business action caused him to consider its perpetrators as "malefactors of great wealth." Indeed, he helped to improve the act's effectiveness and secured twenty-five indictments under it during his two terms. Roosevelt's critics said he wavered in his trust policy, was ambivalent and even capricious. The Chicago newspaper columnist Finley Peter Dunne, who had his bartender character Mr. Dooley make many incisive comments about TR to his customer and dense friend, Hennessy, in an almost unreadable imitation of an Irish brogue, put it this way: " 'Th' trusts,' says Roosevelt, 'are heejoous monsthers built up be th' enlightened intherprise iv th' men that have done so much to advance progress in our beloved country', he says. 'On wan hand I would stamp thim undher fut: on th' other hand not so fast.' "[1] But Dunne wrote before a pattern of action toward the trusts could be detected. Most people were not as discerning as Dunne. Both those who cheered and those who deplored antitrust action spoke of the "trust-buster," seldom noting that Roosevelt never moved against some of the real giants of industry such as International Harvester and United States Steel. TR even privately assured Morgan that his steel combine, the biggest holding company in the world, was safe.

For a president to take any official notice of trusts at all was unusual, and TR set off a bomb with his announcement in February, 1902, that the Department of Justice would institute a suit under the Sherman Act to dissolve the Northern Securities Company. It was the first time in years that the law had been used against a corporation. The law itself had a curious history. It had been enacted by a Republican Congress in 1890 in an unsuccessful effort to prevent a Democratic victory in the fall congressional elections. The law's first effect was to make clearer for corporation attorneys what was legal and what was illegal in the trust field. Several states had antitrust legislation before 1890 and unreasonable restraint of trade was illegal under common law, but the whole legal area was fuzzy. Now, with a supreme federal law, corporations

---

[1] Henry F. Pringle, *Theodore Roosevelt* (New York: Harcourt, 1931), p. 245.

would know what was within the law as soon as the Supreme Court interpreted the act. In 1895, the Court passed judgment on the law in a way that seriously limited the law's application. Cleveland's Attorney General, Richard Olney, argued a suit against the American Sugar Refining Company, commonly called the Sugar Trust, in a way that showed the Court how to exempt manufacturing from the Act. Although the consolidated Sugar Trust was a 98 per cent perfect monopoly, the Court ruled in this case (United States *v.* E. C. Knight) that the Trust's acquisition of the stocks of its component corporations did not constitute interstate commerce and was, therefore, not affected by the Sherman Act. The Court made a distinction between manufacturing and commerce and asserted the federal Constitution's interstate commerce clause did not embrace manufacturing. Mergers and consolidations of all kinds came rapidly after the Knight case. The same year the Court ruled in the Debs case, growing out of the railroad strike of 1894, that the Sherman Act did apply to labor unions.

The Northern Securities Company grew out of a battle over railroads in the Northwest. James J. Hill's Great Northern Railroad and Morgan's Northern Pacific, once competitors in the area between Lake Superior and Puget Sound, combined to buy the Chicago, Burlington, and Quincy to give them access to Chicago. Their action bothered Edward H. Harriman, who controlled the Union Pacific, because he wanted the Burlington for the same purpose. Morgan controlled the Northern Pacific with only a minority interest, and Harriman tried to unseat him by buying up Northern Pacific stock. In the stock market battle between Harriman and Morgan to get majority control of the road, its stock price rose over 900 per cent. This was the kind of competitive economic disorder that Morgan could not abide. He got all parties in the conflict to call off the war and arrange a consolidation. In November, 1901, the principals in the fight formed Northern Securities, a holding company chartered in New Jersey. Its capital stock of $400 million was about one-third water, which indicated the kind of profits it expected to make after it had ended competition. The whole stock battle and the organization of the holding company had attracted considerable unfavorable publicity, and Minnesota had already taken action against Northern Securities.

That the federal government should demand the dissolution of Northern Securities came as an unpleasant surprise to Morgan. Three days after the Department of Justice announcement, Morgan, Hanna, and Depew, among others, went to the White House for what Depew explained was only "a social call." But later in the day Morgan returned for a private conference with Roosevelt and Attorney General Philander Knox at which he told Roosevelt, "If we have done anything wrong, send your man to my man and they can fix it up." Roosevelt went on with the suit and even got Congress to pass the Expedition Act to hasten the progress of antitrust litigation through the federal courts. In 1904, the Supreme Court upheld the government in a five to four decision. Oliver Wendell Holmes, Jr., Roosevelt's first appointment to the Court, wrote the dissenting opinion, arguing that the government had not proved that Northern Securities had actually restrained trade.

Roosevelt claimed too much for the case. In his autobiography he described the effect of the Knight decision and asserted that with the Northern Securities case he had caused its "vicious doctrine" to be "annulled by the Court that had rendered it." This was far too sweeping an interpretation of the facts. Further decisions were necessary to reverse the Knight case completely. For that matter, the Northern Securities dissolution did not even restore competition to northwestern railroading, for Morgan, Hill, and Harriman found other ways to minimize competition. But the case was important nevertheless. It imposed some limitations on business combinations and made clear to both businessmen and the public that the Roosevelt administration would keep an eye on monopoly practices.

Roosevelt initiated another popular antitrust suit in 1902 when he moved against the so-called Beef Trust, an organization made up of the Armour, Morris, Swift, and Cudahy companies that had acquired control of midwestern independent meat packers and dictated prices both to farmers and retailers. In 1905, the Supreme Court upheld the government's suit, although it was not until after World War I that competition in the meat industry became important again. In TR's last two years in office, his Attorney General secured antitrust indictments against the Standard Oil Company and the American Tobacco Company, both important cases, but the final decisions in them were not made until after Roosevelt had left office. Roosevelt instituted these suits while he was trying to get new legislation to regulate business from a recalcitrant Congress. The timing of his waves of antitrust cases—initiated, of course, by the executive branch alone—suggests that TR used the Sherman Act partly as a lever for obtaining regulatory legislation from a Congress more prone to stand pat than he.

Clearly, Roosevelt wanted more regulatory powers than the Sherman Act provided and did not think highly of that law despite the number of times he used it. He urged "Federal control over all combinations engaged in interstate commerce, instead of relying upon the foolish anti-trust law. . . ." His first new regulatory body was the Bureau of Corporations within the new Department of Commerce and Labor. In January, 1903, he asked Congress to create the new department with cabinet rank and to include within it a bureau to "investigate the operations and conduct of interstate corporations." Business was alarmed, utterly failing to see that in time the Department of Commerce would prove a boon to businessmen. The Standard Oil Company wired Congressmen notice of its opposition, but Roosevelt learned of Standard's message and capitalized on Rockefeller's unpopularity by publicizing his opposition. Standard's opposition backfired so badly that the new department bill with the Bureau of Corporations provision became law four days after TR told the press of the telegrams. The Bureau later proved of value in discovering abuses by railroaders and shippers.

Roosevelt appointed James R. Garfield, one of his favorite young officials, to be head of the Bureau of Corporations. In his annual report for 1904, Garfield took a position that smacked of the Rooseveltian philosophy of government and business. To provide adequate control of business, he said, the government's regulatory powers would have to be increased beyond the Bureau's function of investigation. He urged a law that would require federal licensing of businesses engaged in interstate commerce and require licensees to submit annual reports explaining what business they had done and what profits they had made. Roosevelt tried unsuccessfully to get such legislation through Congress in 1906 and 1907. In 1914, President Wilson and Congress moved in this direction, although not so far, with the establishment of the Federal Trade Commission.

In November, 1907, the House of Morgan and United States Steel duped Roosevelt into a widely criticized reversal of his trust policies. In March, a panic had developed on the stock market, particularly in railroad issues. Businessmen, as usual, blamed the situation upon lack of confidence brought about by Washington policies. In the fall, things became worse and threatened to extend into a general depression. The New York brokerage house of Moore & Schley was in difficulty. It had about $5 million worth of stock in the Tennessee Coal and Iron Company, the main firm in the southern steel industry around Birmingham, Alabama, as collateral on loans, and the stock was falling fast. On Saturday and Sunday nights, October 27 and 28, a group of important bankers and steel men met at J. P. Morgan's New York mansion. On Sunday night, Elbert H. Gary of United States Steel telephoned the White House for an appointment the next morning and departed after midnight with Henry C. Frick on a special train. They interrupted Roosevelt at breakfast. They explained to the President that "a certain business concern"—Roosevelt thought they meant a trust company—was threatened with failure because of its Tennessee Coal and Iron holdings. United States Steel would sacrifice and buy Tennessee Coal and Iron at a "price somewhat in excess of its true value" and thereby save the "certain business concern" and other important financial institutions if the President would not prosecute them under the Sherman Act. Roosevelt consented, not knowing the situation fully and fearful of the depression's worsening. United States Steel bought the southern steel firm for $45 million, which one financial expert later described as "the best bargain . . . ever made in the purchase of a piece of property." The holding company giant thus became ever more important in the steel industry with the President's permission. It is significant, however, that in 1907 Morgan thought it advisable to consult the White House before moving ahead; almost exactly six years earlier he had not thought it necessary when he formed the Northern Securities Company.

During the Roosevelt administrations there were important developments in the relationship of the federal government with the railroads. When TR took office, the Interstate Commerce Commission was practically ineffective; when he left the White House, it was considerably stronger, although it fell short still of full effectiveness. The Elkins Act of 1903, sponsored by Senator Stephen B. Elkins of West Virginia, a friend of railroad management, was an antirebate measure. Many railroad managers wanted protection from the more aggressive and powerful shippers. The law affected only legal procedures and made shippers as well as carriers liable for fine. The most famous case under the law was against Standard Oil, in which Judge Kenesaw Mountain Landis of Chicago fined the company $29,240,000 in 1907 for demanding and receiving rebates. A higher court subsequently reversed his ruling on a technicality. Other companies forced railroads to give them rebates through roundabout methods known as "smokeless rebates." A favorite device was to extract extravagant charges for the use of a shipper's own spurs or other tracks. A Kansas salt company, for example, made an arrangement with the Santa Fe whereby one-fourth of the freight charges went to the Hutchinson and Arkansas River Railroad. This unknown railroad was one mile long, had no locomotives or other stock, and was owned by the salt company.

By the beginning of TR's second term, the public clamor for effective railroad legislation became too strong for Congress and railroad management to ignore. Railroad officials recognized that regulatory legislation was inevitable and concentrated on making it as weak as possible. Their friends in Congress stopped the Esch-Townshend bill in 1905, but in 1906 the compromise Hepburn Act went into the statute books. The bill went through the House with little opposition, but Senator Aldrich devised ingenious schemes to delay it and confuse matters in his chamber. He arranged permission for any member of the Interstate Commerce Committee to offer amendments to the bill after it had been reported to the floor and named Benjamin "Pitchfork Ben" Tillman, Democrat of South Carolina, as the bill's floor manager. This complicated TR's life. He strongly wanted the bill's passage, but he and Tillman were personal enemies and did not even speak to one another.

Conservative opponents of regulation concentrated on amending the bill so as to give the courts broad powers of review over both procedural matters and substance, in effect to empower the courts rather than the ICC to set rates. In the past, the courts had all but rendered the Commission helpless. Roosevelt finally compromised, rationalizing that constitutionally the courts would have review powers in any case and that to get any bill through he would have to yield. Advocates of thoroughgoing regulation like Senator LaFollette opposed the compromise and declared that Roosevelt had betrayed the cause. The final law dissatisfied men like LaFollette, but it nevertheless increased significantly the government's regulatory power.

The Hepburn Act enlarged the Interstate Commerce Commission to seven members and empowered it to regulate express and sleeping-car companies as well as pipelines. The ICC also gained power to regulate spurs and switchyards, which had been the root of most "smokeless rebates." Under the law, the ICC could set aside a railroad's rate schedules upon complaint of a shipper and set new rates, effective in thirty days, but subject to review by the courts. To establish a fair rate, the ICC could prescribe a uniform accounting system and see the railroads' books. The "commodities clause" of the Act was aimed at railroads that owned coal mines, as many of them did. It prohibited railroads from carrying in interstate commerce materials which they or subsidiaries owned or controlled except materials for railroad maintenance and operation, but the courts later emasculated this provision. In the first two years of the Hepburn Act's life, the ICC began formal action in over 1,500 cases of the approximately 9,000 complaints filed with it. This was almost double the number of cases it had investigated in its previous nineteen years of existence. The Hepburn Act was not to be the last measure to increase the ICC's power to regulate railroads. As railroad managers grumbled and increasingly appealed to the courts, the public again called for additional legislation. In 1908 the platform of both major parties called for additional railroad legislation, although the Republican demand was not very far-reaching.

Perhaps the Pure Food and Drug Act and the Meat Inspection Act, both passed in June, 1906, afforded the most direct protection of the public's health and welfare by federal regulation of business. For years, a handful of dedicated scientists, the most prominent of whom was Dr. Harvey W. Wiley, chief chemist of the Department of Agriculture, had agitated for government action to prevent food processors and drug manufacturers from adulterating and adding poisonous preservatives to their products. The illnesses and deaths among soldiers during the war with Spain who had eaten "embalmed beef" stimulated

32

demand for action. Two bills on the subject, the first introduced in 1902, passed the House but were stopped in the Senate. Journalists of the "muck-rake" movement hit the issue hard in magazines. Finally, Roosevelt became interested in the issue after reading *The Jungle*, a novel by the Socialist author Upton Sinclair. Sinclair published the novel serially in the Kansas Socialist weekly newspaper *The Appeal to Reason* in 1905 because no book publisher was interested. When circulation of the *Appeal* began to mount, publishers became interested, and the novel appeared in book form in 1906. *The Jungle* was in most ways a routine condemnation of capitalism—the hero, a Lithuanian immigrant, became converted on the last page and joined the Socialist party. But its descriptions of life among the packing house workers rang true. Sinclair had lived among them. Most of all, the book described with sickening detail the filth and carelessness with which the nation's meat was butchered. One of Sinclair's characters fell into a vat of boiling meat juice and ended up in cans of calves' foot jelly. An indignant reading public demanded action.

This time the legislation passed the Senate readily, but James Wadsworth, chairman of the House Committee on Agriculture, delayed the relevant bills and tried to emasculate them. Roosevelt directed his Secretary of Agriculture to make an investigation of the Chicago packing houses, and soon TR had a report prepared by James B. Reynolds and Charles P. Neill that horrified him. When the meat packers, who to a man had supported his election in 1904, now insinuated that Roosevelt's motive was his financial failure as a cattle man, TR released part of the Reynolds-Neill report, which reported gross filth, tuberculosis among the workers, and even pieces of old rope mixed in ground beef. Roosevelt announced that his statement was only a "preliminary report" and that he would release more facts if the meat packers did not call their dogs off Congress. In less than a month the President signed the Meat Inspection Law.

Neither the food and drug measure nor the meat act was fully adequate. Federal meat inspection was perfunctory, and a year later the *New York Herald* made an investigation and found conditions still bad. Roosevelt had dissuaded Senator Beveridge from insisting upon his plan for required dating of meat in the interests of getting a bill through Congress, and, of course, federal inspection did not apply to intrastate meat shipments. Dr. Wiley blamed TR for some of the shortcomings of the food and drug measure, which merely required in some cases that harmful ingredients be named on the label. Another act in 1911 aimed at false claims in patent medicine advertising.

The Rough Rider and Labor

Roosevelt's deep fear and animosity toward socialism, revolutionary disorder, and class violence permeated his whole attitude toward labor. He thought of the Socialist leader Debs as an incipient Robespierre ready to lead a reign of terror. In 1906, he denounced William D. Haywood and two other leaders of the syndicalist Western Federation of Miners, then on trial for the murder of an ex-governor of Idaho, Frank Steunenberg. Roosevelt expressed himself freely while the trial was in progress; by the trial's end it was discovered that the labor leaders had been framed. Fear of radicalism prompted Roosevelt to use his influence to develop the labor movement into peaceful channels and to accept trade unionists who had no quarrel with capitalism as such. Most important, he used the specter of socialism to goad employers and others to yield to an extent to "bread and butter" unionists of the Samuel Gompers type, arguing that if organized capital flatly refused to recognize legitimate labor demands, labor would be driven to the left and ultimately to revolution. As in many other things, Roosevelt was strongly opposed to extremes. The more aggressive and radical labor leaders considered him a dangerous fraud; employers who hated to yield an inch to labor considered him traitorously prolabor.

Roosevelt's handling of the strike in the anthracite coal industry in 1902 was a significant change in the federal government's role in labor disputes. Fifty thousand United Mine Worker members walked out of the pits in May, 1902, demanding recognition of their union, an eight-hour day, a 10 to 20 per cent wage increase, and fair weighing of the coal they produced. UMW president John Mitchell, who had begun his career as a breaker-boy, asked the operators to negotiate long before the strike. They would not recognize him. The strike was peaceful. The first dramatic incident of the strike came in July, when George F. Baer, president of the Philadelphia and Reading Railroad and the operators' spokesman (over three-fourths of the anthracite mines were owned by railroads) made a statement that amounted to a claim of divine right of capitalists. "The rights and interests of the laboring man will be protected and cared for—not by the labor agitators, but by the Christian men to whom God in his infinite wisdom has given the control of the property interests in this country. . . ."

In September, coal began to run short and rise in price. Mark Hanna, who had surprisingly sympathetic views about labor and who, as Republican national chairman, was concerned about the strike's effect on the November congressional elections, sought out J. P. Morgan and requested him to use his influence with the coal operators to effect a compromise. Morgan complied, but Baer flatly refused to consider the idea. Roosevelt, then in a wheel chair as a result of a rather serious accident, called a conference for October 3 at the executive mansion. At the meeting were Attorney General Knox, Mitchell, Baer, and other labor leaders and operators. Perhaps Roosevelt was motivated by the rising demand for nationalization of the hard coal mines. The New York Democratic convention went on record favoring their national ownership and operation, and that political body certainly would not have endorsed such an unconventional resolution unless it thought it would capture votes.

Mitchell told the conference the miners were willing to negotiate with the owners at any time and that, if negotiations brought no settlement, the union would abide by the terms of a Roosevelt-appointed arbitration commission if the owners would agree to abide by such terms. Roosevelt adjourned the meeting until afternoon and asked the operators to consider the offer. At the afternoon session, the owners would not speak either directly or indirectly to Mitchell and the other UMW men. Repeatedly, Baer and the other employers referred to the union leaders as "outlaws" and accused them of murder. They urged Roosevelt to use the army in the coal fields as Cleveland had at Chicago in 1894 and to prosecute the UMW under the Sherman Act. Roosevelt refused and the conference ended. Baer thoroughly irritated TR who said, "If it wasn't for the high office I hold I would have taken him by the seat of the breeches and the nape of the neck and chucked him out of that window." Baer told a reporter, "We object to being called here to meet a criminal, even by the President of the United States." In contrast to Baer, Roosevelt was impressed by Mitchell. Mitchell, he said, was the only man in the room—and that included himself—"who behaved like a gentleman."

When the owners returned to Pennsylvania they had the number of state militia in the coal fields increased to ten thousand and threatened to break the strike with force. Roosevelt heard or thought he heard "ugly talk of a general sympathetic strike which . . . would have meant a crisis only less serious than the Civil War." The old specter of class violence led him to threaten to send in the army to take possession of the mines and operate them. He actually started preparations with the army and, through Senator Quay, had the governor of Pennsylvania ask for troops. Then he sent Secretary of War Elihu Root to see J. P. Morgan. Morgan received Root on the *Corsair*, anchored in the Hudson, and agreed to apply pressure on the operators to accept arbitration or be faced with army seizure. Still the operators balked, insisting that men of certain middle-class occupations but no labor men be represented on the arbitration board. After four days of bickering, during which the owners refused Roosevelt's suggestion that ex-President Cleveland be named to the board on the grounds that he was too radical (a point of view that would have surprised the railroad strikers of 1894) they accepted the appointment of E. E. Clarke, head of the Order of Railway Conductors, to fill their category of "an eminent sociologist." The strikers returned to work.

The following March the arbitration board announced its decisions. The miners received a 10 per cent wage increase, the hours were reduced to eight for a few miners but to nine for most of them, the union was not recognized, and the old system of weighing coal would continue. The board also recommended a 10 per cent increase in the price of coal. Before the awards were announced the Republicans had won the congressional elections. For the first time the federal government had used its power to arbitrate rather than break a strike. For the first time a president had threatened to use troops to seize a struck industry. For the first time the federal government had acted as a third force in a major labor dispute rather than as an auxiliary of capital.

On later occasions Roosevelt used troops in the more traditional manner of a president during a labor dispute. In 1903, he sent army units to Arizona when the governor of the territory requested them, but he withdrew them in eight days, before a mine strike was over, when there was no disorder for the army to quiet. In 1908, he sent the army to Goldfield, Nevada, at the governor's request but again withdrew it quickly when there was no violence. In 1904, during the violent labor strife around Cripple Creek, Colorado, the governor asked for troops to break the strike and the strikers asked for the army for protection from the state militia. Roosevelt refused to comply with either request.

Roosevelt, despite his dramatic intervention in the coal strike, was uneasy about trade unions. He recognized their necessity in the new industrial order, but he did not judge them by the same standards that he did corporations. For example, TR saw nothing inherently wrong in a corporation's monopoly, but he opposed a closed shop for labor. Roosevelt very much reflected the labor attitudes of other middle-class progressives; unions were a necessary evil, likely to threaten the middle class from below as big business ground upon it from above. Nevertheless, TR was fair with labor unions, and, from the unions' point of view, he was a vast improvement over his predecessors.

Roosevelt tried to aid all labor, not exclusively union labor, when he helped push legislation through Congress making employers in the District of Columbia and in common carriers liable for accidents and deaths of their employees inflicted at work. The Employers' Liability Act became law in 1906, only to be struck down by the Supreme Court two years later. Nevertheless, the law was legislative recognition of the unjustice of the common-law "fellow servant" principle, which relieved employers of liability if the negligence of a fellow employee could be shown to be relevant to the accident, and Congress subsequently enacted a law that met the Court's objections. The law's importance may be seen in the great number of industrial accidents. In 1907, there were 11,839 persons killed and 111,016 injured on the railroads, most of them employees. Only about three times as many people per year died from motor vehicle accidents in the late 1950's.

Roosevelt and Conservation

Perhaps Roosevelt's most lasting contribution was in the field of conservation of natural resources, the one area of his activity that reformers more militant than he, such as Senator LaFollette, did not feel he hedged and compromised. Vigorous conservationists saw their mission as urgent because, from the beginning, the American people had been profligate in their exploitation of the continent's unparalleled natural wealth. Soil exhaustion from unwise farming methods had begun to be a problem even during the colonial period. By 1900, the federal government had transferred to private ownership all but a little of the public land that could be farmed profitably by traditional methods. About 80 per cent of the forests were gone, hydroelectric sites were going fast to private ownership for exploitation for profit, and mineral lands were disappearing quickly. America's tremendous natural endowment had been a primary source of America's wealth, its advantage over less fortunate nations of the Old World. Now the day when this advantage would be over seemed imminent.

In 1894, Congress had enacted a measure designed to reclaim irrigable western land. The federal government agreed to give irrigable land to the states if they would permit cooperatives and private companies to construct irrigation facilities. The land itself was cheap, but irrigation was expensive and little land had been reclaimed under the act. In the summer of 1901, senators and representatives of seventeen western states met at Cheyenne, Wyoming, and approved the irrigation plan of Democratic Senator Francis G. Newlands of Nevada. The following year Roosevelt worked hard to help the proposal through Congress over the opposition of Uncle Joe Cannon. Under this Reclamation Act of 1902, frequently called the Newlands Act, the federal government itself built dams and other irrigation facilities from a fund created by setting aside the revenues from sale of other public lands. Farmers who moved into the reclaimed areas could get tracts of up to eighty acres after five years' residence and cultivation of at least half of their land by paying the irrigation construction cost, about $20 to $30 an acre. These funds then financed the reclamation of more land. By 1920, about 1,200,000 acres had been reclaimed under the law.

The President was concerned about hydroelectric sites and ordered the Bureau of Corporations to make a survey of the nation's water-power resources. The Bureau concluded that America had potential power adequate for an electric age if the sites were wisely used. In 1903, in a then little publicized incident that became important later in the century, Roosevelt vetoed a bill that would have permitted a private investor to build a dam and electric power station at Muscle Shoals on the Tennessee River. TR held that natural power sites belonged to all the people and should be exploited in their interest, "not be practically given away" for private profit.

A law of 1891 had empowered the president to withdraw timber lands in the public domain from sale. Presidents Harrison, Cleveland, and McKinley had used the law sparingly. Gifford Pinchot, chief of the federal Forestry Service and a fanatic crusader for conservation, easily persuaded Roosevelt to use the law more intensively. During his two terms TR set aside about 150,000,000 acres of forest, more than three times as much as his predecessors had done. Furthermore, he appointed a special federal prosecutor to protect the national domain from poachers of its riches.

Drying up government largesse is hardly ever accomplished without political opposition, and Roosevelt's conservation policy was no exception. Timber companies, mining concerns, and electric utilities lobbied against TR's policies, and they found a sympathetic ear among many western congressmen who argued that conservation retarded their region's economic development. Senator Charles W. Fulton of Oregon spearheaded the opposition to Roosevelt's program. The fact that Roosevelt's special prosecutor had sent or was sending a considerable part of the Oregon Republican organization to prison, including the other Oregon senator, undoubtedly was one of Fulton's motives. In 1907, Fulton successfully attached a rider to the Department of Agriculture appropriations bill that denied the president power to create new forest reserves or extend old ones in six western states without the consent of Congress. Roosevelt was on the spot. If he signed the bill, his timber program was wrecked; if he vetoed it, the Department of Agriculture would be without funds. He saw one way out of the dilemma. He delayed doing anything until he had added millions of acres to the forest reserves, and then he signed the bill. Pinchot, shorn of any other device for setting aside hydroelectric sites, resorted to designating such sites as ranger stations and sequestered over 2,500 sites from the power companies. Congress fumed, but it was powerless.

In Roosevelt's last year in office, he called a conference of governors and conservation experts to meet at the White House. He impressed upon them and the public the necessity of conservation, and soon most of the states had established conservation commissions. He also created the National Conservation Commission without seeking congressional sanction and enjoined it to survey the whole problem. Through such devices and numerous speeches, Roosevelt vastly increased public support for conservation. After his presidency, although private interests still sometimes successfully executed raids on the public domain, in any showdown fight between conservationists and private exploiters, majority public opinion supported conservation.

The Election of 1908

Roosevelt clearly would have liked to remain in the White House for another term, but after his 1904 electoral victory he had said, "Under no circumstances will I be a candidate for or accept another nomination," and he abided by his statement. The two-term tradition was involved but not absolutely, since TR had succeeded to the presidency six months and ten days after McKinley's second inauguration. If he could not be president, Roosevelt would do the next best thing and name his successor. As early as 1906, Roosevelt had decided upon William Howard Taft, who had become his Secretary of War in 1904. By using the patronage for that purpose, Taft's nomination at the 1908 Republican convention was practically a foregone conclusion.

The convention nominated Taft on the first ballot, but almost nothing else worked out according to plan. The vice-presidential nomination went to a New York conservative, James S. Sherman. Conservatives wrote the platform, whose only shred of progressivism was a promise of a postal savings system. Taft wanted a plank calling for a lower tariff, but the platform promised only tariff revision, not specifying what kind. LaFollette, who had been defeated in efforts to amend the platform, was publicly critical of it.

The Democratic convention went back to its old war horse, Bryan, and placed him upon a progressive platform that called for an end of labor injunctions. (The American Federation of Labor departed from its tradition of political neutrality and endorsed his candidacy.) Bryan campaigned vigorously and took a more radical position than he had in 1896 or 1900, calling for government ownership of the interstate railway systems, gradual abandonment of tariff protection until duties should be for revenue only, government guarantee of bank deposits, and dissolution of all business combinations that controlled one-half or more of the domestic market. But the Democratic candidate, not surprisingly, had little money for the campaign, and he did not succeed in provoking the excitement that had characterized his earlier races. Nor did Taft create much excitement for he was not an exciting man. He went beyond his platform and pledged downward revision of the tariff and a continuation of Roosevelt's policies.

Roosevelt was actually the most popular figure in the campaign, and to many voters the question was whether Taft or Bryan would be the more like him. Roosevelt vigorously supported Taft, who won easily with an electoral count of 321 to 162. Taft's popular plurality was less than Roosevelt's in 1904, Bryan receiving about 1,375,000 more votes than had Parker. The Republicans retained control of each house of Congress, but slipped in their majority of representatives and lost the governorships of North Dakota, Minnesota, Indiana, and Ohio. Taft ran ahead of his ticket in these states. Throughout the Midwest, agrarian and progressive Republican candidates fared better than their more conservative colleagues.

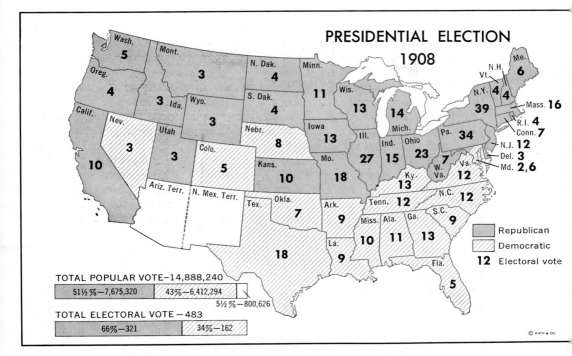

PRESIDENTIAL ELECTION
1908

Wash. 5
Mont. 3
N. Dak. 4
Minn. 11
N.H.
Vt.
Me. 6
Oreg. 4
Ida. 3
Wyo.
S. Dak. 4
Wis. 13
Mich. 14
N.Y. 39
Mass. 16
Calif. 10
Nev. 3
Utah 3
Colo. 5
Nebr. 8
Iowa 13
Ill. 27
Ind. 15
Ohio 23
Pa. 34
R.I. 4
Conn. 7
N.J. 12
Del. 3
Md. 2,6
Ariz. Terr.
N. Mex. Terr.
Kans. 10
Mo. 18
Ky. 13
W. Va. 7
Va. 12
N.C. 12
Tex. 18
Okla. 7
Ark. 9
Tenn. 12
Miss. 10
Ala. 11
Ga. 13
S.C. 9
La. 9
Fla. 5

Republican
Democratic
12 Electoral vote

TOTAL POPULAR VOTE—14,888,240
51½%—7,675,320   43%—6,412,294   5½%—800,626

TOTAL ELECTORAL VOTE — 483
66%—321   34%—162

William Howard Taft, from an important and fairly wealthy family of Cincinnati, represents something of a puzzle to historians, who are far from agreement about how to interpret the man personally and how to explain the disintegration of his party during his administration. Taft had gone to Yale and returned to practice law in Cincinnati. He became a state judge, then federal Solicitor General, then a federal circuit judge. Before 1908, he had been a candidate in only one election, a race for a state judgeship. From the judiciary he moved to public administration, being chairman of the Philippines Commission, Governor General of the Philippines, and then Secretary of War. He did not like politics and was not a politician, in one sense of the word; he himself attributed his political success to the fact that he served his party regularly and well and kept his "plate the right side up when offices were falling." He did not want to be president; he wanted to be a justice of the Supreme Court. But Mrs. Taft, the political member of the family, wanted to be First Lady. Three times before Roosevelt decided to make Taft president, he had offered him a seat on the Court; but Mrs. Taft had persuaded her amiable, easy-going, 320-pound husband to decline. An important aspect of Taft's personality was that he disliked fighting and intrigue, and as president he was to have almost nothing else. Ideologically, Taft's instincts were conservative. As a judge he had attracted national attention for his antiunion decisions and his frequent use of the labor injunction. He did not like the zeal that characterized most reformers. An able administrator, he had served Roosevelt well and loyally, not questioning his policies. But even during the years he was closest to Roosevelt, he found most of his Washington friends among those who resisted reform.

The Taft Administration and a Divided GOP

If one based an account of the Taft administration solely upon statute books and court records, the four years would appear, in most ways, to be a continuation of the Roosevelt terms. But the most important aspect of the Taft years was inner-party struggle, and his administration can be understood only against the background of serious and deep division within the Republican party. The GOP came apart at the seams and left three fragments, the Old Guard, midwestern agrarian radicals, and Rooseveltian nationalistic progressives. President Taft was the central figure in the disintegration of his party. Time and again he made political blunders, and he moved to the right ideologically while much of his party, particularly in the Midwest and West, moved to the left.

Difficulty within the GOP became sharp during Taft's first month in office over the question of overthrowing Uncle Joe Cannon and amending the House rules so as to limit the Speaker's powers. Cannon used his power to appoint committee members and his position on the House Rules Committee to buttress the *status quo*. Taft did not like Cannon personally and decided to help in his overthrow as Speaker soon after the 1908 election when Cannon gave a high-tariff speech. The President-elect announced he would call a special session of Congress in March to write a new tariff law, and it became common knowledge within the party that he wanted to cut Cannon's powers. On March 9, Cannon, Senator Aldrich, and Sereno Payne of New York, chairman of the House Ways and Means Committee, called upon Taft and informed him that if he did not support the regular party organization, meaning Cannon, his tariff policy would be in danger. If he did support Cannon, they would follow the President's lead. Taft supported Cannon. Congressman George W. Norris of Nebraska led the insurgent fight to clip Cannon's wings but lost when a group of Tammany Democrats deserted their party discipline. The insurgents felt Taft had betrayed them. The following March, in 1910, Norris succeeded in keeping the Democratic-insurgent Republican coalition together and, in a stirring session that lasted thirty-six continuous hours, succeeded in changing the House rules so as to reduce Cannon's leverage. This the House insurgents accomplished without Taft's help. Taft first had joined the insurgents on the question of Cannon, then backed out under pressure when he thought Cannon would win, and then eventually lost with Cannon. Backing a loser, especially under the circumstances that Taft backed Cannon, was not good politics.

Taft's handling of the Payne-Aldrich Tariff of 1909 was a fiasco. The House, where tariff bills must originate, put a new tariff through very quickly. Its rates were not as low as Taft wanted them, but they were lower than those in the existing law. Then Aldrich went to work in the Senate, adding over eight hundred amendments that raised the rates for iron and steel and their products, textiles, and lumber. As Mr. Dooley sarcastically noted, such economically unimportant commodities as hog bristles, curling stones, and bird seed went on the free list. The Senate knocked out a provision in the House bill that provided for an inheritance tax. Senators LaFollette, Beveridge,

Jonathan P. Dolliver and Albert Cummins of Iowa, Moses Clapp of Minnesota, and Joseph L. Bristow of Kansas fought the Aldrich amendments, but Taft supported Aldrich even though the insurgents' tariff views were closer to his own than were Aldrich's. The insurgents lost. There had to be a Conference Committee to reconcile the House and Senate bills, and Cannon stacked the House delegation with protectionists. It is difficult to say whether the new tariff was higher or lower than the previous one; it was not much different in its general level. It certainly was no "downward revision" such as Taft had campaigned for. It had no inheritance tax provision, but it imposed a 1 per cent tax on the net earnings of corporations in excess of $5,000 and provided for the establishment of a tariff commission.

The Midwest was up in arms over the tariff, and Taft made the situation worse on a national speaking tour in the late summer of 1909. On his summer vacation he played golf and bridge and neglected his speech writing, and when he left for the tour he had not one speech prepared. On the trip he praised Old Guard leaders but said nothing about the insurgents. At Winona, Minnesota, he blunderingly defended the Payne-Aldrich Tariff. In the heart of midwestern opposition to the act, instead of saying that it was the best tariff he could get under the circumstances, which it might have been, he called it "the best tariff ever passed by the Republican party."

Soon Taft was to suffer in the Midwest over another tariff matter. In 1910, Secretary of State Philander Knox negotiated a reciprocal tariff treaty with the Canadian Liberal ministry headed by Sir Wilfred Laurier, and Taft submitted the treaty to the Senate in January, 1911. In general, the agreement reduced duties on agricultural products that would come from Canada and manufactured exports to Canada, no bargain for midwestern meat and wheat farmers. Taft rammed the treaty through the Senate by getting the votes of southern Democrats. Canada had no cotton or tobacco to export. Some supporters of reciprocity, including Democratic Speaker of the House Champ Clark of Missouri, made public statements to the effect that in time the United States would absorb Canada, and in Canadian politics the issue became much wider than a merely economic one. The Canadian voters removed the Laurier party, and the treaty collapsed. Thus, Taft did not get reciprocity; he got only the opposition of the Midwest for trying to get reciprocity. When a Democratic-insurgent coalition began to pass special small tariff bills to reduce duties on iron and steel products, shoes, and woolens, Taft met them with vetoes.

Immediately after the Payne-Aldrich turmoil, Taft found himself in an even stickier mess over an issue involving conservation. When he had come into office, he had appointed as Secretary of the Interior Richard A. Ballinger, a conservative lawyer from Seattle whose political sponsors were vigorous opponents of TR's conservation policies. Roosevelt's Interior Secretary from 1907 on, former director of the Bureau of Corporations James R. Garfield, had wanted to stay on, and had the support of his friend Gifford Pinchot. Ballinger persuaded Taft to reverse the Garfield-Pinchot policy of creating ranger stations at water power sites and to stop further commitments of the Reclamation Service. Back in 1907, when Ballinger had served briefly as Commissioner of the General Land Office, he ruled on some complicated claims to Alaskan coal fields made by a group of Seattle businessmen. An investigator of the claims, Louis R. Glavis, charged that the claimants had broken the law and were planning to sell their claim, if validated, to a Morgan-Guggenheim syndicate. Ballinger validated the claims anyway, but Garfield overruled him. After Ballinger returned to Seattle in 1908, Glavis pursued the matter further and became further convinced that Ballinger had been wrong. Meanwhile, as an attorney, Ballinger agreed to represent the Seattle claimants before his former colleagues in Washington. When Ballinger became Secretary he removed Glavis from the investigation on a pretense. Then Glavis went to see Pinchot, still chief forester in the Department of Agriculture. Pinchot, who already disliked Ballinger, believed Glavis' story, sent it to the President, and arranged for Glavis to see Taft.

Taft weighed the extremely complicated evidence, upheld Ballinger, defended him as a conservationist, and fired Glavis. Pinchot declared war. He provided information on the matter to the press and eventually, through Senator Dolliver, brought matters to a head in Congress. Taft recognized that to dismiss Pinchot, the symbol of conservation to the nation's progressives and a personal friend of Roosevelt's, was political dynamite, but when Pinchot pressed the issue Taft had to choose between him and Ballinger. He chose Ballinger. Congress began an investigation, and for much of 1910 its disclosures made headlines. The congressional committee exonerated Ballinger of criminal action, but Ballinger lost in the court of public opinion. Glavis' attorney, Louis D. Brandeis, skillfully revealed that Ballinger was not a conservationist crusader and that the Seattle claimants to the Alaskan coal lands had indeed had an arrangement with the Morgan-Guggenheim syndicate. The whole affair did not necessarily prove anything about Taft's conservation views because, when Ballinger resigned in 1911, Taft replaced him with a friend of Pinchot's. But the public in general, particularly Roosevelt's following and the midwestern insurgent Republicans, saw Taft as a repudiator of the vigorous conservation policies begun in the previous administration.

Taft's proposal on railroad legislation, which eventually became the Mann-Elkins Act of 1910, was an example of the President's failure to keep up with, indeed his resistance to, the leftward drift of a considerable part of his party. Taft and Attorney General George Wickersham proposed that new power be given to the ICC to set rates and to supervise railroad stocks and bonds as well as to create a special Commerce Court to review ICC decisions. The insurgents by this time, however, had moved past Taft's proposal. They were skeptical of the broad review powers of the Commerce Court, which barely gained approval. They demanded that rates be based upon a physical evaluation of railroad property, which the Taft proposal ignored. They particularly disliked the provision in Taft's bill, inserted at the last minute, which would exempt railroads from the Sherman Act and allow them to acquire competing systems. In the House and then in the Senate, they amended the railroad bill so that it had to be withdrawn and rewritten. While it was being redrafted, Aldrich made a deal with enough Democrats to insure its passage. In return for a statehood bill for New Mexico and Arizona, both expected to be Democratic states, a group of Democrats would support the railroad bill. The bill succeeded. The Mann-Elkins Act clearly constituted an advance of the ICC's power, granting it authority to begin rate-changing procedures without waiting for a complaint and extending its coverage to the telegraph companies. The burden of proof shifted under the Act; railroads now had to prove that a rate was inequitable, rather than the ICC having to prove its contention.

The stock and bond regulation feature of Taft's plan did not pass, but the Commerce Court came into being. Congress abolished it three years later after one of its judges used his position to advance his personal economic interest. But the new law did not mend Taft's fences; even when he got a reform measure through he did it in such a way as to alienate reformers.

Aldrich kept his part of the bargain with the Democrats, and enabling acts to permit New Mexico and Arizona territories to write constitutions passed in 1910. The next year the two territories presented their constitutions for approval. The Arizona constitution provided the initiative, the referendum, and the recall of judges. Only a few western states had recall of judges or judicial decisions. The Old Guard fought these provisions, but Congress accepted them only to run into a veto. Arizona merely removed the offending constitutional clauses, became a state in 1912 (as did New Mexico), and promptly amended its constitution to put the direct democracy provisions back into the document. Again, Taft had chosen the conservative course, further alienated progressives, and ultimately lost. Both states voted Democratic in the next election.

Taft showed, on the other hand, that he was not a thorough conservative by enforcing the Sherman Antitrust Act as no other president had ever done. Especially in his last two years in office he directed Attorney General Wickersham to use the law with vigor. In his four years Taft brought forty-four indictments under the Sherman Act, more than "trust-buster" TR or any other president. Furthermore, he instituted a suit against United States Steel in 1911, which Roosevelt had always avoided, and because of the inevitable bringing to light of the Tennessee Coal and Iron Company aquisition the suit enraged the ex-President and hastened the split in the Republican party. Also, in 1911, the Supreme Court ruled in two Roosevelt-inspired suits, the American Tobacco and Standard Oil cases. The Court upheld the government's position, but maintained that restraint of trade could be either "reasonable" or "unreasonable" and delegated to itself the right to determine which was the situation in any given case. Justice John M. Harlan, then in his thirty-fourth and last year on the Court, dissented, writing that the majority opinion's "rule of reason" usurped a legislative function. The decision in the Standard Oil case did not make much practical difference in the oil industry. The government accepted the dissolution plans made by Standard's attorneys, which created separate but not entirely independent regional Standard Oil companies. That the Standard companies were not entirely independent of one another was indicated in 1929 when John D. Rockefeller, Jr., used his influence in Standard Oil of Indiana to overthrow its president and by a case decided in 1960, in which a federal court ruled that no law was broken if members of an "industrial family" of oil companies such as the Standard group cooperated in its pricing policies.

Insurgency

Taft's troubles within the Republican party eventually led to a full party split and a new party with its own presidential ticket. But actually a party split in all but name occurred long before the bolt from the Republican convention of 1912. A political party, at least a major one, is not monolithic as was noted earlier in the chapter. A national party is a coalition of state and regional political organizations representing, necessarily, different and even sometimes conflicting economic interests and ideologies. It is held together by the political paste of patronage, or the hope of it, which provides a measure of party discipline. During the Taft administration, the economic interests and ideologies within the Republican party became too divergent to hold together, and Taft's attempt to withhold patronage so as to enforce discipline failed in its purpose and widened the cleavage. First the midwestern radicals of the LaFollette type and then the nationalistic reformers of the Roosevelt type became removed from the main organization.

As early as 1909, Cannon told reporters that the national party would use its influence to defeat progressives in the primary elections of 1910. In early 1910, Taft withdrew patronage from those in his party who were not following his program. Taft and some of his cabinet members worked with the conservatives of midwestern states to aid them in their effort to capture control of their state parties. Sometimes Taft's opposition was fully in the open. In Wisconsin, for example, the LaFollette organization controlled the state Republican convention and the conservatives fled, formed their own party, and conducted their own convention. The Wisconsin Old Guard invited Vice-President Sherman to address its convention, and after he had twice declined Taft personally urged him to accept. Sherman publicly bestowed Taft's blessing on the Wisconsin conservatives, although they were no longer the duly constituted state Republican party. In all the midwestern states where insurgency was strong there appeared "Taft Republican Clubs" to represent the Old Guard interests. The insurgents began to call themselves "Progressive Republicans."

The whole situation was complicated by the former President who in 1910 was only fifty-two years old and as spectacularly vigorous as ever. Roosevelt had not been happy about Taft's cabinet choices, but he was quiet and left soon for a hunting expedition in Africa. (A common toast on Capitol Hill was "Health to the lions.") Upon his return in June, 1910, he was drawn back into politics which was inevitable given the political situation and the Roosevelt personality. His partisans filled him with stories of their suspicions and disgust with Taft, but Roosevelt in 1910 frequently, but moderately, praised his successor. He still wanted Taft to be the Republican nominee in 1912, and Taft, obviously, was busy working toward that end just as Roosevelt had worked toward it in 1908. In the 1910 election TR lashed out at the more radical insurgents as much as he did at the most conservative Old Guard, but he revealed in a series of speeches during the late summer that his views were shifting to the left. In a speech at Osawatomie, Kansas, he called his political philosophy the "New Nationalism" and declared "that every man holds his property subject to the general right of the community to regulate its use to whatever degree the public welfare may require it." Some saw in the New Nationalism the influence of Herbert Croly, whose *The Promise of American Life* had appeared in November, 1909. Certainly there was a similarity, but it seems likely that Roosevelt influenced Croly as much as Croly influenced him.

The 1910 elections changed the whole outlook. The Democrats, for the first time since 1892, won control of the House. Republicans retained a bare majority in the Senate, but a handful of insurgents from the Midwest held a balance of power. In general, where the Republican party had been led by the

Old Guard or Roosevelt progressives it lost; where it was represented by LaFollette-type agrarian progressives, it won. In January, 1911, the midwestern insurgents organized the Progressive Republican League, which included eight senators and six governors. Its purpose was to gain the 1912 Republican presidential nomination for LaFollette and to transform the national party into a vehicle for its kind of reform. The LaFollette group was distinctively midwestern. Its leaders were from an agricultural background; LaFollette had been born and reared in Primrose, Wisconsin. They were products of their state universities. They tended to yearn for a preindustrial society that had disappeared. They were less enthusiastic than Roosevelt about government centralization, but they thought that increased government power was necessary to control industrial might. And, quite unlike Roosevelt and most of his followers, they were anti-imperialist and antimilitarist.

Gradually, in 1911, Roosevelt moved toward his decision to battle Taft for the nomination and control of the party. The decision involved complicated and subtle personal relations between Taft and Roosevelt as well as ideological differences and partisan political considerations. Roosevelt was never able to play the second violin part happily, and he felt frustrated without power. Probably there would have been strain between Taft and Roosevelt even if they had agreed fully on political and economic matters. Roosevelt disliked some aspects of Taft's foreign policy, distrusted him on conservation after the Ballinger-Pinchot affair, and regarded regulation rather than dissolution the answer to the trusts. Taft's decision to prosecute United States Steel tipped the balance. Roosevelt ceased to discourage the many Republicans who urged him to declare for the nomination. By January, 1912, it was fairly obvious to all that he would attempt to beat Taft at the convention.

Meanwhile, the LaFollette boom was languishing. He fell far short of matching Roosevelt's national popularity, and Republicans who might have declared for him failed to do so unless Roosevelt clearly removed himself from consideration. LaFollette misinterpreted Roosevelt's cordial editorials in *The Outlook* magazine and his statements in 1911 that he would support no one at all as the former President's tacit approval of his own candidacy. When Roosevelt did not call a halt to his supporters as they began to raise money for a preconvention campaign, it became generally thought that he would make the attempt, and LaFollette felt that TR had betrayed him. Meanwhile, many LaFollette backers were looking for a way to desert the Wisconsin senator and switch to Roosevelt in January, 1912. An unfortunate performance by LaFollette at the annual banquet of the Periodical Publishers' Association in Philadelphia on February 2 provided an excuse. The previous month, LaFollette had had ptomaine poisoning and was not at full strength; he was suffering from anxiety about political matters and his daughter's serious illness. Always prone to make his speeches too long, LaFollette that night went on and on, repeating himself until there began the shouts of "Sit down." Thus ended serious hopes for LaFollette's selection.

In late January, Roosevelt planned for the formal announcement of his candidacy. He arranged to have seven governors from New Hampshire to Wyoming petition him to seek the nomination, and he formally accepted. He told a reporter, "My hat is in the ring." Taft declared that TR's supporters were "political emotionalists or neurotics" who had lost their "sense of proportion." The battle was joined.

CHAPTER THREE

Progressive Democracy

POLITICS IN A GENERAL WAY REFLECTS THE SPIRIT OR MOOD OF A people. Politicians are basically dependent upon votes, and they realize that to get votes they must present a picture of themselves consistent with what the electorate wants. The contrast between the political situation in 1898 and 1910-1912 indicates that the thinking of the American people had changed considerably.

In the earlier period the Republican party had been thoroughly dominated by men who had no quarrel with the *status quo*. Now, between 1910 and 1912, Taft, the most conservative of the Republican leaders but considerably less so than McKinley, was faced by two progressive rebellions represented by Roosevelt and LaFollette. In the 1890's, the Democracy, as nineteenth-century Democrats liked to call their party, had been divided between Cleveland conservatives and Bryan agrarians. Bryan's victory at the 1896 convention had brought a split in the party. Now, from 1910 to 1912, the Democrats were as united as their coalition could be, and it was the Republicans' turn to split.

The election results in 1896 and 1912 showed a tide away from conservatism. In 1896 the conservative candidate had received 52 per cent of the popular vote. In 1912, Taft, the only avowed conservative in the race, received the support of only a little under 24 per cent of the electorate.

The Culmination of Republican Division

Roosevelt was shrewd enough a politician to realize that his only hope for the Republican nomination was to demonstrate such a mass following within the party that the machines at the convention would not deny him. He knew how nominating machinery worked. After all, he had manipulated it for his own nomination in 1904 and for Taft's in 1908. He knew that he could not count upon even his old Republican friends such as Elihu Root and Henry Cabot Lodge. His strategy was to go on the offensive, to arouse as much popular support as possible through speeches, and to make maximum use of the few primary elections for the selection of convention delegates. His supporters, where possible, instituted presidential primaries in 1912 and thirteen states held them. In those states Roosevelt won 278 delegates, Taft only 48, and LaFollette 36.

The preconvention battle soon became personal and vicious. Roosevelt said Taft was "disloyal to our past friendship . . . disloyal to every canon of ordinary decency." He accused the President of "the grossest and most astounding hypocrisy." Taft, who would have given anything to have read newspapers that reported placid politics while he ate his usual breakfast beefsteak, had no choice but to fight back. "I am a man of peace. I don't want to fight. But when I do fight, I want to hit hard. Even a rat in a corner will fight." He pointed out that in previous elections TR had accepted the support of Republican bosses he was now criticizing Taft for accepting, and that William Flinn of Pittsburgh, whom Roosevelt had once called "one of the worst municipal bosses" in the history of boss-ridden Pennsylvania, was now supporting Roosevelt. In May, a few Republicans tried to get Taft and Roosevelt to agree to a compromise candidate, perhaps Charles Evans Hughes. Both refused, Roosevelt saying, "I'll name the compromise candidate. He'll be me. I'll name the compromise platform. It will be our platform."

When the Republican convention met at Chicago in June, Taft's nomination was assured, although a referendum of all Republicans undoubtedly would have selected Roosevelt. Several states had two delegations, one for Taft and one for Roosevelt, contesting for convention seats. Earlier in June, the Taft-controlled national committee had certified most of the Taft delegations. Roosevelt charged Taft with steamroller tactics and dishonesty. He told a mass meeting in Chicago just before the convention opened, "We fight in honorable fashion for the good of mankind; unheeding of our individual fates; with unflinching hearts and undimmed eyes; we stand at Armageddon, and we battle for the Lord." At the first convention session the Taft forces demonstrated their strength when they elected Root convention chairman by a 558 to 502 vote. Taft won the nomination by a wide margin on the first ballot, and Roosevelt and most of his followers bolted the convention. The convention went on to renominate Vice-President Sherman and write a platform that conceded quite a bit to the reform spirit. When Sherman died before election day, the national committee substituted Nicholas Murray Butler, President of Columbia University. The Republican platform called for revision of the currency system, a maximum-hour work law for women and children, and state workmen's compensation laws.

The night of Taft's nomination the Roosevelt forces met in Chicago's Orchestra Hall and issued a call for a convention of a new party to meet in Chicago in August. The Progressive party came into being on August 6 at an unusual convention marked by political amateurism, righteous indignation, and a spirit of religious enthusiasm. The delegates sang "John Brown's Body" and "Onward, Christian Soldiers," both of them appropriate blends of the warrior and Christian impulses. Before Roosevelt delivered an unusually long speech entitled "A Confession of Faith," he told a reporter, who wrote that TR looked "like an amiable orangutan," that he "felt as strong as a bull moose." The name stuck, and the bull moose became the party symbol. About the only routine aspect of the Progressive convention was its nomination of Roosevelt, with Governor Hiram Johnson of California as his running mate.

The Progressive platform well summarized the Rooseveltian principles of that stage of his career and epitomized the era's middle-class reform. It advocated most of the popular extensions of political democracy: the initiative, referendum, and recall; the recall of judicial decisions but not of judges; nationwide presidential primaries; publicity about campaign contributions; and votes for women. (TR was himself lukewarm on the woman suffrage question.) Economically, the Progressive platform called for prohibition of child labor, workmen's compensation, minimum wages for women, and the establishment of a federal regulatory commission to be to industry in general what the ICC was to transportation and communications. It also endorsed a limitation upon labor injunctions, inheritance and income taxes, currency revision, and limitation of naval armaments. Roosevelt clearly could not have sympathized personally with the idea of naval limitation. The Progressives hedged on the tariff, calling for a "scientific" tariff that would protect workers as well as manufacturers. The idea was not new, since the protection of wages had long been a protectionist argument.

The Progressive party was, in the words of one Roosevelt scholar, "a politician's Gothic horror." Its main difficulty was that it attracted few political professionals with state and local organizations. The agrarian radical wing of the GOP, men like LaFollette and Norris, gave the Roosevelt movement a wide berth. The Old Guard of course shunned it, as did many moderate Republican reformers who felt about party regularity the way Roosevelt had in 1884. Its organization did not build up from the precinct level. It was not even able to field a ticket in many local elections. Organized from the top down, built on national issues alone, staffed mostly by perfectly well-intentioned amateurs but amateurs nevertheless, populated mostly by urban middle-class people, the Bull Moosers offered little prospect of success or permanence. They had a strong candidate and enough money—the Progressives came mainly from comfortable urban neighborhoods and they had such backers as George W. Perkins of the House of Morgan and the publisher Frank Munsey—but, lacking local organization, they had little promise of patronage.

A Reorganized Democratic Party

The Democrats looked forward optimistically to the election because of their victories in the 1910 contests and the final split that occurred at the Republican convention. Bryan had removed himself from further consideration as a presidential candidate soon after the 1910 elections, and, with nomination meaning almost sure election, the fight for the nomination promised to be unusually sharp. Two major contenders, Speaker of the House Champ Clark and New Jersey Governor Woodrow Wilson, and one lesser one, Representative Oscar W. Underwood of Alabama, commanded the convention's attention.

48

Clark was an unimaginative party regular from rural Pike County, Missouri (up the Mississippi from St. Louis), who had moved into the Speaker's chair after the 1910 elections as a reward for years of faithful party service in the House. He had attracted little national attention. Knowing that his political talents were those of the congressional cloakroom rather than the lecture platform, he had restricted his preconvention campaign to buttonholing politicians, except for a few recitations of his favorite stock speech. He was not without ability, but he was a residue of the nineteenth century. He had the strong support of the Hearst newspaper chain and came to the convention as the front-runner with 436 delegates in his pocket. Underwood, a rather typical southern Congressman, did not have great strength. He was primarily his region's favorite son and was not seriously expected to win the nomination.

Governor Wilson was a new and exciting force in the Democratic party, which since Bryan's rise in 1896 had not been very exciting, and Bryan had not lent the party much in intellectual distinction. Thomas Woodrow Wilson, as he was called until adulthood, was born in Staunton, Virginia, December 28, 1856. His father was a Presbyterian minister; his mother was the daughter of one. He grew up in the South, and his childhood and youth coincided almost exactly with the Civil War and the tense reconstruction after the conflict. Wilson entered Princeton in 1875, graduated in 1879, and studied law at the University of Virginia until 1882. He then began to practice law in Atlanta. Up to that point Wilson's life had been a typical one for a Southerner of his social position, but it soon changed. He did not like the practice of law and left the profession after a year to embark upon graduate work in political science at the new Johns Hopkins University. His major professor was Herbert Baxter Adams, one of the more famous and popular historians and political scientists of his day. Wilson's Ph.D. dissertation, *Congressional Government*, published in 1885, was a commercially successful book—highly unusual for dissertations—and went through many editions. Upon leaving Baltimore, Wilson taught three years at Bryn Mawr College and two years at Wesleyan University. In 1890, he went back to Princeton, where he was a prolific author and a popular lecturer. Wilson's scholarly gifts lay not in conventional research but in analysis and an unusual ability to popularize scholarship without cheapening it or distorting it. He wrote well; he turned nice phrases. On the lecture platform he was felicitous and forceful. Throughout his work ran a strong stream of idealistic moral fervor, part of the effect of his Calvinistic background.

In 1902, before his forty-third birthday, the trustees of Princeton University named him president of the institution, a fact which in itself indicated Wilson was a man of no mean political ability as well as a qualified scholar and educator. As Princeton's president he enjoyed victories and suffered defeats. He modified the curriculum, attracted outstanding figures to the faculty, and introduced the system, still used at Princeton, of guided study by young scholars known as preceptors. His first defeat came on the issue of the undergraduate eating clubs, which had been attacked as snobbish and antidemocratic. Wilson proposed their abolition and the establishment of undergraduate colleges similar to those at Yale. His motives, however, were educational and intellectual rather than social. At first he had the support of the trustees, but the alumni attacked in force and halted the reform. He then got into a bitter and heated controversy with the dean of the graduate school over a matter of considerable

49

administrative importance. The struggle with the dean was in some ways a preview of events to come. Wilson refused to compromise or yield in the slightest, injected a personal note into an area where it was irrelevant, and eventually lost because the dean was able to rally strong outside support. Thoroughly frustrated, Wilson was ready to listen to the appeals of politicians.

Being president of a university of prestige and a political scientist, Wilson commanded a wide middle-class audience. Being a southerner, he was a Democrat. He wrote and spoke as a Democratic conservative, critical of Bryan's wing of the party, Roosevelt's program of government regulation of business, and of trade union practices. As early as 1906, George Harvey, conservative intellectual editor of *Harper's Weekly*, became enthusiastic about Wilson's ability and conservatism and began a movement to make him president. In 1910, the Democratic boss of New Jersey, the conservative James Smith, Jr., was faced with stirrings of progressive revolt within his organization. Harvey persuaded Smith that Wilson was the man to nominate for the governorship because he was a stand-patter on economic issues, had a name in the state, and would attract the honest middle-class voter who could not be comfortable with typical Democratic machine politicians. Wilson received the nomination, conducted a brisk campaign, and won with a good majority in a year of Democratic sweeps. But Smith learned to rue the day he heard of Woodrow Wilson.

Wilson broke with Smith soon after becoming governor. There had been a preferential primary for the United States Senate in which the main Democratic contenders had been Smith and James Martine. Martine won, but Smith, as the most important Democratic leader of the state, expected the legislature to elect him. (The Seventeenth Amendment to the Constitution, submitted to the states in May, 1912, and ratified in May, 1913, changed the traditional method of selecting senators to direct vote of the electorate.) Wilson backed Martine, and Martine became senator. The following year, Wilson hammered the legislature into passing a notable reform program that included regulation of railroads and utilities, a workmen's compensation law, and the direct primary system of selecting party candidates. He persuaded the legislature to amend its corporation laws, which had been so lax that Trenton had been the legal home of many holding companies and other businesses that operated nationally. Economically, this measure had little national impact, for many New Jersey corporations merely incorporated under Delaware law, still the weakest link in the chain of state corporation law, and moved their legal home bases to Wilmington. In the spring and summer of 1911, Wilson began actively to work for the presidential nomination. He toured the country speaking in behalf of direct democratic reforms (the initiative, referendum, and recall) tariff reform, a new banking and currency law, and trust busting. Although a newcomer to politics, he aroused wide support. By the beginning of 1912, Wilson was the favorite, although few of the party's professionals had yet committed themselves. But by convention time, despite the strenuous efforts of Colonel Edward M. House, a Texas politician who became Wilson's manager and close friend in late 1911, Champ Clark had come forward strongly and had almost twice as many delegates lined up as Wilson had.

The 1912 convention, held at Baltimore, lent credence to the old adage that a Democratic national convention might be stupid but never dull. On the opening day, Bryan, technically only a member of the Nebraska delegation but still a major force, organized a revolt against the selection of Alton B. Parker as the keynote speaker. The Wilson delegates supported Bryan in this objection, but Clark supported Parker and Parker gave the address. Then Bryan threw the convention into an uproar. He took the psychological offensive by introducing a resolution that pledged the convention not to choose a candidate subservient to "J. P. Morgan, Thomas Fortune Ryan, August Belmont, or any other member of the privilege-hunting and favor-seeking class," and he demanded the removal of any delegates of this type. Both Ryan and Belmont were delegates from New York. Bryan's resolution passed in amended form, all delegates being allowed to keep their convention seats.

Clark had a huge lead on the first ballot. On the second day of balloting, Tammany boss Charles F. Murphy switched his ninety delegates from Governor Judson Harmon of Ohio to Clark, which gave Clark a majority of delegates but not the two-thirds majority then needed under Democratic rules. However, it had been decades since a candidate with majority support had not ultimately received the nomination, and Clark's nomination seemed assured. Wilson's managers, however, operated intelligently as they began to undercut Clark's support. Bryan switched to Wilson on the fourteenth ballot. The Underwood supporters stood firm for days. On the forty-second ballot Wilson won the support of Roger Sullivan, the Illinois boss, putting him within reach of the nomination. On the forty-sixth poll of the delegates the Underwood delegations went to Wilson and effected his nomination. The vice-presidential nomination went to Thomas R. Marshall, a conservative from Indiana, a "swing state" that might be brought into the Democratic column by such a maneuver. Marshall is remembered for just one thing, a statement to express his contempt for reform: "What this country needs is a good five-cent cigar."

The Three-Cornered Campaign

The nominees in 1912 presented interesting contrasts. Wilson was almost the stereotype of the scholar in politics—high-minded, idealistic, a good public speaker but inclined to be ascetic, cool, and distant. Roosevelt seemed always on the verge of breaking into a song such as "Stout-Hearted Men." Taft was lethargic. After his acceptance speech he was heard from no more. He did not have a chance of election and knew it.

The campaign settled down to a contest between what Roosevelt called his New Nationalism and Wilson's New Freedom. They were each regarded as progressive, but they epitomized different streams of thought. The New Nationalism was an effort to pin the Hamiltonian tradition of centralized government power, which until the late nineteenth century, at least, had been used for the immediate advantage of the few, to the Jeffersonian tradition of representing the economic interests of the many. Before 1912, Roosevelt had worked out his philosophy of government and its relationship to the economy; a strong, centralized power, with the executive dominant, would be used to regulate the new industrial society in a fashion the chief executive believed to be in the best economic interests of a majority. A nationalist in all ways, Roosevelt believed in the federal government's taking a vigorous course in its

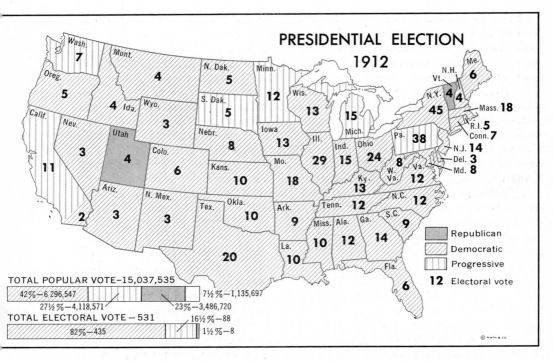

relations with other countries, extending foreign trade and investment, accepting big business operations at home and abroad as inevitable, and regulating big business so that its efficiency's gains would be shared by all. It was a vision of the United States as an internally democratic seat of modern economic empire, plus a dash of what a later generation would call the corporate state. Herbert Croly had given the vision its most articulate expression. In 1912 Roosevelt repeated his earlier formulas, but with a greater emphasis upon social welfare at home—federal workmen's compensation, expanded federal health program, abolition of child labor, and federal intervention in labor conflicts.

Wilson, in time and under pressure, slowly approached Roosevelt's position, but in 1912 he was quite opposed to such a design for America. Indeed, in 1912 Wilson even confused Roosevelt's New Nationalism with socialism, declared it would destroy "free enterprise" (Wilson's phrase) and undermine freedom in general. Wilson was still a Jeffersonian state-rights Democrat in his political philosophy. In his economic thought he was an advocate of competition, but later he met and came under the influence of Louis D. Brandeis, a Boston reform lawyer who advocated a kind of regulated competition. He recognized the historical fact that industrial monopoly had developed during an era of government laissez-faire, that from unbridled competition had come unbridled economic concentration. He proposed that the federal government use its powers, which he did not regard as extensive, to regulate monopoly in order to further competition instead of accepting monopoly as such. America should "restrict the wrong use of competition [so] that the right use of competition will destroy monopoly." Wilson feared in 1912 that an all-powerful national state would be dangerous. He had a Jeffersonian fear that Roosevelt's

52

"noble programme of social betterment" would degenerate into paternalism. In general, these two currents of progressive thought survive today, although since the 1930's the Hamilton-Roosevelt view in economic matters and the Jefferson-Wilson position in matters of conscience and civil liberty have become almost the consensus among those who call themselves progressive.

Roosevelt's campaign lagged in early October. His voice was worn out when, in Milwaukee on October 14, the campaign almost came to a tragic conclusion. As Roosevelt was leaving his hotel on the way to the auditorium, a fanatic shouted his opposition to a third term and shot Roosevelt in the chest. TR did not know how badly he was hurt and insisted upon going on with his speech. Afterward an examination revealed the bullet was lodged in his lung but that his condition was not serious. He was back in action before election day.

Wilson's victory seemed assured long before the balloting, but the actual results were a little surprising. Wilson carried forty states with 6,286,214 popular votes to receive 435 electoral ballots. Roosevelt, with 4,126,020 popular votes for 88 in the electoral college, carried Pennsylvania, Michigan, Minnesota, South Dakota, Washington, and eleven of California's thirteen electors. Taft won only in Idaho and Vermont: 8 electoral and 3,483,922 popular votes. The Socialist candidate, Eugene V. Debs, polled 901,873 popular votes, just under 6 per cent of the total. He even carried two Minnesota counties, one in North Dakota, and one in Kansas. The Democrats won a House majority of seventy-three and had six more senators than the opposition. Yet Wilson did not attract as many voters as had Bryan in any of his three electoral contests, and Taft had polled more in 1908 than he and Roosevelt did together in 1912. Debs's increased vote accounted for the lower major-party totals.

The election results clearly indicated a progressive reform mood among the voters. Roosevelt had been able to attract the progressive Republicans but had been unable to eat into the progressive Democratic bloc. Taft received the conservative vote of his party but was unable to attract the conservative Democrats away from their traditional home. The election doomed the Progressive party. Despite the impressive Roosevelt vote, Progressives won few state and local offices. Such offices are necessary for a party's patronage; professional politicians must have political jobs. Roosevelt understood the situation. He told a friend, "There is only one thing to do and that is to go back to the Republican party. You can't hold a party like the Progressive Party together . . . there are no loaves and fishes." Actually, however, many Progressives did not abandon hope until 1916.

The New Freedom: Tariff and Banking

As president, Wilson carried on and expanded the tradition of a strong executive that Theodore Roosevelt had revived. Wilson, as a political scientist, once had preferred the British system of cabinet government over the Constitution's separate executive, but Roosevelt had shown it was possible for a president to lead Congress. Wilson devised new techniques of exerting influence on Capitol Hill. When Congress met in April, 1913, at Wilson's request for a special session, he delivered his message in person, reviving a tradition that Jefferson had abandoned when he sent his messages in writing because he wrote much better than he spoke. Wilson presented his party leaders in Congress with a full legislative program, and he worked with them closely by frequent letters and conferences, both at the Capitol and the White House. With such techniques and with fair-sized Democratic majorities, Wilson was able to push through a notable series of laws during his first term.

The first order of business was the tariff. During the interregnum between election and inauguration, Wilson had consulted frequently with Oscar Underwood, Chairman of the House Ways and Means Committee. Underwood had worked out a new tariff bill on the basis of extensive hearings conducted during the last two years of the Taft administration and the special "popgun" tariff bills that Taft had vetoed. The Underwood bill sailed through the House without much difficulty. It provided for a significant lowering of the average duty and put many products on the free list. The bill fulfilled the old demand of Iowa insurgent Republican Cummins that protection be removed from trust-produced articles. At the instigation of Representative Cordell Hull of Tennessee, the House wrote into the bill the first income tax, under the Sixteenth Amendment, which Congress had submitted to the states in July, 1909, and which completed ratification in February, 1913.

Prospects in the Senate were dim, however, for a bill such as Underwood's despite the fact that it only decreased protection and fell far short of abandoning it. The Democratic majority of six Senators threatened to dissolve before insistence for more protection of regional commodities and before the intensive pressure of lobbyists. Wilson released a public statement denouncing the lobbies, and Senator Cummins got the Senate to launch a special investigation of them. LaFollette even successfully maneuvered the Senators into revealing their property ownership that had bearing on the tariff. The lobby investigation aroused public opinion for the Underwood bill and united the Democrats behind it. Thereafter it encountered little difficulty, although the Old Guard Republicans stalled its passage in order to rally opposition to the administration's banking measure, which was in the congressional mill at the same time. Senators LaFollette and Norris stiffened the income tax provisions a little. The final measure provided for a 1 per cent tax on all income, personal or corporate, over $4,000 plus a graduated surtax that reached 6 per cent on incomes over $500,000. The income tax provisions were purely for revenue rather than for changing the pattern of income distribution. The Underwood Tariff Act, the first significant lowering of the tariff wall since 1861, went into the statutes in October, 1913.

A little further background is necessary to understand the Wilson administration's banking law, the Federal Reserve Act of 1913. After Andrew Jackson killed the Second Bank of the United States, state-chartered banks issued currency which created considerable confusion because their bank notes were not of equal value. Civil War legislation creating banks with federal charters, "national banks," ended the chaos of several legal currencies but created some problems of its own. The national banks were empowered to issue currency on federal bonds up to 90 per cent of the market value of the bonds. The difficulty with the system was that it reversed the kind of elastic supply of currency needed in a modern economy. During boom times the market value of the bonds increased, thereby enabling banks to issue more currency and further stimulate the boom. When the reverse happened, banks had to recall loans and withdraw currency in order to meet the reduced market value of government bonds. The currency system did not help to compensate for business fluctuations; it made them more severe. Furthermore, under the National Banking Act the government had no control over bank-issued currency; its powers to regulate the currency were extremely limited except for Treasury greenbacks and silver certificates.

The panic of 1907 created a desperate currency shortage. The Aldrich-Vreeland Act of 1908 only partially met the issue of a shrinking currency during times of economic distress by permitting banks to issue bank notes on the security of bonds other than those bought from the federal government and, through national currency associations, even on ordinary commercial paper such as debtors' notes. A complicated tax on these bank notes made impractical their circulation for more than a few months. The Aldrich-Vreeland law also created a monetary commission, which Aldrich headed, to study and report to Congress upon the whole banking and currency system. In 1912 the commission recommended a permanent private reserve association to receive federal government deposits and to act as liaison between the government and the banks.

In late 1912 and early 1913, the House Democrats conducted a sensational investigation of their own, conducted by Representative Arsene P. Pujo of Louisiana. The Pujo Committee's counsel, Samuel Untermyer, dug out evidence showing that during the preceding few years Morgan and Rockefeller had effected an alliance which through interlocking directorates, consolidations, and the purchase of one another's stock had achieved nearly monopoly control over the nation's major credit institutions. The Morgan-Rockefeller group had 118 directorships in 134 banks with total resources of over $2.5 billion, thirty directorships in ten insurance companies with total assets of over $2 billion, and directorships in powerful noncredit institutions such as public utilities, transportation, and manufacturing. In total, the Money Trust, as it came to be called, had effective control of corporations with aggregate resources of more than $22 billion. The Pujo Committee revelations greatly increased the popular demand for regulation or dissolution of such aggregations of capital.

The political problem of what to do about banking and currency was difficult, largely because most people did not understand the whole issue very well, only knowing that the existing system was inadequate and controlled by the Money Trust; those who did understand the issue were largely bankers who had their own special economic interests to consider first. Three alternatives confronted Wilson and Congress. The Aldrich Commission's plan had been drawn by Paul M. Warburg of Kuhn, Loeb and Company, hardly a disinterested institution, and had the support of the American Bankers' Association. It called for one huge central bank, to be called the National Reserve Association, which would have branches all over the country and in many ways be similar to Nicholas Biddle's Second Bank of the United States. The central bank would hold government deposits, issue currency on gold and commercial paper, and hold member banks' reserves. In short, it would perform the activities later to be done by the Federal Reserve Banks but without any government regulation. Bryan and his wing of the Democratic party, plus a few Republican insurgents, demanded thorough government control of banking, a currency system owned and operated by the federal Treasury rather than privately owned banks, and the dissolution of the Money Trust. This group had gotten its views into the Democratic platform of 1912. The third plan came from conservative Democrats, most of them state-rights southerners. They wanted a decentralized scheme—Wall Street horrified them too—but under the private control of local bankers. The three schemes well typified the different points of view of business conservatives, progressives, and rural conservatives on matters of government and business.

Before inauguration, Wilson asked Carter Glass of Virginia, then a member of the House Banking Committee and later to serve in the Senate for many years, to draw up a banking bill. The original Glass bill was of the rural conservative type—private banking and currency but decentralized. Wilson asked him to add a federal supervisory board, which Glass did. When the Glass proposal became publicly known, the progressives were outraged. Secretary of State Bryan told his chief he could not support the measure; nor did Treasury Secretary William G. McAdoo or Robert L. Owen, Chairman of the Senate Banking Committee, like it. Wilson apparently did not fully understand the issues; he knew only that some kind of compromise would have to be made. In June, he consulted Brandeis who told him that Bryan was right. Throughout the summer of 1913, the congressional Democrats fought among themselves before Wilson was able to get most of them to agree to a compromise which did not really satisfy any group but was enough to unite the party. The House passed the greatly amended Glass bill in September by an overwhelming vote.

Now it was the bankers' turn to try to stop or emasculate the measure in the Senate. The American Bankers' Association at its convention denounced the Glass bill and had much of the conservative press on its side. Merchants saw the matter differently, however, probably because of remembered banker rebuffs when they tried to borrow money. The United States Chamber of Commerce approved the amended Glass bill. Three Democratic members of the Senate Banking Committee who were resisting Wilson on other issues delayed the bill, but they eventually relented and the Senate passed the bill by twenty votes in December. Wilson signed it December 23, 1913.

The final law provided that all national banks must belong to the Federal Reserve System; state banks were permitted to join if they wished. The act created twelve Federal Reserve Banks—one each in Boston, New York, Philadelphia, Cleveland, Richmond, Atlanta, Chicago, St. Louis, Kansas City, Minneapolis, Dallas, and San Francisco—owned by the member banks and operated by boards of directors, the majority of whom were elected by the member banks. The other directors were appointed by the central Federal Reserve Board, which was the capstone of the whole System. The seven members of the Federal Reserve Board were appointed by the president with the advice and consent of the Senate. The central Board was not empowered to set the discount rate of the twelve regional banks—that is, in effect, the interest rate member banks pay for its loans from the Federal Reserve Banks—but it could veto changes proposed by the regional banks. The regional banks issued currency of a new kind called Federal Reserve notes to member banks in exchange for commercial and agricultural paper and a 40 per cent gold reserve. The twelve Federal Reserve Banks were, in other words, the "bankers' banks." Federal Reserve currency was flexible in the right direction unlike the previous "reverse flexibility," but the government did not have the power to initiate action to compensate for fluctuations in the business cycle.

The Federal Reserve Act was indeed a compromise amongst the political-economic groups concerned. The bankers retained much of their plan, keeping private ownership and substantial private control, plus, at the last minute, a special banker-dominated Advisory Commission to work with the Federal Reserve Board. They yielded a degree of control and their demand for one centralized bank. The progressives gained a measure of government control. The farm conservatives got a degree of decentralization through the establishment of the regional banks. The agrarians won a point when the act empowered the member banks to receive Federal Reserve notes for discounted agricultural paper. (This was not adequate farm credit, however, and subsequently the Wilson administration saw through another rural credits measure.) Yet, with all its compromises, the final law was consistent with Wilson's stated New Freedom principles. Private business retained control, kept most of its "economic freedom," but the government could regulate to a degree, and concentration of power in banking was hampered although not destroyed. Perhaps most important in the long run, the Federal Reserve Act provided the basis of a system which a later generation could build upon to provide more effective federal regulation.

The New Freedom and the Trusts

Wilson got his administration off to a flying start with the Underwood and Federal Reserve Acts in 1913, but then the reform program lagged. During 1914 and 1915 Wilson resisted the efforts of reformers of all kinds to push the program forward. Two half-way measures concerning business, the Clayton Antitrust Act and the Federal Trade Commission Act became law in 1914, and the next year saw the passage, over considerable executive opposition, of the LaFollette Seamen's Act. But progressives were considerably exasperated with Wilson until early 1916, when for special reasons he again assumed the offensive and secured the passage of a spate of social justice measures.

There appear to be two reasons for Wilson's timidity, which became obvious in early 1914. First, the principles of Wilson's New Freedom seriously inhibited bold measures. Wilson at that time viewed the powers of the government as limited in economic matters, and he was not likely to advocate any thoroughgoing policies. A second reason was industrial depression. The business cycle started downward in the fall of 1913, became severe in 1914, and did not recover until 1915. The decline was worldwide, indeed seems to have started in Europe as credit tightened due to fear of war. When war came to Europe in August, 1914, the depression there soon lifted, as it did in the United States a few months later as war orders stimulated the American economy.

The depression was short-lived but rather severe. Unemployment ran as high as 20 per cent in the big cities in late 1914. But Wilson was fearful of alienating the business community, whose confidence in the federal government he deemed necessary for recovery. This accounts partly for his generally cautious attitudes toward the trust legislation then before Congress. He sought the friendship of businessmen; among the welcome guests at the White House were J. P. Morgan and Henry Ford. Attorney General James C. McReynolds with Wilson's approval began a program of showing corporations how they might operate to stay within the legal limits of the antitrust laws. A corporation that was apprehensive about some aspect of its structure or its operations being legal could go to Washington and receive the friendly advice of Department of Justice lawyers. Among the corporate giants that availed themselves of this free antitrust suit insurance were the New York, New Haven, and Hartford Railroad and the American Telephone and Telegraph Company. Wilson rewarded McReynolds for his services by making him his first appointment to the Supreme Court, where for twenty-seven years he wrote the kind of probusiness opinions that in the mid-1930's would precipitate a constitutional crisis.

Several bills concerning trusts were before the House in early 1914. The Clayton bill, sponsored by Representative Henry D. Clayton, would outlaw several unfair trade practices and make interlocking directorates and holding companies illegal. Another, identified with Representative James H. Covington, would create an interstate trade commission that would perform little more than the functions of Roosevelt's Bureau of Corporations to investigate business practices and aid the Antitrust Division of the Department of Justice. The third, sponsored by Representative Sam Rayburn of Texas and drawn with the help of Louis D. Brandeis, would have empowered the Interstate Commerce Commission to regulate the issue of new railroad stocks and bonds. The Clayton and Covington bills fell far short of the demands of a large minority of more radical Democrats and the insurgent Republicans. They wanted legislation to destroy the trusts rather than, at best, hamper their further development. They introduced a bill that would have brought the stock exchanges under strict government supervision and further proposed that any corporation or holding company that controlled more than 30 per cent of the production of its industry be presumed to be restraining trade and therefore illegal. The House of Morgan apparently believed these radical suggestions had political strength. On January 2, 1914, it announced its withdrawal from thirty directorships in other corporations.

Meanwhile, still another bill had been introduced in the House by Raymond B. Stevens, Democrat from New Hampshire, which had been drafted with the aid of Brandeis. It called for the creation of a Federal Trade Commission with powers to supervise business and prevent unfair business practices. It was a step in the direction of Roosevelt's New Nationalism and was not consistent with New Freedom principles. The United States Chamber of Commerce wanted something similar but different in intent: a federal commission to pass upon the legality of business practices in a friendly way such as Attorney General McReynolds was doing.

Wilson waited until the Clayton, Covington, and Rayburn bills passed the House in early June, 1914, and then summoned his leaders to the White House and announced that the Stevens trade commission bill would be the keystone of his trust program. Wilson had to use his persuasive powers to get conservative Senators to approve the section of the Federal Trade Commission bill that empowered the body to issue orders to business to cease and desist certain practices, but he did not fight Senate amendments which gave the courts broad review of FTC orders. The bill passed the Senate by an overwhelming vote, the House passed it a month later, and it became law in September. Wilson appointed the first commissioners in February, 1915. That Wilson did not intend for the FTC to be a vigorous regulator of business can be seen from his appointments, only one of whom, George Rublee, an associate of Brandeis, would have been a competent and militant regulator, and the Senate refused to confirm his appointment. Wilson's Secretary of Commerce, William C. Redfield, was happy that Wilson "hoped and expected" the FTC's restraining powers "to be of minor rather than of major use."

After endorsing the FTC idea, Wilson let the antitrust bills the House had passed be emasculated in the Senate. The Covington bill, of course, was irrelevant after the decision to enact the FTC. The Senate never passed the Rayburn bill at all, and considerably watered down the Clayton bill without protest from the White House. The more radical Democrats in the House had considered it weak brew even before the Senate's amendments. The Senate amended the Clayton bill by adding the words "where the effect may be to substantially lessen competition or tend to create a monopoly in any line of commerce" to its prohibitions of interlocking directorates, holding stock of a competing corporation, and exclusive selling or leasing contracts. Senator James A. Reed exaggerated when he called the original House bill "a raging lion with a mouth full of teeth," but he was not far from wrong when he called the final law "a tabby cat with soft gums, a plaintive mew, and an anaemic appearance." The Clayton Act became law in October, 1914.

The traditional historical view that the Clayton Act exempted labor unions from the operation of the antitrust acts persists in the face of the evidence. True, Samuel Gompers of the American Federation of Labor hailed the law as "labor's Magna Carta," but he must have known better even before the courts whittled away the minor concessions the act did grant labor. The Democratic platform in 1912 had promised unions and farm organizations exemption from the antitrust laws, but Wilson refused to go farther than a slight restriction upon the court's power to grant injunctions in labor disputes, a trial by jury in contempt of court cases, and agreement that unions did not illegally restrain trade when their procedure was lawful and in pursuit of a legal end. When these labor provisions of the Clayton bill passed the House, the AFL threatened to oppose the whole antitrust bill unless labor received more benefits. It put pressure on the Senate when the bill was in that chamber but won only a sentence added to the law that stated, "The labor of human beings is not a commodity or article of commerce." This amendment did not change trade unions' legal status despite the acclaim labor leaders gave the "labor commodity" sentence. The labor provisions of the Clayton Act did not alarm antiunion employers. The general counsel of the employers' American Anti-Boycott Association analyzed the labor provisions of the Clayton Act more acutely than did Gompers when the employers' spokesman said the measure "makes few changes in existing laws relating to labor unions, injunctions and contempts of court, and those are of slight practical importance." At any rate, the Supreme Court in the Duplex Printing case (1921) and the Coronado case (1922) made it clear that the Clayton Act was of no real value to organized labor.

Until 1916, organized labor actually had little to be happy about with the Wilson administration. In 1915, it won the LaFollette Seamen's Act but narrowly escaped a veto. The old law applying to sailors on merchant vessels reduced them to a status less than that of free labor. A ship's captain was its master. Violations of his orders were liable to interpretation as mutiny. Sailors were bound to their jobs by contract. Andrew Furuseth, an American sailor of Norwegian origin and president of the small Seamen's Union, had struggled for years to get Congress to change the law. In 1912, he won the support of Representative William B. Wilson of Pennsylvania, who became Secretary of Labor the next year, and Senator LaFollette. They got a bill through Congress, but Taft killed it with a pocket veto as he left the White House. LaFollette started the bill again in the new Congress and it passed the Senate in October, 1913. The bill would have released all sailors from labor contracts, including those who were the nationals of other countries when they were in American ports. This proposal was in violation of treaty agreements with all the maritime powers. Furthermore, an international conference on safety on the seas at London in November, 1913, established international safety standards not so high as those demanded by the LaFollette bill. The President thereupon reversed his original support of the seamen's measure and applied pressure on the Senate to ratify the safety Convention adopted at London. Ratification would have meant the end of the LaFollette measure. Progressives in the House went ahead and passed the LaFollette measure, and LaFollette persuaded his fellow Senators to ratify the London Convention only after making reservations that allowed Furuseth's measure to stand. The bill went to the White House. Wilson was inclined to give the bill another pocket veto when Secretary of State Bryan urged such action. LaFollette took Furuseth to meet Bryan, and the Secretary was much moved by Furuseth's account of the legal hardships of sailors. LaFollette agreed that Congress would allow the Department of State sufficient time to abrogate the old treaties and negotiate new ones, and Bryan changed his position. Still, Wilson very nearly let the bill die without his signature.

At the end of 1915, progressives could not find much beyond the Underwood Tariff to gratify them in the Wilson administration. The Federal Reserve Act had fallen short of progressive expectations, as had the antitrust measures. The President stated his opposition to a long-term rural credit bill which agrarians were demanding. He thought a child labor law would be unconstitutional and thus refused to support the one that had been introduced. He would not urge Congress to prepare a constitutional amendment to guarantee women the right to vote. His southern-dominated administration adopted policies that increased segregation in the Civil Service and limited Negroes to menial jobs. And, in November, 1914, Wilson made public a letter that declared the New Freedom had been consummated; this almost made explicit his belief that the era of progressivism had ended. But the politics of 1916 were to show that the progressive era was not yet dead.

The New Freedom Shifts toward the Roosevelt Vision

Wilson reversed his field in the winter of 1915–1916, and by election day in November, 1916, only a hair-splitter could see important differences between the New Freedom and the New Nationalism. In roughly the year before the 1916 elections the differences one by one disappeared—the differences between them about the federal government's powers and the differing views on social welfare legislation, trusts, labor legislation, and nationalism.

The political situation lay behind the Wilson administration's shift. As the presidential election approached, Wilson was forced to remember that in 1912 he had been elected by a minority (about 42 per cent of those voting) and that he had won because of the split in the GOP. Now it appeared that the Republican division was, if not actually healed, no longer bleeding. No astute politician expected a Bull Moose ticket in 1916. Furthermore, the Democrats had not done well in the 1914 congressional and state elections. Their majority in the House had been cut from seventy-three to twenty-five, although their margin in the more stable Senate remained the same, and they had lost the governorships of such important states as New York, New Jersey, Pennsylvania, and Illinois. Knowing they would be unable to capture the conservative Republican vote, the Democrats calculated that their best chance for re-election lay in trying to get as much of the 1912 Roosevelt vote as possible. To achieve that aim a program with a different emphasis was necessary.

Difficulties within the Democratic party also had to be resolved. The Bryan wing had become disenchanted with Wilson. In May, 1915, Bryan had resigned as Secretary of State over an honest difference of opinion with the President on a matter that Bryan feared would involve the United States in the European war. In the fall of 1915, Wilson determined on the preparedness program, as the strengthening of the military and naval establishment was generally called, and, early in 1916, he stumped the country to stimulate support for armament. This program, in itself Rooseveltian, encountered the opposition of Bryan, who wrote that he might oppose Wilson's renomination. Wilson feared Bryan might bolt the party altogether. Many of the militant advocates of social welfare legislation and woman suffrage also opposed the preparedness program. The way, obviously, to prevent possible disruption of the Democracy was to appease the dissenters with some of the domestic legislation they had long demanded.

Wilson indicated the direction in which he was moving on January 28, 1916, when he nominated Brandeis to fill a vacancy on the Supreme Court. He had considered appointing Brandeis as his Secretary of Commerce in 1913 but had been dissuaded by fears that the reaction of conservatives would be overwhelming. Their opposition in 1916 was formidable, but the White House brought pressure upon the Senate and in four months won Brandeis' confirmation.

Agrarian Democrats had long vigorously advocated a system of federally financed and operated credit institutions to make long-term loans to farmers at low interest. The agricultural paper provisions of the Federal Reserve Act had covered only short-term loans and provided no farm credit alternative to the banks. In 1914 and 1915, Wilson had successfully blocked the Hollis-Bulkley bill which embodied the rural credits demand. In late January, 1916, he called the bill's sponsors to the White House and informed them that if they would cut the government's maximum financial obligation to each of the twelve proposed federal farm loan banks to $250,000 he would use his influence to gain the plan's passage. They agreed, and the bill went through Congress with few dissenting votes. The Federal Farm Loan Act of July 17, 1916, created twelve regional farm loan banks controlled by the Farm Loan Board, composed of the secretary of agriculture and four others appointed by the president. The regional banks dealt with their farmer borrowers through national farm-loan associations, regular banks, or joint-stock land banks. Farmers were able to get mortgages of up to 50 per cent of the value of their farms at moderate interest. In the next fourteen years, the regional banks lent over $1.6 billion.

Related to farmers' interests was the passage of the Federal Highways Act, also in 1916. This measure, representing an assumption of federal power quite inconsistent with Wilson's earlier views, provided for federal control of expenditures for "national highways" and a system of financing in which the federal government matched dollar for dollar the appropriations of the states. The first highways to be built under the Act were the Lincoln Highway, now Highway 30, linking the two coasts, and the Dixie Highway, now Highway 41, linking the Great Lakes with the Gulf states. Two other dollar-matching schemes bear mention. In 1914, Congress passed the Smith-Lever Act which provided for federal-state cooperation in agricultural extension work, and in 1917, it passed the Smith-Hughes Act which established a scheme of federal dollar-matching for the costs of public school instruction in agriculture, commerce, and the so-called industrial arts. Both measures were a natural outgrowth of the Country Life Commission, appointed by Roosevelt in his last weeks in office, which was led by a remarkable agricultural scientist of Cornell University, Liberty Hyde Bailey.

Bryan Democrats and other social reformers who opposed preparedness were also mollified by the Revenue Act of 1916. An increase in revenues was necessary to pay for the armament program. Progressives insisted that the costs be financed by taxes based upon ability to pay and not be a burden to the poor. As one Congressman put it, "If the forces of big business are to plunge this country into a saturnalia of extravagance for war purposes in a time of peace . . . the forces of big business should put up the money." Some progressives advocated a surtax on incomes as high as 50 per cent. The final measure tax law fell far short of that, but it was high enough to bring cries that its framers wanted to "soak the rich." The act raised the normal tax to 2 per cent and increased the maximum surtax to 13 per cent. It also imposed a special tax on the capital and undistributed profits of corporations, a tax of 12.5 per cent on the gross income of munitions manufacturers who made more than 10 per cent profit, and an inheritance tax of up to 10 per cent.

The new Wilson program still lacked much to satisfy the left wing of the reform movement, those who demanded federal social welfare legislation. Wilson handled that matter with dispatch during the summer. The American Association for Labor Legislation, a typical reform organization, had long before drafted a model of a workman's compensation bill for federal employees. It had been introduced in Congress as the Kern-McGillicuddy bill and then forgotten. Wilson dug the bill out of the dead file and mustered support for it; it became law in August. He then moved on the question of child labor. Early in the Wilson administration the National Child Labor Committee, another typical progressive group, had prepared a model bill to outlaw child labor by prohibiting the interstate shipment of manufactured goods produced by firms employing children under fourteen years old, or products of mines employing people under sixteen, or any product made by companies that worked employees under sixteen for more than eight hours a day. In January, 1914, Representative A. Mitchell Palmer of Pennsylvania introduced the bill in the House where it died of inattention. Wilson held that the bill was unconstitutional. Representative Edward Keating of Colorado and Senator Robert L. Owen of Oklahoma reintroduced the bill in the new Congress, and it passed the House in February, 1916. It seemed likely to die again in the Senate. Few Senators were willing to work for the bill, and southern textile manufacturers and the National Association of Manufacturers strenuously opposed it, arguing it would violate their economic freedom to employ whomever they wished. Wilson said nothing about the Keating-Owen bill one way or another until mid-July when a group of Democrats informed him that progressives regarded the President's position on the bill as the litmus paper of his progressivism. The next day Wilson went to Capitol Hill to tell his Senate leaders that he wanted the bill passed and their action or lack of it might make a vital difference in the election. The Senate passed the bill twenty days later. Incidentally, Wilson's original view that the Supreme Court would not find the law constitutional proved to be correct. In 1918, in Hammer v. Dagenhart the Supreme Court voided the measure as exceeding the federal government's powers under the Constitution's interstate commerce clause. In 1919, Congress passed a second child-labor law, one that imposed a 10 per cent tax on the receipts of factories and mines employing children and engaging in interstate commerce. The Supreme Court overturned this second law in 1922 in Bailey v. Drexel Furniture Company. Thereafter opponents of child labor unsuccessfully fought for an antichild labor amendment to the Constitution.

But it was not only in the field of welfare legislation that Wilson moved toward Rooseveltian policies. At Wilson's insistence two economically nationalist provisions were added to the Revenue Act of 1916. One, insisted upon by business leaders, created a nonpartisan tariff commission to make close studies of imports and domestic production and make recommendations for tariff action to Congress. It was an effort, Wilson said, "to take the tariff issue out of politics." Actually, to remove the tariff question from politics was quixotic; the idea was really to make the tariff "scientific." The second provision also had to do with international trade, a prohibition of foreign manufacturers' "dumping" their surplus product in the American market in competition with domestic manufacturers. Just when competitive international commerce becomes "dumping" involves subtle and complicated semantics. It is easy for a manufacturer to cry "dumping" when he encounters foreign competitors in his domestic market. Still another, and in the long run more important, aspect of Wilson's 1916 program of economic nationalism was his sponsorship of a bill introduced by Representative E. Y. Webb of North Carolina that would have amended the antitrust laws to allow firms engaged in selling their products abroad to be exempt from antitrust suits so far as their international commerce was concerned. In 1916 this idea was too close to the Roosevelt vision of big state, big government, and big economic empire to be passed by a Democratic Congress. In 1918, however, another Democratic Congress passed it as the Webb-Pomerene Act.

Death of the Bull Moose: The Election of 1916

Although he was technically not even a Republican at the time, Theodore Roosevelt loomed largest in Republican thoughts when they considered the 1916 convention. In 1914, the Progressive party had made a feeble effort in the off-year elections and reaped even feebler results. Without Roosevelt to head their ticket, the Progressives had little appeal. Roosevelt quite obviously still wanted to be president, but few Republicans thought he would ride the Bull Moose again, so moth-eaten had it become in four years. Nor would GOP leaders grant their highest candidacy to a man who had committed the supreme sin of politics by bolting his party. Roosevelt's efforts to arrange a draft fell flat. Aside from Roosevelt's unforgiveable break with the GOP, his nomination would have been extremely risky because of his unusually belligerent attitude about the war. Roosevelt hated Wilson for what he considered his "spineless" support of "professional pacifists, the flubdubs and the mollycoddles." The ex-President was close to explicit demand for intervention as an ally of England and France. Such a candidate would not run well in the Midwest and West.

The Republican convention at Chicago nominated Charles Evans Hughes without incident. Many Republican leaders considered Hughes too much of a reformer for their tastes, but his nomination headed off any serious effort of less regular convention delegates to try to nominate Roosevelt. The distinguished looking Hughes had first held the national limelight in 1905 when he had led an investigation in New York of insurance companies. He was elected governor of New York in 1906 and again in 1908; in that office he had led an honest, efficient, and reforming administration. In 1910, Taft appointed him an associate justice of the Supreme Court where he remained until his nomination.

The Progressive party, or what was left of it, held its national convention in Chicago at the same time. Roosevelt actually was using the Bull Moose organization in an effort to influence the Republican convention to nominate him. The Progressives nominated Roosevelt once more. Roosevelt promptly declined the nomination and urged the Progressives to disband their party and support Hughes. Two weeks later the Progressive national committee declared the organization dead. Many of the Bull Moosers, however, did not return to the GOP. A small group of them met later and declared for Wilson. The week before the election, eleven of the nineteen members of the platform committee of the 1912 Progressive convention urged Wilson's re-election on the grounds he had fulfilled the 1912 Bull Moose platform. The whole Progressive rebellion and death had a major effect upon the Republican party. Roosevelt led many of the rebels out, but he could not lead them all back into the fold. The net result was that the Republican party lost just that much political progressivism. Despite the nomination of Hughes, the Republican Old Guard had won the battle with the Bull Moose and emerged stronger than ever.

The Democratic convention at St. Louis renominated Wilson and Marshall as a matter of routine. Wilson received the nomination by acclamation; there was not even a vote. The nomination, of course, was planned that way, but in another respect the convention did not behave according to plan.

Wilson had instructed his convention managers to make "Americanism" the theme of the convention. The keynote speaker dutifully began on that note but by accident set off an antiwar demonstration when he referred to Wilson's success at maintaining neutrality. Neutrality was obviously more popular than war among the Democrats. The campaign would demonstrate that in this respect the Democrats were representative of the wider public.

The campaign got off to a slow start. Hughes made a series of dull speeches and aroused little enthusiasm. Then in late August it got a stimulus from a threatened railroad strike and a new piece of labor legislation. In the spring of 1916, the railroad brotherhoods had presented management with a demand for an eight-hour day with no reduction in wages for employees who operated trains and time-and-one-half for all overtime. Management refused. Mediation attempts at regular collective bargaining sessions failed to get results. In mid-August, Wilson held two conferences with railroad presidents at the White House and pleaded with them to accept a formula which had already won union acceptance: an eight-hour day, no special overtime pay, and a special commission to study the problems of railroad labor. The railroad managers refused despite Wilson's somewhat emotional presentation of his case. The brotherhoods set September 4, Labor Day, for a national rail strike.

The day after the strike call, Wilson went to Capitol Hill and strongly urged a law providing for his formula for all train-operating railroad labor in interstate commerce. Four days later, Wilson had the Adamson Act, and the railroad unions called off the strike.

Needless to say, the Adamson Act strengthened Wilson's attractiveness to labor, but it also united the business community against him more solidly than it had ever been before. Hughes rode the issue hard, asserting that Wilson had surrendered to a class interest in pursuit of votes. Wilson defended himself by saying that a rail strike would be economic disaster and that the railroad workers deserved an eight-hour day. Indeed, Wilson vigorously defended all the progressive measures of his administration, most of which were only recently enacted. Hughes, torn between fear of losing his conservative support and failure of attracting the progressive vote, hedged on the Wilson social welfare measures and thereby lost the support of most progressives.

On election night, the returns from the East indicated a Hughes sweep. The Republican candidate went to bed thinking he was the next president of the United States. When he awakened the next morning, however, the issue was in doubt. In the Midwest and West the vote was exceedingly close. Hughes, for example, carried Minnesota by only 392 votes. When all the returns were in Wilson had won by a narrow margin. He had 277 electoral votes with 9,129,606 popular ballots; Hughes had 254 electoral votes and 8,538,-221 popular ones. The Democrats gained two seats in the Senate, but they did not have a House majority; neither did the Republicans have a majority in the House. The balance of power was held by five Representatives: two Progressives who no longer had a party behind them, one Socialist (Meyer London of New York City), one Prohibitionist, and one independent.

How to account for the Wilson victory? He gained almost 3 million votes over his 1912 poll. It appears that he received much of the vote that had gone for Roosevelt in the previous election. He also received, probably, the votes of most of the 315,000 voters who had marked their ballots for Debs in 1912 but had not seen fit to support the weak Socialist candidate of 1916,

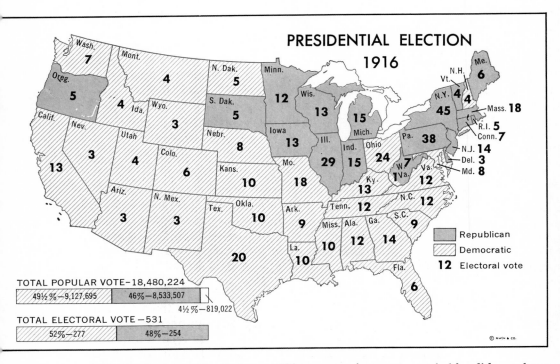

PRESIDENTIAL ELECTION
1916

Republican
Democratic
12 Electoral vote

TOTAL POPULAR VOTE—18,480,224
49½%—9,127,695   46%—8,533,507
4½%—819,022

TOTAL ELECTORAL VOTE—531
52%—277   48%—254

Allen L. Benson. The Debs-to-Wilson vote, however, probably did not have much bearing in the electoral college. Hughes carried most of the states where the Socialists had strength, except for Oklahoma which was traditionally Democratic. Some historians have made much of an alleged snub that Hughes gave Hiram Johnson when he toured California. Hughes and Johnson stayed at the same hotel in California. Hughes did not know Johnson was there, and the two did not confer. When Hughes later discovered the situation, he wrote Johnson to apologize, and Johnson accepted it. California went Democratic by a small margin, and its thirteen electoral votes provided the margin of victory. It appears, however, that it was not the supposed snub but the San Francisco labor vote that decided the California poll.

But why did Wilson get more of the vote of independents and progressives in 1916 than in 1912? Surely, the progressive record of his White House term was an important factor. Whether it was more important than the peace issue is impossible to say. Wilson did not himself ride the neutrality issue during the campaign. His party, however, recognized the good political capital that could be made of the fact that the United States had not become involved in the war which had been in progress in Europe for twenty-seven months before election day. It raised the slogan "He kept us out of war," and the slogan clearly won many votes. Every time Roosevelt stumped for Hughes and demanded more vigorous national action in the European conflict he helped Wilson's election. In sum, Wilson won on both issues with a progressive-peace combination. He won because he had moved close to Roosevelt's position on domestic policies but was not identified with the Rough Rider on foreign policy.

CHAPTER FOUR

Business, Agriculture, and Labor, 1900-1917

IN THE PREVIOUS TWO CHAPTERS THERE NECESSARILY WAS DISCUSSION of certain economic developments that occupied the limelight of national politics. But such incidental discussion of economic history is insufficient to understand the early twentieth-century economy. We must focus on the economy itself in order to get a fuller understanding of American society at that time. Let us observe the businessman, the farmer, and the laborer, the people who made and distributed the wealth that was the material basis of American life.

Business: The Corporation and "Finance Capitalism"

Any count of all the businessmen in the country any time during this period would have shown that the great majority of them were proprietors or associates in small enterprises. Most retail establishments were small operations of little capital, and these small businesses dominated retail trade. In towns of under ten thousand population practically all retail businesses were individually owned and operated. The mail-order house, the department store, and the chain store, however, were beginning to make inroads in the retail field. Mail-order retailing had begun in 1872 when Montgomery Ward and Company was founded; Sears, Roebuck, and Company came soon thereafter to sell primarily to farmers. Conventional retail merchants found it difficult to compete with mail-order houses for many commonplace articles because they could not buy in such large lots. The costs to the mail-order customer were cut further in 1912 when post offices began to accept parcels. Department stores were limited to the larger towns and the cities; but the proprietors of small shops in competition with them deeply resented such huge stores as those of John Wanamaker in Philadelphia and New York and Marshall Field in Chicago because they were inherently unable to match the big store with its greater choice of merchandise at prices as good or better than the shopkeepers'. Chain stores were not yet important except in the "five and dime" and tobacco fields, but chain grocery and meat retailing had made a start. The Kroger chain had started in the early 1880's, and when George Hartford died in 1917 he left over three thousand branches of his A & P.

Outside the distributive and personal service fields, however, the small businessman was economically unimportant. The corporation dominated manufacturing, extractive industries, and transportation. In the last generation of the nineteenth century, the corporation had surpassed individual ownership in these fields. The census of manufactures of 1909 found that corporations produced just under four-fifths of the nation's total manufactured product, and in the basic industries and those that required large amounts of capital, corporations turned out practically all the goods. Corporations completely dominated railroads, the primary means of transportation. The amount of capital required in railroading was far beyond any individual's power to raise.

Outside the basic industries, it is true, many—in fact, most—of the manufacturing corporations were relatively small. Their stock, or most of it, was held by only a few investors, sometimes by two or three families. Frequently their stock could not be bought through the stock exchanges. Although the number of such corporations was great, together they accounted for only a small part of the total manufactured product. In 1909, to repeat a census statistic, 1 per cent of all the manufacturing firms in the nation, corporate or otherwise, produced 44 per cent of all manufactured goods.

The drive toward bigness in manufacturing was inexorable. The corporation with huge capital resources could buy the machinery and make other technological innovations that enabled it to mass produce. Mass production cut the cost for each unit produced, and the saving could either be passed on to the consumer or accrue to the manufacturer in greater profits or both. The small manufacturer without matching technology simply could not compete. The machines necessary to match his competitor were expensive because, there being usually no mass market for such products, there was no mass production of them. Open-hearth furnaces could not be bought from a catalogue, and even such standard items as drill- and punch-presses were not produced in huge numbers, let alone special-order machinery. The small manufacturer, therefore, had five choices. Two of them took him out of the field of small manufacturing: he could raise the capital necessary to become as efficient as his competition, which made him a big manufacturer and which made him dependent upon bank credit or Wall Street firms that raised capital by selling stocks and bonds; or he could combine with his competitors through any of several ways to eliminate or minimize their competition. His third choice was to escape competition by finding some niche of the market that was small enough for his big competitors to ignore. For example, if he were in the steel spring business, he might arrange contracts to supply surgical instrument manufacturers with some items of special specifications. His fourth choice was to get out of the business, sell out for the best price he could get and invest his capital elsewhere. His fifth alternative, trying to meet his competitors on their terms until he was bankrupt, was really no choice at all.

The depression of 1893 and thereafter intensified competition. As the market shrank, firms had to scratch harder for enough orders to keep going. Many were unable to do so and quit altogether. But the really huge firms, the "trusts" such as Standard Oil and American Sugar Refining, not only came through the depression but made good profits. The lesson was obvious: consolidate. The task was made the easier by the bankruptcy of the weakest firms during the depression. The five years from 1898 through 1903 saw an unprecedented growth of huge industrial combinations, many of them taking advantage of an 1899 New Jersey law that made the holding company easily and legally formed. At the beginning of 1904, 236 of the nation's largest 318 corporations, representing more than $6 billion in capital, had been formed since the beginning of 1898. Put in another way, only about one-fourth of the biggest 318 corporations were more than five years old. In certain industries the degree of concentration, most of it recently formed, was more striking. In 1898 and 1899, almost two hundred independent steel firms combined through a complicated chain of eleven mergers; then in 1901 came the creation of United States Steel. By the end of 1901, almost all the nation's railroad systems had become consolidated into the control of six groups. Railroad consolidators had no intention of stopping where they were. Harriman frankly told the Interstate Commerce Commission in 1906 that his goal was to get control of all the railroads. Morgan and Rockefeller, through the New Haven Railroad, in the next decade came very close to getting a full monopoly of all freight transportation in New England, not only of railroads but of electric interurbans and coastal shipping as well.

The frequency of Morgan's name in this discussion points to another important development: the growth of what usually is called "finance capitalism," or the shift of control from manufacturers, those who actually produced material things, to investment bankers who bought and sold stocks and bonds. High finance was complicated and even its vocabulary puzzled the ordinary outsider, but the methods by which investment bankers achieved control of huge corporations were essentially simple. When a manufacturing or railroad corporation needed large amounts of capital, the only place it could turn was to big commercial banks, most of them in the East, and to investment banking firms like J. P. Morgan and Company; Kuhn, Loeb and Company; Lee, Higginson and Company; or Kidder, Peabody and Company. These firms had large amounts of capital of their own to invest, and they raised money for corporations by selling securities to the public. The banker used his control of the necessary capital to get one or more seats on the corporation's board of directors and thereby gained a voice in its management. The banker well understood the advantages of industrial combination, and, again using the leverage his capital or access to it provided him, brought competing corporations together into huge industrial empires.

A brief sketch of some of the activities of the House of Morgan from the beginning of the century to the war will indicate the power a big investment company could acquire. In railroads Morgan controlled the Northern Pacific and the Great Northern from Chicago to the Pacific Northwest, the Southern, the Reading with its rich coal holdings, the Erie from the Atlantic coast to Chicago, and the New Haven. His railroad holdings were almost one-fourth the nation's rail capitalization. The House of Morgan had directorships in United States Steel, International Harvester, General Electric, and lesser manufacturing corporations. The National Bank of Commerce was fully under Morgan control, and the First National Bank of New York was partially controlled by Morgan. Morgan control extended to three of the largest life insurance companies, New York Life, Mutual Life, and Equitable Life, which bought millions of dollars in stocks and bonds each year and provided Morgan a ready place to sell corporation securities.

Rockefeller's Standard Oil Company made such great profits—40 per cent a year for each year of the century's first decade—that he was not dependent upon bankers for capital. Indeed, he reversed the process and got control of banks, the most important ones being the National City Bank and the Hanover National Bank, both of New York. He then went on into other industries: Colorado Fuel and Iron Company and Amalgamated Copper Company in mining and smelting, Public Service Corporation of New Jersey in interurban electric trolleys, and the Union Pacific and Southern Pacific railroads. The Rockefeller interests had allies in Edward H. Harriman and the Kuhn, Loeb and Company investment house. When the Morgan and Rockefeller interests began to work together in 1907—the Money Trust—their power was shockingly great to a generation that could remember when a million-dollar corporation was a wonder of the world.

Manufacturing, Transportation, and Technology

The Ford Motor Company was a striking exception to finance capitalism. Henry Ford, born on a Michigan farm in 1863, had absorbed some of the agrarian ideas of his generation such as pacificism and militant opposition to bankers and Wall Street. He believed that bankers, in the interest of immediate profits, would force him to abandon his purpose of producing an inexpensive car for the mass market. Ford, therefore, avoided getting his capital from regular credit institutions. He even managed to keep the ownership of most of the company's stock and plowed the profits back into expansion.

Ford's contribution to the automobile industry was to develop a car within the price range of millions of consumers and to develop mass production to a fine point through the assembly line. The two contributions were dependent upon one another. By 1900, the automobile, mostly a European invention, had developed to the point that it began to look more like a contemporary car than a horseless buggy. The engine was in front, the transmission carried the power to the back wheels, and it was steered by a wheel instead of a tiller. Steam and electric battery powered cars were popular, but the internal combustion engine had evolved into a fairly reliable power plant. But automobiles were still for the rich. Ransom Olds had experimented briefly with a standard, mass-produced car, but his financial backers forced him back to the conventional market. By 1908 Ford had developed a car that he thought capable of being mass produced for a modest price, the Model T. The next year he announced he would produce Model T's exclusively. By concentrating on one inelegant but utilitarian model with no choice of color, he could sell the first Model T's for $950. In 1913-1914, Ford adopted the assembly-line technique and quickly developed it to a high degree of efficiency. The system was tricky because a failure at any point in the intricate system stopped production entirely, but Ford made it work, and the saving in cost per unit of production was striking. By the war a Model T cost only $360.

By any reasonable esthetic standard the Model T was a failure. It also had mechanical deficiencies. The owner ran the risk of breaking his wrist when he cranked it (self-starters were optional equipment at extra cost); it had a fiendish capacity to break down at inconvenient moments; its fuel lines worked by gravity, and the driver had to go up steep hills in reverse if his gasoline supply was low; it had a tinny, flapping noise that made conversation difficult. But the Model T was cheap, easy for the amateur to repair, and got passengers where they wanted to go, after a fashion. Other manufacturers began to mass produce, although they concentrated on slightly more expensive cars of better quality, and automobiles soon became common. Car registration statistics are not accurate reflections of car ownership because many states did not bother to register cars and issue licenses until years after their citizens drove autos, but they nevertheless give some indication of the automobile's growing popularity. In 1900, there were 4,000 cars manufactured and 8,000 registered; 1905, 25,000 and 78,000; 1910, 187,000 and 468,000; 1915, 970,000 and 2,446,000; 1920, 2,227,000 and 9,232,000. In 1916, one-sixth of the cars on the road were Fords. Mass production had brought the automobile age, and the social implications of this transportation revolution were endless.

The assembly line system was only one aspect of the movement early in the century of mechanizing industrial production and making it efficient. The emphasis upon industrial efficiency is sometimes called "Taylorism" after a pioneer of efficiency engineering, Frederick W. Taylor. Taylor began his career with the Bethlehem Steel Company in 1898 and soon had a host of industrial "efficiency expert" colleagues. Their basic idea was to improve efficiency by eliminating waste motion through the proper placing of steps in the production process in the factory, through training the worker to make all his motions apply to the production task at hand, and, later, through simplifying design. The principles of efficiency engineering were valid methods of increasing total material wealth by achieving maximum use of machine and human resources in a minimum amount of time. Where the principles were applied they brought the results Taylor said they would. Working men, however, mistrusted and resented the "efficiency expert," who timed workers with a stop watch and made notes on their work motions. They felt that he was spying upon them and that his methods amounted only to a "speed-up." Certainly, Taylorism did tend to dehumanize work and to reduce the worker to a machinelike cog while on the job.

American and European inventors brought the airplane into being in the first decade of the century. Samuel P. Langley, secretary of the Smithsonian Institution in Washington, received a $50,000 grant from the War Department to work on a heavier-than-air plane powered by a small steam engine. He previously had successfully flown miniature models of such a craft. In the fall of 1903, Langley made two unsuccessful attempts to fly his plane across the Potomac River. In December of that year, the brothers Orville and Wilbur Wright, bicycle mechanics from Dayton, Ohio, made man's first successful flight in a heavier-than-air plane. Their craft was powered by an internal combustion engine. The first flight at Kitty Hawk, North Carolina, where they had gone to take advantage of the strong winds, lasted only twelve seconds, the second flight only fifty-nine seconds. They returned to Dayton and within two years had developed their plane until they had made several flights of thirty minutes. Not until they returned to Kitty Hawk for further demonstrations in 1908 did they receive much publicity. By the war, Europeans had developed the airplane into a serviceable but still dangerous means of transportation. It was not until the 1930's, however, that airplanes were mechanically reliable and powerful enough to be used for commercial passenger traffic on a significant scale.

Far more important than aviation during the early years of the century was greater efficiency in the generation and transmission of electric power and in using this power for lighting, industry, and transportation. By 1900, the basic inventions had been made; the problem was to perfect them, to make electric power inexpensive enough to be practicable, and to transmit it greater distances. By 1914, there were five thousand power stations over the country and electric power could be carried 150 miles or more. It was not cheap by today's standards, but for many uses it was less expensive than other kinds of energy.

By 1919, almost one-third of the power used in industry was electric, but only a few factories used electric power exclusively. Steam power is incapable of being transmitted great distances, a fact which forced industrial management to build large factories and cluster all of their power equipment around one steam plant, rather than to decentralize. This situation, plus dependence upon railroads for freight transportation, led to the concentration of factories in relatively small districts.

Electric lighting was fairly common in factories, offices, and the homes of the wealthy city dweller by 1900. The urban worker, however, was much slower in getting electricity in his home because of the initial expense of wiring and high electric rates. High rates led to a demand for public regulation of power companies similar to the demand for railroad regulations. Virginia in 1901 was the first state to establish a public utility commission to set electric rates; New York, Wisconsin, and Georgia followed in 1907. A few cities and towns took matters into their own hands and built municipally owned power stations. Most farmers simply did without electricity until the mid-1930's.

Electric streetcars were the main means of public transportation in the cities throughout this period. Richmond, Virginia, in 1888 became the first American city to have an extensive streetcar system, but other cities followed the example of the Confederate capital in the 1890's. In the early 1900's, trolleys became something of a craze, and traction companies, which frequently corrupted city officials for street franchises, overbuilt. Real estate men connived with traction officials to extend their lines out to their edge-of-town developments. Then the electric railway men began to build lines between cities, especially from large cities into the suburbs. By 1914, it was possible to travel from New York City as far as Sheboygan, Wisconsin, north of Milwaukee, by "interurban," if one were willing to put up with innumerable changes of cars. The regular railroads moved against this competitor when possible and bought up interurban electric lines. About the same time, New York City exerted pressure upon the New Haven and the New York Central to use electric locomotives on trains coming into Grand Central Station because of the steam engine's smoke nuisance. Railroaders found the electric trains cheaper to operate and quicker to accelerate.

New York, Chicago, and Boston had elevated steam railroads by the beginning of the century, but they too were a nuisance because of their dirt and their sprinkling of oil and cinders upon the streets below them. During the first decade of the 1900's, all three cities changed to electric elevateds. At about the same time, New York began its subway system. Construction on the Seventh Avenue subway began in 1900, and in 1904 it was open from City Hall Park to 145th Street and Broadway. The next year, Brooklyn became connected to Manhattan by a subway under the East River.

The Farmer, 1900–1917

In dealing with history of agriculture, one should remember that American agriculture is startlingly diverse and that what may be true of agriculture in general may not be valid for some special kind of farming. The New Jersey truck farm owner growing vegetables for the New York City market, the Mississippi cotton sharecropper, and the Iowa corn and hog farmer may have no more in common economically than the board of directors of General Motors, the United Mine Workers of America, and a manager of a small factory manufacturing mattresses for a local market. The American farmers' production methods, capital, and market arrangements differ enormously.

In general, these years were prosperous ones for American farmers, quite in contrast to most years from the Civil War to the war with Spain. So good was this period on the farm that the period 1909 to 1914 was later regarded as being a time when agricultural prices were in proper balance with other prices, and the goal of federal agricultural subsidies was to achieve that balance again. Farm prices increased nearly 50 per cent from 1900 to 1910. The prices farmers had to pay for their purchases also increased but not so rapidly. As farming became more profitable than it had been, the value of farm property increased. The average price of farm land increased from just under $20 an acre in 1900 to almost $40 in 1910. The value of farm land and buildings increased from $16,614,647 in 1900 to $34,801,126 in 1910 and to $66,316,003 in 1920. Much of the increase in farm commodity prices was attributable to a great increase in the population, particularly the nonfarm population, which provided a larger domestic market for farm produce. Between 1900 and 1910, the population increased almost 16,000,000, and in the next decade it rose another 13,738,354. In both decades the increase was greater than it had been in the 1890's. During the first twenty years of the century the number of farms, the total acreage of farms, and the farm population also increased, the latter, however, at a much slower rate than the urban population. Indeed, the percentage of the national population classified as rural by the Bureau of the Census declined from 60 in 1900 to 54.2 in 1910 to 48.6 in 1920. Since the Bureau classified towns of under 2,500 as rural, the decline of the percentage of the actual farm population to the total was actually greater.

Some of the increase in the number of farms was due to reclamation of marshes in the Midwest. To drain a marsh required a great deal of capital, but the rich muck land reclaimed would for several years produce surprisingly large yields. Since muck land was expensive, much former marsh land was owned by land companies rather than individuals. The companies frequently worked the land with poorly paid labor from Mexico and the more depressed parts of the Appalachian South, with the anomalous result that some of the worst rural poverty was to be found on the richest land. Much of the increase in farms was due to the federal government's liberalizing the laws pertaining to the federal domain. In 1909, Congress passed the Mondell Act, which increased the maximum homestead size from 160 to 320 acres for land which had no timber or known valuable minerals. This Act was a recognition of the fact that the old Homestead Act of 1862 with its quarter-section grants was not applicable to dry farming, which required a larger tract of land to support a family. The Mondell Act did not require the homesteader to live on the land, as had the original measure, but the homesteader had to show evidence of successful cultivation to "prove up." In 1912, Congress lowered the residence requirement for other homesteaders from five to three years. Late in 1916, Congress passed the Stock-Raising Homestead Act, which increased the size of a homestead to a full section, 640 acres, in areas that were suitable for grazing but not for irrigation. There was no residence requirement, but the homesteader had to improve the grant by adding $800 to its value. The government reserved to itself mineral rights, cattle paths, and water holes. The wide use of the Homestead Act as amended indicates that the western frontier did not actually close in 1890 as is generally thought. From 1898 to 1918, the federal government granted more land to farmers of various kinds than it had from 1878 to 1898. Furthermore, many United States farmers from the Great Plains moved north into the Canadian prairie provinces, where exceptionally fertile virgin soil was still available for nothing.

Despite the decline in the number of farmers relative to domestic consumers of farm products, the farmers continued to raise more than the rest of the American population could consume. The United States remained an exporter of agricultural products, although such exports declined from early in the century until the war which sharply reversed the situation. The fact was that relatively fewer farmers were producing relatively more than they had when they were proportionately more numerous. The trend continued after 1920, when the absolute numbers of farmers began to decline. By mid-century a sharply decreased number of farmers produced far more than ever before. Increased production came from scientific agriculture, such as improved breeds of plants and animals and better fertilizer, and from the mechanization of farming, which tremendously increased the amount of work a farmer can accomplish in a day. Scientific farming and mechanization, both of which began long before, became more generally used from 1900 to the war. Government, state and federal, played a major role in developing more productive plants and animals and in diffusing knowledge of new methods among the farmers. The Department of Agriculture, after the Smith-Lever Act of 1914, brought its extension work directly to the farmer through county agents and farmer institutes. Schools of agriculture in the state universities not only conducted important agricultural research which directly affected farm production, but each year turned out increasing numbers of young men who were far better informed farmers than their fathers had been. Some university schools of agriculture established special "short courses" to teach scientific farming methods directly to dirt farmers.

Tractors began to be used in significant numbers during this period. In 1916, American manufacturers made nearly thirty thousand gasoline-powered tractors and sold most of them in the United States. Earlier, there had been experiments with steam tractors, huge machines which could pull forty plows. But they had serious disadvantages. They required a ton or two of coal and two or three thousand gallons of water for a day's work, which had to be hauled to the tractor by horse and wagon. But even the early gasoline tractors were less than satisfactory. They were very large by today's standards, their horsepower was not commensurate with their size, their steel wheels were equipped with lugs or cleats that chewed up roads but still did not provide good traction, and they were expensive. The farmer had to debate long and seriously whether or not it would pay him to buy a tractor. He could buy two or three teams of horses for the price of a tractor and he already had the equipment he needed for horses. Horses also could be used for many more jobs around a farm than the early tractors could. On the other hand, a tractor would enable him to take land out of pasture and feed and use it for his cash crop. Only a few farmers bought tractors before the war. The farm horse population reached its peak in 1918, and in 1920 fewer than 250,000 tractors were in use. But although the number of tractor-operated farms was fairly small, they produced a significant part of the total crop, particularly of wheat. Even with the tractor's disadvantages, operators of wheat farms of a thousand acres or more of fairly flat land found that tractors cut their production costs, and the big farmers, though not numerous, produced an increasing share of the annual production.

The lower production costs of mechanized farms made it difficult for the farmer of marginal land farther east to compete. New England farm acreage decreased about 10 per cent in the first decade of the century and more rapidly thereafter. At the same time, the rural population of the eastern part of the Midwest declined by the Census Bureau's classification of rural, as did the rural population of the Middle Atlantic states in the next decade, but this may tell us as much about the growth of small towns as it does of farming population.

Farmers continued to engage in politics after Populism died out in the late 1890's. Even before Populism was dead such organizations as the Farmer's Union, which was strong from northwestern Wisconsin to the Rockies, the American Society of Equity, the Equity Union, and the Gleaners had come into being, mostly to lobby for their interests in state politics. Farmers of several states organized state associations, and the Grange remained strong here and there throughout the country. In 1910, representatives of several state organizations organized the Farmers' National Headquarters in the nation's capital for lobbying purposes. This organization embodied some of the old Populist demands such as government ownership and operation of the railroads as well as such principles as direct election of senators, parcel post, and federal rural credit, all very much a part of the progressive movement. In 1917 still another national farm lobby, the National Board of Farm Organizations, began operations in Washington. The purpose of these organizations was to create a powerful political voice for the farmer, to be for agriculture what the National Association of Manufacturers, the United States Chamber of Commerce, and the American Federation of Labor had become for business and labor. The American Federation of Farm Bureaus, founded in 1919, became a most powerful spokesman for agricultural interests.

The American Federation of Labor

American workingmen had formed themselves into trade unions since the late eighteenth century. Efforts to unite local and craft unions into a single national labor organization, however, were quite unsuccessful before the Civil War and less than fully accomplished after the sectional conflict. The National Labor Union, founded in 1866, disappeared in the panic of 1873. The most noteworthy national labor union of the period was the Knights of Labor, organized in 1869, which became a force of considerable proportions after it won a railroad strike against Jay Gould's lines in the early 1880's. In the late 1880's, however, the Knights also began to fade and by 1900 were of no significance. The American Federation of Labor had replaced it as the primary organization of American workers.

The AFL organized as the Federation of Organized Trades and Labor Unions of the United States and Canada in 1881 by uniting into one body the several independent national trade unions already in existence. It reorganized and adopted its new name in 1886. The prime mover of the AFL and its president each year but one until his death in 1924 was Samuel Gompers of the Cigar Makers Union. The son of a Dutch-Jewish tailor, Gompers was born in London in 1850. His education had been achieved through the cigar makers' practice of paying a fellow worker to read aloud to them while they worked at their silent craft. Gompers left his stamp on the American labor movement as did no other person. His principles of labor organization were the AFL's until long after his death in 1924, and the labor movement still has essentially the Gompers view of its mission.

Under Gompers' leadership the labor movement changed both its objectives and its methods. The shift in objectives was particularly significant. Previous national labor organizations had reform of the economy as one of their primary goals. Under the existing capitalist economy, labor had reasoned, the workingman got less than his fair share of his product, and, therefore, it should be the objective of labor organizations to change the economic system to one more consistent with their interests. In the late 1820's and early 1830's, labor had advocated various kinds of pre-Marxian socialism. The Knights of Labor had encouraged the spread of producer and consumer cooperatives to create a labor and farmer island in the rest of the economy. Gompers held that labor should accept the existing economy but endeavor to get from it a larger share for labor in the form of better wages, better hours, and better working conditions. Reform was illusory, he argued. The goal of a fundamental economic reorganization probably would fail, and even if it should succeed the day of victory could not be soon. Better, he thought pragmatically, to take from the existing order all that could be obtained. So long had American labor worked toward a noncapitalistic or anticapitalistic goal—and labor elsewhere in the western world continued to do so—that many people outside of the labor movement found it difficult to believe that the AFL's only objective was an ever-improving status for labor within the existing economic framework. Many employers saw the AFL's "pure and simple" trade unionism—sometimes called "bread and butter" unionism—as the opening wedge of some kind of socialism. But it was not. Indeed, the traditions of American labor have been a major factor in the maintenance in the United States of a capitalist economy, although a usually flexible kind of capitalism that has been modified as material conditions have changed. When the labor movements of Britain, Scandinavia, and the Continent continued their socialist objectives, the ultimate abandonment or extreme modification of their capitalist economies was perhaps inevitable.

With the AFL's goal being what it was, it logically followed that it should put its emphasis upon economic action—upon collective bargaining—rather than political action. The idea of a labor party or a farmer-labor party, such as the Knights had worked for, became irrelevant. This did not mean that the AFL had no interest in politics at all; it meant that its political activities would be restricted to advancing or protecting organized labor's "pure and simple" economic activities. As Gompers put it, labor's political role should be "to reward its friends and punish its enemies," and the touchstone of friendship and enmity was the politician's willingness to allow unions to operate in the economy without governmental handicaps, and, sometimes, his willingness to use government's powers to help labor in its "pure and simple" economic goals. Gompers and the AFL, actually, saw government in much the same way that most businessmen saw it: as a force to be used opportunistically for a practical purpose and not as a vehicle to utopia.

AFL unions sought their members' economic improvement through control of the job. This was a goal to be achieved through bargaining with the employer, the union representing the employees. Bargaining was to be terminated with the mutual acceptance of a written labor contract, which would set the terms of all matters affecting labor in the shop. The union would be in its best bargaining position if it had a monopoly of the industrial skills the employer needed. The AFL, therefore, worked to establish union-controlled apprenticeship systems, state and local government licensing of labor in certain trades where there was a conceivable public health and welfare interest, and immigration restriction. To secure future monopoly control of the job, unions sought to obtain from employers in their contracts a "closed shop" agreement, which would require the employer to hire only union members. Next best from the union's point of view was a "union shop" agreement, which gave the employer latitude as to whom he would employ but required all employees to join the union. Many employers sought to maintain "open shops," which granted no rights or privileges to the union.

Almost all the AFL affiliates were "craft unions" of skilled workers because control of the labor supply was easier to effect when the required industrial skills automatically eliminated most men. In an industry with a simple production process, such as cigar making, a craft union might represent practically all employees, and the same might be true in a more complex production process characterized by subcontractor employers, such as building construction. But the craft system of organization broke down for an industry with a complex process and large number of unskilled or semiskilled employees. In an automobile factory, for example, there were some skilled workers (*e.g.*, tool and die workers) but the vast majority were relatively unskilled employees on the assembly lines. The unskilled were difficult to organize for several reasons: they were easily replaced, a large proportion of them did not speak English and were difficult to communicate with, and many of them were of a rural background, either European or American, without trade union tradition and frequently with an animosity to unionism. Women workers (19 per cent of all females over ten years old were gainfully employed in 1900) were also difficult to organize, primarily because they did not expect their jobs to be their long-term careers. It is not true that Gompers and other AFL leaders opposed organizing unskilled workers, but they did not try hard to do so. As they saw labor's long-term goals limited to improvement within the existing economic order, they felt the need to organize the unskilled was not as great as it would have been had the goal been to change the rules of the economic game. The only important "industrial unions"—those which embraced all the employees of an industry no matter what their trade or lack of it—in the AFL were the United Mine Workers, founded in the 1880's and the International Ladies' Garment Workers Union, formed in 1910. The Amalgamated Clothing Workers of America, an industrial union in the men's clothing field formed in 1914, was not admitted to AFL membership because parts of it had seceded from the United Garment Workers, an AFL affiliate.

The AFL was organized in a decentralized, federal manner. The American *Federation* of Labor was a loose coalition of almost autonomous national unions (or "international" unions if there were Canadian locals) without power to direct the decisions of its constituent parts. It was organized somewhat like the British Trade Union Congress. The main advantage of decentralization of power was that decisions were made in each union where the leaders knew the situation. The AFL thereby avoided the worst blunders that the highly centralized Knights of Labor sometimes made in strike strategy. On the other hand, the disadvantages of decentralization were that the central body was almost powerless to settle disputes between unions—usually "jurisdictional disputes" over whether workers at a given task should be members of one union or another—and to discipline organizations that were unethical and whose poor reputation damaged labor generally.

In 1900, the total membership of AFL unions was 548,000. In the next four years unionism grew rapidly; AFL membership was about 1,000,000 in 1902 and 1,676,000 in 1904. Employers at this point let loose a massive counterattack and prevented further union membership gains until 1911; indeed, total union membership declined slightly. By 1917, the AFL's membership stood at about two million.

Outside the AFL, but similar to it in philosophy and tactics, were the four railroad unions: the Brotherhood of Locomotive Engineers and similarly named organizations of trainmen and firemen, and the Order of Railway Conductors. When the railroad brotherhoods wrenched the Adamson Act from Wilson and Congress in 1916 (see p. 65), they had about four hundred thousand members.

Trade unions were not able to enroll more than a very small part of the total labor force, never more than 8 to 12 per cent of the gainfully employed during this period. A few industries, however, were well organized, especially railroads and breweries. The International Typographical Union had only about one-third of all printers, and in large and basic industries such as iron and steel, textiles, and automobiles union membership was almost nil.

In well-organized industries labor was able to earn a decent living; in the least organized industries the living conditions of most workers were quite poor. In 1915 the majority report of the President's Commission on Industrial Relations stated that from one-third to one-half of the families of workers in mining and all manufacturing "earn in the course of a year less than enough to support them in anything like a comfortable and decent condition." Hours of work were long. In 1914, the average of all workers was 55.2 hours a week. Industrial accidents were frequent. In 1913 an estimated twenty-five thousand workers were killed and seven hundred thousand seriously injured while at work. The states were slow to enact laws to provide safety and health regulations in industry, and what laws existed frequently were ignored. A great tragedy such as the Triangle Shirtwaist Factory fire in New York City in 1911 was necessary to stir government to action. In that fire 148 women were burned or trampled to death in a loft building without adequate fire escapes. If the fire department regulations had been observed, it is unlikely that there would have been a fire at all.

The Employers' Counterattack

A rather small number of businessmen looked upon trade unions, if not with favor, at least with a feeling that they were inevitable. Recognition of organized labor and the labor contract, they argued, was the best way to industrial peace and uninterrupted production. If American labor adopted the Gompers view and accepted capitalism, then capitalists, they believed, should accept labor organizations. In 1901, a group of employers with such views met with labor leaders and founded the National Civic Federation. Its president was Marcus A. Hanna, whose business credentials were unimpeachable. One of its vice-presidents was Samuel Gompers. The National Civic Federation, through its publicity, worked to bring about better harmony between capital and labor and volunteered to serve as a mediator in labor disputes. Labor radicals, such as Eugene Debs, had only contempt for the Hanna-Gompers alliance, holding that conflict between capital and labor was inherent. To Debs, Gompers' role in the National Civic Federation amounted to a sell-out of the working man. Most businessmen regarded the National Civic Federation as Debs regarded Gompers.

Most employers, and, indeed, a large part of the public in general, had views of the relationship of capital and labor that had been formed in a pre-industrial, precorporate age. All decisions in the operation of a business, according to them, were the exclusive prerogative of the man or men who owned and operated the business; this included all decisions affecting labor such as hours, wages, and working conditions. Neither employees, whether individually or collectively, nor government had any proper right to inhibit management in any of its decisions. Critics of their point of view asserted that if such laissez-faire ideas ever had any relevance and justice it was in an age before large concentrations of capital employed large concentrations of labor. Antiunion employers replied that their views were consistent with natural law; the Reading Railroad's George F. Baer even argued, as we have seen on p. 34, that employers' prerogatives were divinely inspired. A Pennsylvania employer well summarized these views about business and labor and business and government when he had carved in stone on a building he had given to LaFayette College the quotation, "Is it not the law that I may do what I will with mine own?"

In the early years of the century, employers counterattacked labor unions in a variety of ways. First they organized. In 1900, employers of Dayton, Ohio, formed the first citywide employers' association to fight what it called "restrictive" trade union practices. It fought the closed shop with such success that within two years it had routed organized labor from Dayton. Its most effective weapons were its propaganda program for the open shop, dubbed "the American plan" in its literature, and the blacklist. The blacklist was a boycott of individual laborers. An employee suspected of union activity would be fired and put on the blacklist, and other employers thereafter refused to hire the man. The "Dayton Plan" found imitators elsewhere. Soon there were similar organizations in Chicago, Indianapolis, Louisville, and other midwestern cities. By 1903, these antiunion employers had become a national organization. They assumed control of the National Association of Manufacturers, organized in 1895 to encourage exports of manufactures. The NAM lobbied for its position in Washington and the state capitals with considerable success, especially in the states. It poured money into political campaigns to defeat candidates it considered too prolabor. In 1904, two of its targets, a Senator and a Representative, went down in defeat.

Employers also made increased use of professional labor espionage and strikebreaking companies. The most important of these, the Pinkerton Detective Agency and the Burns Detective Agency, had come into being in the late nineteenth century. These companies had other functions, such as the detection of theft of company property, but a large part of their work was against union activity. The labor spy sought any union office which had access to membership lists and turned the names over to employers for the blacklist. Sometimes the detective became an *agent provocateur* and incited union men to illegal activities that brought in the police. If these methods were not successful and a union did come into being and strike, the companies provided professional strikebreakers whose strongarm methods often insured the success of a "back to work" movement.

Employer associations used their influence in state legislatures to create an antiunion state police system or to convert an already existing police organization into an antiunion weapon. Municipal police usually could be counted upon to "preserve law and order" successfully, which for all practical purposes meant to use their force on the employer's side in a labor conflict. The most efficient and best known of the new state police systems was the Pennsylvania State Constabulary, founded in 1905, a mounted police whom coal miners called the "Cossacks" and generally known as the "coal and iron police." Pennsylvania employers found the state organization desirable since many labor disputes occurred in tiny coal mining communities which had no more than a skeleton police system. Union men nearly universally found government's police power arrayed against them. Particularly obnoxious to unions was the frequent use of state militia, and sometimes even the federal regular army, to break strikes.

In such an atmosphere of determination and desperation in industrial relations, it was not surprising that a great deal of violence accompanied labor disputes. Labor relations were particularly violent in the West where the law of the six-shooter was still a sharp memory. The ordinary citizen who relied on the usual newspaper for his information thought that violence came altogether from labor's side, from "trouble makers" and "agitators," but actually both sides were guilty of gross violence. Labor resorted to violence, for example, when two professional dynamiters, the brothers John and James McNamara of the International Association of Bridge and Iron Workers, blew up the Los Angeles *Times* building in 1910, killing twenty-one people. In the long series of conflicts between miners and operators in Colorado's Cripple Creek district, both sides used violent methods as a matter of course. Management in Cripple Creek had greater firepower in the state militia and won. At Ludlow, Colorado, in 1914, in a strike against Rockefeller's Colorado Fuel and Iron Company that became a small civil war, state militiamen machine-gunned and set fire to a strikers' tent colony, killing eleven children, two women, and six men. These were among the more celebrated cases of violence. Lesser conflicts aroused no more than local attention. A writer for a religious magazine in 1904 calculated that in the preceding thirty months, a period of relative quiescence, 180 union men had been killed and 1,651 injured in labor disputes.

Unions had little recourse in law as usually interpreted by the judiciary. Indeed, the courts became one of management's most effective weapons, both defensive and offensive, in its resistance to labor organization. The labor injunction—that is, an order by a judge enjoining labor unions and leaders from doing certain things or ordering them to do others—was a formidable weapon. The two most famous labor cases during this period were the Danbury Hatters' case and the Buck's Stove and Range case. In 1902, the United Hatters of North America called a strike against a Danbury, Connecticut, hat manufacturer, D. E. Loewe and Company, and then organized a national boycott among their members against Loewe's products. Loewe got the money to finance a law suit from the American Anti-Boycott Association, formed in 1902 largely by the Dayton employers' association. The employer brought suit against the union and its officers in the federal courts, charging violation of the Sherman Antitrust Act. The case was in the courts for fourteen years before it was finally settled. It went to the Supreme Court three times. The Supreme Court held that an interstate boycott was a conspiracy in restraint of trade contrary to the Sherman Act. Loewe won triple damages from the union and its officers totalling $252,000. The company attached the bank accounts and homes of the local union officials, but before the properties could be sold in satisfaction of the judgment, the AFL persuaded the company to accept $235,000 in cash and call an end to the affair. It was because of such cases as the Danbury Hatters' that labor eagerly sought congressional exemption from the antitrust laws but won only a token victory in the Clayton Act of 1914.

In 1906, long before the Danbury case was settled, metal polishers of the Buck's stove factory in St. Louis struck for a nine-hour day. They appealed for help from AFL headquarters, which investigated and added the Buck's Stove and Range Company to its "We Don't Patronize" list in the AFL's magazine, *The American Federationist*. The president of the stove company, James W. Van Cleave, a union-hating small manufacturer of the old school, obtained a labor injunction from the District of Columbia court of Judge Daniel W. Wright. Wright enjoined Gompers and his fellow AFL officers, John Mitchell and Frank Morrison, not only to remove the stove company from its "We Don't Patronize" list but also not to express themselves about the case either in writing or orally. The stove company came off the list, but the enjoined officers expressed themselves about the case in no uncertain terms. Thereupon, Judge Wright sentenced Gompers to a year in jail and the others to lesser terms for contempt of court. The AFL appealed to the Supreme Court. Van Cleave died while the case was still under appeal, and the new officers of the company, eager for industrial peace, requested Judge Wright to dismiss the injunction. Wright did so, but held that the power of the courts to punish the contempt was not prejudiced by the dismissal. He then appointed a committee of three lawyers whose labor views he knew well to recommend whether the contempt punishment should be prosecuted or dismissed. The carefully selected committee recommended prosecution. In 1914, the Supreme Court finally dismissed the suit on the grounds that the statute of limitations had expired, leaving the constitutional questions involved unanswered.

The labor injunction, when combined with another device, the "yellow dog" contract, could practically outlaw efforts to organize labor. A "yellow dog" contract was an agreement between an employer and an employee that the employee would not join a union. Occasionally the contract was written; usually it was verbal. Sometimes it was no more than a notice on the wall of the foreman's office. Researchers in labor history have found no employer suits against an employee for breach of a "yellow dog" contract. That was not their purpose. The "yellow dog" provided the legal excuse for an injunction to prevent labor organizers from doing anything whatsoever to organize employees under such contracts, for to attempt to organize would be, in law, an effort to break a contract. It was a preventative rather than a punitive antiunion device. At one time, coal mine operators and judges in West Virginia so blanketed their state with "yellow dogs" and labor injunctions that United Mine Worker organizers could be in the state legally only if they stayed on the public roads.

Confronted at almost every turn by hostile government power, the AFL slightly modified its nonpartisan politics rule. Gompers had steered the organization clear of politics during the Populist era, but now he saw no other alternative. In 1906, the AFL supported union members who ran for the House of Representatives and helped elect six of them. But labor support could hurt as well as help. Employers came to the financial aid of opponents of labor-backed candidates, and frequently their support was enough to provide victory. Also in 1906, the AFL presented President Roosevelt with a Bill of Grievances which asked for labor exemption from the Sherman Act and limitation upon judges' power to issue labor injunctions. In 1908, Gompers went to the Republican national convention to ask the platform committee for a plank promising exemption from the antitrust law. He was told to "go to Denver," where the

Democrats were soon to meet. The Democratic platform committee inserted a not altogether acceptable labor plank, and in the campaign the AFL constantly attacked Taft's labor record, thereby aiding Bryan. In 1912, Gompers and other AFL leaders campaigned for Wilson. Not until the war, however, did the AFL gain anything significant from the Wilson administration, and not until the 1930's did labor gain encouraging federal laws. It is easy, however, to make too much of the AFL's political activity early in the century. Its monetary support of candidates was always small, it never organized a political action committee to get out the labor vote, and it was, in general, ambivalent about labor politics because of Gompers' fear that political action would only fail and result in government antiunion action.

Left-Wing Unionism and Socialism

Gompers' views on labor's acceptance of capitalism, craft unionism, and political action were anathema to a considerable number of working men and intellectuals in the political and trade union left wing. The most important left organizations of this period were the Socialist party and the Industrial Workers of the World.

Marxian socialism of some kind or another goes back in American history to as far as 1857, and for a while in the early 1870's, Karl Marx's First International maintained its headquarters in New York City. Not until the 1890's, however, did socialism attract more than a handful of people to its organizations. The Socialist Labor party, under the leadership of Daniel DeLeon, began to grow and made an unsuccessful effort to capture the AFL. Socialist Laborites and other AFL dissidents were able to depose Gompers from the AFL presidency for the year 1894–1895, but the cigar maker came back so strongly that DeLeon gave up on the AFL and established a separate organization in 1895, the Socialist Trade and Labor Alliance. DeLeon was dogmatic in his social theories and difficult to work with personally, and he soon faced a rebellion in the Socialist Labor party led by Morris Hillquit, a young immigrant labor lawyer. At the same time, a quite separate socialist movement was growing in the Midwest. When Eugene Debs was in jail serving the contempt of court sentence that grew out of the 1894 Pullman strike, Victor Berger, an Austrian immigrant high school teacher who led a socialist group in Milwaukee, visited Debs and converted him to the socialist vision. When Debs was released he announced he was a socialist although he actually behaved like a left-wing Populist for another three years. In 1900, the Hillquit group from New York and the Berger-Debs group ran Debs for president, and he received about ninety-five thousand votes, roughly twice the Socialist Labor party's poll. The following year these socialists met at Indianapolis and formed the present Socialist party.

The Socialist party enjoyed a remarkable growth its first few years. Debs ran for the presidency in each election until 1920 except for 1916 and received a larger popular vote each time. His highest percentage of the vote came in 1912. In that year, thirty-three American cities had Socialist mayors, the most important cities being Milwaukee, Schenectady, New York, and Berkeley,

California. In 1910, Milwaukee elected Berger to the House of Representatives. Several national unions and locals in the AFL had Socialist leadership and a fair following in the rank and file, especially among the brewers, the machinists, and the needle trade workers, but the Socialists were never able to control national AFL policy. The Socialists, however, were badly divided among themselves, and, lacking the patronage and professional politicians of the major parties, were constantly in danger of flying apart. Within the party were a remarkable number of outstanding intellectuals, urban trade unionists who were both radical and relatively conservative, and a considerable group of Populistic farmers. Their emphases and their styles were vastly different. Their ideological range was wide. Among them were extreme revolutionists not averse to industrial sabotage. Others were urban intellectuals not much different from the more radical progressives. Still others were tub-thumping Great Plains agrarians who spiced their socialism with a kind of social evangelism.

It was largely the forceful personality of Eugene Debs that held the party together. Debs, originally a locomotive fireman from Terre Haute, Indiana, was an unusually warm-hearted, generous, and impulsive man whose socialism was more of the heart than of the mind. Whether among poor farmers at a Socialist camp meeting in Oklahoma (which had a larger dues-paying Socialist membership in 1910 than any other state), addressing a mass meeting of immigrant needle trade workers in Manhattan's Union Square, or spending a social evening with a small group of party intellectuals, he charmed those about him and inspired political devotion. Yet, in the end, not even Debs could keep the Socialists together. After the 1912 party convention, when the Socialists amended their constitution to exclude those who advocated violence and sabotage, the organization began to crumble.

The Industrial Workers of the World, generally known as the IWW or the Wobblies, had their founding convention at Chicago in 1905. At first the IWW was a conglomeration of the left. Debs was one of the founders, as was DeLeon. But Debs dropped out soon and DeLeon was expelled in 1908. The main leader of the Wobblies was William D. "Big Bill" Haywood, a one-eyed, fire-eating revolutionist miner from Montana. He had led his Western Federation of Miners out of the AFL and formed the American Labor Union, a radical competitor to the AFL, before he helped establish the IWW. After 1908, the Haywood leadership dominated the Wobblies.

The main core of IWW strength was among transient workers, those who worked in the threshing crews that followed the wheat harvest north through the Great Plains, the lumberjacks, other agricultural workers, and casual laborers of the West. Exploited, homeless, apart from the routine of family and community life that makes conformists of most men, these Wobblies had a militant hatred of capitalism and its institutions. Unlike most Socialists, who believed in attaining their goal through elections and then legislative action, they had only scorn for the ballot box; their goal was to organize all workers into "one big union," strike simultaneously and thereby stop the capitalistic productive process, and then establish an economy run entirely by the workers. Until the day of reckoning arrived, they would fight the bosses, organize the unskilled, and militantly defend their rights to speak and be heard. Over and over again the Wobblies became involved in "free speech fights" in western cities. They would descend on a town and begin to hold street meetings. If the police arrested them, more would come into town, conduct meetings, and invite arrest until the jail was full. When the jail expenses became high enough, the local authorities would relent, whereupon the Wobblies would pick a free speech fight in another city.

The IWW probably never had more than about sixty thousand members at the peak of its strength, but it proved in two big strikes in the East that it made up in militancy what it lacked in numbers. In the textile mills of Lawrence, Massachusetts, more than twenty thousand workers, most of them immigrants, struck against a pay cut in 1912. Their appeals to the AFL craft unions to help them organize got them nowhere, and they turned to the IWW. Haywood and Joseph Ettor, another IWW leader, went to Lawrence and took over direction of the strike. Management and the police were frightened by the IWW's reputation and soon resorted to desperate measures that brought death and bloodshed. A Lawrence businessman had dynamite placed around the city, "discovered" it, and charged the IWW leaders with terrorism. Ettor and another strike leader, Arturo Giovanitti, were arrested. When the "frame-up" was discovered, public opinion swung toward the strikers. The IWW also shrewdly exploited public opinion by arranging to send the children of strikers out of the city to sympathizers elsewhere, saying the children's safety required it and their parents did not have the money to feed them adequately. The Lawrence police roughly, but unsuccessfully, tried to stop "the flight of the children" with clubs when the youngsters were assembled at the railroad station, which again rallied public opinion against the factory owners. Eventually management raised wages, and the strike was won. The next year, the IWW led a strike of the silk mill workers of Paterson, New Jersey. All the advantages lay with the owners in this battle, but for five months the IWW was able to keep the strikers in line and stop production. In the end, short rations among the strikers forced them to accept defeat.

Even when the IWW won a major strike, as it did at Lawrence, it was unable to maintain itself. The Wobblies scorned a wage contract as a bargain with the devil, and after they won a fight they lost interest and moved on to look for another promising conflict. A few months after the Lawrence victory, the IWW was practically gone from the city and conditions in the mills were almost what they had been before the strike. Had there been a blend of the AFL unions' businesslike approach to labor questions with the Wobblies' eagerness to fight, business would have been confronted with a strong adversary indeed.

The IWW began to fade after the Paterson strike, although it maintained most of its strength in the Far West. The war and its aftermath practically killed the organization. The IWW opposed the war, and the government responded with repression and prosecution which deprived it of its most effective leaders.

The IWW and the Socialist party were the high tide of American radicalism. Neither of them attained major power nor majority support, although each was stronger than is generally remembered. The reasons for their failure are complex, and one can best study the reasons by comparing American society to other industrial nations of the western world where socialism and labor syndicalism ran a different and more successful course. But failures though they were, each of them left an imprint on America. The Socialists brought social questions and new ideas to the intellectual marketplace and succeeded in modifying others' opinions. In time, people who by no means accepted the Socialist position and assumptions about society came to accept the less radical demands of the prewar Socialists. The IWW's impact on the labor movement worked both to advance and retard labor organization. On the one hand, it thoroughly alarmed many people, some of whom thought it best to make concessions to more conservative labor and some of whom reacted by stiffening their resistance to all labor organizations. The IWW also confused the whole idea of industrial unionism with radicalism, and the two did not necessarily have a relationship. On the other hand, the IWW's record indicated that it was possible to organize unskilled, poorly educated, and ethnically divided workers into an effective union. Another generation would build strong industrial unionism for a purpose quite different from the IWW's goal.

CHAPTER FIVE

The People
and the Quest
for Social Justice

MANKIND, PERHAPS FORTUNATELY FOR HIS MENTAL HEALTH, HAS A great capacity to blur the memory of past unpleasantness. If one would believe fully the memories of many people who came to maturity between 1900 and 1917, they would think that those indeed were the good old days. The girls were prettier, the men were more manly, moral standards were higher, life had little discord, and people went their idyllic ways to the accompaniment of a picturesque barbershop quartet softly singing "In the Good Old Summertime" or "The Shade of the Old Apple Tree." Certainly, the picture is not altogether false. The pace of life was slower, war did not weigh upon the national consciousness, most people believed the world, and particularly the United States, was steadily becoming a better place to live and had some evidence to support their contention, and people had greater confidence than they have had since World War I about what the balance of their lives had in store. The literary historian, Van Wyck Brooks, had justification for naming the period from 1885 to 1915 *The Confident Years*.

But memory distorts. Historical evidence indicates no idyll, no utopia, for the early twentieth-century years or any other time. American life was full of tension and anxieties, and conflicts were many—between immigrants and Americans of riper vintage, between Negroes and Caucasians, between capital and labor, and between reformers of all kinds and standpatters. American life also, particularly in the cities, was beginning to acquire a frenetic and commercial quality.

Immigration and Immigrants

America had always been a land of immigrants. Every American family, except for the few Indians, sometime or another had come from abroad, and from the late seventeenth century forward, America had been peopled by families from several parts of Europe and Africa. First there had been English, then Scotch-Irish and Germans, and always a sprinkling of people from other European nations. By the time of the American Revolution, foreign travelers remarked that one characteristic which set Americans off from other nationalities was that they were a heterogeneous people, a mixture of cultures. In the pre-Civil War generation there had been a huge wave of immigration. Much of this influx was composed of British whose backgrounds were not greatly different from those of Americans, but there were also many Germans and swarms of Irish. After the Civil War had come another immigrant wave, and nations who had previously sent only a scattering of people to America's shores vastly increased their contribution. Hundreds of thousands of Scandinavians debarked at eastern ports in the 1870's and 1880's. Immigration from Germany reached its peak in the 1880's, when 1,450,000 Germans came to the United States.

But with the twentieth century came the largest immigration wave of all time. Between 1860 and 1900, the total number of immigrants had been slightly less than 14,000,000. Between 1900 and 1915, the total was over 14,500,000, close to one-fifth of what the total population had been in 1900. In 1907 alone, the peak year, immigration amounted to 1,285,000, and in six of the years between 1905 and 1914 the total was over 1,000,000. In 1910, about one-seventh of the total American population had been born abroad and about as many more were offspring of immigrant parents. In New England and the Middle Atlantic states, more than half of the inhabitants were either foreign born or second generation. In the big cities, where most of the immigrants settled not necessarily from choice but because they did not have the capital to begin farming, the ratios were higher. In 1910, 78 per cent of New York City's population was first- or second-generation immigrant, Chicago's percentage was the same, and in Boston, Philadelphia, Pittsburgh, and St. Louis more than half of the population was no more than one generation away from Europe.

In the 1880's, there began a shift in the source of immigration. Great Britain, Germany, and the Scandinavian countries sent more people to America than ever before, but for the first time large numbers began to arrive from eastern and southern Europe, from areas that on today's maps are marked as Russia, Poland, Czechoslovakia, Jugoslavia, Hungary, Bulgaria, Rumania, Albania, Greece, and Italy. In the 1890's and thereafter, immigrants from the former traditional sources declined in number, and the human tide from eastern and southern Europe became a flood.

The change in the nature of immigration alarmed many Americans, including some of those whose families had only recently come from northwestern Europe. They were fond of pointing out that the "new immigration" was overwhelmingly non-Protestant, mostly Roman or Orthodox Catholic or Jewish. Most of the "new immigrants" were desperately poor and had been since birth which in the lands from which they had come doomed them to little if any formal education. They were ignorant of formal culture, had little in their background to equip them for work in industry or life in a city, and many were illiterate. About 27 per cent of all immigrants between 1899 and 1909 were unable to read or write their native language; over half of the new

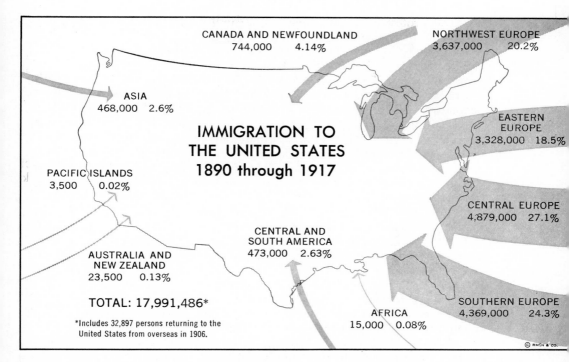

IMMIGRATION TO
THE UNITED STATES
1890 through 1917

CANADA AND NEWFOUNDLAND
744,000   4.14%

NORTHWEST EUROPE
3,637,000   20.2%

ASIA
468,000   2.6%

EASTERN
EUROPE
3,328,000   18.5%

PACIFIC ISLANDS
3,500   0.02%

CENTRAL EUROPE
4,879,000   27.1%

CENTRAL AND
SOUTH AMERICA
473,000   2.63%

AUSTRALIA AND
NEW ZEALAND
23,500   0.13%

SOUTHERN EUROPE
4,369,000   24.3%

TOTAL: 17,991,486*

AFRICA
15,000   0.08%

*Includes 32,897 persons returning to the
United States from overseas in 1906.

© RM N & CO.

Americans from southern Italy were illiterate. Perhaps a third of them intended to be "birds of passage": spend a few years in American factories, save their money, and retire to the old country to live on a plane somewhat higher than they had before emigrating. Large numbers of them did in fact return, sometimes disillusioned, sometimes satisfied. Interestingly, many of those who returned to what is now Jugoslavia took new last names to indicate their American experience, and names like Chicagovich became not uncommon. Nativists made much of the "differences" between the "old" and "new immigration," but what differences existed were greatly magnified. Practically none of the "old immigrant" Irish had been Protestant, almost all were poor and ignorant, and many of them regarded the United States as only a place to strike it rich for a return to the "auld sod." The same was true of many of the south Germans, indeed of many of those who had been peasants anywhere in Europe. But whether based on fact or not, nativists insisted that the "new immigrants" were impossibly and dangerously different, and immigrants of the new wave faced far greater opposition, discrimination, and injustice than had any previous immigrant group with the possible exception of the Irish.

The roots of nativism were many and deep. Some of the opposition to immigrants sprang from sheer irrational prejudice against the unfamiliar and unknown. Some of it arose from religious conviction. Since the Reformation, the Protestants of Europe had regarded Catholics *ipso facto* as either dangerous agents of reaction if they were educated and powerful, or superstitious, fawning dupes of "papistry" if they were not. And America had become, despite the Irish, an overwhelming Protestant nation. Since long before the Reformation, the Jews had been frequent victims of prejudice, and after that religious upheaval Protestants and Catholics, both in America and Europe, had perse-cuted and discriminated against Jews solely because they were Jewish. Some nativism grew from the ideas of race that were then considered established by the best scientific investigation. It was an age when anthropologists ranged over Europe with calipers and notebooks recording the ratio between the length and width of men's heads. Their conclusion was that long-headed people were inherently superior to round-headed unfortunates. Southern Euro-peans, so the supposedly best scientists of humanity said, were given to shifti-ness, untruthfulness, and crimes of passion; Jews were inherently sly and crafty, hated physical work, and were greedy; Slavs were basically stupid and stoic. Such racial stereotypes were widely and firmly believed, and examples of such thinking are easily found in the literature, both scholarly and fictional, of the early twentieth century.

Some of the opposition to immigration was as much a fear and distrust of the poor as it was anxiety about nationality. Related to this thinking was alarm that immigration furnished the votes for corrupt political machines. Still another and by no means insignificant source of nativism was the economic motive. Organized labor consistently supported immigration restrictions be-cause its leaders believed that only by stopping the flow of new labor which would work for lower wages than were prevalent could the American work-ing man achieve a decent living standard. Thus nativism ran from many dif-ferent parts of American society. The Boston Brahmin Henry Cabot Lodge, erstwhile Harvard history professor and a powerful United States Senator, helped to organize the Immigration Restriction League in 1894. Samuel Gomp-ers, himself an immigrant and the antithesis of Lodge, lobbied to stop the immigration flow. Chauncey Depew asserted that immigrants were dangerous radicals, prepared to "cut our throats and divide our fortunes," and some agrarian radicals argued immigrants were reactionary agents of Rome or of "Jewish international bankers." A conservative intellectual like Madison Grant could agree with a radical intellectual like the sociologist E. A. Ross that immigration was deplorable and that as the immigrants married and mixed their genes with native Americans there would be a "Great Dilution" of American strength and character.

The situation of millions of immigrants arriving in a nativist society created tensions that easily exploded into violence. Fist fights, minor riots, and street gang conflicts growing from immigrant-nativist animosity were com-mon, and sometimes especially ugly incidents developed. Violence arising from prejudice further deepened prejudice. The generation felt intensely about what it called "the immigrant question."

Advocates of immigration restriction gradually moved toward their legis-lative goal. First to be seriously restricted were the Chinese and Japanese. In 1882, Congress, primarily at the urging of Californians, passed a ten-year ex-clusion measure later extended and made permanent in 1902. The 1902 act also denied Chinese already in the United States the right to become naturalized. As a consequence of Chinese immigration becoming illegal (although certainly some Chinese came despite the laws) and of a preponderence of males in the Chinese-American population, the numbers of Chinese declined. The census of 1890 showed 107,000 Chinese in America, and the next two counts showed 90,000 and 70,000 respectively. Labor had led the fight for Chinese exclusions,

J. P. Morgan, Sr.
(1837–1913)

William Jennings Bryan

Philadelphia & Reading Railway Company.
Presidents Office.
Reading Terminal, Philadelphia. 17th July 1902.

My dear Mr. Clark:-

I have your letter of the 16th instant.

I do not know who you are. I see that you are a religious man; but you are evidently biased in favor of the right of the working man to control a business in which he has no other interest than to secure fair wages for the work he does.

I beg of you not to be discouraged. The rights and interests of the laboring man will be protected and cared for - not by the labor agitators, but by the Christian men to whom God in His infinite wisdom has given the control of the property interests of the country, and upon the successful Management of which so much depends.

Do not be discouraged Pray earnestly that right may triumph, always remembering that the Lord God Omnipotent still reigns, and that His reign is one of law and order, and not of violence and crime.

Yours truly,
Geo. F. Baer
President.

Mr. W. F. Clark,
Wilkes-Barre,
Pennsylvania.

George F. Baer's "divine right" views
during the anthracite coal strike
STATE HISTORICAL SOCIETY WISCONSIN

Theodore Roosevelt in a characteristic pose   BROWN BROTHERS

Senator Robert M. LaFollette about 1915   STATE HISTORICAL SOCIETY WISCONSIN

Coeds in the dormitory of a state university, 1900   STATE HISTORICAL SOCIETY WISCONSIN

Climbing into America. Slavs arriving at Ellis Island, 1905
LEWIS W. HINE FROM THE GEORGE EASTMAN HOUSE COLLECTION

Eugene V. Debs speaking at a Socialist meeting   UNITED PRESS INTERNATIONAL

Low Library, Columbia University   CULVER PICTURES, INC.

Child labor in a South Carolina textile mill, 1909
LEWIS W. HINE FROM THE GEORGE EASTMAN HOUSE COLLECTION

Immigrant family making artificial flowers at home, 1912
LEWIS W. HINE FROM THE GEORGE EASTMAN HOUSE COLLECTION

The streets of New York, 1912
LEWIS W. HINE FROM THE GEORGE EASTMAN HOUSE COLLECTION

A well-equipped saloon

An industrial suburb before World War I

Woodrow Wilson

Ford's first assembly line, November, 1913
STATE HISTORICAL SOCIETY WISCONSIN

A part of the Armory Show, New York, 1913
COURTESY THE MUSEUM OF MODERN ART, NEW YORK

Marcel Duchamp, *"Nude Descending a Staircase"*
COURTESY PHILADELPHIA MUSEUM OF ART, LOUISE AND WALTER ARENSBERG COLLECTION

A rather good ungraded school, 1914   STATE HISTORICAL SOCIETY WISCONSIN

Samuel Gompers testifying before Industrial Commission, 1915
UNITED PRESS INTERNATIONAL

but West Coast farmers were in the vanguard against Japanese immigration. The Japanese-American population was never large. The Japanese government prohibited emigration until 1885. The census takers counted 24,326 Japanese in 1900 and 72,157 in 1910. But West Coast farmers, particularly in California, were afraid of the Japanese farmers' competition and without much difficulty aroused a "yellow peril" excitement. In October, 1906, the San Francisco school board segregated all Japanese, Chinese, and Korean school children into one building. Only ninety-three Japanese children were involved, but the school board's excuse was that they were crowding the whites out of school. Public opinion in Japan became outraged, and President Roosevelt, afraid for the future of American relations with Japan, exerted pressure on the Californians to rescind their action. Roosevelt made an arrangement with a delegation of San Franciscans led by Mayor Eugene Schmitz, then under indictment for graft, in which the school board agreed to rescind its action and Roosevelt agreed to bring an end to Japanese immigration. In a series of notes between the two nations in 1907 and 1908, the so-called Gentleman's Agreement, the Japanese government agreed to issue no more passports to its subjects coming directly to the American mainland. Federal legislation hampered Japanese emigration from Hawaii. In 1913, California passed a law which had the effect of making it illegal for Japanese to own land.

The first legislation on European immigration was also in 1882, but it affected very few people. The law imposed a fifty cent head tax on each immigrant, to be paid by the shipping company, and excluded idiots, criminals, and potential paupers. Additional laws in 1893, 1903, and 1907 raised the head tax until it reached $4 and excluded polygamists, prostitutes, anarchists, the feeble-minded, and those whose passage had been paid by a corporation or association. In 1896, Senator Lodge introduced a bill that would prevent the entry of all illiterates. The literacy test, as he pointed out, would "bear most heavily upon the Italians, Russians, Poles, Hungarians, Greeks, and Asiatics, and very lightly, or not at all, upon English-speaking immigrants. . . ." Lodge's bill passed, but Cleveland vetoed it as he was leaving office. President Taft vetoed another literacy test bill in early 1913. In early 1915, Congress passed another immigration bill providing for a literacy test, and again the President vetoed it. Wilson argued that a literacy test discriminated unfairly against those whose educational opportunity had been limited rather than those who were mentally deficient. But soon the pressure for restriction was too great to be denied. When a similar bill went to Wilson in January, 1917, and met his veto again, Congress passed the literacy test over his objection. By that time, immigration had been seriously cut anyway by the European war.

The Negro in the Age of Booker T. Washington

Some nineteenth-century background in Negro history is necessary to understand the developments of the early twentieth century with regard to these people. The abolitionist impulse had died rather quickly after the Civil War and Reconstruction; the Negro had few powerful white friends willing to use their strength to help the Negro advance his interests or protect the political rights granted him in the Fourteenth and Fifteenth amendments to the Constitution. What aid the southern Negro received consisted mostly of financial subsidy for Negro education from northern philanthropists. The education of southern Negroes by 1900 was still very poor compared to national educational standards, and there was little of it at all beyond the elementary level, but Negro literacy had been much improved since emancipation. In 1865, about 95 per cent of the Negroes had been illiterate. The percentage fell to 44.5 in 1900 and to 30.4 in 1910. Negroes still lived mostly in the South. In 1900, almost nine-tenths of the Negro population resided in the former slave states, mostly in the former Confederate states. Much of the northern Negro population lived in the large cities; New York's Negro population was sixty-seven thousand in 1900, Philadelphia's was only slightly less, Chicago had about thirty thousand, and Boston had about twelve thousand. Nationally, Negroes constituted 11.6 per cent of the population; ever since the Civil War they have represented 10 to 12 per cent of the total population.

Most Negroes in the late nineteenth century were sharecroppers, trapped in the box of the crop-lien system. They owed both their degradation and what stability and livelihood they had to large white landowners, most of whom were on the conservative side of the political struggles of the Populist era. Some Populists had at first hoped to improve the conditions of all southern agrarians, white and black alike, but the Negro generally had allowed himself to be used by the white conservatives. The Populists' main strength was among the poor whites whose attitude toward the Negro had always been less liberal than that of his richer white cousins, and agrarian demagogues began to exploit the anti-Negro sentiments of that part of the electorate for political ends. Tom Watson of Georgia, who had once tried to effect a Negro-white agrarian alliance, turned bitterly against Negroes, as did such rabble-rousers as Cole Blease of South Carolina, James K. Vardaman of Mississippi, and Jeff Davis of Arkansas. Such politicians as these set about systematically to disfranchise the Negro. Since the Fifteenth Amendment said quite explicitly that no state could deny or abridge the right of any citizen to vote "on account of race, color, or previous condition of servitude," disfranchisement had to be done by subterfuge, some of which was ingenious.

Also during the 1890's and early years of the present century, southern states and municipalities began to codify Negro segregation and make it rigid through Jim Crow laws. In 1883, the Supreme Court ruled that the Constitution did not forbid privately imposed separation of the races in such places as theaters and hotels. In 1896, in Plessey v. Ferguson, the northern-dominated Supreme Court concluded that a state law that segregated Negroes in public schools and public transportation did not violate the Fourteenth Amendment so long as the facilities provided for Negroes were equal to those provided for others. Behind this "separate but equal" doctrine, which remained the Court's constitutional interpretation until 1954, southern whites made their region thoroughly Jim Crow. Whether southern whites actually wanted to provide equal facilities for Negroes in, for example, education or not, they did not. The South was a poor region, then unable to provide one, let alone two, adequate sets of schools, and the Negro schools received the dregs of the school budget. Unable to vote, barred from jury duty, and in general having only what political rights whites were willing to grant him, the Negro easily became the victim of violence. And some whites could be violent indeed. In the 1890's, lynchings averaged over two hundred a year and about one hundred a year from 1900 to 1914. In 1906, Atlanta had a serious race riot that left ten Negroes dead and sixty wounded.

Until 1895, Negroes had no national leader. In that year, Booker T. Washington emerged as the Negro's national leader and remained in that position until his death in 1915. Washington had been born a slave in Virginia in 1856 and had been educated at the Hampton Normal and Agricultural Institute founded by the American Missionary Association in 1870. He founded Tuskegee Institute in Alabama in 1881, a school at that time much like Hampton which emphasized vocational training in agriculture, elementary school teaching, and the trades. In 1895, Washington received an invitation to speak at the Cotton States Exposition at Atlanta, an affair organized and conducted by white men. The evidence indicates that, until his 1895 speech, Washington was but little known by most Negroes. At least, Negro newspapers granted him little space when he made a long tour through southern cities immediately before the Atlanta speech. In his speech Washington offered a compromise in racial relations which most whites and Negroes accepted. His Atlanta Compromise stated that: "In all things that are purely social we can be as separate as the five fingers, yet one as the hand in all things essential to mutual progress."

Estimates of Washington's leadership vary widely, yet certain facets are clear. In economic matters Washington was a thorough conservative; Bourbon whites certainly had nothing to fear from his leadership in that respect. In his thought on racial matters Washington was neither a militant nor an Uncle Tom. He never explicitly denied the long-term goal of Negro equality, but he was willing, at least for his generation, to give up demands for political and social equality and to play down even discriminatory legal injustices. Furthermore, he was willing to flatter southern whites and to deal harshly with Negro intellectuals who dissented from his opinions, especially by failing to endorse them to the northern philanthropists for whom he served as an educational advisor. But Washington made these accommodationist concessions for a price, and the price was a degree of economic integration and material support for the Negro's training so that he could assume a more important role in economic matters. In neither economic matters nor education, however, did he demand equality. He accepted the southern white contention that the Negro's "place" in these fields was to be inferior to the white's. In the short run in the South, Washington's philosophy was probably realistic. Not much more, perhaps nothing more, was possible for southern Negroes but to accept Washington's advice to stop thinking of equal rights and to "cast down your buckets where you are." In other parts of the country, however, Washington's views fell far short of Negro aspirations, and in time even in the South his position would seem extremely timid.

The new century had no more than opened when a few northern Negroes began criticizing the "Washington Compromise." In 1901, two Negro intellectuals, Monroe Trotter and George Forbes, began to publish the militant Boston *Guardian*. Two years later W. E. B. DuBois, a light-skinned Negro from Great Barrington, Massachusetts, who had earned a Ph.D. in history at Harvard, assumed the leadership of dissenting Negroes with the publication of a chapter critical of Washington in his *The Souls of Black Folk*. Washington, DuBois charged, was too timid and his educational practices would fail to develop the "talented tenth" of the Negro population necessary to give Negroes leadership in a struggle toward real equality.

In the summer of 1905, DuBois organized the Niagara movement. He and twenty-eight other Negro intellectuals met at Niagara Falls, Canada, after they had met discrimination at the Buffalo hotel where they had made reservations, and laid plans to develop a national protest organization to battle against all forms of discrimination and segregation. The Niagara movement had two other conferences, one at Harper's Ferry, West Virginia, and one at Oberlin College, both of them sites of abolitionist significance, but it was unable to arouse more than a feeble following. Washington's approval meant too much for the careers of young and ambitious Negroes, and they steered clear of the Niagara movement for fear of encountering the opposition of what DuBois called "the Tuskegee Machine." DuBois, however, earned a hearing, and in Washington's last years he modified his positions to minimize the northern Negroes' stinging criticisms.

In the summer of 1908, a race riot broke out in Springfield, Illinois, ironically within a few blocks of the home of the Great Emancipator. William English Walling, a wealthy, white, left-wing intellectual then living in New York, was in Chicago at the time and went down to Springfield to investigate the situation. Alarmed at the prospect of the racial tensions of the South growing into other parts of the nation, he wrote two magazine articles in which he described the Negro's situation and called for a revival of the old abolitionist spirit. Walling and two other white reformers, Mary White Ovington and Henry Moskowitz, a New York physician, called a series of informal meetings to discuss what should be done. In time, the Walling discussion group linked up with the Niagara movement, and in 1910 they founded together the National Association for the Advancement of Colored People to try to do with white help what the Niagara group had been unable to do alone. At first, the NAACP was a predominantly white organization. DuBois, its salaried Director of Publicity and Research, was its only Negro officer. He also edited *The Crisis*, the NAACP magazine, which soon became popular among Negroes. Within a few years, however, Negroes had assumed most of the responsible positions in the organization which became interracial at the top level but almost altogether Negro in its mass following. In time, the NAACP was to grow to be the most effective voice of the Negro's aspirations. It did not begin with a wholesale campaign to win the Negro his full constitutional rights; it picked the objectives it thought could be won and fought militantly to achieve them.

Another interracial group that grew to prominence was the National Urban League, founded in 1911, which merged three smaller organizations concerned with social work and wider economic opportunity for Negroes. Its first president was an eminent Columbia University economics professor, E. R. A. Seligman. It came into being to help in the adjustment of Negroes when they moved to northern cities, as they began to do in a small way before 1917. By 1910, the Negro population of New York had grown to over 90,000, Philadelphia's to 84,000 and Chicago's to 44,000. As Negroes increasingly moved to northern and southern cities during and after the war, the Urban League expanded.

Muckraking and Middle-Class Reform

In the first decade of the century, a number of inexpensive magazines of national circulation published many articles exposing the seamy side of business and politics. In 1906, after magazine literature of exposé had been commonplace for some time, President Roosevelt tagged the writers of such articles as "muckrakers," a term he used with derision. He likened the writers to the character in John Bunyan's seventeenth-century *Pilgrim's Progress* "who could look no way but downward with the muckrake in his hands." Roosevelt misunderstood most of these writers whose desire was to clear away the stench of muck so that people could look to the sky, but the term stuck. Frequently the muckrakers were given the credit for arousing public opinion about social problems and thereby making reform and progressivism possible. Certainly, muckraking did stimulate and crystalize opinion, but it also reflected opinion. The muckrakers did not create progressivism.

The publisher S. S. McClure is usually thought to have begun the muckraker movement when he published in *McClure's* in October, 1902, Lincoln Steffens', "Tweed Days in St. Louis," and followed the next month with the first installment of Ida Tarbell's, "The History of the Standard Oil Company." Actually, muckraking of a sort had gone on for years, especially in the *Arena* published in Boston by B. O. Flower. McClure, however, perfected that kind of journalism, and his success, both intellectual and financial, prompted many imitators. McClure set high standards. He assigned Miss Tarbell the Standard Oil piece in 1896, expecting her to have material ready for publication in a few months. Her research was slow and painstakingly careful, and she was five years preparing the series; but, as McClure put it, he paid writers "for their study rather than for the amount of copy they turned out." Her five years' research and writing produced only fifteen articles, and Lincoln Steffens produced only about four articles a year, but they and McClure are remembered when hastier writers and publishers are forgotten.

Some of the better or more influential muckraking works deserve mention. Steffens followed up his St. Louis article with similar ones about other cities, such as "Pittsburgh—Hell with the Lid Off," later collected in book form as *The Shame of the Cities* (1904). Ray Stannard Baker, later to be President Wilson's secretary and biographer, was one of McClure's writers until 1906, when he, Steffens, and Miss Tarbell took over *The American*. Baker wrote a five-part article for *McClure's*, "Railroads on Trial," that exposed their practices and helped to mobilize support for their regulation. In 1907, he wrote an important series on Negro-white relations called "Following the Color Line," published the next year in book form. *McClure's* also published Burton J. Hendrick's, "The Story of Life Insurance," based largely on the investigation of insurance companies in New York that Charles Evans Hughes had made in 1905. George Kibbe Turner wrote an article on Chicago for McClure that exposed the connection of Chicago politicians and police with organized prostitution and led to one of that city's ever-recurring and ever-needed reform surges. Charles Edward Russell's articles on the Beef Trust in *Everybody's* in 1905, coming with Upton Sinclair's almost contemporary *The Jungle*, led to federal inspection of meat packing, and Samuel Hopkins Adams' articles in *Collier's* on patent medicine and advertising frauds stimulated the passage of the Pure Drug Act. One of the most sensational muckraking series was Thomas W. Lawson's articles called "Frenzied Finance." During the time *Everybody's* ran this series, 1903–1905, its circulation rose from under 200,000 to 735,000.

Some muckrake articles sacrificed accuracy and fairness for sensation. This was particularly true of the articles in William Randolph Hearst's *Cosmopolitan*. David Graham Phillips' series called "The Treason of the Senate," while accurate enough in its broad accusations, distorted facts and invented others. Nevertheless, it contributed to public demand for the direct election of Senators.

Muckraking died out in 1910–1911 almost as quickly as it had begun. The public appetite for sensation became a handicap. Publishers were just unable to make each issue more sensational than the last, and magazines began to seem anticlimactic. Then, too, large-circulation publishing required large investment, and when publishers sought credit they were sometimes forced to soften their policies. A few publishers yielded to pressure from advertisers. Businessmen also, almost for the first time, began to be concerned about what they called their "public relations" and hired publicists to improve their public reputation. Ivy Lee, one of the first public relations counselors, worked for the Pennsylvania Railroad, Armour and Company, and Bethlehem Steel before he made a permanent association with Standard Oil, eventually becoming a director of the company.

Muckraking was the journalistic aspect of a much wider wave of reform and demand for social justice. One should make a distinction between middle-class progressivism and the labor movement. Labor was not antiprogressive by any means, and many progressives were prolabor. Some individuals are difficult to classify in one camp or the other. But there clearly were two camps. Workingmen concentrated on unionism; most of them were politically apathetic. Persons from the middle classes embraced a wide range of reforms, from clean government to social work to wage and hours legislation.

To generalize about these reformers, as distinct from the labor people, is difficult. They were individuals, highly individualistic many of them. Yet most of them had remarkably similar backgrounds and shared certain fundamental assumptions about life and society. Most of them came from middle-class backgrounds of material comfort; some were quite wealthy. Most of them had university degrees, many of them from the prestige institutions. The labor leader who wrote, "Scratch a champion of the plain people and you will find an aristocrat," surely exaggerated, but he was perceptive enough to see that the progressives were from a different background from himself and his associates. Why so many people in comfortable situations should depart from the usual pattern at about the same time is a question that has fascinated historians. Some have interpreted the rise of big business and the increasing prestige of the very rich as creating a kind of social crisis among what were known as "good families." These families did not suffer economically; in fact, most of them increased their wealth. But the gap between them and the richest elements in society widened as Rockefellers, Fricks, Garys, Morgans, Harrimans, *et al.*, acquired their wealth and power. But to document that this phenomenon motivated their reform activities is difficult at best.

Most of the middle-class reformers were Protestants or religious nonconformists from Protestant families. A few were Jewish, but usually not religiously orthodox. Catholic reformers were fairly rare, although there were some in the priesthood. Catholics, who were then usually of immigrant background, were far more likely to be found in the labor movement than associated with the middle-class reformers. This breakdown by religious affiliation reflects not only the social-economic origins of the reformers; it also relates to an interesting development within Protestantism, the social gospel.

Protestant ministers in the late nineteenth century began to notice that conventional church activities did not have the appeal among industrial workers that they had in small towns and on the farms. The rural church-goer could still sing hymns testifying that the "old time religion" was good enough for him because it had been good enough for his father, but many industrial workers in the large cities did not agree. And neither did many of the reformers, ministers among them, who demanded a less dogmatic religion and a church with an active concern for social welfare. As one of the most radical of the social gospel clergymen, Walter Rauschenbusch of the Rochester Theological Seminary, put it, "It is not a matter of getting individuals to heaven, but of transforming the life on earth into the harmony of heaven." A few social gospel ministers, such as George D. Herron of Grinnell College, Iowa, found that their consciences led them to the Socialist party, but most of them were content to work for reform within the existing system. The social gospel movement, which had begun in the 1880's, as well as the contemporary ecumenical movement looking toward Protestant unity, came to a climax in 1908 with the establishment of the Federal Council of Churches of Christ in America. At its first meeting the Federal Council adopted a sort of religious social platform entitled "The Church and Modern Industry" that placed the organization, with its thirty-three large church-body affiliates, on record in favor of legislation to effect social justice.

The number of reform organizations not only on record but actively working for some aspect of social justice was striking. In the field of labor, but not from the labor movement itself, were the National Women's Trade Union League (1903), the National Consumers League (1898), and the American Association for Labor Legislation (1906). Particularly interested in the problems of urban children were the National Federation of Day Nurseries (1898), the National Child Labor Committee (1904), and the Playground and Recreation Association of America (1906). Margaret Sanger, a singularly single-minded reformer, launched a reform organization in a new field when she founded the American Birth Control League in 1914, but the New York Committee of Fifteen, which fought prostitution, then politely called "the social evil," was concerned with a very old field indeed. The ferment for organizing against evil went so far that in 1910 the president of the General Federation of Women's Clubs, originally an association of women's literary circles, took pride in her organization's work for child health in her presidential address.

Many of these middle-class reformers had an "uplift" or "lady bountiful" attitude toward the poor. Their goal seemed more to teach the poor to follow their own more respectable ways of life than to learn from those less fortunate than themselves or to create a society in which poverty was insignificant. But this was not true of a dedicated band of reformers, practically all of them from upper-middle-class homes and from universities or the new women's colleges, who moved into the slums to establish and work in settlement houses. Jane Addams returned from a visit to English settlements in 1889 and established Hull House in Chicago. Associated with her were Julia Lathrop and Florence Kelley, who later joined Lillian Wald at the Henry Street Settlement in New York. Other prominent settlement centers were the University Settlement in New York and South End House in Boston. Many a young man and woman of means went directly from the campus to the settlement house, there to become aware of how complex and vast were the problems created by poverty, to help as best he or she could at a personal level, and to move on into reform political action. From the settlement house there grew the whole field of social work, and, because the slum dwellers around the settlements were mostly immigrants who needed a special kind of practical education to cope with their new environment, the settlement workers developed new educational ideas which slowly found their way to the public schools. Among the young settlement house workers of the early part of the century who later became prominent in politics were Frances Perkins and Harry Hopkins.

City and State Reform and the Courts

Some of the progressive movement's greatest achievements were at the city and state level where reformers did a remarkable amount of tinkering with constitutional forms and passed a number of important social welfare laws, many of which a generation later were to be adopted by the federal government. Since opposition to political corruption united reformers of varying degrees of dissatisfaction with the *status quo* more than anything else, much of the state and local action was aimed at "throwing the rascals out" and instituting government changes which, they hoped, would impede the rascals' return.

Several American cities elected reform mayors who attracted national attention. Here and there a reform mayor had come to office in the late 1800's, such as Hazen S. Pingree, who was so successful as mayor of Detroit for two terms that he was elected governor of Michigan in 1896. A more colorful figure with a more lasting impact was Samuel M. "Golden Rule" Jones, who became mayor of Toledo in 1897. A small manufacturer of oil equipment who had attracted local attention by giving his employees a profit-sharing system, the eight-hour day, paid vacations, and the right to keep their own work-time records, Jones was essentially a philosophical anarchist who sincerely believed the Golden Rule. "I don't want to rule anybody," he said. "Each individual must rule himself." As mayor he instituted free kindergartens, night schools, public playgrounds, free lodging for tramps, and higher wages for city labor. When he declared himself against private ownership as "a high crime against democracy," both parties denounced him and Toledo newspapers refused even to publish his letter accepting nomination on an independent ticket. Nevertheless, he won office each of the four times he ran, and, when he died in office in 1904, he was succeeded by his secretary, the novelist Brand Whitlock, who served four more terms.

Seth Low, who became mayor of New York City in 1901, represented only a short hiatus in the city's control by Tammany, but Joseph W. Folk, first as district attorney and then as governor of Missouri, was more successful in his attempts to clean up St. Louis politics. San Francisco encountered unusual difficulties in overthrowing the regime of Boss Abraham Ruef and Mayor Eugene E. Schmitz despite gross malfeasance of office, but with the aid of Governor Hiram Johnson, who was elected in 1910, the reformers finally won. In 1902, a grand jury revealed the corruption of Mayor A. A. Ames of Minneapolis, and the city sent him and his clique to prison.

Cleveland, under the administration of Tom Johnson, earned the reputation as the nation's best-governed large city. Later, Milwaukee, which elected Mayor Emil Seidel, a Socialist, in 1910, received that distinction. Johnson had been a financially successful traction company official when in the late 1880's, according to his own account, he completely reversed his career and economic opinions upon reading Henry George's classic *Progress and Poverty*. Persuaded to the single tax and opposition to business privilege, Johnson ran for Congress as a Democrat and was twice elected. In 1901, he was elected mayor of Cleveland on a platform which demanded more equitable taxation of railroads and public utilities and a three-cent fare on streetcars. His enemies now were his former associates. Johnson's program was balked at many points by the state courts and the conservative Republican organization that controlled the legislature, but he nevertheless had corruption and privilege on the run in Cleveland until his defeat in 1909. Two years later, Newton D. Baker, one of Johnson's aides and later Secretary of War under Wilson, won the mayoralty election.

Many cities during this period experimented with new forms of government. In 1900, the National Municipal League urged a program of municipal home rule—freedom for a city to change its governmental structure without special action by the state legislature. By the war, twelve states had passed general home-rule legislation, most of them in the West, and cities began extensively to change their structure. In 1900, Galveston, Texas, was hit by a tidal wave that destroyed one-third of the city and drowned one-sixth of the population. The city administration proved unequal to the crisis, and responsibility for rehabilitation was put into the hands of five commissioners. A new city charter the following year made the commission structure of government permanent. It was efficient, and in 1905 nearby Houston adopted a similar reorganization. In 1907, Iowa enacted permission for cities of over twenty-five thousand to adopt the commission scheme, and Des Moines soon did so with conspicuous success. Another favorite new form of municipal administration was the city manager plan, begun at Staunton, Virginia, in 1908 but coming to national attention in 1913 when Dayton, Ohio, adopted the scheme to make rehabilitation more efficient after a disastrous flood. Much of the tinkering with municipal government was only to make it more efficient, actually to introduce business managerial techniques to city administration. But simultaneously many cities also extended democratic forms. In Toledo, Whitlock secured a new city charter that provided for the initiative, the referendum, recall, and direct nominations, and numerous other cities adopted some or all of these direct democracy techniques which were at the time widely regarded as magic tools for democracy.

In 1898, a Democratic-Populist government in South Dakota became the first to adopt the initiative and the referendum. Utah followed in 1900 and Oregon in 1902. By the end of the war, nineteen other states had adopted these direct democracy devices in some form. The recall of elected officials, a device to keep administrators honest by empowering the citizenry to remove them from office before the end of their terms if they strayed too far from public acceptance, was not so widely adopted. Oregon accepted the idea in 1908. By 1914, California, Arizona, Idaho, Washington, Colorado, Nevada, Michigan, Louisiana, North Dakota, and Kansas had followed Oregon's example. The nomination of candidates by primary elections spread rapidly after LaFollette introduced the idea in Wisconsin in 1903. By 1915, every state had primary elections for at least some offices, and in most of them candidates for all offices were chosen through primaries. In some southern states, Democrats distorted the primary into a device for disfranchising Negroes; officially, in several southern states the primary was operated by the parties rather than the government, and the parties thereby determined who could and could not vote without technically violating the Fifteenth Amendment. Since the Democratic party, except for a few southern counties, was the only party and Democratic nomination assured one of final election, Negroes were effectively shut out of state politics.

The states sucessfully undermined the old system of electing United States Senators and forced the passage of the Seventeenth Amendment. The Constitution quite explicitly required Senators to be chosen by the state legislatures. The Populists had demanded direct election of Senators, and, by 1912, twenty-nine states had adopted a scheme for statewide senatorial elections to be rubber-stamped by the legislature. Thus, when Congress submitted the Seventeenth Amendment to the states in the spring of 1912, almost the two-thirds of the senators necessary to adopt the amending resolution had been actually elected by direct vote of the electorate.

The political reform that brought perhaps the most passionate arguments during this period was votes for women. Advocates of women's suffrage had begun their agitation before the Civil War in a small way and, led by Susan B. Anthony and Elizabeth Cady Stanton, had increased their activity after the North-South conflict. It was not until 1919 that Congress submitted the Nineteenth Amendment to the states which forbade states to deny the suffrage because of sex, and it was not ratified until 1920. But the years before the war saw a tremendous women's suffrage campaign which was successful in several states. Only four western states, Wyoming, Utah, Colorado, and Idaho, granted full suffrage to women before 1900. By 1915, seven other states, all of them western, had granted full women's suffrage, and many others had passed laws providing for partial suffrage, usually for school board elections. The men in the tier of states from Pennsylvania south to Georgia and Alabama held out to the bitter end in 1920.

After 1912, women suffragists increasingly adopted the tactics of their English sisters such as button-holing politicians and giving them vigorously blunt lectures, parading, picketing, and even hunger striking. The leadership of the National Woman Suffrage Association, led by Carrie Chapman Catt and Anna Howard Shaw, discouraged such tactics and removed Alice Paul, a militant, from the chairmanship of their committee to lobby in Congress. But militant suffragists continued their more extreme methods and eventually forced a reluctant Wilson to support their cause.

But the reform movement in the states was not restricted to clean government and extension of political democracy; these years saw a great agitation for state laws prohibiting child labor, insuring workers against industrial accidents, and regulating the wages and hours of women workers, and many states enacted such laws although of widely varying effectiveness. As the century opened, the condition of children who labored in factories, mines, and fields approached the degradation of labor in the early days of the industrial revolution in England. Reformers documented cases of children in southern textile mills being kept awake by throwing cold water on them as they worked at night, of boys as young as ten working ten-hour days on coal breakers, and children as young as four working in New York sweat shops. By 1914, however, every state but one had adopted a minimum age for labor, usually twelve in the South but as high as sixteen in Montana. Several states put limits on the working day for children, usually ten hours, and most of them forbade the employment of children in certain dangerous occupations. Even if the laws had been well enforced they would not have met the demands of opponents of child labor, and in many states they were not well enforced. Enforcement was difficult because too many employers were willing to take the economic advantage of cheap child wages and too many children and their parents found it necessary to add to the meager family income the wages of as many workers as possible. Federal control of child labor was necessary to eliminate such exploitation of children except for the worst cases, and the Supreme Court consistently struck down federal legislation in this field. Not until the 1930's was constitutional federal legislation enacted, although in the 1920's several states indirectly got at the problem by raising and enforcing the compulsory school attendance age.

In Chapter 4 we saw how common-law doctrines worked to employees' disadvantage in industrial accident cases. By 1910, most states had enacted legislation to modify the common law of employee injury, but the laws were of little actual utility because to recover for damages the employee still had to instigate a legal suit which frequently was beyond his financial means. Then states began to demand that employers carry insurance policies against injuries to employees or stand ready to assume full responsibility and liability in the courts. Maryland enacted the first such law, not a very effective one, in 1902. By 1916, all but eighteen of the states had enacted some kind of an industrial insurance and liability law. Since frequency of accidents determined the size of insurance premiums, employers found it advisable to reduce the hazards of work and to institute safety education programs for employees.

Illinois became the first state to enact an enforceable law limiting hours of work for women in 1893, after an agitation campaign by Florence Kelley of Hull House. In 1895, the state supreme court nullified the law which provided for a maximum eight-hour day. By 1908, when the Supreme Court approved Oregon's law regulating the hours of work for women, only eight states had such laws in their statutes, but after the Court gave the green light most of the other states enacted such legislation. Efforts to establish minimum wage rates for women by law were less successful. Massachusetts in 1912 created a wage commission with power to recommend minimum wages for women and to publicize the employers who refused its recommendations. In the next few years, however, only a few other states pursued the idea, although usually with stronger laws than the Bay State one. These states were mostly in the Midwest or West. Wage-hours laws for men were rare and limited to certain occupations.

By 1913, twenty of the states had passed measures providing pensions for women with dependent children. However, only one state, Arizona, had established a full old-age pension system, and the state supreme court voided that law.

Getting such welfare legislation by the courts proved almost as difficult a job for reformers as getting the acts passed by state legislatures. Even when a state welfare law cleared the state courts it faced the prospect of invalidation by the United States Supreme Court. The Supreme Court had accepted the arguments of corporation attorneys whose view of the Fourteenth Amendment was such that it prompted Mr. Dooley's remark that what looked like a stone wall to an ordinary citizen was an arch of triumph to a corporation lawyer. In Santa Clara County v. Southern Pacific Railroad and in the Minnesota Rate case in the 1880's, the Court accepted the view that a corporation was a person and, therefore, protected by the Fourteenth Amendment's prohibition upon the state to "deprive any person of life, liberty, or property, without due process of law." Through this constitutional arch marched regiments of corporation lawyers who argued that state laws setting minimum wages and hours for labor deprived their clients of liberty.

The Supreme Court was not always consistent in its application of the Fourteenth Amendment to state welfare laws because it also recognized that the states had certain police powers. In Holden v. Hardy in 1898 the Court had upheld a Utah law setting a maximum eight-hour day for miners as being within the police powers of a state. Mining, however, was clearly a dangerous occupation, and not until Lochner v. New York in 1905 could the states know how far they could go with hours regulation. The Lochner case severely limited the states. The New York law in question had set ten hours a day or sixty a week as the maximum for bakers. The Court's majority of one issued a sweeping opinion holding that the liberty to make labor contracts for any length work-week was "part of the liberty of the individual protected by the Fourteenth Amendment." Justice Holmes dissented, saying that "a constitution is not intended to embody a particular economic theory" (meaning laissez-faire), and that "the Fourteenth Amendment does not enact Mr. Herbert Spencer's Social Statics."

In 1908, social reformers won a significant victory in Muller v. Oregon. That state had enacted a law setting ten hours as the maximum work day for women in factories, and an employer contested the law's constitutionality. The Court upheld the statute, and following its decision many other states adopted Oregon's example. The most unusual aspect of the case was the argument that Louis D. Brandeis presented for Oregon. Until the Brandeis argument in the Muller case, legal briefs had restricted themselves to legal precedent and abstract legal logic. Constitutional legal arguments were conducted in a real-life vacuum. Brandeis presented a brief that paid but scant attention to the traditional constitutional arguments and concentrated upon the social and economic results of long work days for women. When the Court decided in favor of Brandeis' client, it, in effect, recognized for the first time the social consequences of its decisions. Thereafter, and especially after Brandeis joined the Court, the "Brandeis brief" came increasingly into use. In 1917, the Court fully reversed its decision in the Lochner case on the matter of maximum hours for men when in Bunting v. Oregon it upheld an Oregon statute that established a ten-hour maximum for all workers, men or women.

The Court, however, had only yielded. It continued to strike down state and federal legislation in other fields. In general, conservatives defended the courts' powers to review and nullify acts of the other branches of government as a necessary and proper safeguard of liberty and property, and progressives, seeing their popular measures struck down by judicial conservatives, urged for a judiciary more responsive to the public will. Each side failed to see that the courts could be a weapon and a shield for either side of the dispute and that by mid-century it would be the progressives who would defend the courts from conservative attack. Meanwhile, it appeared that the judges over a long period, to cite Mr. Dooley again, did indeed follow the election returns, although sometimes they seemed to be several elections back in their homework.

The New Leisure

In 1918, a commission of professional educators drew up a list of aims of public education. Among these "Seven Cardinal Principles," studied assiduously by a generation of students in education courses, was "worthy use of leisure time." The inclusion of such an objective indicated that by the end of the period considered in this chapter leisure time had grown sufficiently to be a matter of concern to thinking people. Of course, millions of Americans had little or no more time for other than working, eating, and sleeping than they had ever had, and the total amount of leisure in the whole society was much less than it is today. Nevertheless, for the first time in the world's history, great numbers of ordinary people, both in Europe and America, had a significant number of hours each week which they could spend as they wished. Both the "leisure class" and the classes that had some leisure were beginning to grow. To enumerate, let alone to describe, the multitude of ways that people used their leisure is impossible. We can only deal with certain activities that took a large part of the total leisure man-hours.

Women of the early twentieth century enjoyed more free time than had their mothers and grandmothers, especially if they were of the middle class. Middle-class families of the cities became smaller and easier to care for as gas and kerosene stoves replaced the coal-burning range, commercially canned fruits and vegetables began to be used extensively, and service industries began to do some of the jobs housewives had once done themselves. The presence of large numbers of poor immigrant women made servants or "help" in the home inexpensive, and far more middle-class families then than now could afford to have much of the work of keeping house done by others. Women, of course, did all kinds of things in their new-found leisure. Many of them devoted much of their time to political causes, such as woman suffrage, or to church work. Women's clubs proliferated. In 1889, the General Federation of Women's Clubs federated about four hundred women's societies, most of them literary in their interests. In 1898, the organization had fifty thousand members, and by 1914 it had over a million. As the clubs grew in number, they widened their range of interests to include art, political questions, and feminism. Furthermore, as the educational level of the members rose steadily, they lost much of their superficiality.

More people spent more time reading newspapers than they had in times past. In the 1890's, William Randolph Hearst and Joseph Pulitzer had begun the newspaper in its modern form, and the wire associations had come into being. As Hearst and Pulitzer demonstrated the financial advantages of the new journalism, publishers in other cities began to imitate at least some of their practices. By the war, almost all city dailies had become a kind of journalistic department store with a host of special features such as recipes, bedtime stories for children, crossword puzzles, and columns of the order of Beatrice Fairfax's "Advice to the Lovelorn." The daily editions had a special page or pages each day for sports, the theater, "society," and business. Most city dailies had a page devoted to the "funnies." Richard F. Outcault had established the first successful comic strip in the 1890's with his "Yellow Kid." He soon had many imitators. Millions of adults as well as children followed them with avid interest, although they were crude both artistically and humorously like "The Katzenjammer Kids," "Mutt and Jeff," "Buster Brown," and "Happy Hooligan." The Sunday edition became a large, awkward magazine, with each special daily page expanded into a special section plus a "Sunday supplement" filled with cheap fiction and articles about the activities of the celebrated rich, curses upon famous diamonds, and shop girls who married millionaires. Hearst's *New York American*, perhaps the most sensational paper in the country, had a Sunday circulation of 739,000 in 1914. The more dignified New York *Times*, which aimed at a more highly educated readership, had a Sunday circulation of 217,000.

People of varying political opinions expressed concern about the power of newspaper publishers to mold public opinion. Conservatives distrusted Pulitzer's New York *World*, the most progressive of the eastern big newspapers, and progressives accused the Associated Press of withholding and distorting the news. Owners of newspaper chains, such as George H. and Edward W. Scripps, who owned more than twenty papers in the West and Midwest, controlled the primary source of public affairs information for millions of readers. More alarming were the activities of Hearst, who owned newspapers in New York, Chicago, Los Angeles, San Francisco, Boston, and Atlanta. Hearst had political ambitions, and his newspapers afforded him access to the electorate denied other political figures. Hearst was elected to Congress from a Tammany district in 1902 and 1904, was defeated by Charles Evans Hughes for the New York governorship in 1906, and was an aspirant for the Democratic presidential nomination in 1904 and 1908.

Perhaps American men read no part of a newspaper with greater interest than the sports page. Led by a President who urged the "strenuous life" and glorified physical strength, stamina, and competition, the American people during the Roosevelt years acquired an intense interest in sports. Men and boys had long played outdoor games, but, in the early twentieth century, sports became more organized and commercialized—as did entertainment in general—than ever before. Men of all ages, particularly in the cities, while becoming more sports-minded, came to watch games as spectators more than they played themselves. Wealthy men might play golf or tennis, but the ordinary man got his sports by buying his way into a stadium to watch professional athletes or school and college teams.

Professional baseball, far and away the most popular game, organized itself into the pattern it was to have for decades. The National League of Professional Baseball Clubs had been organized in the 1880's. In 1900, the American League organized and soon thereafter began to move into the larger cities, including ones where there was already a National League club. The two leagues raided one another's players; at one time the New York National League club hired away practically all the Baltimore American League club and its manager, John McGraw, in midseason. In 1903, the National League accepted the American organization as its partner, and the two "big leagues" thereafter worked harmoniously in business matters and agreed to meet each year in a postseason "world series" that soon became an annual national crisis comparable to the Tour de France or a British Empire Test Match.

Boxing and horse racing were the other great professional sports of the day. Professional football then consisted only of some small-city midwestern teams that played before small crowds, and professional basketball, a new game, did not exist at all. Fighting and racing each attracted hundreds of thousands of paying customers every year, and each faced the opposition of middle-class reformers. New York barred both for a few years. These two sports also indicated some unusual twists in social class interests. Professional boxing had once been a field for the poor, to a considerable extent for the underworld, and horse racing had been exclusively a wealthy man's pastime. Now in the twentieth century, people of all classes began to follow their favorite fighters with interest, and "the sport of kings" became largely the sport of gamblers with residues of the aristocratic "horsey set."

Until the late nineteenth century, American schools and colleges had followed the customs of their European counterparts in athletic matters. Students played games among themselves and occasionally with teams from other institutions, but their games attracted little attention outside the student bodies, there were no professional coaches, and admission to games was free. Toward the end of the century, the larger and best known eastern universities, particularly Harvard, Yale, and Princeton, began an emphasis upon intercollegiate athletics, especially football, that later became typical of American colleges. Until the war or after, the Ivy League, itself a term that came from the sports page, consistently played the best football in the nation. The All-American teams, an idea begun by a Yale alumnus, were filled with players from these eastern institutions. As the eastern colleges led the rest of the nation's campuses in athletic matters, so did the eastern private preparatory schools lead the public secondary schools of the rest of the country. Not until

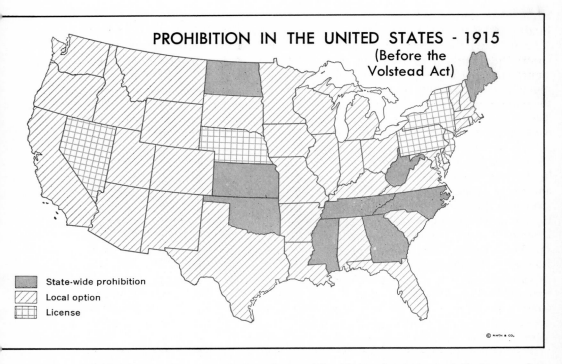

PROHIBITION IN THE UNITED STATES · 1915
(Before the Volstead Act)

State-wide prohibition
Local option
License

after the war did more than a few public high schools have full-time professional coaches and athletic instructors such as the "prep" schools had long been able to afford. A generation later, the eastern institutions were to lead a movement for "de-emphasizing" football and other intercollegiate sports, but the practice they had begun proved difficult to undo.

Motion pictures were no more than a technological novelty in 1900, but by 1917 they were common even in small towns and millions of people attended them regularly. The first movie theaters were only stores equipped with folding chairs and a ticket booth. The usual price of a ticket was five cents, and this kind of theater was known as a "nickelodeon." By 1910, thousands of movie exhibitors had constructed special buildings and prices went up slightly. The first movies did not even tell a story, the marvel of pictures that moved being sufficient to interest viewers. "The Great Train Robbery" in 1903 was the first motion picture with a plot, however crude, but it was not until D. W. Griffiths produced "The Birth of a Nation" in 1915 that there was a full-length feature film with close-ups, fade-outs, and other techniques suitable to motion pictures that were impossible on the stage. "The Birth of a Nation" was important in the technical history of films, but its subject matter was unfortunate. Based upon a novel about Reconstruction, *The Clansman*, by Thomas Dixon, the film portrayed the Ku Klux Klan in a very favorable way and the Negro as ignorant and vicious. Undoubtedly the picture contributed to a deterioration in racial relations. Griffiths later tried to rectify matters with a film that urged brotherhood, "Intolerance."

The saloon took a great deal of the leisure time of workingmen in the cities. Saloons differed tremendously just as contemporary drinking places do.

Some were quiet places, the "poor man's club," similar in some respects to English pubs, where the workingman enjoyed a drink or two and conversation with his friends. Others were honkytonk establishments that were as much fronts for houses of prostitution as they were liquor businesses. Others concentrated upon getting as much liquor down the customer and extracting as much money from him in a minimum of time as was possible. In some saloons the extensiveness and intensiveness of drunkenness were appalling. Such establishments worked to the advantage of the prohibition movement which may have taken as much of the leisure time of some people as drinking did of others.

The temperance and prohibition movements had begun before the Civil War, received a setback during the conflict, and come back to life strongly in the late nineteenth century. By 1900, five states had statewide prohibition and many others had local option laws. The main prohibitionist organizations were the Women's Christian Temperance Union, the Anti-Saloon League, and the Temperance Society of the Methodist Episcopal Church. The Anti-Saloon League, ably and somewhat ruthlessly led by Wayne B. Wheeler and William H. Anderson, was the most effective dry organization in the political field. Its goal was national prohibition. If it could not get that, it worked for state prohibition; if that proved inaccessible, it worked for local option; and, if that objective failed, it worked for high saloon license fees. The League became a political force of major proportions, and its sole criterion of what constituted a desirable candidate was his position on alcohol. By 1915, not a state was left that did not have at least local option laws and eleven of them had statewide prohibition. The big cities held out against prohibition the longest. By the time the United States entered the war, saloons were outlawed in roughly three-fourths of the nation's area where there lived about one-half the population. In 1913, the prohibition forces got the Webb-Kenyon bill through Congress to prohibit the transportation of liquor into any area where it was outlawed, and when Taft vetoed it the prohibitionists mustered enough votes to override the measure. Prohibitionists then made national prohibition the next goal, but such a federal law required a constitutional amendment, and it was not until wartime that the antiliquor people could rally enough support to get such an amendment through Congress.

CHAPTER SIX

American Culture in the Early Twentieth Century

THE EXCITEMENTS AND ENTHUSIASMS OF A SOCIETY AFFECT ITS INTEL-
lectuals and artists as they do other social elements. Indeed, frequently it is
the intellectuals and artists who create the new ideas that influence a civilization, and they thus both reflect and stimulate widely held ideas, interests, and
values.

American culture from the 1890's until the war was much influenced
by the general spirit of experiment and revolt and contributed to that mood.
Many themes can be ascertained if one closely examines various aspects of
culture in this period, but there were two that were apparent in practically
all cultural fields: first, there was a revolt against the traditional, the formal,
and the genteel; second, there was a tendency for the artist and intellectual
to create works that had a relevance to the problems facing society and
thereby make formal culture more a living part of American society than it
had been in the previous generation.

Education

When Americans looked at their schools as the new century opened they
could find little to boast about but the accepted principle of free public
education. Most Americans in 1900 had been to school for less than six years.
In the nation's poorest region, the South, just under 12 per cent of the white
population over ten years old was illiterate. The southern Negro population
was even worse. About 16,300,000 children were enrolled in elementary
schools, public, private, and parochial. Nearly every community outside the

South had an elementary school, but many of them were poor both intellectually and financially. The one-room "little red schoolhouse"—actually, by 1900 it was usually a white frame building—may be fondly remembered, but few people today would want to subject their children to such an education. The average school year for elementary schools in 1900 was only 143 days. The average attendance was only 68 days. Elementary teachers, usually women and sometimes very young women, were poorly prepared. Very few states required their elementary teachers to be high-school graduates, and in most states teacher preparation consisted of brief "teachers' institutes" or brief attendance at a normal school. The average salary of women teachers was $38 a month. By 1914, the national averages had considerably improved. The average school year was up to 158.7 days and attendance average up to 86.7 days. The average woman teacher's salary increased to $66 a month.

Much of the improvement in the national picture was due to an unusual improvement in the schools of the South. North Carolina led the southern states in an educational revival, as she did in many other fields, when, in 1902, the Tarheels raised school taxes and campaigned for better schools. Most of the other Dixie states followed as best they could. School appropriations doubled in ten years, and the school year extended to six months. But there was improvement in the North and West at the same time, and the South still lagged behind the rest of the nation. Southern schools received a great deal of help from private philanthropy. Rockefeller established the General Education Board in 1903 and thereafter contributed to it generously. Much of the Board's funds went for southern education, both white and Negro. Rockefeller also helped the South's regeneration by helping to finance a campaign against hookworm, an intestinal parasite that entered the body through bare feet and left victims anemic and listless. Between 1909 and 1913, the Rockefeller Sanitary Commission examined 415,000 southern children and found nearly half of them harbored intestinal worms.

High schools had a relatively greater growth early in the century than elementary education. In 1900, there were about six thousand high schools in the nation with a total enrollment of about five hundred thousand. By 1914, the number of high schools had almost doubled, and the total enrollment was about 1,200,000. By 1920, the total enrollment had grown to about 2,500,000. The high school had traditionally prepared students for the college or university, both in Europe and America. Although many of the students in high school had no intention of carrying their formal education past a high school diploma, if that far, the curriculum remained primarily one of college preparation. The curriculum changed, it is true, but mostly as the requirements of the colleges changed. Thus modern languages came to replace Greek, although Latin remained strong for years. In some respects the high schools before 1920 had higher standards than they have today. The student who was unable to do consistently passing work simply was dropped, and, since even some high school education gave him an advantage in finding a job, he and his family, while perhaps disappointed, did not object strenuously. On the other hand, most secondary-school teachers were not so well prepared either in their subject matter or in their teaching methods as they later became, and much high school teaching was uninspired and mechanical, a situation which the usual dreary textbook did not help.

Although the minimum standards of preparation required of teachers still fell short of desirability—as did minimum standards for physicians and attorneys—there was improvement between 1900 and 1917. Most states raised their requirements for a permanent license to teach in city schools, particularly in high schools. By the war, most young high school teachers were college graduates. An increasing number of state teachers colleges in the Midwest and West began to offer four-year courses and a baccalaureate degree which those in Indiana and Iowa had done since the 1870's. Many state universities and private colleges instituted schools or departments of education. As minimum standards became higher and salaries improved a little, teaching gradually became more of a profession and less a means for the poor and ambitious young man and woman to escape from the farm or factory. The new Teachers College of Columbia University, which offered graduate work in education during this period, played a major role in the process of making education a profession.

In fact, Teachers College was very much in the center of exciting new developments in education, especially after John Dewey moved from the University of Chicago to become professor of philosophy in another part of Columbia University in 1904. Dewey is usually thought of as the father of "progressive education," but the term has come to mean so many things, some of them contradictory, that Dewey's contribution needs elaboration. His educational ideas were many and any effort to condense them necessarily distorts, but we may summarize them under two main heads. First, he believed that the role of the school within society in general was somewhat more important than others had believed. The school, being one of the primary forces that affected a child during his growth to maturity and thus molding him for society, inevitably played an important part in determining what the society would be. This being the case, argued Dewey, the school should endeavor to develop desirable social attributes, and since Dewey was himself a progressive democrat, these attributes were democracy, social consciousness, a sense of individual responsibility toward society collectively and a sense of collective social responsibility to the individual. Second, Dewey sought to change the curriculum and teaching methods, what happened within the school as apart from the school's relationship to the rest of society. The aims of education extended beyond the acquisition of knowledge alone. Knowledge of facts was necessary, but it was an instrument to be used, he argued, not an end in itself. He held that rote learning was ineffective and useless. Instead, the education of the child should be made meaningful to him, and this could be achieved by the child's "learning by doing," by making the classroom a part of life itself rather than a preparation for life. Dewey's educational ideas divided educational thought both in the profession and the public generally. The assault upon them was sometimes rabid, and they only gradually came to be put into practice in the nation's schools. Nevertheless, Dewey largely set the terms for the debate on education.

Contemporary with Dewey's contributions was important new thought in psychology. Professor Edward L. Thorndike of Teachers College developed the field of educational psychology, scrutinized generally accepted educational theories with scientific objectivity, and opened the whole area of learning theory to further research. Perhaps his most important substantive contribution was to call into question the idea of "transfer of training," that a youth's training in the logic of algebra, for example, would necessarily make him think more logically in other fields. Professor G. Stanley Hall of Clark University was the father of what came to be called developmental psychology, the study of the child's mental and physical growth quite necessary for effective education because students' capabilities and interests necessarily condition what they can learn.

Dewey and the new education had little effect upon colleges and universities except for those parts of them especially concerned with the preparation of teachers, but higher education too was in flux. One of the most startling campus developments was a great growth in enrollments. The number of college students increased from 250,000 in 1900 to 400,000 in 1917. Yet the increase was small compared to what was to come in later decades. The number of degree-granting colleges declined slightly during this period, as regional accrediting agencies came into being and found some institutions far below their standards. Some of these below-grade colleges then became junior colleges, although about all of the institutions of this new type, most numerous in the Far West, built upon their own foundations. The growth of junior colleges was part of a more general tendency to bring higher education to an ever broadening section of the population. Pennsylvania State, the University of Chicago, and the University of Wisconsin pioneered in university extension work. In 1914, Wisconsin had over seven thousand students enrolled in extension courses, and the president of the University, Charles Van Hise, a geologist and prominent conservationist, was fond of saying that "the boundaries of the campus are the boundaries of the state." This assertion might have surprised some of the backward farmers of marginal land in the northern part of the state, but Wisconsin, as did other state universities, clearly added service to the state generally to its older functions of education of the young and the advancement of knowledge.

Many universities added new professional schools during this period. Beside the traditional schools of law and medicine, both graduate and undergraduate, there now came schools of education, journalism, and business administration or commerce. The two best known schools of journalism at the University of Missouri and Columbia began in 1908 and 1912, respectively. The Wharton School of Finance at the University of Pennsylvania had been established as an undergraduate school in 1884, but in 1908 Harvard established the first such center for graduate study with the Graduate School of Business Administration. Several other universities and colleges began undergraduate business majors, and a few of them offered graduate instruction.

Graduate instruction had greatly increased its magnitude since The Johns Hopkins University began the first real American graduate school in 1876. By 1917, graduate degrees were offered not only at the major eastern universities but by most of the state universities as well, and such institutions as Michigan, Wisconsin, and California had produced a considerable number of excellent doctoral dissertations. In 1910, about six thousand graduate students enrolled in American universities which awarded that year 409 Ph.D. degrees. American graduate instruction was modeled after the research seminars of German universities where American scholars had gone for their advanced work until the late nineteenth century. But by 1917, one or another of the

American universities had a graduate program for almost all fields of research that was the equal of anything Europe had to offer, and the exchange of scholarly information began to go both ways across the Atlantic.

Many universities underwent a crisis during this period over whether control of the institution would reside with the faculty, the board of trustees and the economic interest it usually represented, or, in the case of state institutions, with the legislature. The problem was not altogether new. In an earlier era clergymen had dominated boards of trustees and had sometimes taken positions quite in opposition to the faculties. Now businessmen had largely replaced the clergy. No clear pattern emerged from the several conflicts. In some privately endowed universities, Harvard for example, the faculty maintained its control over fundamental matters despite huge grants from businessmen. The pipers in Cambridge continued to select their tunes. In some other private institutions, however, such was not the case. Several state universities became deeply involved in state politics and suffered as a result. In others, the faculties were able quite successfully to resist the pressures exerted upon them. Economic and political radicalism rather than religious unorthodoxy became the root of most academic freedom and responsibility disputes. Sometimes the alleged radical was protected, as in the case of Professor Richard T. Ely, an economist at the University of Wisconsin, who not only retained his position but won a stirring statement of academic freedom from the University regents. Sometimes the dissenter found himself dismissed or forced to resign, as in the cases of Scott Nearing, a young teacher at the University of Pennsylvania in 1914, and a professor of economics at Wesleyan University, Willard Clark Fisher. In order to protect and extend the area of academic freedom, a group of professors in 1914, led especially by two professors of philosophy of quite different philosophical points of view, John Dewey and A. O. Lovejoy of Johns Hopkins, met and founded the American Association of University Professors. Though the fundamental law of colleges and universities remained—statutory power vested in the board of trustees, the president and other administrators the board's agents, and the faculty its employees—the AAUP successfully over the years achieved agreements between faculties and trustees that greatly modified both campus practices and the legal situation.

The Progressive Spirit in Literature

Tastes and practices in literature do not change overnight, and many of the great writers of the late nineteenth century continued the techniques and themes they had earlier found successful. Mark Twain lived until 1910. William Dean Howells lived until 1920 as the accepted dean of American letters, and several important novelists continued in his genteel realist tradition. Indeed, Edith Wharton, best known for *Ethan Frome* (1911), and Willa Cather were productive during this period and for years later. Miss Wharton lived on to 1937 and Miss Cather until 1947. Ellen Glasgow, a Virginia novelist in many ways similar to these two women, lived until 1945. The later writings of these women, however, struck most people as unusually mild and old-fashioned. Two immigrant novelists of this tradition bear mention: Ole Rölvaag, professor of Norwegian literature at St. Olaf's College, whose masterpiece was *Giants in the Earth* (1927) but whose other novels about Norwegian and Irish immigrants on the northern Great Plains were powerful, and Abraham Cahan, publisher and editor of a Socialist New York Yiddish-language newspaper who wrote a strong but neglected novel, *The Rise of David Levinsky* (1917).

But despite the strong survival of this older tradition, two vigorous and almost new developments in American literature pushed to the foreground: experiment with technique and form together with new and harsher themes, and social literature, or the literary expression of social criticism and revolt. In the novel the main new form was the so-called naturalist school. Naturalism has been a rather loosely used term sometimes meant only to apply to harsh realism with a special emphasis upon a candid treatment of sex, poverty, and violence and sometimes to signify an element of social determinism in the handling of fictional characters. Stephen Crane is usually regarded as the first important American novelist in the naturalist tradition. Crane died in 1900 before he was thirty, but he had already written *Maggie, A Girl of the Streets* (1892), and *The Red Badge of Courage* (1895).

The naturalist trend merged with social criticism in the novels of Theodore Dreiser, one of the most important of American novelists of all time despite the fact that he never learned to write with even a touch of grace. A German-American from Terre Haute, Indiana, who had moved to Chicago to make his literary career, Dreiser had his first novel, *Sister Carrie*, published in 1900. He very nearly did not have it published at all. Harper's turned it down, and after Doubleday refused it, Page accepted the manuscript and tried to back out of the obligation. Since the firm was legally committed, it published the book in as small a way as possible, issuing a small edition without a name on the cover. Dreiser went back to working for pulp magazines. Ten years later, when he submitted his second novel to Harper's, the publishers believed the public's attitude toward fictional sex had changed sufficiently for them to issue it, and *Jennie Gerhardt* appeared in 1911. In *The Financier* (1912) and *The Titan* (1914) Dreiser wrote powerful indictments of capitalists and their business and political methods. But the way of the uncompromising rebel is difficult, and Dreiser did not win acceptance until the 1920's. Until even later Dreiser worked in the shadow of his better known but intellectually inferior brother, the popular song writer Paul Dresser ("My Gal Sal" and "The Banks of the Wabash").

Social criticism and rebellion characterized many of the important novelists of the prewar twentieth century. Frank Norris, who with *McTeague* (1899) had written one of the first American naturalistic novels, contributed two of the strongest social novels, *The Octopus* (1901) and *The Pit* (1903). Norris intended to write a trilogy to be called *The Epic of Wheat*, but he died at the age of thirty-two before he finished the cycle. The Octopus was the Southern Pacific Railroad, whose many tentacles strangled California wheat farmers and labor. *The Pit* was a novel about speculation on the Chicago grain exchange. Elements of naturalism appeared in Norris' epics, but they also contained strong strains of sentimentality and supernaturalism. In *The Octopus*, for example, the treatment of the railroad engineer and his little daughter was nothing more than old-fashioned tear-jerking, and the mystic character who saw beyond the horizon was out of keeping with the rest of the novel. The muckraking journalist David Graham Phillips wrote several strongly felt but easily forgotten social novels, such as *The Great God Success* (1901) and *The Plum Tree* (1905) before he was shot and killed on the street by a mad violinist in 1911. Robert Herrick, an instructor at the University of Chicago, wrote damning accounts of American men of wealth in *The Memoirs of an American Citizen* (1905) and *Clark's Field* (1914). Brand Whitlock drew upon his experience in municipal politics for *The Thirteenth District* (1902). Two Socialist novelists, Upton Sinclair and Jack London, wrote perhaps the most severe and revolutionary novels that attacked capitalism or aspects of it and, surprisingly, were among the most popular of such writers. Sinclair's *The Jungle*, mentioned in Chapter 5, was his best-known work of this period. London, a left-wing Socialist who signed his letters for several years with "Yours for the Revolution," was a violent and often confused social critic who had been an Alaskan gold seeker, a sailor, a tramp, and a casual laborer before he enrolled as a student at the University of California. Through both his social novels and his adventure books like *The Call of the Wild* (1903) and *The Sea Wolf* (1904) ran a stream of mystic glorification of the primitive. In *The War of the Classes* (1905) and *Revolution* (1910), he preached the usual left Socialist line, but in *The Iron Heel* (1908) and a short story inappropriately named "The Dream of Debs" (1908) he seemed to despair of conventional socialism and leaned toward anarchism, nihilism, and syndicalism.

As always, of course, many of the novels and novelists that were a rage in their day were deliberately popular things tailored to demonstrated mass taste. Such books as Alice Hagen Rice's *Mrs. Wiggs of the Cabbage Patch* (1902), John Fox's *The Little Shepherd of Kingdom Come* (1903), and Harold Bell Wright's *The Winning of Barbara Worth* (1912) became almost unreadable to a later generation brought up on stronger stuff. But these and other spasms of sentimentality like them were the big sellers of the earliest part of the century, and for years thereafter some high school English teachers tried to foist off such books as contemporary American fiction for a relief from the *Silas Marner* and *Ivanhoe* diet. Perhaps as good a measure of the strength of the social novel as any was that some deliberate best-seller writers such as Booth Tarkington and Winston Churchill (not to be confused with the English statesman) occasionally wrote political novels during this period, although their effect was soothing rather than inflammatory and they oozed gentility. Churchill turned from his usual historical romances to *Mr. Crewe's Career* (1908) which clucked mildly at railroad management. Tarkington chose the relatively safe position of opposition to political corruption in *The Gentleman From Indiana* (1899) and just after this period wrote *Turmoil*, a novel about factories in cities that seemed to suggest that their smoke constituted their greatest social problem. But that such writers had turned to political subjects at all and had been in the least critical of railroad officials and manufacturers indicated that the reading public had changed its social values considerably.

One of the giants of the American novel, Henry James, did not fit well into the new currents. Revolted by the new America, James fled to the milder climes of upper-class England in 1877, while still in his thirties, where he wrote intellectual novels that contrasted the naive and crass Americans with rich, cultured, and educated Europeans. Later in his career he became more acid. Americans read James and appreciated him more after his death in 1916 than during his lifetime. He was not easy to read, and during his life most readers preferred the more vigorous realists.

Just as Harold Bell Wright was one of the era's most popular novelists, James Whitcomb Riley of Indianapolis, a dialect versifier and professional Hoosier, was its most popular poet. Riley's sentimental verses caught the Indiana farmer's speech quite accurately, and although few people today would consider him a poet of stature, many of his contemporaries did. Yale and the University of Pennsylvania awarded him honorary degrees.

Edwin Arlington Robinson and William Vaughn Moody commanded more esteem than other poets of the age, although each of them confined himself to traditional techniques. Robinson concerned himself with the individual's psychological and spiritual problems. President Roosevelt, rather oddly, liked his work and granted the down-and-out poet a sinecure in the New York Customs House so that he could write without concern for his daily bread. Moody, a professor at the University of Chicago, spoke out on the issues of the day and was a vigorous anti-imperialist. His "On a Soldier Fallen in the Philippines" remains a strong poetic reaction against colonialism. It was not Moody's fault that the public preferred the chauvinistic verses of Rudyard Kipling.

Late in this period there developed a remarkable experimentation with poetry forms. Poetry that did not ryhme and that employed an unusual imagery was slow to achieve general public acceptance, but the cognoscenti found the new poetry exciting, and some of the less subtle new poets who used strong rhythms, such as Vachel Lindsay, attracted a wider following. Lindsay was one of the Chicago poets, a group that spoke loudly and often in a new idiom in behalf of and for the ordinary man. Lindsay, whose sympathy for the plain people showed forcefully in "Bryan, Bryan, Bryan," was a self-appointed people's troubadour who made his living, such as it was, by reading his poetry in small towns over the country. Carl Sandburg, whose first volume of poetry appeared in 1916, was a Chicago newspaperman and a son of Swedish immigrants from Galesburg, Illinois, who gloried in the roughness and toughness of Chicago, "the city with the broad shoulders." Edgar Lee Masters, a Chicago attorney, used conventional techniques for a poetically unconventional purpose in his *Spoon River Anthology* (1915), in which he sympathetically and humorously yet thoroughly explored the ways of a small Illinois town. The Spoon River people who came out best in Masters' verses were the rebels and the outcasts. Chicago also became the home of one of the first "little magazines" which were to become legion in the 1920's when Harriet Monroe began *Poetry* in 1912. The new poetry in 1914 acquired further impetus and respectability when Amy Lowell, a sister of Harvard University President A. Lawrence Lowell, published *Sword Blades and Poppy Seeds*. In Miss Lowell's hands the poetic experimentation began to move toward preciousness and obscurity of meaning and away from the outspoken democratic sympathies of the Chicago group.

The theater remained commercialized and imbued with the idea that its sole function was to entertain, which it did fairly well with conventional musical comedies and vaudeville. Broadway produced a few "problem dramas," but they lacked great merit. One of the problem plays that succeeded commercially was Israel Zangwill's *The Melting Pot*, a rather optimistic view of immigration. Zangwill, a British Zionist, was also a leader in the "little theater" movement which began late in this period. Distressed by the artistic timidity of Broadway producers, who were dependent upon mass appeal for their livelihood, many rebels of the theater turned to the small budgets of the "little theater" as a means of producing a theatrical art that would not be dependent upon popularity. Zangwill saw the idea as a natural for his specialty, the one-act play. Many actors saw it as a way to escape from the "star system" and develop a repertory theater that would better develop the young actor to professional maturity. Beginning about 1910, these people began to establish professional "little theaters" all over the country. The most successful were the Provincetown Players and the Washington Square Players, both of which began in 1915. Most of the others eventually had to become primarily amateur companies because the public failed to support even their limited budgets.

The Ferment in Art and Architecture

It was art more than any other aspect of American culture that underwent a revolutionary renaissance in the prewar twentieth century. In 1900, there was little art being produced in America that was worthy of the name, and of excitement in the art world there was almost none. By 1917, several artists of recognized lasting value had come forward, and American art was aflame with excitement. Most of the ferment in art was a revolt against the traditional and formal; it had relatively little social criticism during this period.

In 1900, Winslow Homer, Thomas Eakins, and Albert Pinkham Ryder, each a painter of major importance, were still alive and actively painting. Their influence in their time, however, was small. Homer had retreated in disgust from the New York art world to the coast of Maine, Eakins lived in obscurity in Philadelphia, and the pathetic half-mad Ryder worked in psychological isolation in Manhattan's Greenwich Village. John Singer Sargent, James A. McNeill Whistler, and Mary Cassatt were painters of merit, but they had left their American homes and lived almost altogether in Europe. The American art scene was dominated by the academies, particularly the National Academy of Design in New York. Academic painting was a weak and watered-down version of older European traditions. A few Academy artists such as William M. Chase and Childe Hassam occasionally produced an interesting canvas and most of them were technically quite proficient, but in general academic art was deficient in boldness, interest, and originality. But relative mediocrities had virtual control of exhibits, and there were few other ways for an artist to bring his work to the public. The galleries in New York and elsewhere specialized in old masters, for at that time the new millionaires, who were almost the only art purchasers in the country, were assiduously buying up Rembrandts, El Grecos, and the like, much to the alarm of Europeans. Anyone who was not in the Academy found it extremely difficult to exhibit in the annual shows and thereby sell his works. Academy members could exhibit what they wished. The New York Academy was limited to 125 self-perpetuating members. If an artist did not conform to academic standards, his chances of membership were remote.

In the atmosphere of revolt that produced new ideas in almost all fields of thought, a rebellion against the static, dull, and semimonopolistic art system was almost inevitable. The Establishment, as the English call it, was doomed in such an era of intellectual unrest. The forces that overthrew the Establishment in American art were two: a native school of realism led by Robert Henri and, a little later, a modernist movement with its roots in Paris, led by the New York photographer Alfred Stieglitz.

Robert Henri, born in Cincinnati, had studied art in Philadelphia, gone on to Paris, and returned to Philadelphia in 1891 fired up with enthusiasm for contemporary French painting, particularly with Eduard Manet. He attracted a group of newspaper illustrators—George Luks, William Glackens, John Sloan, and Everett Shinn—and interested them in selecting Philadelphia slum life for their subject matter. By 1904, these five artists had moved to New York where most of them continued to work for newspapers and magazines. Henri continued teaching which was his great contribution. He never himself developed into a great artist, but many of his students did, and he can truly be labelled the father of modern American realistic painting. To Henri and his followers, beauty in the sense that a rose is beautiful was not important in painting. What was important was to reproduce life realistically. If life were ugly or crude, the painter's task was to recreate its truth. Beauty would take care of itself if painting was true.

In 1908, the Macbeth Gallery in New York asked a young painter, Arthur B. Davies, to help select and arrange an exhibit of young American painters. Davies chose the five realists originally from Philadelphia and Ernest Lawson, Maurice B. Prendergast, and himself. Lawson, Prendergast, and Davies were not realists. The exhibition of "The Eight" was a landmark in the history of American art. The public was repelled but fascinated by the work of the realists who were quickly labelled the Ash Can School and called such things as "a revolutionary black gang." But the Ash Can School was revolutionary only in the artistic sense. Its art was not sharp enough to use as a social weapon except for a few sketches that some of its artists, Sloan for example, made for *The Masses*, a left-wing magazine of the day. Its artistic rebellion was part of the wider social rebellion, but these artists worked as sympathetic reporters of the life of the poor rather than as indignant preachers or agitators.

Of "The Eight" John Sloan was the most lasting painter. His work had a sympathetic warmth unmatched by his colleagues. His subjects were the ordinary people of New York City, shop girls, truck drivers, housewives going about their shopping. One of his best paintings, "Sixth Avenue and 30th Street," is typical of his subject matter with its shop girls strolling in the shadows of the El. When he later left New York for the artists' colony of Taos, New Mexico, much of the life went out of his work. Luks was a colorful and gay swashbuckler who found his forte in representations of show-business people whose personalities were similar to his own. Glackens was more detached in his painting than others of his school. He also differed from the others in that his canvases frequently told a human interest story in the manner of Pieter

Brueghel, the elder. Later he came under the influence of the French impressionists. Shinn was the least important of the Philadelphia group and soon drifted away from realism to turn to portraits, murals, theater design, and interior decoration.

George Bellows was certainly the most popular Ash Can painter and the one who brought the group its greatest public acceptance. Bellows was an athlete, the only major American painter who might have chosen to be a major league baseball player. A star infielder for The Ohio State University nine, he left Ohio State in his senior year in 1904 to go to New York to study with Henri. He learned quickly and painted rapidly, using his strength and vitality to produce as much as he could. One of his favorite subjects was prize fighters, and his "Stag at Sharkey's" has become one of the country's favorites. The public took to Bellows partly because he was the opposite of its false preconception of an artist: a pale Gallic fellow with a beret who was desperately poor and lived in a garret. Some critics in recent years have minimized Bellows as a painter, but whatever the long-term judgment, his role of popularizer is secure. Death from a ruptured appendix cut short his career at the age of forty-three in 1925. Among the artists that might be considered as akin to Bellows in a school of strenuous Americans were Rockwell Kent, Gifford Beal, and Leon Kroll. Two other American realists worthy of mention were Jerome Myers and Guy Pene du Bois.

While "The Eight" and other realists were concentrating on truth in the slums, another group was going back and forth between New York and Paris and importing enthusiasm for the new French art movements, particularly fauvism and cubism. Fauvism was a style of vivid colors and simplified and slightly distorted shapes of which Matisse was the outstanding exponent. They were labelled les fauves (the wild beasts) by their detractors after a famous Paris exhibit in 1905. Cubism was less concerned with emotion than with form, and in its simplest form broke down physical reality into its basic structural elements: cubes, cones, and cylinders. The American modernists found even greater difficulty than the realists in breaking the grip of the Academy over exhibitions.

Alfred Stieglitz, a successful photographer and proprietor of the Photo-Secession Gallery at 291 Fifth Avenue, New York, took up the modernists' cause. Stieglitz was a tremendously vital person who thought that the fulfillment of an individual's creative powers was the highest human value and that the artist should be nurtured and sheltered from the rebuffs of a hostile, philistine public. He made "291" a stimulating haven for modern artists where they could meet with one another, exhibit their work, and receive his financial help when they needed it most. The artists forgave Stieglitz his great ego. Before the war modernists clustered about him who were to become the great names of the 1920's and later such as John Marin, Max Weber, Arthur Dove, Charles Demuth, Charles Sheeler, Georgia O'Keeffe (whom Stieglitz married), Marsden Hartley, Oscar Bleumner, and Alfred Maurer. But in 1913 these artists and others jolted the public out of its artistic complacency as it had never been jolted before with the famous Armory Show, probably the most important art exhibition in American history.

The Armory Show—it took that name because it was held in the 69th Regiment Armory in New York—was the idea of a group of modernists plus a few realists who wanted to bring their work before a wide American public. They formed a radical rival to the Academy, the Association of American Painters and Sculptors, of which Arthur B. Davies became president. The Association decided to add a European section to its show in order to educate the public in avant garde modernism. Walt Kuhn, Maurer, Walter Pach, and the sculptor Jo Davidson arranged for the imports, and Bellows did most of the hanging. The final show included 1,600 pictures and sculptures, representing 307 American artists.

When the Armory Show opened in New York on February 17, 1913, it was as if a bomb had been exploded in the Academy and among the art critics who favored the academicians. The European section caused the greater uproar, particularly a cubist painting by Marcel Duchamp, a not very great painter, entitled "Nude Descending a Staircase." A yellow and brown composition of rectangular shapes arranged to suggest the kind of action that a camera would later capture with a stroboscopic photograph, the painting looked very little like either a nude or a staircase. Someone suggested it should have been entitled "Cyclone in a Shingle Factory." Theodore Roosevelt visited the show and pronounced that modern art was retrogressive and that the Navajoes painted better. Better informed viewers were equally outraged. The most eminent art critic of the day, Royal Cortissoz of the *New York Tribune*, wrote that the purpose of the modernists was "to turn the world upside down." Others asserted their purpose was to overturn morality and Christianity. Matisse drew considerable ridicule when it was discovered that one of his nudes in the exhibit possessed six toes. Critics dismissed Van Gogh and Cézanne as "unbalanced fanatics."

But despite the critical uproar the public went to the Armory. About one hundred thousand people paid admission, and untold numbers of school children entered free. New Yorkers bought 235 of the pieces; the Metropolitan Museum of Art became the first American museum to own a Cézanne. The show went on to Chicago and Boston. Chicagoans reacted to the exhibit, which was at the Art Institute, as had the New Yorkers. Matisse, Brancusi, and Pach were burned in effigy, but an eccentric Chicago lawyer, Arthur Jerome Eddy, defied the world and bought the controversial Duchamp painting. Only in Boston did the show fall flat. The Boston Irish and Brahmins simply ignored it; Boston was the only city where the show failed to meet its expenses. Altogether, about 250,000 people had paid money to see the show and bought over 300 of the paintings.

The academicians and the critics were sure that modern art was only a temporary madness, but they soon proved to be wrong. Thereafter, the market for academic paintings, either American or European, began to slip. Even the realist school was cut short. Cubism with its logical and geometric analysis of reality and fauvism with its simplified forms and brilliant colors sent many a young artist away from the Armory Show to experiment at his easel. Some artists modified their work only slightly and some went all the way; some were successful with the new ideas and some failed utterly. American artists soon went off into short-lived radical experiments of their own. One of these developments, synchronism, became completely abstract and concerned itself only with gradations of color. The leaders of synchronism were Morgan Russell, S. Macdonald-Wright, and his brother, the critic W. Huntington Wright who later became a highly popular detective novel writer under the name S. S. Van Dine. Another result of the show was that it brought to America a group of French modernists, among them Duchamp, who went so far as to predict that New York would soon replace Paris as the world's art center. They were fascinated by the vigor and vitality of America, but the hostility of most of the critics and the relative lack of a market for their works soon drove them back to the Left Bank.

American taste in art, at least among educated people in the cities, was changing very rapidly. Realism had seemed shocking in 1908 and modernism disgraceful in 1913, but a large comprehensive show of all kinds of new American art in New York in 1917 aroused little critical comment and caused no burnings in effigy. By the time the war brought practically a complete halt to the art world, metropolitan and cosmopolitan Americans were accepting the artistic revolution. The millions who lived outside the biggest cities were hardly concerned. What little art they saw was still of the painted-dishes and *Saturday Evening Post* variety, and it would be another generation before the new art became national. But the new art had established its crucial bridge-heads by World War I.

Architecture, fully as much in the doldrums as art in the late nineteenth century, underwent a renaissance of its own. Two related but separate prewar developments in architecture in time came radically to change the face of the American city: the use of a structural steel skeleton for large nonresidential buildings and the slow development of functionalism for all kinds of building.

A group of Chicago architects, notably Louis Sullivan, Daniel Burnham, and John W. Root, led in the abandonment of huge masonry wall structures and the adoption of a steel skeleton enclosed by a sheath of other material. The new technique opened up many possibilities: big buildings could be built higher into the air at less cost, they could be covered with more interesting materials than brick or stone—even with glass—and they enabled buildings to be lighter, more graceful, and less of a mass of rock. Steel skeletons made the modern skyscraper possible, and the skyscraper was a natural way out of the high land prices and lack of room for expansion that plagued New York's Manhattan. Though developed in Chicago, the skyscraper came into its own in New York because of the greater need for it and because the soft clay geological structure under the midwestern city made a very tall and heavy building more expensive than the same building would be on Manhattan's granite base. The first real skyscraper, although not tall by later standards, was Burnham's Flatiron building in lower New York completed in 1902. The peculiar requirements of the small triangular site required the steel skeleton technique. Other very tall buildings soon thrust up above the New York skyline. The Singer building was completed in 1908 and the Metropolitan Tower the next year. Cass Gilbert's Woolworth building, a tall one even by contemporary standards (785 feet and still a Manhattan landmark) was finished in 1912. The skyscraper presented social problems of its own, as a later generation would learn while it fretted about commuting from its suburban bedroom communities to the central work city with its dark man-made canyons, but it provided a building solution that seemed plausible at the time.

Sullivan and a young colleague of his, Frank Lloyd Wright, began experimenting with functional designs in architecture in the late nineteenth century. Their motto, "form follows function," was the reverse of the dominant architectural thought of the period, especially for public buildings. The firm of Mead, McKim, and White was the most highly esteemed design group in America in the early part of the century. Men like Charles F. McKim had rescued American architecture from the horrors of the pseudo-Gothic—such as the towered red brick armories and college buildings which still exist in considerable numbers—only to create a pseudoclassical school of their own. Their emphasis was on reproducing "the grandeur that was Rome"—McKim himself was a leader in the establishment of the American Academy at Rome in 1905—and to design monumental buildings that were impressive by ancient esthetic standards. A building's function, the uses to which it was to be put, seemed not to concern them at all. Seth Low Library of Columbia University is a case in point. Low Library is an impressive building, especially from the outside, with its heavy columns, its exceptionally wide stone steps, its fountains, and its great dome. As a library it was impossible. The acoustics of the reading room under the dome magnified a whisper into a reverberating roar, and the awkward-sized rooms around the periphery of the building proved too large for offices and too small for library stacks. Columbia had to abandon it as a library in the 1930's. Sullivan and Wright, on the other hand, argued that a building should be designed around its function and that so long as the necessary lines were kept clean and unadorned by "gingerbread" the beauty of the structure would follow automatically.

It took time for even such rebels as Wright and Sullivan to break free of architectural clichés, but Wright's so-called prairie houses in Chicago in the century's first decade came close to the functional ideal. The public was slower to accept the new architecture than the architects, but by midcentury practically all new public buildings and many new residences had at least made concessions to the functional ideal. Wright, who was active in architecture until his death in 1959, moved on to an occasional romantic striving to be unique and sometimes violated his basic functional precepts, but no other figure in architecture, in Europe or America, did more to jolt the public out of its traditional architectural values.

American Music in the Early Twentieth Century

The United States matured more slowly in music than it did in most of the other cultural forms. In 1900, the nation was not quite a musical wasteland—there had always been folk and church music—but the opportunities to hear serious music played or sung by professional musicians were few and limited to some of the biggest cities. The person who lived in a smaller city might never be exposed to good music, except perhaps for an occasional touring musical organization, unless he was a member of an immigrant group that had brought a musical tradition across the Atlantic. Furthermore, music even in the big cities was dependent upon Europeans. For musical performers, conductors, and composers, the United States was an importing nation.

In 1917, America still imported its serious music for the most part, although progress had been made in the development of American composition and training of native artists. The biggest change in the field of music between 1900 and 1917 had been a considerable extension of the musical audience. Far more people had opportunities to hear live concerts by professional musicians, and the phonograph made it possible for millions to hear at least a scratchy and thin reproduction of the best music of the world. The phonograph was to music almost what the invention of printing had been to literature.

Several cities established or re-established symphony orchestras during this period. The Philadelphia Symphony began in 1900, and after 1912, when it took Leopold Stokowski from the Cincinnati Orchestra, it became one of the great orchestras of the world. Minneapolis founded its symphony in 1903, Detroit in 1914, and Baltimore in 1916. In 1904, the Russian Symphony Orchestra of New York began a fifteen-year career of specialization in Russian music. Two older symphony organizations improved vastly during this period, the Chicago Symphony under the direction of the German-born Frederick Stock and the New York Philharmonic. The New York organization, founded in 1842 and the nation's oldest permanent orchestra—indeed, only two European orchestras have a longer unbroken history—was until 1901 a cooperative enterprise of the musicians who paid the expenses and retained what profits there were for their compensation. In that year a group of wealthy New Yorkers agreed to underwrite the orchestra and guarantee the musicians a salary.

The prewar years in retrospect were "the golden age of opera," due largely to the competition offered the staid Metropolitan Opera by another New York opera company, the Manhattan Opera begun by Oscar Hammerstein in 1906. After four financially disastrous years, Hammerstein sold out to the Metropolitan and much of his company moved to the Chicago Opera, which combined with Philadelphia to support a first-rate organization that split its season between the two cities. While Hammerstein was still offering competition, the Metropolitan brought Giulio Gatti-Casazza from Italy as its new manager, and he raised its standards until it became recognized as one of the great companies of the world. Enrico Caruso had made his debut with the Metropolitan in 1903 and the beloved Ernestine Schumann-Heink had been with the company since the 1890's, but Gatti-Casazza attracted such stars as Emmy Destinn and Feodor Chaliapin.

Thomas Edison and others had invented the phonograph in the 1880's, but it was not until soon after 1900 that one could purchase discs with great music recorded by the world's best performers. In 1903, Columbia Records began its "Celebrity Series," and in 1904 Victor began its "Red Seal" recordings. The Victor Talking Machine Company with its dog and phonograph-trumpet trademark and its crank and spring powered Victrola (a trade name so general it became a widely used generic term) had practically a monopoly in the American phonograph market. By the war, thousands of middle-class homes had a Victrola and a collection of Caruso, Schumann-Heink, Fritz Kreisler, and Ignace Paderewski records. Caruso's great voice and colorful personality made him America's first musician folk hero.

American composers of serious music were far behind their counterparts in painting and other visual arts. Edward MacDowell, the nation's first native son to receive world recognition as a composer—whatever the eventual estimate of him—left Columbia University in a huff in 1904 after a dispute with

122

President Nicholas Murray Butler. He died four years later. Other than MacDowell's work there was little native composition played that was of lasting interest. Anton Dvořák had lived and worked in the United States from 1892 until 1895 when he returned to Bohemia. Dvořák was a musical nationalist who strongly urged the nation's composers to concentrate on their culture's unique folk-music themes. He himself composed his "New World Symphony" in America, but few of the others who tried to adapt Negro and Indian music to a more ambitious medium achieved much success. Victor Herbert's operetta music, somewhere between grand opera and Tin Pan Alley in its quality and ambition, flowed from his pen with ease and became very popular. The experimental music then being composed in Europe by Igor Stravinsky, Arnold Schoenberg, and Claude Debussy attracted no like-minded musical rebels in the United States. Only Charles Ives, whose musical career was most unusual, wrote experimental music, and he did so without knowledge of what was being done in Europe. Ives had received his early musical training from his father, a music teacher of Danbury, Connecticut, and at Yale. Upon leaving New Haven he went into the insurance business and quickly became a leader in the business when he developed the so-called estate-planning idea. He worked hard at his business by day and at composition by night and on weekends. The few musicians who read his music dismissed it as too bizarre for serious consideration. Not until 1919 did he publish any of his work, and not until 1939 was any of it performed in the United States. By then the experimental music of Europe had been played enough in America partially to break down the hostility toward it, and Ives, in his old age, was hailed as a composer of the first rank.

The early history of jazz remains partially obscured because the earliest such musicians went unnoticed by people interested in the history of music and because there has since been such a spectacular amount of commercialized nonsense on the subject. In the 1890's, ragtime began to be popular and some ragtime music was published. Ragtime was primarily piano music characterized by a march rhythm with the left hand and complicated syncopated figures with the right. Irving Berlin's "Alexander's Ragtime Band," frequently played as an example of rag, was not ragtime at all. The best known composer of rag music, Scott Joplin of St. Louis and Kansas City, had great ambitions for the form and even wrote two rag operas, one produced in St. Louis in 1903 and the other in New York in 1915. About 1910, the blues began to be popular beyond the Negro population and a few musicians, many of them Negroes, began to elaborate the basic blues, which was vocal music, and adapt it for instruments. W. C. Handy wrote "Memphis Blues" in 1909 and "St. Louis Blues" in 1914. The blues had a basic structure of twelve measures and was characterized by the "blue note," a slightly flattened tone between an ordinary flat and a natural that the singer or instrumentalist slid into rather than hitting suddenly. Upon the instrumental versions of ragtime and the blues and some of the practices of New Orleans brass bands, there grew what gradually came to be known as Dixieland jazz. When the first Dixieland bands played in Chicago and New York in 1915 and 1917 respectively, they caused a sensation, although it was not until the 1920's that, except for a few cities, jazz became well known among whites.

The Work of the Scientists and Scholars

Much of the outstanding work done by American scientists during this period was in medicine and related fields. The new scientific investigation of nutrition, of which W. O. Atwater of Wesleyan University was a pioneer, in time led to a great improvement in the health, strength, and vitality of the American people. Thomas B. Osborne of the Connecticut agricultural experiment station, Elmer V. McCollum of Johns Hopkins, and Lafayette B. Mendel of Yale began a series of experiments in 1909 that indicated the existence and importance of vitamins. Beginning with this basic knowledge, scientists within a generation had found nutritional cures and preventatives for rickets, scurvy, pellagra, and beriberi, and public health workers and publicists had disseminated nutritional knowledge that greatly improved the nation's well being.

The successful campaign against yellow fever illustrated forcefully the value of medical cooperation among scientists of several nations. An army physician, Major William C. Gorgas, had worked without success in Cuba during and immediately after the war with Spain to eliminate this tropical disease. He operated on the assumption that the disease spread by personal contact. A special yellow fever commission headed by Walter Reed in 1900 tested the theory of a Cuban physician, Carlos J. Finlay, that the fever was spread by the mosquito and found it valid. Thereafter, antimosquito measures successfully prevented yellow fever epidemics. Workers on the Panama Canal from 1906 to 1914 had not a single case of it, and a New Orleans epidemic was nipped in the bud in 1905. Progress in treating a person who had contracted the fever, however, had to await the discovery in 1919 by Hideyo Noguchi, a Japanese scientist with the Rockefeller Institute, of the yellow fever spirochete. French medics in North Africa and American scientists in Mexico, led by Howard T. Ricketts of the University of Chicago, discovered that body lice were the carriers of typhus. This 1906 discovery proved valuable during World War I in controlling the disease in Europe.

Americans led in the western world's campaign against tuberculosis. In 1898, Theobald Smith of Harvard differentiated between the tubercule bacilli that infected cattle and the ones that struck down human beings, and early in the new century Edward L. Trudeau of Saranac Lake, New York, who had demonstrated that rest, fresh air, and a good diet frequently effected a cure for tuberculosis of the lungs, led in the establishment of the National Tuberculosis Association. This organization, the first of many like it in the United States, raised money to subsidize medical research on the disease and to educate the public about how best to prevent it. The results were excellent. The annual death rate from lung tuberculosis in the United States dropped from 166.7 per 100,000 in 1900 to 92.2 in 1920, and similar improvement was made in Great Britain and Scandinavia where the disease had been even more prevalent.

Tuberculosis was largely a public health matter, and during this period the field of public health became for the first time a major and respectable part of medicine. Not until 1912 was there a professional magazine in the field. But public health work in quarantine precautions, public health nursing for the poor, particularly in childbirth, and education were largely responsible for extending the average life expectancy at birth from forty-nine years in 1901 to fifty-one in 1910 and to fifty-six in 1920.

During this period, European mathematicians and physicists, notably Albert Einstein and Max Planck, developed new theories that were soon to revolutionize man's view of the universe, but few American physicists contributed to the earliest thought in the new physics. The main exceptions were Albert A. Michelson of the University of Chicago, whose contribution was measuring the speed of light, and Joseph Henry of the Smithsonian Institution, who contributed to electromagnetic theory.

American geneticists, however, had an international reputation in their relatively new field. Not until after 1900 was the research on heredity by the Austrian monk Gregor Mendel discovered, but the work of such American scientists as Jacques Loeb and Thomas Hunt Morgan soon carried the work far. In the late nineteenth century, the Darwinian theory of evolution had been the center of popular controversy. Now the theory was widely accepted but Americans turned to debate over eugenics, or the application of genetics to mankind. While students and others debated endlessly, and on the whole meaninglessly, over the relative importance of heredity and environment in molding the individual, a few states, notably Indiana, accepted the extreme eugenecists' theories at their face value and sought to improve the breed by wholesale sexual sterilization of habitual criminals.

But if Darwinian evolution was not as often a subject for hot public debate in the twentieth century as it had been in the 1870's and 1880's, it nevertheless had a great impact on thought beyond the fields of biology and religion as increasing numbers of people began to grasp its full implications. Philosophers, for example, led by Charles S. Peirce, William James, and John Dewey, began to abandon the idea of the superiority of the fixed and final and to view life and thought as an experiment in constant process with no prospect of ending. This philosophical school, known as pragmatism, instrumentalism, and experimentalism, in abandoning fixed and absolute standards for "truth," was left with the problem of establishing another standard. Peirce, a Harvard mathematician and philosopher, had emphasized in 1878 in a paper entitled "How to Make Our Ideas Clear" that the test for clarity of ideas was their consequences in practice. An idea, then, was akin to a scientific hypothesis, its validity to be tested by actual life. James built upon Peirce and erected individualist pragmatism. Each individual had to establish for himself what was true and false, and the test was how well an idea "worked" in practice. He was much interested in individuals' religious experiences, and to him the validity of a religious idea, no matter how wildly inconsistent with the modern scientific temper, depended upon the degree of emotional satisfaction the idea in practice gave to the individual. Dewey went beyond James and applied the instrumentalist test to social ideas. To Peirce, pragmatism had to do with abstract logic. James gave it a personal and emotional emphasis. Dewey raised it to a rule for social action. And to the common query of Dewey's critics about what standard to apply when measuring whether or to what degree a social idea "works," Dewey in practice applied democratic concepts as well as the Benthamite view of "the greatest good for the greatest number."

Technical philosophy is a complex and difficult field no more than hazily understood by a vast majority of people. Yet Americans, without actually knowing it, had long in actual practice been pragmatists in meeting routine and practical problems in their lives. Older absolute social doctrines, however, did not and have not yielded fully to relativism and pragmatism, and many people continue to judge social ideas by a dogma—"rugged individualism," capitalism of the Adam Smith age or some other model, and for only a few, Marxism. Yet Americans have been pragmatic in their social actions to a considerable degree and by thousands of pragmatic decisions, both governmental and otherwise, have created a society that is necessarily internally inconsistent but workable and amenable to further experiment. And as Americans look at some other nations which have been more inflexibly doctrinaire, most of them are gratified by their own methods of determining social policy, illogical in the absolute sense though they may be.

Scholars in history and the social sciences to a remarkable extent broke from traditional ideas and methods and turned their minds to problems in their fields that were relevant to contemporary issues. A few historians, but only a few during this period, widened the focus of their backward-looking lenses to include a larger part of man's experience than his political, diplomatic, and military activities. James Harvey Robinson of Columbia University argued for a "new history," and Frederick Jackson Turner and his students, both at Wisconsin and Harvard, investigated not only the social history of people on the frontier but also the social and intellectual life of other parts of the nation's past. Those whose primary concerns remained with political history began to look at past politics in a new and more exciting way that both reflected the ferment of progressivism and contributed to it.

A political scientist from the University of Washington, J. Allen Smith, in 1907 published *The Spirit of American Government* in which he stressed economic groups rather than political forms and organizations. He also suggested that the writing and adoption of the federal Constitution itself had been the work of an interested economic group. Six years later, Charles A. Beard, then a professor of history and government at Columbia, published his epochal *An Economic Interpretation of the Constitution*. The book created a furor. Beard brought forth evidence to support Smith's interpretation and described in considerable cool detail how men of property had written and secured the ratification of the Constitution in order to protect and extend their economic interest against a more democratic opposition. To attribute an economic motive to the founders of the Republic, a group of men who had become more the object of hagiography than of historical method, was an outrage to conservatives. To progressives, Beard offered an historical basis for their belief that the basic document of American government and law should be flexibly interpreted to allow government a greater degree of control over the economy. The irreverent were delighted with the consternation that Beard's book caused stuffy standpatters, such as Columbia's President Butler, who when asked if he had read Beard's last book replied, "I hope I have." Butler was to be disappointed. In 1915 Beard's *The Economic Origins of Jeffersonian Democracy* carried the story on through the Republic's earliest years.

Sociology, a new academic field still fighting to establish itself, was still largely concerned with establishing its boundaries and methods. By the end of this period, most sociologists had abandoned their earlier efforts to write all-encompassing abstractions about society and settled down to a systematic investigation of the relationships between individuals and social groups. Economists, however, wrought a revolution in their discipline. The classical economists of the nineteenth century had built elaborate and abstract models of supposed universality from which, they believed, could logically be deduced the solution of any economic problem. But the economy in fact did not behave according to the classical economists' models. As the economy itself changed, an increasing number of economists abandoned their older scholastic approach and began to study actual economic practices and institutions. Richard T. Ely of Johns Hopkins and later of Wisconsin and his colleague John R. Commons studied the history of labor. Wesley C. Mitchell of Columbia concentrated on actual fluctuations of the business cycle rather than armchair theories and economic abstractions. Easily the most original and radical of the economists of the period was Thorstein Veblen, a son of Norwegian immigrants who ranged far and wide through economic thought challenging the traditional assumptions, particularly that man was primarily an economic animal. His *The Theory of the Leisure Class* (1899) advanced the thesis that a primary motive for acquiring wealth was to be able to impress others with "conspicuous consumption" rather than to gratify economic wants. Veblen's influence was not so great in his time as it was after his death in 1929, but he shared with other economists of his own generation a tendency to widen the scope of economic studies and make them relevant to actual life and to favor economic reform.

CHAPTER SEVEN

Beyond the Continental Boundaries, 1898-1916

DURING THE CENTURY FROM THE END OF THE NAPOLEONIC WARS TO the outbreak of World War I in 1914, there was a major change in the line-up of world powers although the period had no wars of world proportion. After the Congress of Vienna, the major powers were Great Britain, France, Russia, Austria, and Spain. In the late nineteenth and early twentieth centuries, Germany, Japan, and the United States had moved into the small circle of powerful nations. Spain had dropped from the small circle by the gradual loss of her Latin American empire and her defeat in 1898. Russia had declined relatively as she failed to industrialize as fast as the West and had yielded much of her Asian strength to Japan. Austria had become relatively less important as her culturally similar neighbor, Germany, had come to the fore. This chapter's subject is the rise of the United States to a position as one of the major powers.

The United States did not suddenly in the summer of 1898 emerge from obscurity and impotence to major-power status, important as the imperialist victory over Spain was. The economic base of America's strength had slowly developed, first in agriculture and commerce and then, in a late nineteenth-century rush, in industry. American imperialism even did not emerge suddenly and without precedent in 1898. An enormous piece of valuable land had been wrested from Mexico by force in the 1840's, and the purchase of Alaska in the 1860's had been the first major acquisition of non-contiguous territory. Nor had the United States been economically isolated. Yankee traders had been active as far away as Asia even in the days of wood sailing ships. The years 1898 and immediately thereafter were a culmination of earlier forces and developments, ones that saw the United States accelerate its older tendencies and thereby burst into recognition as a world power.

The term "imperialism" needs clarification and some subdividing distinctions. In this book the term "colonialism" or "colonial imperialism" signifies a nation's territorial acquisition and rule of an area and a people. America's acquisition of the Philippines was an example of colonial imperialism. For the economic penetration of an area with sufficient strength substantially to influence the area's governmental policies and to assume a major role in the area's economy, the term "informal imperialism" or "economic imperialism" will be used. United States policy toward Mexico, Venezuela, and most of Latin America in general north of the equator was an example of informal or economic imperialism. The distinction between the two is useful and valid, but the two kinds of imperialism should not be regarded as hard and fast categories or as mutually exclusive. Economic considerations were very important in colonialism, and sometimes the United States—and other nations as well—exercised policies generally thought of as colonialism, such as the employment of military or naval force, to effect an informal or economic imperialist end. From 1898 to 1916 the United States pursued both colonial and informal imperialist policies.

The Administration of the Colonial Empire

The debate over the Spanish treaty of 1898 provoked a heated discussion. Many citizens were particularly hostile to the idea of the United States becoming a colonial power on the grounds that it was a reversal of the nation's ideals when it became independent, that such a colonial empire would be expensive to administer, and that it would probably involve the country in needless disputes with other powers that might lead to war. The anti-imperialists pointed out that it was not consistent to go to war to free Cuba from Spain and then annex the Philippines, eight thousand miles from American Shores. Had the war been fought for or against imperialism?

The Philippine Islands were the crux of the controversy as the Senate debated the treaty in January, 1899. In order to reject the acquisition of the Philippines, the Senate would have had to reject the treaty entirely. Bryan went to Washington and urged his followers in the Senate to accept the treaty and then grant independence to the Filipinos. Enough Democrats voted for the treaty to pass it fifty-seven to twenty-seven, two more votes than necessary for ratification, on February 6. On February 4, perceiving at last that they were only exchanging Madrid for Washington, the Filipinos began a revolt led by Emilio Aguinaldo. Ten days later, the first clear-cut vote came in the Senate on the matter of Philippine independence. A resolution looking toward Filipino independence ended in a tie vote, and Vice-President Garret A. Hobart cast the deciding vote against independence. The Senate then went on to hedge with a resolution that declared American annexation of the Philippines was not permanent and that the nation would "in due time" "make such disposition of said islands as will best promote the interests of the United States and the inhabitants of said islands."

There the issue stood for years, but first there was the matter of quelling the Filipino insurrection. Over two years were required to crush the rebellion. The army used about seventy thousand men, four times as many as had been necessary to wrest Cuba from Spain. Before the affair was finished, the army invoked the kind of methods against the Filipinos that the Spanish had used in trying to crush the Cuban insurrection.

Even before Aguinaldo's capture in March, 1901, the United States began to lay plans for a permanent government of the islands. In July, 1901, a civilian administration with William Howard Taft as governor took over from the military. Thereafter, Congress made several modifications of the Philippine governmental structure, but in general the government remained one with a governor appointed by the president as the executive, a Philippines Commission appointed by the president as a Cabinet and upper house of the legislature, and a White House–appointed judiciary. After 1907, Christian Filipinos were allowed to elect a lower legislative chamber, and usually the president appointed some Filipinos to the Commission. Both by changes in the law and changes in appointments and practices the Filipinos gradually acquired a greater degree of self-government, but the ultimate constitutional power remained in Washington. The first major change in American administration of the islands came with the passage of the Organic Act for the Philippines of 1916, usually called the Jones Act. The Democratic party had consistently in its platforms advocated Philippine independence, but Wilson and his administration were not willing to grant what the party had long favored. The Jones Act provided for Filipino election of both houses of the legislature and reduced the powers of the governor-general. Wilson's governor-general, Francis B. Harrison, played only a small role and handed most responsibility and power over to Filipino leaders of the legislature and to his appointed Filipino officials. This situation obtained until 1921, when a Republican administration in Washington appointed General Leonard Wood to be governor-general.

The material situation of the Filipinos significantly improved under Washington's administration. Americans built roads, schools, sewage plants, and hospitals. The American market for Philippine products, sugar, cocoanut oil, and hemp, brought the islands a degree of prosperity. Perhaps most important, Washington effected a basic land reform. When the United States acquired the Philippines, various orders of the Roman Catholic church owned about four hundred thousand acres of "friar lands" greatly desired by the Filipino people. During the insurrection many tenants on this land attempted to appropriate it by force. In 1902, Roosevelt sent Taft to the Vatican to negotiate for a settlement. The United States paid $7 million for the land in question and later disposed of it through land grants to Filipinos.

Cubans also soon discovered that the Spanish-American War had not entirely freed them from colonial status. Two years after the end of hostilities in Cuba, the army still governed the island, and Democrats during the campaign of 1900 charged that the McKinley administration planned to keep Cuba for the United States in defiance of a pledge made when Congress declared war. McKinley issued a call for a Cuban constitutional convention which met soon and devised a frame of government with the advice of the American military commander. The constitution did not grant suffrage to Cubans who were illiterate (about two-thirds of the population) or who owned less than $250 in property unless they had served in the Cuban army against Spain. Then in March, 1901, Congress enacted the Platt Amendment to an army appropriations bill that in effect made Cuba a United States protectorate. The Platt Amendment stipulated that the republic of Cuba agree in a special treaty with the United States that the United States should have the right to intervene in Cuban affairs to maintain its government, that Cuba should never by treaty with another power impair its independence, that it should keep its public debt within its capacity to repay, that the acts of the American military government not be abrogated, that the United States plans for public sanitation be continued, and that it should sell or lease to the United States what lands were necessary for naval bases. Cuba really had no choice but to accept such a treaty. Furthermore, Washington pressured Cuba into adding the Platt Amendment provisions as an appendix to its constitution.

American troops withdrew from Cuba in May, 1902, after having been there nearly four years. A reciprocity treaty the following year stimulated the market for Cuban sugar, some of which was produced on American owned plantations, and brought a measure of prosperity to the island. In 1906, a revolt broke out against the Cuban government and the threatened Cuban president asked for American intervention. Roosevelt sent Secretary of War Taft to Cuba to try to bring about a reconciliation between the factions, but when Taft failed in that purpose he assumed governmental authority. Roosevelt soon established a provisional government under the control of the governor of the Canal Zone, Charles E. Magoon, which governed until the troops pulled out again early in 1909. In 1911 and 1917 there were further brief American troop interventions.

Puerto Rico and Hawaii were administered by territorial governments similar in pattern to the Philippine system. The navy governed Guam, Samoa, and Wake. A series of Supreme Court cases in 1901 known collectively as the Insular cases determined that American territorial possessions were not in law fully a part of the United States although belonging to it, or, to use the popular phrase of the day, "the Constitution did not follow the flag" unless Congress so legislated. The Foraker Act of 1900 established a system of government for Puerto Rico and levied a tariff, to be effective until 1902, against Puerto Rican imports of 15 per cent of the regular rates then charged under the Dingley Tariff. The first Insular case concerned an importer of Puerto Rican sugar who had been required to pay the full Dingley Tariff duties on a shipment made after the acquisition of the island but before the Foraker Act. The Court ruled that the importer's duty payment should be refunded since Puerto Rico was not a foreign country. Another Insular case had to do with an importer who had paid the 15 per cent requirement of the Foraker Act and sued for a refund of his payment on the grounds that Puerto Rico was part of the United States and that the Constitution declared that "all duties, imposts, and excises shall be uniform throughout the United States." The Supreme Court denied the refund in a five–four decision since Puerto Rico, it said, was not precisely a part of the United States. Subsequent cases applied the same doctrine to the Philippines and Hawaii.

The United States rounded out is colonial empire in 1917 with the purchase from Denmark of the Virgin Islands in the Caribbean. In 1902, Denmark and the United States agreed to a treaty by which the islands would go to the

United States for $5 million but the upper house of the Danish parliament rejected the treaty by one vote. The 1917 price was $25 million. This time the Danish parliament did not ratify the treaty until the Danes had overwhelmingly supported it in a national referendum.

The Open Door Notes and Informal Imperialism in Asia

In September, 1899, while the debate between imperialists and anti-imperialists was still going strong, McKinley's Secretary of State, John Hay, a man of letters who had once been one of Lincoln's personal secretaries, sent Germany, Great Britain, and Russia the first Open Door note. He subsequently dispatched the note to Japan, Italy, and France. After a war with Japan in 1894–1895 in which China had demonstrated her weakness to the world, the European powers had moved into China and wrested leases and spheres of influence from the weak imperial government to further European commercial interests. The idea for the Open Door in China came originally from the British largely through Alfred E. Hippisley, an Englishman who had worked in the Chinese customs service and who had consulted frequently in 1899 with Hay and W. W. Rockhill, who held the State Department's Far Eastern desk. A group of American exporters to China also influenced Hay by organizing a powerful propaganda campaign against European dismemberment of the Chinese Empire. On the whole, however, the vast amount of research that has gone into the origins of the Open Door policy might better have been spent on the policy's effects.

The first Open Door notes, which had solely to do with Chinese commercial matters, asked the powers to whom the notes were addressed to reply with assurances on the following points: (1) that within its leasehold or sphere of influence no power would interfere with any treaty port or already established vested interest; (2) that Chinese treaty tariffs would apply within each sphere of influence and would be collected by the Chinese customs service; and (3) that no power within its sphere would charge the merchants of any power more for harbor fees and railroad charges than it did its own nationals. Since to oppose openly the Open Door idea was rather like taking the stump in favor of sin, the other powers, except Russia (and Italy, which had no spheres of influence), did not state their opposition but were equivocal and evasive and replied their acceptance was contingent upon the acceptance of the other nations. Russia politely refused which, if its refusal had been known by the other powers, would have released them from any commitment. But Hay decided to bluff and in March, 1900, announced that all powers had accepted.

At this point the so-called Boxer Rebellion broke out in China. A large number of fanatically nationalist Chinese attempted to throw out the westerners and massacred over two hundred of them. The others took refuge in the diplomatic quarter of Peking where the Boxers besieged them. The Manchu government, aware of the popular dislike of the "foreign devils" but afraid of western retaliation, hedged and managed only to prevent worse massacres. The western powers organized an international expedition of about twenty thousand soldiers to rescue the besieged westerners and put down the rebellion.

The United States eventually had about five thousand troops with the expedition.

While the rebellion was still in progress, Hay, on July 3, 1900, dispatched a second series of Open Door notes. He now declared that the United States opposed any violation of the territorial integrity of China and that it favored commercial equality in all parts of the Chinese Empire, not merely within the spheres of influence. In other words, the second notes extended the geographic area of commercial equality and put the United States on record as opposing colonial imperialism at China's expense.

The western powers exacted stiff terms on the Chinese for the rebellion, although probably not so harsh as they might have been if Hay had not urged moderation. The protocol of September, 1901, called for the execution or exile of Chinese officials who cooperated with the Boxers, the erection of monuments at the sites of massacres, the protection of communications between Peking and the coast, and an indemnity of $333 million. The United States share of the indemnity, $25 million, was far more than necessary to pay the claims of American nationals, and Washington returned the balance to China, which in time amounted to about $17 million. The Chinese earmarked the fund for the education of young Chinese, both in China and the United States. A considerable number of young people who later became prominent Chinese government officials attended American colleges and universities financed with Boxer indemnity funds.

These, then, were the essential facts of the Open Door notes, but what were the implications and effects of the policy? Hay himself seems not to have fully realized the implications of his new policy. Indeed, in November, 1900, five months after the second note, he succumbed to Navy Department pressure and secretly tried to get a naval base at Samsah Bay in southern China, a violation of China's territorial integrity. The Japanese, who had prior rights to the area, learned of Hay's effort and reminded him of his own policy. But despite Hay's aberration, the Open Door policy became tremendously important. The United States had declared itself to the world as opposed to colonial imperialism without hampering, indeed while furthering, its own informal or economic empire. The United States later implicitly extended to the rest of the world, especially to Latin America and the Middle East, this particular kind of anticolonial imperialism. If the advocates of old-fashioned colonialism in Europe and America, the Kiplingesque Colonel Blimps, blustered and fumed, the manufacturers, bankers, and export-import merchants of the western world understood the situation and gladly pursued in foreign parts the dollar, pound, guilder, mark, franc, kroner, and ruble.

One immediate effect of the Open Door policy was to start the development of an informal British-American alliance. Britain at that time was fearful of growing German might and was seeking powerful friends, and it had been the British who started the State Department thinking along Open Door lines. At that time there were two disputes dividing the United States and Great Britain; treaty rights for construction of a canal across the Central American isthmus to connect the Atlantic and Pacific, and the boundary between Alaska and Canada. There was no explicit diplomatic bargain, but Britain yielded to America on both disputes—to the chagrin of Canadians on the Alaskan boundary question—and soon even withdrew her fleet from the Caribbean, leaving it in control of the American Navy. One effect of the Open Door policy was that Britain got out of the Caribbean and America got into Asia.

Another important effect of the announcement of the Open Door was that it virtually ended the debate between imperialists and anti-imperialists and brought about almost a bipartisan foreign policy. Democrats and Republicans still divided over the issue of colonialism with most Democrats opposing such colonialism as the United States practiced in the Philippines and most Republicans, particularly urban progressives of the Roosevelt persuasion, favoring retention and even extension of colonial holdings. But they did not disagree over informal imperialism. Secretaries of State under the Republicans Roosevelt and Taft vigorously pushed and protected American investments abroad and sought overseas markets for the products of American industry. When the Democratic Wilson became president and appointed the political symbol of anticolonialism, Bryan, as his Secretary of State, the policy of informal empire did not change. Secretary Bryan told a national convention of the American Manufacturers Export Association in 1914, ". . . my Department is your department; the ambassadors, the ministers, and the consuls are all yours. It is their business to look after your interests and to guard your rights."

The basic force behind American informal imperialism was the desire of businessmen for profitable investments and markets and, to a lesser extent, sources of raw materials. Some historians have tried to minimize the importance of foreign operations to the domestic economy by pointing out that in 1900, for example, Chinese trade accounted for only 2 per cent of American foreign trade, that in 1915 all overseas activities equalled only 10 to 12 per cent of the gross national product, and that it was not until World War I that American investments abroad totalled more than foreign investments in the United States. Actually, however, these statistics mean little because they apply to all business activities, and any given firm or industry that had vital overseas interests was not concerned about national statistics but its own profit and loss statements. If Chinese trade was insignificant to total foreign trade, that did not detract the Chinese trade's importance to a powerful company like Standard Oil which moved into China in strength in the 1890's. Nor did the relative smallness of that trade alter the fact that Chinese life was being significantly changed by American and other western trade. Standard Oil, for example, produced millions of small kerosene lanterns called Mei Foo Lamps ("beautiful confidence") which it sold for the equivalent of ten cents in Asia. The five-gallon Standard Oil kerosene cans became common Chinese household utensils and, after being flattened, provided roofing for many a Chinese peasant's hut. An old treadle Singer sewing machine became the prized family possession of thousands of poor Chinese, and during World War II the one article that was invariably to be found strapped to the backs of poverty stricken refugees.

Japan proved to be the greatest threat to the operation of the Open Door in China. Early in 1902, Japan and Great Britain made an alliance in which they agreed to maintain Open Door policies in Asia (although in 1905 Britain agreed to give Japan a free hand in Korea and Japan chose to ignore British activities in Tibet) and, in case either of them became involved in war with a third power over Asian interests, to go to the other's aid if a fourth power should enter the war against either party to the alliance. This move enabled Britain to concentrate its naval power in European and North Atlantic waters where it was fearful of growing German strength, and it strengthened Japan's hand against Russia. Japan regarded Korea as her own preserve and looked greedily at Manchuria; Russia regarded Manchuria as her own and looked optimistically toward Korea. Before any declaration of war, Japan struck at the Russians at Port Arthur on February 5, 1904. The war was fought on the seas and supposedly Chinese soil. Americans sided with the Japanese, and Roosevelt declared "Japan is playing our game" by trying to prevent Russia from closing the door in Manchuria, a door American as well as Japanese interests wanted to enter. Roosevelt let the Japanese know that he thought they deserved Korea, and he later asserted, although there is no evidence that his assertion was not another of his after-the-fact exaggerations of the situation, that he notified Germany and France to stay out of the Russo-Japanese war upon pain of encountering American opposition. The Russian forces were inefficient and took a licking from the aggressive and well-organized Japanese. Although victorious, the Japanese had used their resources to the limit and were ready for peace, but the rest of the world and even most Japanese did not know the true situation. On May 31, 1905, the Japanese secretly asked Roosevelt to use his position to serve as a mediator and bring the war to an end. Roosevelt by then had second thoughts about the balance of power in northern Asia and feared that Japan might prove the threat that he had once thought Russia was. Roosevelt agreed. On June 8, he issued formal invitations to Japan and Russia for a conference to be held at the naval yard in Portsmouth, New Hampshire.

In July, Secretary of War Taft, then on a Philippine mission, negotiated with Japanese Prime Minister Taro Katsura. The result was the secret Taft-Katsura memorandum by which the Roosevelt administration approved Japan's "suzerainty over" Korea, and Japan declared it had no designs on the Philippines. The agreement was not a treaty; it bound only the Roosevelt administration. On August 9, the Russians and Japanese met at Portsmouth under Roosevelt's auspices. Russia had consented to peace negotiations because revolution was spreading within her empire, she had not demonstrated strength against the Japanese, and her ally France had urged peace. The Japanese at Portsmouth demanded all the Russian island of Sakhalin and a big financial indemnity. The Russians refused. American opinion swung from Japan to Russia, and Roosevelt urged the Japanese to compromise. The Japanese gave up their monetary claim and accepted the southern half of Sakhalin. The delegates signed the treaty September 5. Now Japanese opinion swung sharply against Roosevelt and the United States. Roosevelt's efforts to play world balance of power politics were not conspicuously successful. After first siding with Japan, he eventually lost Japan's good will. His role of peacemaker, however, increased his world reputation and the following year the militaristic hero of San Juan Hill received the Nobel Peace Prize.

At the height of Japanese dissatisfaction with the Treaty of Portsmouth and anti-American feeling, the San Francisco school board adopted the Oriental school segregation program described in Chapter 5. Japanese hostility toward America became inflamed. Roosevelt, with difficulty, brought the Californians to rescind their order. Then Roosevelt became anxious that the Japanese might think he was afraid of them. He decided to wield the "big stick." Roosevelt had once given the advice "to speak softly and carry a big stick," and he was as prone to follow the latter part of the injunction as he was constitution-ally unable to observe its first part. He then decided to "big stick" Japan by sending the fleet on a round-the-world cruise. When the chairman of the Senate naval affairs committee protested and said he would not approve appropriations for such a cruise, Roosevelt reached for his "big stick" again and informed the Senator that he would send the fleet to the Pacific anyway and Congress would have no choice but to appropriate the funds to bring it back. The "great white fleet" left Hampton Roads, Virginia, in December, 1907, rounded Cape Horn, came north to California, visited Australia and Japan, and steamed home through Suez and the Mediterranean to arrive back on the Atlantic coast in TR's last two weeks in office. Whether or not the Japanese were impressed by this show of force—they received the fleet with great celebrations—depends upon how one interprets the Root-Takahira executive agreement of November 30, 1908. In this agreement the United States and Japan agreed to maintain the *status quo* in the "region of the Pacific Ocean," to respect one another's territories in that region, to uphold the Open Door, and to support peacefully the "independence and integrity of China." Did the "region of the Pacific Ocean" include Manchuria? Did the agreement give Japan a free hand in Manchuria so far as the United States was concerned or did it only recognize the position Japan already had there? Historians disagree in their interpretations. At any rate, the agreement was binding only on the Roosevelt administration, and Taft had already been elected. It was soon clear that Taft and his Secretary of State, Philander C. Knox, did not intend to grant Japan carte blanche in Manchuria.

Taft himself referred to his foreign policy as "dollar diplomacy," meaning a distinction with what might be called "bullet diplomacy," but the public then and historians since have seen something sinister in the concept and used it as a term of opprobrium. But actually Taft pursued "dollar diplomacy" no more than his more swashbuckling predecessor or his morally righteous successor. Roosevelt, Taft, and Wilson did not see eye to eye on colonialism or balance-of-power international politics, but they did not substantially disagree on informal or economic imperialism.

Willard Straight, a young man who had served two years as American consul general at Mukden, Manchuria, returned to Washington in 1908 to be Acting Chief of the Division of Far Eastern Affairs in the State Department. Straight believed strongly that Manchuria must be opened up for American bankers' investments. A consortium of British, French, and German bankers had been formed to build the Hukang railroad in central and southern China. With Straight's urging, Taft and the State Department insisted that American bankers be admitted to the group. Straight resigned from the State Department to become the American bankers' agent which meant, practically, an agent for J. P. Morgan. The final arrangement admitting Morgan and the others to the consortium was signed in May, 1911. In 1912, Russian and Japanese bankers joined the consortium. After negotiations for American participation in the consortium were underway, Taft and Knox made a further proposal. In communications to Britain in November, 1909, and to France, Germany, Russia, Japan, and China the next month, they suggested that the countries then in the consortium plus Russia and Japan lend China a large sum to purchase all the railroads, including those in Manchuria, or alternatively to build a new north-south railroad in Manchuria. Russia already controlled the Chinese Eastern railroad in northern Manchuria and Japan the South Manchuria Railway, and these two nations objected. Both nations continued to expand their Manchurian influence.

The consortium did not turn out to be the financial success its American participants, at least, had hoped it would be. American bankers had only $7,290,000 invested. In early 1913, they were considering participating in a $125 million six-power loan to China, but they had misgivings and consulted with Wilson who had just been inaugurated. Wilson announced that they would not have the support of the government, and the next day the bankers withdrew. This reversal is sometimes interpreted as a retreat from informal empire, but it was only a tactic to pursue that policy. Wilson feared that the loan compromised China and might lead to its actual territorial division, he regarded exports as more important than foreign investments, and he and Bryan thought that the American bankers did not have enough control of the consortium. In November, 1917, Wilson reversed himself and urged a new bankers' consortium of American, British, French, and Japanese bankers which signed formal articles of agreement in October, 1920.

The new consortium was part of an arrangement worked out between the United States and Japan about China and the Open Door after the outbreak of World War I. In 1913 and early 1914 American-Japanese relations became severely strained when Californians again offended the new Asian power, this time by enacting a state law designed to prevent Japanese from owning land in the state. For a time it looked as if an American-Japanese war were possible, but Wilson realized the Japanese did not really want war and took a conciliatory attitude until the crisis had passed. When war began in Europe, Japan saw the opportunity presented her in China by the European powers' engagement elsewhere. She entered the war on the Allied side and seized the German naval base and concession in Shantung Province, China. In January, 1915, Japan tried to get China to agree to a treaty containing the so-called Twenty-one Demands, which if accepted would have made China practically a Japanese puppet state. In May, the United States sent notes to Japan and China asserting it would not recognize any such agreement contrary to the Open Door, and Great Britain brought pressure upon Japan. The Japanese ceased to push the treaty, but Wilson was eager to rush American capital into China to take up the slack left there while Europe was at war. Therefore, Wilson reversed himself on the consortium idea. In the fall of 1917, Secretary of State Robert Lansing and Japanese envoy Kikujiro Ishii conversed in Washington about the whole Chinese situation. Ishii wanted America to recognize Japanese "paramount interests" in China; Lansing wanted Japanese assurances about the Open Door and the integrity of China, or, in other words, American commercial opportunity in China. They could come to agreement only by resort to vague and ambiguous language, which they employed in the Lansing-Ishii Agreement of November 2, 1917. By that time the United States was also in the war, and Lansing was at a disadvantage because the Japanese held the threat of leaving the Allies and joining Germany, as Germany had asked her to do. The Agreement stated that "Japan has special [the word paramount was avoided] interests in China"; in exchange Japan endorsed the Open Door.

"*I Took Panama*"

A canal through the Central American isthmus to connect the Atlantic and Pacific had been a dream at least as early as the California gold rush. In 1850, the United States and Britain had signed the Clayton-Bulwer Treaty which enjoined each power from building such a canal without the other's participation. During the war with Spain, the strategic advantage of a canal came sharply to the public mind when the battleship *Oregon* had to sail around Cape Horn to get from Puget Sound to Cuban waters. In 1899, McKinley appointed an engineering commission to recommend the best canal route. In February, 1900, the United States and Great Britain signed the first Hay-Pauncefote Treaty which abrogated the treaty of 1850. America could now build and own an isthmian canal but could not fortify it. The Senate objected to the ban on fortifications and amended the treaty to provide for them. Britain would not accept the Senate amendments but reconsidered and signed the second Hay-Pauncefote Treaty in November, 1901, granting the United States the right to fortify such a canal. Britain's concession was part of her campaign to win America's friendship and potential alliance.

Also in November, 1901, the engineering commission recommended a canal route through Nicaragua, holding that such a route was the least expensive. The other alternative was a route through Panama which belonged to the Republic of Colombia. In 1879, a French company headed by Ferdinand DeLesseps, builder of the Suez Canal, had received construction rights for the Panama route, but the company had gone bankrupt without completing a canal and had reorganized in 1894 as the New Panama Canal Company. Philippe Bunau-Varilla, a French citizen who had been chief engineer of the old company, was its main stockholder. Alarmed by the engineering commission's report, Bunau-Varilla dropped his price for the purchase of his company's rights from $109 million to $40 million. Roosevelt calculated that the saving made the Panama route the better bargain and pressured the engineering commission to change its recommendation which it did in January, 1902, but not before the House of Representatives had voted in favor of the Nicaraguan route with only two dissenting votes.

Bunau-Varilla now began a powerful lobby action in the Senate. His chief lobbyist was William Nelson Cromwell, partner in the influential Wall Street law firm of Sullivan and Cromwell. In 1900, Cromwell had contributed $60,000 to the Republican party to prevent its favoring the Nicaraguan route in its platform, for which sum he billed his French client. Cromwell's total efforts, he calculated, were worth $800,000 to the French organization. Fortunately for the lobby, a Nicaraguan volcano erupted in May, and in June, Congress urged the President to secure a right of way through Panama from Colombia. The administration then put pressure upon the Colombia *chargé* at Washington, Tomás Herrán, and on January 22, 1903, three days before Herrán received instructions from home not to do so, he agreed to the Hay-Herrán Treaty granting the United States the canal right of way for $10 million in cash and a $250,000 annual payment. Two months later the Senate ratified the treaty.

The dictator of Colombia called his Congress into session for the first time in several years and presented the treaty for ratification, knowing full well that Colombian public opinion required the treaty be rejected. The Colombian Senate rejected it in August, 1903. Colombia wanted more money. Furthermore, the French company's concession was to expire in October, 1904, and its assets would go to the Colombian government. Roosevelt was furious. He even drafted a message to Congress suggesting that the canal territory be taken by force but did not send it. Roosevelt did not have to send the message; Bunau-Varilla arranged another scheme.

The French engineer arranged a "revolutionary army" of Panamanians through his agents in Panama, a force that consisted of 500 bribed Colombian soldiers and 441 members of local fire departments. But Bunau-Varilla had to ascertain what position Roosevelt and the State Department would take toward an 1846 treaty between Colombia (then called New Granada) and the United States in which the northern republic had agreed to maintain the neutrality of Panama so that "free transit" would not be stopped. Seven times before 1903 American troops had gone to Panama to assure "free transit," each time with Colombia's blessing. Without giving specific assurances, Roosevelt gave Bunau-Varilla to understand that he would not allow Colombia to crush a Panamanian revolution.

Bunau-Varilla telegraphed his agents in Panama that a United States warship would reach Colon, Panama, on November 2, 1903. The next day the Panamanian "revolutionary army" revolted and on November 4 proclaimed Panamanian independence. Within two hours after receiving the news, Roosevelt authorized recognition of the new state, and official recognition came on November 6. The American naval force prevented the landing of Colombian troops who had sailed for Panama to put down the uprising. Things were moving fast. On November 13, Washington received Bunau-Varilla as a representative of the new Republic of Panama, and six days later Bunau-Varilla signed a treaty with the United States which the cagy Frenchman had persuaded the real Panamanians to approve sight unseen. The Hay–Bunau-Varilla Treaty granted the United States in perpetuity a zone ten miles wide across the new republic and made the zone virtually a United States military outpost; in exchange, Panama was to receive $10 million and $250,000 a year. Hay rushed the treaty to the Senate for ratification because two bona fide Panamanians were coming to Washington to try to get better terms. They arrived on February 23, 1904, six hours after the Senate had ratified the treaty. Since Panama's independence from Colombia depended upon the presence of American forces, she had no choice but to ratify the Hay–Bunau-Varilla Treaty. The United States took legal possession of the Canal Zone in May, began construction in 1906, and sent the first ship through the Panama Canal in January, 1914.

Roosevelt did not stretch the facts of the case very far when he declared in 1911, ". . . I took the Canal Zone and let Congress debate." But besides taking the zone, Roosevelt had created a considerable amount of bad feeling toward the United States in Latin America. In 1914, Wilson negotiated a treaty with Colombia in which the United States declared "sincere regret" about the Panama affair and agreed to pay Colombia $25 million for its loss. John Hay had suggested a payment for Colombia to Bunau-Varilla, but that modern statesman of the Spanish Main rejected the notion as "blackmail."

139

Roosevelt stated his unalterable opposition to a payment to Colombia, his friend Senator Lodge opposed the treaty in the Senate, and it was not ratified. When Wilson revived the issue in 1917, Roosevelt's friends blocked ratification again. In 1921, after the Republican Warren G. Harding had become president, Roosevelt had died, and American oil companies were eager to overcome Colombian opposition to concessions for American companies in the newly discovered oil fields there, a treaty providing for a $25 million payment without expression of regret was signed and ratified.

Stretching Mr. Monroe: The United States and Latin America

Between the Spanish-American War and World War I, the United States vastly increased its influence in the governmental affairs of the nations south of Florida and the Rio Grande and north of the bulge of South America. Some of the once-independent republics of this area became virtual American protectorates, policed internally by American military forces. The economic strength of the United States and its economic expansionist impulse were the basic causes of these Latin American developments, plus strategic considerations for the Panama Canal. Much of the international legal justification was found in new interpretations of the Monroe Doctrine of 1823.

During the Monroe administrations, much of Latin America had declared its independence from the Spanish and Portugese empires. The United States was anxious about the possibility of European powers taking advantage of the turmoil and weakness of the new Latin American republics to extend their imperial designs. In his annual message to Congress in December, 1823, Monroe stated that the United States would do nothing to interfere with the European colonies of Latin America but would regard as an unfriendly act any European nation's interference with the nations that had declared their independence. The United States would keep hands off European affairs, such as the contemporaneous Greek war for independence, but expected a policy of European hands off in Latin America. By the twentieth century, the Monroe Doctrine had become an object of folk veneration, confused in many people's minds with the federal Constitution and the Ten Commandments.

That European powers recognized the Monroe Doctrine was clearly indicated in 1901, when they ascertained Washington's attitude toward the use of force against Venezuela to collect debts for their nationals. Investors from many countries, but primarily Germany and Great Britain, demanded payment of their Venezuelan debts, but the dictator of that country, Cipriano Castro, refused to consider or arbitrate any of the claims. When the United States made no objection, Germany and Britain, later joined by Italy, began a blockade of Venezuela. The Germans were particularly truculent and bombarded a Venezuelan fort and destroyed the village around it. The blockade made Castro buckle, and he asked Washington to arrange arbitration. When Venezuela signed the protocol in February, 1903, the three-month-old blockade ended. Then the question arose whether or not the creditors of the nations that had participated in the blockade would receive preferential treatment in the payment of the debts. The question was referred to the Permanent Court of Arbitration at The Hague, Holland. The Hague Court ruled in favor of the blockading powers, which had the effect of putting a premium on the use of force in collecting international debts.

In 1904, a similar situation threatened to develop when the Dominican Republic defaulted on its bonds. The Dominican Republic occupied roughly the eastern half of the island of Santo Domingo or Hispaniola; Haiti occupied the western part of the island. The Dominican Republic looked to Washington for a solution to avoid what had happened to Venezuela. The island republic had already turned over to an American the responsibility of collecting customs at its main port in order to satisfy the debt owed a New York corporation. Now the State Department prepared an agreement which provided for the establishment of an American operated customs service which would apply 55 per cent of the revenues collected to the payment of foreign debts on an equal basis. Although the Senate did not consent to the agreement for two years, Roosevelt went ahead with the plan. United States warships anchored in Dominican harbors. The American Receiver General persuaded the foreign creditors to accept lower interest rates and thereby scaled down the debt from $22 million to $17 million. At the time, the arrangement did not cause cries about "Yanqui imperialism," as later it would. In fact, the Dominican Republic enjoyed a brief era of peace because outside control of the customs made the usual revolutions unprofitable.

During the Dominican debt affair, Roosevelt in his annual message to Congress in December, 1904, enunciated what later came to be called the Roosevelt corollary to the Monroe Doctrine. "Chronic wrongdoing . . . may in America, as elsewhere, ultimately require intervention by some civilized nation [the implication for Latin American civilization was clear], and in the Western Hemisphere the adherence of the United States to the Monroe Doctrine may force the United States, however reluctantly, in flagrant cases of such wrongdoing or impotence, to the exercise of an international police power." In the hands of Roosevelt and his successors, then, the Monroe Doctrine, whose original purpose was to prevent European intervention in Latin America, would be used to justify United States intervention there.

Roosevelt then moved to stabilize Central America. Washington united with Mexico City to bring about a truce in the war between Guatemala and El Salvador. There followed a Central American peace conference at San José, Costa Rica, which adopted a series of treaties pledging the signatory countries to arbitrate disputes between them and to refrain from supporting one another's revolutions. But the dictatorial president of Nicaragua, José Zelaya, had only contempt for the treaties. When war came between Nicaragua and Honduras, he succeeded in bringing about a revolution in Honduras that supported his regime. Then the United States and Mexico persuaded the little republics to attend a conference at Washington in 1907. Another series of treaties written there under Washington's guidance, which looked toward a degree of Central American federation, soon went the way of the earlier agreements.

In 1909, a revolution broke out against Zelaya in Nicaragua, and United States firms supported the revolutionists. The Taft administration sent cruisers

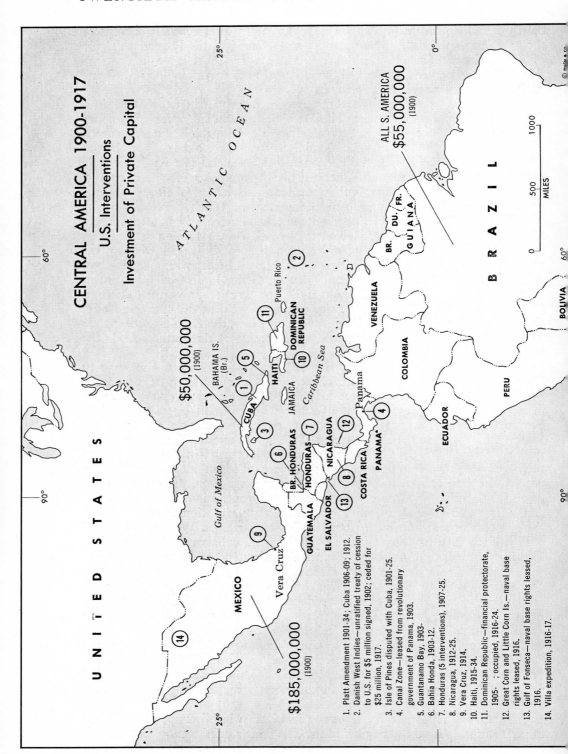

CENTRAL AMERICA 1900-1917

U.S. Interventions

Investment of Private Capital

ATLANTIC OCEAN

$55,000,000
(1900)
ALL S. AMERICA

$50,000,000
(1900)

$185,000,000
(1900)

UNITED STATES

Gulf of Mexico

MEXICO

Vera Cruz

BAHAMA IS.
(Br.)

CUBA

HAITI

JAMAICA

Puerto Rico

DOMINICAN
REPUBLIC

Caribbean Sea

BR. HONDURAS

GUATEMALA

HONDURAS

EL SALVADOR

NICARAGUA

COSTA RICA

PANAMA

Panama

COLOMBIA

VENEZUELA

ECUADOR

PERU

BOLIVIA

BRAZIL

BR. DU. FR.
G U I A N A

MILES
0   500   1000

60°

90°

25°

25°

90°

60°

0°

1. Platt Amendment 1901-34; Cuba 1906-09; 1912.
2. Danish West Indies—unratified treaty of cession
   to U.S. for $5 million signed, 1902; ceded for
   $25 million, 1917.
3. Isle of Pines disputed with Cuba, 1901-25.
4. Canal Zone—leased from revolutionary
   government of Panama, 1903.
5. Guantanamo Bay, 1903-
6. Bahia Honda, 1903-12.
7. Honduras (5 interventions), 1907-25.
8. Nicaragua, 1912-25.
9. Vera Cruz, 1914.
10. Haiti, 1915-34.
11. Dominican Republic—financial protectorate,
    1905- ; occupied, 1916-24.
12. Great Corn and Little Corn Is.—naval base
    rights leased, 1916.
13. Gulf of Fonseca—naval base rights leased,
    1916.
14. Villa expedition, 1916-17.

and Marines to Nicaragua for the ostensible purpose of protecting American nationals and their property, and with their aid Adolfo Diaz, a Nicaraguan who had been an official of an American firm, became president in 1911. Secretary Knox arranged the Knox-Castrillo Treaty which provided for two New York banks to refund the Nicaraguan foreign debt and for the establishment of an American Receiver General on the Dominican pattern. When the Senate refused to ratify this protectorate arrangement as well as a separate but similar one Knox worked out with Honduras, the State Department and the bankers proceeded with out a treaty. The New York banks lent $1.5 million to Nicaragua and in return received majority control of the railroads and the Nicaraguan national bank. Later the banks nominated and Nicaragua appointed an American Receiver General of Customs. In 1912, the Nicaraguans supported Zelaya in a revolt against the Diaz government, and Washington dispatched 2,700 Marines to protect its puppet. A Marine garrison remained in Nicaragua until 1925.

The bankers' loan and the customs proved insufficient to pay off the Nicaraguan European debt, and in early 1913 Knox negotiated another treaty. This one would have had the United States government pay Nicaragua $3 million and in return receive an exclusive option of the canal route (so that some other nation would not build another canal), the right to build a naval base in the Gulf of Fonseca on the Pacific side of Nicaragua, and a ninety-nine-year lease on the Great Corn and Little Corn Islands on the Caribbean side. There was not time for this treaty to be ratified before the Taft administration left office. The Wilson administration went farther. The Bryan-Chamorro Treaty of August, 1914, accepted the Knox provisions and added an explicit statement of the right of American intervention in Nicaraguan affairs similar to the Platt Amendment. The Senate struck out most of the Platt Amendment-type provisions before it ratified the new treaty, but Nicaragua remained for all practical purposes a United States protectorate. The article of the ratified treaty providing for the naval base granted the United States the right "to take any measure necessary" to protect the Panama Canal and its "proprietary rights" to the Nicaraguan canal route. This provision left Nicaragua far short of full sovereignty.

These Central American excursions into informal imperialism, which sometimes came close to colonialism, were taken in the name of the Roosevelt corollary and the defense of the approaches to the Panama Canal. In 1911–1912, the United States Senate added still another corollary to the Monroe Doctrine. In 1911, a Japanese company negotiated with a syndicate of American investors for purchase of a large tract of land near Magdalena Bay in Lower California, Mexico. The United States was interested in Magdalena Bay as a potential naval base, lying as it does between California and the Pacific end of the Panama Canal. When Secretary Knox learned of the negotiations, he protested through diplomatic channels, and the Japanese company dropped its plans. That would have been the end of the matter had not Senator Lodge introduced a resolution which declared that the nation disapproved of the transfer of strategic positions to non-American private companies which the Senate passed fifty-one to four. This resolution, the Lodge Corollary, extended the Monroe Doctrine to apply to an Asian power and to private companies as well as governments. Since the Senate resolution's passage, the

143

State Department has upon four occasions invoked the doctrine to stop the sale to Japanese of Mexican property owned by United States nationals.

The Wilson administration sent troops to both republics on the island of Santo Domingo when revolutions broke out there, although in neither case were European loans a major consideration. In 1915, President Guillaume Sam of Haiti ordered the slaughter of 167 political prisoners. A revolutionary mob chased President Sam to the French legation, caught him hiding inside the building, and literally tore him to pieces. Wilson sent Marines and part of the fleet which took control of the republic. The State Department forced the acceptance of a twenty-year treaty which made Haiti a United States protectorate. Americans not only took over the customs service and financial control of the government but gained possession of the native constabulary. An indication of the Navy Department's control of Haiti is seen in a message of a naval commander sent to Washington: "Next Thursday . . . unless otherwise directed, I will permit the Haitian Congress to elect a president." Marines remained in Haiti until 1934, when Franklin D. Roosevelt ordered their withdrawal. Interestingly, it was he who as Assistant Secretary of the Navy had written from his desk in Washington the Haitian constitution of 1916.

In 1914, when revolution broke out in the Dominican Republic, Wilson sent a warship there and urged the various Dominican factions to stop their fighting and establish a provisional government under American control of finances and police. The Dominicans consented but would not sign a Platt-Amendment type of treaty. Fighting broke out again in 1916, Wilson sent Marines in force, and they took control of the government. Still the Dominicans refused a treaty, and they remained under an American military government until 1924.

Anxiety about the Panama "life line" prompted such actions as these on Santo Domingo which left a bad taste among Latin Americans for decades. The Panama Canal also precipitated a crisis in Anglo-American relations from 1912 to 1914. The second Hay-Pauncefote Treaty stipulated that the tolls charged to users of the still-to-be-completed Panama Canal would be the same for all nations, but when Congress in 1912 established the toll schedule it exempted American ships engaged in coastal shipping from paying any tolls whatsoever. Both the Democratic and Republican parties in 1912 approved of the Panama tolls act, and soon after the election the British Foreign Office sent a strong protest to Washington suggesting arbitration of the question. Secretary Knox refused to take any action, arguing there could be no arbitration case until the canal opened and the British paid the tolls; then they would have a claim for damages. During the campaign, Wilson had supported exemption of American coastal vessels from canal tolls, but during his first year in office he changed his mind on the issue. Being a moralist, Wilson surely was concerned about the ethics of the 1912 toll act and the Hay-Pauncefote Treaty; but the Panama tolls question was tied in with other considerations. Wilson seems to have had a tacit understanding with the British that if he could bring about the repeal of tolls discrimination they would support his policies in Mexico. Repeal of the toll discrimination was politically difficult, but Wilson in a personal appearance before a joint session of Congress asked for the change. After considerable debate, especially in the Senate, Congress repealed the exemption in June, 1914.

Wilson and Mexico

In considering the complicated relationships between the United States and Mexico from 1911 until after World War I, it is necessary to keep certain things in mind. First, Mexico was not Nicaragua or Honduras, and its revolution was not just the action of one group of politicians to overthrow another. Mexico was, and is, a large and important nation with long-standing independent traditions of its own. Its revolution, beginning in 1911 and lasting for many years, now erupting and now quiescent, was a social revolution, partly against the main institutions that oppressed the Mexican people (corrupt professional politicians, the Church, and the army) and partly against informal or economic imperialism. Mexico can be best understood if considered a nation endeavoring to overthrow the influence of foreign capital and to emerge from the status of an "economically underdeveloped area" while at the same time fighting for internal reforms.

Next, we must understand Woodrow Wilson and his attitudes toward Mexico. Wilson was an idealist and a reformer, and in foreign affairs he had a missionary complex. He approved of the Mexican revolutionists' efforts to eliminate internal corruption and curtail its own oppressive institutions. Often he wished that Mexican revolutionists would observe the forms of the middle class in the United States, but on the whole he supported their efforts at internal reforms and thought that the United States had a special mission toward its southern neighbor to help them execute their plans. He did not, however, support the revolutionists' efforts to block informal imperialism, whether exercised by the United States or one of the European powers. Wilson summarized his whole Mexican policy neatly in talks with a British envoy, Sir William Tyrell, in November, 1913. He assured Tyrell that: (1) he would "teach the South American republics to elect good men"; (2) he would try to establish a Mexican government "under which all contracts and business and concessions will be safer than they have been"; and (3) he would endeavor to protect all foreign property, not merely that of American nationals, during the Mexican revolution.

Except for four years in the early 1880's, Porfirio Diaz was President of Mexico from 1877 until 1911. Diaz ruled with a strong arm and handed out generous economic concessions to foreign interests. What economic benefits for Mexicans there were in these concessions accrued to a small group of lawyers, engineers, and other professional groups, most of whom lived in Mexico City. The peasants, fully 90 per cent of the population, lived in ignorance and poverty. United States investors had more money in Mexico than all other nations combined. In 1913, there were about fifty thousand United States nationals living in Mexico, and about $1 billion in American capital was invested there. The main American companies with holdings were the Mexican Petroleum Company, Phelps, Dodge and Company, the Greene Cananea Copper Company, and the Southern Pacific Railroad. Although British investments in Mexico were much smaller, they were just as important to her, more so from the standpoint of national security. Mexico was at that time almost the sole source of oil for the British fleet.

The Mexican revolution began in May, 1911, when a force led by a reformer, Francisco Madero, succeeded in driving Diaz into exile. Madero attempted to change the power structure of Mexican society and was betrayed by his chief general, Victoriano Huerta, in February, 1913. Huerta took control of the government and arranged for Madero's murder. The American Ambassador, Henry Lane Wilson, approved of Huerta and probably helped to arrange his coup. Ambassador Wilson urged Taft, then in his last month of office, to recognize the Huerta government. Taft did not, hoping he could use recognition as a weapon to be used in bargaining on some other disputes. This was the situation when Wilson took office.

Wilson would not recognize Huerta's government because he disapproved of his butchery in coming to power. From the time of Jefferson it had been American policy to recognize a *de facto* government, that is, one that actually was in power. Wilson changed the policy, and in Mexico and later in Russia, he withheld recognition of a government of which he disapproved. He maintained his nonrecognition policy in the face of considerable pressure from American financial interests which saw Huerta as a new Diaz and were eager to get on with the economic show. Ambassador Wilson remained in Mexico City and only informally dealt with the Huerta government.

Wilson came to place his hopes with the Constitutionalist movement led by Venustiano Carranza, Maderista governor of the northern state of Coahuila which began a revolt against Huerta as soon as he (Huerta) took office. Carranza and his second in command, Francisco (or "Pancho") Villa, had their main strength in the northern Mexican states. In the summer of 1913, Wilson accepted the advice of the American companies with large investments in Mexico and proposed to the Mexicans through his special representative in Mexico, John Lind, former governor of Minnesota, who replaced Ambassador Wilson, that the United States serve as a mediator between the Carranza and Huerta forces, that the Mexicans establish a constitutional government which Wilson would recognize, that the elections scheduled for late October be moved forward, and that Huerta eliminate himself as a candidate. When Huerta refused and the Constitutionalists supported him in his refusal, the surprised Wilson declared a policy of "watchful waiting."

Then in the fall of 1913, the British, anxious about their naval oil supply, got busy in Mexico. Huerta arrested the Maderista members of the Chamber of Deputies and abandoned all pretense of constitutional government. Wilson suspected, probably rightly, that the British were behind Huerta's last move. It was at this point that Wilson conferred with Sir William Tyrell. Wilson made it clear that the British would have to choose between Huerta and the United States; they could not have both as friends. It was apparently also the understanding that in exchange for British cutting off support for Huerta, the United States would endeavor to protect British property in Mexico and amend the Panama tolls question. Having isolated Huerta, Wilson now moved to support Carranza. At a conference with Constitutionalist leaders at Nogales just south of the Arizona border, Wilson's agent proposed that the United States back the Constitutionalists in exchange for Carranza's promise for participation in new elections and the establishment of a provisional government. Carranza made it clear that all his forces wanted from the United States was the right to purchase arms, that the Mexican revolution was none of Wilson's business, that he would not cooperate with the Huerta government in any elections, and that if the United States sent troops across the Mexican border they would encounter his armed resistance.

Wilson was dismayed and for two months did nothing but make threats against Huerta. Seeing that he was in a position of either having to use force to overthrow Huerta or play the Constitutionalists' game, Wilson in early 1914 lifted the ban on arms to the rebels that Taft had imposed. The additional arms did not immediately bring the Carranza success that Wilson had hoped for and expected. In April, 1914, Huerta was as well entrenched as ever. Then on April 10 came an incident at Tampico that precipitated first a ridiculously comic impasse and then a tragedy at Vera Cruz.

An Huerista colonel arrested the paymaster and part of the crew of the *U.S.S. Dolphin* while they were loading supplies into a small boat at Tampico. The navy men were soon released, and the Huerista commanding officer sent a personal apology to the commander of the squadron off Vera Cruz. Instead of considering the incident closed, the officer demanded a twenty-one-gun salute to the American flag. Wilson backed his demand. Huerta asserted he would provide the booming salute if the American navy would return the salute, boom for boom. Wilson refused, holding that to salute the Mexican flag would be tantamount to recognizing the Huerta regime. The logic escaped Mexican realists. For ten days the situation was only ridiculous. Then on April 20 it became dangerous. While the warlike cheered, Wilson went to Congress and asked for authority to use force in Mexico. Congress gave its assent on April 22.

But other things happened on April 22. In the early hours of April 21, Washington learned that a German freighter with arms for Huerta was soon to land at Vera Cruz. Wilson ordered the fleet to take Vera Cruz and prevent the arms from being landed. On April 22, the fleet bombarded and captured the Mexican port city, killing 126 Mexicans and wounding 195 others. American losses were 19 dead and 71 wounded. Carranza condemned the seizure of Vera Cruz almost as vigorously as did Huerta; Carranza even wrote Wilson that the invasion "will drag us into an unequal war which until today we desired to avoid."

At this point the ABC powers (Argentina, Brazil, and Chile) offered mediation, and the United States gratefully accepted the opportunity to get out of the mess. The ABC conference met at Niagara Falls, Canada, May 20 to July 2, 1914. As the talks went on, Carranza's forces pushed nearer and nearer to Mexico City, and Huerta informed the conference that it looked as if he was finished and would have to abdicate. Carranza's representatives at the conference made it clear that the Constitutionalists would not accept any ABC mediation to end the civil war. They were too close to victory to allow Wilson a voice in the proceedings. The conference settled nothing. It only offered the United States the opportunity to step out of Vera Cruz and avoid a war that neither side really wanted. On July 15, Huerta abdicated, and on August 20 Carranza and his army entered Mexico City.

Soon after the Constitutionalists routed Huerta in the summer of 1914, Villa turned against his chief, Carranza, and tried to take over the whole revolutionary movement. Villa issued a declaration of war against Carranza even before the convention that was to draw up a new civil government. Wilson supported Villa against Carranza which, as it developed, was betting on the losing horse. Why did the Washington administration make this blunder? It could hardly have been a sympathy of Wilson's for Villa's personality. Villa was ignorant and illiterate and had been a bandit until he joined his bandit gang to the revolutionary forces in 1911. The reason appears to be that the administration thought it could control Mexico through Villa and that it could not through Carranza. Villa had always left the impression with the Wilson administration that if he controlled affairs, Washington would have considerable influence in Mexico City. Villa had even approved the bombardment and capture of Vera Cruz, the only Mexican leader of either side to do so.

Carranza instituted a series of reform measures that rallied popular support behind him and began military operations against Villa that drove the ex-bandit to his stronghold in the northern states. Carranza's forces destroyed Villa's offensive power in a major battle in April, 1915. Washington then shifted to a supposedly neutral position, hoping to persuade Carranza to form a coalition government and stop the civil warfare. Within the United States there was considerable demand for military intervention. Roosevelt vigorously urged sending the army to Mexico, and spokesmen of the Roman Catholic church, alarmed by Carranza's anticlericalism, similarly urged intervention. On June 2, 1915, Wilson told the Mexican leaders to stop fighting or be faced with United States intervention. Villa, who was being defeated in the warfare, agreed to make peace with Carranza, but Carranza stuck to his position that Mexican politics was the Mexicans' and not Wilson's affair. Carranza continued to press the fighting and in September won another major victory that drove Villa farther to the north.

Lansing succeeded Bryan as Secretary of State during a crisis with Germany over submarine warfare. Lansing was convinced that the German question was more important than the Mexican troubles, and since Germany sought to stimulate a war between the two American republics, the United States should avoid war there at all costs. In October, 1915, the administration in Washington reversed itself and recognized the Carranza government as the *de facto* power of Mexico.

For the rest of 1915, Mexican-American relations were without serious incident. Then in January, 1916, Villa began a guerilla campaign against Americans that nearly brought a Mexican-American war. He apparently was attempting to provoke American intervention so as to weaken Carranza. After killing sixteen Americans he took off a train in Chihuahua without provoking intervention, Villa went north of the international border on March 9 and burned the little town of Columbus, New Mexico. This brought the results he wanted. The administration on March 13 reached an agreement with the Carranza government granting each side the right to pursue bandits across the border, and on March 15 the Punitive Expedition led by Brigadier General John J. "Black Jack" Pershing crossed the border to pursue Villa. The Mexican government had not yet ratified the bandit-pursuit agreement when Pershing crossed the border—and the agreement provided for only temporary incursions into one another's territory. The Mexicans, at least, had thought any bandit-chasing expedition would be small in numbers, but Pershing had five thousand men when he started and over twice that before he withdrew.

Villa shrewdly led the Pershing expedition deeper and deeper into Mexico. In three weeks it was over three hundred miles south of the international border and still had not caught the wily Villa. Carranza demanded the withdrawal of the expedition in mid-April after a clash at Parral when

Mexican soldiers opened fire on an American patrol and in the return fire suffered forty deaths. Wilson refused, holding that the Carranza government was neither willing nor able to control the bandits. Carranza feared that the United States meant permanently to occupy northern Mexico. Meanwhile, Villa slipped behind Pershing's lines and raided Glen Springs, Texas.

In June war seemed imminent. Carranza sent a note to the State Department, received May 31, that charged the United States with bad faith in keeping the Pershing expedition in Mexico and demanded its removal immediately. He ordered his commanders to resist any new expeditions from the north and any movement of the Pershing force, except retreat toward the border. On June 18, Wilson called into federal service almost the entire National Guard, sent one hundred thousand soldiers to the border, and ordered additional warships to the squadrons patrolling both Mexican coasts. On June 19, a clash came between Mexican soldiers and American sailors at the port of Mazatlán on Mexico's west coast. On June 21, there was a conflict between two troops of American cavalry and a Mexican detachment. Wilson's first report on the incident—at Carrizal, roughly 150 miles south of El Paso—was to the effect that the cavalry had been tricked and ambushed. Wilson prepared a message to Congress that probably would have precipitated war, but he did not send the message because American newspapers published a report of the conflict by the captain of one of the American cavalry troops that indicated that the Americans, rather than the Mexicans, were the aggressors. American pacifists were outraged, and Wilson was bombarded with appeals to keep the peace. By the end of June, Wilson was making conciliatory statements, and on July 4 Carranza proposed negotiation by a Joint Commission of Mexican and American officials.

The Commission met in United States cities from September, 1916, until mid-January, 1917. The Mexican delegation pressed for immediate evacuation of the Pershing expedition; the United States delegation insisted upon talking about taxes on mining properties owned by its nationals and the protection of American and British oil interests. In November, the Mexican delegation agreed to a protocol calling for withdrawal of the expedition within forty days if peace prevailed in northern Mexico. Late in December, Carranza rejected the protocol and announced he would agree to nothing unless the United States troops were withdrawn. But meanwhile the tensions between the United States and Germany were becoming increasingly serious, and Wilson was eager to bring the Mexican impasse to an end. By the end of February, 1917, the withdrawal of the Pershing expedition was complete.

Carranza and the Mexican Constitutionalist movement had won the showdown with the United States with the aid of the northern neighbor's troubles in the North Atlantic. The Mexicans were now able to proceed with their internal reforms and to begin to change their nation's semifeudal economic and social order by constitutional means. Actually, Wilson had helped the Mexican revolution by his opposition to Huerta, by getting the British to cease their support of Huerta, and by refraining at the last minute from full war against Mexico in the face of a considerable war sentiment in the United States. Yet Wilson left no legacy of good will in Mexico. Quite the reverse. His interventions, both diplomatic and military, into Mexican domestic affairs left a distrust of the gringo that has not yet disappeared.

Part II

WAR AND BOOM
1917–1929

CHAPTER EIGHT

The War Comes — and the Yanks Who Went

AMERICANS HAVE MANY LEGENDS ABOUT THEIR PAST. ONE OF THEM is that the United States was "isolated," at least from Europe's affairs, until it entered World War I. The previous chapter indicates clearly that America was not isolated from Latin American and Asian affairs, either diplomatically or economically, before World War I. Neither was it remote from, and disdainful of, strictly European matters, and it never had been. During the colonial period, Americans had participated in three wars with the French and the Indians that were the American theater of "world wars." During the Napoleonic wars, the new republic fought on both sides, first against the French in an undeclared naval war in 1798 and then against the British in the War of 1812.

Although most Americans in the nineteenth and early twentieth centuries regarded the quarrels of the European powers as little more than exotic curiosities (unless they had to do with the western hemisphere), the United States had participated in European diplomatic conferences during this time. Roosevelt had played the peacemaker role between Japan and Russia in 1905. Almost simultaneously, Roosevelt was engaged in bringing about an international conference of the major European powers. Germany coveted the trade of North Africa which the French were attempting to keep for themselves. In the spring of 1905, the Kaiser delivered a warlike speech at Tangier, Morocco, and European tension was such that war was entirely possible. The Kaiser requested that Roosevelt use his good offices and call a conference of the great powers, and in June, Roosevelt received the acceptances of France and England to meet with Germany at Algeciras in southern Spain. The United States had two official representatives at the conference which began in January, 1906. The Anglo-French alliance had the power to prevent Ger-

153

many's demands at the Algeciras Conference, and Germany accepted the diplomatic results rather than go to war. The point is that the President of the United States had twice, once for the Russian-Japanese war and then for the Moroccan crisis, arranged an international conference to deal with matters in which the United States had little or no direct national security interest. Clearly, this was not "isolation."

The United States as a Neutral Power, 1914–1915

Americans were not excited when news came that a Serbian nationalist had assassinated the heir to the Austrian throne on June 28, 1914, at Sarajevo, in what today is Jugoslavia. It was too bad the man had been killed, but Americans thought that Balkan nationalists were crazy, and they had no love for the Hapsburg monarchy. But the nation was thoroughly shocked by the diplomatic chain reaction to the assassination. Austria declared war on Serbia on July 28. Russia mobilized, and Germany declared war on Russia on August 1. France was Russia's ally and itching to regain Alsace-Lorraine. When France replied unsatisfactorily to a German message, Germany declared war on France August 3. When the Belgians resisted the movement of the German armies on their way to France, Germany declared war on Belgium. Great Britain had an alliance with France dating from 1904, and Britain declared war on Germany August 5. The war was not only international madness, it was the bloodiest international war in the world's history. To say that Americans were shaken is an understatement. Europe, the seat of the world's richest culture, had gone berserk.

On August 4, Wilson issued an official proclamation of neutrality and offered to mediate the conflicts but his suggestions were rejected. Fearful that the large number of foreign born would have unusual sympathies one way or the other, Wilson on August 19 made a personal appeal to the people to "act and speak in the true spirit of neutrality. . . . The United States must be neutral in fact as well as in name during these days that are to try men's souls. We must be neutral in thought as well as in act. . . ." Practically everyone in the nation agreed that neutrality was the nation's only true course. Yet, thirty-two months later Wilson asked Congress for a declaration of war against Germany. What happened in the administration, in the changing international situation, and in American public opinion that led to the decision to abandon neutrality and become a full belligerent?

American sympathies for one side or the other existed despite Wilson's plea and were to become stronger as the war continued. Most Americans were more for the Allies—Britain, France, and Russia—than they were for the Central Powers—Germany and Austria. German-speaking Americans, particularly first-generation immigrants, hoped for a Central Power victory, but they were few in number compared to the general population which spoke the English language, had been brought up on English literature and history, and remembered with gratitude France's help to the colonies during the American Revolution. Russia was unpopular among Americans because of its autocratic Czar, its repression of internal dissent, and its anti-Semitism, but anti-Russian sentiment abated after the March, 1917, revolution. Britain was extremely unpopular among Irish-Americans, especially after its ruthless crushing of the Dublin uprising during Easter week of 1916.

Both the British and the Germans directed extensive propaganda campaigns in America. German propaganda was on the whole crude and ineffective. An official of the German embassy even left a briefcase of propaganda plans on a New York elevated train, and German efforts to foment strikes in munitions industries and a few efforts at sabotage caused more harm in public relations than they were worth to the German armies. Respected British scholars such as James Bryce wrote accounts of German atrocities to the Belgians, and the English supplied scores of competent speakers for American audiences and, to a considerable degree, controlled the journalistic reporting of the war after they cut the cable from Germany to the United States. Yet, all of the propaganda efforts probably did no more than intensify sympathies and hostilities that already existed. American public opinion was outraged by the German invasion of Belgium in defiance of a long-standing treaty which a high German official called "a scrap of paper." The Allies were on the defensive, the war was on French soil, and American sentiment usually goes to the underdog.

Economic considerations were more important to both sides than public opinion, and here the Allies because of Britain's naval power had the upper hand. Part of Britain's strategy was to strangle Germany with a naval blockade. The British navy effectively prevented American trade with the Central Powers. American industry was eager to sell abroad—there was a depression in this country when the war began in Europe—and the Allies were able to get practically all of the American war production. American trade with Britain, France, Italy, and Russia grew from $824.8 million in 1914 to $3 billion in 1916, an increase of roughly 390 per cent. During these same years, American trade with the Central Powers declined from $169.3 million to $1.2 million, a decline of over 99 per cent. The British navy also controlled the shipment of goods to neutrals such as Holland and the Scandinavian nations from which war material from America might have been transshipped to Germany and Austria.

Soon after the declaration of war, American exports to the Allies far exceeded its imports from them, thereby creating a need for the Allies to get loans or some kind of commercial credit in America. The month the war began, the Wilson administration imposed a ban on loans by American bankers to belligerent governments. In Wilson's mind the reason for the prohibition was concern for the domestic economy which was momentarily disrupted with the outbreak of war; to Bryan the reason for the no-loan policy was to maintain absolute neutrality, although one might argue that the policy favored Germany, because only England had the physical means to transport American goods across the Atlantic. Wilson began to reverse the decision two months after it was made when he let it be known that he would not oppose extending short-term foreign credits. In March, 1915, the House of Morgan requested Washington's permission to grant a $50 million commercial credit loan to the French government. Wilson and Bryan approved. In September, 1915, after Bryan had resigned and Lansing had replaced him as Secretary of

State, the administration approved a $500 million loan to an Anglo-French commission. Thereafter, private loans to the Allies became common. By the time the United States entered the conflict, American bankers had lent $2.3 billion to the Allies and only $27 million to Germany. These loans directly stimulated the American economy because the money was spent in the United States. The American economy thus became inextricably intertwined with the Allied war effort.

In the first months of the European war, practically all of the American diplomatic difficulties over the rights of neutrals in international waters were with Great Britain rather than Germany. Several issues divided the United States and the Allies, particularly Britain, about neutral rights: definition of contraband, rights of search and seizure, British freighters flying the American flag to avoid German attack (an old ruse that the United States had employed during the Civil War), and censorship of mail. Britain, though a legalistic nation, was struggling for her life and frequently went beyond the bounds of accepted international maritime law, saying that the new warfare rendered the old customs irrelevant. Britain refused to accept the Declaration of London, a code of maritime law adopted by an international conference at London in 1909, when Wilson suggested she accept it, because the code would have put greater limitations upon her than the older international law.

Britain gradually extended the contraband list to include commodities that had theretofore not been included: cotton, gasoline, and, most important, food. In April, 1916, Britain abandoned the distinction between absolute and conditional contraband, and for the next year practically all goods shipped from America were considered contraband. Britain also departed from custom with her blockade techniques. Instead of erecting a blockade near the German coast where her ships would have been vulnerable to coastal batteries, she took the more efficient alternative of blocking the entrances to the North Sea and then instead of searching American ships for contraband on the spot, taking them to English ports. British and French censorship of mail particularly irked American businessmen, who argued that censorship delayed the delivery of their letters occasionally causing their bids on contracts to arrive too late and that the British used the trade information in their letters for their own advantage.

At the very outset of the conflict, Wilson was prone to take a stern position with Britain on American neutral rights, but Colonel House persuaded him to be moderate. Once Wilson accepted the general principle of the maritime system imposed by the British, saying that all differences could be arbitrated after the end of the war, the essentials were beyond further dispute. Wilson could only object to certain specific practices and incidents. Usually when Wilson objected he did so in a mild manner; even when he did send a strong note to London the American ambassador there, Walter Hines Page, a strongly pro-British literary man, often softened the blow by conciliatory statements to British officials. Page even told the British Foreign Office that he did not himself agree with the substance of some of Wilson's messages, that the messages were motivated by domestic politics, and that the British could find some way to circumvent Washington's objections without affecting the naval strangle on Germany.

On the whole, Americans, although annoyed with the British, did not feel nearly as strongly about British disregard for conventional neutral rights as they did about Germany's because of vital differences in British and German strategic positions and weapons. Britain's infringements of international law caused inconvenience, delay, and sometimes loss of profits to American shippers. Germany, who had to rely upon the submarine, cost American lives rather than business disadvantage when she tried to effect a stranglehold on the Allies.

German Submarines, American Lives, and American Ships

On February 4, 1915, the German Admiralty announced a submarine blockade of the British Isles. She said the use of submarines was necessary to counteract the recent British addition of food to the list of contraband and that if the British would revoke their food-as-contraband order she would call off the U-boats. The German announcement stated it would destroy all Allied ships within the blockade zone around Great Britain "although it may not always be possible to save crews and passengers." The statement also warned that neutral ships would be endangered because of the British practice of flying flags of neutrals on her merchantmen.

On February 10, Wilson sent a note to Berlin that was both strong and weak. It was strong in that he declared that if American ships were lost by submarine action the United States would hold Germany to "strict accountability." This was a harder position than Wilson ever took with the British. But the note was weak in that it said nothing about the question of Americans who might be working as sailors or traveling as passengers on Allied ships, and it was here that most of the difficulty came. Wilson also tried to persuade the British to rescind their ruling on food as contraband. Ultimately, the British complied with important reservations, but by that time the activity of German submarines had created serious tensions between the United States and Germany.

Wilson's note was effective so far as submarine attacks on American ships were concerned. German forces attacked only two American vessels before February, 1917. Both attacks were in 1915. The *Cushing*, which was plainly marked as an American ship, was attacked by a German plane without loss of life. Soon thereafter, a German submarine torpedoed the *Gulflight*, a Gulf Oil Company tanker, which did not fly the American flag until just before the torpedo was fired and which was near a British ship. Two men on the *Gulflight* were killed and the captain died of shock. The ship reached port. Germany quickly apologized and offered compensation.

But loss of American lives on British ships was another matter. On March 28, 1915, a German submarine sank the British steamer *Falaba* which was carrying passengers and munitions, killing one American passenger. The submarine commander had warned the *Falaba* to unload its passengers. Before the administration could settle differences within it about how to deal with the *Falaba* affair, the whole situation was changed. On May 7 a German submarine without warning sank the *Lusitania* off the south coast of Ireland just within the German submarine zone. The ship, the largest Atlantic liner then afloat and owned by the British Cunard Lines, sank in eighteen minutes with a total loss of 1,198 lives, 128 of whom were American citizens. The *Lusitania* was carrying many cases of rifle cartridges, and the German embassy in Washington had advertised in New York newspapers that anyone sailing on British flag ships did so at their own risk.

There is no question but that the sinking of the *Lusitania* greatly turned American opinion against Germany, but there was considerable disagreement about what the United States should do about the sinking. On May 10 in a speech at Philadelphia, Wilson said, "There is such a thing as a man being too proud to fight." Being "too proud to fight" was a concept unfathomable to the furious Roosevelt, who declared Wilson was surrounded by "flubdubs," "mollycoddles," and "flapdoodle pacifists." Important Democrats in Congress, however, warned Wilson that the American people were not ready to go to war over the *Lusitania*. The first *Lusitania* note went out May 13 over Bryan's signature. The note virtually demanded that Germany refrain from submarine attack on unarmed merchant vessels. Bryan cautioned moderation and persuaded Wilson to issue a statement advocating arbitration of the *Lusitania* affair, but Wilson yielded under great pressure from less cautious advisers and recalled the statement which had already been cabled to Germany. The German Foreign Office replied to the first note evasively. Bryan resigned rather than sign the second note, which denied that Germany had a right to ignore "the rights of humanity, which every Government honors itself in respecting" because the British violated property rights on the high seas. A third note appealed to Germany to try to safeguard neutral lives and stated that a repitition of sinkings of unarmed vessels would be "deliberately unfriendly," a sharp diplomatic phrase that might lead to recalling of diplomats and possibly war. Finally, in February, 1916, the German government implicitly admitted liability and offered to indemnify the United States for the loss of American lives, but since Germany would not admit the sinking was illegal, Wilson refused to accept the German offer as adequate and the affair remained unsettled.

On August 19, 1915, the British *Arabic*, a ship that had been carrying contraband consistently, was sunk on a westbound crossing. Two American passengers were killed. Wilson resolved to settle the issue, and the tensions in German-American relations were extreme in both Berlin and Washington. Six days later, Germany announced that the submarine commander must have gone beyond his orders and that if investigation showed that it was a torpedo from a German submarine that sank the *Arabic*, Germany would immediately fully apologize and offer indemnity. It became known that more than two months before the *Arabic* sinking submarine commanders had been ordered not to sink large passenger liners. The Kaiser ordered the abandonment of unrestricted warfare against all passenger ships. On September 1, the German ambassador to the United States, Count Johann von Bernstorff, gave a written promise to Lansing that came to be known as the *Arabic* pledge: "Liners will not be sunk by our submarines without warning and without safety of the lives of noncombatants, provided that the liners do not try to escape or offer resistance."

The *Arabic* pledge was a major diplomatic victory for the United

States, although it did not settle the question of American seamen aboard belligerent freighters. It apparently did not settle the question in Wilson's mind either. According to Colonel House, in September, 1915, the President told him "he had never been sure that we ought not to take part in the conflict and if it seemed evident that Germany and her militaristic ideas were to win, the obligation upon us was greater than ever." The best way to maintain American peace, Wilson apparently reasoned, was to try to end the war in Europe.

Attempts at Mediation, 1915–1916

Wilson made his first real attempt to end the war by mediation only a few months after the declaration of war. German Ambassador von Bernstorff hinted that the Kaiser might be receptive to mediation, might withdraw from Belgium, and give the Belgians an indemnity. After preparatory talks with Allied and Central Power diplomats in America, Wilson dispatched Colonel House to London, Paris, and Berlin in late January, 1915. House received the most encouragement from Berlin, but the terms the Germans wanted— parts of Belgium, a slice of the Belgian Congo, and an indemnity from France —were unacceptable to the French, and the British were in no mood for mediation after the sinking of the *Lusitania*.

In the fall of 1915, the Wilson administration embarked on another effort to bring a negotiated peace, but the effort was inept, less than candid with the American people and congressional leaders, not fully open and above board in its dealings with the belligerents, and finally, marked by contradictions and confusion within the administration. On October 8, 1915, Colonel House proposed to the President that the United States compel a settlement of the war or, should that fail, enter the war on the Allied side. Wilson did not veto the idea, and House took his silence as consent. Soon thereafter, House received letters from Sir Edward Grey, the British foreign minister, which implied that the Allies might consider a negotiated peace if America would join a League of Nations to prevent future wars. Wilson collaborated with House on a reply to Grey's letter. The reply asked Grey to inform House when he thought an American move for a negotiated peace would be propitious, and he promised that when so informed he would urge the President to begin action. House, upon getting Wilson's approval, would then confer with the British and go to Berlin to tell the German officials that Wilson wanted to stop the fighting but would not tell the Germans of the earlier understanding with the British. "If the Central Powers were still obdurate, it would probably be necessary for us to join the Allies and force the issue." Wilson inserted the "probably." Grey replied seeking some clarification and asking for a pledge to a League of Nations. Wilson approved the League idea.

In December, 1915, without any word from Grey that the time was ripe, Wilson decided to send House on a peace mission. At that time, relations between Washington and Berlin were sorely strained—Germany was requested to recall Franz von Papen and Karl Boy-Ed, its military and naval attachés

159

in Washington, for plotting against American neutrality, and a complete break in relations seemed possible. House arrived in London on January 6, 1916. He received no commitments from the English but was encouraged nevertheless and went on to Berlin. The German leaders said they would participate in no peace negotiations that did not include assurances of French and British indemnities and German control of Belgium and Poland, harder terms than they had laid down a year before. Actually, both sides expected major victories in the summer campaigns and neither was eager to bring peace. House went on to Paris and back to London where he and Grey in February prepared a memorandum of the Anglo-American understanding. The House-Grey memorandum stated that when France and England declared the time opportune, Wilson would propose a peace conference. Should the Allies accept and Germany refuse, "the United States would probably enter the war against Germany." If both sides accepted a conference, the peace meeting would secure "terms not unfavorable to the Allies; and, if it failed to secure peace, the United States would leave the Conference as a belligerent on the side of the Allies, if Germany were unreasonable." Again, Wilson had the "probably" inserted. Within a few months after this memorandum, Britain became quite optimistic about its chances of success on the battlefields of France and in August flatly rejected House's suggestion of a conference. House's negotiations were not known outside the Wilson administration, not even by the Democratic leadership in Congress.

While House was in Europe seeking a kind of pro-Allied peace, Lansing and Wilson were taking actions in Washington that, at first, brought Germany and the United States more closely together. Consistency was not among Wilson's virtues in early 1916. The White House also precipitated a major explosion on foreign policy in Congress.

The main issue was over the arming of merchant ships. Early in the war, before the beginning of the German submarine campaigns, the State Department had classified armed merchant ships as peaceful and therefore free to enter neutral America's ports. In the summer of 1915, the British began to arm her freighters and even her liners and ordered them to attack submarines. For America to insist that German submarines observe the same rules toward these armed merchantmen that naval surface craft observed—warning and search for contraband—was to expose the relatively defenseless surfaced submarine to great danger. On January 18, 1916, therefore, soon after House arrived in London, Lansing proposed in notes to the Allies a new *modus vivendi*, or implicit working arrangement for maritime warfare: the Allies would remove arms from their nonnaval vessels and the German submarines would observe the rules of surface craft. The British could not understand the House negotiations and the new Lansing proposal coming at the same time, for they considered that to disarm the merchant ships would serve Germany's advantage.

Soon Lansing and Wilson would back off from their new proposal but only in such a way as to heighten German-American tensions and bring about a congressional crisis. On January 26, Lansing told an Austrian diplomat in Washington about his proposal to the Allies. The Austrian replied that the Central Powers were contemplating a declaration of unrestricted submarine warfare against armed merchantmen and asked Lansing if he thought such a declaration advisable in view of his proposal to the Allies. Lansing answered that he thought such a German and Austrian declaration should be issued soon. On February 10, the Germans made the following announcement: beginning on February 29 their submarines would attack armed Allied freighters without warning. Having led the Central Powers to issue the declaration, Lansing now reversed himself and on February 15 told the press that although he still thought it best for the Allies to disarm their merchantmen, if they did not do so the United States would not press the issue and would not warn its citizens against traveling on armed Allied ships. Two days later, Lansing and Wilson rejected the German proposal for indemnity for the American lives lost on the *Lusitania*.

Now Democratic leaders in the Senate and House concerned with foreign affairs became alarmed and had an interview with the President. They wanted to know what Wilson would do if a submarine without warning sank an armed Allied ship on which American citizens were traveling. Wilson replied he would hold Germany to strict accountability but would not press the Allies to disarm their merchant ships. This was too warlike for Congress. The House Foreign Affairs Committee unanimously agreed to bring to the floor a resolution already offered by Representative Jeff McLemore of Texas which warned Americans against traveling on armed ships of countries at war. Senator Thomas P. Gore introduced a similar resolution in his chamber. The resolutions were strongly supported. House Speaker Clark said the McLemore resolution would carry by two to one if it came to a vote. But Wilson pressured Congress not to pass the resolutions by using his patronage powers extensively and succeeded in having both of them tabled.

The German government refused to revoke its declaration of unrestricted submarine warfare, even though Lansing was by this time unsuccessfully urging Wilson to break off diplomatic relations. On March 24, a German submarine torpedoed the *Sussex*, an unarmed French passenger ship, in the English channel. The boat made port, but there was a heavy loss of life. None of the American passengers was killed, but several were injured. At first the German diplomats, misinformed by their naval people, evaded responsibility for the attack. Lansing and House urged severe measures upon Wilson. On April 16, 1916, a note to Berlin declared that unless Germany "should now immediately declare and effect an abandonment of its present methods of submarine warfare against passenger and freight-carrying vessels," the United States "can have no choice but to sever diplomatic relations." Wilson went before Congress and repeated the ultimatum. This was a long way from Lansing's proposal about disarming merchantmen three months earlier.

The Germans were then eager to avoid war with the United States and backed down part way. On May 4, the German government replied to the note of April 16 saying that it would thereafter observe the rules of visit and search before sinking merchant vessels, but that if the United States did not make the British cease violations of prewar international law "the German government would then be facing a new situation in which it must reserve itself complete liberty of decision." Wilson replied to this so-called *Sussex* pledge on May 8 by saying that friendly relations between the two powers depended upon German observance of its statement and the United States did not recognize the conditional provision that it should hold the British to compliance with international law. There the matter stood. The tension abated. But Wilson had placed himself in a position that required a diplomatic break if the Germans resumed unrestricted warfare.

For the balance of 1916, German-American relations were relatively peaceful. But Anglo-American relations deteriorated badly. The suppression of the Irish rebellion in April heightened American popular disapproval of the English, and Wilson was distressed by the final British refusal to accept a peace conference at that time. Furthermore, in July, 1916, the British published a list of eighty-seven American companies with whom British subjects were forbidden to deal because they had done business with the Central Powers. In retaliation against this blacklist, Wilson secured legislation that empowered him to refuse American port facilities to ships that discriminated against the forbidden American companies. These difficulties with the English, however, were not so emotional as had been the situation with Germany in the spring, and the elections of 1916 were held without a threat of imminent war.

Preparedness

Almost from the beginning of the European conflict there had been demands for strenghtening the American military and naval establishment from both economic conservatives such as Henry Cabot Lodge and from followers of the chip-on-shoulder Roosevelt. In the fall of 1914, the Army League, the Navy League (both old militaristic organizations), and the new National Security League urged Congress to increase American armed strength. Most people were apathetic or opposed, and the White House was then opposed to an increase in armaments. The advocates of preparedness argued that America could best preserve her neutrality by building strong defenses.

But the thousands of people in peace organizations believed that the argument of neutrality through strong defenses was specious because its proponents frequently urged intervention when there was a crisis in relations with Germany or Mexico. Furthermore, with the exception of the Roosevelt group, the advocates of preparedness were conservatives in domestic affairs, and most of the peace organizations were dominated by Democratic progressives or Republican agrarian progressives. They feared that preparedness would mean militarism and an end of progressivism at home.

As the German submarine disputes became serious in 1915, Wilson began to shift ground toward preparedness. He also was surely not unmindful of the fact that he and his party would be in an advantageous position for the 1916 elections if he yielded some to the preparedness advocates and yet preserved the peace. In July, 1915, he asked the Secretaries of War and of the Navy to prepare recommendations for strengthening national defense. Their reports recommended building a navy to be the equal of Britain's by 1925, increasing the size of the regular army, scrapping the state-controlled National Guard, and erecting in its place a national reserve force, the Continental Army, of four hundred thousand men. The President made the program public in November, and when Congress met the next month Wilson made patriotism and preparedness the main topics of his annual message. The Democratic leader of the House, Claude Kitchin, and a considerable group of Democratic congressmen from the South and West sharply opposed Wilson on preparedness and controlled the House military affairs committee. Wilson went on a speaking tour of major cities of the Midwest to whip up enthusiasm for preparedness but he failed to excite much support. In March, the House passed a bill to increase the regular army from 100,000 to 140,000 men but killed the Continental Army idea, which had aroused widespread opposition as a militaristic notion, in favor of granting War Department control of the state National Guard units. The next month, however, the Senate added to the limited House increases against the background of the *Sussex* crisis, and the final law passed in May raised the regular army to 11,327 officers and 208,338 enlisted men. The law also integrated the National Guard into the War Department and authorized total National Guard strength of 17,000 officers and 440,000 enlisted men. On the whole, the Army Reorganization Act was a substantial step toward preparedness, although Kitchin regarded the bill as a personal victory and extreme preparedness advocates such as Roosevelt denounced it. The National Security League even urged Wilson to veto the bill and demand stronger legislation.

The congressional naval affairs committee postponed action until the army bill went through. Then the House ignored the executive request for a five-year building program but authorized more tonnage the next year than the White House had requested. The Senate put the five-year program back in and stepped up the schedule to three years. Wilson pressured the House into concurring in the $500 million plus measure. The act provided for the construction the first year of four battleships, four battle cruisers, four cruisers, twenty destroyers, and thirty submarines. The White House also obtained passage of the Merchant Marine Act of 1916 which created a United States Shipping Board empowered to spend as much as $50 million on building or purchasing merchant ships suitable as naval auxiliaries, to operate shipping lines, and to charter its ships to private companies. Shipping companies objected to the bill, calling it "socialism," never dreaming that the Shipping Board in time would be a tremendous subsidy to them.

The opponents of preparedness had lost almost everything on the defense program except for omitting the proposed Continental Army. At the same time, however, Wilson urged a series of domestic reform measures and acquiesced in the progressive demand that the cost of the armament program be paid for by higher taxes on big incomes of individuals and corporations, as described in Chapter 3. It is difficult to say with any certainty if a majority of the people supported the preparedness program or not. Washington sponsored several "preparedness parades" and other patriotic demonstrations in 1916, but much of the enthusiasm for these spectacles seemed synthetic. Wilson's efforts to turn the Democratic national convention into a patriotic preparedness rally backfired completely, and it actually became more of a peace demonstration. Undoubtedly, the fact that the nation was still at peace on election day had more to do with Wilson's re-election than the fact that he had led the struggle for greater armament.

The War Comes

When Wilson could again turn his full attention to foreign affairs after the election, the situation in Europe had changed. The German offensive at Verdun in the spring of 1916 had failed, as had the Allied Somme counteroffensive, but in the late fall of 1916 the Germans gained on the eastern front and occupied Rumania. The Germans, of course, did not know that the first Russian revolution would come the following March and that Russian resistance would collapse soon thereafter. In the immediate situation it seemed to both sides that they must intensify the use of their best weapons: for Germany, the submarine campaign to disrupt the economic base of British strength; for Britain, the stranglehold of economic blockade.

The British tightened their hold through bunker agreements; neutral shippers agreed to adhere to the regulations of the British Admiralty in exchange for the privilege of buying British coal at ports of the world. From November, 1916, until the end of January, 1917, Anglo-American relations were their most strained.

At a high-level conference of German leaders in late August, 1916, the naval officials had urged an all-out submarine campaign, arguing that they could knock out about 40 per cent of the British sea freight capacity within five months and that the campaign would meanwhile keep many neutral vessels at home. Civilian and army leaders, however, argued that a submarine campaign probably would bring the United States into the war and vetoed the German Admiralty's suggestion for the moment. Germany first would try direct negotiations for peace.

Wilson also decided that another effort to bring peace was in order. He realized that the House-Grey memorandum was dead, and to Colonel House's question as to what he would do if the Germans accepted peace overtures and the Allies did not—House even suggested the Allies might declare war on America—he replied that he did not think the Allies would declare war but that if they did he would not back away. The Germans had already urged Wilson to take the initiative for peace, and in late November, 1916, Wilson began to draft a note to urge a peace conference.

Wilson's first draft of the note is interesting in view of later developments. He wrote that the reasons for the war were obscure, that neutrals still did not know what the war was all about, and that the belligerents ought to state their war aims. Lansing and House persuaded Wilson to redraft and tone down the note which went out on December 18. It asked only that the belligerents state their objectives.

Both the Allies and Germany were evasive, dilatory, and less than candid in stating their war objectives. The day after Wilson sent his note, the British prime minister, David Lloyd George, told the House of Commons that the Allied peace terms were "complete restitution, full reparation, and effectual guarantee" of peace in the future. The British foreign secretary, Arthur Balfour, in a confidential memorandum whose contents did not become known until years later, was more specific. The objectives were to weaken the Central

Powers by breaking up large parts of Central Europe into several nations on the basis of nationality—Alsace-Lorraine back to France, Constantinople for Russia, a semiautonomous Poland with close Russian connections and to include parts of Germany and the Austrian provinces—and to secure reparations for the submarine sinkings and war damages in Belgium, France, and Serbia. The Germans were reluctant to reveal their aims until after they had already made the decision for an all-out submarine campaign, and further made clear they did not want Wilson at any peace conference that might develop. To the Germans, his function was merely to force the Allies to a peace conference. The German war objectives Wilson received on January 31, 1917, were territorial changes in East Europe to protect Germany from Russia, additional colonies, indemnity from the Allies for war damages, and German withdrawal from France and Belgium but with financial compensation and redrawing the boundaries to Germany's advantage. Clearly, neither side in the winter of 1916–1917 was willing to settle for a draw, a "peace without victory" such as Wilson urged in a speech to the Senate on January 22, while delicate negotiations were still in progress.

When Wilson gave his "peace without victory" address Germany had already decided, on January 9, 1917, that a negotiated peace on the terms she wanted was out of the question and that she would begin her attempt at a knockout blow by submarine on February 1. The German government informed its ambassador in Washington, Bernstorff, on January 16, of its decision and instructed him not to notify the Wilson administration until January 31. Bernstorff presented both the notice of the submarine campaign and the final statement of German war objectives at the same time. The submarine note declared that effective February 1 German submarines would attack all ships, Allied or neutral, in a war zone around Great Britain, France, Italy, and the eastern Mediterranean. The United States would be permitted to send one passenger ship a week to Falmouth, England, if it bore certain designated markings. In other words, Germany had revoked not only the *Sussex* pledge of May, 1916, but the practice observed since the spring of 1915 of avoiding attacks on American ships. The German government took this decision with recognition that it would probably mean American military intervention on the side of the Allies. Germany's hope was that the submarine campaign and an offensive on the western front would end the war before American military power could tip the balance for the Allies.

Wilson had committed himself to breaking diplomatic relations with the resumption of intense submarine warfare at the time of the *Sussex* crisis. On February 3, Wilson announced in a speech to Congress that he had taken steps to end all diplomatic relations with Germany. The immediate economic effects of his action are worth noting. The stock market, which had been depressed during the peace efforts, immediately started up, and Wilson received messages of congratulations from the House of Morgan, United States Steel, Bethlehem Steel, and the Remington Arms Company. But Wilson's support was far wider than just among the interests that stood to profit from a war. On the whole, he had the support of the Midwest and the West, which theretofore had been primary centers of neutralist sentiment. Only very few people, however, called for a declaration of war.

Wilson was by no means ready for war. In fact, he made an unsuccessful and desperate attempt to divide Austria-Hungary from Germany and to bring peace by a promise it could retain its prewar empire, an attempt which was interesting in view of Wilson's ultimate peace conference position. He also made it clear to the British that the United States was still neutral when, on February 17, he notified them that international maritime law was still unsettled and that America reserved the right to enter claims for damages to American citizens incurred by British action. Wilson was waiting for an overt act by German submarines. The first attacks on American ships did not come until March 12.

On February 7, Wilson refused to use the navy to convoy ships through the war zone. Shipping companies began to cancel sailings, and, as material began to pile up in Atlantic ports, there was considerable pressure on the administration to arm merchant ships. In cabinet meetings Wilson resisted a decision to ask Congress for authority to arm them until February 25. He then changed his mind upon learning from Ambassador Page in London the contents of a note from the German foreign minister, Alfred Zimmermann, to the German minister in Mexico City which the British had intercepted and decoded.

On January 17, Zimmermann had sent to his minister in Mexico via Ambassador Bernstorff in Washington instructions to be followed in the event of war between the United States and Germany. Upon a declaration of war, the minister should propose to the Mexican government an alliance in which Mexico would declare war upon the United States and recover Texas, New Mexico, and Arizona. Mexico was also to ask the Japanese to join the new alliance. Ironically, the German foreign office had asked for and received permission to send the message over the wire connecting the American embassy in Berlin with the State Department. After the British had intercepted and decoded the note, it delayed informing the United States of its contents until an advantageous moment. The day after learning of the proposed German-Mexican alliance, Wilson went to Congress and asked for authority to arm American merchant ships.

Wilson's speech was not warlike. He did not mention the Zimmermann note, pointed out that there had not yet been a submarine attack on an American ship, and expressed a hope for peace. Yet he asked for authority to arm the merchant ships and for broad authority to use "any other instrumentalities or methods" to safeguard lives and commerce. There was little sentiment in either house of Congress for arming the merchant vessels, but the extreme neutralists in the Senate, led by LaFollette and Norris, threatened to filibuster the whole armed ship bill if it granted the President broad powers. Congress was then in a "lame duck" session which had to disband by March 4, and a filibuster could be successful. Indeed, a group of Republican senators had already decided to filibuster an appropriations bill so that the "lame duck" session would be ended and Wilson would call the new Congress, elected in November, 1916, into a special session. The Republicans called off their filibuster plans and let the LaFollette-Norris group bear the odium of the delay. The House foreign affairs committee would grant the power to arm merchantmen but not the broad powers, despite great White House pressure.

When it appeared that neither house would give him the powers he asked, Wilson released the Zimmermann note to the Associated Press which published it on March 1. A great wave of hostility to Germany swept the country, and immediately the House passed the armed ship bill by an overwhelming margin but without a broad powers provision. Senate majority leaders urged the passage of a grant of broad authority, but the neutralists talked the bill and the session of Congress to death. On March 9, Wilson announced he would arm the merchant ships upon the authority of an antipiracy law of 1819. The gun crews on the ships were ordered to fire upon any submarine that came within range. He also called the new Congress to meet on April 16. On March 12, a German submarine sank the *Algonquin*, an unarmed American merchantman, without warning. The same day, there came the first revolution in Russia. American public reaction was quite favorable, partly because it gave a greater aspect of democracy to the Allied cause, and the United States officially recognized the new government on March 22. On March 18, German submarines sank three more American merchant vessels.

At a cabinet meeting on March 19, Wilson did not announce a decision for war despite the cabinet's urging of a war message. When Lansing argued at the meeting for a war declaration upon ideological grounds, to save democracy from German militarism, Wilson replied that he did not see how he could invoke democracy in a war message to Congress. The next day, however, Wilson moved up the opening date of the new Congress to April 2 "to receive a communication concerning grave matters of national policy." His decision to deliver a war message became clear when he called the National Guard of the eastern, midwestern, and Pacific Coast states into federal service and authorized the Secretary of the Navy to begin working out plans for coordinating American and British naval operations. He went to work on his war message, but only with a heavy heart and well aware of what war would mean for the country. On April 1, he sent for his friend Frank Cobb, editor of the New York *World*, to tell him of his decision. He saw no way out of war, he told Cobb, but the consequences would be severe. "Once lead this people into war and they'll forget there ever was such a thing as tolerance. To fight you must be brutal and ruthless, and the spirit of ruthless brutality will enter into the very fibre of our national life, infecting Congress, the courts, the policeman on the beat, the man in the street."

Wilson delivered his war message to a joint session of Congress the evening of April 2. He asked Congress to recognize that a state of war already existed between the United States and Germany. He had changed his mind since the cabinet meeting of March 19 about putting the message on ideological grounds and declared, "The world must be made safe for democracy. Its peace must be planted upon the tested foundations of political liberty." The Senate adopted a war resolution on April 4 by an 82 to 6 vote; the House passed the resolution on April 6 at 3:12 in the morning by a 373 to 50 vote. Wilson signed the resolution the afternoon of April 6, and the United States was officially at war. America did not declare war on Austria-Hungary until December 7, 1917, hoping meanwhile it might divide the Central Powers. The United States never declared war on Germany's other two partners, Turkey and Bulgaria, although it broke diplomatic relations with Turkey. An era of American history had ended.

Why did the United States go to war with Germany? Few people would assert that there can be a simple or definitive answer to the question. The submarine campaign of early 1917 triggered American intervention, but the gun was already cocked. What cocked the gun? Many things. One was majority sentiment for the Allied cause, a belief that German victory was inimicable to democracy and that an Allied victory, while not necessarily cause for democratic jubilation, was at least more desirable. Akin to this underlying cause of the war was American belief in a right, even a duty, to set the world aright—a missionary impulse which for many meant molding the rest of the world in the American image. Economic factors were certainly another basic cause. Loans and sales to the Allies, long before the war declaration, had been the basis of American prosperity, and the United States had a considerable economic stake in an Allied victory. This does not imply a banker–munitions manufacturer plot to trick the nation into war; it merely means that societies are basically conditioned by their economic foundations. American national security in the sense of protection of its shores from foreign attack was not truly a major consideration, although many people regarded the Zimmermann note, which was to be executed only in the event of a declaration of war, as a threat to national security.

Could American entrance into the war have been avoided? In other words, what would have happened if different decisions had been taken from the time of the outbreak of war in Europe? No one can ever know for sure, and the conditional tense is not the one for historians. One can only speculate. Some have speculated that if the Russian revolution had come earlier, thereby encouraging German victory, Germany would not have resorted to all-out submarine attacks and the United States would not have become involved. One can speculate that if the United States had placed its very highest priority on remaining neutral and submerging other considerations it could have avoided war. The grounds for this speculation lie in the relatively small amount of damage incurred by the United States as a result of German naval attack which was the factor that precipitated the final declaration. Between the outbreak of war in 1914 and April, 1917, 209 American citizens died as a result of German attack, more than half of them on the *Lusitania*. Only 28 Americans lost their lives on American ships. The contrast with the Scandinavian nations, which remained neutral, is striking. Norway lost over 3,000 sailors and about half of its merchant marine, and foreign commerce was more important to that small nation than it was to the United States. Yet to expect the complicated and vast nation that was the United States to have unitedly submerged all else for neutrality would be unrealistic.

The Yanks Who Went to War

The first United States contribution to the ultimate Allied victory was on the seas. (America, incidentally, was careful not to make any permanent alliances and always referred to herself during the war as an "Associated Power" rather than as one of the Allies.) Admiral William S. Sims conferred with British naval officers in London even before the declaration of war, and thereafter the United States navy worked as an integral part of British operations rather than independently.

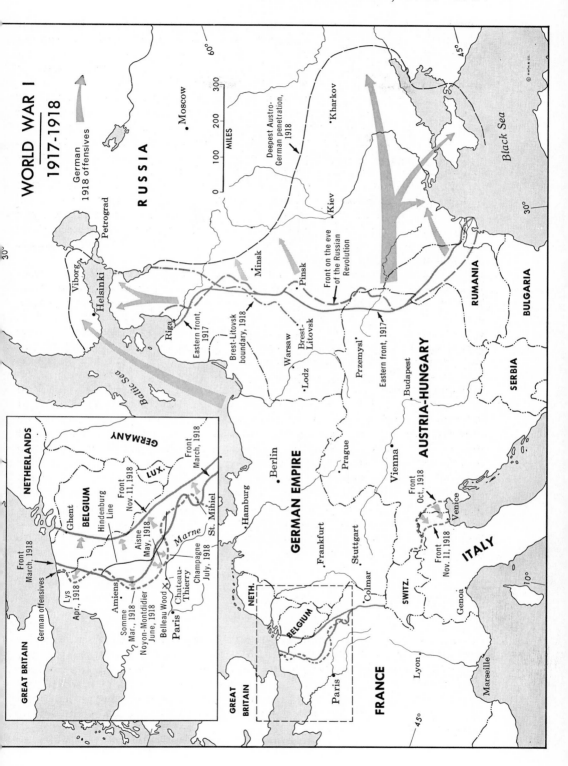

WORLD WAR I
1917-1918

German
1918 offensives

Deepest Austro-
German penetration,
1918

Front on the eve
of the Russian
Revolution

MILES
0   100   200   300

Moscow

RUSSIA

Kharkov

Black Sea

Petrograd

Viborg

Helsinki

Riga

Eastern front, 1917

Brest-Litovsk
boundary, 1918

Minsk

Pinsk

Kiev

Baltic Sea

Warsaw

Brest-
Litovsk

Lodz

Przemysl

Eastern front, 1917

Budapest

RUMANIA

BULGARIA

SERBIA

NETHERLANDS

GERMANY

LUX.

BELGIUM

Ghent

Hindenburg
Line

Front
Nov. 11, 1918

Front
March, 1918

St. Mihiel

Aisne
May, 1918

Marne

Champagne
July, 1918

Chateau-
Thierry

Belleau Wood

Paris

Amiens

Somme
Mar., 1918

Noyon-Montdidier
June, 1918

Lys
Apr., 1918

German offensives

Front
March, 1918

GREAT BRITAIN

Berlin

GERMAN EMPIRE

Hamburg

Frankfurt

Stuttgart

Prague

Vienna

AUSTRIA-HUNGARY

Front
Oct., 1918

Venice

Front
Nov. 11, 1918

ITALY

Genoa

SWITZ.

Colmar

NETH.

BELGIUM

Paris

GREAT
BRITAIN

FRANCE

Lyon

Marseille

169

The primary naval tasks were to protect the sea lanes and transport troops, which meant that the main enemy was always the submarine. There were no major naval battles such as the British had fought with the Germans at Jutland in the spring of 1916. In May, 1917, therefore, the United States abandoned its general shipbuilding program and concentrated on destroyers and other antisubmarine craft. It was important that the American navy get into the war against the submarine quickly. In April, 1917, alone, German submarines sank over 880,000 tons of shipping. In May, the first American destroyers began operating with the British, and by the end of the year losses to submarines had been cut in half. After the first year of American naval operations, shipping losses never amounted to more than two hundred thousand tons a month.

The United States navy made two main contributions to Allied naval strategy: the convoy technique for trans-Atlantic merchant and troop shipping and a partial blockade of the entrance to the North Sea by a mine field. The British had not had enough destroyers to protect convoys and had thought it impossible to keep merchant vessels in formation in the foggy North Atlantic, but American officers insisted that the trick could be done and ran the first convoy to Britain in May, 1917. From the summer of 1917 until the end of the war, Allied shipping went by convoy. The British navy at first rejected the American suggestion of a mine field between the Orkney Islands and Norway, but cooperated in the venture in early 1918 after the development of an improved mine. The two navies had not completed laying the field by the end of the war, but the mines nevertheless destroyed about 10 per cent of the German submarines that tried to go through the huge sea gate, and many others suffered damage.

When the United States first declared war, few citizens thought that American participation would go beyond naval support, shipping, and material. French and British army missions, however, explained that the Allies were getting low on manpower and had to have American troops. Wilson and his Secretary of War, Newton D. Baker, were determined that the raising of the army would be somewhat more efficient than had been earlier American efforts, when individuals were allowed to raise volunteer units such as the Rough Riders and conscription had been only a last resort. The administration asked for a conscription law soon after the war declaration, but the bill ran into considerable opposition in Congress. Speaker of the House Champ Clark vigorously opposed the draft, remarking that where he came from conscripts and convicts were regarded as remarkably similar. Congress opposed the War Department demand for conscription of men aged nineteen to twenty-five and set the registration for all men between twenty-one and thirty. Congress also authorized volunteer units, although it did not force the administration to take them. The prohibitionists showed that they were going to use the war to their advantage by banning the sale of liquor at or near army camps, but, as French bistro keepers soon learned, the dry camps did not diminish the American doughboy's taste for alcohol. Roosevelt wanted desperately to raise his own division and take it to France although he was fifty-eight years old and blind in one eye. When Wilson and Baker refused him and all other volunteer units, the ex-President was convinced that Wilson acted only from personal malice.

The draft bill became law on May 18, 1917; the first registration under it was on June 5. The administration remembered the opposition to the draft during the Civil War, anticipated violence on registration day, and obtained the cooperation of local sheriffs and police, but 9,500,000 men registered that day without major incident. On August 31, 1918, conscription was extended to all men between eighteen and forty-five. No enlistments were permitted after August 9, 1918. By the end of the war, 24,234,021 men had been registered and 2,810,296 drafted. On April 2, 1917, there were 378,619 men in all the armed forces; on Armistice Day the figure had increased to 4,791,172.

To get men in the armed forces was easier than training and equipping them. In June, 1917, construction began on 16 new army camps, each one to be a complete unit for the training of 48,000 new soldiers. They went up remarkably quickly but were far from ready when the first draftees arrived in September. Training officers was more difficult than training enlisted men, and the system used at Plattsburg, New York, and other such centers where college students and a few others became "ninety-day wonders" was never fully satisfactory. Although American industry performed miracles during the war, it was never able fully to meet the demands of the services. Most of the artillery used by the American Expeditionary Force in France was of French manufacture, and only a small proportion of the aircraft used was produced in the United States.

Wilson bypassed General Leonard Wood to make General Pershing commander of the American Expeditionary Force (AEF). Pershing arrived in Paris in mid-June, 1917, to announce, "Lafayette, we are here," but "we" consisted of only about 14,500 troops, whose chief immediate value was for Allied morale. Pershing insisted to the British and French commands that the AEF be an independent unit, working with the Allies in general strategy of course, but a unit unto itself with its own independent function at the front. There was little the Allies could do under the circumstances but submit to Pershing's demand, and they grudgingly granted the AEF a quiet sector to defend near Verdun in the fall of 1917. Some battalions had already had some battle experience serving with the French.

In the fall of 1917, the German armies began a series of attacks which became increasingly serious as the Germans shifted divisions from the eastern front. The second, or Bolshevik, Russian revolution came in November, 1917, and the Russians were soon out of the war altogether. Not until the Germans concentrated on the western front did the Allies create the Supreme War Council to direct all western military operations. During the winter of 1917–1918, Pershing and Wilson were under considerable pressure from the Allies to allow elements of the AEF to be used as replacements in defense against the German attacks, but they successfully held to their demand for an independent American command.

On March 21, 1918, the Germans launched a series of attacks which they hoped would end the war. The first attack, against the British on the Somme sector, rolled thirty miles the first week, a greater gain than either side had made in such a short period since 1914. The Allies and Wilson then named Marshal Ferdinand Foch as supreme commander of the western forces, and Pershing offered him all of his resources. At the time, Pershing had four divisions plus necessary supporting units. By the Armistice on November 11, he had forty-two divisions and slightly over two million men.

The AEF First Division went into the Somme sector in late May with

171

orders to take the village of Cantigny. This was the first rough action American troops had been in, and the Allies were eager to see how the doughboys acquitted themselves. They did well. They captured Cantigny on May 28 and successfully defended the strategically important village at the tip of the German offensive against seven counterattacks in three days.

On April 9, the Germans unleashed a major attack on the British toward the northern end of the front, and although they made advances and captured many prisoners the British held their lines. Then on May 27, the Kaiser's army unleashed a dangerous campaign against the French between Soissons and Rheims. In three days, the Germans were at Chateau Thierry on the Marne River, only fifty miles from Paris. Foch threw in the AEF Second Division and American marines. They pushed the Germans back across the Marne and in June cleared them out of Belleau Wood.

A word needs to be said about the nature of the fighting on the western front, which was different from most subsequent American military action. Each side in times of relative quiet settled down to trench warfare, a dirty, cold, and thoroughly unpleasant life for the soldier, which only got worse when either side made an attack. Preceding an attack the artillery would lay down a terrific barrage, and then the infantry would go "over the top" in an effort to dislodge the enemy from its stronghold. Casualties were concentrated and very heavy.

Finally, on July 15, the Germans made a desperate attack on the sector between Soissons and Rheims, the Marne offensive. About 85,000 American troops were in the Marne pocket, and in three days the Germans had been stopped. The Germans had spent their last offensive strength in one final effort. Pershing and the Allied commanders realized the German position and soon began a series of offensives that finally ended the war.

The offensives extended the length of the front; American troops were engaged in two drives near the southern end, the St. Mihiel salient southeast of Verdun and the Meuse-Argonne sector west of Verdun. The Germans had been dug in at the St. Mihiel salient since 1914 and were well fortified. The AEF attacked it on September 12 and within four days had control of the area. Pershing wanted to push on to Metz, but Foch moved the AEF's main strength to the Meuse-Argonne sector, where the objective was to capture the railroad behind the German lines upon which the Kaiser's armies depended.

The battle for the Argonne was one of the bloodiest of the whole war. The AEF had twenty-four miles of the two-hundred-mile front when the counteroffensive opened on September 26. It sputtered at first and had to be reorganized eight days later. Then one sustained and hard push for the rest of the month pushed the quickly weakening Germans back to the Meuse River and beyond at some points. Allied arms had similar success in other sectors, and the Germans were on the run.

The Central Powers began to fall apart. Bulgaria agreed to an armistice on September 29 and Turkey on October 30. On November 3, Austria gave up, and the end was in sight for Germany. On November 7, a German detail of officers passed through the lines to discuss armistice terms, and on November 11 at 11:00 A.M. the long and horrible war ended at last.

For years after 1918, Americans fruitlessly argued with British and French citizens over who won the war. It was easy for Americans to say they had won because victory came after they had thrown their full force into the battle. Indeed, American power was decisive although it was only the straw that broke the German camel's back. When the Germans began their last offensives in the spring of 1918, they had a numerical superiority. By the fall, the heroic measures taken to get American soldiers across the Atlantic and to the front had given the Allies superiority in numbers and firepower.

The statistics were appalling. Slightly more than 50,000 American soldiers lost their lives in battle. Another 75,000 died from other causes, largely the influenza epidemic that swept the world and killed about 10,000,000 people. Over 200,000 American troops were wounded; about 85 per cent of the wounded, thanks to efficient medical services, returned to active duty. Yet the American losses were minor compared to those of the other belligerents. Germany lost 1,600,000 men and Austria 800,000. On the other side, the Russians suffered the worst losses, 1,700,000 killed, a fact that was no small factor in bringing about the Bolshevik revolution. The French lost 1,385,000 and the British, with her empire troops, 900,000. It was no gross exaggeration to say that the flower of the western world's young generation lost its life blood on the soil that fertilized European nationalism. And, as everyone soon would see, the war had not made the world safe for democracy.

CHAPTER NINE

The Home Front and the Peace

THE HISTORY OF A WAR IS NOT COMPLETED WHEN THE MILITARY AND naval action has been described. Success or failure in battle underlies all a nation's decisions and policies during wartime, of course, and to the men engaged in battle nothing else in the world is as important. Yet, apart from the basic condition of victory or defeat, what happens to a nation economically, politically, socially, and diplomatically during a war has a more lasting impact than the events of conflict. What happens at home has even a more permanent effect upon the soldier himself, provided he survives in reasonably good condition.

The United States that returning servicemen found in 1919 was not the United States they had left in 1917. Nor would it ever be again. Progressivism was all but dead. Intolerance had replaced freewheeling dissent and rebellion. The economy had changed significantly and was to change still more. And the peace that was made held little promise of preventing another war.

The Economic Impact of War

The stimulus of war contracts, both for American use and for the Allies, brought a high level of prosperity. Unemployment, which had not been any serious problem since mid-1915, when sales to the Allies ended the 1914 recession, practically disappeared, and women and young people who had theretofore not been on the labor market took jobs in industry. Work was regular, and the take-home pay of industrial workers rose considerably. High prices wiped out a large part of the gain in money income, but not all of it; real wages—wages in relation to cost of living—improved. With a better market in the cities and a huge market for their products abroad, farmers' real income increased by about one-fourth. Furthermore, a speculative boom in farm property made it possible for those who sold their farms to make huge returns on their investment. On the other hand, those who bought farm acreage at inflated prices incurred large debts that would later bring agricultural disaster.

Before the war, the federal government's annual budget had never exceeded $750 million, but the average for fiscal 1918 to 1920 (July 1, 1917 through June 30, 1920) was $12.5 billion. Increased taxes and borrowing—at a ratio of about twice as much in bond sales as in taxes—paid for the war. Left progressives wanted the war to be paid entirely from increased taxes, and business wanted at least four-fifths of the cost to be financed by bonds. Congress passed the first War Loan Act two weeks after the war declaration. It authorized government borrowing of $2 billion in short-term notes and $5 billion in Liberty Loan bonds. Later in the war, there were three other Liberty Loan drives, and a Victory Loan came after the armistice. Altogether these bond sales brought the Treasury about $21 billion.

The Treasury was eager for the Liberty bonds to have a wide general sale, both to prevent banks and other financial institutions from holding all the debt and for propaganda purposes. The Department organized huge bond-selling drives and publicized them extensively. Local Liberty Loan committees organized brigades of "four-minute men" to give speeches at public gatherings to boost bond sales, and frequently the committees resorted to high pressure tactics and intimidation to reach their quota. People who did not purchase as many bonds as the community thought they should were likely to be labelled "slackers," the great smear word of the era, and, especially, if they had a German name, might find their home smeared with yellow paint during the night. School boards cooperated by selling students thrift stamps in small denominations.

The revenue measure adopted soon before the war declaration had to be buttressed with a new tax law in October, 1917. The new law levied excise taxes on tobacco, liquor, insurance, transportation, automobiles, and other less revenue-producing items. The act lowered income tax exemptions to $1,000 for single people and $2,000 for married couples, raised the normal tax to 4 per cent, and increased the maximum surtax (on incomes of over $2 million) to 63 per cent. It also increased the inheritance tax to a maximum of 25 per cent and levied an excess profits tax on corporations that ranged from 20 to 60 per cent. Late in the war, the administration asked for an increase in taxes, but the next revenue act did not become law until soon after the armistice. It raised the normal income tax to 6 per cent (on incomes up to $4,000), hit receivers of huge incomes a little harder by lowering the highest income bracket level to $1 million and increasing the maximum surtax to 65 per cent, and increased the excess profits tax slightly. Although families with unusually large incomes paid far greater taxes under the war tax laws than they had ever before, families with low and moderate incomes provided the bulk of revenues for the war.

Before the war, it was apparent that an unusual amount of federal direction of the economy would be necessary even to meet the demands of the preparedness program. When the war came, the government realized that the nation's economic system was far from adequate to produce and transport what was necessary. The administration only gradually and piecemeal took over direction of the economy and never fully controlled it, but by the end of the war the federal government had become the nation's economic coordinator and regulator. World War I was the United States' first experiment with a planned economy.

Congress created the Council of National Defense in 1916 as part of the preparedness program. The Council, composed of six cabinet members and its Advisory Commission, which did most of the actual work and which consisted of transportation, engineering, mercantile, financial, and labor specialists, made an inventory of the nation's productive capacity. In late March, 1917, it created the Munitions Standards Board to standardize munitions production which after the war declaration was renamed the General Munitions Board and empowered to supervise the purchase of all munitions for the services.

It became obvious, however, that government control would have to go farther than munitions, and on July 28, 1917, the Council of National Defense abolished the General Munitions Board and created the War Industries Board (WIB) to coordinate all relevant production, allocate materials and power, and supervise labor-management relations. The new system did not work at first because the WIB had insufficient power. The first WIB director, Frank A. Scott, broke down and resigned in October, and his successor, Daniel Willard of the Baltimore and Ohio Railroad, left the position in January, 1918, just as a Senate committee revealed chaotic inefficiency in the industrial war effort. Instead of resorting to laissez faire as the Senate committee suggested, Wilson drafted a bill that granted him very extensive powers to reorganize the war agencies and to direct the nation's industrial effort. The bill became the Overman Act in April, 1918. In March, Wilson named Bernard M. Baruch, a highly successful Wall Street speculator who was a member of the Council of National Defense, to be director of WIB and granted him emergency powers.

Baruch used his great powers to rationalize American industry, something that had to be done to get material produced and transported. Some individual firms, most of them large ones, had already rationalized their production, but Baruch found it necessary to rationalize whole industries and coordinate the various industries into an efficient national production system. The WIB accomplished a great deal of efficiency merely by standardizing sizes and reducing them to a minimum. For example, it reduced the number of sizes and types of automobile tires from 287 to 9, steel plows from 312 to 76, and buggy wheels from 232 to 4. It also experimented successfully with regulating the size of packages so that box car space would be most fully put to use. Businessmen frequently grumbled at taking orders from Washington bureaucrats, but they made good profits. "Dollar-a-year men," businessmen who gave their services to the government for a nominal salary while they remained on the payroll of their corporation, frequently were not above the temptations of their conflict of interest. "Cost plus" government contracts, which allowed a fixed percentage of profit on the gross costs of production, encouraged reckless spending and, sometimes, dubious accounting methods.

Wilson and the Council of National Defense in April, 1917, brought Herbert Hoover, who had been director of the Belgian Relief Commission during the neutrality period, into the administration to serve as chairman of the committee on food production and distribution. His function was at first only advisory, but in May he became Food Commissioner and was granted slightly more power. The Lever Act of August, 1917, created the office of Food Administrator with broad powers over the production and distribution of food, feed, fertilizer, farm implements, and fuel. The law also forbade the manufacture from foodstuffs of all alcoholic beverages.

Hoover's main food problems were with wheat, sugar, and pork. The wheat crops of both 1916 and 1917 were poor. The Lever Act set a minimum price of $2.00 a bushel for wheat, but Hoover offered to buy the 1917 crop, through the new United States Grain Corporation, at $2.20 a bushel. This price encouraged greater wheat production in 1918, but it was short throughout 1917, and families were urged to observe "wheatless Mondays and Wednesdays," as well as "meatless Tuesdays" and "porkless Thursdays and Saturdays." Practically every day was "sugarless," as the price of sugar soared beyond reason and grocers were ordered not to sell more than two pounds per person per month. Hoover urged families to grow "war gardens" even in their front yards. Hoover did as good a job of efficient food distribution as could be done under the law. But the distribution of food would have been more equitable had the federal government been empowered to control prices and ration critical items.

Coal became seriously short in the winter of 1917–1918. In August, 1917, Wilson established the Fuel Administration and named his friend Harry A. Garfield, president of Williams College, to head it. Garfield was able to bring about an increase in coal production by raising its price, which made it profitable for operators to work mines that had become marginal. But coal soon ran into a major transportation problem during the unusually cold winter. Some steel plants ran short of fuel and had to cut back production, and, in January, thirty-seven freighters laden with munitions were stranded in New York harbor by lack of coal. Garfield ordered all manufacturing plants except those engaged in vital war production to close down for five days in mid-January and to observe nine subsequent "heatless Mondays." Businessmen roared but the drastic action, plus a far-reaching railroad reorganization, got the economy past the crisis.

Wilson put all rail transportation under the control of the United States Railroad Administration in the closing days of 1917. McAdoo resigned as Secretary of the Treasury to become its head. The railroads were in a terrible mess at the time. Eastern freight yards were jammed to capacity and manufacturers elsewhere needed empty cars. Heavy snows and frozen switches created chaos throughout the transportation system. To meet the crisis, McAdoo operated all the nation's railroads as if they were one integrated system and cut back passenger schedules to a minimum. When it became evident that the railroads' equipment and facilities were inadequate—sometimes actually dangerous—the federal government spent over $500 million on improvements.

The production of ships was not satisfactorily solved before the armistice. The Emergency Fleet Corporation was created as a subsidiary of the United States Shipping Board in April, 1917, but the chairmen of the two bodies argued with one another over wooden ships versus steel ships and accomplished little. Wilson fired them and appointed Edward N. Hurley of the Federal

Trade Commission to head both agencies. Hurley pressed ahead on the construction of both wooden and steel ships and even some concrete vessels. Despite great efforts, however, ship production did not become adequate until the end of the war. The shipping agencies accomplished more in the prosecution of the war by rationalizing schedules and putting into service the German ships that had been caught in American ports by the declaration of war. The administration also took command of ships under construction in private shipyards.

Efficient war production was dependent upon peaceful labor relations. Wilson recognized the importance of labor when he appointed Samuel Gompers to the Council of National Defense in 1916. Gompers and other AFL leaders were so impressed by being treated as respectable members of the nation that they perhaps overdid their cooperation with the President. For example, the lengths the AFL leadership went to in order to minimize the influence of Socialists in the labor movement were sometimes absurd. AFL leaders even rented all of the meeting halls in some cities so that Socialist trade unionists would have no place to meet.

Throughout 1917, the federal agencies to deal with labor relations were scattered and uncoordinated. Perhaps the most effective was the President's Mediation Commission, led by Felix Frankfurter. In April, 1918, Wilson created the National War Labor Board under the joint chairmanship of ex-President Taft and Frank P. Walsh, a prominent labor attorney. The Board served mostly as a labor disputes court, although it lacked real authority to do so. It averted many strikes by informing both management and labor, after a hearing, what it thought the terms of agreement should be. If the executives and labor leaders involved did not heed the Board's recommendations, Wilson could resort to his emergency powers. When the management of Smith and Wesson Arms Company refused a Board recommendation, the War Department simply took over the Smith and Wesson Springfield, Massachusetts, plant. When a local of the International Association of Machinists at Bridgeport, Connecticut, threatened a strike against a Board decision, Wilson announced that he would revoke the draft deferments of the war production workers and put them into the army.

The National War Labor Board's tasks were too great for it to accomplish alone, and in May, 1918, Wilson established the War Labor Policies Board with Frankfurter as head. Its function was to determine general war labor policy, standardize wages and hours, and, insofar as it could, allocate manpower. Its most effective allocation of manpower was through the newly established United States Employment Service in the Department of Labor, which placed 3,700,000 workers in war industries.

America's World War I experience indicated that an essentially laissez faire economy was inadequate in a national emergency. It indicated, furthermore, that planning and central direction, while difficult, nevertheless could produce and distribute the necessary goods and services, but that half-way measures could not do the job. In order to meet the demands, the Wilson administration increasingly had to resort to greater federal action. Where it fell short it was because it never took the next obvious step, such as rationing and price control, or took it too late to avert an industrial bottleneck, as in the transportation crisis of the winter of 1917–1918. The experience also indicated that the economy could be directed without gravely injuring individual freedom. Liberty and freedom received body blows during the war and immediately thereafter, but the centralized economy was not the reason for them.

Public Opinion and Civil Liberty

No one has ever known what percentage of the American people supported the war and what proportion thought the decision to intervene was a serious mistake, and no one has ever known how many of those opposed to the war were prepared to do anything against the war effort. Probably a majority of the people favored the war declaration, although many of them reluctantly, and it is clear that support for the war increased as the conflict progressed, particularly after Wilson stated the nation's war aims in January, 1918. But there is considerable evidence that a sizeable minority was lukewarm or even opposed.

A total of fifty-six Representatives and Senators voted against the war resolution, and, although some of them probably voted their convictions against the wishes of a majority of their constituents, surely some of their districts supported their vote. Some citizens of recent German and Austrian background undoubtedly opposed the war, although their opposition was never as open as that of the Socialists and other radicals, few of whom were of German background. The Socialist party, in a convention that met as Congress declared war, stated its opposition but did not state what the party would do about it. A referendum of the membership overwhelmingly supported the convention. Some members quit the party over its antiwar position, but they were relatively few. In the municipal elections of 1917, the Socialists in several midwestern and eastern cities polled the best votes in the party's history. The fact of considerable opposition to the war led to an unusually shrill prowar propaganda campaign and a widespread disregard of constitutional rights.

A week after the war declaration, Wilson created the Committee on Public Information with George Creel, a Denver journalist, as its chairman. Creel conceived his task to be "to sell the war to America" and to publicize the American cause abroad. The extent of the CPI's activities was tremendous: more than 7,500,000 speeches, and thousands of pamphlets and magazine articles in several languages. The Creel committee endeavored on the one hand to picture the American war effort as eminently Christian, decent, and democratic and to picture "the Hun" as depraved, bloody, and cruel. The CPI whipped the war spirit to a fever. Many schools abolished the teaching of the German language, and at least one college allowed students to acquire credits in German by cultivating war gardens. There was an unsuccessful effort to rename sauerkraut "liberty cabbage." A popular song of the day was entitled "I'd Like To See the Kaiser with a Lily in His Hand." The regents of the University of Wisconsin rescinded an honorary degree they had once awarded the German ambassador, Johann von Bernstorff, and many Wisconsin faculty members signed a public letter condemning Senator LaFollette for his vote against the war declaration. Even before the war declaration, Professor Charles A. Beard resigned at Columbia University over a matter pressed by the "patriotic" university administration.

In this atmosphere, words such as "traitor" and "disloyal" were thrown about recklessly, and vigilante organizations came into being in every state. The National Security League and the American Protective League sent voluntary agents to meetings of radicals and German-American organizations and received the cooperation of the Department of Justice. Wilson's administration proved the validity of his prediction to Frank Cobb that war would bring intolerance. Three wartime laws were the authority for most of the prosecutions of war objectors. The Espionage Act of June, 1917, provided penalties of up to twenty years' imprisonment and fines of up to $10,000 for convictions of inciting rebellion in the armed forces, obstructing recruitment of servicemen or operation of the draft, or making false reports to aid the enemy. The law also authorized the Postmaster General, Albert S. Burleson of Texas, to deny the use of the mails to materials which in his opinion advocated treason, insurrection, or resistance to law. The Trading-with-the-Enemy Act of October, 1917, was primarily to control foreign trade, but it gave the Postmaster General wide powers to censor the domestic foreign-language press. An amendment to the Espionage Act in May, 1918, often called the Sedition Act, extended the ban to the spoken word and provided that a conviction under the Espionage Act would be legitimate if words or actions "tended" to bring violations of law, whatever their actual consequences.

The most famous cases under these laws were the conviction of the Socialist leader Eugene V. Debs in 1918 and the conviction in a mass trial of one hundred leaders of the IWW. The speech for which Debs was convicted, before the Ohio state convention of the Socialist party at Canton, was actually rather mild. Debs's appeal to the Supreme Court was futile, and he went to prison in early 1919. Wilson refused to commute his sentence and release him despite considerable support in the cabinet for such action, and Debs remained in an Atlanta penitentiary—even ran for president from there in 1920—until Wilson's successor commuted his sentence on Christmas, 1921. In the IWW trial the jury took only four hours to find all guilty as charged, and the judge, Kenesaw Mountain Landis, sentenced fifteen of the leaders to twenty-year terms, thirty-five others to ten years, and imposed fines totalling $2.3 million. Judge Landis also presided at the trial of the Socialist leader Victor Berger; a higher court found his conduct of the trial prejudiced and set Berger free. Higher courts, however, upheld nearly all the convictions under these laws, and the Supreme Court after the end of the war found the laws constitutional. The opinion of Justice Oliver Wendell Holmes in the Schenck case in 1919 deserves special consideration because he introduced a judicial concept in free speech cases that later was to have wide application. Schenck admitted advising resistance to the draft. Speaking for a unanimous Court, Holmes was faced with the problem of squaring the Espionage Act with the First Amendment which states, "Congress shall make no law . . . abridging the freedom of speech, or of the press. . . ." Holmes ruled that Congress had the constitutional power to prevent speech and publication that constituted a "clear and present danger." Schenck's activities, he ruled, did in fact constitute such a danger. Holmes apparently intended the "clear and present danger" doctrine to hamper the prosecution of persons whose violations of the laws were minor. Critics of the doctrine have pointed out that it, in effect, said that a person could say whatever he pleased only so long as he was ineffective.

Postmaster General Burleson greatly hampered radical organizations by denying their publications the use of the mails, even sometimes of first-class mail. He banned the IWW weekly newspaper as well as several publications with Socialist connections: *The Appeal to Reason, The American Socialist, The Masses,* and Berger's daily *Milwaukee Leader.* He also suppressed anti-British Irish nationalist publications and even forbade the circulation of one issue of a Henry George single tax journal. (The producer of a Hollywood film about the American Revolution learned it was almost as dangerous to be critical of the British as to criticize the American government when he was sentenced to ten years.)

Surely no administration in American history ever went farther in suppressing dissent and prosecuting critics. Wilson himself was as unrestrained as his less constitutionally minded subordinates. In 1918, he suggested to Attorney General Thomas W. Gregory that something be done to "bring to book" the editor of the Kansas City *Star* for publishing a letter from Mrs. Rose Pastor Stokes, wife of a prowar millionaire Socialist, that said "the government is for the capitalists." Gregory assured the President that the editor had violated no law. Mrs. Stokes was later imprisoned for the Kansas City speech her letter to the newspaper was intended to clarify.

War passions did not cool with the end of hostilities in France. If anything, the public and the federal administration became even more intolerant in 1919 and early 1920 than it had been during the war. Wartime hostility to "the Huns" was now directed exclusively against "the reds," and the wave of hysterical fear and intolerance is usually called the Red Scare.

The Bolshevik revolution of November, 1917, divided the American Socialist movement. The extreme left wing of the party wanted to redesign the Socialist party along Bolshevik lines; a majority and practically all the leaders, while not opposing Bolshevism for Russia, wanted to keep the organization oriented toward democratic socialism to be achieved by parliamentary means. At a convention of the Socialists in the summer of 1919, the party split forever, the minority bolting and constituting themselves as the Communist Labor party. Another group called itself merely the Communist party. Several months later they merged, under Moscow direction, as the Workers' party, later renamed the Communist party. Even in 1919, before the Communists of various kinds suffered serious reverses, total membership of all the left parties was less than .2 per cent of the population. But the Communists, seeing the success of their idols in Russia and their idea spreading in eastern Europe, were convinced that revolution was just around the corner, and many conservatives hysterically agreed with them on this point. Both far left and far right interpreted the 1919 steel strike in terms of revolution.

A general strike in Seattle, Washington, in February, 1919, and a series of bombs in April set the country aflame. The Negro maid of a Georgia senator had her hands blown off when she opened a package addressed to her employer. A search of the mails uncovered thirty-six bomb packages addressed to prominent political and business leaders. The guilty person or persons were never caught, but everyone assumed it was "the reds," and the public rarely made any distinctions among the many kinds, who fought one another usually more vigorously than they did those contented with capitalism. Antiradical mobs became common. Sometimes the mobs rounded up local radicals, roughed them up, and forced them to kiss the flag. Others were somewhat more serious.

On May Day, 1919, a mob of servicemen invaded the offices of the Socialist daily newspaper in New York City, *The Call*, and destroyed the equipment. On Armistice Day, 1919, gunfire from an IWW hall in Centralia, Washington, killed three paraders in an American Legion demonstration. The Legionnaires said the attack was unprovoked; the IWW members said they were defending their hall from attack and destruction as it had previously been attacked. Twelve IWW members were arrested. A mob lynched one of them, and the others received sentences of from twenty-five to forty years. Other mobs elsewhere in the Pacific Northwest destroyed IWW halls and local police arrested over one thousand members. Mobs, federal prosecution during the war, and so-called criminal syndicalism laws adopted by thirty-two states outlawing membership in revolutionary organizations practically killed the IWW. Twenty-eight states also forbade the display of red flags.

As it had during the war, the Wilson administration led in the postwar drive against dissenters. A law passed in the last month of the war authorized the Secretary of Labor to arrest and deport any alien who advocated revolution or belonged to a revolutionary organization. During 1919, Secretary William B. Wilson rounded up a considerable number of such alien radicals, and the *Buford*, popularly called "the Soviet ark," left the United States with 249 radicals bound for Finland, there being no regular relations with Russia. Attorney General A. Mitchell Palmer, who succeeded Gregory in 1919 and had his eyes on the White House, soon made Secretary Wilson seem a model of restraint by comparison. Palmer had turned the Federal Bureau of Investigation into a red-chasing organization, but despite horrifying reports he sent to Congress he had been unable to get Congress to enact a bill that would have made it illegal to say or write anything that tended to incite sedition. Without the knowledge of Secretary Wilson or the Assistant Secretary, Palmer obtained from an agent in the Department of Labor warrants for the arrest of three thousand alien radicals. On the night of January 2, 1920, the "Palmer raids" rounded up thousands of radicals in thirty-three cities from coast to coast. (The Republican District Attorney of Chicago, hoping to steal some limelight from the Democratic Attorney General, jumped the gun by twenty-four hours.) A second series of raids came on January 5. Everyone found in the offices of revolutionary organizations, whether citizen or alien, warrant or not, was put under arrest. In some cities even those who visited the arrested persons in jail were locked into cells. Altogether more than five thousand people were arrested. Secretary Wilson took over the deportation proceedings, weeded out thousands of innocent victims of Palmer's ambition, and deported 556. The states prosecuted about one-third of the others. Both Communist parties went underground.

In this hysterical mood, the Vice-President of the United States saw evidence of subversion in the fact that the Radcliffe College debating team had taken the affirmative in an intercollegiate debate on the subject, "Resolved, that the recognition of labor unions by employers is essential to successful collective bargaining." It was inevitable that legislative branches of government would reflect the popular intolerant mood. A special joint committee of the New York legislature headed by Clayton R. Lusk investigated radicalism, and its fat four-volume report, *Revolutionary Radicalism*, amply revealed how broadly it defined its terms. The legislature passed several sweeping laws against radicalism, but Democratic Governor Alfred E. Smith vetoed them. The New York legislature also refused to seat five assemblymen from New York City solely because they had been elected on the Socialist ticket. Congress refused to seat Victor Berger after his election to the House in November, 1918, actually because he was a Socialist, ostensibly because he was then under indictment under the Espionage Act. When the House declared the seat from Berger's Milwaukee district vacant and ordered another election, Berger entered the second election and defeated a candidate who had combined Democratic and Republican support. Still the House refused Berger. After Berger won again in 1922, the House seated him without incident.

In early 1920, it seemed that the Red Scare might go on forever, but it faded quickly during the year, especially after lawyers of unimpeachable respectability, many of them conservative in economic matters, denounced intolerant excess. Charles Evans Hughes in a New York Bar Association report denounced the refusal of the legislature to seat the five Socialists as a denial of representative government. A committee of twelve distinguished lawyers and law professors in May issued a severe denunciation of Palmer's administration of the Department of Justice, charging that "the office of the Attorney General . . . has committed continual illegal acts" and regularly denied due process of law. So quickly did the immediate manifestations of intolerance fade that when by far the most outrageous bombing of the era occurred in September (the detonation of a wagonload of explosives outside the offices of the House of Morgan on Wall Street, killing thirty-eight, injuring two hundred, and destroying $2 million in property) the reaction was surprisingly slight. But intolerance itself did not disappear by any means, and the war and demobilization period left a legacy of distrust, reaction, and violence that was to plague American society for years. One famous case begun during the Red Scare involving two Massachusetts anarchists, Nicola Sacco and Bartolomeo Vanzetti, was to divide the nation and arouse hostility to the United States abroad for several years.

The Peace: Diplomacy During the War

Long before the United States entered the war, Wilson made public statements about the kind of peace he hoped would be created. In a speech to a meeting of the League to Enforce Peace in May, 1916 (the League was an American organization founded by ex-President Taft and A. Lawrence Lowell, president of Harvard, in 1915 to work for a postwar international organization), Wilson committed himself to American participation in a postwar organization of nations. In his "peace without victory" speech to the Senate in January, 1917, Wilson reiterated his belief in an international organization and further made clear he was opposed to indemnities.

Wilson's failure to get all he wanted from the Allies at the peace conference began when he blundered in bargaining, or failing to bargain, with the Allies immediately after the American declaration of war. The decision to become a belligerent did not commit the United States to military participation in France. It would have been quite possible for the United States to have restricted her operations to the seas. This the Allies realized when they came to Washington in April, 1917, to seek American military intervention. Arthur Balfour, the British foreign minister, headed his Washington delegation. Balfour apparently expected to have to make concessions to Wilson on the peace conditions to get military help, and he informed Wilson and Colonel House about the secret treaties and agreements the Allies had made since the outbreak of fighting in 1914. Summarized, these agreements were as follows: (1) Russia was to get Constantinople and the Asian shore of the Bosporus and the Dardanelles, reserving the right of transit of the straits for all nations; (2) Italy was to get control of the Adriatic, the Alpine passes to Austria, parts of Albania, and parts of the Turkish empire; (3) Rumania was to get some Serbian-populated areas in the Austrian-Hungarian empire, but these were abrogated by her defeat and separate peace with Germany in 1918; (4) Great Britain was to get the conquered German islands in the Pacific south of the equator, Japan was to get those north of the equator plus the German rights in the Chinese province of Shantung; and (5) Russia and France were to have a free hand in drawing their boundaries with Germany, which meant that France would get Alsace-Lorraine at least and Russia at least a slice of German Polish provinces. But Wilson did not press Balfour for a postwar agreement, apparently on Colonel House's advice, and committed the United States to military action without guarantees. Wilson rationalized that by the end of the war the Allies would be so much in debt to the United States that he could force them to accept his peace terms.

The Bolshevik revolution in November, 1917, not only created a new situation so far as the conduct of the war was concerned but for the peace as well—and, when the Bolsheviks in time showed they were going to survive and retain control of Russia, for the whole shape of the postwar world. Hoping that the people of the world would overthrow their governments, stop the war, and form communist governments when they became aware of the hypocritical secret treaties, the Bolsheviks published the treaties in December, 1917. The publication did not bring the expected reaction, and the Bolsheviks began peace negotiations with Germany.

Wilson's reply to the publication of the secret agreements was his Fourteen Points address, a statement of war aims intended not only for shaping the peace but as a propaganda weapon, delivered before Congress January 8, 1918. To the Germans, Wilson held out the hope of a just peace. Summarized, the Fourteen Points were as follows:

1) No secret diplomacy—"Open covenants of peace, openly arrived at."
2) Freedom of the seas during both peace and war.
3) "The removal, so far as possible, of all economic barriers and the establishment of an equality of trade conditions among all the nations consenting to the peace and associating themselves for its maintenance." (The Open Door, in other words, for nations adhering to point 14.)
4) Reduction of armaments.
5) Impartial adjustment of all colonial claims, "the interests of the populations concerned" to have "equal weight with the equitable claims of the government whose title is to be determined."

6) Evacuation of Russian territory and opportunity for Russia to develop herself however she sees fit without foreign interference. "The treatment accorded Russia by her sister nations in the months to come will be the acid test of their good will, of their comprehension of her needs as distinguished from their own interests, and of their intelligent and unselfish sympathy." (This point would be ironic before the end of 1918.)

7) Evacuation of Belgium and full Belgian sovereignty.

8) Evacuation of French territory and "the wrong done to France by Prussia in 1871 in the matter of Alsace-Lorraine . . . should be righted."

9) Redrawing of the Italian boundaries "along clearly recognizable lines of nationality."

10) Free opportunity of autonomous development of the nationalities within Austria-Hungary.

11) Evacuation and restoration of the Balkan nations and access to the sea for Serbia.

12) Sovereignty for the Turkish parts of the Ottoman empire, but opportunity for the autonomous development of other nationalities within the empire and the Dardanelles to be open to the commerce of all nations.

13) An independent Poland with access to the sea.

14) A League of Nations. "A general association of nations must be formed under specific covenants for the purpose of affording mutual guaranties of political independence and territorial integrity to great and small states alike."

Liberals everywhere regarded the Fourteen Points as a great manifesto. Creel had thousands of leaflets containing these war aims dropped by airplane behind the lines in Germany and Austria. They undoubtedly were a factor behind the Central Powers' decision to seek an armistice.

In early October, 1918, Germany and Austria-Hungary approached Wilson, not the Allies, to propose an armistice based upon the Fourteen points. The German generals hoped to trick Wilson into a cessation of hostilities during which they could regain their strength and attack again. Wilson headed off this possibility by dilatory tactics and insistence upon a German civilian administration. The Central Powers' position was deteriorating badly, both on the western front and at home, where communism was growing rapidly, especially in Berlin and Hungary. On October 20, Prince Max of Baden, the new German chancellor, informed Wilson that Germany accepted all of Wilson's conditions. Wilson replied three days later that he would transmit the appeal for an armistice to the Allied governments and implied that Germany would be well advised to abandon its monarchy and establish a republic. The Kaiser abdicated on November 9 and fled to Holland.

Colonel House dealt with the Allies on the armistice terms in Paris. They at first professed not to know what the Fourteen Points were, and House informed them. The British prime minister, David Lloyd George, flatly rejected Point 2 on freedom of the seas. The French insisted upon the right to impose reparations for German-inflicted damages to civilian property. House headed off further Allied objections by raising the threat of a separate peace between the United States and Central Powers. The Germans agreed. Thus on November 11, 1918, each side laid down its arms and agreed to a peace to be negotiated between the Allies and Associated Powers on the one side and Germany on the other on the basis of Wilson's peace pronouncements, with the two exceptions of the abolition of Point 2 and German reparations to France.

Point 6 of the Fourteen Points, pertaining to Russia, had already disappeared. After the Treaty of Brest-Litovsk in the spring of 1918, chaos enveloped Russia. Civil war broke out at many points between the supporters of the old Czarist government—the Cossacks or Whites—and the Bolsheviks' Red armies. A band of fifty thousand Czechs, formerly Russian prisoners of war, formed themselves into a military unit and began to beat their way to Vladivostok, Russia's port on the Pacific, hoping ultimately to get to the western front. Neither the Reds nor the Whites effectively controlled Siberia, and Japan was preparing to take the territory for herself. The Allies were eager for the overthrow of the Bolsheviks. After weeks of hesitation, Wilson consented in the summer of 1918 to participate in Allied expeditions in Russia, one in Siberia and one in northern European Russia around Murmansk and Archangel. Wilson's concern for Siberia had as much to do with heading off the Japanese as protecting the Czech force, the ostensible reason for the Siberian intervention. The ostensible reason for the northern intervention was to prevent the Germans from getting the military supplies in the port cities. The United States had 9,000 troops under the command of General W. S. Graves in Siberia before they began to leave in January, 1920. There were 4,500 American troops in the northern expedition, which had no justifiable strategic reason for being there after the armistice but which remained until May, 1919. The United States did not participate in an Allied intervention into Russian territory near the Black Sea made after the armistice. Actually, the Allied armies aided the efforts of the Russian Whites. The Allied policy of helping the anti-Bolsheviks, which was not vigorous enough to defeat the Bolsheviks, only left an understandable Soviet legacy of hostility toward the West.

The Peace Conference

Wilson, who had on the whole displayed political finesse in his first five years in office, yielding when he had to, pushing and demanding when he had to, committed a series of political blunders beginning in the late fall of 1918 that were to make most of his second term a personal nightmare and insure the doom of his peace program. In politics, at least, nothing succeeds like success and failures snowball; Wilson's failures came all at once.

First, Wilson injected partisan politics into the peace issues. If, eventually, it was partisan politics that defeated his program, it was Wilson who first tried to make political capital from international policy. During the campaign for the congressional elections in 1918, Democratic hopefuls asked him to lend their candidacies a helping hand with public endorsements. Wilson was busy with the war and early armistice negotiations, and he decided to make a blanket appeal for his party's candidates. This decision was probably mistaken, but he made it worse in the way he did it. On October 25, 1918, the newspapers carried this statement from the White House:

> If you have approved of my leadership and wish me to continue to be your unembarrassed spokesman in affairs at home and abroad, I earnestly beg that you will express yourselves unmistakably to that effect by returning a Democratic majority to both the Senate and the House of Representatives. . . . The return of a Republican majority to either house of the Congress would . . . be interpreted on the other side of the water as a repudiation of my leadership.

If Wilson's primary purpose was to have a cooperative Congress, he would have been wiser to have asked the voters to elect men who supported his position, irrespective of party; if his main concern was to have a Democratic Congress, he would have been politically more astute if he had not spelled out so clearly what a Republican victory would mean. Why the voters cast their ballots the way they did was of course a multiple mystery. Local issues, vague dissatisfaction with the war, and discontent about wartime restrictions played a part in causing citizens to vote Republican. It also should be remembered that the GOP was then the majority party and Democratic victories depended upon Republican division and the cross-over vote. At any rate, the new Congress was Republican, 49 to 47 in the Senate and 237 to 191 in the House. By Wilson's own terms, the citizenry repudiated his leadership.

A week after the armistice, Wilson announced that he would head the American peace conference delegation and go to Paris. Republicans raised an outcry against his decision (no president had ever gone to Europe before during his term of office nor had personally conducted peace treaty negotiations), but, if his decision to participate personally was a blunder at all, it was not so serious as his failure to include a prominent Republican in the peace commission. The other commissioners were Secretary of State Lansing, Colonel House, General Tasker H. Bliss, and Henry White. White was an experienced diplomat and a Republican voter but not an influential Republican politician. If he had wanted to avoid Senator Henry Cabot Lodge of Massachusetts, which was understandable, he still could have named Taft, Elihu Root, or Hughes. Besides not naming a Senator to the commission, Wilson did not even confer with Senators about the appointments. And, as Senator Lodge pointed out, the Senate would have to ratify the treaty.

Wilson also assembled a large body of experts, largely from university faculties, to advise him and the other commissioners at Paris. On European technical questions, such as ethnic boundary lines, The Inquiry (as the experts were called collectively) was of great utility. For years later The Inquiry members bored their classes with stories of how they personally had been responsible for a boundary being drawn around some obscure Balkan village.

On arriving in Europe, Wilson made a tour of Paris, London, and Rome which demonstrated he had considerable popularity among the European masses, but it is doubtful that his popularity made much difference to his skilled and cynical adversaries at the conference, Lloyd George, French Premier Georges Clemenceau, and Italian Prime Minister Vittorio Orlando. These three and Wilson constituted the Big Four which made most of the important decisions at the conference. The peace conference cannot be fully understood without seeing its background. There were the Allied representatives, in varying degrees old-fashioned nationalists and colonial imperialists, trying to establish a postwar world as much as possible like the prewar world minus German power. There was Wilson, a middle class liberal idealist with something of a Messiah complex, who wanted to amend the old order considerably and reform it along the lines of Open Door empire. Not represented at the conference, but very much in the minds of the peace negotiators, was a new force, symbolized by the new Soviet government, which wanted to create a communist world. Marx had exaggerated a bit when he wrote in the Communist Manifesto in 1848, "The specter of Communism is haunting Europe" but the specter very much haunted the conference at Paris and Versailles. It haunted Wilson as much as it did the Allies. The Allies and Wilson had their differences, important differences, but they were united in their opposition and fear of the new force and endeavored to create a fresh era which would minimize it. The peace conference did not come to terms with Bolshevism or with the conditions which created it. The conference only shut it out and tried to isolate it. For decades to come, communism and various reactions to it were to be the main issues of world politics.

The first plenary meeting of the conference was on January 18, 1919. Twenty-seven nations, all enemies of the Central Powers during the war, had representatives. Such a large group was unwieldy, and a Council of Ten, representing the United States, Britain, France, Italy, and Japan, met separately and made the important decisions. Sixty commissions, in which small nations were represented, attended to details of special questions. Wilson returned to the United States early in the conference and was not at the conference from February 15 to March 14. Lloyd George was gone part of this time, and Clemenceau was incapacitated by an anarchist's attack. Orlando went home in a huff in late April. The Council of Ten was abandoned on March 24, and the Big Four decided important questions until it became the Big Three with Orlando's departure. The Treaty of Versailles was completed by the end of April and presented to Germany in early May. Germany made some written objections and counterproposals, and the conference made some minor changes in the document. In June, the German cabinet resigned rather than approve the treaty. General Foch was ordered to march on Germany, which had continued to suffer under the blockade over the winter, unless she accepted within three days. On June 23 the Germans capitulated and signed the treaty in the famous Hall of Mirrors at Versailles.

These are the bare bones of the conference. What did the treaty provide? How did Wilson and his Fourteen Points fare at the peace table? In summary, he won his objectives or partially won them on several points and lost badly on others. The treaty was a Wilson-Allies compromise.

Wilson partially lost Point 1, "open covenants openly arrived at," on the first day of the conference when the press was shut out from the meetings. At the end of each day the press received a bare, very brief summary of the day's activities. His main victories were the redrawing of the map of Europe along general lines of "self-determination of peoples" and the League of Nations. Ethnic boundaries and political boundaries were by no means identical after the treaty, but the lines were more nearly coterminous than they had ever been before. At least some of the new national states were created to serve as buffers between Central Europe and the Soviet Union.

The League was Wilson's primary desire. He won assent to the League in principle and presented a draft of the League constitution or covenant to the conference before his brief return to America. He later had the League thoroughly tied into other treaty provisions so that to accept the treaty meant necessarily to accept the League. The League covenant called for an Assembly in which each member nation, no matter what its size, would have one vote and a Council consisting of four small nations on a rotating basis and five permanent seats for the United States, Great Britain, France, Italy, and Japan. The League was empowered to create a Permanent Court of International Justice and deal with several matters such as disarmament, world health, and labor conditions, but its main function was to preserve peace. The covenant provided that members of the League would submit any controversy between them (not with non-League members) likely to lead to war to arbitration or investigation by the Council and not resort to war until at least three months after a report or award had been made. If all League members other than the interested parties agreed to certain recommendations, no League member would go to war with a nation that complied with the recommendations. A League nation that went to war in defiance of the covenant would be liable to economic sanctions, and the Council could recommend joint military action against the offender. Wilson regarded Article 10 as "the heart of the Covenant": "The Members of the League undertake to respect and preserve as against external aggression the territorial integrity and existing political independence of all Members of the League. In case of any threat of danger of such aggression the Council shall advise upon the means by which this obligation shall be fulfilled." This provision was to be central in the battle over Senate ratification.

Now for the other main provisions of the treaty. Great Britain and the dominions of the empire wanted to keep the German colonies they had won in Africa and the Pacific. This involved Point 5 of the Fourteen Points. The upshot was that the former German colonies would be governed by League of Nations mandates, the nation to hold the mandate to be named by the League. In every case, the League awarded the mandate to the nation that had conquered the colony or had been promised it by a secret treaty. At best, Wilson won only a paper, legalistic victory on the issue; at worst, there was little difference between governing a colony under mandate and ruling it by outright possession. The decision was not between colonialism and anticolonialism but who should have colonies and how. The colonial people were not granted the right of self-determination.

The mandate scheme was used to settle the question of Japan and Shantung. Japan wanted two things: an explicit statement of racial equality in the League covenant, which she did not get, and Shantung, promised her by a secret treaty, which she got by mandate. Wilson did not like the Shantung settlement but agreed to it, which, as one of the historical specialists on the conference, Professor Thomas Bailey, has written, "lent point to Clemenceau's alleged remark that Wilson 'talked like Jesus Christ but acted like Lloyd George.' " At another point in the conference the cynical Clemenceau was supposed to have remarked, in reference to Wilson's Fourteen Points, that even *le bon dieu* had but ten.

Wilson grossly violated his "self-determination" principle in assenting to a secret treaty that awarded Italy the Alpine passes to Austria, areas populated by Austrians. Wilson resisted Italian demands for the port city of Fiume, necessary for the new state of Jugoslavia. The conference ended with the Fiume question unsettled. A 1920 treaty between Italy and Jugoslavia made a compromise, and four years later, after Benito Mussolini became Italy's Fascist dictator, Italy took Fiume by force.

The toughest opposition Wilson faced was Clemenceau's insistence upon French security against Germany in the Rhineland and huge German reparations. Wilson, with Lloyd George's help, gained a compromise with Clemenceau on the boundary question but lost nearly everything on reparations with hardly a fight. France demanded removing Germany from the west side of the Rhine and creating French-controlled buffer states there. In the end, France had to be satisfied with the return of Alsace-Lorraine, demilitarization of a zone of Germany extending thirty miles east of the Rhine, and a fifteen-year joint Allied occupation of the west bank of the Rhine. Clemenceau agreed to this arrangement only if the United States and Great Britain would sign a treaty with France pledging them to come to her aid if Germany attacked. Wilson and Lloyd George agreed and signed such a treaty which provided that the alliance would not become effective unless ratified by all three parties. Britain and France ratified. The United States Senate never put the treaty to a vote, and Wilson did not push the issue.

The reparations matter was to be an international issue for years. The Allies would have liked to have made Germany pay the whole cost of the war. The final provisions were not so harsh as that, but they were severe. The armistice understanding had left open the possibility, which under the circumstances meant the probability, of German reparations for civilian damages to the Allies. Now Wilson further agreed that Germany should pay the Allies a sum sufficient to pay their servicemen's separation payments and pensions and to extend the responsibility on damages to include damage to Allied government property as well as civilian property. France also got ownership of the coal mines in the Saar province of Germany, the Saar to be governed by a League commission for fifteen years. At the end of that time there would be a Saar plebiscite to determine whether the area would be German or French. Finally, the treaty itself did not determine the size of the reparations or set a maximum amount. The reparations bill would be drawn up by a special commission instructed to make a report no later than May, 1921. When Germany signed the Treaty of Versailles, she in effect signed a note of unknown size. The reparations commission in 1921 set the bill at the astronomical figure of $33 billion.

Was the Treaty of Versailles consistent with the Fourteen Points? Clearly, it violated them in several respects but did not wipe them out completely. Was it the best that Wilson could have achieved? The question has been debated at length but remains unanswered, as it must, because one can only speculate. Was it a more equitable treaty because of Wilson's role in its writing? Probably France would have imposed a more Carthaginian peace without Wilson's restraint, but, again, one can not say what might have happened. It has been argued that the treaty was neither harsh enough to prevent a German resurgence of strength nor fair enough to prevent German demagogues from exploiting popular dissatisfaction with it. Certainly, the treaty did not bring stability and peace, but one cannot lay the blame for the growth of Hitlerism and extreme German nationalism entirely upon the Treaty of Versailles. The most valid criticism to be made of the treaty was that it was based upon a conception of the world that was no longer relevant, if indeed it had ever been. It failed to treat constructively the questions of communism and nationalist revolt of colonial peoples. If the Treaty of Versailles and the thinking behind it were ever suitable to the facts of the world, it was the world sometime between 1815 and the 1890's.

The United States Rejects the Treaty

The most common interpretation of the Senate's rejection of the Versailles Treaty and the League of Nations is that the defeat of the treaty instituted an era of "isolationism" that lasted for about twenty years. The term "isolationism," however, is too broad and vague to be useful as a tool of communication. It is far more accurate to say that the treaty's defeat was a victory for the opponents of collective security. Certainly, the United States was not "isolated" economically between the two World Wars. For that matter, despite America's refusal to enter the League of Nations, the nation was not entirely aloof even from the idea of collective security during the two interwar decades.

The reasons why opponents of the treaty and the League took the position they did were many. Most were alarmed by the degree of collective security implicit in the League and feared that membership entailed a limitation on the power of the United States to make its own decisions. A few were true "isolationists," who believed America should concentrate on its own problems, ignore the rest of the world, and withdraw from it. A few were critics of Open Door empire and thought that the new wave of communist revolution and nationalist revolts of colonial peoples required a fundamental revision of American policies and that the treaty only solidified the old policies. Some represented special interests which were slighted by the treaty. Here, for example, were many Irish-Americans, who were aroused by the treaty's failure to provide Irish independence, as well as Zionists disappointed by the absence of provisions for a Jewish national state in Palestine. Still others were motivated by Republican partisanship and hatred of Wilson as a Democratic leader. But the sharpness of the conflict over the League—and it was bitter—should not obscure the fact that Wilson and most of his opponents were in fundamental agreement about the basic shape of American foreign policy. They nearly all agreed implicitly in Open Door empire or informal imperialism. Wilson and his enemies differed more over means than ends, the opponents of the treaty holding that the League jeopardized American economic opportunity abroad.

Wilson's difficulties with the Senate over the League began well before the treaty had been entirely drafted. Wilson, rather belatedly, conferred with the Senate and House foreign relations committees during his brief return to Washington in late February, 1919. He did not satisfy the objections of some of the Republican Senators to his League proposals. The Democratic "lame-duck" Congress was then in session, and Republicans in the Senate filibustered an important appropriations bill in order to force Wilson to call a special session of the Republican-dominated Congress that had been elected in November. On the last day of the old Congress, Senator Lodge released a round robin signed by thirty-nine Senators or Senators-elect, well over the one-third plus one needed to reject a treaty, that declared "it is the sense of the Senate that . . . the constitution of the league of nations in the form now proposed to the peace conference should not be accepted by the United States. . . ." The letter also stated that the United States should first conclude a peace with Germany and then consider a league. The main stated objections to the League at that time were that the League covenant contained no procedures for a nation to withdraw, made no explicit recognition of the Monroe Doctrine, and provided no specific guarantees that the League would not consider member nations' internal affairs. Wilson revealed how uncompromising he would be on the League issue on the night the round robin was released by telling a Madison Square Garden audience, "When that treaty comes back, gentlemen on this side will find the covenant not only in it, but so many threads of the treaty tied to the covenant that you cannot dissect the covenant from the treaty without destroying the whole vital structure." And upon his return to Paris Wilson did inextricably tie the League into the rest of the treaty, although he arranged for some modifications in the covenant to meet a few of the objections. The final covenant expressly stated that nothing in the League affected the validity of "regional understandings like the Monroe Doctrine" and provided a method for a nation to withdraw from the League with two years' notice.

The revised League covenant, however, did not satisfy Senator Lodge, and he was chairman of the Senate Foreign Relations Committee in the new Congress. Furthermore, nine of the ten Republican members of the committee supported Lodge's position, as did one of the seven Democratic members. When the Senate began to consider the treaty in July, 1919, public opinion seemed to be for the League. Two-thirds of the state legislatures and governors had gone on record supporting it. A *Literary Digest* poll of newspaper editors in April had shown overwhelming League support. The odds against Lodge in the Senate were long, for more than two-thirds of the members of the upper chamber were for membership in some kind of a league. Only seven of the forty-seven Senate Democrats were unwilling to support Wilson on the League issue to the hilt. A group of twelve to fifteen so-called irreconcilables, led by Senators Hiram Johnson, William E. Borah of Idaho, and Robert LaFollette were opposed to the League altogether. Another group of Republicans, led by Senator Lodge, were for strong reservations to the League covenant, some of which, in the eyes of Wilson's supporters, practically emasculated the document. Most Republican Senators favored ratification with only mild reservations.

This being the situation, Lodge saw that his best strategy was to stall for time until League opponents could muster greater support. He even consumed two weeks by reading aloud the 246 large pages of the treaty at committee meetings. Extensive hearings took another six weeks. Meanwhile, anti-League propaganda, financed by Henry Clay Frick and the Pittsburgh banker and majority stockholder in the monopolistic Aluminum Corporation of America, Andrew Mellon, began to make inroads in public opinion.

After Wilson conferred with several Republican Senators on August 19, he realized that Lodge was gaining. Most of the Republicans who conferred with the President were mild reservationists concerned about Article 10 of the covenant. Wilson pointed out that Article 10 provided only that the League could "advise upon" means to be taken against an offending power and that, unless the United States were a party to a controversy, the permanent American seat on the League Council provided a veto. And although Wilson had said in the past that Article 10 was the "heart" of the covenant— he sometimes changed his anatomic figure of speech and called it the "backbone"—he told the Republican leaders that Article 10 provided only "a moral, not a legal obligation." He also told the conference that he would not object to resolutions that stated the Senate's interpretation of the treaty, but that he did not approve of amendments to the treaty itself because they involved acceptance by the other signatory nations. When Lodge continued to oppose, Wilson decided that an appeal to the people was necessary to carry the day.

On September 3, he began a speaking tour of the Midwest and Far West that in twenty-two days took him eight thousand miles. He delivered thirty-seven major addresses. His health had not been good when he started the tour, and he left Washington against his physician's advice. He had been very sick with influenza while in Paris and had suffered from headaches during the summer. At Denver, on September 25, he was so near collapse that his physician ordered his immediate return to Washington. One week later he suffered a stroke that left his left side paralyzed and nearly killed him. For weeks he was unable to perform personally the responsibilities of the presidency. Besides raising the serious constitutional problem of how to proceed when the president was incapacitated, a problem not yet solved, Wilson's stroke and slow recovery was a serious handicap to the treaty's chances in the Senate.

The Senate Foreign Relations Committee reported the treaty on September 10. Ten of the seventeen members of the committee signed the majority report, which called for forty-five amendments to the treaty; the minority report recommended ratification without change. A coalition of Democrats and mild reservationist Republicans voted down the forty-five amendments, the main argument against acceptance of the amendments being that they were so sweeping that the peace conference would have to reconvene and begin over again if they were adopted. On November 6, Lodge, acting as committee chairman, presented fourteen reservations. Most of them were unimportant, but one declared that the United States would assume no obligations under Article 10 of the covenant or use its armed forces under any article of the treaty unless Congress authorized such action by joint resolution. Another withheld approval of the treaty provisions for Shantung. The Senate approved the Lodge reservations by an almost solid party division. There was not yet a vote on the treaty itself. Thus the ball was tossed to Wilson and the Democratic Senators.

Democratic friends of the League urged Wilson to accept at least some of the Lodge reservations in order to get ratification. Colonel House urged Wilson to compromise but with no effect. The Democratic leader in the Senate, Gilbert M. Hitchcock of Nebraska, twice visited Wilson in his sickroom and twice found him unwilling to yield. Illness seemed only to strengthen Wilson's Calvinist will. On November 18, Wilson released a public letter to Hitchcock that declared the Lodge reservations do "not provide for ratification, but, rather for the nullification of the treaty. I sincerely hope that the friends and supporters of the treaty will vote against the Lodge resolution of ratification."

The following day the Senate voted for the first time on the treaty itself with the Lodge reservations. The Democrats were almost solid against Lodge's ratification resolution and were joined by the "irreconcilables." The Senate defeated ratification, fifty-five to thirty-nine. Hitchcock then offered a resolution of ratification with five reservations which embodied the critical Lodge objections, but this too went down, fifty-one to forty-one. Then the Senate voted on the treaty without reservations at all, and the vote was fifty-three to thirty-eight.

There the matter stood at the end of 1919, but no one yet considered the treaty and League issue dead. After all, almost four-fifths of the senators were for the League either with or without reservations. How many of the strong reservationists really hoped to defeat the treaty is impossible to say. One cannot even be certain what Lodge's objective was. But, in any case, it was apparent that to get ratification, Lodge's reservations, or most of them, would have to be accepted. Wilson was under considerable pressure from his party to bend and accept the inevitable, but Wilson was not a man to bend when he thought the right was entirely on his side. The British sent former foreign secretary Sir Edward Grey to Washington as a special ambassador to urge Wilson to compromise, and Wilson refused to see him. When Grey wrote a letter to the London *Times* saying that failure of the United States to join the League would mean the wrecking of the international body and that the Allies would accept the Lodge reservations without new negotiations, Wilson only became angry. Public opinion demanded that the Senate reconsider the treaty and that ratification in some form or another be made.

The Senate began debate on the treaty again in mid-February, 1920. By this time Wilson had recovered his health sufficiently to lead a more active life, and he used much of his regained vigor to hold out against compromise. On March 19, ratification came to a vote again. This time there were fifteen reservations, one having been added that advocated Irish independence. Twenty pro-League Democrats who figured that ratification would either be with the Lodge reservations or not at all braved White House wrath and voted for the resolution. Most Senate Democrats remained in line. Ratification failed, forty-nine voting for the resolution and thirty-five against it. If seven more Democrats had joined the twenty who deserted Wilson on the vote, the treaty would have been ratified and the United States would have been a member of the League of Nations.

Technically, the United States still was at war. To remedy this situation and to curb Wilson's wartime powers, Congress, on May 15, passed a joint resolution, the so-called Knox resolution, that merely rescinded the declarations of war. Wilson vetoed it. Treaty ratification was thereafter practically dead. Wilson had in effect demanded total victory or total defeat. He received total defeat.

There remained one anticlimactic chapter to the treaty fight. In January, Wilson had sent a message to a Jackson Day dinner in Washington in which he said that if the Senate refused to ratify the treaty without reservations the election of 1920 would be a "great and solemn referendum" on the issue. This was a serious lapse on the part of the former professor of political science, for American presidential elections are not referendums on a single isolated issue and certainly they are not "great and solemn." The issues of 1920 were many. The Democratic canditate endorsed the League. The Republican platform was deliberately vague, and the Republican candidate was evasive. Republican friends and opponents of the League both thought that he agreed with them, and the Republicans won a landslide victory. The Senate did not consider the treaty again. On July 21, 1921, Congress passed a joint resolution declaring the war was over.

CHAPTER TEN

The Politics
of Business,
1919-1929

AMERICA IN THE 1920's BELONGED TO THE BUSINESSMAN. IT WAS
a business civilization. The business community had always been extremely
influential, and it had at times so thoroughly controlled national politics that
it regarded Washington as a branch office. But never before in American
history had business influence been so unhampered and so pervasive. Politics,
economic affairs, foreign policy, social relationships, and the life of the mind all
reflected the triumph of the businessman. Two Republican slogans, each of
which was taken as a profound statement of social philosophy, indicated
the pedestal of prestige that business basked upon: Harding's slogan, "Less
government in business, more business in government" and Coolidge's statement, "The business of America is business."

The Republican party installed three of its figures in the White House
during the decade, Warren Gamaliel Harding, Calvin Coolidge, and Herbert
Clark Hoover. Coolidge was Vice-President under Harding, and Hoover was
Secretary of Commerce and one of the most important cabinet advisers under
both Harding and Coolidge. The differences among the three men reflected
three evolutionary stages in the relationship of government to business. Harding was first and foremost a politician, not a businessman. He had no serious
disagreements with the business community, and he accepted business as an
ally, but he owed his career to his political activities. In many ways, Harding
was the last of the nineteenth-century presidents—a political figure who usually
did what business expected of him but was actually more interested in the
political spoils of office. Harding let business down because he was too much
of a political wardheeler; the scandals of his administration, revealed after
his death in office, jeopardized the stability of business control of government. Coolidge, too, was from a political background and business's agent,

but he had even less personal force than Harding, surrounded himself in Washington with business rather than political figures, and smacked less than Harding of the political clubroom. Hoover was the ultimate in business and government. Rather than the agent of business, he was business. Himself an experienced engineer and a highly successful mining investor, Hoover, as Secretary of Commerce and then as President, used his positions to further the business community's interests in a more positive way than had the earlier business agents. Hoover brought the economic traditions of Alexander Hamilton to twentieth-century fruition. As cabinet member and chief executive, he instituted a new order. And when the crisis of 1929 came it was the new order's responsibility. Rather than the old order of politics and business represented by U. S. Grant and Daniel Drew, or William McKinley and Mark Hanna, or Warren Harding and Harry Sinclair, it was a new order symbolized by Herbert Hoover and anonymous corporation executives.

Demobilizing the Economy

Conservative reaction to the Progressive Era, both in economic matters and civil liberties, began long before the election of a Republican president in 1920. The last two years of Wilson's second term, when there was a Democratic executive and a Republican Congress, was a period of bipartisan conservatism.

During the war, left progressives had regarded the federal government's transportation and communications role with approval and hoped that with the coming of peace the government would stay in these businesses, as was the general practice in Europe. Businessmen, however, decried government operation of the railroads and the communications industry as socialism and demanded the return of their properties. In communications, railroads, and shipping, the federal government got out of business on terms quite favorable to the property owners. Telegraph and telephones were simply returned to private operation on August 1, 1919, with only the condition that rates should not be raised for four months.

The return of the railroads could not be accomplished so simply. Never before had the nation's railroads operated as efficiently as they had under government operation, and many people demanded that the government stay in the railroad business. McAdoo, Railroad Administrator until January, 1919, and his successor, Walker D. Hines, recommended that Washington continue to operate the railways for another five years and that meanwhile an investigation be made of the whole transportation problem. The railroad brotherhoods threw their weight behind the Plumb Plan, a scheme for the socialization of the railroads worked out by the brotherhoods' legal counsel, Glenn Plumb. Plumb suggested that the government buy the railroads with funds to be raised through bond sales and operate them through a board representing the public, labor, and management. Half of the earnings of the roads would be used to pay off the bonds, the other half would be divided among all employees, labor and executive alike, as a bonus to wages and salaries.

While the public debated the question, Wilson announced on Christmas

Eve, 1919, that he would return the railroads to private management on March 1, 1920, no matter what action or lack of it there was in Congress. Congress passed the Esch-Cummins Act (sometimes called the Transportation Act of 1920) on February 28. The law and its operation were complex, but in general it returned the roads to private operation on terms favorable to management. For six months, the government guaranteed the railroads a profit equal to the rent they had received from the Railroad Administration, and during this period all rates and wages were to remain as they were. The government financed improvements were to be paid for by the railroads over several years, and the law established a fund of $300 million to be lent to the railroads on liberal terms. The Interstate Commerce Commission, enlarged from nine to eleven members under the Act, received greater powers to regulate railroads, but railroad law was changed in such a way that the ICC's new power did not necessarily cause opposition from railroad managers. Although the ICC now had power to ban the issue of new securities and the construction of new facilities, it also could set aside the rates fixed by state regulatory commissions, which in many cases in the past had been tougher on the railroads than the ICC. The law also empowered the ICC, in an effort to build consolidated railroad systems, to lift the ban on long haul–short haul price discrimination and permit pooling. Indeed, the feature of the act that aroused the most controversy, the "recapture clause," involved a kind of pooling. The commission divided the nation into districts and fixed rates at such a level as to bring railroads within the district a fair return on their investment, in practice 6 per cent. An efficient railroad would make a higher return at a given district rate than an inefficient one. The "recapture clause" met the situation by providing that half of the profits in excess of 6 per cent should be set aside for the road's reserve fund and the other half turned over to a general contingent fund, supervised by the ICC, from which loans to inefficient railroads could be made or from which the ICC could purchase new equipment to be leased. The stronger railroads objected to the plan, and eventually the "recapture clause" was repealed and the contingent fund returned to its contributors. The Esch-Cummins Act provided that the ICC should evaluate railroad properties and use that figure as a basis for calculating a fair return on investment. Agrarians had long demanded that the worth of railroad property should be determinated by its original cost, and railroads had pleaded that the evaluation should be in terms of contemporary replacement cost. Because of generally rising costs, the later the base year for figuring replacement costs the higher the total and, therefore, the higher the rates allowed to meet a fixed percentage of profit. The ICC set 1914 as the base year for calculating replacement costs; the railroads argued for current replacement costs. In 1929, the Supreme Court, in a case involving the St. Louis and O'Fallon Railroad, accepted the railroad's contention. One final provision of the Esch-Cummins Act: it created a Railroad Labor Board representing labor, management, and the public to settle labor disputes. The board failed to prevent a shopmen's strike in 1922, and in 1926 Congress abolished the board and established a Federal Board of Mediation with less power.

The problem of what to do with merchant ships was somewhat different because some two thousand ships totalling fifteen million tons had been built and operated by the federal government rather than rented from private companies as in railroading. The experience of the war had shown that an efficient merchant marine was vital to national defense. The crux of the issue was: should a merchant marine be maintained, as it had been built, through government enterprise, or should it be turned over to private hands and subsidized? Subsidies seemed necessary if shipping was to be private; unsubsidized shipping before the war had resulted in only a feeble merchant fleet.

Congress and the President chose to turn the fleet over to private business and to subsidize it. The Jones Merchant Marine Act of June, 1920, directed the Shipping Board to sell its ships quickly and on easy terms to American-owned corporations and ordered the Emergency Fleet Corporation to operate the ships until they could be sold. The law also stimulated private shipping by setting up a $25 million loan fund to be lent to American shipping companies, providing extremely liberal mail contracts, exempting marine insurance companies from the operation of the antitrust laws, excusing shipping companies from excess profits and corporation income taxes if the money thus saved were used for the construction of new ships in American shipyards, and, reminiscent of English mercantilism during the colonial period, granting American ships a monopoly on shipping between colonial territories and the mainland. Under the act, shipping companies purchased wartime built ships at ridiculously low prices. A fleet of two hundred wooden ships brought what it had cost to build one. Henry Ford bought 199 ships and used them for steel scrap. But even with these generous government subsidies, American shipping was unable to compete with the merchant marines of other nations, and in 1928 Congress passed the Jones-White Act. This law restricted the bargain-basement sales of government ships but provided government loans of up to 75 per cent of the construction costs of new ships and increased subsidies for mail carrying. Under this law the American merchant marine flourished briefly, but it was hard hit by the depression of the 1930's and was in poor condition at the outbreak of World War II.

Government with the public's support was generous to business in its economic demobilization, but labor organizations found both government and the public cold to their demands. With the end of the war most working men had less regular work and therefore less income, but prices continued to rise until the fall of 1920. In 1919, the cost of living was 77 per cent higher than it had been in 1913, the last full prewar year; in 1920, the figure rose to 105 per cent. Labor in many industries sought higher wages, and when it found almost universal resistance among employers resorted to strikes. Over four million workers were on strike sometime or other during 1919, but labor won no important victories and suffered some major defeats. The public confused labor unionism with Bolshevism, and employers took advantage of the Red Scare to advance their own interests.

In the fall of 1919, three strikes held the nation's front pages: the strike of the Boston police, not very important economically but psychologically and politically significant, and strikes in the basic steel and coal industries. In the summer of 1919, the Boston police, disturbed by their low pay, asked the AFL to grant a charter to their Boston Social Club. Police Commissioner Edwin U. Curtis had previously warned the police against any union affiliation and now threatened to suspend nineteen officers of the policemen's organization. Democratic Mayor Andrew A. Peters offered a compromise, but Curtis refused to yield anything and proceeded to suspend the police leaders. After a vote in which only two policemen dissented, the police went on strike on September 9. That evening gangs of youthful vandals disrupted Boston's peace and there was some looting, but losses amounted to only an estimated $34,000 for the entire strike. On the second day of the strike, Mayor Peters called out Boston residents of the state guard for street patrol, and Harvard students put on arm bands and served as auxiliary policemen. Order returned to Boston with this action, but Mayor Peters publicly criticized Governor Calvin Coolidge, a candidate for re-election, for inactivity. Coolidge then called out the rest of the state guard and asked Washington for federal troops if the strike should spread. On the fourth day, the striking policemen saw they were defeated and prepared to return to duty, but Commissioner Curtis refused to reinstate any of the strikers and prepared to recruit practically an entire new force. Samuel Gompers tried to intercede against the lockout, but Governor Coolidge supported Curtis and sent a public telegram to Gompers in which he said, "There is no right to strike against the public safety by anybody, anywhere, any time." The nature of public opinion in 1919 was such that this statement not only helped Coolidge's re-election, for which he received congratulations from the Democratic President, but lifted him into contention for the 1920 Republican presidential nomination.

Hours, wages, and working conditions in the steel industry were more than usually bad. Roughly one-half the nation's steel workers received wages below those considered by the federal government to be the minimum necessary to maintain a family with a minimum decent living standard, and the average hours of work in the entire industry was 68.7. The industry operated on a two-shift basis, and many steel workers worked a twenty-four-hour shift every other Sunday when they changed from the day to the night shift. In the summer of 1918, Gompers created a National Committee for the Organizing of the Iron and Steel Industry and named William Z. Foster, a former Socialist and syndicalist who supported the war and was then a Chicago AFL official, as its chairman. In 1921, Foster joined the Communist party and later became its national leader. By the summer of 1919, the steel workers' committee claimed one hundred thousand members and demanded an end of the twenty-four-hour shift, an eight-hour day, and a six-day week. Judge Elbert H. Gary, chairman of the board of United States Steel and leader of the whole industry, refused to negotiate with Foster or Gompers or any other union official and dismissed known union members. The union voted to strike on September 22. Wilson urged the AFL to postpone the strike. Gompers was willing to do so, but Foster and the steel workers were not. On the appointed date, 343,000 steel workers walked off the job, most of them in the Chicago-Gary steel district, but some in the Ohio, Pennsylvania, and New York steel centers.

The strike was never fully effective, and steel management found that crying communism and exploiting nationalistic rivalries among the predominantly immigrant steel workers both brought public opinion to its side and created dissension among the strikers. Violence broke out at Gary in November when United States Steel imported thousands of southern Negroes to break the strike. The governor of Indiana sent the state guard to Gary to protect the entrance of the strikebreakers into the plant, and when violence persisted he appealed to Washington for federal troops. General Leonard Wood arrived in Gary with an army contingent and declared martial law. The strike in Gary was defeated. The steel workers' committee gave up entirely in January, 1920, and the steel industry was not to become organized until 1937.

During the strike, the Industrial Relations Department of the Interchurch World Movement made an extensive investigation of the strike and working conditions in the industry and issued a report that supported labor's contentions. The report was not issued in time to influence public opinion during the course of the strike, but in subsequent months public opinion turned against steel management. The steel companies denied the accuracy of the churchmen's conclusions, but in 1923 it partially surrendered to public opinion and, upon President Harding's urging, abolished the twelve-hour day.

The coal strike of 1919 was interesting due to the attitude of the Wilson administration and the emergence of a new personality in the labor movement, John L. Lewis, who had just become president of the United Mine Workers. Bituminous coal miners had not had a wage increase since 1917 despite the soaring cost of living. A convention of the UMW in September, 1919, called for the termination of the 1917 wage agreement and negotiation for a thirty-hour week and a 60 per cent wage increase. Coal mine operators refused these terms, and despite Wilson's assertion that a strike would be "morally and legally wrong," the miners left the pits on November 1.

Attorney General Palmer, acting upon Wilson's recommendation, secured a sweeping labor injunction from a federal judge, citing the wartime Lever Act. Lewis called off the strike, saying, "We cannot fight the government." But most of the miners refused to return to work. In December, Palmer conferred with UMW leaders and achieved agreement with a compromise solution of an immediate small wage increase and arbitration of other issues. Ultimately, the miners received a 27 per cent pay increase but no change in the hours of work.

Harding and the Election of 1920

Republican victory in the congressional elections of 1918 and Wilson's unpopularity heartened the GOP and heightened the struggle for the 1920 Republican nomination. The front runner for the nomination was General Leonard Wood, who wore the mantle of the deceased Roosevelt as much as anyone and was a militaristic nationalist, independent of the bosses of the party. Just behind him was Governor Frank Lowden of Illinois, a former Congressman whose main support was in the Midwest. There was a host of other hopefuls: Hiram Johnson, Senator LaFollette, Governor Coolidge, Hoover, Nicholas Murray Butler, and Senator Warren G. Harding of Ohio. A Senate investigation, prompted by Senator Borah, revealed just before the convention that Wood had spent $1.8 million in working for the nomination, much of it raised by the soap manufacturer William C. Procter, and Lowden had spent $414,000.

In the first balloting at the Chicago Republican convention the Wood and Lowden forces battled to no conclusions, and the convention seemed likely to deadlock. Senator Lodge, the convention chairman, successfully maneuvered an adjournment of the convention early in the evening of Friday, June 11, and

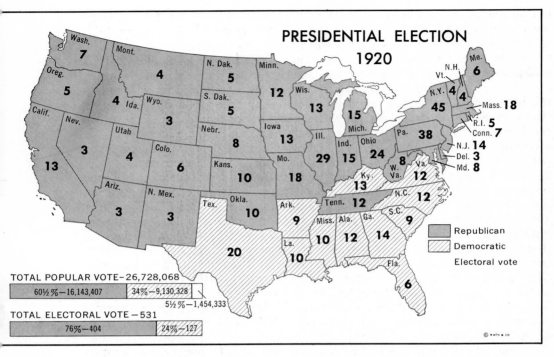

PRESIDENTIAL ELECTION 1920

Wash. 7
Oreg. 5
Calif. 13
Nev. 3
Ida. 4
Mont. 4
Wyo. 3
Utah 4
Ariz. 3
N. Mex. 3
Colo. 6
N. Dak. 5
S. Dak. 5
Nebr. 8
Kans. 10
Okla. 10
Tex. 20
Minn. 12
Iowa 13
Mo. 18
Ark. 9
La. 10
Wis. 13
Ill. 29
Mich. 15
Ind. 15
Ohio 24
Ky. 13
Tenn. 12
Miss. 10
Ala. 12
Ga. 14
S.C. 9
N.C. 12
Va. 12
W. Va. 8
Fla. 6
Pa. 38
N.Y. 45
Vt. 4
N.H. 4
Me. 6
Mass. 18
R.I. 5
Conn. 7
N.J. 14
Del. 3
Md. 8

Republican
Democratic
Electoral vote

TOTAL POPULAR VOTE—26,728,068

| 60½ %—16,143,407 | 34%—9,130,328 | 5½ %—1,454,333 |

TOTAL ELECTORAL VOTE—531

| 76%—404 | 24%—127 |

© swin & co

a group of Republican bosses met in George Harvey's suite at the Blackstone Hotel to pick a dark horse. Harvey was the publisher who had first sponsored Wilson for the presidency and then turned strongly against him. Others in the famous "smoke-filled room" were Lodge, Senator Boies Penrose of Pennsylvania, and Republican National Chairman Will Hays of Indiana. Late that night the group decided upon Harding because he had always been a party regular, made a good personal appearance, was extremely pliable, and had been so inconspicuous in the Senate as to make no strong enemies. The bosses summoned Harding and asked if there were any reason the GOP should not nominate him. Harding adjourned to an adjoining bedroom, thought for ten minutes, and emerged to say that his record was clean. Later it would be charged that he was only recently the father of an illegitimate child. The next day the powers of the GOP easily put across Harding's nomination. The convention balked at the inner-group's attempt to force the nomination of Senator Irvine Lenroot of Wisconsin as vice-president, but the measure of its rebellion was indicated by its choice of Governor Coolidge as Harding's running mate. The platform was evasive on the League but promised support of the World Court. It endorsed the recent railroad and merchant marine laws and promised aid to the farmers, lower taxes, higher tariffs, and reduced government expenditures.

The Democrats met at San Francisco later in June. The race for the Democratic nomination had been confused. Wilson had acted as if he were a contender for a third nomination without ever saying so which put the front runner, his son-in-law McAdoo, at a disadvantage. Attorney General Palmer and the three-term governor of Ohio, James M. Cox, had considerable preconvention strength. McAdoo led for the first thirty-seven ballots, but Palmer was not far behind. On the next ballot Palmer withdrew and most of his delegates went to Cox, who was the favorite of the city bosses because he opposed prohibition. The nomination went to Cox on the forty-fourth ballot. Cox chose the Assistant Secretary of the Navy, Franklin D. Roosevelt, for the vice-presidential place on the ticket.

Cox and Roosevelt campaigned hard and supported the League, but the Republicans were ahead throughout the campaign. Harding had made a statement before the convention that proved popular and indicated the way the Republican nominee saw the presidency. What the country needed, said Harding, was "not heroism but healing, not nostrums but normalcy [Harding always suffered from acute suffix trouble], not revolution but restoration, not agitation but adjustment, not surgery but serenity, not the dramatic but the dispassionate, not experiment but equipoise, not submergence in internationality but sustainment in triumphant nationality." Precisely what that meant was anyone's guess, but obviously Harding did not want much action—and neither did the electorate. Harding conducted a front-porch campaign reminiscent of that of McKinley in 1896 and won in a landslide. He received 16,152,200 votes for 404 electoral votes to 9,147,353 popular and 127 electoral votes for Cox. Cox carried no state outside of the former Confederate states except Kentucky and lost even Tennessee. In twenty states, among them Massachusetts, New York, Michigan, and California, Cox failed to carry a single county. The GOP also won overwhelmingly in the congressional elections. It had a majority of 22 seats in the Senate and 167 in the House.

Harding's tragedy—and the country's—was that he had risen in politics far above the level his abilities warranted, and he knew it. Raised on an Ohio farm, he had married a widow of moderate wealth and strong will and become owner and publisher of the Marion, Ohio, *Star*. A hearty extrovert, Harding had gone into local politics, then served in the state legislature and as lieutenant-governor. He was defeated for the governorship in 1910. He went to the Senate in 1914. His chief political manager and supporter was Harry M. Daugherty, leader of the "Ohio gang" who aspired to play the role of president-maker. Harding was not an evil man; he was only a weak one.

Harding's cabinet revealed the blend of political mediocrity and big business conservatism that characterized his administration. Harry Daugherty became Attorney General and Senator Albert B. Fall of New Mexico, around whose person there had long been the political odor of oil, became Secretary of the Interior. The most distinguished member of the Harding cabinet was Charles Evans Hughes, who became Secretary of State only after the outcry against Harding's suggestion of Fall for that post proved overpowering. Two able businessmen-politicians, Hoover and Andrew Mellon, became Secretaries of Commerce and the Treasury, respectively. The appointment of political hacks was to ruin Harding and make his administration second only to Grant's for political scandal and corruption.

With its huge majorities, the Republican party was able to enact a series of important measures that lowered taxes, raised tariffs, and restricted immigration in the first two years of the Harding administration. These laws will be considered in greater detail later. The Budget and Accounting Act of 1921, first urged by Wilson and then vetoed by him when Congress severely limited executive power, also became law. This measure introduced the present system of an executive budget and established the Bureau of the Budget. But the business reaction to the progressivism of the preceding decades received a temporary setback from the short but sharp depression of late 1920 to early 1922, the resulting formation of a farm bloc in Congress, and Democratic and insurgent Republican gains in the 1922 congressional elections. After these elections, Republican majorities were cut to eight in the Senate and eighteen in the House.

Most of Harding's worries, however, were caused by the friends he had appointed to office rather than his political opponents. In June, 1923, Harding left Washington for a speaking trip through the West and a vacation in Alaska. He was worried and exhausted, and he could not get his mind off of his treacherous friends in Washington. Upon returning to Seattle in late July, he nearly collapsed on the platform while making a public address. His physician reported that he was suffering from ptomaine poisoning from eating spoiled crabs. The ship on which he traveled from Alaska did not report any crabs on its manifest. The presidential party went on to San Francisco, where Harding got pneumonia. When the pneumonia crisis seemed over, he had a stroke and died on August 2. The close-mouthed rural Yankee, Coolidge, then on a vacation at his father's Vermont farm, took the presidential oath of office. His father, a rural justice of the peace, administered it.

Soon the causes of Harding's worries would become public knowledge. A woman named Nan Brinton wrote a book entitled *The President's Daughter* in which she alleged that Harding was the father of her illegitimate child. Senate investigators revealed graft and corruption in the Harding administration so startling that it was years before Harding's hometown could persuade a prominent Republican to dedicate its Harding Memorial. There were unsubstantiated charges that Mrs. Harding had poisoned the President; there was better evidence that Harding's health broke from worry caused by his cronies in office. He told the Kansas publisher William Allen White before he left on his last trip that he had no trouble from his opponents, "But my damned friends, my God-damn friends, White, they're the ones that keep me walking the floor nights!"

Coolidge and the Collapse of Progressivism

Although Harding's friends in the "Ohio gang" were involved in a wide variety of corrupt practices, some of them as petty as bootlegging liquor from government warehouses, the main cases brought to light were in the Veterans Bureau, the Department of the Interior, the Department of Justice, and the office of the Alien Property Custodian. Harding knew at least part of the Veterans Bureau scandal before he died. The head of the Bureau, Charles R. Forbes, a Harding appointee, had enriched himself and some close friends by about $250 million of Bureau funds. One of his practices was to label certain veterans hospital goods as worthless, sell them to friends at a low price, and have the Bureau buy them back later at a high price. Another was to accept bribes and grant special favors to contractors engaged in building veterans hospitals. Honest contractors who were discriminated against began to talk of

Forbes's corruption and rumors reached Harding. Harding called in Forbes, got some of the story from him, and allowed him to go abroad and resign in February, 1923. The following month, the Senate heard the rumors about the Veterans Bureau and began an investigation, whereupon the Bureau counsel, Charles F. Cramer, committed suicide. After Harding's death, the Senate revealed much more of Forbes's corruption. Forbes was convicted of fraud and was sentenced to two years in the penitentiary.

The most famous of the Harding scandals involved the naval oil reserves at Elk Hills, California, and Teapot Dome, Wyoming. Presidents Taft and Wilson had set aside these oil lands for the navy's future use. Soon after Harding's inauguration, Secretary of the Interior Fall, upon a pretext, got Harding secretly to transfer administration of the two reserves from the Navy Department to his jurisdiction. The Secretary of the Navy, a nonentity from Michigan named Edwin Denby, did not protest. He apparently did not know of Fall's plans. In 1922, Fall leased, again secretly, the Elk Hills reserve to the Pan-American Petroleum Company, owned by Edward L. Doheny, and the Teapot Dome reserve to the Mammoth Oil Company, owned by Harry Sinclair. News of the leases leaked out, Senator LaFollette demanded a Senate investigation, and the Senate named Thomas J. Walsh, Democrat from Montana, to head the inquiry.

Walsh investigated the existing situation thoroughly before he began open hearings in October, 1923, two months after Harding's death. Witnesses conveniently suffered attacks of bad memory and resorted to unusually evasive replies, but Walsh slowly and painfully dug out the story. Doheny's son had given Fall a "little black bag" containing $100,000 in currency as an unsecured "loan." Sinclair had given Fall $223,000 in Liberty bonds, $85,000 in cash, and some prize cattle for Fall's New Mexico ranch. Fall's inability to explain how he had recently spent $170,000 on his ranch from his $12,000 salary had given Walsh his opportunity. Fall resigned, and the government began prosecution, circumventing the Department of Justice because Attorney General Daugherty was already in trouble in another scandal. Conspiracy and bribery indictments were charged against Fall, Sinclair, and Doheny in June, 1924. Delays and appeals of various kinds postponed final action for years, but Fall was finally convicted of accepting a bribe and sentenced to a year in prison and a fine of $100,000. Doheny and Sinclair, the bribers, managed to get acquitted, but Sinclair got three months for contempt of the Senate and six months more for contempt of court when he hired detectives to shadow the jurors. The government, after carrying the case to the Supreme Court, got the Doheny and Sinclair leases invalidated.

Fall and Denby resigned from the cabinet; Daugherty not only refused to resign but set the FBI to investigating Senators who were investigating executive corruption. Daugherty's downfall came in 1924 in a case involving the American Metal Company, a $6.5 billion German corporation the government had seized during the war. Early in the Harding administration, a German representative paid John T. King, a prominent New York Republican, $441,000 in the hope that the company would be returned. King turned over $50,000 to the Alien Property Custodian, Thomas W. Miller, an "Ohio gang" member who had been prominent in the American Legion. Another $50,000 in Liberty bonds was deposited to a joint account held by Daugherty and his close Ohio friend, the "unofficial attorney general" Jesse Smith. When the case broke in March, 1924, King had already died and Smith had committed suicide in Daugherty's Washington apartment, thinking he was about to be discovered in another fraud. Daugherty refused to testify before a Senate investigating committee, citing the Fifth Amendment right to withhold testimony that might be self-incriminating. Coolidge then demanded and received Daugherty's resignation. In 1926, Daugherty refused to testify at his trial, saying that his silence was to protect the confidence of the late President. He was acquitted. The next year Miller was convicted.

The surprising thing about the Harding scandals was that they did not significantly harm the Republican party. The public, in general, took the attitude that only the individuals involved were responsible. The fact that Harding had died and that the puritanical, tight-fisted, taciturn Coolidge occupied the White House had a great deal to do with the public's reaction. Harding's views of government and business had been consistent with the majority public mood. His only trouble, thought most people, was that he surrounded himself with crooks, and they regarded Coolidge as a kind of honest Harding, New England division. Indeed, there were similarities between Harding's and Coolidge's careers. Both were country boys who had moved to small towns, pursued professional careers, and slowly worked their way up through local and state politics more because of their party regularity than their ability. Coolidge had been born in rural Vermont in 1872, had gone to Amherst College, and had settled down to practice law in Northampton, Massachusetts. He had gone to the state legislature (called the General Court in Massachusetts) where in the course of time he became speaker and then governor. There was nothing distinguished nor colorful about him. A sour man who said little, probably because he had little to say, Coolidge was always essentially a narrow, inhibited, conservative, rural Vermonter, almost the stereotyped Yankee of jokes. The title of William Allen White's biography of Coolidge well summarized the man: *A Puritan in Babylon.*

The Election of 1924

Coolidge's nomination by the 1924 Republican convention was entirely predictable. He received the nomination at the Cleveland convention on the first ballot, and all that prevented his nomination by acclamation was the opposition of the Wisconsin and North Dakota delegations. The Coolidge demonstrations lacked fire and conviction because it was difficult to get excited about the man. Charles G. Dawes, a Chicago banker and former Director of the Budget who swore masterfully and smoked a peculiar underslung pipe, received the vice-presidential nomination and lent color to the ticket. The platform was a safe, conservative document, adopted when the convention defeated a more progressive platform submitted by the Wisconsin delegation.

The badly divided Democratic convention at New York's Madison Square Garden offered far more fireworks. Prohibition and the anti-Catholic Ku Klux Klan widened already existing Democratic cleavages. The eastern urban wing of the party supported Governor Alfred E. Smith of New York, a son of Irish immigrant parents, a Roman Catholic, and, in the language of

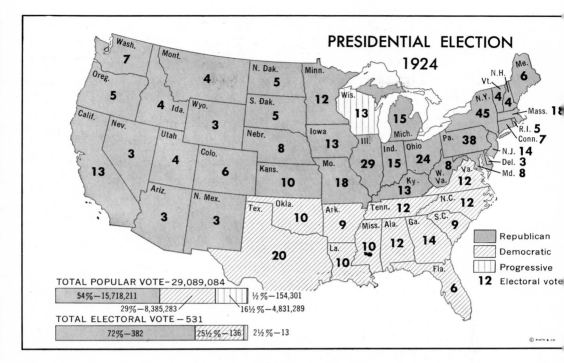

PRESIDENTIAL ELECTION
1924

Wash. 7
Oreg. 5
Calif. 13
Nev. 3
Mont. 4
Ida. 4
Wyo. 3
Utah 4
Ariz. 3
N. Mex. 3
N. Dak. 5
S. Dak. 5
Nebr. 8
Kans. 10
Okla. 10
Tex. 20
Minn. 12
Iowa 13
Mo. 18
Ark. 9
La. 10
Wis. 13
Ill. 29
Miss. 10
Colo. 6
Mich. 15
Ind. 15
Ohio 24
Ky. 13
Tenn. 12
Ala. 12
Ga. 14
N.C. 12
S.C. 9
Fla. 6
Pa. 38
W. Va. 8
Va. 12
Me. 6
N.H. 4
Vt. 4
N.Y. 45
Mass. 18
R.I. 5
Conn. 7
N.J. 14
Del. 3
Md. 8

Republican
Democratic
Progressive
12 Electoral vote

TOTAL POPULAR VOTE—29,089,084
54%—15,718,211   ½%—154,301
29%—8,385,283   16½%—4,831,289
TOTAL ELECTORAL VOTE — 531
72%—382   25½%—136   2½%—13

© •win • co

the day, a "wringing wet" on the prohibition question. He was anathema to
the southern and western wings of the party, which supported McAdoo.
McAdoo might have received the nomination had he not lost the support of
progressives in the party who disapproved of his serving as Doheny's lawyer
in the oil scandals. The balloting went on for days while the noisy Tammany
galleries thoroughly alienated the rural delegates. Smith and McAdoo withdrew after the ninety-fifth inconclusive ballot. On the one hundred and third
ballot the nomination went to John W. Davis, an able and prominent Wall
Street lawyer originally from West Virginia. To placate the agrarian wing of
the party, the convention nominated Governor Charles W. Bryan of Nebraska,
brother of the Great Commoner, for the vice-presidency. The platform, except
for criticism of the last Republican tariff and a promise of Philippine independence which the Democrats had failed to enact in 1916, was as conservative and
conventional as the Republican platform. The biggest fight within the platform
was over a resolution sponsored by Smith's followers which called the Klan an
un-American organization. The convention defeated the resolution by one vote.

The only real excitement in the 1924 campaign came from the independent candidacy of Senator LaFollette. Progressivism had by no means died out
completely among the agrarians of the upper Mississippi Valley. The National
Non-Partisan League had spread from North Dakota into neighboring states.
Founded in 1915 by an ex-Socialist named Arthur C. Townley, the League had
won the governorship of North Dakota in 1916 and the legislature as well in
1918. It partially enacted its semisocialistic program, creating a state-owned
flour mill and grain elevator. In 1920, the League had made common cause
with agrarians in Minnesota and North Dakota and nominated a Farmer-Labor
party ticket headed by Parley P. Christensen. Most farmers gave up on old-

fashioned agrarianism in the postwar depression and supported the American Farm Bureau's farm bloc tactics, but in early 1922 a group of agrarians, railroad brotherhood officials, Socialists, and a few urban reformers met in Chicago and formed the Conference for Progressive Political Action. The CPPA considered launching a third party, but abandoned the idea in favor of working for selected candidates in the major parties in the 1922 congressional elections. CPPA-endorsed candidates did very well.

Had the Democrats not been so badly divided and had they not neglected economic issues for prohibition and the Klan, they might have been able to capitalize on the agrarian movement of the upper Midwest. They did not, however, and after the agrarians were thoroughly repudiated at the 1924 Republican convention, there was nowhere for them to turn. The CPPA met in convention at Cleveland on July 4. It decided to defer the question of the formation of a permanent third party until after the election, but it nominated LaFollette for the presidency and later named Senator Burton K. Wheeler, Democrat of Montana who had been prominent in investigating Harding scandals, as its vice-presidential candidate. LaFollette dictated the platform. It was for elimination of monopolies, federally owned water power, direct election of federal judges, the child labor amendment, and a prohibition of the labor injunction. The Socialist party, the Farmer-Labor party, and the AFL endorsed the LaFollette-Wheeler ticket, although the AFL did practically nothing to help LaFollette and Gompers all but withdrew the endorsement just before the election. The Communists, who had been denied seats at the CPPA convention, offered their support, but LaFollette vigorously repudiated them.

Most of the electorate was disinterested in the campaign. The Republican slogan, "Keep Cool with Coolidge," was well adapted to the majority mood. Coolidge campaigned little, and Davis' speeches were dull. LaFollette worked hard in the Midwest and the Far West, but much of his potential vote was scared away by the Republican argument that a strong LaFollette vote would produce no electoral majority and throw the election into the House of Representatives, as had happened in 1824. Only half of the qualified voters bothered to go to the polls on election day. Coolidge received 382 electoral votes and 15,725,003 popular votes, Davis 136 and 8,385,586, and LaFollette 13 and 4,826,471. The new Senate was composed of 50 Republicans, 40 Democrats, and 6 LaFollette Progressives; the House of 232 Republicans, 183 Democrats, and 20 Progressives. Davis carried only the eleven former Confederate states and Oklahoma. LaFollette carried his home state of Wisconsin and ran ahead of Davis in eleven other states, all of them in the West. Davis faded to political obscurity. In 1954 he was the attorney for the segregationists in the school integration cases before the Supreme Court.

Although the LaFollette Progressives did very well for an independent candidacy, a meeting of the CPPA early in 1925 decided not to attempt to form a permanent third party. LaFollette died a few months later, to be succeeded in the Senate by his elder son, Robert M. LaFollette, Jr. With the collapse of the LaFollette movement, independent political Progressivism receded to its lowest ebb since the Civil War. Both parties were under the control of standpatters, and most of the public did not seem to care. Yet it is easy to exaggerate the strength of political conservatives in the 1920's. A handful of progressives from each party remained in Congress, especially in the Senate, and in combination with farm bloc congressmen who frequently stood pat on nonfarm issues, these progressives were able to block or modify part of the conservatives' legislative program. Their position was strengthened after the 1926 elections, when the GOP majority was cut to forty in the House and the new Senate contained forty-eight Republicans of various hues, forty-seven Democrats of similar variegation, and one Farmer-Laborite.

The progressives were able to give Coolidge and the regular Republicans a great many headaches. For example, early in 1925, the Senate twice rejected Coolidge's appointment of Charles B. Warren to the Attorney Generalship. In 1927, led by Senator Norris, the Senate progressives blocked the seating of two conservative Republicans, William S. Vare of Pennsylvania and Frank L. Smith of Illinois, who had been elected with huge campaign funds. They also were able to defeat the Coolidge administration's plan to sell the power site at Muscle Shoals on the Tennessee River and thereby save the area for development by the Tennessee Valley Authority in the 1930's. But the most the progressives could do in the Coolidge administration was to throw an occasional monkey wrench into the conservative gears, and business had good reason to be happy with Coolidge and his cabinet.

The Republican Administrations and Business

It frequently is said that the Republican administrations of the 1920's favored laissez faire. This is true only if one defines "laissez faire" as the absence of government restraint on business. In many areas, these administrations used the power of the federal government to aid business enterprise. Some of the aid was by the executive branch of government alone; some was through legislation.

Needless to say, the Department of Justice in the 1920's did not embark upon any trust-busting campaigns, but in this respect it did not differ from the Wilson administration. In fact, the government instituted more antitrust actions during the eight years of the Harding and Coolidge administrations than it did during Wilson's eight years. Indeed, in many ways the attitude of the executive branch toward business in the 1920's was the logical extension of Wilson's policies. For example, Wilson never intended the Federal Trade Commission to be a militant regulator of business, and his appointees to the FTC were safe conservatives. Under Harding and Coolidge, the FTC became only more active in its probusiness activities. From 1921 until 1925, however, the FTC was more restrained in its aid to business than was the Department of Commerce under Secretary Hoover. Then in 1925 Coolidge appointed William E. Humphrey of Washington to the FTC, and he was able to convert it to an all-out aid for business agency. As late as 1924, the FTC could issue a report critical of Mellon's Aluminum Corporation of America, but after 1925 its regulation consisted of no more than clamping down on the most flagrantly fraudulent of advertisers.

The FTC after 1925 worked closely with Secretary Hoover in helping business to minimize competition through trade associations, so much so that Senate progressives like Norris demanded that the FTC be abolished. Hoover had accepted the Commerce post from Harding only on the condition that he be given a free hand on all matters pertaining to business and that he have an unofficial veto in foreign policy. Both under Harding and Coolidge he operated without White House restraint, a kind of subpresident for business affairs. The trade association, of which there were already about two thousand in existence in 1921, was Hoover's favorite device for achieving business stability and minimizing competition. Hoover called many industrial conferences and explained to them the advantages of the device for businessmen, published a handbook that explained how to organize a trade association, and helped the associations gather statistics and other information—even published it at government expense—that was necessary for businessmen efficiently to restrict production, maintain prices, and divide markets, as well as to rationalize production and distribution. The FTC worked closely with the trade associations to advise them what was and what was not contrary to the antitrust laws. In other words, the FTC conceived its function, after Humphrey joined it, as showing business how legally to minimize competition. When the courts changed interpretations of antitrust law, the FTC and the Department of Justice advised business of the effects of the new judicial interpretations on their operations. Operating from shared information supplied by Washington and the trade associations, business in the 1920's, as we shall see in greater detail in Chapter 11, was enabled to become practically self-governing and to establish an oligopolistic structure in the important industries.

The main legislative aids to business in the 1920's were the traditional ones of tariff protection and a tax structure favorable to wealthy individuals and corporations. Wilson and his three Republican successors did not see eye-to-eye on the tariff, although they substantially agreed that the purpose of tariff revision was to benefit American business; they disagreed on the tariff as a means, not as an end.

With the advent of the postwar depression, the Wilson administration was under considerable pressure to increase tariff duties, especially on agricultural products. Farmers, subjected to generations of high-tariff propaganda, were blind to the fact that with few exceptions foreign farm commodities could not compete with their products in the domestic market even if there were no duties whatsoever. Wilson resisted the pressure for raising the tariff, saying, "If we want to sell, we must be prepared to buy." That was indeed the situation unless another way could be devised to get purchasing power in foreign hands. But it should be noted that Wilson's objection to increased tariffs was that higher duties would hurt American markets abroad. In the last days of the Wilson administration, Congress rushed through a new tariff bill that raised duties on several agricultural commodities. Wilson vetoed it on March 3, 1921, his last full day in office. The new Congress, after receiving a special message from Harding in favor of tariff protection dug out the rejected bill, revised it slightly, and submitted it to Harding, who promptly signed it. This measure, the Emergency Tariff of 1921, raised duties on meat, wool, sugar, corn, and wheat to about the levels of the Payne-Aldrich Tariff of 1909.

But the Emergency Tariff was only a temporary measure until a more comprehensive tariff bill could be prepared. Steered through the House by Joseph W. Fordney of Michigan and the Senate by Porter J. McCumber of North Dakota, the new tariff bill was the highest yet in America's history. In exchange for almost meaningless increases in duties on farm products, Congressmen from rural districts supported increases in duties on manufactured goods. A number of raw materials on the free list of the Underwood Tariff, hides, leather, coal, iron ore, and cotton, were kept without duty since manufacturers did not want to pay a premium on their own imports. The biggest increases in the duties on manufactured goods were for chemicals, textiles, chinaware, toys, and jewelry. Even books printed in the English language were taxed almost 25 per cent, and scientific laboratory equipment had a duty of 40 per cent. The bill enjoined the tariff commission to keep an eye on the relative costs of production of domestic and foreign manufacturing and to advise the president, who under the bill could raise or lower duties by as much as 50 per cent. Coolidge accepted the tariff commission's suggestions only when it recommended an increase in duties. Harding signed the Fordney-McCumber Tariff in September, 1922.

Despite the Democrats' condemnation of the 1922 tariff in their 1924 platform as the "most unjust, unscientific, and dishonest tariff tax measure ever enacted in our history," the act actually removed the tariff from serious political differences during the 1920's. Battles over domestic taxation were much hotter. Many businessmen were beginning to see that, with American industry becoming increasingly dependent upon foreign trade, raising the tariff amounted to cutting one's own throat. They clamored instead for a reduction of taxes, and in Secretary of the Treasury Mellon they found a kindred spirit.

In order to cut taxes there had to be a reduction in government spending. Through ruthless trimming and refusal to undertake new expensive programs, the federal government was able in the 1920's to cut its expenditures to about $3.6 billion each year from 1922 until the depression. This figure was well above the spending of the prewar years—higher prices and a greater population made return to the old budgets impossible—but it was less than one-third of the budgets of the war years. Despite the fact that taxes were cut sharply, the government still spent less than it received and reduced the war debt by about one-third, from about $24 billion to about $16 billion. This record earned Mellon the generally accepted title of "the greatest Secretary of the Treasury since Alexander Hamilton." Certainly his view of who should pay taxes was reminiscent of Hamilton and the whiskey tax.

Almost all political groups urged tax cuts. The question that divided them was who should receive the lion's share of the cuts. Mellon, soon after he came to office, sent Congress a series of messages in which he urged abolition of the excess profits tax, a slight compensatory increase in the regular corporate tax, gradual reduction of individual income taxes until the maximum was 33 per cent, repeal of the wartime excise taxes, and a new tax on automobiles. The House and the Senate finance committee went along with Mellon's recommendation, but a group of agrarian Republicans combined with the Democrats to write their own tax bill and informed Mellon and the White House that they must accept their bill or get none at all. The final law eliminated some of the excise taxes, left the individual income rates where they were, and raised the personal exemption for married couples from $2,000 to $2,500. Some Congressmen asked Mellon why personal exemptions should not be raised to excuse the taxation of incomes less than $5,000. Mellon's Hamiltonian reply was, ". . . nothing so brings home to a man the feeling that he personally has an interest in seeing that Government revenues are not squandered, but intelligently expended, as the fact that he contributes individually a direct tax, no matter how small, to his Government."

In 1923, Mellon urged a reduction of the surtax on large individual incomes and a drastic cut in the inheritance tax. He argued that wealthy people would not invest in industry if income taxes took a large share of their return. He declared that tax-exempt bonds of municipalities were taking such a share of total investment that industry was suffering, an assertion that was hardly borne out by corporate balance sheets. Coolidge urged Congress to amend the Constitution to abolish tax-exempt securities. But again a combination of farm Republicans and Democrats made their point of view prevail. The tax law of June, 1924, cut the maximum surtax on individual incomes from 50 to 40 per cent, but it also cut the normal tax of low and middle incomes by half, left corporation taxes where they were, and raised the maximum inheritance tax from 25 to 40 per cent. In addition, it imposed a new gift tax, a device to prevent the circumvention of inheritance taxes by giving fortunes to heirs before death.

The general prosperity of 1925 to 1929 brought increased tax revenues and surpluses to the federal government and helped Mellon in his program to reduce taxes on large incomes. The Revenue Act of 1926 lowered the normal tax on incomes, reduced the maximum surtax to 20 per cent, reduced corporation taxes, cut the inheritance tax by half, and eliminated the gift tax altogether. The act of 1928 left personal income taxes at the 1926 rates but reduced corporation taxes further. Neither measure raised personal exemptions, consistent with Mellon's theory that the more people who paid taxes the better. But Mellon's tax program reduced taxes on large incomes so much that a million-dollar income after 1926 would pay less than one-third as much in taxes as in 1921.

Conservatives of today's heavily taxed generation look back wistfully to the taxes of Mellon's days and maintain that Mellon was a paragon of fiscal wisdom. Some even favor abolition of the income tax altogether. However, one can make a strong argument that it was economically unwise to reduce taxes on high incomes at all. Much of the income thus saved from the tax collector went into land and stock speculation and contributed to the crash of 1929. If wealth had been taxed at the rate it was during or soon after the war, more of the national debt could have been retired or, possibly, the higher revenues could have been used for a vigorous government farm program and an economically healthier distribution of income. Prosperity might have lasted longer. Part of the responsibility must fall on the progressives, who never seriously put forward better proposals for dealing with the annual government surplus.

The Farm Problem and Politics in the 1920's

Agriculture, in general, did not share in the prosperity of the 1920's. As already described, farmers overextended their investments during the war. When the government withdrew wartime price supports from wheat in May, 1920, agriculture's wartime prosperity came to a sudden end. By the end of 1920, wheat prices had fallen to $1.44 a bushel as compared to $2.15 at the end of 1919, corn from $1.25 to 68 cents, and cotton from 36 cents a pound to 14 cents. Farming never truly recovered until World War II. Although farm prices subsequently rose, they did not go up as much as the prices farmers had to pay for manufactured goods nor as much as local taxes on their land. Total farm income amounted to a smaller percentage of the national income, falling from 16 per cent in 1919 to 9 per cent in 1929. Farm tenancy and mortgage indebtedness became increasingly serious.

The decline of farm prices and income was attributable to a number of factors. An important one was that increased mechanization and use of better seed, fertilizer, and breeding stock greatly increased farm yields. At the same time, there was no compensating increase in farm markets. Indeed, demand for many farm commodities declined during the 1920's. For example, the widespread use of rayon and the fashionable abandonment of numerous petticoats and long, fully cut dresses seriously reduced demand for cotton. Even diet changed. Americans in the 1920's ate less bread and fat than they had before the war. Further, population increase slowed down and less land was needed to produce feed for draft animals.

Thus far we have been considering the total farm picture. The situation of the small farmer was worse than the national average. The small farmer in the 1920's was a victim of the new technology. He could not produce as efficiently nor compete with the bigger farmer whose mechanized efficiency reduced his costs per unit of production. As the optimum farm size and the optimum investment increased, the smallest and least efficient farmers experienced great difficulty. Many left farming altogether; the total farm population decreased by over 3 million in the 1920's.

Farmers tried to meet their new situation through two means: cooperative marketing and politics. Aaron Sapiro, who became general counsel of the American Farm Bureau Federation in 1923, was a strong advocate of cooperative marketing. He had already helped dairy and tobacco farmers to organize cooperatives. To be successful, a marketing cooperative had to be able to force nearly all producers of a commodity for a particular market to agree to work within the organization and not sell privately, and that required law behind the cooperative. Kentucky passed the first Cooperative Marketing Act in 1922, and most other agricultural states soon followed suit. Cooperative marketing worked well—sometimes too well for the public's economic welfare—when the production of a commodity was fairly well concentrated. For example, the California Fruit Growers' Association was able to dictate prices about as it chose. But the scheme did not work for commodities that were produced in large areas of the nation, and the majority of farmers raised such widely produced commodities as wheat, corn, hogs, beef, and cotton. These farmers had to resort to politics.

In May, 1921, at the suggestion of the head of the Farm Bureau, Grey Silver, a group of Congressmen from agricultural states met in the Bureau's Washington office and organized the farm bloc. Senator William S. Kenyon of Iowa was its first leader; he was succeeded by Senator Arthur Capper of Kansas. In the Senate the bloc consisted of fourteen Republicans and twelve Democrats, all from the West and the South. For the next few years the bloc stuck together and was able to pass a series of laws designed to aid the farmer.

The farm bloc got Congress to pass the Packers and Stockyards Act in August, 1921. This law subjected meat packing to the control of the Secretary of Agriculture, who was empowered to issue cease and desist orders to prevent packers from engaging in monopolistic practices such as rigging prices and uniting to charge high stockyard fees. Two weeks later Congress passed the Grain Futures Act to give the Secretary of Agriculture similar powers over the grain exchanges. The Supreme Court, which Harding packed with four conservative appointments in his twenty-nine months in office, declared this act an unconstitutional use of the taxing power but ruled that Congress could achieve the same end through use of the interstate commerce power. Congress rewrote the act. Senator Norris proposed a government corporation to erect warehouses and to buy and export farm products as a means to stabilize farm prices. The administration refused to accept the proposal and got the farm bloc to accept amending the War Finance Corporation, founded in 1918 to lend capital to new war industries, so that it could lend funds to farm associations engaged in exporting. When this scheme expired in 1924, it had lent almost $300 million.

In 1922, the farm bloc pushed through the Capper-Volstead Act to protect the new marketing cooperatives from antitrust actions. The exemption of agricultural organizations from the Clayton Act of 1914 was deemed insufficient, and the new law drew the boundaries of what the marketing cooperatives could do. The following year, the farm bloc successfully sponsored the Intermediate Credits Act. This measure, designed to supplement the Federal Land Banks established in the Wilson administration, established twelve new credit institutions to lend funds to farm associations for periods of from six months to three years. The Federal Reserve accepted only short-term agricultural paper and the Federal Land Banks dealt only in longer-term loans.

These agricultural acts of 1921 to 1923 helped the farmer, but they did not get at the basic problem of low farm prices. Farm economists reasoned that the root of the farmer's problem was the low world price of farm commodities and that the answer was to provide the farmer the kind of protection from world prices that the government had already granted manufacturers with the protective tariff. An ordinary tariff on agricultural imports would not work because the goods imported were only rarely in competition with American farm products. Tariff protection for corn was mythical if no one imported corn, and no one did. The four McNary-Haugen bills of 1924 to 1928 were efforts to build an effective tariff for farm products—to institute a two-price system, one price for the United States and another for the rest of the world.

The McNary-Haugen bills, named for their sponsors Senator Charles McNary of Oregon and Representative Gilbert Haugen of Iowa, can be traced to the ideas of George N. Peek and Hugh S. Johnson, president and general counsel respectively of the Moline Plow Company. Each of these men was to become prominent in the early New Deal. They realized that to sell agricultural implements to farmers, the farmer had to have more income. The McNary-Haugen bills differed in detail, but they all had this rather complicated basic feature: a federal farm board would be established which would buy up the surplus of designated farm commodities at a price based upon prewar averages, when prices farmers received were in better relation to prices farmers paid. This price would be about equal to the world price of the commodity plus the existing tariff. The government-owned surplus could then be stored for a lean year or sold abroad at the world price. Thus the domestic price would be higher than the world price by the amount of the tariff. The loss to the government incurred by selling at a lower price than it had bought would be met by an equalization fee to be paid by producers of the commodity. The net return to the farmers, the plan's proponents argued, would be higher than under the existing practice of selling all the crop at world prices whether at home or abroad. The total equalization fees would not equal the increase of the domestic price unless exports equalled domestic consumption.

McNary and Haugen introduced their first bill in January, 1924. It had the support of nearly all of the farm organizations and of Secretary of Agriculture Henry C. Wallace. When Wallace died later in the year, Coolidge replaced him with a man whose views on farm economics were more nearly like his own. But Congress defeated the first bill, as well as the second one in 1926, largely because the bills covered only commodities produced in the Midwest and West and omitted southern cotton and tobacco. A third bill, which satisfied southern Congressmen, passed in February, 1927, only to run into a veto from Coolidge. In May, 1928, Congress passed a McNary-Haugen bill again and drew a second veto. Advocates of the plan were insufficient to override either veto. Coolidge's second veto, coming in an election year, made farm relief one of the issues of the campaign, but other factors in the election so clouded the picture that the Republican party's continued opposition to McNary-Haugenism did not confront a real referendum.

The National Grange suggested still another scheme, the "export debenture" plan, to give effective tariff protection to farm commodities. It never was able to get its plan through Congress. The idea was for the federal government to pay an export subsidy on designated commodities equal to one-half of the tariff duty on the commodity in the form of "debentures" which would be accepted by customs collectors for any import. After receiving their "debentures," according to the plan, farm associations would sell them at a discount to importers and thereby receive benefit from duties on manufactured goods.

Whether the McNary-Haugen bills or the export debenture scheme would have effected a lasting solution to the farm price problem is dubious. Neither plan provided for an effective means of limiting agricultural production, of eliminating the surplus by growing less. Not even the production controls of the farm laws adopted in the 1930's and later successfully met the problem of the surplus, and it is safe to assume that the plans of the 1920's would not have either. Nor did the farm plans of the 1920's promise much for the small farmer confronted with the superior resources and efficiency of the big-scale farmer. For that matter, no subsequent legislation met that problem either. In the 1920's, "factories in the fields" were beginning to become important economically. The Campbell Farming Corporation of Montana operated over one hundred thousand acres and could plow one thousand acres and seed or harvest two thousand acres in a single day. The farm relief plans of the 1920's and the opposition to them from the eastern wing of the Republican party did, however, have a political impact: they demonstrated conclusively to western farmers that eastern Republicans had a double standard for government aid to business. Eastern Republicans would help commerce and manufacturing but deny real aid to agriculture as a violation of laissez faire. When a general downswing in the business cycle after 1929 made farm conditions much more desperate, the political chickens hatched by the McNary-Haugen vetoes came home to roost.

CHAPTER ELEVEN

The Economics of Business, 1917-1929

THE ERA FROM THE BEGINNING OF WORLD WAR I UNTIL THE GREAT Depression was more prosperous than any the American people had ever known. They had more money and more of the things that money could buy than at any period in the history of the country. There were blemishes on prosperity's beaming face as we shall see, but the period was nevertheless one of unprecedented comfort.

Merely to describe prosperity, however, is to miss some highly important developments in American history, to ignore some facts from the past which helped mold the way Americans live today and the material basis of American society. Put most generally, business in the 1920's brought the big corporation to a new state of development and in so doing modified the whole nature of the economic system. This basic economic change did not develop overnight. It had developed slowly. The large business corporation might be dated from the establishment of United States Steel in 1901. But in the period from 1917 to 1929, big businesses came into their own. When Herbert Hoover and others referred to the economy of the 1920's as the New Economic Order or the New Era, they did not exaggerate. It was new, and it was of overriding importance. One of the most perceptive of scholars, Professor Thomas C. Cochran, writing on the history of American business, has justifiably described the rise of the large business corporation as "one of the major changes in history, comparable to the rise of medieval feudalism or of commercial institutions at the close of the middle ages. . . . Corporate enterprise gradually altered the meaning of property, the circumstances and motivations of economic activity, and the careers and expectations of most citizens."[1]

---

[1] Thomas C. Cochran, *The American Business System* (Cambridge, Mass.: Harvard Univ. Press, 1957), p. 51.

Prosperity and Wealth

Real per capita income (the dollar value of total national income divided by population and adjusted for price changes) increased from $517 for the period 1909–1918 to $612 for the years from 1919–1928. Real per capita income in 1921 was $522; it grew to $716 in 1929. This was a notable gain, but the increase was not steady. One major and two lesser dips in the business cycle during the 1920's interrupted economic growth.

The boom created by war orders sustained itself on reconstruction loans and pent up consumer demand until mid-1920. Then the economy went into a sudden decline that was as sharp a drop as any America had ever before experienced. The postwar depression was at its worst in 1921, when unemployment reached 4,750,000 and national income was off roughly 28 per cent from the previous year. But the economy righted itself rather quickly and by late 1922 the depression was over. Since agriculture did not regain its normal level, the growth of national income by 1923 to the 1919 level indicates how strong the recovery was in industry. Slight dips in 1924 and 1927 were no more than the usual fluctuations of the business cycle, which does not climb steadily in the best of times.

TABLE 1

ECONOMIC GROWTH, 1919–1929

	Industrial Production	Cost-of-Living Index 1929=100	National Income Billions of Dollars	Real Income per Capita, 1929 Prices
1919		101.6	64.2	543
1920		116.9	74.2	548
1921	58	104.2	59.4	522
1922	73	97.7	60.7	553
1923	88	99.5	71.6	634
1924	82	99.8	72.1	633
1925	90	102.4	76.0	644
1926	96	103.2	81.6	678
1927	95	101.2	80.1	674
1928	99	100.1	81.7	676
1929	110	100.0	87.2	716

Construction and manufacturing boomed more than other parts of the economy. The amount of new building was tremendous after 1922. In that year more than $12 billion worth of building materials were used by the industry. In 1928, the figure stood at $17.4 billion, but it dropped over a billion dollars in 1929 to a level below that of 1926. Construction used more new capital than any other industry, employed between 5 and 6 per cent of the labor force, and accounted for 7.5 per cent of total payrolls. A large part of the construction boom was the result of road and bridge building made necessary by the greater number of automobiles. By the end of the 1920's, about one-fifth of America's three million miles of roads were hard-surfaced one way or another. More than eighty thousand miles were paved with concrete. The Portland Cement Association used high-pressure sales tactics on many municipal and township governments, and some of the new roads were unwarranted. Others were poorly constructed—too narrow, improperly drained and banked, and insufficiently reinforced at the edges—and had to be rebuilt in another age. Yet most of the roads were a vital necessity to the new automobile age. The states' share of the costs of new road construction came mostly from registration taxes on cars and on gasoline taxes, which ranged from two to six cents a gallon. In 1930, gasoline taxes totalled nearly $500 million. But residential, hotel, and office building construction also boomed during the decade. Real estate men opened thousands of new suburban developments, usually called something innocuous and homey like Elm Grove or Green Highlands, and Sinclair Lewis was wise to make Babbitt a "realtor." Much of the hotel, some of the office, and a bit of the housing construction was more the result of rosily optimistic speculation than the fulfillment of real need.

Manufacturing increased its output during the decade by 64 per cent. Because of an improvement in labor productivity of 40 per cent, this increased production was the work of fewer workers. There was a small absolute decline in the number of people engaged in manufacturing between 1919 and 1929. It has been estimated that between 1920 and 1929 manufacturing dispensed with the labor of thirty-two men out of every one hundred employed per unit of production, but that twenty-seven of them were absorbed in increased total production. Most, but not all, of the workers displaced from industry found jobs in service or trade, which accounted for a larger percentage of the labor force.

Two trends in manufacturing during the 1920's stimulated speculation, and speculation had doleful implications for the future. Manufacturing corporations, particularly big ones, were able to finance a larger part of their expansion from their own reserves and thus were less dependent upon bankers than they had been before the war. "Finance capitalism" was being undermined in the decade of its greatest success. Corporations kept their reserves in bank time deposits, rather than demand deposits, which enabled banks to lend a greater amount of money for essentially speculative purposes. Brokers' loans, to be considered in greater detail in the discussion of the stock market boom in Chapter 15, constituted a considerable part of the capital for speculation on Wall Street. The other trend was that industry in general invested relatively less money in new physical equipment; there was a decline in the percentage of the national income going into capital formation. This decline in the last five years of the boom was particularly marked, so much so that there was an absolute decline in new investment. In 1924, financing for new physical equipment was 76 per cent of all new financing; in 1929, it was only 35 per cent. The dollar total declined from $3.5 billion in 1924 to $3.2 billion in 1929. This decline occurred despite the great growth of a few industries, such as autos, chemicals, electric power, and electric appliances. At the same time total savings increased. The lag in capital investment, therefore, stimulated speculation of all kinds, primarily in stocks and bonds and in real estate.

The pattern of income distribution had much to do with savings and speculation. The share of income received by the richest 10 per cent of the population had been increasing ever since about 1910. Between 1919 and 1929, the share received by the wealthiest 1 per cent of income receivers increased by 13 per cent. People with low and middle incomes necessarily spent whatever additional income they received for consumer goods, but people with large incomes did not add appreciably to consumption when they received more income. In the 1920's, what happened to the increased share of total income that accrued to the wealthiest families of America was almost the sole decision of the business community. Government played only a small role in investment; its expenditures were low and federal taxes on wealth declined during the period. Business leaders decided not to invest in new capital equipment at the rate they had earlier. They had many reasons for their decisions, but the fundamental one was that the market did not, in their opinion, warrant expansion at the old level; and a basic reason why the market did not warrant expansion was the incomes of the great majority of consumers were not sufficient to absorb the production that would result from a greater rate of investment in capital plant. Thus the pattern of income distribution tended to increase the volume of speculation, both by creating larger discretionary sums and by influencing investment decisions. The resulting speculation was spectacular.

Speculation in securities became major after mid-1924. The stock market climbed rather steadily until 1926, declined slightly, and then from 1927 to 1929 zoomed to unprecedented heights. Salesmen for stocks and bonds scoured even small towns for people with savings and encouraged them to get into the market and get rich fast. John J. Raskob, a member of the Democratic national committee and chairman of the board of General Motors, wrote in *The Ladies' Home Journal*,

> If a man saves $15 a week, and invests in good common stocks and allows the dividends and rights to accumulate, at the end of twenty years he will have at least $80,000 and an income from investments of $400 a month. He will be rich. . . . I am firm in my belief that anyone not only can be rich, but ought to be rich.[2]

If Raskob were right, and a great many people thought he was, this was a return on investment of over 400 per cent. A big electric sign above New York's Columbus Circle declared that every man fifty years old should have $50,000.

Land speculation probably involved more people than stock speculation. Small town promoters appealed both to desire for financial gain and local pride when they organized hotel-building ventures. These economic white elephants, many of them financed with contributions as low as $500 to $1,000, still ornament hundreds of court house squares. Florida had the most spectacular land

---

[2] Samuel Crowther, "Everybody Ought To Be Rich" (An Interview with John J. Raskob), *Ladies Home Journal* (August, 1929), 9.

boom of the decade. If everyone who had a normal amount of sense was going to be rich, thought many speculators, then they would want to vacation in Florida. Promoters put up palatial resort hotels of pseudo-Spanish design, drained swamps and called the drainage ditches lagoons, and fleeced the unwary. One promoter in Coral Gables paid William Jennings Bryan to sit on a raft under a beach umbrella and lecture on the glories of Florida's climate and attracted a crowd for Bryan with the popular dancer Gilda Gray. Speculators bought and sold titles and options for unseen lots and acres, some of which, it later developed, were under a few feet of swampy water. Bubbles like the Florida land boom have their foundation in mass delusion and greed and are easily broken. A disastrous hurricane in 1926 broke the Florida mania. By the early 1930's, when few people could afford Florida vacations, some communities of the state were ghost towns with abandoned hotels and grass in the streets. One Florida promoter then shifted his operations to eastern Long Island. He created a skyscraper office building at Montauk which still stands alone and mostly deserted and tried to persuade trans-Atlantic shipping companies to land at Montauk Point rather than New York. To demonstrate that Lake Montauk could accommodate large ships, he got a friend in the Navy Department to order part of the fleet there. When the shipping companies refused to go along with the venture and thereby spared their passengers the uncertainties of travel on the Long Island Railroad, the project collapsed. How much capital and labor went into such wasteful speculations can never be known precisely, but the total must have been staggering.

Prosperity's record in the 1920's was extremely spotty. On the one hand, total compensation to employees increased from 1922 to 1929 by about 40 per cent while the cost-of-living index rose only from 97.7 to 100. This was probably the best record in improved living standards of any previous eight-year period. But on the other hand, some economic areas were depressed throughout the decade. The trials of the farmer have already been discussed. Coal mining was a sick industry, as was the New England textile industry. Unemployment in 1928, the last full boom year before the crash, was 1,900,000 out of a labor force of 47,900,000, roughly 4 per cent unemployment. A brief description of income distribution in 1929 indicates how far prosperity was from being universal and illustrates how the boom was based upon a narrow foundation. Of the approximately 27,500,000 American families of 1929, 16,-350,000 received less than $2,000 income; 11,653,000 families received less than $1,500; 5,775,000 families received less than $1,000. At the other end of the scale, the most fortunate 1 per cent of income recipients received 14.5 per cent of the total and the top 5 per cent received 26.1 per cent.

New and Expanded Industries

The automobile industry grew more and had more far-reaching effects on the economy and the way people lived than any other industry in the 1920's. The industry introduced no startling new inventions during this period, but it enormously improved its product through better machining and engineering. At the end of the war, machine tools in the auto industry were still so crude and allowed such tolerances that a hand-finished auto engine could develop as much as twice the horsepower as a standard, machine-made one. By the end of the 1920's, due to better cutting tools and the use of the Swedish Johansson measuring blocks, hand finishing offered little mechanical advantage.

The following table indicates the expansion of the industry during the postwar decade. Imports of foreign cars amounted to practically nothing; in 1926, the year of largest auto imports after 1920, only 813 entered the United

TABLE 2

EXPANSION OF AUTOMOBILE INDUSTRY, 1915–1930

Year	Total Automobiles Manufactured	Number Registered
1915	970,000	2,446,000
1920	2,227,000	9,232,000
1925	4,428,000	19,937,000
1929	5,622,000	26,501,000
1930	3,510,000	26,524,000

States. There is no better way to indicate the central position the auto industry began to take in the economy than to cite some statistics. In 1929, the industry accounted for 12.7 per cent of all manufactures, employed 7.1 per cent of all manufacturing wage earners, paid 8.7 per cent of manufacturing payrolls, and used 15 per cent of total steel production. These figures do not include the expansion that autos brought in oil, rubber, glass, textiles, and nickel. According to one estimate, the industry directly or indirectly was responsible for the employment of 3,700,000 workers in 1929. After 1923, when Detroit for the first time produced more closed cars than open models and sales began to boom, financing car purchases became a significant part of the national credit structure. In 1925, 68.2 per cent of all new cars were bought on time.

At about the same time the sale of used cars began to be economically important. The used car market doomed Ford's Model T, for prospective car buyers could buy a larger and more comfortable used car for the price of a new Model T. Ford's dealers pleaded with him to manufacture a fancier model, but he refused to change until his competitors began to eat seriously into the Ford market and Model T sales fell. Ford ended production of the Model T in 1927 and was out of production for a year before he put the Model A on the market. From that time forward until the late 1950's, the industry concentrated on ever bigger and more powerful cars and shunned smaller, less expensive models. Rather than use the savings brought by more efficient production to lower prices—because cutting prices in any important way might bring disastrous competition—the lower costs were absorbed by more complicated and elaborate models. This pattern became the usual one for American production of complicated and durable consumer goods.

The auto industry was a prime example of developing oligopoly. An *oligopolistic* industry is one dominated by a few large firms and characterized by a lack of price competition although competition for sales may be intense.

In the industry's early days, there had been numerous small companies, none of them with a major share of the market. Then Ford concentrated on a mass-produced inexpensive car and became the industry's giant. In 1908, William C. Durant of the Buick Company, a former wagon company executive, organized General Motors with a minimum of Wall Street financing by combining seventeen independent firms. General Motors at first concentrated on medium-priced to expensive cars, the Buick, Oakland, Oldsmobile, and Cadillac. Continental Motors, a mass-production parts maker, provided parts at wholesale prices to small firms, which merely assembled them and sold them under their own brand names. One of these small firms was run by Louis Chevrolet. Small firms could sell a medium-priced car in competition with larger companies but were at a disadvantage nevertheless because they could not afford large-scale advertising campaigns nor attract sufficient dealers to provide a network of convenient service garages.

The DuPont interests, in chemicals and explosives, came into General Motors in 1917 and acquired control of it in 1921. General Motors acquired Chevrolet and made it a competitor to Ford's Model T. Selling for a little more in the early 1920's, it offered much the Model T could not meet, such as four-wheel brakes and a standard gear shift. The growth of Chevrolet sales more than anything else forced Ford to abandon the Model T, but his Model A never caught up with its GM competitor. GM operated as a huge industrial empire governed by a federal system. Executives of its component divisions had considerable autonomy and competed with one another, but a committee of the central organization determined general policy. Despite GM's ties to DuPont, it provided much of its own financing for expansion by plowing back its profits. It reinvested about 47 per cent of its profits between 1909 and 1926. Profits in the industry were high. The profits of the thirty-two auto companies that operated throughout the period 1919 to 1928 ranged from a high of 25.3 per cent in 1922 to lows of 16.1 in 1927 and 1928.

Walter P. Chrysler, a former GM executive, formed the Chrysler Corporation in 1923 when he acquired control of the failing Maxwell Company. He manufactured a line of cars under his own name and acquired Dodge Brothers in 1928. Dodge was in difficulty partly because of its insistence upon retaining an unusual gear shift for its sturdy and utilitarian medium-priced car. In 1929, Chrysler got control of Plymouth and made it a competitor to Ford and Chevrolet.

By 1923, the ten largest auto manufacturers produced 90 per cent of all cars and trucks. By 1930, Ford, GM, and Chrysler produced 83 per cent of the output. Of the 181 auto manufacturing companies of 1903, only 11 survived in 1930. Studebaker, Nash, Packard, and Hudson were secure small manufacturers, but dozens of others slowly died out. Some disappeared altogether, such as the Moon and the Dort. Others were absorbed or turned to specialized production. Reo converted to truck manufacture entirely, but big over-the-road trucking did not begin to become economically important until the late 1920's and early 1930's.

The Big Three and the independents competed vigorously but not in the traditional ways. Because the intricacies of production required planning for changed models far in advance of actual production, each firm knew well what its competitors were planning. Secrets were difficult to keep when thousands of employees were involved. All companies except Ford belonged to the National Automobile Chamber of Commerce and provided the Chamber with monthly reports of sales. Until 1925, the auto companies maintained a patent pool, and any firm could use any patent without royalty. Success in the business depended more upon salesmanship than upon engineering.

The chemical industry received a great stimulus from the war. Military orders for explosives provided good profits, and companies like DuPont invested its increased revenues in new endeavors, frequently using research to develop entirely new products and markets. The war also provided an opportunity to overtake the German chemical industry, which was the most important in the world before 1914. During the war, the federal government confiscated German chemical patents and sold them to American firms. Formulas for dyes were the first German patents exploited, but so far behind Germany was American chemical engineering that it was years before American firms could produce dyes comparable to those of German manufacture at reasonable cost. The Fordney-McCumber Tariff put a high duty on dyes, and ever since the chemical industry has strongly advocated a high tariff, although, since World War II, at least, it has been in a strong competitive position with foreign producers even on a free trade basis.

The most dramatic development in the chemical industry after the war was the proliferation of synthetics. Synthetics were nothing new. Celluloid had been developed in 1869 and was used widely early in the twentieth century for combs, novelties, and even men's collars. Bakelite, also developed before the war, became increasingly important in the 1920's as an insulator in radios and electric appliances. Rayon, another prewar product, was not commercially used to a significant extent until the early 1920's, when it was produced cheaply enough almost to replace silk in women's clothing. Celanese, another artificial silk synthetic, went on the market in the mid-1920's, as did cellophane, first produced commercially by DuPont in 1924. George Washington Carver, the best known Negro scientist of the day, concentrated on finding uses for materials found in surplus farm commodities. From peanuts and sweet potatoes he synthesized a wide range of products from paste to shaving lotion.

Measuring the growth of the chemical industry during the 1920's is impossible because the definitions of the census of manufactures were arbitrary and meaningless. The chemical industry, in a sense, knows no boundaries. Chemistry is universal, like mathematics. One specialist, however, for what his figures are worth, estimated the industry's production in 1929 as worth $3.8 billion, a growth of over 50 per cent since 1914.

The electric industry, both the generation and transmission of power and the manufacture of electrically powered machinery and appliances, was one of the big growth industries in the 1920's. Electric power generated more than doubled between 1920 and 1929. The increasing use of electricity in industry is seen in Table 3.

As more households gained access to electricity—from 16 per cent of the population in 1912 to 63 per cent in 1927—there developed a vast market for home electrical appliances. Two giants dominated the industry. In 1897, General Electric, itself a consolidation of several smaller companies, and Westinghouse Electric signed an agreement to share one another's patents. They were thus enabled to gain practical control over the heavy equipment

223

TABLE 3

CONSUMPTION OF VARIOUS KINDS OF POWER, 1919–1927

Year	Establish- ments Reporting Power	Total* Rated Capacity	Steam* Engines and Turbines	Internal* Combus- tion Engines	Water* Power	Electric* Motors
1919	222,924	29,324	17,034	1,242	1,765	16,252
1923	173,415	33,092	16,700	1,223	1,803	22,185
1925	167,533	35,767	16,916	1,186	1,801	26,120
1927	174,118	38,826	16,924	1,171	1,599	30,352

*1,000 rated H.P.

field, but in the 1920's the market for home appliances became too large for them to keep out competition, although they continued to dominate the appliance industry. In 1926, an estimated four-fifths of homes with electricity had an electric iron, three-eighths had a vacuum cleaner, and one-fourth had a washing machine. Electric refrigerators were uncommon until late in the 1920's. For the working-class housewife, work was cut down considerably by some of these appliances. Certainly, electric ironing was more efficient and easier than lifting the old heavy irons back and forth from the stove, and piloting a vacuum cleaner did a better job more easily than a hand broom or a carpet beater. For middle-class housewives, however, it is dubious that these work-saving appliances actually simplified her life. They may have made it harder. One could send out the laundry and ironing for quite a long time for the price of an electric washer, and hiring someone to do the cleaning was easier than doing it oneself even with an electric sweeper. Rising labor costs for domestic services more than convenience made purchase of electric appliances economical for middle-class families.

Home radio was a completely new postwar industry. Many cities claim to have been the first to have had a radio station. The Wisconsin state station on the University campus broadcast experimentally in 1919, and in the summer of 1920 *The Detroit News* started broadcasting news bulletins for the benefit of local radio "hams." The first commercial station was KDKA operated by Westinghouse Electric from East Pittsburgh. It began broadcasting on November 2, 1920, just in time to give the first election returns by radio. By 1922, three million homes had a radio, usually a battery set, frequently with earphones, that had a bewildering array of dials on its front panel. Sales of radios that year amounted to $60 million. By 1929, about 40 per cent of America's families owned a radio and sales amounted to over $400 million.

General Electric and Westinghouse, through their creation and control of the Radio Corporation of America (1919), held the basic patents and controlled both radio manufacture and one of the national radio networks. In the mid-1920's, RCA created the National Broadcasting Company and arranged with the American Telephone and Telegraph Company to use its long-distance telephone lines to transmit broadcasts to stations in the network.

The Columbia Broadcasting System came into being the next year. When the number of broadcasting stations multiplied—there were over five hundred by 1924—something obviously had to be done by the federal government to prevent broadcasters from using the same wave lengths. The Department of Commerce began to assign wave lengths in 1924, but it ran into an adverse court decision in 1926 and stopped the practice. In 1927, Congress created the Federal Radio Commission to license broadcasters and bring order into the chaos. The new commission soon ran into difficulty with the Los Angeles evangelist Aimee Semple McPherson, a cultural phenomenon who combined sex and religion and called herself "the world's most pulchritudinous evangelist," when that lady declared that her radio wave length came from Divine authority, the government of the United States to the contrary.

Broadcasting was a profitable business after station WEAF in New York City began to sell time to advertisers in 1922. A New York real estate company had the dubious distinction of sponsoring the first radio commercial. Most of the other nations of the western world forbade radio advertising and subsidized broadcasting from revenues gained by a tax on radio receivers. If commercial radio had begun a decade earlier or later than the time it actually did or if the American people could have foreseen singing commercials, perhaps their radio programing would have developed along similar lines.

Supercorporations and the "New Competition"

By the end of the 1920's, the supercorporation was the norm in the critical areas of the American economy: manufacturing, railroad transportation, communications and other public utilities, and finance. The large corporation also was becoming increasingly important even in retail trade. Small and medium-sized businesses were far more numerous than their big brothers, and they remain so today. Big businesses did not even employ a majority of the wage-earners. Only about one-sixth of them, in fact, were on big business payrolls. But large corporations had their grip on the most important parts of the economy. To use military terms, they were the main sources of supply, except for food products (and big corporations were growing quickly there), and they controlled the "narrows" of the economy, the economic bridges, passes, and straits.

In the 1880's, an ordinary citizen might come into contact with a supercorporation only when he purchased Standard Oil kerosene for his lamps. By 1929, he might awaken in a house built of lumber supplied by the Weyerhaeuser Timber Company and financed by a mortgage from the Bank of America, glance over his newspaper published by a unit of the Hearst chain while he ate a breakfast bought at the A & P and prepared on a General Electric or Westinghouse stove which used electric power generated by a link in the Insull empire, and drive to work in a Big Three car burning Standard Oil gasoline. In the evening he and his family might have an Armour ham for dinner and listen to a radio program sponsored by United States Steel and carried to his city over American Telephone and Telegraph Company lines. Like as not, he would then go to bed priding himself on his "rugged individualism" and thankful that he did not live in a centralized society.

Statistics are necessary. In 1929, the two hundred largest business corporations possessed just under half of the total wealth of corporations, just under two-fifths of the total business wealth, and one-fifth of the total national wealth. These two hundred companies grew three times as fast in assets and income as small corporations. A major study of the corporation made by Adolph Berle and Gardiner C. Means published in 1932 estimated that if the two hundred largest corporations continued their rate of growth they would own half of the national wealth and four-fifths of the corporate wealth by midcentury. Thousands of small corporations disappeared as separate entities by merging with others or by selling out to larger corporations, usually for stock in the purchasing company. Between 1919 and 1930, over eight thousand businesses in manufacturing and mining disappeared. In 1926 and 1927 alone, 1,940 public utility firms disappeared as separate businesses. Retail outlets did not disappear, but chain stores steadily accounted for an increasing share of total sales. Chain-store units increased from twenty-nine thousand in 1918 to one hundred sixty thousand in 1929. In 1929, they sold 27 per cent of the country's food, 19 per cent of its drugs, 27 per cent of its clothes, 30 per cent of its tobacco, and 26 per cent of its general merchandise. A & P had about 15,000 retail stores. Drug, Inc. had 10,000 Rexall stores and 706 Liggett stores, as well as control of Bayer Aspirin, Bristol-Myers, and Vick Chemical. Chain stores were to grow even more in the 1930's.

Banking experienced a concentration in the 1920's that made the old "money trust" seem juvenile. In 1921, there were 30,812 banks; in 1929 there were only 25,330. Failures accounted for much of the shrinkage. Bank failures never fell below 367 a year in the 1920's, and 976 banks failed in 1926. Almost all these closed banks were fairly small and in depressed agricultural areas. Branch banking became important in states that permitted it. Branch banks approximately tripled in number during the decade. Far and away the biggest bank chain was the Bank of America, centered in San Francisco and founded by A. P. Giannini. New York banks, many of which merged during the 1920's, remained the most powerful of the country. In 1929, the biggest 1 per cent of the banks controlled 46 per cent of the nation's bank resources.

The holding company was the most common device of concentrating economic control. Of the ninety-seven biggest industrial corporations in 1929, ninety-four were holding companies. Twenty-one were purely holding companies that did not themselves produce anything. Among the prominent companies of this sort were United States Steel, Eastman Kodak, and Allied Chemical & Dye. Most of them were operating companies themselves but owned controlling stock of other corporations in their industries. In manufacturing, the holding company seldom extended above one level. That is, one holding company controlled two or more operating companies. But in public utilities—and to a lesser extent in railroading—pyramid holding companies were the rule. In 1930, ten holding-company structures dominated 72 per cent of the nation's electric power.

The huge and enormously complicated holding-company pyramid of Samuel Insull, an immigrant from London who settled in Chicago, was the nation's biggest. Insull was chairman of the board of 65 corporations, and there were 111 separate corporate entities within his pyramid. The structure was so complicated with its 24 levels of holding companies between the top and the firms that actually generated electric power that it is doubtful if anyone, including Insull, fully understood the giant's anatomy. Owen D. Young, chairman of the board of General Electric from whom Insull sought advice, said of the Insull empire, "It is impossible for any man to grasp the situation of that vast structure . . . it was so set up that you could not possibly get an accounting system that would not mislead even the officers themselves." If Young could not understand the system, certainly the thousands of investors did not. But investors were eager to buy stock in Insull companies because they thought the stock would appreciate quickly—and it did until late 1929. By having a maximum of 51 per cent control of the first-level holding company, whose stock was owned by another Insull-controlled company, and so on up for 24 layers, Insull achieved powerful leverage all the way down through the pyramid. With each dollar he invested in the top company, Corporation Securities Corporation, Insull controlled over $2,000 in assets of a generating company at the bottom, such as Georgia Power and Light.

The Van Sweringen railroad empire was not as big or complicated as Insull's, but it was built with less cold cash. O. P. and M. J. Van Sweringen, Cleveland brothers who had made a fortune in real estate, parlayed $500,000 of their own money and a like sum from a group of associates into control of several railroads with over twenty-nine thousand miles of track. They bought control of the Nickel Plate Railroad from the New York Central for $8 billion, one-fourth in cash which they borrowed through the House of Morgan, the rest payable in ten years. Collateral for the loan was the Nickel Plate stock acquired with the loan. They organized a holding company and sold stock in it to raise the funds for the balance of the Nickel Plate price. Then they branched out. In 1930, just before their whole structure collapsed, the Van Sweringens controlled the following railroads through minority stock holdings: the Nickel Plate, the Chicago and Eastern Illinois, the Erie, the Wheeling and Lake Erie, the Chesapeake & Ohio, the Hocking Valley, the Kansas City Southern, and the Pere Marquette. They also had majority control of the Missouri Pacific, which in turn owned half the stock of the Denver & Rio Grande. Here is an example of Van Sweringen leverage: the brothers owned 80 per cent of the stock of the Vaness Company, which owned 50 per cent of the stock of the General Securities Corporation. The Van Sweringens owned another 40 per cent of General Securities in their own name. General Securities controlled the Allegheny Corporation by owning 8.61 per cent of its stock. Allegheny controlled the Chesapeake Corporation in which the Van Sweringen equity was only 4.1 per cent. The Chesapeake Corporation controlled the Chesapeake & Ohio Railroad of which the Van Sweringen equity was .98 per cent of the stock. The C & O controlled the Hocking Valley. Van Sweringen equity in the Hocking Valley amounted to only .04 per cent of its ownership. Like Insull, the Van Sweringens were dependent upon large numbers of small stockholders to retain their control of the whole structure.

So far in this section we have considered the diminution of full competition only by the acquisition of at least some of the stock of a potential competitor. Competition was also reduced by cooperation of firms completely independent of one another so far as ownership was concerned, and the usual instrument of such cooperation was the trade association. Trade association members competed with one another for markets, but through advertising rather than underselling each other. They sometimes referred to this kind of cooperation as "the new competition," taking the term from a 1912 book by that name by Arthur Jerome Eddy, the same Chicago lawyer who purchased the "Nude Descending a Staircase" at the Armory Art Show. Eddy's book, which went through five editions in three years and favored trade associations, asserted that the main difference between old-fashioned competition and "new competition" was that the old employed secrecy and conspiracy and that the new was open. The new was also usually more efficient because it generally embraced all the economically important firms in a market. The contrast between the methods of a trade association and the older means of price setting may be illustrated by describing the steel industry's Gary dinners and the association "open price" system. Early in the twentieth century, steel executives met irregularly and informally for dinner at the home of United States Steel chief Judge Elbert H. Gary and set prices for their products. Once when a small firm began to cut prices against the Gary dinner set it was warned that if it continued its "unreasonable and destructive competition" the industry would have to resort to the law of the jungle in which only the fittest would survive. The threat was sufficient. The Gary dinner system could not work in an industry with a greater number of smaller firms with less punitive power.

Trade association members furnished the association with their price information, and the association made it available to all either through a publication or letters. Associations also persuaded members to use standard cost-accounting methods and instructed members in the use of uniform formulas to calculate costs for contract bidding. Under the guidance of Hoover's Department of Commerce, associations urged standardization of product sizes and shapes, for such standardization was necessary to achieve price uniformity. Over two hundred sizes and shapes of bottles were cut to ten, varieties of brick shapes declined from sixty-six to seven, and numerous other commodities were similarly standardized. This standardization was only a continuation of War Production Board policies, the benefits of the efficiency now to accrue to manufacturers in the interest of profits rather than in the interest of better prosecution of the war. The Supreme Court in a series of cases in the early 1920's, the American Column and Lumber Co. case in 1921, the American Linseed Oil Co. case in 1923, and the Cement Manufacturers' Protective Association and Maple Flooring Manufacturers' Association cases in 1925, ruled, in effect, that exchanging price information and other knowledge among "competitors" was within the law unless the purpose was explicitly to raise prices. Associations merely refrained from stating that purpose and were legal.

As corporations grew larger and their stock ownership became more diverse and as trade associations increasingly assumed corporate functions of determining price and nature of production, the ownership of a firm became separated from actual control. Let us take an extreme example for illustration. General Motors was a huge corporation with hundreds of thousands of stockholders, most of whom owned only a tiny proportion of the outstanding stock. Each share had one vote in elections to GM's board of directors, and each stockholder was legally entitled to attend the annual stockholders meeting and speak his mind. But in actual fact most stockholders did not care one way or another about the thousands of decisions, big and small, that the corporation had to make each week. Most stockholders were interested only in dividends and appreciation of their shares on the stock market. Most GM owners who did care about the corporation's decisions were ill prepared to make a decision, for example, on whether the 1928 Chevrolet should have wire-spoke or disc wheels, what advertising agency should handle its account, what the FOB Detroit price should be, or what the wage rate should be for tool and die makers. Decisions, major and minor, in all large corporations came increasingly to be made by salaried corporation officials who did not necessarily own any stock at all. If officials did own stock they nevertheless were decision-makers because of their employment rather than their stock ownership. Several corporations in the 1920's sold stock which had no voting rights; owners of nonvoting stock did not have even a legal or theoretical right to participate in making decisions. Owners of voting stock in a company such as the Hocking Valley Railroad were likewise powerless to defy the Van Sweringen interests in the company although the brothers personally had only a very small equity in the firm. Thus the traditional concept of private property, in which the owner was inhibited in his decisions about how to use his property only by law—he could not legally use his gun to shoot his neighbor, for example, nor use his ships in smuggling—became considerably modified. Paradoxically, the ultimate development of American capitalism, based upon private ownership, was to change the nature of property ownership.

The shift of substantial control from owners to corporation executives has been called a "managerial revolution." Business administrators—"corporation bureaucrats"—were a new breed of businessmen. They endeavored to make administration a precise and specialized science and resorted to a complicated division of labor and specialization. At the same time as the blue-collar worker "on the line" in an automobile plant became a human cog, something similar happened to his white-collar colleague in the plant's offices. Some administrators became specialists in personnel work and applied psychological principles to put square pegs in square holes for the benefit of the corporation's efficiency. Others became specialists in some small part of production, or advertising, or cost accounting, or sales, or purchasing of supplies. Top managerial positions tended to go to men who had specialized in some aspect of sales because the decline of price competition heightened the importance of persuading the public to buy the corporation's products by some other means.

One kind of corporation administrator with special implications for society was the public relations specialist. His function was to get the public's good will for the corporation, to mold public opinion so as best to promote his corporation's interest. The best of them, who usually founded independent firms and contracted with corporations much the same way as advertising agencies, were surprisingly successful in forming what they in time came to call a favorable "public image." The wartime Creel committee was a training school for several of the public relations specialists of the 1920's, who now sold a corporation rather than the war. Edward Bernays, one of the cleverest of the image-molders, was a graduate of the Creel committee and a nephew of Sigmund Freud, whose psychological theories sometimes were applied to advance corporate interests.

The question of efficiency of production and distribution is a central one in forming a judgment about corporatism. There is little question that most large corporations produced and distributed more efficiently than most small ones. Because they could achieve greater production with mass methods, they could decrease costs of production. Many of them had huge research departments that developed new products and more efficient methods of producing old ones, and the fruits of some of this research improved the population's material standard of living. Management specialization resulted in miracles of production. Bigness, it was apparent, had its limits. A factory could become too large and complicated to operate at maximum efficiency. Optimum size depended upon markets and the state of technology, both of which changed constantly. But a single corporation could efficiently operate a number of optimum-sized production units. There were dangers of bureaucracy, however, even in a huge corporation that divided its production into efficient separate units. Some became inflexible and unwieldy. In industries with extremely high overhead costs, such as steel, corporations sometimes had to retain production methods that management knew were not as efficient as a new process because too much was invested in the old to make changing to the new profitable.

Sometimes concentration of control had no effect whatsoever on the efficiency of the industrial process. Samuel Insull did not erect his crazy-quilt power empire to improve the generation and transmission of electricity, nor did the Van Sweringens integrate operations of their many railroad lines. The purpose of these businessmen was to profit by shuffling around paper evidences of property ownership. Only the disadvantages of concentration operated in cases such as these.

It should be noted that the growth of supercorporations by no means meant the extension of absolute or total monopoly of a market. Sometimes it did, as in aluminum, but on the whole there was less absolute monopoly in the 1920's than there had been early in the century when Standard Oil stood virtually alone in the oil business and United States Steel controlled a larger proportion of the nation's steel capacity. Indeed, chain stores often broke local monopolies of small merchants, and consumers' burdens had not been lighter merely because they had been exploited by a small monopolist.

But after assuming that large corporations and other forms of economic concentration did increase efficiency with certain exceptions noted, one is confronted with the question of who was the beneficiary of the improved efficiency. The facts indicate that corporation officials and stockholders received the lion's share of efficiency's benefits during the 1920's. Workers' incomes increased 11 per cent from 1923 to 1929 while corporate profits rose 62 per cent and dividends 65 per cent. Prices were fairly stable, but the consumer usually got a better product. A 1929 car was a better machine than a 1923 flivver, and the price was about the same.

The administered prices that came with the "new competition" were to have great implications for the next decade of depression. In classical economic theory, depressed economies right themselves automatically because prices drop, thereby increasing demand and bringing it again into balance with supply. Whether this classical theory ever actually and perfectly described the actual situation is dubious, but it certainly did not apply to the facts of the Great Depression. In industries where the "new competition" obtained, corporations tended to keep prices stable and to restrict production. Restricting production meant unemployment, and unemployed workers had only a minimum of purchasing power.

There were also political issues in the New Economic Order. Was it right, asked some critics, for a relatively small group of corporation directors and salaried officials, who wielded great power without any mandate from the population, to make economic decisions which affected almost everyone? The sum of decisions made by businessmen—whether or not to cut prices, cut production, expand research, move a factory to another part of the country, or expand foreign investments—probably had more to do with the way citizens lived than the decisions of the politicians for whom they could vote. Others replied that the consumer voted every time he made a purchase. To a limited degree this was true. He could vote against Henry Ford by buying a Chevrolet if he did not like black cars. (Ford had once said that a Model T buyer "can have a Ford any color he wants—so long as it's black.") But the consumer's veto power had tight boundaries. If he disliked a firm's labor policies and organized a boycott, he ran afoul the law. Protective tariffs limited his freedom to buy foreign products. An industry that administered its prices left him only the choice of not buying at all. The consumer's veto was at best an imprecise one.

But in the palmy days of the late 1920's few questioned corporate policies or expressed concern about corporate power. Public opinion put top corporation officials upon a prestige pedestal, and neither government nor labor organizations made serious inroads upon their prerogatives.

Labor in the Business Decade

Although working men did not receive as great a share of the economic expansion of the postwar decade as their employers, they made a substantial gain in their living standards. Average real wages in 1919 were 105 on an index in which 1914 was 100; in 1928 real wages had risen to 132. This method of measuring living standards disregards unemployment. Prosperous eras usually stimulate the effectiveness of labor organizations because employers, eager for uninterrupted production when sales prospects are bright, are more likely to make labor concessions than they are when they are pessimistic about business. But organized labor suffered severe defeats in the depression of 1920–1921 and failed to recover thereafter.

Employer associations opened a vigorous "open shop" campaign during the postwar depression in an effort to drive labor unions out of their cities and industries. Employers actually wanted more than the open shop; they wanted elimination of unions altogether. And they had considerable success. Unions in industries only recently organized were the most vulnerable, but well-established unions in the printing and building trades also retreated. Bethlehem Steel Company President Eugene G. Grace announced in late 1920 that his firm would refuse to sell fabricated steel to building contractors in New York and Philadelphia who did not have an open shop and that he would not recognize a union and bargain with it even if 95 per cent of his employees belonged. Businessmen were seldom so extreme in their public statements, but many were equally opposed to unionism.

The failure of the railroad shopmen's strike in 1922 further depleted the ranks of union labor. In July, 1920, just before the postwar depression began, the Railroad Labor Board created by the recently passed Transportation Act awarded a 22 per cent wage increase to the shopmen. Railroad managers counteracted with a publicity campaign against the working agreements that established shop rules. The rules encouraged feather-bedding, claimed management, and in April, 1921, the Labor Board, containing new Harding appointees, abrogated the agreements. Three months later, the Labor Board ordered a 12 per cent wage cut. In June, 1922, the Board ordered a further wage cut that wiped out the 1920 raise, although by the time of the second wage cut the economy had revived. On July 1, the railroad shopmen went out on a nationwide strike.

Harding tried to mediate. The union leaders agreed to a formula, but railroad managers refused to restore seniority rights to the strikers, arguing that they had quit their jobs when they struck. The unions refused to call off the strike unless management accepted the whole Harding formula. On September 1, Attorney General Daugherty obtained a labor injunction from a Chicago federal judge that restrained the unions from doing anything to further the strike. Later in the month, eleven railroads signed new agreements with the shopmen, but the other roads took advantage of their opportunity and banned the union from their shops.

Employers also dampened enthusiasm for unionism through what was commonly called *welfare capitalism*. Welfare capitalism included everything from sports programs, soap in the toilets, and water coolers to good company housing and group insurance. Several companies introduced employee stock-purchase plans in which employees bought the corporation's nonvoting stock on the installment plan. Employers hoped the scheme would lead employees to adopt stockholders' viewpoints rather than those of labor organizations but the idea backfired after 1929 when employees lost not only their jobs but their savings.

By such devices total union membership, both within and outside the AFL, fell from about 5,100,000 in 1920 to about 3,600,000 in 1923. Organized labor had not received such a blow in the twentieth century. From 1923 until the depression, union membership was fairly stable, neither growing nor shrinking significantly. Employers' counterattacks and prosperous complacency had much to do with labor's failure to grow during the boom, but labor's leadership must also share some of the responsibility. Samuel Gompers died in 1924, and William Green, of the United Mine Workers and Chillicothe, Ohio, succeeded to the AFL presidency. Green was not the man Gompers had been. Surely UMW president John L. Lewis exaggerated when he said of Green in the late 1930's, "I have done a lot of exploring of Bill Green's mind, and I give you my word there is nothing there." There was something there, but not much originality nor imagination. He and such colleagues as Matthew Woll, AFL vice-president, and John P. Frey, head of the Metal Trades Department, were far more interested in appearing respectable to the public and in maintaining the economic status of the craft unions' skilled members—"labor's aristocracy"—than they were in extending unionism to the roughly 90 per cent of the working force that had no organization.

Union-sponsored banks, one of organized labor's few experiments during the 1920's, reflected labor's business outlook. At the height of the labor bank movement in 1926, thirty-five labor banks had combined resources of over $126 million. The bank established by the Brotherhood of Locomotive Engineers, perhaps the most "aristocratic" of all unions, got into the Florida land bubble. It invested heavily in what was to be a model project at Venice, Florida. When Venice land values fell disastrously in the general Florida collapse, the engineers' bank went on the rocks. Most of the labor banks were poorly managed, and only a few of them survived the bank crisis of the early depression. Those that did stand the shocks of the Great Depression did so because they operated much as conventional banking institutions. Labor banks made one contribution both to people of little income and to general banking practice. They pioneered in making small loans at reasonable interest rates, thereby saving their borrowers from the much higher rates of finance companies and the usury of illegal "loan sharks." When commercial bankers saw labor banks enjoying a high rate of repayment from small loans, increasing numbers of them followed the labor banks' example. Labor banks also stimulated the growth of credit unions, special associations of employees to receive members' deposits and make small loans.

The most notable exceptions to general timidity and lack of imagination in the labor movement were the activities of the needle trade unions, particularly the two biggest such unions, the Amalgamated Clothing Workers in the men's clothing industry of which Sidney Hillman was president and the International Ladies Garment Workers Union of which David Dubinsky was president. The clothing industry was characterized by sharp competition and a myriad of small entrepreneurs who could start a business on a contracting or subcontracting basis with a minimum investment. Labor usually finds it difficult to organize such an industry because failure to capture the whole industry usually puts the employer who pays union-scale wages at a competitive disadvantage. The needle trade unions largely solved this problem by pioneering in introducing Taylorism in the industry, sometimes even lending employers the funds necessary to introduce new and more efficient methods, and vigorously organizing all firms in the industry. Having much of the brains of the industry as well as its labor and being almost the only industry-wide association in the fragmented field, the Amalgamated and the ILGWU came to provide what stability and leadership the industry had. The needle trade unions were among the first to win the forty-hour week, to build cooperative housing projects, and to gain unemployment compensation. It was largely these unions, composed mostly of Jewish and Italian immigrants, that kept alive the tradition of labor militancy between the setbacks of 1920–1922 and labor's revival in the Great Depression.

Labor conducted relatively few strikes after the immediate postwar strike wave. The most important ones during the 1920's were in coal and textiles. Most coal mining was done in isolated, small communities marked by constant friction between miners and owners. Competition in the industry was sharp, and during the 1920's the whole industry became sick as coal lost ground to natural gas and oil as fuel. Mine operators were in no position to be generous, and miners, the world over a tough breed hardened by back-breaking work and constant danger, were in no mood to compromise. Isolated from the enlightened and pacifying influences of urban civilization, both operators and miners frequently used violence to try to achieve their ends. Violence was particularly sharp in the coal field of West Virginia and eastern Kentucky from 1919 to 1921. When armed battles between striking miners and company guards broke out, the governor of West Virginia declared martial law and called out the state guard. In 1921, battles between guards and miners became serious, and Harding sent the army into the troubled area.

Both anthracite and bituminous miners went out on strike when old contracts expired in April, 1922. Operators had tried to reduce wages during negotiations for a new contract. The strike was peaceful until June, when a large coal company in "Bloody Williamson" County, Illinois, imported strike-breakers and mine guards killed two strikers attempting to keep strikebreakers out of the pits. The strikers retaliated by killing nineteen strikebreakers in a company stockade. In mid-August, about one-fifth of the soft coal operators gave in and most of the other operators soon followed suit, but the United Mine Workers had been unable to make much headway in organizing the West Virginia and Kentucky fields.

The 1922 contracts were due to expire in April, 1924. Before the contract expired, the operators of the central competitive field, Illinois, Indiana, Ohio, and western Pennsylvania, signed the Jacksonville agreement with the UMW. The agreement maintained wages, but the understanding was that the operators of the region would not extend the wage agreement when it expired in 1927 if the UMW had not meanwhile organized the southern or West Virginia–Kentucky field whose coal competed with that from UMW areas. The miners were not only unsuccessful in organizing the southern field, due largely to wholesale injunctions and yellow-dog contracts, but the southern field expanded its production. In 1924, three-fifths of the nation's soft coal came from the central district's union mines; a year later the non-union southern field produced three-fifths of the total. At the same time, Lewis faced a revolt within the UMW in Illinois, and when the 1927 negotiations came up, the UMW, after an unsuccessful strike, had to accept a wage cut. The UMW remained weak until new federal legislation in the 1930's enabled it to organize better the southern field.

Textiles were as sick or sicker than coal. Faced with a shrinking market, textile firms in the North shifted their operations to the cheap-labor southern Appalachian region. Despite appeals from southern AFL organizations, the national AFL and its United Textile Workers made little more than half-hearted efforts to organize the South until 1928. By that time the Communists' National Textile Workers' Union had already made progress. The next year violent and unsuccessful strikes occurred in Elizabethton, Tennessee, and Marion and Gastonia, North Carolina.

Girls in the Elizabethton rayon mill worked a fifty-six-hour week for from sixteen to eighteen cents an hour. They walked out and obtained a verbal agreement for a slight wage increase, but they did not get union recognition. The employer soon violated the verbal agreement. Two AFL representatives who went to Elizabethton were beaten by a mob of businessmen and local civil officers, taken to the state line, and warned not to return. Workers in the Marion mill went out on a United Textile Workers strike against low wages and the "stretch-out" which required employees to tend more machines. Feelings ran high when the company evicted the strikers from their company-owned homes, and the governor sent in the national guard to supplement a large force of deputy sheriffs. In a brawl between unarmed pickets and the national guard deputy force, five unarmed pickets were killed and nineteen wounded. Strike leaders and the responsible law officers were arrested, but the accused killers were acquitted and the most prominent local labor leader sent to prison. The Communist-run strike at Gastonia was the best publicized. The strike, which began in April, collapsed in October when seven Communist strike leaders were convicted of the second-degree murder of the Gastonia police chief. One of the convicted Communists, Fred Beal, jumped bail and went to Russia, but became disillusioned with communism while there and returned to serve his sentence.

CHAPTER TWELVE

The Foreign Policy of a Business Government

FOREIGN POLICY IS THE EXTENSION OF A NATION'S DOMESTIC PROBLEMS and policies. We do ourselves a disservice and make understanding impossible if we conceive of foreign policy as the pursuit of abstract principles separate from other considerations, decided upon by a small group of rarified experts studying and discussing calmly in the foreign offices of the world's capitals, and put into action by suave, striped-trousered, formal diplomats over teacups or cocktail glasses. True, the Department of State and foreign offices of other major powers maintain staffs of experts on various subjects, and, true, diplomatic tradition is more encrusted with protocol established in another century than most other governmental functions. But foreign relations are real, diplomacy is earnest, and the form is not the goal. A nation's policies with other nations are subject to all kinds of domestic pressures, and the overwhelming bulk of foreign policy activities has to do with mundane dollars-and-cents matters.

With corporation businessmen controlling the federal government during the 1920's and less strength in agriculture, labor, and reform than there had been since the 1890's or earlier, American foreign policy was inevitably the policy of American business. The primary molders of the nation's foreign policy, Secretary of State Hughes and Secretary of Commerce Hoover, were confronted, first and foremost, with problems of economic expansion and then war debts, reparations, and maintenance of peace.

Business and Foreign Policy, 1919–1929

The outstanding difference between the postwar and the prewar international balance of power was the tremendous growth, both absolutely and relatively, of American strength. In 1929, United States national income was greater than the combined national incomes of France, Great Britain, Germany, Japan, Canada, and seventeen smaller nations. Before the outbreak of war in 1914, the United States had been, on balance, a debtor nation despite huge investments abroad. On July 1, 1914, nationals of foreign countries had $3.68 billion more invested within the United States, either directly or in loans, than Americans had invested abroad. By December 31, 1919, private investment had shifted until the American advantage amounted to $2.97 billion, and there was a further net foreign debt due the United States government of $9.59 billion. Table 4 gives more detail. Washington's international power, in other words, had become remarkably stronger as a result of the war. New York and Washington had become the world's economic centers of gravity, taking the position that London had enjoyed from 1815 to 1914.

TABLE 4

AMERICA'S INTERNATIONAL CREDITS AND DEBTS

(in millions of dollars)

	July 1, 1914	December 31, 1919	July 1, 1929
Private credits			
Securities	862	2,576	7,839
Direct investments	2,652	3,880	7,553
Short-term credits	...	500	1,617
Private debits			
Securities	5,440	1,623	4,304
Direct investments	1,310	900	1,400
Seized enemy property	...	662	150
Short-term credits	450	800	3,077
Net private debit or credit	–3,686	2,971	8,078
Intergovernmental debt			
Owed to United States	...	9,982	11,685
Owed by United States	...	391	...
Total net debit or credit	–3,686	12,562	19,763

How did the Republican administrations of the 1920's desire to use this new power? What were the objectives of their foreign policy? Actually, they did not differ substantially from the objectives of Democratic administrations either before or after them, although they sometimes differed from the Democratic administrations in methods. Most important during the 1920's was extension of the Open Door empire, informal imperialism, economic expansion abroad, or whatever one chooses to call it. This expansion was necessary to make the domestic economy function smoothly. As Hoover put it, "We must find a profitable market for our surpluses." As Harding put it, American businessmen must "go on to the peaceful commercial conquest of the world." But such expansion was not only an objective; it was partly a means to other ends. As Hoover, Hughes, and their presidents saw it, expansion, peace, and the prevention of revolution were irrevocably dependent upon one another. One of the results of war was revolution, and revolutions could result in war. Peace and stability were necessary for economic expansion. But economic expansion and the use of American strength also could be used to effect a *Pax Americana*. Peace, order, national stability, and expansion of American business opportunity abroad—these were the main objectives of American foreign policy.

Operating on the theory that revolution was an export commodity, American foreign policy makers in the 1920's sought to prevent such disruptive social upheavals partly by isolating the Soviet Union. (Communists too, incidentally, thought revolution emanated only from Moscow and imitated the Bolsheviks' methods. One effect of this conservative-Communist area of agreement was to make every successful revolution in the world enhance the influence of the Soviet Union.) Throughout the 1920's, the belief persisted in America that the Soviet regime would not last. The conclusion of many people in the western world was that the Soviet regime was such a negation of the values of western liberal society that it could not in the nature of things long endure. Disapproval and the assumption of impermanence were behind the American policy of refusal to recognize the Soviet state. The immediate and ostensible reason for nonrecognition was Soviet repudiation of the pre-revolutionary Russian debt and confiscation of about $443 million in American-owned property. The czarist government had sold about $75 million worth of bonds in America, and the government had lent the Kerensky regime $178 million in 1917. Nonrecognition was bipartisan; Wilson had begun the policy, and his Republican successors continued it. Wilson and his successors were under some domestic pressure to recognize the Russian regime, although the pressure did not become strong until after the crash of 1929. Some of the pressure was ideological; some of it was from businessmen who wanted to trade with Russia and thought trade could best be done under normal diplomatic arrangements. During the 1920's, Hughes and Hoover, without publicity, permitted some economic relations between American businessmen and the Soviet Union in the belief that these activities would both undermine the Bolsheviks and increase American influence in the new government to be established after their collapse. Ironically, these economic relations actually helped Russian economic recovery and thereby bolstered the Communists.

Before the war, when the United States had been, on balance, a debtor nation, its exports had exceeded its imports. This was normal for a debtor nation, the only way under ordinary circumstances that, over a period of years, interest and dividends could be paid to investors on the other side of the Atlantic. During the war and immediate postwar reconstruction years, while European investors were liquidating many of their American investments and the federal government was lending billions to European governments, United States exports continued to exceed imports. This was a normal war condition. But even after the war and reconstruction, when the United States was the greatest creditor nation of the world, American exports still exceeded imports, and this was *not* a normal condition. The tariff acts of 1921 and 1922, plus the efficiency of American production and the distance of the American market from Europe, prevented the United States from assuming the normal position of a creditor nation, an excess of imports over exports.

This being the situation, how could nations in debt to the American government and American private investors pay for their imports from the United States and pay their American debts? The answer was that, ultimately, the debtor nations could not pay their debts, even after the United States scaled down the war and reconstruction debts. But meanwhile, such "invisible" American payments as shipping fees to European freighters, American tourist spending abroad (which amounted to a surprising amount in the late 1920's), and remittances from American immigrants to their families in the Old Country helped to lessen the dollar gap but fell far short of closing it. The greater part of the annual European dollar deficit from 1919 to 1929 was covered by further American investments, either direct investments or loans. Thus American capital subsidized American exports. A large amount of world trade was dependent upon the outward flow of American capital. So long as American capital continued to flow, trade went well enough. But with the depression the flow of capital largely dried up and world trade collapsed. The whole western world had become extremely sensitive to fluctuations in the American business cycle. This was the over-all scheme of America's world economic role. Let us now consider various aspects of the scheme, imports and exports, loans abroad, and direct foreign investments.

Imports into the United States increased during the 1920's, although not so much as did American exports. In 1914, imports amounted to $1.9 billion. By 1923, when the abnormal conditions of war, reconstruction, and postwar depression were over, imports totalled $3.8 billion. By 1929, they had grown 16 per cent to $4.4 billion, considerably more than double the 1914 figure. Most imports were raw materials for manufacturing, finished manufactures for American manufacturing use (newsprint for example), and food. Of consumer goods imported in 1929, less than 6 per cent were finished manufactures for direct consumption. These finished consumer imports were mostly luxury items. The main raw material imports were silk, crude rubber, tin, copper, tobacco (for blending with domestic tobacco), and hides and skins. The quantity of imports followed almost exactly the curve of American manufacturing. This fact not only shows American manufacturing's dependence upon foreign sources for many items, but it indicates how dependent were the economies of other nations upon the health of American manufacturing. In 1929, the United States received about one-eighth of the world's total imports. Only Great Britain, a nation lacking many important raw materials, accounted for a larger proportion of total imports.

The pattern of American exports since the Civil War had been characterized by a steady growth in the proportion of manufactured goods to the total. This trend continued throughout the 1920's and accelerated after the postwar depression. From 1911 to 1915, manufactures each year had averaged 30 per cent of American exports; the proportion increased to 36 per cent for the period from 1921 to 1925 and to 45 per cent from 1926 to 1930. When one compares average export figures for the first half of the 1920's with the second half of the decade, one sees that every farm product dropped in dollar volume and that practically every industrial product increased. Oil shipments increased from $405 million to $524 million, machinery from $320 million to $493 million, and autos and auto parts from $177 million to $405 million. In sum, foreign trade increased during the 1920's, and manufacturing took an increasingly important share of both imports and exports.

More than half of the dollar gap was covered by loans and much of the balance by direct foreign investments. From 1925 through 1929, American investors bought foreign bonds totalling about $5.1 billion. The war had accustomed Americans of moderate income to buying bonds, and an estimated one-eighth of the population had an interest in foreign securities of some kind. Banks scoured the world searching for likely borrowers, sometimes resorted to questionable methods to persuade foreigners to take a loan, and then dispatched thousands of bond salesmen to beat the American bushes for bond buyers. One village in southern Germany, bankers discovered, needed to borrow about $125,000; the village burghers were persuaded to borrow $3 million through bonds sold in America. Competition among banks for the privilege of handling bond issues was intense. When Budapest decided to borrow, thirty-six banks, most of them American, competed for the commission; fourteen banks competed for the flotation of a Belgrade bond issue. All too often investment houses floating the bonds were more interested in their underwriting profits than in the wisdom of the loan, either from the point of view of the borrower or the lender. Since many of the loans were risky, interest rates were frequently high, and foolish American investors, attracted by the interest rate, bought bonds unlikely ever to be paid in full. When the whole flimsy international trade structure collapsed in 1929, millions of dollars worth of bonds were defaulted, and broke but wiser American investors muttered about their valueless "Brazilian 6½'s" or their "Peruvian 7's."

The biggest borrowers, in descending order of the total of their loans, were Germany, Canada, Italy, Australia, Chile, Argentina, Brazil, Colombia, Japan, and Poland. Some of these loans, especially those in Canada, went for projects that increased productive capacity; others went for monumental public works that had the effect of bolstering the political regime. Frequently, the regime aided by the loan was utterly undemocratic, such being the case in Mussolini's Italy and several of the Latin American nations. That democratic forces in these countries were disillusioned with America as a democratic force was not surprising.

Direct foreign investments in the 1920's were not as great as loans, but they were more lasting and had greater permanent influence both upon foreign nations and upon United States foreign policy. In 1919, new foreign direct investments amounted to $94 million. Big profits and undistributed corporate earnings during the 1920's—the latter averaged about $2.5 billion a year—enabled industrial corporations to increase their investments abroad independent of bankers. Their investments increased, particularly in the latter part of the decade, until in 1929 new foreign direct investments amounted to $602 million. During the decade, American corporations invested about $3 billion abroad. In general, it was the very big corporations that made most of the foreign investments.

Canada took much of the American corporate expansion in the 1920's. The corporations' motive here was largely to get inside the British imperial preference system. By building factories across the river from Detroit, Ford and General Motors were far better able to compete with British products in Great Britain and throughout the empire. Each company also began production on the European continent itself and vastly increased its sales and service organization there. Separating their domestic production from their foreign market, besides reducing costs by moving nearer to the market and taking advantage of generally lower wage scales, also enabled Ford and GM to tailor their product to the desires of the foreign market.

Oil companies, particularly Standard Oil of New Jersey, made the most dramatic foreign expansions of the decade. Oil companies in the 1920's usually bought into already existing foreign corporations. Thus during the Wilson and Harding administrations American oil corporations got into the Turkish oil field by buying stock in the Turkish Petroleum Company. An Anglo-Dutch petroleum corporation, Royal Dutch Shell, began operations in the United States just before the war. In the late 1920's, this firm and Standard of New Jersey together with another British oil company, formed a cartel that carved out world markets and quotas.

Indeed, cartel arrangements with European companies became not uncommon and enabled large corporations to extend their "new competition" to the world scene. Two sulphur companies, Texas Gulf Sulphur Company and Freeport Sulphur Company, between them controlled practically all American production and sulphur deposits. In 1922, they formed together the Sulphur Export Corporation (not a violation of the antitrust laws after the passage of the Webb-Pomerene Act of 1918) and made a cartel agreement with an Italian firm that controlled most of the supply of the rest of the world. DuPont, through complicated arrangements on patents and sales agencies, had a link with the huge German chemical cartel I. G. Farben.

In nations where American corporate investments were large, it was natural for people to form their idea of what the United States was and what it stood for by observation of the corporations near them. Venezuelans and Mexicans who worked for American oil companies in their countries easily transferred their antagonism for the boss to the United States generally and learned to hate "Yanqui imperialism." Liberians who sweated on the Firestone Tire and Rubber plantations were not blind to the fact that the profits went to Americans rather than Liberians. In general, it is accurate to say that the United States set the main outlines of its economic policy toward underdeveloped nations in the 1920's, and the policies were such that would naturally, perhaps inevitably, make popular political movements in these countries suspicious of America.

War Debts and Reparations

During the war the United States government lent the Allies a total of about $7.08 billion. Soon after the war the government lent another $2.53 billion for reconstruction. A considerable part of the postwar loans went to new countries created after the war. Most of the money had come originally from purchases of government bonds by Americans, and the debtor European governments had spent about 90 per cent of the money for food and war supplies in the United States. Total governmental indebtedness to the United States amounted to $10,350,479,074. Most of the loans had been at 5 per cent interest, the terms of repayment to be worked out after the war with interest to be paid meanwhile. Great Britain ($4.3 billion), France ($3,404,818,945), and Italy ($1,648,034,050) were the biggest borrowers. In addition to these loans from the United States, the Allies had lent one another considerable sums. The whole picture of intergovernmental debt was enormously complicated and further confused by the Soviet Union's repudiation of the debts incurred by previous Russian governments. The United States government had incurred no debts to another power during the war and reconstruction years.

Soon after the war ended, the debtor nations started a campaign to have the war debt cancelled or at least scaled down. They argued that for America to cancel the loans would only make her war contribution more nearly equal to their own, for they had fought longer and lost far more men and property. They also pointed out that most of the money borrowed had been spent in the United States. Further, the Europeans reasoned, how could the debts be paid even if they agreed they should be paid? Payments in gold were impossible for most of the powers. The United States owned much of the world's gold already, and what Europe had was necessary to stabilize its currencies. To pay in goods was difficult because of American protective tariffs. For that matter, American industrialists did not want payment in goods they themselves produced. At the peace conference the British suggested unofficially that all war intergovernmental debts be cancelled or, if that idea were not acceptable, that payment of the Allied debts be tied to collection of reparations from Germany. Wilson refused to consider either idea. His successors down until World War II followed Wilson's policy in the matter. Coolidge summed up the United States view with his typical Vermont spare language: "They hired the money, didn't they?" More articulate Americans pointed out that the Allies had received territory either directly or in mandates from the peace treaty as well as German reparations and that the United States received neither.

Late in 1921, Harding asked Congress for authority to make a settlement of the principal and interest not yet paid, and in February, 1922, Congress created the World War Foreign Debt Commission, authorized to fund the debt and extend the time of payment. Soon the Debt Commission, of which the Secretary of the Treasury was chairman, received delegations from debtor powers and began negotiations. In every debt settlement, the Debt Commission agreed to terms more liberal than those provided by the enabling act, but in each case Congress ratified the settlement. The settlements consisted of extending the time period and reducing the interest rate. At 5 per cent, interest payment of the debts was manifestly impossible; capital at 5 per cent interest compounded annually doubles itself in fifteen years.

Great Britain in June, 1923, was the first to arrange a debt settlement. The old arrangement had been 5 per cent payable over twenty-five years. The new settlement extended the period to semiannual payments over sixty-two years and reduced the interest to 3 per cent for the first ten years and 3.5 per cent for the last fifty-two years. This amounted to about a 30 per cent cancellation of the debt as it stood before funding. The French, who remembered that the United States had never completely paid off the French debt incurred during the American Revolution, were tougher in negotiations. In a 1926 funding settlement, which the Chamber of Deputies did not ratify until 1929, the French interest rate was cut to 1.6 per cent. "Ability to pay" was the principle followed in reducing the interest, and under this principle Mussolini's Italy got the best bargain. Italy's interest was reduced to 0.4 per cent which meant a reduction of 80.2 per cent of the entire debt. The various funding agreements cut the aggregate debt due the United States slightly more than 50 per cent. At the same time the Debt Commission was funding the debt to America, the European powers made funding settlements with one another for the inter-Allied indebtedness.

At no time did the United States agree that the war debt question was in any way connected with German reparations, although as a matter of practical fact rather than legal theory the two matters were thoroughly related. It will be recalled from Chapter 9 that the Reparations Commission set up by the Allies at the peace conference presented Germany on May 1, 1921, with a reparation bill of $33 billion. The payment scheme called for Germany to pay the Allies at the rate of $375 million each year from 1921 to 1925 and at least $900 million a year thereafter. Any interest charge not paid on the bonds Germany had to give the Allies would be added proportionately to the capital indebtedness. The Reparations Commission was to collect by supervision of Germany's foreign trade and controls over her internal economy. Any willful default of reparations was to be punished by military occupation of German territory, a provision of the peace treaty.

In 1922, Germany was unable to pay the next reparations payment and French troops, over the objections of the British, occupied the Ruhr—Germany's coal, steel, and general heavy industry region. Germany's economic condition was desperate. Her currency became wildly inflationary, so much so that German workers demanded they be paid at the end of each hour so that they could pass their wages out the window to their wives who rushed to stores before prices went up again. Nor did France profit from the occupation. The German workers offered passive resistance and production fell sharply. The cost of occupation made French government expenditures exceed revenues which caused a degree of French inflation. The State Department was alarmed at the situation which promised only to get worse. Hughes persuaded the French to agree to work out a new reparations system more nearly consistent with Germany's ability to pay.

The United States officially had nothing to do with the Reparations Commission, but three American citizens, Charles G. Dawes and Henry M. Robinson, both bankers, and Owen D. Young, joined a Commission committee. In April, 1924, the committee presented the Dawes Plan which was ratified in August. Under this scheme Germany was to pay reparations the following year of $250 million and in increasing amounts thereafter as the German economy was able to stand it. American and Allied bankers were to lend Germany $200 million in gold to be used to hasten industrial recovery and to back a new currency issue. As Germany's payments became larger and she saw she had no visible end of reparations, she asked for a further reduction in reparations. Again American citizens, officially without government connection, worked out a plan. The Young Plan, adopted December 22, 1928, reduced the German obligation to $153 million a year until 1988, there also to be additional "conditional payments" depending upon the strength of the German economy. The Allies agreed to leave all German territory and to relinquish controls over the German economy.

The Dawes and Young plans worked well enough in one sense; Germany paid reparations to the Allies. But, on the other hand, the plans started a crazy circular financial motion. The Dawes Plan, by stabilizing German currency, made German bonds attractive to American investors. Between 1924 and 1930, American private investors bought German bonds of the German central government, municipalities, and corporations totalling about $2.5 billion. With these outside loans Germany was able to pay approximately $2 billion in reparations to the Allies. With help from reparations, the Allies were able to pay approximately $2.6 billion on their war debts to America. Thus the money, after unknown numbers of exchanges, interest payments, broker's commissions, and underwriting fees, went from America to Germany to France, Britain, or Italy and then back to America again. European need for American money kept the circle going. The State Department frowned upon private investments to nations in default on their war debts thereby levering them into keeping up their payments. Europeans began to refer to Uncle Sam as Uncle Shylock.

Based ultimately upon American private investment, the whole reparations and war debt system was dependent upon the continuation of American prosperity. When American prosperity came to an abrupt end, the whole structure collapsed.

Japan and the Open Door in Northeast Asia

Japan's desire to control Asia, at least northeastern Asia, ran head on against the American Open Door policy, and the United States was by no means willing to abandon the Open Door, the basis of her foreign policy everywhere. Japan had strengthened her position and expanded her influence and control considerably between the outbreak of war in Europe and the early 1920's, but she had continually run into an American stumbling block. Situations which would lead to war between Japan and the United States two decades later were already beginning to take shape; on both sides as early as 1920 there was talk that war might come to pass.

Japan had become angry with Wilson at the peace conference when he opposed inclusion in the League covenant of an explicit statement of racial equality. Wilson had compromised his stated principles and yielded on the question of a Japanese mandate of Shantung, but the Japanese, in view of their secret treaty on Shantung, did not regard the mandate solution as a total victory. In 1917, Wilson had revived the idea of an international bankers' consortium to keep an eye on the Japanese in China and to keep America's foot in the open door. The Japanese agreed to the consortium only after reserving themselves special commercial privileges in Mongolia and Manchuria, and the final signing of the consortium agreement came in October, 1920.

A large part of the reason for America's participation in the armed intervention into Soviet Siberia in 1918 had been to block the possibility of Japan's taking complete advantage of the power vacuum created in northeastern Asia by the Russian Revolution. A point of conflict in that part of the world was control of the Chinese Eastern Railway which ran across Manchuria toward Vladivostok and had been controlled by Russia until the revolution. Japan coveted the railroad for herself, but the Allied command of the Siberian expedition successfully put it under the control of an Inter-Allied Railway Commission. When the United States and the other western powers evacuated Siberia in the spring of 1920, the Japanese occupation force remained. The Railway Commission continued to control the Chinese Eastern, but the Japanese had the only foreign troops in the vicinity.

In March, 1920, the Japanese also extended their occupation to the rest of Sakhalin, the northernmost island in the Japanese chain just off the Siberian coast. Japan had received the southern half of Sakhalin at the end of the Russo-Japanese war in 1905; Russia retained the northern half. When Bolshevik troops massacred a Japanese garrison in Siberia, the Japanese retaliated by rushing north across the Russian-Japanese border on Sakhalin to hold it, they said, as security until the Russians agreed to a satisfactory restitution for the massacre. They did not leave until 1925, and then only after wresting concessions from Russia for coal and oil rights in northern Sakhalin as well as fishing rights in Siberia.

One other territorial matter disturbed Japanese-American relations: control of a tiny island in the western Pacific with the unlikely name of Yap. This little dot on the map was of potential use as a cable station. Wilson had argued unsuccessfully at Paris that Yap be made international territory. Instead it had become one of the Japanese mandates. Through late 1919 and 1920, the United States had pressed Japan for rights to establish cable operations there, but the Japanese were adamant.

Perhaps the most potentially explosive matter between Japan and America was naval armament, a question made more complicated by the existence of the Anglo-Japanese Alliance of 1902. In 1916, the American government had made plans for building a huge navy as part of the preparedness program. During the war, paradoxically, the plan had been laid aside. The 1916 idea had been to construct a huge, balanced fleet with battleships and other capital ships as the central core. The war had forced the navy to concentrate upon immediately needed destroyers and other smaller craft. With the end of the war, the navy wanted to resume its earlier program and even expand it. The British were not likely to sit back and let the United States build a navy superior to hers, and the Japanese expanded their naval construction. Admirals and other United States big-navy advocates, however, faced strong political opposition to a great naval expansion. Congress in 1919 and 1920 had cut back the navy's plans considerably. In May, 1921, the Senate overwhelmingly passed a Borah resolution that requested the administration to negotiate with Japan and Great Britain on naval disarmament, and the House concurred the following month. If a full-scale naval armament race actually got under way, reasoned the State Department, the United States might well lose the race because of domestic opposition.

Even if no naval race developed, there was the possibility that two of the three naval powers in the Pacific—Japan, Britain, and the United States—might combine to harm the third. The alliance between Japan and Britain provided that if either power became involved in a war brought on by "an unprovoked or aggressive act" anywhere the other should help its partner. When the alliance was renewed in 1911, the British insisted upon including a clause that exempted operation of the alliance in the case of a war with a nation with which either Japan or Britain had a general arbitration treaty. This was the cue for the United States to remove herself from the possibility of war against combined British and Japanese power. President Taft negotiated an arbitration treaty with Great Britain, but the Senate involved the treaty with other matters and did not ratify it. When Japanese-American relations deteriorated, Canada became excited over the possibility that her imperial connection with Britain and the Anglo-Japanese alliance might involve her in a war with her southern neighbor. Britain did not want to be forced into a war with the United States because of her alliance with Japan any more than did Canada. It was high time, thought the British, for clearing the air on the whole matter of naval armament and Pacific questions. It seemed the same to Secretary of State Hughes.

A New Complex of Treaty Arrangements

On July 5, 1921, the British Foreign Office suggested to the American ambassador, George Harvey of "smoke-filled room" fame, that Harding invite the major powers to a disarmament conference. Harvey cabled the suggestion to Washington on July 8. Earlier that same day, Hughes had cabled Harvey with instructions to ascertain if the British would agree to meet at a disarmament conference. Upon receipt of Harvey's cable, Hughes released a statement to the press and issued informal invitations to the other major powers to meet in Washington to discuss not only naval disarmament but general problems of the Far East and the Pacific. Japan qualified and delayed her reply, but Hughes announced that all invited powers had accepted. From the Washington Conference were to come three major treaties—the Five Power Naval Treaty, the Four Power Treaty, and the Nine Power Treaty—as well as a series of small agreements.

The Conference met for its first plenary session on November 12, 1921, in Washington's large Memorial Continental Hall. Quite in contrast to the secrecy and formality of the Paris Conference, the press and hundreds of others who were not delegates, including many Congressmen, were invited to the Washington meeting. The American delegates, led by Hughes, were Senator Lodge, Democratic Senate minority leader Oscar Underwood, and Elihu Root. Harding opened the meeting with the kind of inane welcoming address of which he was a master and yielded the floor to Hughes. The audience prepared for the usual ceremonial opening speech of felicitously phrased banalities.

But Hughes flouted diplomatic convention and came straight to the point. He proposed a ten-year holiday on the construction of new capital ships and the scrapping of some already built or under construction so that the number of capital ships of the three largest naval powers, Britain, the United States, and Japan, would be maintained at the existing ratio of 5–5–3 respectively. Then he declared that the United States was prepared to scrap thirty capital ships with a total tonnage of over eight hundred thousand. He went on to describe just what Japan and Britain should turn to scrap. As an English newspaperman put it, Hughes destroyed more of the British fleet in a few minutes than the armadas of the world had been able to in centuries. Under the plan Britain would discard capital ships totalling about 583,000 tons and Japan about 449,000 tons. The delegates were thunderstruck by the audacity of the proposal, particularly one made so early in the negotiations.

In mid-December, the British, American, and Japanese delegates announced essential agreement. But then the French became difficult when Hughes tried to get them and the Italians to agree to accept their existing 175,000 tons apiece as their maximum. The French, under the illusion they were still a national power of the first magnitude, had already shown they were touchy when they objected to where their delegates were seated at the conference table, and Hughes had not improved matters when he made an aside about France's ability to pay her debts. The French delegates insisted upon a maximum capital ship tonnage of three hundred thousand. The British leaked this demand to the press, and the reaction of the world was strongly against the French. Hughes then appealed over the heads of the French delegates directly to Premier Aristide Briand, who had gone back to Paris after the conference opening, and was able to persuade him to accept the 175,000 ton maximum.

The Five Power Naval Treaty, signed in February, 1922, provided for a roughly 5-5-3-1.7-1.7 ratio of capital ships: for Britain and the United States, a maximum of 525,000 tons; for Japan, a maximum of 315,000; for France and Italy, a maximum of 175,000. In addition, Britain and America could have up to 135,000 tons of aircraft carrier, Japan 81,000 tons, and France and Italy 60,000 tons each. The signatory nations agreed to stop capital ship construction for ten years and, importantly, to maintain the *status quo* on naval bases and fortifications of Pacific islands except for Hawaii and those immediately off the powers' coasts. The treaty limited the size of smaller naval vessels but imposed no restrictions about their number.

Senator Lodge proposed at a plenary session in December, 1921, that Japan, Great Britain, France, and the United States agree to a treaty under which the signatory nations would respect one another's possessions in the Pacific and confer if any disputes among them or with an outside power threatened to break the peace. Lodge, who just two years before had led the fight against the League as an "entangling alliance," surprised the public with his proposal. The resulting Four Power Treaty, signed in February, 1922, also abrogated the Anglo-Japanese alliance effective upon ratification by all powers. The Senate ratified the treaty the following month after making the reservation that the treaty imposed no American obligation to commit armed forces.

The Washington Conference's Nine Power Treaty, also signed in February, 1922, was an international recognition of the Open Door in China. The United States, Britain, Japan, France, Italy, China, Belgium, Holland, and Portugal pledged themselves to respect the "sovereignty, the independence, and the territorial and administrative integrity of China" and to "refrain from taking advantage of conditions in China in order to seek special rights or privileges which would abridge the rights of subjects or citizens of friendly states, and from countenancing action inimical to the security of those states." The Nine Power Treaty did not commit its signatories to action in case of violations.

Two days before the nine powers signed their treaty, China and Japan signed a treaty that Hughes had been strongly urging upon them. Japan agreed to return the Shantung peninsula to China, but China agreed to honor the many private contracts that Japanese businessmen had already made in Shantung and to buy from Japan the railroad the Germans originally had built. Japan also announced that she would withdraw her troops from Siberia and did so in October. Finally, the Japanese allowed the United States to build a cable station on Yap and agreed to abrogate the Lansing-Ishii agreement of 1917, supplanted by the new Nine Power Treaty.

What can one say of the Washington Conference treaties? During World War II many considered the naval limitation idea a mistake, but this judgment was a reflection of war passion. True, the United States sacrificed potential naval supremacy in the Pacific. If Japan and the United States had engaged in a naval armaments race, surely America could have built the more powerful navy because her wallet was thicker. But it is dubious that the United States actually would have built a superior fleet. She did not in fact even keep her fleet up to the limits imposed at the Washington Conference. If Japan gained a little in actual naval strength under the agreement as it was observed, she backed at least part of the way out of Shantung and recognized the Open Door principle more strongly. Of course, the Washington treaties did not get at the root of the difficulty in the Far East: commercial rivalries and the conflict of the American Open Door empire and the British formal and informal empire on the one hand, with Japanese colonial empire ambitions on the other. And they did not prevent war in the long run. But, given the basic policies of the Pacific powers concerned, they clarified the situation, saved a great deal of money by limiting naval armament, and preserved peace for a decade.

In 1927, President Coolidge rather hastily decided to call another international conference to limit naval armament. The Five Power Naval Treaty had not prevented unlimited building of cruisers and other ships smaller than battleships and aircraft carriers, and the three greatest naval powers had begun to build heavy cruisers. The French replied that they preferred to work for naval disarmament within the League of Nations and declined to attend the conference which began at Geneva in June. Italy also declined to participate. Planning for the conference had been inadequate, and Britain, America, and Japan could not agree. The conference broke up in early August with no accomplishments. Two years later, it was revealed that armament and steel manufacturers had retained a lobbyist named William B. Shearer to try to sabotage the conference. The sensational revelation prompted a congressional investigation, but it was not at all clear that Shearer's activities were what had caused the conference to fail.

In 1929, the new prime minister of Great Britain, Ramsay MacDonald, visited Hoover in Washington and at the President's fishing camp at Rapidan, Virginia, and the two agreed to call another naval conference to meet in London the following year. The London Conference extended the ban on capital ship construction for another five years (to the end of 1936) and continued limitations to smaller vessels. Japan objected to the old 5–5–3 ratio for smaller ships but agreed to a compromise that kept the old ratio for heavy cruisers, increased the ratio for light cruisers and destroyers to 5–5–3.5, and granted Japan equality on submarines. France and Italy would not ratify the London Treaty.

Such negotiations and agreements as the naval disarmament treaties suggest that even in international political affairs, the United States did not pursue an isolationist foreign policy during the 1920's. America only drew back from entering any international agreement or organization that might in any way obligate her to use her armed power in a dispute in which she had no immediate interest. The decision of 1919 not to join the League of Nations was never rescinded; the United States never officially joined the organization. Yet America had a great deal to do with the League. In 1922, Hughes sent "unofficial observers" to meetings of special League commissions and agencies, and at these meetings the American participants spoke and argued but could not vote. Two years later, the administration named official delegates to the League's Second Opium Conference. By 1931, the United States had five permanent delegates to League agencies at Geneva and had participated officially in more than forty conferences. American opponents of the League had some justification for their charge that the United States had taken the back door to Geneva; certainly, American policy was not isolationist by any reasonable definition of the term.

In 1927, the State Department led in an international effort—pathetically futile as it turned out a few years later—to "outlaw" international war. In early April, 1927, Aristide Briand, after earlier conversations with Professor James T. Shotwell of Columbia University and the Carnegie Endowment for International Peace, announced that his nation was prepared to agree with America never to war with the other. Secretary of State Frank B. Kellogg, who succeeded Hughes in March, 1925, was at first cool to the idea but yielded to popular pressure. Kellogg extended the proposal to suggest that such an agreement between France and America be made to include other nations. Subsequently, France and the United States drew up a document which declared that "they condemn recourse to war for the solution of international controversies, and renounce it as an instrument of national policy in their relations with one another" and invited fourteen other nations to sign the document with them jointly. The other nations were Belgium, Czechoslovakia, Germany, Italy, Japan, Poland, and Great Britain and her self-governing dominions. These nations agreed and signed the Pact of Paris (usually known by its unofficial name, the Kellogg-Briand Pact) on August 27, 1928. Later the Soviet Union and several other nations signed the pact. The public record of the negotiations made clear that the pact imposed no ban upon a war of self-defense, although, since almost every nation in the world ultimately signed, self-defense would in theory be unnecessary.

After the Pact of Paris, Kellogg went on to make bilateral arbitration treaties with eighteen nations which provided that certain kinds of disagreements between the signatory powers would be submitted to the Permanent Court of Arbitration at The Hague, usually called The Hague Court. The treaties provided that arbitration might be undertaken by any other "competent tribunal." This phrase was a reference to the Permanent Court of International Justice, usually called the World Court and with no connection to The Hague Court. The World Court had been established as a fully independent agency of the League of Nations.

In 1924, public opinion for American participation in the World Court was strong enough that both major parties supported the Court in their platforms. Early in 1925, the House by an overwhelming vote passed a resolution favoring United States adherence to the World Court. Debate in the Senate was extensive, and the upper chamber modified the resolution to include five reservations. The modified resolution passed the Senate in early 1926. At the time the Kellogg arbitration treaties were drawn, it was assumed that the United States would soon be a participating member of the World Court. A committee of the League appointed an international committee of jurists, of whom one was Elihu Root, to revise the World Court protocol so as to meet the American reservations. In 1930 and again in 1935, the revised protocol, already agreed upon by the President and the Department of State, failed to get the necessary two-thirds vote of ratification in the Senate. Thus, the United States never joined the World Court.

Slowly Learning to Behave in Latin America

During the 1920's, the United States improved her relations with the Latin American nations. When Hoover left office early in 1933 the situation was considerably better than it had been when Wilson left the White House in early 1921. Two factors seem to have operated in the gradual growth of better United States manners in Latin America. Public opinion at home turned increasingly against armed intervention south of the border, which by the time the United States entered the war had become a matter of ordinary routine. The newspaper sentence, "The marines have landed and the situation is well in hand," had become a cliché. Part of the reason for the gradual shift in public opinion was that only by the wildest flight of imagination could anyone see a threat to the nation's security in events to the south. The other factor was that businessmen, who greatly increased their investments in Latin America during the prosperity decade, began to learn that over the long run a policy of cordiality with firmness on economic matters was financially wiser than bulling one's way through with reliance upon armed force. One might gain in the short run by resort to force, but the reservoir of ill will that resulted, businessmen learned, would in the long run harm their economic influence. Armed intervention came to be a last resort.

Relations with Mexico and Nicaragua proved the most trying Latin American problems in the postwar decade. Petroleum's pungent odor permeated United States diplomacy in Mexico. During the 1920's, before the Venezuelan and Middle Eastern oil fields were in full production, Mexico was second only to the United States in world oil production, and American and British corporations accounted for roughly two-fifths of Mexican oil output. To protect United States oil investments was the primary objective of the State Department's Mexican policy. As Hughes said in a 1924 public statement, the "fundamental question" was "the safeguarding of American property rights . . . against confiscation."

During the war, President Carranza decreed that Article 27 of the Mexican constitution of 1917 would be put into effect. This article provided that all subsoil rights to land owned or leased by foreigners belonged to the Mexican nation, even holdings acquired before promulgation of the new constitution. Article 27 actually was a return to historic Mexican practice. In Spanish nations it was the common rule that subsoil resources were the property of the nation rather than of the owner of the lands, and Mexico had followed this general rule until the late nineteenth century. Foreign oil corporations would have to seek new concessions from the government, which was likely to be tougher in dealing with foreign interests than had been the prerevolutionary Diaz regime. The State Department and the British Foreign Office protested strongly enough to get Carranza to postpone enactment of the retroactive feature of the article.

In the spring of 1920, a revolutionary movement headed by General Álvaro Obregón overthrew Carranza. Obregón was actually more friendly to foreign oil interests than Carranza, but when he did not immediately agree to keep the *status quo* on foreign oil investments the Wilson administration refused to recognize his regime. This was the situation Hughes inherited in 1921. Two years later, Hughes began negotiations with the Obregón government which ended with the signing in September, 1923, of two claims conventions. In these agreements Obregón conceded that subsoil rights to property held by American firms before 1917 would remain in American control and that American owners of land expropriated under another provision of the 1917 constitution should be granted fair compensation. The numerous monetary claims of American citizens against the Mexican government and vice versa would be settled by special claims commissions. In return the United States diplomatically recognized Mexico again and thereby facilitated private American loans. Soon thereafter, when the Obregón regime was threatened by a revolt led by General Adolfo de la Huerta (not to be confused with Victoriano Huerta with whom Wilson had had difficulty early in his first term), Hughes consented to sell a limited amount of arms to Obregón and deny them to de la Huerta. The Mexican government put down the revolt, and when the new Mexican president-elect, Plutarco Calles, visited Washington in October, 1924, all seemed rosily optimistic for Mexican-American relations and the interests of United States oil companies.

Secretary of State Kellogg and James Sheffield, the new ambassador to Mexico, quickly created trouble again. Sheffield, who was close to the biggest American oil interests in Mexico, reported that the Calles government was not respecting American property rights. Kellogg issued an incredible public statement that implied that if the Calles government did not do the State Department's bidding on oil matters the United States would support any revolution against the Mexican government that might develop. Calles, perhaps figuring that working with Washington was impossible, yielded to Mexican popular opinion in December, 1925, and got laws through the legislature that for all practical purposes rescinded subsoil rights to land held before 1917. The laws were to go into effect January 1, 1927. Throughout 1926, the Mexican government negotiated with American oil companies, regaining oil and mineral rights for the Mexican nation and granting fifty-year leases. Nearly all the American companies but the Mellon-Sinclair-Doheny group complied, but this group remonstrated strongly with the State Department. Kellogg asserted that Mexico was supporting rebels in Nicaragua, where the United States was simultaneously embroiled, and in January, 1927, he charged that the Calles government was Bolshevik-controlled and working with Russian agents to endanger the Panama Canal. The situation was further irritated by the heated opposition of American Roman Catholics to the anticlericalism of the Calles government. Some people even expected war. But in late January the Senate indicated what it thought of Kellogg's charges when it, without a dissent, passed a resolution calling for arbitration of the whole Mexican oil problem.

Sheffield resigned in June, and Coolidge replaced him with Dwight Morrow, a House of Morgan partner who had unusual skills of persuasion and diplomacy. Within a few months Morrow was able to arrange a way in which subsoil rights on pre-1917 holdings would stay in private foreign hands and Calles could appear not to reverse himself. Morrow also brought about a truce in the battle between church and state and thereby quieted anti-Mexican feelings in the American Catholic community. Apparently no small part of Morrow's success was due to his arranging for Charles Lindbergh to make a goodwill flight to Mexico City in December, 1927. The young flier, soon to become Morrow's son-in-law, had become a world hero the previous May when he became the first man to fly solo and nonstop across the Atlantic.

Resolution of the difficulties in Nicaragua was somewhat cruder. Both concern for the Nicaraguan canal possibilities and American investments were behind United States interests in that Central American hotbed of palace revolutions. Marines had been stationed there since the Taft administration. An American collector of customs had stabilized Nicaraguan finances, and in 1923, Hughes promised that if the Nicaraguans conducted an honest election the next year, the marines would be withdrawn. The election was held under a law written by a United States citizen, the Liberal party under Carlos Solórzano was formed, and the marines departed in August, 1925. Soon after their departure, another palace revolution forced Solórzano to resign and Vice-President Juan Sacasa to leave the country. But the State Department refused to recognize the new government led by a Conservative party leader, Emiliano Chamorro. Such was the state of Nicaraguan politics that the Nicaraguan Congress deposed Chamorro and elected another Conservative, Adolfo Díaz, an old friend of American interests, and the State Department promptly recognized the Díaz government.

At this stage of the matter, former Vice-President Sacasa returned, claimed to be president, set up his own government, and began warfare with the Díaz regime. The United States responded by sending in five thousand marines, more than had been there before they left the previous year. Sending the marines back was highly unpopular with most of the American population. In the spring of 1927, Coolidge sent Henry L. Stimson, who had been Secretary of War under Taft, to Nicaragua in an effort to resolve the conflict between the Conservatives and the Liberals, who did not capitulate when the marines arrived. Stimson brought an end to most of the fighting when he persuaded Díaz to accept Liberals in his cabinet and guaranteed fair elections in 1928. The American military forces supervised the election and prevented "repeaters" by requiring every voter to dip his fingers in a red dye upon leaving the polls. The Liberal candidate won. The marines were employed for several months trying to capture a Liberal rebel group led by Augusto Sandino who refused Stimson's terms, but they were gradually withdrawn after 1931.

Elsewhere in Latin America the United States behaved not quite so imperiously as it had before the war, and late in the decade it even repudiated the Roosevelt corollary to the Monroe Doctrine. The last American marines withdrew from the Dominican Republic in 1924, although American control of Dominican finances continued until 1940 and marines remained in Haiti on the other half of Santo Domingo. At a Pan-American Conference in 1923, Hughes supported a proposal for peaceful settlement of disputes among American republics but refused to budge from the traditional United States position that only it could invoke the Monroe Doctrine. But he also said in a speech before the American Bar Association in 1923 that the Monroe Doctrine as he understood it "does not infringe upon the independence and sovereignty of other American states." "Misconception upon this point is the only disturbing factor in our relations with Latin American States." However exaggerated this second statement was, the speech was nevertheless at least a step backward from the Monroe Doctrine as interpreted by Theodore Roosevelt.

At the next Pan-American Conference at Havana in 1928, Hughes again led the United States delegation although he had left the cabinet three years earlier. Representatives of Caribbean and Central American republics pressed strongly for a commitment from the United States that it would not intervene in the affairs of other American nations. Hughes refused even to allow the topic to come into official conference discussions, and with the help of South American nations below the equator smothered discussion. At the same time, Coolidge requested J. Reuben Clark of the State Department to define precisely what the Monroe Doctrine was. Clark's memorandum, not published until 1930, clearly repudiated the Roosevelt corollary.

Just how much difference Hughes's and Clark's interpretations of the Monroe Doctrine actually made would have to be determined by later administrations. It was now official State Department policy that the Monroe Doctrine could not be used to justify intervention into Latin American affairs, but at the same time both Hughes and Clark made clear that intervention could be justified on other grounds, notably self-preservation and defense of the Panama Canal. As shallow a concession as this was, however, it made easier the adoption in the 1930's of what another Roosevelt called the "Good Neighbor policy."

Administration of the Colonial Empire

Thus far in this chapter we have considered America's Open Door empire and its relations with European nations. The country still retained, however, residues of old-fashioned colonial empire in Puerto Rico and the Philippines.

Harding made a disastrous appointment in 1921 when he named a political hanger-on, E. Mont Reily, as governor of Puerto Rico. Reily governed Puerto Rico as if it were a politically corrupted city and he were its political boss and mayor. He fired many Puerto Rican native officials, including judges, and appointed his friends to their offices. Then he raised their salaries. Protests from Puerto Ricans became so numerous that Congress threatened an investigation, whereupon Reily resigned in early 1923. Harding replaced him with Horace Towner, who restored Puerto Ricans to local offices and gained the confidence and respect of Puerto Rican leaders.

Nevertheless, the Puerto Ricans wanted a greater degree of self-government. With Towner's approval they sent a delegation to the nation's capital in 1924 to request the right of the island to elect its own governor with power to appoint local officials. Neither Congress nor Coolidge looked favorably upon the Puerto Rican proposal and neither acted. Coolidge even asserted to the delegation that they had more control over their internal affairs than did any state in the Union, perhaps forgetting that he had been selected as governor of Massachusetts by the vote of its people rather than by presidential appointment. Again in 1928, Puerto Rico petitioned Washington for greater autonomy. Again the islanders were unsuccessful. Coolidge took the position this time that Puerto Rico was better off under Washington's administration than it would be if it were self-governing, a "this is for your own good" attitude often used by parents when dealing with children. To Coolidge's credit is the fact that when a hurricane devastated Puerto Rico in 1928, he was influential in extending government aid.

Harding appointed General Leonard Wood in 1921 to succeed Francis B. Harrison as governor-general of the Philippines. Harrison had granted Filipinos a considerable degree of control over their own affairs, but the swashbuckling Wood put a quick end to the practice. When asked by Harding to report upon the Philippines' readiness for independence, Wood replied not only that the Filipinos were incapable of self-governing independence but that his own powers should be strengthened. Wood used his veto powers so extensively that in 1923 the Filipino legislature passed a resolution asking Coolidge to recall him. Coolidge supported Wood, and for the rest of his term of office —he died in late 1927—he and the legislature were at loggerheads. Coolidge named Stimson to the post early in 1928. Stimson dropped Wood's autocratic policies, but he did not go as far in granting Filipino administration as had Harrison. The issue of Philippine independence would not die, either at home or in the islands, and matters were to come to a head early in the depression.

CHAPTER THIRTEEN

The Business Civilization and Its Critics

BETWEEN WORLD WAR I AND THE DEPRESSION, A WIDE GULF SEPARATED the values of the nation's intellectuals and artists from the rest of the population. Before the war, novelists, for example, had written on political and social themes that both reflected and stimulated a general concern for such matters among less articulate people. Painters, like social workers and progressive politicians, discovered poverty and made it central to their work. But after the war popular tastes and values went one direction while most intellectuals went another. People of an artistic or literary bent frequently referred to more conventional people as "philistines." H. L. Mencken, a Baltimore newspaperman and magazine editor who was extremely popular in the 1920's among young people with intellectual aspirations, called the ordinary, unintellectual, popular mass the "booboisie." The philistines and the booboisie retaliated with condemnations of "long-haired men and short-haired women."

Practically everyone on both sides of the cultural fence agreed that those with conventional values, ideals, and ideas—the philistines—both reflected the dominance of businessmen in American society and set the nation's cultural tone. So, too, did foreign observers, many of whom were fascinated but repelled by American society and wrote books about the country. André Siegfried, a French author (*America Comes of Age*, 1927), Arthur Feiler (*America Seen Through German Eyes*, 1928), and an iconoclastic London philosopher, C. E. M. Joad (*The Babbitt Warren*, 1927), were probably the three best-known foreign authors who wrote about the United States in the 1920's. These men differed on many particulars but were unanimous in commenting that culturally conventional, intellectually shallow, artistically ignorant, and socially primitive businessmen dominated America and set the framework for its formal culture. (Joad, incidentally, the most vivacious but irresponsible of the three, did not think it necessary to visit the United States before writing his book.)

Yet, looking back at the period from a greater time perspective, one is struck by the fact that the creators of enduring works, those who have become accepted as major intellectual or artistic figures, were not in the dominant cultural stream. The major figures divided into two camps, each of them scornful of popularly accepted values. One intellectual camp attacked convention by explicitly criticizing the direction of American life. Sinclair Lewis, for example, brought a new word into the vocabulary with his book about *Babbitt*, a well-meaning but bigoted and culturally hopeless businessman. The other camp revealed its disgust by retreating from American society in one way or another. Many of them actually lived abroad; others of them turned inward into their chosen field, working out their artistic or intellectual problems, ignoring society as much as possible; still others concentrated upon form more than upon content. A popular slogan of this last group, whether they were artists or not, was "Art for Art's sake."

But for all the social critics and *avant garde* bohemians or mandarins, respected by a relative few in their own day but honored by many in a later generation, the 1920's popular honors went to defenders of the cultural *status quo*, particularly to those who glorified the man of business. To be a "go-getter," a "success," a "live wire" was the generally accepted ideal. Writers who enthusiastically supported these ideals reaped large rewards. A book by Bruce Barton, partner in the advertising firm of Batton, Barton, Durstine, and Osborn, entitled *The Man Nobody Knows: A Biography of Jesus*, was a best seller in 1925 and 1926. The dust jacket reprinted enthusiastic endorsements from many of the country's outstanding clergymen. Jesus, according to Barton, was "the founder of modern business." He was the greatest salesman of His age, the "most forceful executive" of His world. He demonstrated His genius for personnel work in the manner in which He chose His disciples. Although Barton's readers in a later day waver from incredulity to dismay to hilarity, he was taken seriously and at face value in the 1920's. Most of his readers were not sure whether Barton's primary purpose was to sanctify the businessmen or to pay Jesus his ultimate compliment, but they disagreed with neither intention.

Most of this chapter will be concerned with those who dissented from the dominant values and thought of the 1920's since these dissenters were the ones who carried formal American culture along through the decade. The next chapter on various aspects of the era's social history will concentrate to a greater extent upon dominant, popular currents. The reader should remember, however, that for every person to whom a Sinclair Lewis or T. S. Eliot was a hero there were a dozen who honored a Barton.

Education

The outstanding development in public education during the 1920's was a tremendous increase in the number of years young people went to school. Increases in enrollments of primary grades were more the result of a larger population than an increased percentage of school attendance. Increases at the junior and senior high school level were due mostly to an increased proportion of that age level continuing their formal education. High school enrollments increased from approximately 2,200,000 in 1920 to roughly 4,400,000 in 1930. By the late 1920's, about half of the population of high-school age was in school, a proportion unsurpassed elsewhere in the world. In Europe as high a proportion of young children went to school as in America—a higher percentage in some of the most advanced nations—but secondary education was restricted to those who had proved academic competence. In most United States communities entrance to high school was routine, although a considerable number dropped or flunked out before graduation.

States and communities increased their school taxes and revenues tremendously. Teacher salaries had lagged far behind the sharp increase in the cost of living from 1917–1920, but after the postwar depression salaries improved. By the end of the decade, teachers' average real income was better than it had been before the war. Yet, teacher incomes did not improve as much as incomes in other fields requiring a similar amount of training. One result of this economic situation was that men teachers became fewer. Those who had families felt obligated to go into fields where they could better support them. Those who remained in the schools were likely to be found in boys' physical education, vocational training for boys, science, or administration. While certainly a teacher's sex makes no difference in his or her ability, the predominance of women in teaching did make it more difficult for the field to acquire the characteristics of other professions. Women frequently taught for a few years and then quit to marry. Many school boards refused to appoint married women and dismissed single women who did marry. But teaching, increasingly during the decade, acquired one of the aspects of a profession—special graduate education. Most of the schools of education in the state universities offered graduate work in the 1920's, and Teachers College of Columbia University almost abandoned undergraduate instruction. Thousands of teachers attended graduate school each summer, and, particularly in the high schools of the cities and larger towns, master's degrees became commonplace.

Better automobiles and roads made it possible for the first time to abandon the rural one-room elementary school and to bring secondary education to country youth. The nation's school transportation bill each year amounted to more than $20 million. Although there was almost unanimity among educators that a consolidated, graded school was superior to a one-teacher, ungraded institution, consolidation frequently faced considerable political opposition. To build the new schools meant higher taxes, and farmers often deplored the loss of the local school because it seemed to them that they thereby lost status to the town or village that had the new school. Some states levered the abandonment of rural schools by rigging the state financial aid system.

With thousands in high schools who in an earlier day would have quit school at the elementary level, the high schools were forced to modify their standards and curriculum. More modification came in the next decade as high school enrollments continued to rise, but by the late 1920's, many schools had introduced ambitious vocational training programs for the students who were poorly equipped for the usual academic program or uninterested in it. The best of these vocational programs turned out young people prepared to take jobs in commercial offices, the building trades, print shops, and automobile garages; others merely taught the students the use of hand carpentry tools

257

and the rudiments of mechanical drawing. The equipment required for vocational education made its costs greater than those of academic courses, and most school systems were unable or unwilling to make a sufficient investment.

Preparation for an occupation was only one of several aspects of the broadening function of the public schools. The school had originally served for intellectual or academic training altogether; no other social institution— the family, the church, the trade union, the social club—was able to fulfill the intellectual training function. But by the end of the 1920's, the school had taken on a number of other social functions. In an agricultural society, the family had provided vocational education and a measure of social preparation, the family and the church had at least endeavored to provide moral training, and the family and the doctor had taught the rudiments of health and hygiene. But in urban and industrial society, the family had tended to become less powerful as a social organization at the same time that life became infinitely more complex and education for that life therefore more difficult. The school, as a result, came to assume functions in the education of the young theretofore alien to it. Pressures for modification of school program came from many directions. Educators themselves brought some of the changes. Patriotic organizations insisted upon nationalistic citizenship training. Society in general demanded that the school become the main agency for Americanization of immigrants. Insurance companies pressured school administrators to set aside student time for instruction in safety. Prohibitionists enlisted teachers in the campaign against alcohol. In the assumption of these many tasks the school often neglected its original academic function.

Many people became alarmed by the changes in the school, saw the changes as all for the worse, and, confusing all change with John Dewey's ideas, lashed out against "progressive education." According to the more old-fashioned intellectuals, the school produced a more inferior intellectual product each year, a deterioration that dated from the educational golden age when the critics themselves had sat at student desks. Actually, most objective comparisons of the academic knowledge of children in the 1920's with that of school children a generation earlier showed no deterioration and sometimes an improvement. But this was because teachers had become more effective rather than because they put an equal emphasis upon academic subject matter. With the better methods, textbooks, and libraries there is reason to believe that a much higher level of achievement could have been reached if the school had retained its academic function exclusively.

Despite all the talk of Dewey and "progressive education," there was relatively little of Dewey's theory put into practice in most school systems. For the most part, one had to go to experimental schools operated by universities or teachers colleges to find Deweyism. Yet there were many innovations, particularly in private schools in the large cities, that went under the name of "progressive education," innovations so wildly different from convention that their label of "progressive" damaged Dewey's popular reputation. Most of these wilder innovations derived more from a revolt against Victorian mores and misunderstanding of Sigmund Freud than they did from pragmatism.

It was the antievolution crusade of religious fundamentalists rather than progressive education that caused the big headlines about schools in the postwar decade. The post-Civil War generation had engaged in an enormous controversy over Charles Darwin's theory of evolution that most people in the cities by 1920 had assumed to be a dead issue. Biological evolution was generally accepted, and the urban churches had accommodated their doctrine to the scientific view of man's origin. But rural America, particularly in the South, revived the controversy in a startling way in the early 1920's. William Jennings Bryan became the popular leader of the fundamentalist crusade against evolution. He engaged in an extended public controversy with E. A. Birge, a biologist and the acting president of the University of Wisconsin, that rallied him strength in the country but only disdainful amusement from the cities. In 1922, the Kentucky legislature came within one vote of passing a bill to outlaw teaching evolution in the schools. Antievolutionists won minor successes in North Carolina, Florida, and Oklahoma, and Governor "Ma" Ferguson of Texas herself blacklisted biology textbooks when the legislature refused to do so. Then in 1925, Tennessee's legislature made it illegal for a teacher in the public schools "to teach any theory that denies the story of the divine creation of man as taught in the Bible." Mississippi and Arkansas soon enacted similar statutes. The American Civil Liberties Union offered free counsel to any Tennessee teacher who violated the act, and a young high school biology teacher of Dayton, Tennessee, accepted the ACLU offer. The teacher, John Scopes, became the least important figure in the trial as the ACLU provided him the services of Clarence Darrow, the most famous criminal defense lawyer of the day, Dudley Field Malone, and Arthur Garfield Hays as counsel and Bryan acted as a special assistant for the prosecution. The "monkey trial" attracted national headlines, and H. L. Mencken wrote brutal attacks upon Bryan, referring to him, among other things, as a "sweating anthropoid." Darrow made Bryan look like a fool, getting him to contradict himself in his defense of his proposition that the Bible was in every respect literally true. The jury found Scopes guilty of violating the law, which clearly he had, but the state supreme court threw out the case on a technicality and thereby dodged a decision on the constitutionality of the law. The heat at the trial, held in July, was oppressive, and Bryan so exhausted himself that he died a few days later. It was tragic that the Great Commoner died when his reputation was at its lowest point, when he appeared to be an ignorant, anachronistic, rural clown rather than the leader of one of the nation's major political parties and a Secretary of State.

The biggest problems confronting the colleges and universities arose from rising costs and a huge expansion of enrollments. In 1920, the campuses were jammed with about six hundred thousand students, many of them war veterans whose education had been interrupted or delayed. But the increased enrollments were not temporary, as they were expected to be. By 1930, there were roughly twice as many students in college. Rising costs of going to college, averaging about $800 a year nationally, but somewhat higher at most private colleges, did not deter youth of the prosperity decade. Although some employers still fumed that college was a waste of time, specialization in engineering and other professions made college attendance a practical necessity. In some lines of business the social polish and associations that one could acquire at certain campuses were more important vocationally than whatever knowledge and intellectual discipline might have been developed within the walls of ivy. Young women and their mothers realized that one's chances of attracting a desirable bachelor improved by pursuing a bachelor's degree. But for whatever reasons, intellectual or otherwise, hundreds of thousands of new students arrived on the campuses each fall, and higher education in the United States became mass education. And as faculties increasingly expected the Ph.D. degree as a condition of appointment and industry began major research laboratories, expensive graduate education became ever more common. In 1920, American universities awarded slightly over five hundred Ph.D. degrees; by 1930 the figure had quadrupled.

Several colleges and universities experimented in an effort to minimize the standardization and mechanical quality that characterized most large institutions. Operating on the not necessarily valid assumption that only the professor's mind is active during a lecture, some institutions did what they could to abandon lectures and introduced tutorial systems. Others attempted to separate the best students from the herd and offered honors programs of various kinds. Antioch College at Yellow Springs, Ohio, began a "platoon" system under which a student was on campus for a period and then worked at a job away from Yellow Springs, all the time reading and studying in his chosen field. Alexander Meiklejohn, first at Amherst until he was released as its president and then at Wisconsin where he directed the Experimental College, endeavored to return education to integrated unity and away from sometimes artificial compartments. None of the campus experiments developed a magic formula, but they did demonstrate that a new program which excited faculty and students and thereby rose above the routine was superior to the usual educational assembly line.

So much has been written and put onto film about campus life in the 1920's, the Charleston, raccoon coats, hip flasks, and Stutz Bearcats, that little need be said. The usual Hollywood account is grossly exaggerated. Men and manners, maidens and morality, differed enormously from campus to campus and from group to group upon a single campus. Some professors thought that there was less drunkenness in the 1920's than there had been before the war, but surely professors were not in the best position to know all that went on in either period. One thing is indisputable about campus life during the boom: never before had football loomed so large as a university activity. Men like Harold "Red" Grange of Illinois, Albie Booth of Yale, Ernie Nevers of Stanford, and Coach Knute Rockne of Notre Dame came to be known to far more people than the professors or presidents of their institutions.

Literature and Prosperity

If there was anything that most major literary figures of the 1920's could agree upon—and there was not much—it was that America was a mess. Harold Stearns, a disgruntled literary critic, edited a volume in 1922 entitled *Civilization in the United States* in which thirty American writers in various fields looked about them and unanimously concluded that American life was esthetically barren, intellectually superficial, and stiflingly oppressive. Middle-class values, worship of technology and material wealth, Victorian morality, and glorification of outmoded ideals had, they said, made it impossible for art and intellect to flourish. That they had a point any objective observer would agree.

Yet by the decade's end any accountant of culture would have to agree that the years had brought forth an unusual burst of creative energy, a frenzy of intellectual and artistic excitement, and a few masterpieces.

A few writers dedicated the decade to documenting the conclusions of the Stearns volume. The most famous and widely read of these were Sinclair Lewis, Sherwood Anderson, and H. L. Mencken. Lewis skyrocketed to national attention in 1920 when he painted a grim picture of a small midwestern town in *Main Street*. Two years later he did a similar job on a larger city in *Babbitt*. In *Arrowsmith* (1925) he was critical of the medical profession, in *Elmer Gantry* (1927) he ripped the clergy to shreds, making them all either fools or knaves, and in *Dodsworth* (1929) he featured the soul sickness of a businessman who had wrecked his life pursuing the dollar and neglecting his own development. In 1930, Lewis became the first American novelist to receive a Nobel prize.

Sherwood Anderson, who had more impact upon intellectuals but less of a popular following than Lewis, was best known for his *Winesburg, Ohio* (1919). A legend about Anderson which he himself encouraged was illustrative of one intellectual fad of the 1920's. Anderson had, it was said, walked out of his paint factory in Elyria, Ohio, one afternoon in 1912, thoroughly sick of his middle-class way of life, set his face toward the sun of culture and art, and never turned back. The fact was that Anderson had a nervous breakdown. But hundreds of young writers treasured the legend and romantically honored him for breaking with convention, and, probably, hundreds of frustrated young businessmen envied him for the courage they thought he had.

Henry Louis Mencken, "the bad boy of Baltimore," was the rage among young would-be sophisticates of the 1920's, a sort of earlier Philip Wylie with guts. Mencken became an editor of *The American Mercury* in 1924 and soon every sophomore who yearned for Montmartre and despised his hometown carried the green-covered magazine. If anything was sacred to Mencken besides beer and Johann Sebastian Bach, he concealed the reverence. Voting was ridiculous, wrote Mencken, and politicians were only "beaters of breasts." He defended prostitution, declared that bootleggers were nature's noblemen, and proposed to sink the Statue of Liberty. The more he shocked dominant middle-class America, the more subscriptions he received. Quite apart from his social and literary commentaries, Mencken was a respectable philologist, and his studies on the American language received critical acclaim.

But most of the major writers of the prosperity decade did not regard America's cultural shoddiness as even worthy of serious direct attack. Henry Adams, a descendent of a great family, in his 1918 autobiography included a perceptive criticism of American culture from the Civil War to the World War and then retreated to the Middle Ages, attracted by that period's spiritual unity and repelled by modern materialism. T. S. Eliot was thinking of more than business when he wrote *The Waste Land* (1922) and *The Hollow Men* (1925), but his despair certainly included the United States. This expatriate, whose poetry forms had a great impact on young people, also retreated to medievalism. Scott Fitzgerald, whose novels became the symbol of "flaming youth" and the "lost generation," occasionally made explicit criticisms of American life but was for the most part concerned with individual and personal matters.

261

Indeed, emphasis upon the individual in one way or another to the almost complete exclusion of concern for society, was an outstanding characteristic of letters during the decade. It was quite a reversal from the dominant pattern before the war and in contrast to what was to come in the 1930's. Even the writers who were expressly critical of America saw the problems of the nation in individual rather than social terms. The same was true of their solutions, to the degree they offered solutions. Most saw no hope whatsoever and, therefore, no possible solution. When Stearns turned in the manuscript for his *Civilization in the United States* he issued no manifesto, called no writers' congress, organized no intellectual school or community. He embarked for France. The drama critic George Jean Nathan, a friend and associate of Mencken, stated the view of most major writers well if in exaggerated form:

> The great problems of the world—social, political, economic and theological—do not concern me in the slightest. If all the Armenians were to be killed tomorrow and if half of Russia were to starve to death the day after, it would not matter to me in the least. What concerns me alone is myself, and the interests of a few close friends. For all I care the rest of the world may go to hell at today's sunset.[1]

Such views, if sincerely held, automatically threw reform out the window. Before the war the arty set, the bohemians, had mingled happily with the reformers and the social radicals. The left-wing *Masses* had combined social radicalism with literary and artistic innovation. Greenwich Village had been a neighborhood for both kinds, and the distinction between artist and radical had been difficult to make. Again in the 1930's radicals and artists were to move back together for a while. But in the 1920's they had little in common. They fused around the Sacco-Vanzetti case but little else. To the artistic temperament, reform was old hat and radicalism was an irrelevant museum piece. John Chamberlain, a newspaper book reviewer, wrote a survey of American social protest movements in 1929 which was vaguely sympathetic but condescending. He buried social protest, he thought, with his title: *Farewell to Reform.* For Chamberlain personally reform was buried indeed; he later became an extreme rightwinger. Max Eastman, a Greenwich Village young genius who before the war was both literary and radical as a *Masses* editor, became exclusively literary for a while in the 1920's. He later became an editor of *The Reader's Digest* and a warrior against the left. Lincoln Steffens, the muckraker who had moved steadily leftward and had hailed the Bolshevik revolution, announced that the Hoover administration would bring all the material goals for the poor that the Socialists had agitated for.

The main tendencies of literature and intellectual life in the 1920's—remembering always that we are here considering relatively few people, not the mass popular Bruce Barton school of thought—flowed naturally from rejection of reform and social problems for concern with the individual and particularly for one's self. The main tendencies, but one can discern others, were hedonistic pursuit of pleasure, Freudianism or distorted forms of it, primitivism, and antidemocracy.

---

[1] William E. Leuchtenburg, *The Perils of Prosperity, 1914–1932* (Chicago: Univ. of Chicago Press, 1958), p. 150.

Edna St. Vincent Millay wrote a short poem, "Figs from Thistles," which became one of the most widely quoted verses of the decade. It well expressed the hedonistic mood that extended far beyond the intellectual, would-be intellectual and artistic community.

> My candle burns at both ends;
> It will not last the night;
> But, ah, my foes, and oh, my friends—
> It gives a lovely light.

Scott Fitzgerald's novels, *This Side of Paradise* (1920), *The Beautiful and the Damned* (1922), and *The Great Gatsby* (1925), and the facts and legend of his career were perhaps the best example of postwar hedonism. Fitzgerald's characters found life meaningless, they had been tragically disillusioned by the war, they conceived of themselves as "the lost generation" and they abandoned themselves to pleasures of the moment. To be "free" and "gay" were their goals. Until the crash, Fitzgerald and his wife even lived the life of their determined-to-be-carefree characters. They were in France much of the time with hordes of other American expatriates. Their money went farther there, and France had no prohibition or puritan tradition. Ernest Hemingway, the best stylist of the "lost generation," also lived in France and developed fictional characters who found their world without meaning and therefore gave up and pursued pleasure for pleasure's sake. His *The Sun Also Rises* (1926) and *A Farewell to Arms* (1929) had a huge impact on young intellectuals of their day and upon successive generations of them, both in America and throughout the western world. Most people, however, were only shocked by his use of four-letter words and his explicitness about sex. "Oh, Mr. Hemingway!" was a catch phrase of the late 1920's almost as popular as "Twenty-three skidoo" had been early in the decade.

A few American intellectuals had discovered Freud before the war, but only a few. After the war Freudianism became widespread, although far less so than it would become after World War II. One of its greatest influences upon literature was through the stream of consciousness technique. The dramatist Eugene O'Neill even used this technique on the stage. His *Desire under the Elms* (1924), *The Emperor Jones* (1920), *The Great God Brown* (1926), and *Strange Interlude* (1928), while they puzzled their audiences, disseminated Freudian ideas to a wide circle. Easily the outstanding American playwright of the decade (perhaps of all time), O'Neill's stature at home and abroad has grown with the years.

Primitivism received a stimulus from the notion that civilization was thoroughly sick and rotten. If man had any dignity at all, primitivists held, it would be found among people whose contact with civilization had been small, for to civilize was to spoil. A strong primitive streak ran through Hemingway's novels. The characters he most admired were men of muscle and violence and unfettered sex urges, people who operated by their emotions rather than by their reason. When they had intelligence it was the cunning of a jungle animal rather than cultivated insight. Thus boxers, hunters, soldiers, rum runners, and bull fighters peopled his pages. One aspect of primitivism of the 1920's was a cult of the Negro. During the decade there was a consider-

263

able Negro literary renaissance. Some white intellectuals sponsored and praised Negro artists, novelists, poets, and musicians mainly because they were Negro. Carl Van Vechten was the leading white sponsor of Negro literature, and Countee Cullen was the best known Negro poet. In some white circles in New York City people prattled of atavism and "earth rhythms" and spent their evenings in the night clubs of Harlem. The Cotton Club soon became too well known for the true connoisseur of Negro life who sought out his jazz and gin in smaller and more esoteric Harlem speakeasies. It is interesting to note that these primitivists did not oppose segregation in one sense; they thought it would be tragic if the Negro became so much a part of American life that he would lose what they considered unique and inherent Negro qualities. France, perhaps through the influence of the expatriates, also had a wave of Negro primitivism. French intellectuals raved about *le jazz hot* until the French masses and American whites also discovered jazz.

Antidemocratic attitudes revealed themselves in a great deal of the decade's literature. In Fitzgerald there was an element of elitist thinking. When one reads today the detective novels of S. S. Van Dine one is astonished by their snobbery and racism. The poet Ezra Pound ultimately became a Mussolini facist, and some who retreated into medieval culture did so largely because they found the democracy of later eras distasteful. Mencken included democracy among the favorite targets of his literary meat axe. The clearest and best reasoned attack upon democracy in literary circles, however, came from a group of critics called the "new humanists." Led by Paul Elmer More of Princeton and Irving Babbitt of Harvard, the "new humanists" rejected the naturalism and sensuality of the literary innovators of the decade as well as old-fashioned progressivism and defenders of the business civilization. They deplored the direction of the modern world since the late eighteenth century. The best of all possible worlds, they at least implied, was one such as pre-revolutionary France where a cultured elite with wealth and leisure patronized unadulterated art and literature.

In a culture as dynamic and diverse as American culture was, however, there were many exceptions to the literary trends noted here. Magazines like *The Nation* and *The New Republic* more than held their own. Reform was not altogether dead even among writers of fiction in the Coolidge era. Upton Sinclair, for example, wrote steadily throughout the decade and had a wide audience, although he was regarded as old hat by many. Theodore Dreiser never lost hope for social regeneration despite his gloominess, and his *An American Tragedy* (1925) was one of the greatest novels of the era. Carl Sandburg's and Edgar Lee Masters' sense of identification with ordinary people never left them, and the same might be said for the more conservative Robert Frost. There even was a considerable amount of good literature in the older genteel tradition. Willa Cather's *Death Comes to the Archbishop*, her best and most famous novel, was published in 1927. Her *The Professor's House* (1923) remains one of the best novels about academic life, although dozens of them were written later. Perhaps the most striking exception to the dominant literary trends of the period by a young man was Stephen Vincent Benét's *John Brown's Body*, a masterful epic poem of the Civil War which won a Pulitzer prize in 1928. Benét, like so many others of his generation, had fled to France. But instead of cursing and despairing of America he wrote a beautiful reaffirmation of old American values without in any sense being old-fashioned.

The Twenties and Music

The history of music in the United States in the twentieth century is largely the story of the development of its own musicians of all kinds, including composers. Then, when the basis of an American music had been laid, much of the story had to do with efforts to produce a distinctively American music, to evolve musical expression less dependent upon European traditions. America's musical history has been roughly analagous to the industrial strivings of economically underdeveloped nations of South America, Africa, and Asia. During the 1920's, however, there were several important developments in the effort both to develop American musical personnel and to create a unique musical tradition.

American musical development was tied in with the growth of an American musical audience. To use an economic analogy again, there had to be a market, a demand, before there could be production. Further, American musicians could not come into being from a musically arid society. In the 1920's, prosperity and technology stimulated the domestic market for music. Phonographs became more widely owned than they had been before the war, and the introduction of electrically transcribed recordings in 1925 considerably improved their fidelity to the sound as it had come from the musicians' instruments or voices. Radio made it possible for millions to hear music who had never heard it extensively before, and the variety of music that one could hear from the radio was much wider than anyone could have from recordings, no matter how much money he could spend for records. Prosperity made possible live music in towns that had previously had a minimum of professionally produced music. In 1920, Henry P. Harrison of the Redpath Chautauqua and Lyceum Bureau of Chicago began to organize groups in several towns and cities that he called Civic Music Associations. The Associations sold subscriptions for a season's concerts, and Harrison supplied the artists. He soon had several imitators. The performers, it is true, had to cater to rather unsophisticated popular tastes and had to feature dramatic selections that involved as much showmanship as music—one will never know how many times Fritz Kreisler and Albert Spaulding, the nation's favorite violinists, had to play Saint-Saëns's "Ghost Dance"—but their programs and musicianship were clearly superior to the old traveling troupes of Swiss bell ringers.

Three major schools of music opened their doors during the decade. The Eastman School of Music at Rochester, New York, began in 1921, founded by an endowment from the photographic equipment manufacturer George Eastman. After Howard Hanson became director of the Eastman School in 1924, it quickly became noted for its vigorous composition department. New York's Julliard School of Music opened in 1923 and a few years later moved to the Columbia University neighborhood where it developed a graduate program and profited from its relationship with the University. Philadelphia's Curtis Institute accepted its first students in 1924. Graduates of these schools, both performers and composers, were to become the equal of their counterparts from Europe within a few years.

By the end of the 1920's, American symphony orchestras contained many American born and educated instrumentalists. The Metropolitan Opera Company still found it necessary to contract with European singers for most of the stars of the company, but during the decade John Charles Thomas, Lawrence Tibbett, and Rosa Ponselle sang important roles on the Metropolitan's stage and were well received. Marion Talley, originally from Missouri, captured the public imagination when she sang her first major role at the Metropolitan in 1926. The Cincinnati summer opera organization, which began in 1921 by staging its productions in the zoo, gave young American singers an opportunity to gain professional operatic experience and more established performers to learn new roles. In 1927, *The King's Henchman*, one of the first American operas to make an impact, was a New York hit. Deems Taylor was its composer, and Edna St. Vincent Millay wrote the book.

American symphony orchestras still had to import conductors capable of leading a first-class orchestra, but they were able to appoint from among the best the world had to offer. Leopold Stokowski, who had gone to the Philadelphia Orchestra in 1912, became world famous for his willingness to introduce contemporary music. Serge Koussevitzky became director of the Boston Symphony in 1924, and Arturo Toscanini moved to the New York Philharmonic in the late 1920's.

Three young American composers in the 1920's became the first to achieve national and world esteem, Aaron Copland (born 1900), Howard Hanson (born 1896), and George Gershwin (born 1898). Both Copland and Gershwin tried to adapt jazz or elements of jazz to symphonic forms. Gershwin was easily the more widely heralded of the two, largely because he was already known as a composer of popular music and songs for musical comedies, but also because he had the backing of Paul Whiteman, a popular orchestra conductor who stood between the jazz and "serious music" worlds. Whiteman, a symphony violinist, endeavored to tame jazz down a little and play it as concert music. At a 1924 New York concert, the Whiteman orchestra first played Gershwin's "Rhapsody in Blue." Ferde Grofé, later to gain a name for himself for his symphonic suites on American themes, orchestrated Gershwin's composition. The same concert introduced a sticky suite entitled "Serenades" which Victor Herbert had especially written for the occasion. The comparative lasting qualities of the two compositions well reveals which kind of music better reflected American interests and characteristics. The New York Symphony, an organization that later merged with the New York Philharmonic, first played Gershwin's "An American in Paris" in 1928.

Hanson soared across the musical sky like a rocket and became a dean of American composers while still a young man. A son of Swedish immigrant parents, reared in Wahoo, Nebraska, Hanson attended Luther College in Nebraska, Northwestern University, and the Institute of Musical Art in New York, a predecessor of Julliard. In 1921, he won an American Prix de Rome and studied abroad for three years, then returned to the United States to direct the Eastman School. He composed his "Nordic Symphony" in the 1920's as well as his symphonic poems "North and West" and "Pan and the Priest."

Jazz, or more precisely, jazz-influenced popular music swept the country after the first years of the decade. Real jazz, unadulterated by Tin Pan Alley, also gained in the decade after the war, but it was little heard on the radio, and the record companies separated it from popular music by creating "pop" divisions in their firms and relegating jazz to what they called "race records" sold mostly in Negro neighborhoods. Neither was respectable in the highest social circles, and jazz devotees were not fully successful in their efforts to make it respectable with concert performances and learned articles in highbrow and middlebrow magazines. But the vitality of jazz and its reflection of the dynamic and disturbing new machine America, a hustling, break-neck urban civilization, made it attractive to young people whose tastes had not been formed by the Victor Herbert version of Viennese music. Sweet string music simply did not fit the America of the second quarter of the century. The brassy, blaring, wailing, and nervous rhythms of jazz did fit modern America, and jazz needed only time to live down older prejudices and become widely accepted.

Prosperity and Art

The business cycle and art are intimately related, although many artists might deny any connection. Prosperity and local civic pride in the 1920's led almost every fair-sized city in the country that did not already have an art museum to establish one. Between 1921 and 1930, sixty new art museums were formed in the United States, and thirteen of them moved into especially constructed new buildings costing a total of $16 million. At the same time there was an expansion of the private art market. Once only a relatively few families of enormous wealth had bought paintings. The greater number of rich families during the boom decade considerably widened the market, and art-buying extended downward a little into less wealthy income groups.

Most of the money, however, went for purchases of old and traditional European painters. Portraits by eighteenth-century English painters became a vogue in the bigger "English manor" style houses that went up in the new suburbs. Probably the most famous painting in the United States was Gainsborough's "Blue Boy" at the Huntington Library at Pasadena. Winslow Homer's "Eight Bells" brought $50,000 at a New York sale, and an Inness brought $60,000 soon thereafter, both new highs for American paintings. Significantly, however, no contemporary American painter ever received more than a small fraction of such prices. French modernism caught on with a relatively small public, and the collector John Quinn, who had a tremendous modern collection by French and American artists, sold it in 1927 for $700,000. Still we must remember that the market for contemporary art in America, either by its own or European artists, was never, in the 1920's, remotely close to the demand for contemporary literature or even music. The French in 1925 asked President Coolidge to send an American exhibit to the Exposition des Arts Décoratifs. Coolidge replied that the United States had no contemporary art to send. He clearly was badly misinformed, but few people knew that he was.

267

Modernists and experimentalists dominated American art in the 1920's. The trend was consistent with the main directions of literature and music during the period. Modernism meant a great many things. There were several modernist schools, but they had certain general similarities. They did not attempt life-like representations, but their subject matter was usually recognizable. Only a few of them were completely abstract. The modernists emphasized formal harmonies, and they expressed subjective emotions. It was a new way of looking at things, a new vision, greatly influenced by new schools of painting abroad, especially in France, and to some extent by new perspectives offered by the camera and the microscope. In New York, where most of the modern painting was done, modernism created a spirit of excitement and exploration in the art colony.

Three major painters with highly individualistic styles who were outstanding in the 1920's were John Marin, Georgia O'Keeffe, and Max Weber. Marin, who was to live until 1953 and become the dean of American artists, specialized in modernist water colors. During the twenties, his style reached its most abstract point, but generally the form was recognizable—usually scenes of New York City or the Maine coast. But the form was not the most striking aspect of his work. It was rather his sweeps of bright color which gave his paintings a dynamic quality that have reminded some of strong lyrical poetry.

Miss O'Keeffe painted with a clean, austere line that heightened reality. Even when she did completely abstract things she kept her edges sharp and clean, almost camera-like. She has been critized for too often becoming merely decorative, but her best canvases, such as her "The American Radiator Building" done in 1929, have been of lasting importance.

Weber is considered here because he first came to attention in the 1920's. He continued to be one of America's foremost painters for many years, especially after World War II. Weber painted in a variety of styles. He was influenced by Oriental art as a student, and when he studied in Paris he became interested in primitive and Middle Eastern art. Matisse was his teacher in Paris, but Cézanne became his idol. Cézanne, incidentally, was the most important single influence on American painters in the 1920's. Back in America, Weber painted in many of the styles of modernism and was criticized for not being himself. He was eclectic, but in all his styles his own distinctiveness was apparent.

Three painters of the 1920's who had a marked similarity in subject matter and in general approach were Charles Demuth, Charles Sheeler, and Joseph Stella. Sometimes called the cubists-realists, they emphasized geometric forms to be found in architecture and machinery. Cubism was a school of painting, originally French, in which emotion was subdued and, in its simplest interpretations, broke down all physical reality into its basic structural elements: cubes, cones, and cylinders. Demuth, who painted in a flat style with little perspective, distorted reality by stripping his vision down to the essentials. The result was a very stylized rendition of a perfectly recognizable building or machine, made more elegant by the distortion. Sheeler's work emphasized depth or perspective. One gets the feeling in looking at them that one is looking through a strong lens. Sheeler first made his living as a photographer, and his emphasis on perspective, light, and shadow learned with his camera carried over to his canvases. In 1922, he made a film entitled "Manahatta" with the photographer Paul Strand who, along with Edward Steichen, was at the forefront of art photography during the decade. One of his most famous paintings, "Church Street El," done in 1920, emphasizes light and shadow under an elevated railway to such an extent that at first glance the composition seems abstract. Later in the decade, Sheeler became increasingly realistic. He did a series of photographs of Ford's River Rouge plant and then painted many of the scenes with the photographs as notes. His work did much to popularize industry as subject matter for painting, and *Fortune* magazine later did many covers in this stylized fashion. Stella's pictures gave more feeling of movement than Demuth's and Sheeler's. He particularly liked to do suspension bridges and port scenes, and the big cables swooping down and across the canvases gave them a dynamic quality. Other painters of the cubist-realist school such as Stefan Hirsch, George Ault, Niles Spencer, and Oscar Bleumner set their cubist buildings on lifeless streets and evoked an eerie feeling of sterility and vacuum.

Several other American painters prominent in the 1920's went through cubist phases. Alfred H. Maurer, who did cubist still lifes, is attributed by some to have done the most interesting and advanced cubist work of any American painter, but he is also known for his sad stylized portraits in the manner of Matisse. Maurer never received the recognition during his lifetime that he deserved, and he committed suicide in 1932. Andrew Dasburg did cubist interpretations of the desert landscapes of the American Southwest which must have amazed the New Mexicans who might have looked over his shoulder. Stuart Davis, who was in Paris for most of the decade, was the most radical of the American cubists. Some of his paintings, for example "Egg Beater No. 1," were such departures from surface reality in their attempt to portray reality in the cubist sense that viewers felt grateful, if puzzled, by their titles.

Arthur Dove had been influenced by cubism, but he did not fit into that school precisely. He was a daring innovator. His colors were on the drab side, but his forms were frequently completely abstract. He also experimented with collage in a manner that was almost surrealist. Dove was so dedicated to the avant-garde that seeing his collages a generation later, with their use of pieces of steel spring, pages torn from old Bibles, fragments of needlepoint, and bits of weathered wood, one is struck by the degree later offbeat artists only repeated ideas he worked out in the 1920's. His collages have rotted and rusted to such an extent that their main interest today is historical.

Marsden Hartley, although he painted a great many mediocre pictures, did some of the most emotionally intense canvases of the decade. Hartley had studied in Germany, unlike most American artists, and his painting showed the influence of German expressionism. He did some powerful pictures of the southwestern desert, featuring twisted trees and barren landscape. Another artist influenced by German expressionism, strangely enough, was a Japanese-American, Yasuo Kuniyoshi. He came to America from Japan when a boy and had all of his training in the United States. Because of his background, many have proclaimed that he combined western and Oriental art, but it is doubtful that a Japanese artist would see anything familiar in his paintings.

Modernist, but far more in keeping with popular tastes, were a group of painters who continued to take the human face and form for subject matter. Walt Kuhn had been a realist associate of George Bellows. He was greatly affected by the Armory Show, which he helped to organize, and for a while experimented with radical modernism. Then in the 1920's he returned to representational portrayal of people only slightly distorted or stylized. His favorite subjects were stage and circus people, but his portraits were of types rather than of actual people. Bernard Karfiol specialized in nudes that were much like Renoir in their style. Alexander Brook, another painter of this school, was for a time assistant director of the Whitney Studio Club, a center for many artists in the 1920's. Gertrude Vanderbilt Whitney, herself a sculptor, sponsored the club, and eventually her collection became the Whitney Museum of American Art.

Realists worked throughout the decade, but they were fewer in number than they had been before the Armory Show or would be in the 1930's, and they did not attract as much public attention. John Sloan and George Luks were active as realists, but had given up their Ash Can tradition. In the late 1920's, a considerable group of realists, including Reginald Marsh, Morris Kantor, and the Soyer brothers, who were to come to national prominence in the depression, had shows in New York. Social protest art during the decade was restricted almost entirely to illustrators for left-wing magazines, and they, too, would attract greater attention with a reversal of the business cycle.

On the whole, American painting during the 1920's was in the art-for-art's-sake tradition, and it was much influenced by Europe, especially Paris. Cubism, fauvism, and other French styles seldom were taken wholly by American painters, but they had a strong impact.

Sculpture and Architecture

In both sculpture and architecture, especially for public buildings, there was relatively little experiment or departure from tradition. Perhaps the economics of these fields made them differ from painting. Paintings usually were purchased by one person to be hung in the home or perhaps given to a museum, frequently for speculation. But it was government commissions, corporations, or civic clubs that instigated public buildings and statues. Committees were involved; purchasing or commissioning a design was an organization enterprise. In such circumstances, daring was the last thing to be expected. So sculptors maintained a safe and diplomatic conformity to precedent—designs which the public would approve. The sculpture in the many World War I memorials of the 1920's differed from the memorials to the Civil War mainly in that they indicated more action than the old general-on-a-horse pose and they were more nationalistic in feeling.

One of the best-loved sculptures of the decade was Daniel Chester French's enormous and romantic statue of Lincoln in the Lincoln Memorial at Washington. The public clearly liked representations of Lincoln consistent with the Lincoln legend. A 1917 magazine poll to determine the public's favorite Lincoln statue rated a realistic work by George Gray Barnard that emphasized the Emancipator's ungainliness at the bottom of the list; Augustus Saint-Gaudens' romantic likeness in Lincoln Park, Chicago, was the easy winner. Gutzon Borglum was the best-publicized sculptor of the 1920's. Borglum agreed to do a monumental chiseling of the side of Stone Mountain, Georgia, and transform its stone front into likenesses of Confederate heroes. After a disagreement with some of the project's sponsors, Borglum temperamentally left the job to be completed by others. He later did an even bigger work of mountain sculpture on Mount Rushmore in the Black Hills of South Dakota. More of a geological and sculptural stunt than a work of art, the Mount Rushmore monument has representations of Washington, Jefferson, Lincoln, and Theodore Roosevelt.

In 1924, Louis Sullivan died broke and broken in a run-down Chicago hotel. Not far away from his death bed was rising Colonel Robert R. McCormick's *Tribune* Tower, about as complete a negation of Sullivan's skyscraper idea as could be possible and still be called a skyscraper. *Tribune* Tower was capped with pseudo-Gothic decoration. To combine skyscraper and Gothic architecture was about as sensible, critics said, as an airplane pilot's wearing a monk's robe, but there were other examples of this combination before the decade ended. The University of Pittsburgh erected in the steel city's Civic Center what came to be known as the "Cathedral of Learning," a hybrid between a Gothic cathedral and an office skyscraper that proved so unfunctional for classrooms that the inside is not yet finished. Other universities, too, taught twentieth-century knowledge and ideas in Gothic surroundings. Yale built its medieval Harkness Quadrangle deliberately dilapidated. The cigarette king James B. Duke endowed Trinity College of Durham, North Carolina; it became Duke University, abandoned its old campus, and built a new Gothic one.

In university schools of architecture, however, students and faculty showed an interest in architectural functionalism and modernism that in a generation's time would make it almost impossible to study traditional architecture in the United States. The commission for *Tribune* Tower had been awarded after a competition that attracted 260 proposed designs from 23 countries. Second prize went to a Finnish architect, Eliel Saarinen. Saarinen's design was far more exciting to architectural educators than Raymond Hood's winning entry and thereafter the University of Michigan invited Saarinen to join its faculty.

Research in Laboratories and Libraries

Between the war and the depression, two tendencies came increasingly to affect research in the United States, whether in the natural sciences, the social sciences, or the humanities. They were a steady drift toward cooperative research projects and a gradual shift in the financial support of research from university funds to corporation earnings, often through philanthropic foundations. As mankind acquired more and more specialized information, it became impossible for any scholar or scientist to keep abreast of all developments in his own specialty, let alone in all science. The old ideal of the universal man had long before become outmoded. Frequently a chemist, a zoologist, a historian, or a literary scholar found that he could not profitably discuss his research problem even with colleagues in his own university department, so fragmented had knowledge become. Often, however, big problems of science or scholarship required competence in many specialties or lay between the traditional lines demarcating disciplines and specializations. Thus, cooperative research became a necessity. Another impulse toward research organizations came from national need. In 1917, scientists had established the National Research Council to make the best use of scientific manpower in the war effort. For somewhat different purposes, scholars in the 1920's founded the American Council of Learned Societies and the Social Science Research Council. While necessary, cooperation and organization had handicaps. Administration took energies away from the research front and always was in danger of becoming bureaucratic. The individual, speculative mind remained the source of genius; a group of scholars or scientists could be no more able than its best member in perceiving new relationships or having the brilliant insights that extend the frontiers of understanding.

Whether or not increased research subsidies from foundations affected the nature of research and the researcher's conclusions was a matter of considerable controversy. Research conclusions in the social sciences especially, some feared, would be distorted by being financially underwritten by wealth that derived ultimately from private corporate enterprise. Even in the sciences there was concern that those who paid for research would favor their pet projects and practical and applied research at the expense of basic theoretical advance. Oddly, both the political-economic left and right have been extremely critical of philanthropic foundations. The officers of such foundations obviously have a great deal of power and, therefore, a special obligation of responsibility, and in most scientists' and scholars' judgment they have seldom seriously misused their might.

Scientists of all kinds acquired a new stature in public esteem during the decade. The layman realized that the scientist was ultimately responsible for many technological and medical advances that made his life more comfortable and convenient. From chemistry laboratories came a host of new products and improvements of old ones. Geologists advised oil companies where it was best to explore for new oil fields. Medical researchers advanced knowledge in their field until, in 1930, the statistical life-expectancy of a newborn American baby was about sixty years, an achievement unprecedented in the world's history. An antitoxin for scarlet fever, once a major killer of children, was developed in 1925. The layman also realized, although he did not very well understand, that scientists in genetics, astronomy, and physics were on the verge of discoveries that would enable man to understand far better than ever before the nature of life and the universe. The general theory of relativity of the German mathematician Albert Einstein received considerable attention in the press, as did the work at California's Mt. Hamilton and Mt. Wilson observatories to test aspects of Einstein's hypothesis.

Of all the sciences, the place of psychology in the public mind was paramount. Between the real advances of psychological knowledge, theories acclaimed by some psychologists, and popular interpretations there were lamentable but ridiculous gaps. Sigmund Freud's theories, first noted in

America by G. Stanley Hall, Dr. A. A. Brill, and Dr. Adolph Meyer, emphasized the nonrational aspect of men and recognized that human beings are motivated at least partly by unconscious drives of which the sex urge is one of the most important. By the 1920's some psychiatrists in the United States were regularly effecting improvement in their patients by use of Freudian concepts and techniques. But some Freudian psychologists were extreme in their claims for the theory, and the man in the street distorted it. Freud and his responsible disciples emphasized that by man's use of his rational powers he could better understand, control, and direct his unconscious forces. At the popular level, people prattled Freudian jargon and used the theory as an excuse for license.

The theories of Professor John B. Watson of Johns Hopkins were perhaps even more widely known to Americans. His *Psychology from the Standpoint of a Behaviorist* (1919) carried mechanistic environmental determinism to a new extreme. Based partly on the research of the Russian physiologist and psychologist Ivan Pavlov, Watson's "behavioristic psychology" asserted that the child's environment could be manipulated so as to develop the individual in any desired direction. Through conditioning, an individual's responses could be controlled, just as at the most rudimentary level Pavlov's dogs had been conditioned by being given food at the sound of a bell and had then increased their saliva flow upon hearing the bell, whether there was food or not. Watson's ideas permeated a government handbook on infant and child care printed and distributed by the hundreds of thousands in the 1920's.

In a business civilization it was natural that psychological concepts should become commercially exploited. Watson himself in 1924 became vice-president of a large advertising agency and endeavored to manipulate consumers' responses. Books appeared by the score on "the psychology of salesmanship." The fetish in the United States about the ideas of Émile Coué, a misguided and untrained but sincere Frenchman who came to America for visits in 1922 and 1923, provided several illustrations of exploiting psychological theory to commercial advantage. Coué was a "mental healer" who preached that for good health one should say to himself several times each morning upon arising and again each evening upon retiring, "Every day, in every way, I am getting better and better." The formula was so popular that Mutt and Jeff said it even in the funny papers. How many people failed to consult a doctor about a dangerous condition in favor of muttering the magic incantation will never be known. Many sales managers assembled their staffs for "Coué sessions" before the men went out to meet prospective customers, and one company sold "Coué rosaries" to help faithful cultists count their utterances.

A more sophisticated understanding of psychological concepts had an impact on several academic disciplines. Literary scholars and critics, as well as writers of fiction, used Freudian ideas in the 1920's, although the movement did not grow to flood proportions until the 1940's and thereafter. The University of Chicago political scientist Harold D. Lasswell was under Freud's influence to a notable degree in his study of propaganda during the war and in his *Psychopathology and Politics* (1930) which put several long-dead political figures "on the couch." Biographers who wrote for a popular audience began to emphasize their subjects' psyches in a way earlier biographers had made their subjects moral paragons as examples for the young. Sociologists and psychologists developed an area between their two fields usually called social psychology.

Sociology as the youngest of the social sciences underwent more changes during the 1920's than more established disciplines. Where once sociologists had displayed a strong reformist attitude, they now at least endeavored to capture the cool detachment of the laboratory scientist; where once they had tended to make deductions from sweeping *a priori* principles, they now turned to amassing a huge body of evidence from which they hoped they could discover basic social principles by induction. Perhaps their striving to be "scientific" reveals as well as anything society's high regard for science.

Historians who wrote of America's past continued to expand their definitions of what was relevant and significant and, perhaps because of their time perspective, were less inclined than writers in other fields of literature to belittle democracy. When novelists, poets, and playwrights turned away from social problems and even from society to focus on the individual and his inner problems, historians usually kept their older approach. In *New Viewpoints in American History* (1922), an admirable series of essays that reflected recent research, Professor Arthur M. Schlesinger of Ohio State, Iowa, and Harvard did not reveal the current intellectual vogue of regarding democracy and reform as old-fashioned, although he did cut through the cant of some professed democrats. Two other great syntheses of the American experience, Charles and Mary Beard's first two volumes of *The Rise of American Civilization* (1927) and Vernon Louis Parrington's history of American literature, *Main Currents in American Thought* (3 volumes, 1927–1930), turned a sympathetic light on the struggles of democrats and reformers. Within just a few years after the publication of these books American democracy was to have one of its greatest crises, and the way Americans interpreted their past had at least something to do with democracy's emergence from the crisis battered and scarred, but vigorously alive.

CHAPTER FOURTEEN

The People
and Their Tensions

THE SOCIAL HISTORY OF THE 1920's OFFERS SO MUCH THAT IS COLOR-ful that it has become a favorite subject of popular writers. Babe Ruth, the Hall-Mills murder case, "Lucky Lindy," flappers, speakeasies, Rudolph Valentino, and Floyd Gibbons receive a full measure of treatment in these accounts, some of which are accurate, well written, and entertaining. It is interesting that the emphasis of popular and nostalgic social history of the 1920's is on aspects of urban life, almost to the exclusion of the country and the small town. Yet a large part of the population lived in rural communities and was not much involved in jazz age life. In many ways the countryside in the 1920's made its last losing battle to preserve its values and traditions as the national standard. Many of the social conflicts of the decade—struggles over immigration, over prohibition, over religion, and over individual morality—were related to urban-rural division.

The decade's prosperity brought little social harmony and stability. Changes in the way people lived, especially in the cities, were greater from 1919 to 1929 than during any decade between the Civil War and World War I. Rapid social change invariably brings anxiety and conflict between those who approve of the new ways and those who resist them. The postwar decade was marked especially by conflict between immigrants and old-stock Americans, Protestants and Catholics, and those who wanted a homogeneous, stable society and those who saw America's greatness in its heterogeneity and dynamism.

Immigration Restriction

For years, a combination of forces as diverse as Boston blue bloods and organized labor had converged in an effort to restrict immigration. Gradually they had been able to get legislation through Congress that excluded certain persons deemed undesirable, the most important law being the illiteracy test act that Congress had passed over Wilson's veto in 1917. Immigration had declined to unimportant proportions during the war because of the regulations of European powers. Immigration's opponents were determined that the stream should not flow again in its former volume when the war ended. Soon after the armistice, however, thousands of Europeans departed for the New World. Immigration figures for 1920 were almost as high as they had been for the peak years from 1905 to 1914. Renewed immigration stirred restrictionists to legislative action, and they received additional public support because of widespread fear of communism. Most people associated radicalism with immigrants.

Restrictionists pushed a bill through Congress in the last days of the Wilson administration. The House passed a bill late in 1920 introduced by Representative Albert Johnson of Washington to suspend immigration for a year while new restrictive legislation was prepared. The Senate amended the bill to provide a quota system. Wilson refused to sign the bill, however. Harding favored restriction, and Congress passed a slightly revised Johnson bill in May, 1921. The new law was a radical departure from previous immigration legislation. It provided that the number of immigrants from any nation who might be admitted each year should be no more than 3 per cent of the number of foreign-born of that nationality living in the United States in 1910. The law further provided that no more than one-fifth of the quota could be admitted in any single month. This led to a ridiculous situation when steamers loaded with immigrants waited outside New York harbor and raced for Ellis Island as the old month expired.

The Johnson Act, sometimes called the Emergency Quota Act, rigorously reduced immigration. In its first year of operation, immigration declined roughly 62 per cent to about three hundred thousand persons. This was still too many for extreme restrictionists, and it did not discriminate sufficiently against southern and eastern Europeans to meet their demands. By the base year of 1910 millions of immigrants from Italy, the Balkans, and the Russian empire had migrated to America. Under the law the maximum quota for eastern and southern Europe was about 160,000 and the maximum for northern and western Europe about 200,000. In the first year of its operation, more than half of the quotas for northern and western Europe had gone unused, but 95 per cent of the other quotas had been filled. Restrictionists demanded a more severe law, as did Coolidge in his State of the Union message in December, 1923. "America," said Coolidge, "must be kept American," by which he meant white, Anglo-Saxon, and Protestant.

The National Origins Act of May 26, 1924, also introduced by Representative Johnson, had two major parts, the first to apply until 1927 (later delayed until 1929), and the second to operate thereafter. For the first years, immigration quotas were figured at a maximum of 2 per cent of the foreign-born population for each nationality as revealed by the 1890 census. This new quota system reduced the total legal European immigration to about 164,000, and it further discriminated against the "new immigration." Putting the base year at 1890 cut back quotas for southern and eastern Europe from the 1921 level because most immigration from there had been after 1890.

The system to go into effect July 1, 1927, was even more restrictive. It put maximum immigration each year at 150,000. The quotas within this maximum were arrived at by figuring the ratio of "the number of inhabitants in the continental United States having that national origin" to the total population in 1920. Note that instead of figuring quota on the basis of foreign-born, as in earlier workings of the quota system, it now was to be on the basis of "national origin." Calculating these quotas, a task of the executive branch, involved genealogical chaos. Who could say what a family's "national origin" was when it had been in America for several generations and had intermarried? This scheme even further reduced quotas for eastern and southern Europe because the new basis included those whose forefathers had come to America as long ago as 1607 and immigration from other than the British Isles had been small until the 1840's. The executive branch of the government wrestled with the genealogical problem unwillingly and tried to get Congress to amend the law to make it administratively more convenient. Congress refused to budge, but it consented to extend the deadline until July 1, 1929. When the new quotas finally were announced there was considerable consternation in some quarters. Great Britain's quota almost doubled, but Germany's and Ireland's declined by half and Sweden's, Norway's, and Denmark's fell by two-thirds. There had been many people of German, Irish, and Scandinavian background who were perfectly willing to exclude Italians, Slavs, and Jews to "keep America American," but they had not foreseen how the new formula would discriminate against their own kind. Their protests availed them nothing. Congress was not particularly happy to see Great Britain get the lion's share of the 150,000 maximum, but it feared that to reopen the whole matter might allow substantial numbers of "new immigrants" to reach American shores.

One provision of the National Origins Act simplified the tasks of officials and removed one source of immigrant hardship. When immigrant ships had raced one another to docking space at Ellis Island, immigrants over the quota had been turned back and families had become separated. Under the new law, United States consuls at European port cities had responsibility for the acceptance of immigrants.

The law provided for no quota whatsoever for Asian countries, not even the token quota of one hundred granted countries such as Luxemburg. The law forbade the entry of any person not eligible for citizenship, and the Supreme Court had only recently reaffirmed that Japanese, for example, were not eligible. The Court had ruled that Japanese, being neither "free white persons" nor persons of African birth or origin, could not be naturalized under existing law. While Congress debated the National Origins bill, Japan sent the State Department a note which reminded the United States of the Gentlemen's Agreement of the Roosevelt administration and stated that absolute exclusion would have "grave consequences." In the conventions of diplomatic note writing "grave consequences" is a strong phrase. Secretary of State Hughes sent the note on to Congress. He had calculated that the Japanese quota would be about 250 a year if she were allowed one at all, constituting something surely less than a "yellow peril" to California. But West Coast newspapers demanded Japanese exclusion, and Congress by an overwhelming vote kept the exclusion clause in the bill. Passage of the law set off anti-American demonstrations in Japan, and when the new law went into effect, Japan observed the day as one of national humiliation.

The law's purpose was to freeze permanently the national composition of the American people, and it has not been altered in any essentials since its enactment. The great tide of humanity that had flowed from Europe to America for a century was now completed. It may have been almost finished anyway. Several European nations restricted emigration in the 1920's and 1930's, and some of those that did not never filled their quotas. The law did not apply to immigration from other American nations. During the 1920's, about nine hundred thousand Canadians moved to the United States, many of them French-speaking Roman Catholics and precisely the kind of immigrants the laws were designed to exclude. Almost a half million immigrants from Mexico went through the formality of being counted. How many others moved across the border without the Immigration Service's knowledge was not known, nor was there an accurate estimate of the number of Mexican laborers who entered the United States on temporary work permits to take stoop-labor agricultural jobs but escaped federal supervision and did not return. In 1930, the Mexican-American population was about two million.

With the practical end of immigration came inevitable changes in established immigrant institutions. The many fraternal organizations of immigrant groups waned in vigor as their source of new members declined to a trickle and children of immigrants felt less identification with the parent nationality. Foreign language newspapers continued to be published by the score in the major cities, but these also changed. First the comics and the school news appeared in English, then the sports page, and eventually much of the general news. Immigrant churches began to conduct two services, one in the European tongue and one in English. One aspect of America's diversity began slowly but steadily to disappear.

The Negro, South and North

The most important development among American Negroes during the war and the 1920's was a huge migration out of the South. In the long run, this migration had tremendous implications. First, it enabled the Negro to receive a better formal education than he would have had in the South, and educated Negroes could give their race better leadership. Second, by moving where he could vote, the Negro in time gained political leverage in national politics that he could use to improve his position. Had there not been the big migrations of the war and postwar eras, surely the subsequent history of the Negro would have been vastly different.

Migration to the North began to become significant in 1915. It grew during the war and increased still more in the 1920's. In 1910, only about 850,000 Negroes lived outside the South; in 1920, the figure was about 1,400,-000; in 1930, it was about 2,300,000. The percentage of nonsouthern Negroes to the total increased from slightly less than 10 per cent in 1910 to 20 per cent in 1930. Various pulls from the North and pushes from the South got the migration under way and kept it going. Prosperity created jobs in the North, although for the most part Negroes got the worst jobs available. Fewer European immigrants provided Negroes the chance to get employment that had formerly gone to "greenhorns." In the South a combination of circumstances made the Negro want to leave more than before and made it possible for him to do so. The boll weevil made cotton farming more precarious than usual, and white men increasingly moved into occupations that had traditionally been reserved for Negroes. More widespread elementary Negro education in the South sharpened Negro aspirations and gave him the literacy necessary for most urban employment. Prosperity created jobs in southern cities as well as northern ones, and thousands of Negroes moved from their rural homes to the nearest city where they got the cash necessary to go north. Most of the northward migration was from city to city, and most of it was to the nearest northern city. Thus Negroes in the southeastern states tended to go to Washington, Baltimore, Philadelphia, and New York, and those in the central South tended to move to cities of the Midwest. Negro migration to the West Coast had not yet become significant.

The war itself wrenched thousands of Negroes from their homes and their old ways of living. Roughly four hundred thousand Negroes served in the armed forces during World War I, and about half of them served overseas. Once moved from behind a one-mule plow and shown something of the outside world (including the racial equality of France) the young Negro was not likely to return to his old life. In fact, many Negro soldiers stayed in France. Far more moved to northern cities.

The immediate disruption of traditional patterns in the South during the war and the appearance of large numbers of Negroes in the North brought an appalling outbreak of violence. In the South most interracial violence was lynching; in the North most of it was rioting. Lynching was usually rural and small-town; rioting was usually urban. Perhaps the main reason why practically all of the rioting was in the North was that only there did the Negro feel secure enough to fight back. Yet there was one serious riot at Houston, Texas, in 1917, which ended in the deaths of thirteen Negro soldiers. Another soldier riot was narrowly averted at Spartanburg, South Carolina. Negro lynchings increased from thirty-four in 1917 to sixty in 1918 and to seventy in 1919. Several of the victims were soldiers or veterans, some of them in uniform. Simultaneously in the South, the Ku Klux Klan revived and terrorized Negroes, sometimes only frightening them but often beating them.

So many riots occurred in the North in the summer of 1919—more than a score—that Negro publications referred to it as the Red Summer. The worst of the riots began in Chicago in late July when a fight began between some young Negroes and young whites at a Lake Michigan beach. The violence went on for almost two weeks before the National Guard and the police restored order. White gangs invaded the Negro neighborhood to beat victims, loot stores, and burn buildings and black gangs ranged out of their ghettos into neighboring slums to do the same. When it was at last over, 15 whites had been killed and 178 injured and 23 Negroes had been killed and 342 injured. In the nation's capital a mob of white soldiers, having saved the world for democracy, roamed Negro neighborhoods to destroy property and beat up those who resisted.

Lynching and rioting were almost altogether a lower-class phenomenon.

Both white and colored leaders deplored violence, and following the 1919 violence, they formed interracial commissions in both the North and the South in an effort to prevent further outbreaks. The National Association for the Advancement of Colored People undertook a campaign for the enactment of a federal law against lynching, violators of the law to be tried in federal courts. When lynchers were arrested at all, and they seldom were, their trials in state and local courts were farces. In 1921, in the face of strong public opinion, the House passed an antilynching law, but southern Senators filibustered it to death. Their stated reason for opposition was that a federal law on the subject would be an invasion of state rights.

It was against this background of strife and bloodshed that millions of Negroes enlisted in the only Negro nationalist movement that had ever amounted to anything in the United States. The leader was Marcus Garvey, a remarkable Negro from Jamaica who saw himself as the Moses of his people. In 1914, Garvey founded the Universal Negro Improvement Association, but when he moved to Harlem two years later his group and idea struck little response. He went to Europe until 1918, and when he returned his organization caught on and spread quickly. It was at its height in 1920 and 1921, although it did not die out until the mid-1920's. He claimed to have six million followers; four million was a better estimate.

Garvey was a thorough nationalist who exalted all things black and had contempt for all things white. Even God and Jesus Christ were black, said Garvey, and it was humiliating for Negroes to worship a white God. He vigorously opposed integration, declaring that it was a scheme of the whites and that Negro leaders who worked for assimilation were accommodationist Uncle Toms. He proposed a kind of Negro Zionist movement. American Negroes should flee to Africa and establish a strong Negro empire. To do so meant that the white rulers of Africa would have to be driven out, and he organized the Universal African Legion, the Black Eagle Flying Corps, and the Universal Black Cross Nurses complete with uniforms and officers. Transportation would be needed, and he organized the Black Star Line and purchased ships. In 1921, he proclaimed the Empire of Africa and was inaugurated as its provisional president. He tried to get the "nation's" acceptance into the League of Nations and negotiated with Liberia as a fellow state. If all these plans seemed ridiculous it was only because Garvey ultimately failed. Had he been as successful as the Zionists or the Czechs or the Latvians, his grandiose plans would have indicated great foresight.

Garvey as a political leader was an interesting phenomenon, but his tremendous reception by American Negroes was even more interesting. And this was over almost unanimous opposition from the Negro press, the churches, and the leaders of the racial organizations. Negro intellectuals, both educators and others, were particularly outraged. But when he counterattacked, asserting that these Negro leaders were traitors to their race and worse, hundreds of thousands of his followers believed him. Part of the explanation of the Negro response to Garveyism lay in the techniques of the movement. The uniforms and ritual had appeal for people who led drab lives. But apparently it was an illusion of probable success that was Garvey's greatest attraction. The established Negro organizations had not yet achieved startling success with their programs. Nine years after the NAACP's foundation had come the worst wave of lynchings since the 1890's. The achievements of the Negro labor movement were still pathetic. Most Negro ministers still emphasized only salvation after death. Negro educators had done a great deal to help the race to lift itself by its bootstraps, but at late as 1929 there were only about 15,000 Negro college graduates and only forty who held a Ph.D. The momentum of the Garvey movement made quick success seem possible.

The movement died out rather quickly, probably because it became apparent that the difficulties facing the Empire of Africa were insurmountable. Garvey's several business ventures either failed or involved him in legal tangles. The Department of Justice prosecuted him for using the mails to defraud in selling stock in the Black Star Line. Garvey foolishly conducted his own case at the trial. After a long series of legalistic holding actions, he went to prison in 1925 for a two-year term. Upon his release he was deported back to Jamaica. The Universal Negro Improvement Association collapsed. Garvey himself faded into obscurity and died in London in 1940, forgotten and broke.

Negro history for the rest of the war-to-depression period offered nothing as spectacular as the immediate postwar violence and the Garvey movement. A few Negro leaders moved into left-wing politics during the decade. A. Philip Randolph, who was later to become an outstanding and effective leader of his people, published a left-wing magazine and joined the Socialist party which was extremely weak in the 1920's. The Communists began to make a determined effort for Negro support in the late 1920's, but they met with little success. Perhaps the strongest reason for Communist failure among Negroes was the Negro's suspicion that he was being used. Nor did the Communist program of "self-determination for the Negro people in the Black Belt" make much sense to American Negroes. An attempt to transplant Josef Stalin's theory, but not his practice, on the various nationalities in the Soviet Union, "self-determination" meant to establish an autonomous black republic in the most densely Negro-populated area of the South. This involved a kind of supersegregation, and Negroes came to call the plan "Red Crow."

Two Negro intellectual movements attracted considerable attention among American Caucasians. The "new Negro movement" among Harlem intellectuals, which produced the so-called Negro Renaissance, became a special fad among some white intellectuals, as described in Chapter 13. White interest in the movement created a market for Negro talents, and several writers and entertainers were thereby able to work at their special crafts and make a living at it. The other movement, while not so well publicized, was more lasting. In 1915, Dr. Carter G. Woodson, a Negro historian, brought about the founding of the Association for the Study of Negro Life and History. He became editor of its chief publication, *The Journal of Negro History*, a learned quarterly. The *Journal* undoubtedly stimulated research and writing in the field. In 1926, the Association began to push an annual Negro History Week. At first the Association endeavored to reach only Negro school children during this special week, and it provided teachers in dominantly Negro schools with material and lesson plans. Later, the Association enjoyed considerable success in getting special study units taught in all schools and gained the cooperation of newspapers and magazines. As a result of the Association's work, American Negroes are far better acquainted with their history than other minority groups are with their pasts.

Prohibition: Wets, Drys, Crime, and Politics

We have already seen in Chapter 5 how the prohibition movement gained strength and how, by 1917, it had succeeded in banning the sale of liquor in a large part of the United States. In 1917, the Lever Act prohibited the manufacture of alcoholic beverages in order to conserve grain for food. The prohibition movement had strength and momentum, and the wartime mood with its special kind of idealism further strengthened the prohibitionist principle.

It should be noted that prohibition movements were not unique to the United States. Most of the nations of the western world in the first third of the twentieth century had at least a temperance movement, and several of them legislated prohibition. Great Britain's dry movement was of considerable proportions, and it succeeded in cutting down the hours that pubs could remain open and creating a chaotic schedule of opening and closing hours that defied reason. Sweden, Norway, and Iceland imposed absolute prohibition. The Soviet Union, under quite a different rationale, outlawed liquor. Even the French, for all their professed amazement and amusement by American prohibition—"But, yes, next *les américains* will regulate the marriage bed"—had a modest temperance movement and outlawed the manufacture of absinthe.

On December 17, 1917, Congress passed the Eighteenth Amendment to the Constitution and submitted it to the states. "After one year from the ratification of this article, the manufacture, sale, or transportation of intoxicating liquors within, the importation thereof into, or the exportation thereof from the United States and all territory subject to the jurisdiction thereof for beverage purposes is hereby prohibited." (Congressmen in 1917 did not write as clearly as the founding fathers did in 1787.) The amendment further provided that it should become inoperative if three-fourths of the state legislatures did not ratify it within seven years. Given the pitch of prohibitionist sentiment, the seven-year provision did not give wets even a sporting chance. The thirty-sixth state ratified the amendment in January, 1919. In October, 1919, Congress passed the Volstead Act over Wilson's veto. The law extended wartime prohibition until the Eighteenth Amendment went into effect the following January and defined "intoxicating liquors" as any beverage that contained as much as 0.5 per cent of alcohol by volume.

Prohibitionists were ecstatic in their victory over what they called John Barleycorn or The Demon Rum. The new Prohibition Commissioner promised that his administration would be so strict that no liquor would be manufactured "nor sold, nor given away, nor hauled in anything on the surface of the earth or under the earth or in the air." He was wrong on almost all counts, although not much was given away. Actually, it is impossible to say precisely how well—or how badly—the law was observed and enforced. It was observed best in rural areas and small towns that were overwhelmingly Protestant. But it was possible in even the dryest of regions to buy a bottle if one used some ingenuity. In the rural upper South and the southern Midwest, both predominantly Protestant, it was possible in several places to leave some money on a special stump in the woods and return after a respectable interval to get the moonshine that an obliging "alky cooker" had provided. Doctors reported fewer deaths from alcoholism and police blotters recorded fewer arrests for drunkenness than there had been before prohibition. But, obviously, the Eighteenth Amendment was the most widely disobeyed part of the Constitution—unless maybe the Fifteenth Amendment, which forbade racial discrimination in the right to vote, received more violations. Paradoxically, on another level, Constitution worship was a major fetish of the decade.

Particularly in the late prohibition period, one could buy liquor and beer without difficulty. Patrolling the whole Mexican and Canadian border was impossible. Whole fleets of boats imported Canadian whiskey across the Great Lakes. Running rum from Cuba was more difficult but was commonly done. Bootleggers in many cities offered delivery service, and the saloon merely became more or less secretive and known as a speakeasy. In cities with a large foreign-born population speakeasies operated fairly openly. Strangers sometimes asked policemen for the address of the nearest one. Much of the stuff that was sold had only an alcoholic similarity to what it was labelled. Burnt sugar and iodine added to watered pure grain spirits looked similar to bourbon. Some of the concoctions were dangerous, and blindness, paralysis, and internal bleeding were their consequences. Making one's own beverages was common. Copper stills were for sale in many hardware stores, and one could buy drops or powders at drug stores which flavored the distillation however one wished —gin, rum, bourbon, or scotch. Making beer in the basement became a great indoor sport. Crocks, bottles, and bottle cappers were easily purchasable; malt companies took full-page advertisements in national magazines and sold their product through groceries. Families sometimes bought equipment cooperatively, and children hauled it about from family to family in their toy wagons.

In the nation's big cities, gangsters consolidated the bootlegging business upon the same economic principles as general business. But since they operated altogether outside the law and had no resort to conventional legal procedures for enforcing contracts, they used their own private force as a business auxiliary. In 1920, Al Capone, a New York hoodlum, moved to Chicago and began a bootlegging business. He became the most important of the Chicago beer barons who divided the market amongst themselves. By 1927, Capone had a $60 million business with a private army of nearly one thousand gangster troops to protect the market and raid other territories. Bootlegger gangsters thoroughly corrupted the administration of Republican Mayor William H. Thompson. In 1926 and 1927, there were 130 gang killings in Chicago; not a single one of the murderers was caught and brought to trial. A group of Sicilian brothers, the six Terrible Gennas, sought to underprice their competitors and engaged the services of five police captains and four hundred policemen. Their corruption of the police, however, was not enough to save three of the brothers from being killed in typical gang fashion. Dutch Schultz's organization in New York collected protection money from speakeasy operators and had an alliance with Tammany Hall and the Democratic Jimmie Walker administration. Bootleggers of Philadelphia, long a center of commercial propriety, organized their own court system with a "judge" who held bootlegger court, complete with attorneys and precedent, and whose decisions were enforced by thugs. Prohibition has sometimes been blamed for indirectly creating this kind of organized crime, but the allegation is unfair. Organized crime existed before prohibition and after repeal; it only moved into the liquor business during prohibition because of the fat profits to be made. And if organized crime flouted the law more openly and successfully during prohibition than at other times it was because of the venality of public officials and lack of moral indignation in the public at large rather than the fact of the Eighteenth Amendment.

Popular support for prohibition was clearly at its greatest in 1918 and early 1919 when the amendment was before the states and when wartime faith in the millennium was high. Its popularity waned steadily thereafter. A poll of almost two million people in 1926 indicated that less than one-fifth supported the Volstead Act completely, almost one-third were for outright repeal ("wringing wets" in the parlance of the day), and half wanted the law modified to permit light wines and beer. Yet prohibition of all liquor remained on the law books for another seven years. Why? Basically, because the prohibition question had become involved in partisan politics and a number of other social conflicts, between city and country, Catholic and Protestant, Negro and white. Thousands of people who regularly used bootleggers' services and grumbled about the poor quality and high price of their purchases voted for candidates who were politically dry—and sometimes also personally wet. The most outspoken opponents of prohibition, both before its adoption and after, were immigrants and those of recent immigrant background. Among Germans, beer at meals was as routine as salt; among Italians, wine was the table beverage. These immigrants, for the most part, lived in industrial cities of the North and West.

Many middle-class persons privately violated prohibition but approved of it as a means to keep liquor away from the working class, either out of compassion for working-class wives and children whose breadwinner might drink away his wages or from vague fear that liquor might unleash class violence. Again, the industrial working class lived mostly in the northern cities. Because the Republican party's main strength was rural or small town and urban middle-class, that organization remained steadfastly for prohibition until the bitter end. The Democratic party divided badly over prohibition. The urban parts of the party were wet, from slightly damp to wringing wet. The western rural Democrats usually agreed with their Republican neighbors on the issue. The South remained firmly dry, not because the term "bourbon" for a southern Democrat did not have a logical linguistic basis, but because white supremacists wanted to keep liquor from the Negro. A drunken Negro was less likely to be docile than a sober one. As the comedian Will Rogers, a man who made many shrewd political observations, said, "Mississippi will vote dry and drink wet as long as it can stagger to the polls." The Democratic party compromised in 1924 and did not put repeal into its platform, but in both 1928 and 1932 its platform advocated the end of prohibition. In both 1928 and 1932, differences between wets and drys played such an important part in the campaigns that more important issues were obscured and submerged, although prohibition was by no means the only issue in the campaign. John Dewey exaggerated only a little when he wrote after the national convention of 1932, "Here we are in the greatest crisis since the Civil War, and the only thing the two national parties seem to want to debate is booze."

Ironically, prohibition faded quickly while Hoover, who called it a "noble experiment," was in the White House. Soon after he took office, he appointed a commission headed by former Attorney General George W. Wickersham to investigate prohibition's enforcement and to make recommendations. Testimony given to the commission indicated that enforcing a widely unpopular law was next to impossible short of police-state measures. The Commission, however, refused in its 1931 report to recommend repeal. It instead offered several suggestions to make federal enforcement more efficient. But enforcement was already deteriorating quickly. Three states, New York, Maryland, and Wisconsin, had already repealed their "baby Volstead Acts" and ceased state enforcement. Other states practically abandoned enforcement as the depression cut into state government revenues seriously. After the electorate overwhelmingly elected a Democrat on a repeal platform in 1932, the end was in sight. On February 20, 1933, a lame-duck Congress passed the Twenty-First Amendment which repealed the Eighteenth. A new Congress made the manufacture and sale of weak beer legal the next month, and the thirty-sixth state ratified the repealing amendment on December 5, 1933. Prohibition on a national scale was finished.

Manners and Morals

Many writers have concluded that standards of behavior changed so radically during the 1920's that the change amounted to a "revolution in morals." They point out that older people whose standards had been formed in a more sedate society expressed considerable dismay about "flaming youth" and "flappers." The automobile, they suggest, offered young people greater freedom from social supervision than they had once enjoyed. Rudolph Valentino, a rather oily film star who played great-lover roles in desert "sand and sex" pictures, was the most popular male Hollywood figure of his day, and thousands of women rioted at his funeral in 1926. These writers often assert that popular songs of the day indicated drunkenness and passion—"Show Me the Way To Go Home," "Makin' Whoopee," "Hot Lips," and "Hot Mama."

That there were significant changes in manners is clear, but it is not at all clear that society in the 1920's underwent a "revolution" in sexual morality. Each generation from time immemorial has regarded the next one as more degenerate than itself. Statistics on sexual matters are elusive at best. The questionnaire studies of Dr. Alfred Kinsey of Indiana University done a generation later indicated, for what they were worth, that women who matured in the 1920's had only a slightly higher incidence of premarital and extramarital sexual relations than those who matured in an earlier day. In general, it seems that the "revolution in morals" has been grossly overstated and overemphasized, but the whole truth is impossible to discover.

Obviously, there was less prudery in the most commonly accepted code of manners and dress after the war than there had been previously. Where mother would never have said the word sex, at least in mixed company, and might even have referred to the legs of a table as its limbs, daughter tossed around Freudian terms as if she understood them. Women's figures were far less concealed. Dresses at the end of the war were fully cut tent-like garments that extended to the ankles. Stockings were dark, petticoats numerous, and corsets forbiddingly hard. By the late 1920's, skirts came to slightly above the knees, stockings were flesh colored, and corsets were reserved for dowagers. Certainly there was less prudery in the subject matter and language of fiction, although it was fairly tame in comparison with what was to come after World War II. But what, if anything, the new code signified about personal morals is moot.

When one makes class and urban-rural distinctions and considers feminism as a relevant factor, the thesis of a "revolution in morals" seems even less justifiable. The main changes in behavior were most pronounced in the urban middle-class. Except for women's fashions, rural and small-town life had little of the jazzy flapper age. The ways of working class youth, male and female, changed less than their wealthier neighbors. Prudery had never been as strong among immigrant working people as it was in more comfortable circles with rural and Protestant backgrounds. The way older critics referred to the behavior of "flaming youth" as "common" suggested an impression of blurred class mores. Much of the change in manners can be explained in terms of feminism, the gradual adoption of a single standard of conduct by middle-class urban girls. If society was not shocked by the young men's drinking, smoking cigarettes, and general lack of parental control, feminist young women figured they too should have a similar freedom.

Indeed, the fashions and ideal feminine types of the 1920's suggest that feminine equality rather than sex was the main factor in changing manners. The flapper costume was anything but sexy, with its sackish lack of waistline, a roll of stocking just below the knees, and hat that looked like a too large Viking helmet. Women looked like dressed up little girls, or even little boys, especially when they wore their hair bobbed. Florenz Ziegfeld chose flat-chested girls for the nudes in his famous Follies, a fact the Freudians of the age could have speculated upon gaily. Nor were the famous dances of the period erotic in any sense. The Charleston and the Black Bottom were boisterous but hardly bawdy. Only one thing is certain: sex was more freely discussed in the 1920's than it had been before the war.

Rural and small-town people resisted the new folkways more than their more hedonistic city cousins. Rural people did not enjoy as much prosperity or as much leisure. When rural youths revolted they were likely to move to the city and thus be less subversive of traditions in their home communities than city young people were to theirs. The automobile and better roads, to be sure, changed rural life, but lack of money, the necessity of hard work and long hours, the family, and the church braked the speed of rural social change. The city changed rapidly, the country changed slowly, and the differences in their ways of life broadened.

"One Hundred Percentism"

Rural America and urban America had one important social-political trait in common during the 1920's: extreme nationalism, "one hundred per cent Americanism." Twenty years of Theodore Roosevelt on the national scene and the forced-draft patriotism of the war had had their effects. Nationalism in the United States or in other countries has two aspects: externally, a strident chip-on-the-shoulder attitude toward other nations and other peoples of the world; internally, a glorification of national institutions, superpatriotism, lack of toler-ance, and efforts to bring about conformist unanimity. During the 1920's, the government itself pursued economically nationalist policies, and the electorate displayed a generally hostile attitude toward the rest of the world. But "in-ternal nationalism" was even stronger. Nationalism in the cities differed in its emphases from that of the country, but each was nationalistic.

Perhaps William Hale Thompson, mayor of Chicago in the 1920's, got more political mileage from a nationalistic stance than any other urban figure of the period. By any standard Thompson's administration was disgraceful. The Chicago schools suffered badly from lack of funds and political inter-ference. Its officials' alliances with bootlegger gangsters made it the most law-less large city in the United States. Chicago acquired a deserved reputation abroad for corruption and violence which has not entirely dissipated yet. But despite the gross inadequacies of his administration, Thompson's political op-ponents were ineffective because the mayor's political organization was good and his flamboyant nationalism was popular. He led a campaign to remove "pro-English" history textbooks from the schools. He gained international notice when he offered to "punch King George on the snoot." Such state-ments, designed especially for the Irish vote, had a much wider appeal. Patriot organizations such as the Daughters of the American Revolution and the American Legion were as popular and as powerful in all but the biggest cities as they were in small towns. City dwellers, perhaps more than people in the country, had great praise of the Italian dictator Benito Mussolini, primarily because of his extreme nationalism, his anticommunist policies, and the sup-posed efficiency of his government. Not until the 1930's was Mussolini's fascism regarded as a menace by most American publications. The historical novelist Kenneth Roberts wrote a highly laudatory series on Italian fascism for the Saturday Evening Post, and the American Legion invited Mussolini to address its 1923 convention at San Francisco. (Mussolini declined.)

Both rural and urban nationalism contained a great deal of racism, but anti-Semitism was clearly stronger in the cities, where most Jews lived, than on the farms and in small towns. The American Farm Bureau Federation, as a case in point, appointed a Jew, Aaron Sapiro, as its general counsel in 1923. The most important sources of anti-Semitism in America were upper-middle-class Yankess and Polish and Irish immigrants; most of them were urban. The amount and intensity of racism in general but of anti-Semitism in particular that came forth in the arguments for immigration restriction was similar to what would soon be revealed in Germany. Madison Grant, author of the pop-ular and virulently racist The Passing of the Great Race (1916), wrote, "The man of the old stock . . . is to-day being literally driven off the streets of New York City by the swarms of Polish Jews." Kenneth Roberts referred to East European Jews as "human parasites." Henry Ford published the anti-Semitic Dearborn (Michigan) Independent and had his dealers put copies of it in their new cars. Among other hate pieces, the Independent published a famous forgery, "The Protocols of the Elders of Zion," an alleged plan for Jewish conquest of the world.

The Ku Klux Klan, most important hate organization of the decade, however, was overwhelmingly rural. During Reconstruction the Klan had come into being as a means to terrorize newly freed slaves. In 1915, a romantic history teacher at Lanier College, William J. Simmons, a man who worshipped at the shrine of the "lost cause," founded a new Ku Klux Klan. Simmons' purpose apparently was more to glorify the memory of past white supremacists than to preach hate, but he built more than he knew. It was Simmons who gave the organization its fantastic terminology. Simmons gave himself the title of Imperial Wizard. Local units were called Kleagles and other terms began with the letter K. Under Simmons the KKK was only an unimportant lodge, however. In 1920, it had only about five thousand members, most of them in Georgia and Alabama. Then two professional fund-raisers, Mrs. Elizabeth Tyler and Edward Y. Clarke, took hold of the lodge, raised its initiation fee to $10, and began to high-pressure its growth. In two years it had grown to one hundred thousand members. At this point a Texas dentist, Hiram Wesley Evans, became Imperial Wizard and changed the nature of the Klan. It went into politics and quickly demonstrated its strength. A Klan-supported politician in Texas defeated the incumbent in the 1922 Democratic primary. The following year, when the governor of Oklahoma, J. C. "Our Jack" Walton, opposed the Klan and declared martial law in an effort to suppress it, the Klan was active in bringing about his successful impeachment.

The Klan was different things in different parts of the country. In the South it was primarily anti-Negro; in the Midwest and the Far West it was primarily anti-Catholic; in the East, although it was never very strong east of Pennsylvania, it was primarily anti-Semitic. Everywhere it opposed the immigrant and immigration as a national policy, persecuted bootleggers and preached the dry gospel, railed against divorce, and tried to enforce monogamy. In general, it upheld what rural, old-fashioned, white, Anglo-Saxon Protestants held to be "the American way of life." Everywhere its strength was its conspiratorial secrecy—members wore white masked hoods and gowns at meetings and were supposed never to reveal membership—its working as a bloc in politics, and its terror devices. Klansmen several times beat people horribly and killed upon a few occasions. Usually it found it necessary only to burn a cross conspicuously or conduct a masked parade to intimidate its victims. The Klan, which violated both Christian and American principles, published a periodical called *The Cross and the Flag*.

Politically, the Klan was bipartisan. In Oregon it moved into the Democratic party, elected a Democratic governor by a huge plurality, and in a state initiative brought passage of a law designed to abolish parochial schools by requiring that all school-age children attend public schools. In 1925, in Pierce *v.* Society of Sisters, the Supreme Court found the Oregon law unconstitutional. In Indiana the Klan was primarily Republican, but it had strength in the Democratic party as well.

The Klan reached its heights and started its downfall in Indiana. Both its rise and its decline there were due to the extraordinary activities of D. C. Stephenson, leader of the Klan in the entire Midwest. Through rallies that were masterpieces of showmanship—Stephenson liked to arrive at rallies by airplane—and appeals to dark and latent prejudices easily exploited because of the rapid changes that were occurring in the half urban and half rural state,

Stephenson built an Indiana organization of an estimated three hundred fifty thousand members. In small towns practically all men of social consequence were members, and they became so bold they frequently marched with their white hoods thrown back. In 1923 and 1924, the Indiana Klan got control of the state legislature, both the United States Senators, and most of the congressional delegation. In the 1924 elections, Stephenson had his friend Ed Jackson elected governor on the Republican ticket. But late in 1925 the Klan, at its height with an estimated national membership of five million began to crumble.

One night in the summer of 1925 at a party in Indianapolis, Stephenson picked up a twenty-eight-year-old Sunday school teacher who worked as a secretary at the state house, plied her with bootleg liquor, got her on a Pullman bound for Chicago, and assaulted her. Humiliated, the girl took poison and became extremely ill. Stephenson and Klansmen friends got her off the train before it crossed the Illinois line—thus avoiding a federal offense—and got her to a hotel without undue notice. For several days they denied her medical aid for fear of discovery. A month later she died. Many Indiana politicians who had joined the Klan and cooperated with it only to save their political lives saw the chance to get off the Klan's hook. They saw to it that Stephenson was prosecuted for his crime, and in November, 1925, a jury found him guilty of manslaughter. The most powerful figure in the Klan had been found guilty of a sordid crime that violated the organization's principles and was lodged in the state prison of what had been the Klan's strongest state. Thereafter the KKK fell apart quickly, holding on longest in the South. (Incidentally, when Stephenson's puppet, Governor Jackson, refused to pardon him, the convict told something of the political corruption he knew about, and others went to jail. Jackson was indicted for bribery but escaped under the statute of limitations. For fear that he would talk even more, Hoosier politicians kept Stephenson imprisoned for almost his full term, not usually done in manslaughter cases, and then made his parole conditional upon his leaving the state.)

The Ku Klux Klan was the strongest terroristic, essentially fascistic, organization in the nation's history. Fascist organizations of the next decade never began to approach its strength, largely because they imported their unpopular ideas and methods whereas the Klan was entirely homegrown. Not all rural states succumbed to Klan rule, at least partly because state political leaders and newspaper editors fought it and exposed it for what it was. Although cooperating with the Klan might prevent political suicide, many Indiana politicians learned that going along with it could also mean political death. Speaking out on one's convictions proved not only the most honorable but the most expedient alternative in the long run.

The Election of 1928: The Tension's Climax

In the summer of 1927, President Coolidge issued a puzzling statement to the press: "I do not choose to run for President in 1928." Did he mean he would not run under any circumstances, would reluctantly accept a draft, or would look favorably upon a draft? He did not encourage the draft-Coolidge move-

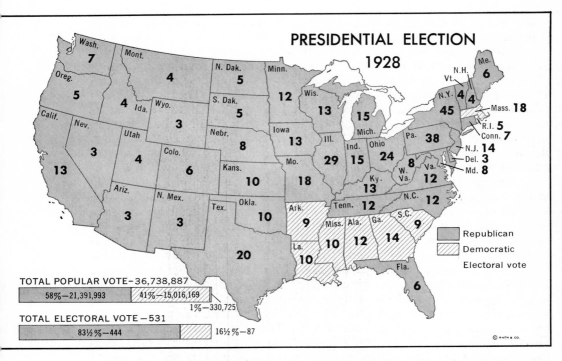

PRESIDENTIAL ELECTION 1928

Republican
Democratic
Electoral vote

TOTAL POPULAR VOTE—36,738,887
58%—21,391,993   41%—15,016,169
1%—330,725

TOTAL ELECTORAL VOTE—531
83½%—444   16½%—87

ment that developed, and the movement lost steam. Democrats and progressive Republicans in the Senate passed a resolution which stated it would be "unwise" and "unpatriotic" to depart from the two-term tradition. The poker-faced Coolidge may have been disappointed by the absence of a draft, but he later stated in his autobiography that he declined to seek the nomination because of the two-term tradition.

Although Senator Borah, former governor of Illinois Frank O. Lowden, and Vice-President Charles G. Dawes were talked of as Republican candidates, Herbert Hoover was the politically proper and logical man for the nomination. Popular with the country at large and seemingly "above" politics, Hoover was the symbol of prosperous Republicanism, of the businessman in government. The Kansas City convention nominated him on the first ballot and named Charles Curtis of Kansas, Republican majority leader in the Senate, as his running mate. The GOP platform pledged "vigorous enforcement" of the Eighteenth Amendment, praised the accomplishments of the Coolidge administrations, and promised action on the farm problem.

Several men contended for the Democratic nomination, among them Senator Thomas J. Walsh of Montana and Governor Albert Ritchie of Maryland. But Governor Alfred E. Smith of New York, who had come close to nomination in 1924, was not to be denied. He not only had the delegates from Tammany Hall behind him at the Houston, Texas, convention (many of the New Yorkers pronounced the city "Howston," the proper pronunciation of Houston Street in lower Manhattan), but those from practically all the states with big cities in them. He received the nomination on the first ballot. His nomination, however, did not sit well with the southern delegates because he was a wet, a Roman Catholic, and a New Yorker. To placate the southern delegates, Senator Joseph T. Robinson of Arkansas received the vice-presidential nomination, and the platform promised "an honest effort" to enforce prohibition. Smith said as president he would enforce the Eighteenth Amendment but that he would also work for the amendment's repeal. Using Dixie arguments, he declared prohibition was a matter for the states to decide. The Democratic platform differed little from the Republican. It urged enactment of a law prohibiting injunctions in labor disputes and was for public control of hydroelectric power, but it approved tariff protection and only criticized the Republican party for its lack of an agricultural program without outlining one of its own.

The main issue of the campaign became the background and personality of the Democratic candidate. Smith was born in 1873 in a tenement in New York's lower east side, the son of Irish immigrant parents. When he was seven years old he became an altar boy at the parish church. At fifteen he had to quit school to help support the family, and at nineteen he went to work as a salesman and bookkeeper at the Fulton Street Fish Market. When he was old enough to vote he joined the local Tammany organization, a natural thing for any ambitious Irish boy from his neighborhood to do. Soon he was rewarded with an appointment as a process server, a routine task he performed for eight years. In 1903, he was elected to the state assembly. There his competence soon attracted attention; he was generally regarded as the best-informed man in the state on legislative matters. In 1918, he was elected governor, but he was defeated in the Republican landslide in 1920. He won again in 1922, as he did also in 1924 and 1926. No previous New York governor had been elected four times. As legislator and governor, Smith was fair, efficient, and mildly progressive. He managed the bills that came from Hughes's investigation of life insurance companies, investigated the Triangle Shirtwaist Factory fire, and defended the assemblymen who had been elected in 1920 on the Socialist ticket. He was by no means a radical; he never went beyond the public opinion of his urban constituents.

In one way, Al Smith was the personification of the American dream—the poor boy who rose above humble origins to a position of responsibility and acclaim. But the American dream in politics was a rural dream, from a log cabin and one-room school to the court house and eventually the White House, not from a tenement and a fish market. And, very important, no Roman Catholic had ever before run for president on a major-party ticket.

Smith had to face powerful odds against him in 1928. Republican politicians basked in the decade's prosperity, and Smith could only promise that as president he would do nothing to upset the business cycle. He appointed John J. Raskob as his campaign manager. Raskob had been a Republican, had voted for Coolidge in 1924, had been a top official of General Motors, and had listed his occupation in *Who's Who in America* as "capitalist." He was prominent in Roman Catholic lay organizations. Raskob's appointment and the generally conservative platform were attempts to leave the impression that Smith was "safe." On the other hand, Smith tried to capitalize upon what discontent there was with the GOP's record. He attempted to attract urban votes with his stand on prohibition, liberals with his speeches on electric power (for which he gained the endorsement of Senator Norris), and farmers with his support of McNary-Haugenism. Hoover, on the other hand, campaigned as a bone dry and condemned government power projects and the McNary-Haugen bills as dangerous deviations from "rugged individualism" which would lead to a slave state. Hoover did not need to campaign hard. All that was necessary was to identify himself with prosperity and respectability.

Hoover won easily. He won 444 electoral votes and received 21,392,190 popular votes. Smith received only 87 electoral and 15,016,443 popular votes. Besides sweeping all of the northern and western states with the exception of Massachusetts and Rhode Island, Hoover cracked the Solid South and carried Virginia, North Carolina, Tennessee, Florida, and Texas. He also carried the border states: Delaware, Maryland, West Virginia, Kentucky, and Missouri. He nearly won in Alabama. Republicans won majorities in each house of Congress. Minor party candidates showed little strength. The Socialists nominated Norman Thomas for the first time, and the former Presbyterian minister received 268,000 votes. William Z. Foster received 48,000 votes on the Communist ticket.

After the election it was commonly said that Smith had lost the election because he was a Roman Catholic. How accurate was the assertion? Final answers are not possible, but certain conclusions can be made. Smith's religion, obviously, was a prominent feature of the campaign. A year before his nomination he had been asked by the editor of *The Atlantic Monthly* to write an article on the implications of a Catholic president. A Methodist bishop, James Cannon, Jr., of Virginia, mobilized Protestant opinion in the South against Smith. Thousands of scurrilous pamphlets and leaflets full of forebodings about the influence of the Pope in Washington if Smith should be elected were passed hand to hand and mailed anonymously. Responsible Republican officials did not circulate hate literature, but they did not actively try to prevent its circulation. An examination of a collection of such pamphlets in the Columbia University library—the so-called Book of Horrors—shows that the 1928 anti-Catholic literature repeated the same old discredited stories that had circulated as far back as the 1830's. It must be remembered that the Ku Klux Klan was not long dead. That it had faded in influence was apparent in the fact that a major party had nominated a Roman Catholic for president, but most of its members presumably did not discard their prejudices along with their white hoods.

Yet, did rural Protestant opposition to Smith exist because he was Catholic or because he was a symbol of an urban immigrant? Smith was almost the stereotype of the Irish urban politician. He wore a brown derby hat, gave campaign speeches to his "friends of the 'raddio' audience," and made his theme song "The Sidewalks of New York." His wet campaign intensified his rural opposition. Bishop Cannon said the issue of the campaign was "Shall Dry America elect a 'cocktail President?'" Whether Smith's opposition to prohibition provided religious bigots with a mask for prejudice or whether it only intensified their opposition to Smith cannot be determined, but obviously Smith's lower-class New York speech and mannerisms were inextricably entwined with rural Protestant opposition to him. Urban-rural division embraced the Catholic, prohibition, and immigrant issues. But it is doubtful if the Democrats could have won in 1928 with a Protestant candidate who was a combination Abraham Lincoln and Davy Crockett. Smith undoubtedly suffered worse defeat than a Protestant, rural, and dry candidate would have—such a candidate would have carried the traditionally Democratic South—but prosperity gave Hoover a tremendous advantage.

An analysis of the election returns reveals that Smith polled a better vote in northern and eastern cities than had any Democratic presidential candidate in modern times. In 1924, Coolidge had beaten Davis by 1,300,000 votes in the nation's twelve largest cities; in 1928, Smith led slightly in these same cities. Democratic success in northern cities was a new phenomenon. Wilson in 1916, Cox, and Davis had been unable to carry the big urban counties of the North, but Smith's success in these counties was to build a new strength for the Democrats which in the 1930's and later was to be an important force. In the South the rural-urban division was the reverse. Hoover ran better in southern cities than in southern rural regions, with the exception of traditionally Republican east Tennessee, as have Republican candidates since then. Given their gains in industrial cities and the depression that was soon to settle over America like a life-killing fog, the Democrats could take solace in the election results.

Part III

THE GREAT DEPRESSION
1929–1941

CHAPTER FIFTEEN

The Great Crash
and the Hoover
Administration

FEW PRESIDENTS EVER ASSUMED OFFICE UNDER SUCH HAPPY CONDITIONS
as did Herbert Clark Hoover on March 4, 1929. There were no serious crises
in the nation's foreign relations and none seemed to be on the horizon. At
home the American people were enjoying unprecedented prosperity. Business
was good. Industry was thriving. The skies over the cities were dark with the
smoke of industrial prosperity. So confident of America's economic future
were those who played the stock market that the price of speculative stocks
went ever higher.

Not all Americans shared in the general prosperity, however. Agriculture generally had been depressed for most of a decade. There were a few sick
industries, notably coal and textiles. Nebraska farmers or western Indiana coal
miners and the retail businessmen dependent upon their trade could not agree
with the dominant view that all was right with the world and that conditions
would become even better. But these dissenters were a distinct minority. The
United States was bathed in optimism.

The figure of the new President himself evoked optimism and confidence.
Hoover, born in a Quaker community in eastern Iowa in 1874, had been in the
public eye for years. After graduating from Stanford University he had been
a very successful mining engineer and investor, making a fortune in foreign
mining enterprises. He had first come to national attention early in the European war as director of Belgian relief and then as food administrator under
Wilson after the United States entered the fighting. As Secretary of Commerce under Harding and Coolidge he had fostered the growth of trade associations and sought to increase sales of American products overseas. He seemed
to be the epitome of the successful businessman-engineer in public office, an
efficient but humane spokesman and symbol of the New Era. Even his appear-

ance suggested conservative solidity, caution, and stability. He continued to wear high stiff collars years after most men had adopted less formal but more comfortable neckwear.

The Hoover who left the White House four years later was the same man. His ideas changed very little during his administration. Indeed, his memoirs, published in 1952, indicated that he never changed his political-economic ideas significantly. There is nothing in the memoirs to suggest that Hoover would have followed a different course if he could have relived his presidency.

But by the time Hoover left the White House, the happy conditions which had surrounded his inauguration had disappeared and the man who for almost eight months had been one of the nation's most popular presidents had become an object of ridicule, scorn, and even hatred. There was a great deal of bitter irony in the situation. During the election campaign in 1928, Hoover had said that if the Republican policies of the preceding two administrations could only be continued, "we shall soon, with the help of God, be in sight of the day when poverty will be banished from this nation." There had been loose talk of two chickens in every pot and two cars in every garage. But in 1932 and 1933 the shack towns, constructed of packing crates, old tin cans, and other junk which sprang up on the fringes of industrial cities were bitterly known as "Hoovervilles," and the newspapers under which homeless men slept on park benches were called "Hoover blankets." The man who had been the symbol of the New Era was still the symbol of it, but by 1933 the symbol evoked a different emotional response.

The Wall Street Crash

When Hoover took office, the biggest stock market boom in the history of the United States was almost five years old. The boom got under way in the last half of 1924; by the end of 1925, the New York *Times* average of twenty-five selected industrial stocks, which had been at 106 at the end of May, 1924, was at 181. The market skidded in early 1926 but recovered by the end of the year. The big bull market began in earnest in 1927 and soon got out of hand. The *Times* industrial index stood at 245 at the end of 1927 and at 331 at the end of 1928. In 1928, Radio Corporation of America rose from 85 to 420. The year 1929 saw an even wilder speculative market. By early September, the *Times* industrials had climbed to 452, an increase of about 85 per cent in twenty months. Radio reached a high of 505 on September 3; that is to say, if a person invested in Radio on January 1, 1928, and sold on September 3, 1929, he would have increased his capital by about 530 per cent. This increase occurred despite the fact that the company had never paid a dividend.

Dividends had little to do with the bull market. Indeed, the rate of return upon capital through dividends was quite low because of the excessive price of stocks. It was a speculator's market. People bought stocks at prices they might really have thought excessively high in the belief that before long they could sell at a still higher price. And they were generally right—until the fall of 1929.

298

The practice of buying stocks on margin facilitated speculation. The market player who did not want to pay cash for the full amount of what he wanted to buy could put up margin, or a down payment, and borrow the balance from his broker, using the purchased stocks as collateral. The brokers, in turn, received the money from the so-called call money market, money provided mostly by bankers. The call market was a most lucrative and safe investment. The interest rate was as high as 12 per cent, and the loan was relatively safe because the lender had only to demand more margin from the borrower if the value of the stocks used as collateral should fall. So advantageous were such call money investments that money from all over the world poured into Wall Street, thereby stimulating margin buying and speculation. A few manufacturing corporations even invested in this fashion, preferring easy interest to the problems inherent in producing goods. In 1929, Standard Oil of New Jersey poured money into the call money market at an average of $69 million a day, thus lubricating stock speculation as well as automobiles.

The total of such brokers' loans is a rough indication of the volume of speculative stock buying. In 1926, brokers' loans amounted to about $2.5 billion. Just before the crash they totaled $6.63 billion, evidencing a very large—and, as it turned out, unhealthy—amount of speculation. Yet margin requirements were 45 and 50 per cent in 1929 which is not unusually low. Had the margin requirement been lower, we may assume the market would have been even wilder; but if the margin requirement had been as high as 75 per cent, it is not likely that the speculative bubble would have become so inflated.

The stock market began to behave erratically in September, 1929. But after each break in the market there was a recovery. Then on October 24— Black Thursday—came the beginning of the end. A few hours after the market opened there was a panic to sell and get out of danger. As more speculators wanted to sell rather than buy, the prices of stocks, of course, fell even lower. For some stocks there were no purchasers to be found at all, a phenomenon which, in its own way, indicated a crisis in financial capitalism. So many shares of stock traded hands—a new record of 12,894,650 during the day— that the ticker was hours behind the actual situation on the floor of the Exchange where the scene was one of panic and confusion.

At 1:00 P.M. on Black Thursday representatives of four big New York banks met in the office of Thomas W. Lamont of the J. P. Morgan firm. The bankers agreed to pool some of their resources, go into the market and buy, and thereby indicate to the panic-stricken speculators that they, the pillars of the financial community, were not alarmed. Lamont, in a model of understatement, told reporters after the meeting, "There has been a little distress selling on the Stock Exchange." At 1:30, Richard Whitney, vice-president of the Exchange and floor operator for the Morgan firm, jauntily walked to the post where United States Steel was traded, and ostentatiously placed an order for ten thousand shares at 205. The highest bid at that moment was 193½. The effect was electric. Whitney's action was taken to mean that the bankers had moved in to peg the market, that the bankers would not allow the market to hit rock bottom. The market became firmer and many issues made strong recoveries before the end of trading. The *Times* industrials came back enough so that there was only a twelve point loss for the day. On

Friday and Saturday, trading was heavy but prices were steady. Asked for a comment on the economy, President Hoover said that "the fundamental business of the country, that is production and distribution of commodities, is on a sound and prosperous basis."

On these two fairly steady days the bankers who had shored up the market on Black Thursday quietly sold some of their recently acquired shares. When the market dropped precipitously again on Monday and Tuesday the twenty-eighth and twenty-ninth, no group of bankers again brought confidence with ostentatious buying. The prices went on down, down, down, and sometimes there were no purchasers at any price. The *Times* industrials fell ninety-two points in two days.

Thereafter, although there were occasional days when the market gained, the course was downward. Important business and political leaders issued statements on the soundness of the economy designed to be reassuring, but their incantations were without economic effect. (They were in time to have political effect: their statements were quoted against them later.) By mid-November, the stocks listed on the Stock Exchange had shrunk in their market value over 40 per cent, and prices continued to go down. A brief summary of stock prices indicates the extent of the wreckage. All the following prices were from the Dow-Jones index, in September, 1929, and January, 1933: thirty industrials dropped from $364.90 to $62.70, twenty public utilities fell from $141.90 to $28, twenty railroads declined from $182 to $28.10.

The New Era on Wall Street had been short lived.

The Course of the Economy, 1929–1933

Had the whole economy, as apart from the stock market, been as sound as Hoover thought it was—in November, 1929, he said, "Any lack of confidence in the economic future or the basic strength of business in the United States is foolish"—it is possible that the Wall Street catastrophe would not have seriously affected most Americans. But the economy was not sound. There were several indications before the market crash that there was economic difficulty ahead. The rate of increase of consumer spending slipped badly in 1929, well before the crash. Residential construction in 1929 lagged behind, off about $1 billion from 1928. Business inventories increased from about $500 million in 1928 to about $1 billion in 1929. By mid-century such conditions as these would be red danger flags, crying for some kind of remedial action. But in 1929, so optimistic was the administration and so thoroughly ingrained was the laissez-faire ideology demanding a minimum of governmental "interference" in business that the administration did not act.

One of the important ways in which the stock market crash widened out into a general depression was through bank failures. Banks had many of their assets in stocks which shrank in value after the crash. Furthermore, they held devalued stock as collateral on loans. For banks to fail or suspend operations was nothing new to Americans in the 1920's. In the year beginning July 1, 1928, a year of "prosperity," 549 banks had closed their doors, freezing the funds of thousands of depositors. Bank failures in Florida had been com-

TABLE 5

THE STOCK MARKET, 1929-1936.

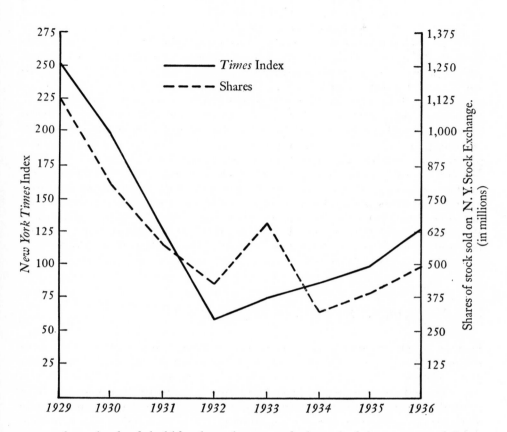

mon when the land bubble there burst, and there had been many failures throughout the postwar period in depressed agricultural areas such as the Dakotas. But after the crash, bank failures became more frequent. In the twelve months following July 1, 1929, 640 banks closed. The figure rose to 1,553 in the next year, and over $1 billion in deposits became inaccessible. In the first ten months of 1932, 1,199 banks suspended operations.

Bank failures and the stock market crash reduced the total of purchasing power and shattered economic optimism. The outlook for the economic future being dark, people with capital were hesitant to invest in new or expanded ventures. And because there was less purchasing power to buy goods and services, management adjusted its production downward to match the decreased effective demand. A cut in production involved putting labor on a shorter work week or laying off employees, or both. Thus, a cut in production further reduced the total of purchasing power, which further brought a decrease in production, and so on, down and around the vicious circle. The

301

depression tended to snowball; the adjustments of business to depressed conditions brought even worse conditions.

Any series of economic indices for the years 1929–1933 tell a dreary tale. The New York *Times* "Weekly Index of Business Activity," based upon the physical volume of electric power, steel, lumber, cotton textile, and automobile production, as well as freight car loadings, reached its peak of 114.8 in late June, 1929, months before the crash. The index went down fairly steadily until it reached its low of 63.7 in mid-March, 1933, the month that Franklin D. Roosevelt became President. There was one slight gain during this period. This index climbed—if that is the word—from 66.2 in early August, 1932, to 73.8 in early January, 1933. Hoover and his defenders interpreted this slight gain as self-justification, arguing that the economy was in the process of righting itself when Roosevelt's election ruined everything by causing the business community to be fearful of the new administration's economic policies. The argument cannot be proved or disproved, but it did not persuade many voters at the time or many economists since then.

Other statistics tell a similar story. Gross national product (GNP, the total of goods and services produced) fell from $104.4 billion, or $857 per capita, in 1929 to $74.2 billion, $590 per capita, in 1933. This was less GNP per capita than there had been for the five years, 1907 through 1911. (The above figures are all in terms of 1929 dollars.) National income (the aggregate earnings of labor and property) declined from $87.8 billion in 1929 to $40.2 billion in 1933. The total income from labor dropped from $51.1 billion to $29.5 billion, while the total paid to salaried employees fell 40 per cent. Business failures in 1932 were almost one-third more numerous than in 1929. Exports declined from $5,240,995,000 in 1929 to $1,611,016,000 in 1932 and imports from $4,399,361,000 to $1,322,774,000. Farm prices, which were not good even in 1929, fell 61 per cent in those terrible four years. Total farm income fell from about $13 billion in 1929 to $5.5 billion in 1932. Dividends declined 57 per cent, but interest paid on long-term debts declined only 3.3 per cent.

The economic statistics most important in human terms were those on unemployment. The following figures are those issued by the Bureau of Labor Statistics of the Department of Labor, but they were not universally accepted. In 1929, there were 1,499,000 unemployed persons, constituting 3.1 per cent of the total civilian labor force. These figures rose in 1930 to 4,248,000 and 8.8 per cent, in 1931 to 7,911,000 and 16.1 per cent, and in 1932 to 11,901,000 and 24.0 per cent. The low came in 1933, when, according to BLS figures, there were 12,634,000 unemployed, constituting slightly over one-fourth of the labor force.

But other statisticians, using other definitions of employed and unemployed and other techniques, differed with the BLS mathematicians. The American Federation of Labor estimated there were 13,271,000 unemployed in 1933, the generally pro-business National Industrial Conference Board put the figure at 11,842,000, and the Communist Labor Research Association claimed 16,138,000. We shall never know which, if any, of these estimates was accurate. Furthermore, even if we knew the total for certain, we would not know the answer to such pertinent questions as how many people were unemployed at one time or another during the Great Depression, how many people went how long without work, and how many people who were employed were working at occupations well below their capacity. We shall never know, for example, how many physicists were employed as dishwashers or how many teachers were selling encyclopedias—or trying to sell them.

The work of statisticians is extremely useful, but statistics cannot tell us how much pain and suffering there was in the nation as a direct result of the Great Depression. How much it hurt to be hungry, how much distress there was among parents who could not afford to clothe their children decently, how many personalities and bodies were warped as a result of poverty, and how much they were warped are questions beyond the ken of the statisticians. No one knows the answers to them.

But even a quick look through the newspapers of the early 1930's reveals some idea of the dimensions of misery resulting from the depression. Two stories from the New York *Times* in early 1932 bear repeating, and the "good, gray *Times*" was certainly not a newspaper given to sensationalism. An interview with the director of the nursing bureau of the New York City Department of Health summed up some of the observations of nurses who visited homes in the nation's largest and richest city. The nurses reported that due to doubling up to save rent, it was not at all unusual to find twelve or thirteen relatives living in a three-room apartment that today would be considered too small for a family of five. They found that children who attended schools with free lunch programs were better fed than children not in such happy circumstances and that schools that served lunch had a lower absentee rate than those that did not. A quick survey of newspapers also reveals that it was not only unskilled workers and their families who were suffering. The *Times* of May 4, 1932, told the story of a forty-four-year-old unemployed civil engineer who in 1929 had earned $450 a month but who three years later was arrested for vagrancy when found sleeping in a Brooklyn vacant lot. For forty-six days the engineer had made the lot his home, living on handouts of food from neighboring housewives and children. A graduate of the University of Colorado with twenty years' experience in his profession, he had been unsuccessful in finding work of any kind.

Multiply stories such as these by thousands and the magnitude of the Great Depression will be seen. How large exactly was the mountain of misery we shall never know. We know only that the Great Depression was the greatest economic calamity in the history of the American people.

Why the Great Depression?

Why this economic desolation and decay had come about was a question that perplexed millions. Certain matters were obvious. The potential of a decent living for all still existed. The natural resources of the nation had not disappeared. The machinery for converting those resources to usable goods was unimpaired. The manpower and the brainpower to operate the machinery still existed. And the need for economic goods certainly existed. College students of the present generation often find it difficult to appreciate fully how badly people in the 1930's needed such basic goods as shoes, sweaters, and food. The resources, the means of production, and the need were there. Yet there was stagnation.

At the time there were several foolish and ignorant explanations that seemed to satisfy a few shallow minds but that should not be regarded seriously. Some fatalists regarded the depression as the work of inscrutable destiny and quoted Nostradamus as mystic confirmation. Some Puritan souls saw the hard times as the necessary reaction of the good times of the 1920's, assuming that for every pleasure there is an inevitable retribution. And still others saw the depression as the inevitable aftermath of World War I.

President Hoover interpreted the nation's economic difficulties as being only part of a world depression. The United States had been dragged down by the economic failure of Europe. The beauty of this interpretation for the Hoover administration was that it shifted responsibility for hard times away from Washington and from the American business civilization. Certainly there was a relationship between the American depression and the depressed economy of the western world, but one could have argued as well that the American experience dragged down Europe. Other conservatives argued that the stock market crash had caused the general depression and that the decision of the Federal Reserve Board in August, 1929, to raise the discount rate (the interest rate charged member banks for their loans from the Federal Reserve Banks) had caused the stock market crash. In other words, these people argued, governmental bungling had caused the depression, bungling in an area where, they felt, government should not have operated at all. At the other end of the political spectrum were the Marxists of various kinds who, although they differed among themselves, agreed that such calamities as the Great Depression were an inherent and unavoidable feature of a capitalist economy. The only way to end the depression and prevent future ones, they declared, was to abandon capitalism and establish a socialist economic order.

There can be no certainty about the causes of the Great Depression, but most economists think along the following lines. They assume, first of all, that in a capitalist economy there must be expanding capital investment and a high level of consumer spending to maintain economic health. If the one declines, it should be compensated by an increase in the other. From 1919 until the depression, workers' productivity in American manufacturing increased about 43 per cent. That is to say, the volume of goods produced by any given number of man-hours of labor increased by about two-fifths. But wages and salaries did not increase appreciably and prices on the whole did not decrease. The increased productivity of labor, therefore, resulted in an increase in profits. Until 1929, these profits encouraged capital expansion. The market crash of October, 1929, brought a lack of confidence in the economy and a consequent decline in the rate of capital investment. But there was no compensating increase in consumer spending. Indeed, consumer spending declined along with capital investment.

The question arises, why was this economic dislocation of 1929 so much more serious than earlier and later downswings of the American economy? The answer seems to lie in certain deep-seated weaknesses in the economy throughout the 1920's, the prosperity period once regarded as the New Economic Era.

Most importantly, there was a very poor distribution of income during

304

the supposedly palmy days of Republican prosperity. It was not a case of the rich getting richer while the poor got poorer, but it was a case of the rich getting tremendously richer while the poor got only slightly less poor. In 1929, the top one-twentieth of all receivers of personal income received about one-third of the total. With such a distribution of income, either a high level of investment or a very high level of luxury spending, or both, was necessary to keep the economy going. The spending of the very rich is much more erratic than the steady purchasing of the poor who necessarily spend all they receive for the necessities of life. After the crash, the spending and the investments of the rich declined and the whole economy collapsed. Had there been a compensating increase in the spending of the great masses of people (farmers and workers on low incomes) presumably the economy would have rolled along unscathed or only slightly damaged after 1929. But ordinary people could not spend more because they were already spending all, or nearly all, the money they received.

This poor distribution of income during the 1920's was at least partly the result of governmental policies. Certainly, federal tax policies during that decade did nothing to rectify inequitable income distribution. Income taxes were extremely low by recent standards and were easily avoided. Assuming that a vigorous organized labor movement would have brought to industrial workers a greater share of the advantage of increased labor productivity, the antilabor policies of the federal, state, and local governments tended to maintain the kind of income distribution that later proved disastrous. And obviously the federal government's farm policy during the 1920's did not serve to increase the income of thousands and thousands of poorly compensated farmers.

Although poor income distribution was probably the greatest weakness of the American economy, it had other faults. One weakness was the banking system. The failure of one bank naturally caused people to rush to withdraw their deposits from other banks. Bank runs became commonplace, endangering fairly sound banks as well as dubious ones. And when a bank failed, needless to say, its depositors were in no position to increase their spending and investments. Most economists also would agree that the complex structure of holding company pyramids made the economy of the 1920's unduly sensitive to business recessions. In the public utility field, for example, continued failure of an operating company to pay dividends meant default on the bonds of the holding companies stacked on top of the operating company. The situation was akin to what happens if one saws off one leg of a top-heavy stool.

Finally, another weakness was the inadequacy of even the supposedly best economic thought. Where economists today would have seen danger signals in abundance in the summer of 1929, the economists of that day saw only reasons for optimism. Even after the crash, the economists remained optimistically reassuring. In November, 1929, the Harvard Economic Society declared that "a serious depression . . . is outside the range of probability." At the end of the year, these Harvard professors expected a business recovery soon. In 1930, the widely respected Irving Fisher, professor of economics at Yale, wrote that the "outlook is bright" for the immediate future. The judgment of these foggy prophets was as widely trusted as the estimates of our economists today, perhaps more so.

The Hoover Administration and the Depression

As the depression deepened, the view grew among voters that Hoover was a "do-nothing" President, a kind of modern Nero. Certainly the Democratic party then and since did nothing to change this fairly common impression. And Hoover suffered in comparison with his successor because Roosevelt's pace was faster and his scope was broader. Yet the impression of Hoover as a "do-nothing" President was a false one. He did attempt to combat the depression. Indeed, Hoover's administration did more in its attempt to bring about recovery than had any previous administration, either Republican or Democratic, in earlier economic depressions. And it should be noted that Roosevelt continued some of Hoover's policies—the Reconstruction Finance Corporation was a notable example—although in an expanded form. Yet Hoover's policies did not succeed in effecting recovery. Neither he nor anyone else did enough fast enough to reverse the downward spiral from 1929 to 1933.

Hoover's economic philosophy, as well as that of most of his fellow Republicans and huge sections of the Democratic party, greatly inhibited his attack on the depression. And he was so much on the defensive politically that he appeared sometimes not to realize fully the depression's terrible impact. Years later in compiling his memoirs he wrote some of the most surprising sentences in American politics:

> Some Oregon or Washington apple growers' association shrewdly appraised the sympathy of the public for the unemployed. They set up a system of selling apples on the street corners in many cities, thus selling their crop and raising their prices. Many persons left their jobs for the more profitable one of selling apples.[1]

His most important inhibition was his conception of the role of the federal government in the economy. Hoover was not a follower of pure Adam Smith laissez faire. He believed it proper for the federal government to stimulate business. In 1931, he said, "The sole function of government is to bring about a condition of affairs favorable to the beneficial development of private enterprise." But he held tight to the view that for the federal government to reform or reorganize the economy, even when the economy obviously did not function well, would mean inevitably a loss of individual freedom. He was so committed to the kind of relationship between business enterprise and the federal government he had promoted as Secretary of Commerce that even when the crash and the depression proved that relationship's inadequacies he had no alternative scheme. All he could do was work within his fundamental framework and hope for economic improvement. His political-economic philosophy failed its great pragmatic test.

He quite firmly believed that direct aid to poverty-stricken people was

---

[1]Herbert Hoover, *The Memoirs of Herbert Hoover: The Great Depression, 1929–1941* (New York: Macmillan, 1952), p. 195.

not a legitimate function of the federal government. All aid to the needy, he maintained steadfastly, was the responsibility of state and local government and of private charity. So far as the federal government's activities were concerned, he placed a higher value on the security of private property than on the welfare of human beings.

It is true, of course, that the welfare of human beings benefited from some of the Hoover policies. But individual welfare improved only indirectly. Hoover believed in a "trickle down" theory of federal aid. For example, the Hoover administration lent huge sums to banks and railroads, on whose condition the welfare of thousands of individuals was partially dependent. But Hoover stuck firmly to his conviction that federal aid directly to individuals would be a "dole" (a favorite smear word of that day) which would "injure the spiritual responses" of the American people. Some of Hoover's critics described his policies accurately, if somewhat bitterly and inelegantly, when they charged that Hoover believed in "feeding the sparrows by feeding the horses." But all humanitarian considerations aside, considering only economics, the "trickle down" method of federal aid was not as effective in combating depression as direct aid to low-income groups would have been. The poor, after all, would have spent their aid very quickly and thereby lubricated the economy.

Agriculture and the Tariff

During the election campaign of 1928, Hoover had recognized the need for bettering the condition of American agriculture and had promised a farm relief program and "limited" upward revision of the tariff. He mentioned these subjects in his inaugural address and soon thereafter called a special session of Congress, which met April 16, 1929, months before the crash, to consider these matters.

The Congress took months to write a tariff act because such distribution of federal largesse was inevitably accompanied by large-scale backstage bargaining, but after sharp but brief debate the national legislature passed an agricultural relief measure similar to the one the President had requested. Hoover signed the Agricultural Marketing Act on June 15. The Act created the Federal Farm Board and granted it fairly wide powers to supervise the marketing of agricultural commodities. Board members represented various agricultural interests. The major exception was cotton; most people in cotton production were Democrats. The chairman of the board was Alexander Legge, president of International Harvester, whose appointment evoked criticism from agrarians. One magazine critical of the Hoover administration commented, "As a farm reliever Mr. Legge is an incomparable machinery manufacturer." Under the terms of the law the board had $500 million available on a revolving fund basis to buy agricultural surpluses, store them, and establish "stabilization corporations" and other agencies for marketing.

Some economic historians have asserted that the wording of the Marketing Act was loose enough to permit the board to limit agricultural production much as the Agricultural Adjustment Administration did under Roosevelt's leadership. Other historians hold that the board's power to restrict production was dubious. In any case, Hoover's political philosophy would not have countenanced enforced crop restriction, and the board never did more than encourage farmers to reduce their production in order to raise farm prices. Individual farmers, fearful that they might be alone in reducing their output and thereby be in the position of having little to sell but having to sell at low prices, ignored the advice. Indeed, farm production was greater in 1932 than it had been in 1929.

Unable to restrict production but directed to buy agricultural surpluses, the stabilization corporations soon found themselves with mountains of surplus commodities on their hands. By mid-1931, the Grain Stabilization Corporation, which had been buying wheat, held over 257,000,000 bushels. The Cotton Stabilization Corporation held 1,300,000 bales of cotton. When the deepening financial crisis in Europe in 1931 made it more difficult to dispose of these surpluses abroad and drove the world price even lower, the whole program floundered. Farmers received as little as thirty cents for a bushel of corn and a nickel for a pound of cotton, far below their costs of production.

The Hoover farm program may fairly be judged a failure. Had there been no general economic depression, the Federal Farm Board might have stabilized and relieved agriculture appreciably. But the program was wholly inadequate for a generally declining economy. Perhaps Hoover's expressed distaste for the whole idea of the federal government's participation in that part of the economy doomed the program to ineffectiveness: "Even indirect purchase and sale of commodities is absolutely opposed to my theory of government."

No more successful was the Hoover program of aiding agriculture through tariff manipulation. Except for a few agricultural products such as wool and sugar, a protective tariff was of dubious help to the American farmer because he competed little with imported products in the domestic market. But tariff protection, even for farmers, was part of the popular economic mythology of that day. Republican Congressmen from industrial areas were willing to grant the empty gesture of increased imports for agricultural commodities while receiving higher rates on manufactured products in return. And most farm leaders believed an agricultural protective tariff was not an empty gesture.

In early May, 1929, Willis C. Hawley of Oregon, chairman of the House Ways and Means Committee, introduced a tariff bill which passed the lower house within a month. Amendments to the original bill considerably increased the proposed tariff schedules even before it went to the Senate. There Reed Smoot of Utah, chairman of the Finance Committee, teamed up with Joseph R. Grundy of Pennsylvania to make the measure the highest tariff bill of the twentieth century. Special interest lobbying and log-rolling were intense. Lobbyists and Congressmen bargained and compromised for nearly a year. The extent of their maneuvering can be seen in the final vote in the Senate. The Hawley-Smoot bill passed the Senate forty-four to forty-two, the dissenters being thirty Democrats, eleven Republicans, and one Farmer-Laborite. If the Democratic Senators of Florida, Louisiana, and Wyoming had not voted for the bill after log-rolling to get special favors for fruit, sugar, and wool-growers, the bill would have been defeated. The bargaining had been closely calculated.

Many economists were legitimately apprehensive about the effect the new tariff measure would have on foreign trade and thereby on the economy in general. Paul Douglas, then of the economics department of the University of Chicago and a United States Senator after World War II, drafted a statement urging Hoover to veto the bill and within a few days got 1,028 members of the American Economics Association to sign the statement. Hoover defended the bill, however, and signed the Hawley-Smoot Act on June 15, 1930. The Act raised the average of all duties from 33 per cent under the old Fordney-McCumber Tariff of 1922 to 40 per cent. The average of duties on agricultural commodities increased from 20 per cent to 33 per cent.

The precise economic effects of the Hawley-Smoot Act are impossible to determine since there were other forces operating that tended to decrease international trade. Surely Franklin D. Roosevelt exaggerated for political advantage when he charged in 1932 that the new tariff was "one of the most important factors in the present world-wide depression." But surely Republican Senator James E. Watson of Indiana was even more wrong when he predicted in 1930 that if the Hawley-Smoot measure were passed, "within a year of this date we shall have regained the peak of prosperity." After the United States, one of the world's leading industrial and commercial powers, adopted a clear policy of economic nationalism with this tariff, other powers of the world followed suit. In 1932, Great Britain fully abandoned her free trade principles, and other countries raised their trade barriers. Indeed 1930 was an inauspicious year to heighten tariff walls.

Politics and the Early Depression

Although Hoover publicly expressed confidence in the fundamental health of the economy just after the stock market crash, he was worried enough to call a series of conferences with business and labor leaders. In November, 1929, Hoover urged business leaders to maintain wages and expand their industrial construction. The business leaders agreed, contingent upon assurance from trade union officials that they would not strike or demand higher wages. A subsequent conference of trade unions assured the President on this point. That same month, Hoover telegraphed the nation's governors and mayors urging them to expand their public works programs.

In the first winter of the depression, industrialists did not appreciably cut wage rates, but they did not undertake any substantial amount of industrial construction. Labor honored its pledge. But in the spring and summer of 1930, industrial management seriously began to cut production, thereby reducing the national payroll, although they still did not reduce hourly wage rates importantly. The administration responded to this situation with an increase in its public works program. Federal public works increased from about $250 million in the last predepression year to about $725 million in Hoover's last year in office. State and local public works increased to a lesser degree. In the fall of 1930, Hoover created the President's Committee for Unemployment Relief which, with Colonel Arthur Woods of New York as chairman, sought to co-ordinate the relief activities of local agencies. Hoover was adamant in his conviction that relief for the unemployed was the responsibility of the states, counties, and municipalities rather than the federal government. Colonel Woods, unable to persuade the President to accept a bolder relief program, resigned the following April.

In August, 1931, Hoover appointed a new organization, the President's Organization on Unemployment Relief (POUR), with Walter S. Gifford, president of the American Telephone and Telegraph Company as chairman. Most of the sixty-two members of POUR were businessmen. Its main effort was an advertising campaign that urged citizens to give to local community chests. In January, 1932, a Senate committee called Gifford to the witness stand and asked him if he knew the relief needs of rural districts and of towns too small to have a community chest. He admitted ignorance. When asked if he knew the total relief needs of the nation, he again admitted that he did not know. Congress, upon the warranted assumption that the Gifford committee was woefully inadequate for its task, refused Hoover's request to appropriate further funds for it.

By election time of 1930, the depression was not nearly as severe as it was soon to become, but the times were hard enough to put the Republican party at a bad disadvantage. Even before the elections, Hoover was confronted with a sometimes hostile Congress because a handful of progressive Republicans from the Midwest and the West frequently voted with the Democrats. The Senate nearly refused to confirm Hoover's appointment of Charles Evans Hughes as Chief Justice of the Supreme Court and did defeat his appointment of Judge John J. Parker of North Carolina to the nation's highest bench. After the 1930 elections, the Republicans held the slimmest of margins in the Senate. There were forty-eight Republicans, forty-seven Democrats, and one Farmer-Laborite. Since the Republican Old Guard had been unsuccessful in purging such Republican progressives as Senator George Norris of Nebraska, Hoover had a hostile upper house on his hands. The Democrats had a majority of four in the new House of Representatives.

In December, 1931, Hoover asked Congress for a whole series of acts having recovery as their purpose. Congress passed many of these proposals, usually in stronger form than the President had requested. Among these measures were the Glass-Steagall Act of 1932 (not to be confused with a more important banking act of the same name the next year), which expanded the currency by making new classes of commercial paper and government bonds collateral for Federal Reserve notes; a measure of January, 1932, furnishing additional capital for the Federal Land Banks, which had been established in the Wilson administration; and the creation of the Federal Home Loan Bank system in July, 1932, an on-the-whole ineffective plan to ease the hardship of homeowners who could not pay their mortgages.

The Hoover administration's most important antidepression measure was the establishment of the Reconstruction Finance Corporation in January, 1932. The RFC was a government owned and chartered corporation, capitalized at $500 million, with authority to borrow three times that amount. Its purpose was to lend money to businesses which were in danger of collapse. Most of its funds during the Hoover administration went to support banks, railroads, and insurance companies, all institutions which would bring thousands of individuals down with them should they fail.

The way the RFC disbursed its funds caused political uproar. RFC officials issued statements during the agency's first few months calculated to leave the impression that it was aiding small business. In the summer of 1932, Speaker of the House John N. Garner of Texas pushed through legislation which required the RFC to report its loans to Congress. The reports made good ammunition for the Democratic party. A major political row involved Charles G. Dawes, the colorful former Vice-President who was the first president of RFC. In June, 1932, Dawes resigned from the RFC, announcing that he had to give full time to the affairs of the Central Republic Bank of Chicago. A few weeks later this bank received an RFC loan of $90 million. At that time, the bank's deposits were only $95 million. The loan did not save it. The bank reorganized, and the RFC later had to resort to the courts to collect the loan. Dawes's successor, former Senator Atlee Pomerene of Ohio, authorized a $12 million loan to a Cleveland bank of which he was a director. The Democrats made a telling point when they charged that Hoover objected to federal relief to the poor but allowed the RFC to become "a rich man's dole."

Democrats and progressive Republicans sponsored several measures which Hoover either vetoed or had stopped by his friends in Congress. Among these was Senator Norris' proposal to start up the turbines at the Muscle Shoals power installation in Tennessee under federal operation. This dam had been built during the war and Norris had fought an almost one-man campaign to save it for the government throughout the 1920's. Under President Roosevelt, Muscle Shoals was to grow into the mighty Tennessee Valley Authority, but President Hoover vetoed Norris' bill in 1931 with the comment that for the federal government to operate the power plant there would mean the break-down of "the initiative and enterprise of the American people . . . destruction of equality of opportunity of our people . . . the negation of the ideals upon which our civilization has been based." Hoover also vetoed a bill sponsored by Speaker Garner and Senator Robert F. Wagner of New York which would have appropriated $2 billion for a public works program, declaring that "never before" in the history of the United States had anyone made "so dangerous a suggestion." Another bill of Senator Wagner's, one which would have created a federal system of employment bureaus, also met one of Hoover's vetoes. The frankly inflationary Goldsborough Bill, which would have directed the Federal Reserve System and the Treasury Department to expand credit and paper currency until prices rose to the average level of the 1920's, passed in the House but was defeated in the Senate. Still another such proposal to widen the attack of the federal government on the depression, a measure suggested by Senators Robert M. LaFollette of Wisconsin and Edward P. Costigan of Colorado that would have granted the states $375 million for poor relief, failed of passage because of Hoover's opposition.

Hoover compromised his federal relief position ever so slightly when in July, 1932, he signed the Emergency Relief and Construction Act, a compromise measure submitted by Senator Wagner in an attempt to get something through that Hoover would approve. The law established a Reconstruction

Finance Corporation fund of $300 million to be lent to the states for relief of the unemployed. It also appropriated $322.2 million for public works from general federal revenues. The states would have to repay the loans beginning in 1935, and no state would be permitted to borrow more than 15 per cent of the total loan fund. Governor Gifford Pinchot of Pennsylvania, in applying for the maximum loan of $45 million, reported that even if he could borrow 33 per cent more his state would have only enough to provide thirteen cents a day for a year to each of its unemployed workers. Pennsylvania actually received only about $11 million. In fact, by the end of 1932 the RFC had actually lent only one-tenth of the $300 million. The RFC had lent three times as much for Dawes's Chicago bank as for relief loans to the states. Actual expenditures for public works were even less.

The only real victory of progressives in either party was the enactment of the Norris-LaGuardia Anti-Injunction Act in March, 1932, sponsored by Senator Norris and Representative Fiorello LaGuardia of New York City. The act seriously inhibited the power of federal courts to issue injunctions in labor disputes and thereby rendered "yellow-dog" contracts ineffective. The "yellow-dog" was an agreement, frequently only oral, between employer and employee that the worker would not join a labor union. When trade union organizers tried to organize workers under such contracts, the employer was able to get an injunction from a federal court against all organizing efforts on the grounds that such efforts jeopardized an existing contract. There is evidence that Hoover did not really approve of the measure despite his signing of it. His Secretary of Labor, "Puddler Jim" Davis, worked behind the scenes to prevent its passage in Congress. That Hoover signed reluctantly the only important reform measure of his administration, a bill sponsored by two progressive Republicans, indicates a great deal about the confused but heated political struggles of the last two years of the Hoover administration.

Will There Be a Revolution?

As the depression became worse and worse in 1931 and 1932, and as people in desperate financial condition read of RFC loans to banks and presidential opposition to federal relief for individuals, the popular mood became understandably somewhat angry and ugly. Here and there, there were outbreaks of class violence.

The nation's farmers, who in good times were usually on the side of conservative political respectability, were perhaps the most violent part of the population during the early depression. At forced farm auctions, held by a creditor in order to pay off a farmer's debt, farmers sometimes terrorized prospective buyers from bidding, bought the property at a small fraction of its value, and returned it to the original owner. In at least one case, a mob of farmers beat a local judge who refused to stop issuing foreclosure orders.

In their desperation, farmers in the western part of the Midwest organized in 1932 what they called the Farm Holiday Association. Milo Reno, a former president of the Iowa Farmers Union, was its leader. The idea of the movement was a strike against economic relations with urban people. The farmers would refuse to sell their products. They hoped this action would bring their urban opponents to heel and result in higher farm prices.

> Let's call a "Farmers Holiday"
> A Holiday let's hold
> We'll eat our wheat and ham and eggs
> And let them eat their gold.

The first "farmer's strike" was around Sioux City in extreme western Iowa in August, 1932. The farmers blocked off the highways entering Sioux City with logs bristling with railroad spikes and turned back all shipments of food. They poured fresh milk, which would spoil soon anyway, into ditches. The farmers of the area were at that time getting two cents a quart for their milk and Sioux City consumers paid eight cents. The Farm Holiday idea spread in a sporadic fashion over the northern Great Plains, mostly in 1932 and early 1933, but there were a few farm strikes in the winter of 1933–1934. Some governors refused to use the militia against the striking farmers.

The Farm Holiday movement had little economic effect. Here and there the price of fluid milk increased, but in general the tendency was to flood the unblockaded cities with goods and thus depress prices. Total livestock shipments to Iowa packing houses declined, but shipments to Chicago increased and the prices remained very low. Even had the Farm Holiday action been entirely successful and farm prices raised, there would have been a price problem when the products temporarily held back were released for sale.

The greatest effect of the Farm Holiday movement was to dramatize the plight of the farmers. Their "strikes" made headlines all over the country and helped to crystallize opposition to the already unpopular Hoover. When Hoover visited Des Moines during the 1932 campaign, distressed Iowa farmers staged a demonstration and parade against him carrying signs which declared, "In Hoover we trusted; now we are busted," and "Hoover, Hyde [Hoover's Secretary of Agriculture], Hell and Hard Times. The Republican Four-H Club." Among the demonstrators at Des Moines was Republican Senator Smith W. Brookhart, who had campaigned for Hoover in 1928.

An even more dramatic and potentially explosive expression of widespread economic discontent was the march of World War I veterans on Washington in the summer of 1932. After the Armistice, Congress had passed legislation granting veterans "adjusted compensation certificates," a kind of bonus which was to be paid in 1945. A former army sergeant and unemployed cannery manager of Portland, Oregon, one Walter W. Waters, spread the idea of a Bonus Expeditionary Force march on Washington to pressure Congress and the administration into paying off the certificates immediately. In May, 1932, the veterans started for Washington, riding the rails, hiking, and living on handouts. Other unemployed veterans joined the BEF along the way, and by June there were about 15,000 bonus marchers in Washington, bivouacked in shacks and tents on Washington's Anacostia Flats. The marchers were unarmed, disciplined, and orderly; they made a vigorous effort to minimize the effectiveness of the small group of Communists who attached themselves to the movement. But the presence of so many desperate men in the nation's capital was potential dynamite. The superintendent of the Washington police, Pelham D. Glassford, a retired army general, did his best to be understanding and helpful with the BEF and to prevent an outbreak of violence.

Representative Wright Patman of Texas had introduced a bill embodying the BEF's demands. The bill passed the House on June 15. But the administration's opposition buttressed the opponents of a bonus in the Senate and the Senate defeated the Patman bill on June 17. Some of the marchers then left Washington but thousands of them, having no better place to go, remained in the Anacostia "Hooverville." President Hoover refused to receive a delegation of the veterans. He and his administration did nothing for the marchers other than to secure passage of a bill which would lend money to the veterans for transportation home—if they had a home—the loan to be deducted from the bonus payable in 1945.

Late in July, six weeks after the defeat of the Patman bill, the first outbreak of violence came. When the Washington police were clearing some veterans out of abandoned buildings, a policeman panicked and fired into a crowd of veterans. Two veterans were killed and others were wounded. At this point the administration moved with dispatch. Secretary of War Patrick J. Hurley ordered the army chief of staff, General Douglas MacArthur, to take action. MacArthur sent cavalry, infantry, and tanks into the Anacostia settlement. Two of MacArthur's subordinate officers were Dwight D. Eisenhower and George S. Patton, Jr. The troops drove the veterans, some of whom had their wives and children with them, from the camp with bayonets and tear gas and then burned the tents and shacks. The bonus army straggled out of Washington.

General MacArthur issued statements to the effect that the army's action had saved the capital from revolution, but the nation was hardly impressed. Instead, the nation was distraught and bitter that social and economic conditions had reached such a low point that the force of the United States government had been used against unarmed men and their families, men who had been victorious heroes only fourteen years earlier. Many people who opposed the idea of a bonus were sickened by the inhuman efficiency with which the army dispersed the bonus marchers.

General MacArthur clearly overestimated the danger to the nation's stability represented by the bonus army, but the question of how close the country was to a revolution was a moot point. Conservatives were aware that the situation was explosive and were fearful. When they contemplated the fact that it was the farmers and the veterans, normally on the side of conservative social policies, who were creating the greatest violence, they had cause for concern. Yet the fear of conservatives was exaggerated. There was widespread discontent with the *status quo*, but there was little popular demand for a thorough overhaul of the economic and political structure, the abandonment of capitalism and of representative democracy. When the bonus marchers, assembled on the steps of the nation's Capitol on June 17, heard the news that the Senate had just defeated the bonus bill, they did not storm the Senate chamber in the traditional manner of European revolutionists at the barricades. Instead, they sang "America" and marched off quietly.

The depression prompted many people to revise their political-economic opinions and to reassess their old social values, but the extent of social revolt in 1932, aside from such exceptions as the bonus army and the farm strikes, was to turn the Republican party out of national power and install a Democratic Congress and administration. The American people seemed to agree with Thomas Jefferson, who had included this sentence in the Declaration of Independence: "Prudence, indeed, will dictate that Governments long established should not be changed for light and transient causes; and accordingly all experience hath shown, that mankind are more disposed to suffer, while evils are sufferable, than to right themselves by abolishing the forms to which they are accustomed." But there was a question in 1932 and early 1933 as to how long some evils were sufferable and what were light and transient causes.

CHAPTER SIXTEEN

The Early New Deal

IN EARLY JULY, 1932, THE DEMOCRATIC NATIONAL CONVENTION AT Chicago nominated Governor Franklin Delano Roosevelt of New York for the presidency. The next day Governor Roosevelt captured the imagination of the American people. Instead of waiting to make an acceptance speech weeks later as was customary, he flew from Albany to Chicago in a Ford three-engine airplane, a craft today considered a curious aberration in the history of aviation. To deliver one's acceptance speech at the convention was unusual; to fly to the convention was in 1932 unprecedented and daringly dramatic.

The public was eager to hear what the new nominee had to say because it was almost a foregone conclusion that the Democratic candidate would defeat President Hoover, whom the Republicans had nominated in Philadelphia in mid-June. In April, Roosevelt had created a generally favorable popular impression with a radio speech about the "forgotten man": the Hoover administration "has either forgotten or does not want to remember the infantry of our economic army." Roosevelt's 1932 acceptance speech seems a curious document to a later generation. On the one hand, he promised greater economy in government and warned against extremism, either reaction or radicalism; on the other hand, he criticized the Republican administration for "putting its head in the sand" and ignoring the "large number of destitute people in our midst who need food and clothing," deplored the pre-1929 "obeisance to Mammon . . . profits of speculation, the easy road without toil," and urged a "more equitable opportunity to share in the distribution of national wealth." But it was the climax of Roosevelt's speech which has lived:

> I pledge you—I pledge myself to a new deal for the American people. Let us all here assembled constitute ourselves prophets of a new order of competence and of courage. This is more than a political cam-

paign; it is a call to arms. Give me your help, not to win votes alone, but to win in this crusade to restore America to its own people.

The term "the New Deal" had been born, and the newly ordained prophets went forth in quest of disciples, which proved an easy task.

Roosevelt's Background

Fifty years old when nominated for the presidency, vigorous, possessed of a magic voice, confident, gay, warm, lucky, and clever, Franklin D. Roosevelt— or FDR as he was commonly called in the headlines—was to dominate the political scene more intensely and for a longer time than any previous president. He was a figure about whom it was difficult to be neutral or dispassionate. He evoked strong loyalties among a majority of citizens, but he evoked bitter animosity among a large minority. He was both well loved and well hated.

Roosevelt was born January 30, 1882, at Hyde Park, New York, to a family of wealthy landowners whose Dutch and English ancestors had settled the Hudson Valley in the seventeenth century. There was little about his father, James Roosevelt, to distinguish him from other Hudson squires other than that he was a Democrat, surely a distinct eccentricity in the circles in which he moved. Young FDR received his early education from private tutors at home and on European tours until he entered Groton in 1896. He went on to Harvard four years later. In his freshman year, he joined the Harvard Republican club, presumably because his fifth-cousin Theodore was the GOP vice-presidential candidate. Popular with his classmates and a good although not brilliant student, he finished his undergraduate course in three years, but he returned for a fourth year in order to serve as editor of *The Crimson*, the college newspaper. In the fall of 1904, he entered Columbia University Law School and announced his engagement to Anna Eleanor Roosevelt, one of his distant cousins and a niece of the President of the United States. Theodore Roosevelt went to New York to give the bride away, her father having died when she was a small child. The couple had five children: a girl and four boys. FDR passed the bar examinations before his third year of law school was over, and he quit school at that point and worked for a Wall Street law firm. Most of his work there consisted of the preparation of briefs for cases involving corporations, an intellectual task he did not enjoy, but he delighted in the opportunities he had to appear in municipal court where he had his first real contact with ordinary people, with working men and immigrants.

Young FDR had an itch for politics. In 1910, he ran on the Democratic ticket for the New York State Senate from Hyde Park, campaigning vigorously from an automobile, something of a novelty in that slowly paced day. In the Democratic trend of that year he squeaked by his opponent to be the second Democrat elected from that district since the Civil War. He won re-election in 1912.

Early in 1912, FDR visited Governor Woodrow Wilson at Trenton and came away enthusiastic for the former Princeton president. He organized Wilson for president clubs in New York, thereby earning the opposition of Tammany Hall which denied FDR the opportunity to be a delegate to the

1912 national convention. The young state senator—he was only thirty—campaigned for Wilson, and after Wilson's victory William Gibbs McAdoo, who was to be Wilson's Secretary of the Treasury, asked FDR to be his assistant secretary. FDR declined. But when Secretary of the Navy Josephus Daniels offered him the post of second in command of that department, young Roosevelt leaped at the chance. Theodore Roosevelt had been Assistant Secretary of the Navy under McKinley and had risen to the governorship of New York, the vice-presidency, and the presidency. Young FDR may have seen himself following in his distant cousin's footsteps.

As Daniels' assistant secretary during the Wilson years of war and peace, FDR gained valuable administrative experience and built his contacts within the Democratic party. In 1920, the Democratic convention nominated him for the vice-presidency as James M. Cox's running mate in order to give balance to the ticket. Before he left Washington after Harding's electoral victory, he had impressed Supreme Court Justice Oliver Wendell Holmes as "a good fellow with rather a soft edge." The judgment seems valid for the young Roosevelt. But through personal tragedy he was soon to gain in maturity and internal strength, to harden the soft edge.

Polio struck Roosevelt in August, 1921, while he was vacationing at the family's summer place on Campobello Island off the coast of Maine. At first improperly diagnosed, the disease left Roosevelt paralyzed from the waist down. Although he had sufficient wealth to retire, he apparently never considered such surrender. He gamely fought his way back to an active and useful existence, but he wore heavy steel braces on his legs for the rest of his life and could not walk unaided. By 1924, he had recovered sufficiently to nominate Al Smith at the Democratic national convention with his famous "Happy Warrior" speech—and to demonstrate to the nation's Democrats that infantile paralysis, as it was then commonly called, had not knocked him out of politics.

In 1928, he proved his ability as a vote getter when he won election as governor of New York. Presidential candidate Al Smith lost his own state by 100,000 votes, but FDR won by 25,000. In 1930, he won re-election by a staggering 725,000 votes, unprecedented in New York's history. A humane and progressive governor as well as a popular one, FDR in 1931, through his political adviser James A. Farley, began to line up delegates for the 1932 convention.

When the Democrats met at Chicago, Roosevelt was clearly in the lead over other contenders for the nomination, the main ones being Al Smith, John N. Garner, and Governor Albert Ritchie of Maryland. The nominating and seconding speeches began in the stifling and sweltering auditorium the afternoon of Thursday, June 30. Orator after orator and demonstration after demonstration went on into the small hours of the morning. The first ballot began at 4:30 the next morning. Roosevelt received 661.25 votes to Smith's 201.75 and Garner's 90.25 and a scattering of "favorite sons" with lesser support. But under the rules of Democratic conventions of that time, FDR was about one hundred votes short of nomination because a two-thirds majority was necessary, a rule that in effect gave the South a veto power over nominations. Two other ballots that morning brought no real change. FDR gained only a little. The convention adjourned at 9:15 A.M. for a day of hotel-room bargaining. That evening the California delegation, controlled by the newspaper publisher William Randolph Hearst and the Texas delegation, supporters of Garner, swung to FDR, giving him the nomination. Garner's reward was the vice-presidential nomination. In 1936, the Democrats abolished their two-thirds rule.

The End of the Republican Era

Roosevelt and his political advisers realized that, having the political advantage over Hoover because of the depression, the best strategy was to keep the various factions and interests within the Democratic party as harmonious as possible, avoid words and actions that might alienate many voters, and let Hoover and his record be self-defeating. Roosevelt stuck to generalities usually and avoided making a blueprint of what his New Deal would be. By the end of the campaign he had indicated in a rough way that he supported crop controls for agriculture, government regulation of stock exchanges, and co-operation of businessmen to combat the depression. He was silent on foreign policy and made no promises to organized labor.

The 1932 Roosevelt campaign makes the most sense when it is interpreted against the background of antagonistic interests and divisions within the Democratic party. During the course of the campaign, FDR displayed considerable agility as a broken-field runner on the gridiron of Democratic discord. Immediately after the convention, when Roosevelt was fearful he had alienated conservative Democrats, he ran toward the right and conducted a series of well-publicized conferences with important business leaders. When Senator Huey Long of Louisiana, a demagogic radical, objected strenuously (and profanely) to the direction of Roosevelt's campaign, FDR invited Long for lunch at Hyde Park, at which Roosevelt's patrician mother acquired a strong personal dislike for the Senator, and began to run to the left. The break toward the left sideline reached its peak on Roosevelt's swing through the West, culminating in his speech to the Commonwealth Club of San Francisco in late September. In this speech, one of his clearest statements of political philosophy, he spoke "of distributing wealth and products more equitably, of adapting existing economic organizations to the service of the people." And then Roosevelt ran to the right again, coming near to the right sideline in October in a speech at Pittsburgh in which he condemned the Hoover administration for failure to balance the budget, pledged himself to carry out his party's platform plank to reduce federal expenditures by 25 per cent, and called the Hoover spending policies "the most reckless and extravagant . . . I have been able to discover . . . of any peacetime Government anywhere, any time." This Pittsburgh speech was to haunt him in later days.

Hoover's campaign was in sharp contrast to his 1928 race against Al Smith. In 1928, Hoover never indulged in personal attacks; indeed, he never deigned even to speak his opponent's name in public addresses. But in 1932 Hoover's campaign speeches were bitter. He referred to prominent Democrats and progressive Republicans as "exponents of a social philosophy different from the traditional American one." And if the Republican protective tariff were altered, he warned, "The grass will grow in the streets of a hundred cities, a thousand towns; the weeds will overrun the fields of millions of farms. . . ."

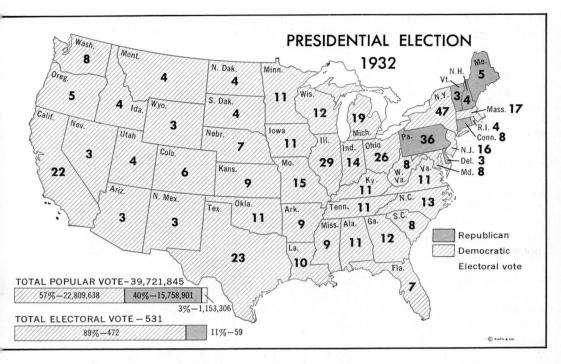

PRESIDENTIAL ELECTION 1932

Washington 8, Montana 4, Oregon 5, N. Dak. 4, Minn. 11, Wis. 12, Mich. 19, Me. 5, N.H., Vt., N.Y. 47, Mass. 17

Calif. 22, Nev. 3, Ida. 4, Wyo. 3, S. Dak. 4, Iowa 11, Ill. 29, Ind. 14, Ohio 26, Pa. 36, R.I. 4, Conn. 8, N.J. 16, Del. 3, Md. 8

Utah 4, Colo. 6, Nebr. 7, Mo. 15, Ky. 11, W. Va. 8, Va. 11

Ariz. 3, N. Mex. 3, Okla. 11, Kans. 9, Ark. 9, Tenn. 11, N.C. 13

Tex. 23, La. 10, Miss. 9, Ala. 11, Ga. 12, S.C. 8, Fla. 7

Republican
Democratic
Electoral vote

TOTAL POPULAR VOTE—39,721,845
57%—22,809,638   40%—15,758,901
3%—1,153,306

TOTAL ELECTORAL VOTE—531
89%—472   11%—59

© Rand & Co.

The voters, figuring that Hoover had not been conspicuously successful about grass in the streets, overwhelmingly repudiated their President. Hoover received 15,761,841 votes for 59 electoral votes, and Roosevelt received 472 electoral votes with 22,821,857 popular ballots. Hoover carried only six states —Maine, Vermont, New Hampshire, Connecticut, Pennsylvania, and Delaware. After the election, the Democrats had 59 Senate seats to 36 for the Republicans and one for the Farmer-Labor party, and 313 House seats to 117 for the Republicans and 5 for independents. The Socialist party's presidential candidate, Norman Thomas, received 884,781 votes, and 102,991 voters marked their ballots for the Communist nominee, William Z. Foster.

The four months between Roosevelt's election and his inauguration were perhaps the longest four months for Americans in the present century. Throughout the 1920's, there had been a considerable movement for a constitutional amendment to reduce the time lag between elections and taking office. Until the Twentieth Amendment, ratified in February, 1933, the president was inaugurated on March 4, four months after his election, and the new Congress met in December the year after the election, thirteen months later, unless called into special session. The Lame Duck Amendment eliminated the ridiculous situation.

There were efforts during the interregnum to effect a degree of cooperation between the old and new administrations. Hoover and Roosevelt had conversations—very strained ones—and corresponded with one another. But Roosevelt legitimately feared that Hoover was trying to commit him to policies which might tie his hands when he became president, and Hoover legitimately was uneasy about adopting new policies which might be repudiated after March 4. Meanwhile, the economy continued downward. The international economic situation deteriorated badly, and American banks faced the worst crisis in their history.

Roosevelt's cabinet appointments offered something of a glimpse into what the New Deal would be, a curious mixture of tradition and unorthodoxy, of conservatism with experiment. The State Department went to Senator Cordell Hull of Tennessee, a plodding, hard-headed, sixty-one-year-old conservative who had championed the League of Nations, low tariff policies, and prohibition. The Secretary of the Treasury, William H. Woodin, was a charming, violin-playing industrial magnate, president of the American Car and Foundry Co., who had been a Republican until 1928 and who had been a beneficiary of the House of Morgan's "inside lists" which gave prominent figures the opportunity to buy new issues of securities at reduced rates before they were offered to the public. Henry Morgenthau succeeded him in December, 1933. The new Attorney General was Homer Cummins of Connecticut, a conservative who had been slated for a lesser post until Roosevelt's designated appointment, the western Democratic progressive Senator Thomas J. Walsh of Montana, died before inauguration. Senator Claude Swanson of Virginia, an amiable and ancient party hack and big navy enthusiast, became Secretary of the Navy. Governor George Dern of Utah became Secretary of War, the politician James A. Farley became Postmaster General, and the conservative Daniel Roper of South Carolina became Secretary of Commerce. Roosevelt made three unorthodox appointments: Frances Perkins to Labor, Henry A. Wallace to Agriculture, and Harold Ickes to Interior. The appointment of Miss Perkins, a woman with a social work background who had served with Roosevelt in Albany, was the most unusual. She was not at first well received by the AFL leadership. Wallace and Ickes were each former Republican progressives, and Wallace's father had headed the Department of Agriculture under Harding and Coolidge. This was hardly a radical collection: three former Republicans (two progressive and one conservative) and three southern Democrats.

It is difficult today to understand fully how desperate was the nation's predicament on inauguration day, Saturday, March 4, 1933. The nation's banks, the very heart of American capitalism, had closed their doors, and business generally was at a standstill. The first "bank holiday" had begun just before the election when the governor of Nevada closed the banks of that state for twelve days to prevent the failure of a banking chain. The first major state to close its banks was Michigan, whose governor issued a "bank holiday" proclamation on February 10. In order to prevent further runs and failures, the governors of Indiana, Maryland, Arkansas, and Ohio took similar action before the end of the month. In the first three days of March, seventeen other states closed their banks. The flow of gold from the banking nerve center in New York both to banks in the interior and to foreign depositors was alarming, and the Federal Reserve System's gold reserves were falling dangerously fast. The gold reserve declined from about $1.4 billion in January to $400 million by March 3. The night before inauguration, Treasury officials, both old and new, worked together appealing to the governors of the states where banks were still open to close them immediately. The new governor of New York, Herbert M. Lehman, himself a banker, reluctantly took the step in the early morning hours of March 4, as did twenty-four other governors.

The weather in Washington on inauguration day matched the grim status of the economy: rainy, gray, cold, and blustery. The atmosphere was not warmed by Hoover's chill attitude toward Roosevelt. In the limousine on the way to the ceremonies Hoover was aloof and quiet and looked as if he genuinely and firmly believed that the inauguration of the president-elect on the seat beside him meant the end of all that was good in American society. When Chief Justice Hughes read the presidential oath of office, Roosevelt surprised the country, listening on the radio, by repeating the entire oath rather than uttering the customary "I do." Then the new President turned and with an air of confidence but yet great seriousness, delivered his inaugural address with the memorable words, "This great Nation will endure as it has endured, will revive and will prosper. . . . Let me assert my firm belief that the only thing we have to fear is fear itself—nameless, unreasoning, unjustified terror which paralyzes needed efforts to convert retreat into advance." The "unscrupulous money changers" had failed and abdicated, Roosevelt declared. He went on to say that he hoped the "normal balance of executive and legislative authority" would be adequate to meet the problems of the economy's halt, but that if such conventional authority were inadequate he would ask Congress for "broad Executive power to wage a war against the emergency, as great as the power that would be given to me if we were in fact invaded by a foreign foe."

Roosevelt then called a special session of Congress to meet March 9, and the New Deal began. Executive orders and new legislation came with such rapidity and covered such a range of public affairs, particularly for the first few weeks of the new administration ("the hundred days") that the ordinary newspaper reader was more than a little bewildered. The citizen perceived that FDR provided action, a frontal attack on the depression that he had long hoped for, but the action came with such speed and against a background of such desperation that he was unable to see the New Deal in an organized and coherent fashion. Before the graduating classes of 1933 had received their diplomas, Congress had passed and the President had signed basic measures on banking and monetary matters and had created a host of new agencies generally known by their initials—"alphabet soup" FDR's critics called it—such as NRA, AAA, PWA, FDIC, and CCC. When these graduating classes had registered for the second semester of their senior year, the discredited Hoover had still been President and inactive despair had been the Washington mood.

It is necessary to organize a description of the early New Deal into its component parts—banking, industry, agriculture, and relief—for purposes of intellectual orderliness and clarity. The reader should remember that the citizen of 1933 was usually unable to see the New Deal as it unfolded with the organized hindsight afforded to a subsequent generation.

Banking and Stock Exchange Legislation

At 1:00 A.M. on Monday, March 6, Roosevelt issued an executive order declaring a national four-day bank holiday. For his statutory authority Roosevelt stretched a point and used the long-forgotten Trading-with-the-Enemy Act of 1917. While the new Congress made its way to Washington, Treasury Department officials hurriedly wrote a banking bill to be enacted as soon as possible. They finished their draft at 2:00 A.M. the day Congress convened, March 9. Most members of Congress had little more than a rough idea of the bill's provisions, but they pushed the Emergency Banking Act of 1933 with unprecedented speed. The House allowed only forty minutes for debate on the bill, but even so there were cries of "Vote, vote." Such was the bipartisan panic over the banking crisis that during this forty minutes the Republican floor leader of the House Bertrand H. Snell said, "The house is burning down, and the President of the United States says this is the way to put out the fire." The Senate took only a little more time. At nine that evening, Roosevelt signed the measure into law, only nineteen hours after its drafting had been completed.

The Emergency Banking Act granted the President authority for the banking orders he had already issued, established a means to help banks in distress, and provided a scheme for the reopening of the closed banks. The Act permitted the Reconstruction Finance Corporation, begun under the Hoover administration, to buy the preferred stock of banks and empowered the Federal Reserve Banks to lend money to state-chartered banks, which were not members of the Federal Reserve. The Act authorized the issue of additional Federal Reserve bank notes with commercial "paper" for support. The Act divided the closed banks into four categories. Those that government examiners thought to be fully sound were to resume normal operations. By March 15, half of the nation's banks, which held 90 per cent of the nation's deposits, were open for regular business. A second category, about one-fourth of the total, were authorized to pay out a fraction of their deposits. The third group of banks, in worse condition, were allowed to reopen under the supervision of "Conservators" but could not pay out old deposits. They were allowed to accept new deposits, in effect to begin operations anew. The fourth category, about one thousand banks in all, were in such poor condition they were not allowed to reopen at all.

When the banks began to reopen, much of the fear and panic began to subside. Business was not yet as usual, but the economic heart of the economy had begun to beat again. On Sunday evening, March 12, only eight days after inauguration, Roosevelt addressed the country in the first of his radio "fireside chats." He explained the government's banking program in laymen's terms, and the confidence of his voice was contagious. The worst had ended.

The measures against the banking crisis in Roosevelt's first few days in the White House were very much a one-man show. Such was the crisis that he could have successfully put through almost any kind of banking program, and there were several alternatives. He conceivably could have nationalized American banking; he could have done nothing, allowed the banks to wallow in their own failure. The alternative Roosevelt chose was a middle way and essentially a conservative one since it preserved the essence of capitalism—private investment for profit. Professor Raymond Moley, one of Roosevelt's advisers whose economic conservatism later prompted him to leave Washington and become an opponent of the administration, wrote in his *After Seven Years*, a book generally critical of Roosevelt, that FDR was

intent upon rallying the confidence, first, of the conservative business and banking leaders of the country and, then, through them, of the public generally. . . . If ever there was a moment when things hung in the balance, it was on March 5, 1933—when unorthodoxy would have drained the last remaining strength of the capitalistic system. Capitalism was saved in eight days. . . .[1]

In time, capitalism's savior was to draw the hostility of the capitalists, but they were grateful recipients of his relief in March, 1933.

Capitalists, particularly bankers and stock market speculators, had never been more unpopular with the American public than they were in the early 1930's, and the headlines about the revelations of the so-called Pecora investigation were important in shaping this public opinion. The Senate Committee on Banking and Currency had begun an investigation of Wall Street practices in April, 1932, while Hoover still was President. In January, 1933, Ferdinand Pecora, a former Roosevelt Republican then a Democrat and a Sicilian immigrant who had worked himself up to become an assistant district attorney in Manhattan, became chief counsel for the committee. Pecora's research and sharp questioning of important financial figures brought sensational results. Among the disclosures were that the House of Morgan had maintained a "preferred list," friends of the firm who were occasionally offered an opportunity to buy stocks well below the market price; that there had been stock market pools and other devices to rig the market; that commercial banks had engaged in dubious financial practices to advance the interests of their affiliated investment firms; and that several prominent financiers had employed deception in order to reduce substantially their federal income taxes or even to avoid payment of them altogether. The list of prominent persons who had profited from the "preferred list" scheme was shocking. Among the recipients of these favors in 1929 were: Calvin Coolidge; Newton D. Baker, Wilson's Secretary of War; John W. Davis, Democratic presidential candidate in 1924; Bernard Baruch; Owen J. Roberts, whom Hoover appointed to the Supreme Court; William H. Woodin; John J. Raskob and William G. McAdoo, both prominent conservative Democrats; General John J. Pershing; and Charles A. Lindbergh. And the fact that J. P. Morgan had paid no federal income tax whatsoever in 1930, 1931, and 1932 dismayed less wealthy persons who had sent checks to the Collector of Internal Revenue. The wave of public resentment against bankers and Wall Street that grew from the Pecora investigation—it continued until June, 1934—expressed itself in a modification of tax law, a new banking act, and two pieces of legislation regulating the activities of the stock market.

The plugging of several income tax loopholes was a relatively simple matter—a series of amendments to the Revenue Act of 1934 called a halt to the tax deception devices the Pecora committee had revealed—but legislation to cope with banking malpractices was somewhat more complicated. The Glass-Steagall Banking Act of June, 1933, increased the powers of the Federal Reserve Banks to regulate the activities of the member banks, greatly inhibited member banks' opportunity to provide credit for speculation, called for all commercial member banks to divorce themselves utterly from any affiliated investment companies, and created the Federal Deposit Insurance Corporation (FDIC). The FDIC guaranteed depositors' accounts up to $2,500. (This guar-

---

[1] Raymond Moley, *After Seven Years* (New York: Harper and Brothers, 1939), p. 155.

antee was raised to $5,000 in 1935 and to $10,000 in 1950.) Although the principle of government guarantee of deposits was an obvious method of promoting public confidence and lessening the likelihood of bank "runs," the eastern bankers who controlled the American Bankers Association used their organization to oppose the bill, which was carried only by the insistence of the South and the West. The FDIC proved very effective: all the bank failures of the rest of the 1930's amounted to less than 8 per cent of the failures of 1933.

In May, 1933, Congress enacted the Truth-in-Securities Act which required that investors in new stock issues be fully apprised of the issuing company's financial condition, but the Act did not establish any regulatory body to police the exchange of stocks. The situation was remedied by the Securities Exchange Act of June, 1934, which established the Securities Exchange Commission and which extended regulation not only to new issues but to all securities traded. Most Wall Street leaders fought the bill vigorously, but the overwhelming vote for passage in both the House and the Senate indicated how far the mighty had fallen in public prestige. Characteristically, Roosevelt, having won a round with Wall Street, then appointed Joseph P. Kennedy, a Boston millionaire who had himself been a securities manipulator, as chairman of the new SEC. Kennedy, however, turned out to be somewhat firmer than warm New Dealers feared he would be, although his successors, James M. Landis (1935) and Professor William O. Douglas of Yale (1937), strengthened the Commission. As with much other New Deal legislation, businessmen not only learned to live with the new law but thrived under it, thereby wrecking their own original pessimistic predictions of ruin before the law was passed.

Four Strands of New Deal Thought

The immediate banking crisis over within a few days after inauguration, the Democratic party, through its firm control of the Congress and the administration, was ready to move on to the larger problem of bringing about economic recovery and providing relief. But what was the Democratic party? Certainly it was not a cohesive organization representing a particular political-economic point of view. It was a coalition of various regional economic and political interests, interests whose desires were sometimes, but not always, in conflict with one another. Within the party in 1933 can be seen four main economic positions with many subclassifications. First, there was an agrarian interest, stronger on the Hill than in the administration, that believed recovery lay in the direction of monetary inflation. Some nonagrarians also wanted a degree of inflation. This was an old and honorable tradition in the Democratic party, dating back to the days of William Jennings Bryan and even earlier. Second, there was a small but influential group of economic conservatives, whose Democratic godfather may be said to be Grover Cleveland, and whose greatest concern was economy in government and a balanced budget. Third, there was a group to whom liberalism meant restoring industrial competition. The hero of this group was Louis D. Brandeis, and the early days of the Wilson administration had been its period of glory. Finally, there was a group whose intellectual debt was to Herbert Croly, who saw the federal government playing a strong and positive role in the economy. Within this group were some who were essentially conservative—Raymond Moley, for example—and who were seeking a collaboration between government and business in industrial planning in which the business community would play the paramount role. Rexford Tugwell, another industrial planner, would have had government be paramount. Others, often considered radical but certainly not radical in the sense that they rejected capitalism, were thinking along the lines of the British economist John Maynard Keynes, even though they by no means disapproved of government-business collaboration. To summarize Keynes briefly leads to oversimplification, but in essence Keynes argued that governments should play the role of stimulator and regulator in capitalist national economies, that they should stimulate the economy during depression by deficit government spending and that they should slow down dangerous booms by a government fiscal surplus. Keynes's direct influence in the New Deal, however, has often been overstressed. His great work, *The General Theory of Employment, Interest and Money*, was not published until 1936, after the New Deal had already adopted "Keynesian" measures. Some of the "Keynesians" in the New Deal, for example, Marriner S. Eccles of the Treasury Department and later the Federal Reserve Board, had not even heard of Keynes until after they had already arrived at conclusions similar to his on their own.

It is in the nature of things in American politics that any president must play the role of conciliator and leader of the various factions and power groups within his party and the nation. The success of a president depends upon his ability to keep his coalition harmonious and yet move ahead. FDR proved remarkably successful in this respect, first yielding to this pressure, then to that pressure, and then, through his power to shape public opinion, aiding still another group to increase its pressure. Roosevelt was a most adroit political broker and manipulator. The New Deal will not be understood if one is looking for a consistent economic philosophy behind it or a logical development of a grand plan. But the New Deal administration was willing to experiment, and it accepted the idea of using the power of the federal government to help the economy crawl and scratch its way back to normal health while reforming glaring wrongs and providing relief along the way.

During the so-called First New Deal (until early 1935), the administration had something for all four main economic philosophies within the coalition. For the Bryan tradition, there was inflation; for the Cleveland tradition, there was an effort to balance the budget (an effort not abandoned, and then only reluctantly, until the winter of 1933–1934); for those concerned about Wall Street there was the banking law and the SEC; for the planners of various kinds there were, among other things, the National Industrial Recovery Act and the Tennessee Valley Authority.

Monetary Manipulation

At least as far back as the late eighteenth century, American farmers had occasionally demanded monetary inflation with great political vigor. In the late nineteenth century, they had been at the forefront of the greenback and free silver movements, both of them inflationary proposals which had the alleviation of debtors' burdens and higher prices in view. In 1933, with heavy Democratic majorities in each house of the Congress, the Bryanite agrarian wing of the party was determined to get an inflationary monetary policy.

Roosevelt was prepared to go part way with the Bryanites, for certainly the prices of early 1933 indicated a severe deflation. Through a series of executive orders and laws in March and April, 1933, the United States in effect abandoned the gold standard. On March 6, Roosevelt prohibited the redemption of currency in gold coin, and by the end of April, gold had been nationalized and its export prohibited without the consent of the Treasury. Subsequently, Congress by joint resolution declared void all clauses in either public or private contracts that required payment in gold. (The Supreme Court upheld the validity of this action in the Gold Clause cases of 1935.) With this tacit abandoning of the gold standard, the value of the dollar fell to eighty-five cents on foreign exchanges, thereby making it 15 per cent easier for foreigners to buy American products, and domestic wholesale prices increased. A degree of inflation, in other words, proved advantageous for the American economy.

In the spring of 1933, FDR had to come to a decision: on the one hand, further inflation seemed salutary at the moment and inflationists had large majorities in Congress; on the other hand, FDR had pledged support of the World Economic Conference, to meet at London in June to seek international agreements on monetary stabilization, lowering of tariffs, and encouragement of international trade. Roosevelt was in the kind of position he did not like: he had two mutually exclusive alternatives before him. He could not choose both inflation, even controlled inflation, and support of the Conference.

The inflationists in Congress were impatient with the President. In April, Senator Burton K. Wheeler of Montana proposed the old 1896 Democratic plank of free and unlimited coinage of silver at the ratio of sixteen to one, and the Senate defeated his proposal by only ten votes. Senator Elbert D. Thomas of Utah then introduced a broad amendment to the Emergency Farm Relief bill (the first Agricultural Adjustment Act). Through pressure from the White House, the inflationary schemes were only made available for the President's use, rather than made mandatory for him. When this measure passed, the President was authorized to pursue any or all of six inflationary schemes: (1) issue $3 billion in fiat "greenbacks"; (2) adopt bimetallism, the President being free to fix the ratio of gold to silver; (3) reduce the weight of the gold dollar by as much as 50 per cent; (4) persuade the Federal Reserve Banks to buy government bonds in the open market up to $3 billion in order to increase the lending power of banks; (5) accept, for a period of six months, silver at not more than fifty cents an ounce in payment of debts from foreign governments.

Roosevelt eventually decided in favor of the United States "going it alone" instead of cooperating with other powers in seeking to stabilize currencies. His radio message to the Conference, to use his own words, "fell upon it like a bombshell." The American delegation was deeply embarrassed, but John Maynard Keynes, in disagreement with his own government, declared that Roosevelt was "magnificently right."

But after the Conference "bombshell" Roosevelt refrained from further inflationary actions until it could be seen how far the dollar would decline in international exchange of its own accord and how far the upward turn of the domestic economy would go. Economic health did improve markedly during June and July, although the improvement was by no means solely attributable to monetary manipulation. In the fall, however, the business index fell sharply —sometimes referred to as "the first Roosevelt depression"—and FDR resolved to move ahead with further inflationary measures. In October, he ordered the Reconstruction Finance Corporation to begin buying gold at a price above the world market. The first RFC purchases were at $31.36 an ounce when the world price was $29.80, which meant that the dollar was worth seventy-two cents in international exchanges. The price paid for gold kept rising and the value of the dollar kept declining until the end of January, 1934. On January 15, Roosevelt asked for the Gold Reserve Act, which became effective January 31, and which authorized the President to fix the gold content of the dollar between fifty and sixty cents. Roosevelt fixed the price of gold at an even $35 an ounce. When Roosevelt took office the price had been $20.67. In other words, the dollar had been devaluated roughly 40 per cent.

The whole gold price manipulation left the United States in an odd status so far as the gold standard was concerned. There was no unalterably fixed gold content to the dollar, no gold was coined, one could not demand gold in exchange for currency, and gold could not be exported without permission. Yet gold was available for foreign payments, the federal government continued to buy and store it at Fort Knox, Kentucky, and the dollar had at least a theoretical gold content. The arrangement was certainly not the conventional gold standard, but it was not altogether on a paper basis either.

To assess the Roosevelt gold policy is a difficult task. This much is clear: prices, although they did rise, did not increase to the point desired. Certainly there was no economic magic in such manipulation. The decision to manipulate the dollar rather than to cooperate with other world powers in currency stabilization is also difficult to assess. Some experts have gone so far as to say that the London Conference "bombshell" laid the foundations for economic nationalism that ended in World War II; others point out that a managed money system can be used either to further world trade or to promote national self-containment, and that United States policy promoted international commerce. One further effect was that with the banking legislation and the control of stock purchase margin requirements, the new monetary policy tended to shift the locus of power over monetary policy from Wall Street to Washington.

The silver fiasco remains to be explained. Silver and gold had, over the course of decades of political-economic conflict, come to be symbols for more than they actually were. In general, conservatives tended to equate an orthodox gold standard with all that was desirable in western civilization, and agrarians thought of gold as the rich man's metal and of silver as the poor man's saviour. The Congressmen from the western silver states, of course, had an obvious economic interest in providing a better market for silver, which had declined from $1.12 an ounce in 1919 to only twenty-nine cents in 1931. In early 1934, despite FDR's objections, the silver steamroller began to move in Congress, well supported by agrarian interests generally. In March, a silver-purchase bill introduced by Martin Dies of Texas passed the House by an overwhelming majority, and the Senate Agriculture Committee gave a version of the Dies bill unanimous endorsement. Since Roosevelt had failed to use the silver powers granted him by the Thomas Amendment to the Emergency Farm Relief bill, the silverites did not trust him with another permissive piece of legislation. Finally, FDR capitulated in May and asked Congress for silver legislation that would grant the executive a little discretion. The measure passed in June.

The Silver Purchase Act of 1934 enjoined the Treasury to purchase silver at home or abroad until its supply of silver equaled one-fourth the value of all its metal or until the market price of silver reached $1.29 and to put silver certificates, redeemable in silver dollars upon demand, into circulation. The silver purchase program was a vast handout to a special interest group, the western silver mine operators, but, contrary to the expectations of agrarians, it had no significant effect upon prices in general. The goal was to raise prices to the 1926 level, but despite all of the many New Deal measures, prices did not reach that level until after America entered World War II.

Budget Balancing and Relief Spending

When FDR entered the White House, he held quite orthodox and un-Keynesian views about budget balancing and governmental economy. When he criticized Hoover's deficit in his 1932 campaign speech at Pittsburgh, he was not cynically exploiting the situation for political advantage; he was genuinely alarmed by the slowly growing national debt. At the same time, however, Roosevelt realized that federal relief had to be increased. Throughout 1933, he was torn between a desire for a balanced budget and the necessity for more relief.

His first week in office FDR sent a message to Congress urging greater governmental economy, to be accomplished through a cut in federal salaries and veterans' pensions. Congress, sensitive to the powerful veterans' lobby, was hesitant, but Roosevelt insisted and the Economy Act became law on March 20. FDR sweetened the medicine with a proposal to amend the Volstead Act to permit the manufacture and sale of beer with an alcoholic content of 3.2 per cent, thereby increasing federal revenues with a beer tax and soothing the boys in the nation's American Legion halls. This light beer became legal before the end of the month. (In February, 1933, the Lame Duck Congress had submitted the Twenty-first Amendment to special state conventions, and the required number of states had ratified it, eliminating the Eighteenth Amendment by December 5, 1933.) With such measures, federal spending at first actually decreased; the deficit for the first five months of the New Deal's first year was approximately 25 per cent less than the deficit for the corresponding five months of Hoover's last year.

The strongest voice for orthodox economy within the administration was that of the Director of the Bureau of the Budget, Lewis W. Douglas, from an important Arizona copper-mining family. Roosevelt leaned heavily on Douglas in the first months of his administration, much to the annoyance of less orthodox New Dealers whose emphasis was relief and recovery rather than economy. At the opposite pole from Douglas was a small group within the administration, of which Marriner S. Eccles was later to be the chief spokesman, which advocated deficit spending as a positive good under the circumstances. Big spending would, they argued, not only prime the economic pump, but would bring a degree of inflation ("reflation," Eccles called it) desirable at that time by expanding bank credit.

Roosevelt never fully accepted this Keynesian idea (he was to call for a reduction of spending and deficit in 1937) but he gradually abandoned the emphasis on a balanced budget in favor of greater relief spending. In the summer of 1934, Douglas, tired of rather unsuccessfully inhibiting federal spending, gave up the task as hopeless and resigned, leaving Treasury Secretary Morgenthau as the primary spending brake.

After the first few months of the New Deal, the gross federal debt began to climb. Under Hoover the debt had increased from $16.2 billion in 1930 to $19.5 billion in 1932, largely the result of seriously lower revenue collections. In 1933 the debt rose to $22.5 billion, to $27 billion in 1934, to $28.7 billion in 1935, to 33.8 billion in 1936, and to $36.4 billion in 1937. (For further details, see Table 6.) Thereafter, military expenditures drove the figure beyond the wildest fears of the budget balancers, but they did not complain as much about the enormous debt brought about for bombs and battleships as they had about the smaller debt incurred for relief and civilian public works. One cannot avoid the conclusion that the political debate over the federal debt had more to do with how the money was spent than the fact that it was spent. In the worst years of the Great Depression, only a fairly small but extremely vocal minority of citizens opposed the principle of great federal spending for relief of the poverty stricken.

The first significant New Deal relief measure, and one that evoked relatively little opposition, was the act of March 31, 1933, creating the Civilian Conservation Corps (CCC). The CCC with an initial appropriation of $300 million quickly took two hundred and fifty thousand young men from relief families and put them to work under direction of the War Department at soil conservation and reforestation projects. The young men in "the C's" received board and room at the work camps and $30 a month, of which $25 automatically went home to their families. By 1940, when the CCC came to an end, more than 2,225,000 young men had worked in the program, and their labors had significantly improved the condition of the countryside.

The Federal Emergency Relief Administration came into being in May, 1933. FERA granted relief to the needy indirectly through the states, one-half of its $500 million being used to match state relief expenditures for the previous three months at a one to three ratio. Roosevelt brought in Harry Hopkins, a New York social worker, to head FERA, and he brought imagination to his task. Hopkins greatly preferred work relief to cash relief and persuaded the state relief agencies he coordinated to inaugurate work relief programs.

In the fall of 1933, the administration abandoned FERA for the Civil Works Administration (CWA), which had a strange origin. Title II of the National Industrial Recovery Act of June, 1933, had created the Public Works Administration (PWA) with a huge appropriation of $3.3 billion. FDR placed Interior Secretary Harold Ickes in charge of PWA, and so careful was "Honest Harold" that no money was wasted that he spent it very slowly and without immediate economic effect. In November, Roosevelt created CWA, put Hopkins in charge, and transferred $400 million from PWA. Within two months,

CWA had four million people on its rolls busily building and repairing schools, highways, sewer systems, and airports. The goal of CWA had been to provide work relief fast, and that it did. Within two months, more people were on CWA than there had been in the armed services during World War I, and they received a higher average wage. But Hopkins' boldly unorthodox meth-

TABLE 6

PUBLIC DEBT OF THE FEDERAL GOVERNMENT, 1929–1939
(In thousands of dollars)

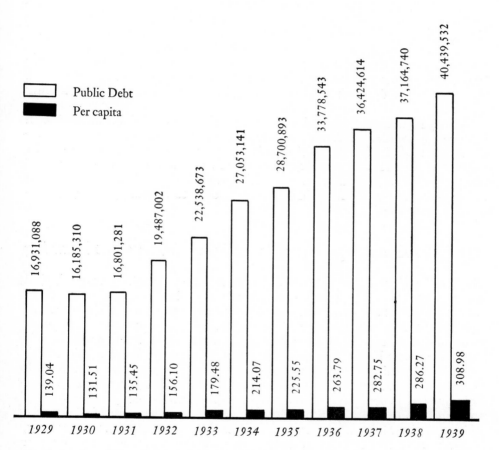

ods—jobs for three thousand writers and artists, for example—aroused considerable opposition, and in the late winter of 1933–1934 Roosevelt closed out CWA. Congress then reinvigorated FERA with a $500 million appropriation. One can fairly conclude that the New Deal's relief activities in 1933 and 1934 were a great help to the needy, although far below what was necessary for a decent standard of living, and that the program was erratic. The PWA, however, under Ickes' direction slowly grew into a major achievement. In its six years of existence, it helped in the construction of thousands of school buildings and gymnasiums, dams, bridges, postoffices, and courthouses, creating about four million man-hours of work.

There was aid for the middle classes also in the form of mortgage relief. Mortgages contracted before the crash, of course, were not scaled down to meet the new economic conditions and worked a considerable hardship on home owner–debtors. In June, 1933, Congress created the Home Owners Loan Corporation, which in time bought up approximately one-sixth of the total urban home mortgage debt and refinanced the loans at lower interest rates on long terms. The following June, Congress established the Federal Housing Administration (FHA) to stimulate the all-but-idle residential construction industry. The FHA, instead of lending money for mortgages directly, guaranteed mortgages contracted by the usual lending agencies. This agency revolutionized home financing and made home ownership feasible for many families by lowering down-payment requirements and setting up an amortized long-term mortgage system that was rare before the depression. Most lending institutions at first resented this "intrusion" into their domain, but they soon learned that the different mortgage practices opened up a vast new lending market.

The New Deal expanded considerably the scope of the Reconstruction Finance Corporation's activities, and its loans and stock purchases can be considered as a kind of relief to the business community, although some of its funds were lent for projects that aroused the opposition of business. An RFC report of 1941 revealed that the powerful economic engine had lent over $15.7 billion since its establishment in 1932, much of it to railroads, banks, and insurance companies.

The NRA: Experiment in Business-Government Planning

The irrationality of the whole industrial depression appalled many logical minds. After all, such prerequisites for economic health as a vast industrial plant, an efficient transportation and distribution system, and an abundance of competent manpower still existed. There had been no war or physical calamity to wreck the material foundation for a thriving economy. Many people concluded that some kind of planning was necessary to make the economic wheels resume their turning. Some of the more imaginative businessmen began to think in terms of planning. Naturally, they believed such planning should be done by businessmen cooperating through trade associations. In 1931, Gerard Swope, president of General Electric, and the United States Chamber of Commerce each came forward with plans for "industrial self-government." Such plans, however, required at least the consent of the federal government for they ran afoul of the antitrust laws. Before the 1932 elections, Roosevelt had indicated interest in such schemes, and on June 16, 1933, when he signed the National Industrial Recovery Act creating the National Recovery Administration (NRA), these ideas came to fruition in modified form.

But the legislative origin of NRA was somewhat different. In December, 1932, Senator Hugo L. Black of Alabama had introduced an AFL-sponsored bill to prohibit interstate shipment of goods produced by labor working more than thirty hours a week. The idea was to spread the available employment. On April 6, 1933, the Black bill passed the Senate. FDR disapproved of the bill and rushed Labor Secretary Frances Perkins to the House labor committee to head it off. Secretary Perkins urged minimum wages and government control of production. Business objected, and the administration worked the rest of April and early May on drafting a bill. Administration spokesmen presented the draft of the measure to the convention of the United States Chamber of Commerce in early May, and that group was enthusiastic for the central idea but wary of the labor provisions.

The final bill had within it something from each of several schools of economic thought. For business, there was a section providing for codes of fair competition and exemption from the antitrust laws; for the national planners, there was a scheme of government licensing of business through government approval of the codes written by industry; for labor, there were minimum wages, maximum hours, and Section 7a which promised collective bargaining; for the advocates of a large public works program, there was the whole of Title II of the bill which established the Public Works Administration. Still, the bill had some rough sailing in Congress, and the Senate adopted the conference report on it by only a seven-vote margin. The Act was to be in effect for only two years. It could, of course, be renewed.

The NRA proved to be far less than a success. In the first place, industries could not write the codes quickly, and while the codes were in preparation many businesses practiced a kind of "chiseling in advance" by expanding production to the limit while there was no floor under wages, so that they could build up inventories to be sold after the codes became effective and brought higher prices. In order to head off this self-defeating action, the NRA asked all employers in late July, 1933, to accept the President's Re-employment Agreement (PRA), commonly called the Blanket Code, which established minimum wages and maximum hours. But much damage had already been done. Industrial production in July rose slightly higher than the 1923–1925 average, only to fall roughly 35 per cent by October as PRA became effective and inventories were built. Inventory building during the summer was a major factor in the "first Roosevelt depression" in the fall of 1933. In the second place, the writing of the codes fell mostly to the bigger businesses within each industry. Labor's role in code writing was small except for the clothing industry, where there were large unions and small entrepreneurs. Consumers never had more than token representation in the drafting of codes. In the third place, there was confusion in the administration of the Act. There was constant conflict among the NRA administrators, the chief of whom was General Hugh S. Johnson, a blustering probusiness ex-cavalryman whom FDR eventually eased out. Some of the administrators believed in giving business its head, some became ineffectually concerned about protecting the consumer, and some conceived their role as business regulators. In the fourth place, the labor provisions and interpretations of those provisions proved quite inadequate from labor's point of view. By early 1935, labor leaders were saying that NRA stood for "National Run-Around." In the fifth place, small businessmen complained of the red tape inherent in the NRA and of domination by big business. As the economic historian Broadus Mitchell has put it, "A code was something between a charter of a medieval guild and the agreement of a modern cartel," but small businessmen—and trade unionists, too—saw their codes as closer to a cartel agreement than to a guild charter.

The President was understandably distressed when a unanimous Supreme

Court declared NRA unconstitutional in the Schechter case on May 25, 1935, less than a month before the statute was due to expire. And it is true that immediately after NRA died unemployment increased, hours of work increased, and wages decreased. Yet few deeply mourned the passing of the experiment which, as some intellectuals noted, had similarities to European syndicalism. As will be described more fully in Chapter 18, many industries continued to practice the anticompetitive devices NRA had sanctioned even after the Schechter decision. NRA had brought a psychological lift and a sense of national solidarity in the summer of 1933. By 1935, the immediate economic crisis had passed. The first flush of NRA-inspired confidence and feeling of purpose had helped, but it had not brought recovery. Greater institutional changes and vastly greater federal spending proved necessary to bring recovery.

The First New Deal and Agriculture

Agriculture received legislative attention from the very beginning of the New Deal. Two problems confronted agriculture: farm mortgages, which were rapidly being foreclosed and provoking violence in the Corn Belt; and the more general problem of raising farm prices to an equitable ratio with the prices farmers had to pay for industrial goods.

Roosevelt began the attack on the mortgage problem in late March, 1933, by consolidating all of the existing federal farm credit agencies into the Farm Credit Administration, and in May and June, Congress enacted the Emergency Farm Mortgage Act and the Farm Credit Act. With this legislation the FCA in time refinanced one-fifth of the total farm mortgage indebtedness. The agricultural bloc demanded further relief, which Congress provided in June, 1934, with the Frazier-Lemke Farm Bankruptcy Act. This unusual law enabled a farmer who had lost his farm through foreclosure to buy it back at a figure determined by a federal district court, the payment to extend over six years at just 1 per cent interest. In 1935, the Supreme Court found the Frazier-Lemke law unconstitutional, but the next year a revised version of the law passed Congress and was later upheld in the courts.

The first week of the new administration Agriculture Secretary Henry A. Wallace began a series of conferences with farm leaders on the general problem of raising farm prices. From these meetings came the Agricultural Adjustment Act (AAA) of May 12, 1933. The AAA was not a new idea; it was the culmination of farm measures and proposals that went as far back as the Populists. The purpose of AAA was to bring about a balance between the production and consumption of farm products so that farm income would have the same relative purchasing power—"parity"—that existed from 1909 to 1914. The law empowered the Secretary of Agriculture to use several methods to achieve that goal. For seven basic farm products (wheat, cotton, corn, hogs, tobacco, milk, and rice—later amended to include beef and sugar), AAA could enter into agreements with individual farmers by which the AAA would pay the farmer to limit his production by taking some acres out of cultivation. The AAA also was empowered to buy up agricultural surplus, or to lend money to farmers and accept their crops as collateral, until prices rose. This method was

A loyalty parade, 1917   STATE HISTORICAL SOCIETY WISCONSIN

American first aid station in trench in France. Photo released by the
Committee on Public Information   STATE HISTORICAL SOCIETY WISCONSIN

Henry Ford, Thomas A. Edison, Warren G. Harding, and Bishop W. F. Anderson
CULVER PICTURES, INC.

A high school typing class, 1920–1921   STATE HISTORICAL SOCIETY WISCONSIN

Warren G. Harding, Mrs. Harding, Mrs. Coolidge, and Calvin Coolidge,
March 3, 1921   UNITED PRESS INTERNATIONAL

Nicola Sacco and Bartolomeo Vanzetti

Ku Klux Klan members in 1923   CULVER PICTURES, INC.

Daytona Beach, Florida, during the land boom   STATE HISTORICAL SOCIETY WISCONSIN

A small midwestern town in 1911   STATE HISTORICAL SOCIETY WISCONSIN

The same town, 1925. Note the advent of automobiles and the disappearance
of the saloon   STATE HISTORICAL SOCIETY WISCONSIN

Radio broadcasting in the 1920's. The second from the left is Charles Coburn
CULVER PICTURES, INC.

Vilma Banky and Rudolph Valentino in "Son of the Sheik"   BROWN BROTHERS

Hemingway impressed
with the importance
of being Ernest
CULVER PICTURES, INC.

The novelist of
"flaming youth,"
F. Scott Fitzgerald
BROWN BROTHERS

Georgia O'Keeffe,
"The American Radiator Building"
COURTESY ALFRED STEIGLITZ
COLLECTION FOR
FISK UNIVERSITY

The Bath Club,
a flossy New York speakeasy,
by Al Hirschfeld
STATE HISTORICAL
SOCIETY WISCONSIN

Charles Lindbergh and the plane he used on his 1927 trans-Atlantic flight
BROWN BROTHERS

A campus hangout after a dance in the mid-1920's
STATE HISTORICAL SOCIETY WISCONSIN

Al Smith and F. D. Roosevelt at opening of Empire State Building,
May 1, 1931   UNITED PRESS INTERNATIONAL

Al Capone (at the right) with friends

put to work in the fall of 1933 with the newly created Commodity Credit Corporation acting as the lending agency. Finally, AAA granted the Secretary power to subsidize agricultural exports. The whole program was financed from revenues acquired from a special tax on food and fiber processors, who, of course, passed the tax on to the consumer.

AAA got off to a bad start so far as public relations were concerned. Alarmed by reports of a bountiful crop of cotton already planted and a redundancy of baby pigs, the AAA had about one-fourth of the cotton acres plowed under and over six million young pigs slaughtered. Coming at a time when thousands were hungry and in rags, besides traditional opposition to waste, there was a loud public outcry. The Socialist Norman Thomas pointedly suggested that Wallace was trying to solve the paradox of poverty in the midst of plenty by eliminating the plenty. The later prevention of production by letting land lie fallow was far greater than the destruction of 1933, but it was not so dramatic as the killing of baby pigs and evoked far less opposition.

Trying to restrict production by taking land from cultivation was by no means fully effective. Farmers merely fertilized more extensively, got higher yields per acre, and still received payment for keeping some of their land idle. The cotton crop of 1933, despite the plowing under in the spring, was actually slightly larger than it had been in 1932. Congress corrected this situation with the Bankhead Cotton Control Act of 1934, which put cotton production on a marketing quota basis rather than acreage allotment.

Crop restriction, plus serious droughts in the Midwest in 1933 and 1934, brought some of the effects desired before the Supreme Court declared the law unconstitutional in 1936. The price of cotton, wheat, and corn approximately doubled from 1932 to 1935, total farm income rose from $4.5 billion to $6.9 billion, and total farm mortgage indebtedness declined. Farmers complained about the program at times, but in AAA referendums they voted overwhelmingly to continue the program, at least until they had a better plan. Perhaps they were chagrined that agriculture had become a subsidized industry, although industrialists had never shown much embarrassment about the government subsidies they received.

Not all farm people benefited from AAA by any means. Cotton tenant farmers directly suffered from the program. Benefit payments went to the landlord rather than the tenant, and the landlord, having cold cash in his pocket at last, bought tractors and other equipment which diminished the demand for tenant labor. This feature of AAA, plus the dust storms, displaced thousands of southern tenant farmers. John Steinbeck later publicized the plight of these people in his *Grapes of Wrath* (1939).

An Assessment of the Early New Deal

By the end of the winter of 1934–1935 (the New Deal was implicitly to change its emphasis in the spring) there was much that the administration could point to with pride, to use a cliché of politicians. On the other hand, there remained much to be viewed with alarm, to use another. Certainly the economy showed improvement. Unemployment was down about 1,700,000 from 1933. The physical volume of industrial production was up about twelve index points from 1932. Farm problems were not as acute. Most of all, the banking system had been stabilized and the sense of panic that characterized February and March, 1933, had vanished.

Yet about eleven million workers remained without jobs, and the relief situation, although improved, still left millions of people in desperate and deplorable condition. The effectiveness of the monetary manipulation program had been dubious, and the silver purchase program was an enormous boondoggle. Organized labor and workers who wanted to become organized were justifiably distressed with the New Deal's labor policies.

In sum, recovery had not been achieved, relief had improved only a little, and reform had largely concentrated on financial institutions. Yet, in the congressional elections of 1934, the electorate returned even greater Democratic majorities, perhaps because the Republicans presented no attractive alternatives. The Democratic share of the popular vote increased slightly, an unprecedented development for a majority party in an off-year election. GOP representation in the House shrank from 117 to 103, and the Republicans lost 26 of the 35 contested Senate seats. After the elections the Republicans had only seven governorships left.

CHAPTER SEVENTEEN

The Later New Deal

FOR THE FIRST SEVERAL MONTHS OF THE FIRST ROOSEVELT ADMINIS-
tration, the usual political tugging and hauling between political parties and
amongst economic interest groups was considerably subdued. The business
community, with some important exceptions, had supported Hoover in 1932,
but Roosevelt did not alarm most businessmen at the beginning of his first
term. So great was the sense of urgency arising from the economic calamity
and so discredited was conventional business leadership that Roosevelt enjoyed
at first an unusual degree of unanimity. The Democratic party was as united
as ever it can be, the Republicans were in a bewildered daze, and most of the
nation's press gave the administration at least critical support. The New York
Daily News, the nation's most widely circulated tabloid and usually a Republican supporter, even sponsored a campaign to raise funds for a swimming pool
in the White House for the President's recreation.

But the spirit of the first of the New Deal was not to last long. As
FDR put it, "Now that these people are coming out of their storm cellars
they forget that there ever was a storm." After the banking crisis was past,
after the economy stopped its downward skid, and after the Republicans began
to recover from their depression shell shock, criticism of Roosevelt and his
associates began to become sharp. The Roosevelt haters came into being. By
1935, the vehemence of their almost hysterical attacks on "that man in the
White House" was greater than that against any American president since
Andrew Johnson.

"Polarized Politics"

The formation of the American Liberty League in August, 1934, symbolized
the new conservative opposition to the New Deal. Fronting for the Liberty

League was a group of conservative Democrats who had dominated their party in the 1920's but who had been pushed aside by the Roosevelt forces: Al Smith; Jouett Shouse, former director of the national committee; John J. Raskob, millionaire former chairman of the national committee; John W. Davis, Democratic presidential candidate in 1924; and Bainbridge Colby, once Wilson's Secretary of State. Behind these Democrats was an impressive array of rich and powerful businessmen who usually voted Republican. Most of these tycoons were of the DuPont family or in businesses in which the DuPonts had a large interest, such as General Motors which was represented in the Liberty League by Alfred P. Sloan and William S. Knudsen. But there were others: Sewell L. Avery of Montgomery Ward, J. Howard Pew of Sun Oil, and Ernest T. Weir of National Steel. The League was ostensibly a nonpartisan organization, but it required no particular political insight to perceive that it was primarily an anti-Roosevelt organization. Its millions of dollars were devoted to propaganda, mostly in a long series of pamphlets, which attacked the New Deal as a violator of the Constitution, state rights, and "free enterprise." But despite its great energy, the voters ignored its arguments in the 1934 congressional elections.

But the voters, or large numbers of them, displayed a mood in 1934 and 1935 that seriously disturbed Roosevelt. They returned a heavier Democratic majority to Congress, but they did so partly because the Republicans had not provided what they considered acceptable alternatives. Large numbers of voters were attracted to ideas and leaders more radical than the New Deal had been. All over the country people were responding to a variety of left-of-center but non-Communist political leaders, and, if some of their notions were strange indeed and some of the leaders were demagogues, fanatics, or crackpots, the basic dissatisfaction with what the Roosevelt administration had been was still apparent.

The novelist Upton Sinclair, who had been a Socialist most of his life except during World War I, led a radical movement in California that momentarily won control of the state Democratic party. In 1933, he published *I, Governor of California and How I Ended Poverty*. The next year, he entered the Democratic primary for governor and won a clear majority in a field of nine candidates. The McAdoo machine's candidate was George Creel, Wilson's wartime propaganda chief, who received 288,106 votes to Sinclair's 436,200. Sinclair's EPIC program (End Poverty in California) included a $50 a month pension for poverty-stricken people over age sixty and a "production for use" system for the state's unemployed in some ways similar to cooperatives and in some ways similar to state socialism. The campaign against Sinclair in the fall was bitter and dirty. FDR refused to support Sinclair, even though he was the Democratic candidate, and the Socialist party repudiated him. The state's newspapers were solidly against Sinclair, and prominent Hollywood figures contributed a big campaign chest to his Republican opponent, Frank Merriam. Merriam won the election by 260,000 votes. A middle-road candidate received over 300,000 votes. EPIC collapsed as quickly after the election as it had grown; by 1936 it was almost extinct.

California was also the home base of the Old Age Revolving Pension, or the Townsend Plan. Francis E. Townsend of Long Beach, a retired physician, urged that the government pay a pension of $200 each month to all unemployed people over sixty and that the pensioners be required to spend the entire sum within a month in order to be eligible to receive the next $200. Dr. Townsend was not as clear with his arithmetic about the scheme's financing as he was in his exposition of the benefits that would flow from the Plan, but the necessary funds, he explained, were to come from a 2 per cent tax upon all financial transactions. The Townsend Plan was very popular among the indigent aged, who formed Townsend Clubs all over the country and pressured their Congressmen.

From Louisiana came Senator Huey Long and his Share Our Wealth plan with its slogan "Every Man a King." Long, the "Kingfish," was from poverty-stricken northern Louisiana, and he had long been the champion of the "wool hat boys" in that state's politics. A vulgar corruptionist and a demagogue he surely was, but he used his political machine to get for the poor of his state many of the things they needed: better schools, highways, and hospitals. After he moved from the governor's mansion to the United States Senate in 1930, he increasingly became a national figure. He supported FDR strongly in 1932 but turned against him in 1933 to organize the Share Our Wealth society. He promised every family a $5,000 homestead and a $2,500 annual income, the funds to come from the confiscation of great fortunes. There was about Long and many of his followers much that was illiberal and antidemocratic—anti-Semitism, contempt for civil liberty, disregard for democratic political process—but it is significant that a demagogue in the 1930's gained his popularity with economic radicalism. After Long was assassinated in September, 1935, the Reverend Gerald L. K. Smith of Kansas became the movement's leader. Smith emphasized the fascist aspect of the movement and subdued economic unorthodoxy; the movement soon shrank to political insignificance.

Similar to Long in some respects was a Roman Catholic priest, the Reverend Charles E. Coughlin, who ranted each Sunday from his radio station in Royal Oak, Michigan, a Detroit suburb. Father Coughlin capitalized upon agrarian suspicion of "international bankers" to build up his National Union for Social Justice, although most of his radio listeners were in the big eastern cities. He first supported the New Deal and then turned against it with most extreme language. As did the Long movement, he later became primarily antidemocratic and anti-Semitic.

Besides these groups that Theodore Roosevelt would have called the "lunatic fringe" there were more respectable political developments that threatened to undermine the Roosevelt camp. In the upper Mississippi Valley, the LaFollette Progressives in Wisconsin and the Farmer-Labor party in Minnesota made overtures to labor and farm groups in neighboring states with a view to forming a new national party if the New Deal did not move in the directions it wanted. Organized labor in 1934 had become thoroughly disgruntled with the President and had begun to try to get what it wanted through sympathetic Congressmen such as Senators Wagner and LaFollette.

Under the circumstances, there was only one thing for Roosevelt or any other politically sensitive chief executive to do: move to the left and urge reform measures. With the political right having shifted to powerful attack and with large numbers of farmers, laborers, and the down-and-out increasingly flirting with political leaders to Roosevelt's left, pursuing the old direction or standing still would have been political suicide. This situation being the political reality, Roosevelt urged action upon the Congress elected in November, 1934. The first session of that Congress enacted a very large and important body of reform legislation that significantly altered the American economic and political structure, and this second New Deal took the steam out of the left-of-FDR movements.

Fundamental Reforms: Progressivism's High Tide

Of the many reforms enacted by the Seventy-Fourth Congress, the two most far-reaching were the National Labor Relations Act and the Social Security Act. The legislative history of the labor measure, generally called the Wagner Act, was a curious one. Despite the tone of reverence with which the labor movement today recalls Roosevelt, the Wagner Act, which did more for trade unionism than any other federal law at any time, was not Roosevelt's idea. Indeed, he did not state his support of the law until its passage was practically assured. All through 1934, Senator Wagner had worked fruitlessly for legislation more favorable to trade union growth than Section 7a of NRA. In February, 1935, he reintroduced his measure into the new Congress and successfully resisted efforts of a few Senators to amend the essential features of the bill. On May 16, 1935, eleven days before the Supreme Court declared NRA unconstitutional, the Senate passed the bill sixty-three to twelve. Still Roosevelt kept silent. On May 24, three days before NRA went down, at last FDR announced his support. Less than a month later the House, over the practically unanimous opposition of business, passed the bill without even a roll call.

The new labor law declared that employees engaged in interstate commerce had the "right" to join or form labor unions and to bargain collectively with their employers through representatives of their own choosing. A union which won majority support from the workers in any plant, company, or industry in a secret-ballot election conducted by the National Labor Relations Board, which was established by the law, became the sole bargaining agent of the employees. The law required employers to recognize and bargain with the union in good faith. The law also, in a list of "unfair practices," prohibited employers from interfering with employees in the practice of their union rights, from aiding or financing a company union, and from discriminating against employees as a means to defeat a union. The passage of the Wagner Act coincided with a great wave of labor militancy, and with this law behind them workers soon became organized in American industry as they had never been before.

The idea behind the Social Security Act of August 14, 1935, went back several years. The Bull Moose platform of 1912 had advocated old-age pensions, and by the time Congress passed the Act of 1935 about half of the states had enacted old-age pension or unemployment compensation laws, although few of them were adequate. In 1934, two separate social security bills were before Congress, and FDR asked for a special Committee on Economic Security to study the problem and formulate a plan. The committee reported the following January, and their proposed bill moved easily through both houses, delayed only by disagreements over details. Senator Wagner sponsored the bill in the Senate; Congressmen David J. Lewis of Maryland and Robert L. Doughton of North Carolina were its co-sponsors in the House. Though businessmen growled that Social Security was the opening wedge of socialism and the end of American self-reliance, only thirty-three Representatives and six Senators voted against the bill.

The Social Security law was one of the most complicated ever passed by Congress. Old-age pensions under the law were to be administered by the federal government. All employers and employees except those in certain categories (public employees, domestic servants, farm and casual workers, and employees of educational, philanthropic, and religious institutions) were required to pay a payroll tax of 1 per cent on all wages under $3,000 a year, the tax to be increased gradually until it reached 3 per cent in 1949. The revenues thus gained would go into a reserve fund from which, beginning in 1942, retired workers over sixty-five years old would receive monthly payments of from $10 to $85, depending upon how much they and their employers had contributed. For people already retired and sixty-five, the federal government would share the cost of pensions with the states, the federal contribution being limited to $15 per month.

The other main part of the law had to do with unemployment compensation. Here the scheme involved federal-state cooperation. A federal unemployment tax was placed upon all employers except those in certain categories. Employers, however, would be allowed a credit up to 90 per cent of the tax for contributions made to state unemployment compensation funds. This was the lever Congress used to encourage the passage of state funds; within two years all of the states had established such programs. The federal law required minimum standards of the states, but the states varied widely in the adequacy of their unemployment programs. Other parts of the Social Security Act provided funds to be granted to the states on a matching basis for the blind, for occupational training of those who were otherwise physically handicapped, and for indigent dependent children.

Although the law was one that a majority of the public clearly wanted, it drew a great deal of criticism about its details. Employers objected to its costs. The unemployed objected that to get unemployment benefits one had first to get a job and then lose it. Others were dissatisfied that there were so many employees in the exempted categories. Some economists warned that the growth of a large reserve fund, taken from active circulation, would be deflationary. But the proponents of the law argued that at last social security was recognized as a legitimate function of the federal government and that the law could be improved in the future. And it was. A 1939 amendment to the law moved the beginning date for old-age pensions forward to 1940, and since then the law has been amended several times to extend the coverage and increase the amount of the payments.

Another indication of the New Deal's new direction was a changed emphasis in taxation policy. On June 19, 1935, FDR urged Congress in a special message to revise the federal tax system with a view to accelerating progressive income taxation and "encouraging a wider distribution of wealth." Congress quickly responded with a new tax law that sharply increased inheritance taxes, imposed a new surtax on net incomes over $50,000 (which went up as high as 75 per cent on incomes over $5 million), and initiated a graduated net income tax on corporations. The following year's revenue act experimented with a tax upon the undistributed profits of corporations. Had this special tax been continued long, it might have brought about some major changes in corporation policy.

The Banking Act of 1935 was, in the words of the *Federal Reserve Bulletin*, "the most fundamental revision of the Federal Reserve Act since its adoption . . . in 1913." The banking measures of 1933 had been taken primarily with a view to getting the banks open and functioning again; the law of 1935 was a reform measure designed to centralize control of national banking in Washington. The 1935 law was the idea of Marriner S. Eccles, a maverick Utah banker who had become chairman of the Federal Reserve Board. Eccles argued that centralized control of the Federal Reserve's monetary powers was necessary in order to make the supply of money compensatory to fluctuations in the business cycle, a necessary weapon in the federal arsenal in the battle for economic stability. Eccles did not get from Congress all he wanted, but the law did give the Federal Reserve Board increased authority, including power to fix the discount rate directly, to set reserve requirements for member banks, and to control the System's open market operations. The law also extended the classifications of commercial paper against which Federal Reserve notes could be issued. Finally, the new law made some changes in the Federal Deposit Insurance Corporation's arrangements, the one raising the limit of deposit insurance up to $5,000 being the most important.

Actions of both the Congress and the President in 1935 had great effects upon powerful public utility companies. Public utility holding company empires, such as the one Samuel Insull built in the 1920's, had been under public attack since some of them collapsed with the depression. In 1935, a demand came for a "death sentence" for holding companies in this field. The companies lobbied intensively, but their effect was mitigated by an investigation led by Senator Hugo Black of Alabama which brought forth the information that the flood of telegrams that had beseiged Congressmen had emanated from lobbyists rather than their ostensible senders. The law finally passed in August, 1935, contained a modified "death sentence." The law required the Securities Exchange Commission to limit each holding company to a single integrated system. In other words, holding companies above the first level were illegal. The SEC also received complete powers to supervise the financial activities of these holding companies. The public utilities fought back with a vengeance in the courts after they had lost in Congress, but in 1938 the Supreme Court upheld the constitutionality of the law.

On May 11, 1935, Roosevelt established the Rural Electrification Authority (REA) and granted it $100 million from already appropriated funds. At that time, only one-tenth of the nation's farm families had electricity which was necessary not only for a modern home but for the new farming technology. The next year, Congress passed the Rural Electrification Act which encouraged farmers without electric power to form themselves into co-operatives and with low-interest REA loans to acquire the necessary generating and distributing facilities. Where sufficient electric generating power already existed in private companies, the REA co-operatives were to buy their power at wholesale rates and distribute it to their members. The private companies became alive. They went about building power lines to remote rural areas as they never had before. Between the co-ops and the new efforts of the private companies, America's farms rather quickly became electrified. Although city people paid little attention to this movement and most historians have slighted the subject, the REA did perhaps more than any other New Deal measure to raise the living standard and ease the physical work burden of a large number of people. One further electric power measure was that in 1935, Congress amended the legislation establishing the Tennessee Valley Authority, to be described in a later chapter, to clarify and expand its statutory power to generate and sell electricity.

Expanding Federal Relief

The Works Progress Administration (WPA), created by executive order on May 6, 1935, under authorization of the Emergency Relief Appropriation Act of April 8, 1935, was the biggest, most ambitious, and generally most successful relief program the federal government has ever undertaken. Since the idea behind WPA was to put the unemployed to work on public works programs in unprecedented numbers, the administration denied that WPA was a relief measure. Indeed, FDR had said in January that the federal government "must and shall quit this business of relief." But the public quite properly identified WPA with relief, and its administrators ran the program with an eye toward relieving distress among the unemployed. What Roosevelt had in mind with his somewhat Hooverian statement was a distinction between the federal government's giving direct payments to the poverty stricken and employing them for useful work. WPA shifted to the state and local governments responsibility for relief to "unemployables" and endeavored to hire the "employables" on its projects. Actually, as the record of industry would show during World War II, thousands of the "unemployables" handed back to the states were capable of gainful employment.

By 1941, over eight million different persons, almost one-fifth of the labor force, had been on WPA. The average number on the monthly payroll from 1935 to 1941 was 2,112,000. Their wages depended upon their degree of skill and their geographic region. The average monthly wage of all classifications was $52.14 in 1936. In its first six years, the total WPA expenditures was $11.4 billion. When one considers that, because of their poverty, the receivers of this money spent it quickly, the stimulation to the economy in general can be realized.

Most of the money went for construction and conservation projects—highways, streets, levees, airports, schools, hospitals, and other public buildings. About one-fifth of it went for various kinds of community service programs which employed people with all kinds of skills—musicians, actors, dentists, historians, and painters. Secretary of Interior Ickes, who was chief of the WPA planning division, concentrated on permanent and material public works; WPA Administrator Harry Hopkins, who was the more powerful figure in WPA, operated on the assumption that painters and actors had to eat even if they could not build bridges and dams.

WPA became one of the major targets of New Deal critics. Some of the

343

charges were true, others were false, and still others depended upon one's basic assumptions. One charge was that too many of the WPA construction projects were of peripheral utility. The answer to this was that if WPA administrators had undertaken projects conventionally in the domain of private enterprise the outcry against "socialism" would have been even greater. Many people objected to the projects that employed artists, writers, and actors. Congress in 1939 eliminated the WPA Federal Theater Project altogether. A very widespread and heated charge was that WPA laborers loafed on the job. Others replied just as heatedly that, although some did shirk, most WPA workers gave more than full value for the wages they received. The most serious charge was that the Democratic administration used WPA for its partisan advantage. This charge is difficult to assess. Certainly it is true that most WPA employees supported the Democratic party, but most of them came from classes of society that usually support that party and, furthermore, they probably felt that the Democratic party had done more for them in their struggle with the depression than had the Republicans. There were some real cases of local WPA officers using their power for corrupt political purposes in Pennsylvania, Kentucky, and Tennessee. Congress responded with the Hatch Act of 1939, which prohibited political activity for all employees of the federal executive branch below the policy-making level and made it unlawful for anyone to coerce a voter to influence his vote in any federal election. All things considered, one could build a better case against WPA for its failure to end economic distress among the depression's victims. Still, the record of WPA was remarkable in that it provided at least some income to millions who would otherwise have been destitute and, by employing thousands of skilled workers of hand and brain, helped to preserve skills for a later day.

Two other congressional actions of 1935 expanded relief for young people. Congress doubled the appropriation for CCC, inaugurated in 1933. In August, 1935, there were a half-million young men in the one thousand five hundred CCC camps over the country. When the program ended in 1940, there had been over 2,250,000 members in the Corps at some time or another. The National Youth Administration (NYA) came into being under the same act that had provided for WPA. The main purpose of NYA was to provide part-time employment for high school and college students, enabling them to continue their studies and remain off the labor market, but there was a smaller out-of-school NYA program for people age eighteen to twenty-five. In June, 1940, the average monthly wage of the over 200,000 high school NYA students was $4.74; the average for the 100,000 college undergraduates was $12.68, and the average for the 1,655 graduate students was $21.72. The selection of students for NYA jobs was on the basis of need, and the schools, rather than the federal government, directly controlled selection. In colleges and universities the faculty officer who administered the student loan system usually was in charge of NYA. NYA students as a rule worked in libraries and laboratories, did clerical work, and assisted faculty members in research projects. Some research projects, such as the Lorge-Thorndike *Semantic Count of English Words*, highly important in the teaching of reading and in compiling dictionaries, could not have been completed without the large quantities of skilled manpower that NYA made available.

One final reform measure. The Resettlement Administration, headed by

Rexford Tugwell and created by FDR's executive order in April, 1935, was a Department of Agriculture unit whose functions were both relief and reform. RA consolidated all the various rural relief activities previously handled in the Department. The biggest part of its job was to continue and expand the program, begun in the previous year, of buying up submarginal land and resettling the destitute families on this poor land in more promising areas. RA managed to remove about nine million acres of submarginal land from cultivation and move the families. It also built three "greenbelt" towns near Washington, Milwaukee, and Cincinnati as experiments in suburban planning. The very nature of RA's work involved government planning and paternalism, and it drew a considerable amount of fire from administration critics. In 1937, the White House consolidated RA into the new Farm Security Administration.

The Election of 1936: A Champion Political Coalition

As November, 1936, approached, both parties regarded the presidential election as a political showdown. The public would have its first chance to express itself directly about Franklin D. Roosevelt, whose renomination was a foregone conclusion. Roosevelt and the New Dealers would see how politically wise their shift to the left had been. Republicans and old-line conservative Democrats would see how effective their increasingly bitter attacks on FDR had been.

The Republican party did not have an obvious candidate. Ex-President Hoover had his supporters, but the voters seemed to have spoken clearly about him in 1932 when he ran against the same man. Senator Arthur H. Vandenberg of Michigan, who had won in 1934 despite the Democratic landslide, looked promising but he did not seek the nomination. Old Senator William E. Borah of Idaho was willing enough, but he was too unorthodox for most members of his party. The Cleveland Republican convention decided on Alfred M. Landon, governor of Kansas who had also survived the 1934 elections. Landon had attracted attention for balancing the Kansas budget and had the support of the Hearst newspapers, which in 1932 had supported FDR. Landon had done nothing recently to disturb seriously the more dyed-in-the-wool conservatives in his party, and the more liberal Republicans were gratified that he had supported Theodore Roosevelt in 1912. He was a man of little flair and color, but the nomination of Colonel Frank Knox, publisher of the *Chicago Daily News*, for the vice-presidency lent glamour to the ticket.

The Republicans also had difficulty in writing their platform. The problem was how to denounce the New Deal as a whole and yet appear sympathetic to those parts of it that seemed popular. Their platform criticized the Roosevelt administration for being bureaucratic and appealing to class prejudice, but it asserted that the Republicans supported labor's right to organize, aid to the unemployed, regulation of business, and subsidies to farmers. The Republicans promised if elected to repeal the Reciprocal Trade Agreements Act and to balance the federal budget.

Even the more conservative Democrats had little alternative in their convention at Philadelphia but to renominate FDR and endorse his administration.

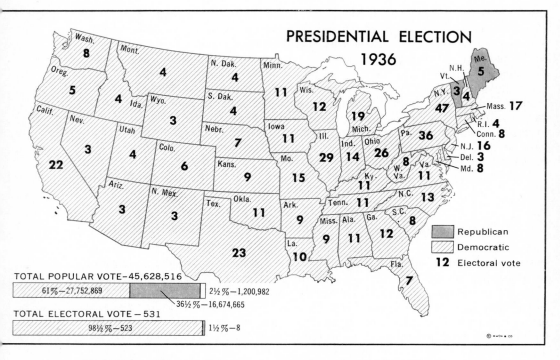

PRESIDENTIAL ELECTION
1936

Republican
Democratic
12 Electoral vote

TOTAL POPULAR VOTE—45,628,516

61%—27,752,869   2½%—1,200,982
36½%—16,674,665

TOTAL ELECTORAL VOTE—531

98½%—523   1½%—8

Both Roosevelt and Garner were nominated amid huge demonstrations on the first ballot. The platform was a reaffirmation of the ideas of the later New Deal. As he had done in 1932, Roosevelt went to the convention to accept the nomination, and in his speech he condemned "economic royalists" who would bring the American people into "industrial dictatorship." In his conclusion he became a little mystical, but his thought was widely acclaimed: "There is a mysterious cycle in human events. To some generations much is given. Of other generations much is expected. This generation of Americans has a rendezvous with destiny."

Both Roosevelt and Landon campaigned hard. Landon seemed unable to excite people's imagination, but he did a good job of what a later generation of advertising men would call "projecting an image" of a sincere, hard-headed, homespun, flexible conservative. Roosevelt met the attacks of his critics by asserting that, instead of being the opponent of capitalism that his opponents charged he was, he was that economic system's savior. "It was this administration which saved the system of private profit and free enterprise after it had been dragged to the brink of ruin by these same leaders who now try to scare you," he said in one campaign speech. On another occasion he told the story of an old man with a top hat who had fallen off a pier. He was rescued from drowning but lost his hat in the process, whereupon the old man berated his rescuer for not saving the hat as well.

The flood of Roosevelt votes in November was bigger than almost anyone expected. Roosevelt received 27,476,673 popular and 523 electoral votes; Landon received only 16,679,583 popular votes with just 8 commitments in the electoral college. Landon lost his own state and carried only traditionally

346

Republican Maine and Vermont. He received less than 40 per cent of the popular vote.

An analysis of the campaign and the vote reveals several significant developments. Important for later political history was labor's role in the Roosevelt victory. John L. Lewis and Sidney Hillman, leaders of the newly formed CIO, and George L. Berry of the AFL Pressmen's Union formed Labor's Non-Partisan League in the spring of 1936. Compatible with the Gompers tradition of rewarding political friends and punishing enemies, the League participated actively in several congressional races. But the League also supported Roosevelt with campaign speeches and financial contributions (about $1 million) to a far greater extent than organized labor had ever before supported a presidential candidate, far greater than the AFL's aid to LaFollette in 1924.

Another development with long-term significance was a shift in the Negro vote. Traditionally, Negroes who voted, which meant northern and western Negroes, had favored the Republican party, the Grand Old Party of the Great Emancipator. But in 1936 a majority of the Negro vote went to Roosevelt and the Democratic party.

Interesting also was the degree to which the Roosevelt and Landon votes reflected social-economic class. Traditionally, both major parties received support from all income groups. In 1936, certainly, many people with lower incomes voted Republican and some of the rich voted Democratic. But the vote in 1936 indicated more of a "horizontal" division than there had been previously. The story of the *Literary Digest* pre-election poll was revealing. That magazine, which died soon after the election, conducted a post card straw vote from mailing lists drawn from telephone directories and automobile registration records. Upon this kind of a sampling the magazine predicted that Landon would win. People who did not have the money for telephones and autos drastically upset the prediction. Nor did newspaper support make any difference. In 1936, an overwhelming majority of the nation's metropolitan dailies not only supported Landon but attacked Roosevelt with fury. The voters ignored the editorials.

Roosevelt's 1935–1936 program had well undercut the upsurge of the political left that had seemed strong two years before the election. In June, 1936, the followers of the late Huey Long, Father Coughlin, and Dr. Townsend formed the Union party, whose symbol was the Liberty Bell. The organization nominated a relatively little-known Republican Congressman from North Dakota, William Lemke—"Liberty Bell Bill"—and Father Coughlin predicted that he would receive twelve million votes. Roosevelt strategists feared Lemke might run well. But on election day he received only 892,000 votes, less than Debs received in 1912 or 1920 and far less than LaFollette in 1924. Norman Thomas, running again on the Socialist ticket, lost ground with 187,000 votes; the Communist nominee, Earl Browder, received only 80,000.

Roosevelt's victory was unprecedented in the history of modern politics. Not since James Monroe, before the days of modern political parties, had a candidate received such an endorsement. Nor has any presidential candidate since 1936 won by such a margin. If any presidential election could be regarded as a mandate, it seemed in November, 1936, that the electorate had given the signal for another four years of the later New Deal. Roosevelt had overwhelming Democratic support in Congress—328 House seats and 77 in the Senate. But no sooner had this champion political coalition been formed of city and country, North and South and East and West, farmer and laborer, than it began to come apart at the seams.

The deterioration of the Democratic coalition was the most important political development of the next four years. The battle over the Supreme Court, the "recession" of 1937–1938, and the intrusion of foreign affairs into domestic politics seriously divided and weakened the Roosevelt camp.

The Supreme Court Fight

Roosevelt said nothing in his second inaugural address of January 20, 1937—the first inauguration on this date provided by the Twentieth, or Lame Duck, Amendment—to indicate that he planned any action concerning the Supreme Court. His second inaugural, one of his most widely quoted speeches, called for a continuation of the New Deal to meet the problem of poverty: " . . . here is the challenge to our democracy: In this nation I see tens of millions . . . who at this very moment are denied the greater part of what the very lowest standards of today call the necessities of life. . . . I see one-third of a nation ill-housed, ill-clad, ill-nourished." But the second term was to have fewer benefits for the "one-third of a nation" than the six months from March through August, 1935.

On February 5, 1937, less than three weeks after the second inauguration, FDR sent a message to Congress calling for the reorganization of the federal judiciary. The message triggered a political and constitutional crisis. To understand the uproar over the judiciary reorganization bill one must know the background of the relations between the New Deal and the Supreme Court.

Roosevelt had made no appointment to the Court. Clearly, the Supreme Court's political complexion was far more conservative than the executive, the Congress, and the mood of the electorate. Four of the nine justices were confirmed conservatives who found their social philosophy in Herbert Spencer and their legal philosophy in John Marshall's sanctity of contract cases. They would not have been out of place on the late nineteenth-century bench. The four were Willis Van Devanter, appointed by President Taft in 1911; James C. McReynolds, appointed by President Wilson in 1914; and George Sutherland and Pierce Butler, each appointed by President Harding in 1922. At the other end of the Court was a group of three progressives: Louis D. Brandeis, appointed by Wilson; Harlan F. Stone, appointed by Coolidge; and Benjamin N. Cardozo, appointed by Hoover. In between these two groups were two other Hoover appointments: Chief Justice Charles Evans Hughes and Owen J. Roberts. Six of the justices were over seventy years old.

The Supreme Court had begun to thwart the legislative and executive branches early in 1935. In the "hot oil" cases, decided in January, 1935, the Court held Section 9c of the NIRA unconstitutional on the grounds that it bestowed an undue amount of legislative power upon the President in the regulation of the oil industry. Only Cardozo dissented. On February 18, the Court ruled in the gold-clause cases. It agreed with Congress and the President that clauses in private contracts that called for payment in gold need not be honored, but it ruled that gold clauses in government bonds must continue in force. On May 6, the Court struck down the Railroad Retirement Act of 1934 by a five to four decision on the grounds that a compulsory retirement and pension system denied due process of law "by taking the property of one and bestowing it upon another."

Then on May 27, 1935, "Black Monday," the Court unanimously struck down three actions. It found the Frazier-Lemke Farm Mortgage Act unconstitutional. It ruled that Roosevelt had acted illegally in removing William E. Humphrey from the Federal Trade Commission because independent regulatory commissions were responsible to Congress rather than to the president. And, most important, the Court declared all of NIRA unconstitutional in Schechter v. United States. The Court found two faults with NIRA: the law conferred too much legislative power to the executive branch and went too far in its assumption of what constituted interstate commerce. FDR retorted that the Court's view of interstate commerce was a "horse-and-buggy definition."

In 1936, the Court went even farther. On January 6, the Supreme Court in Butler v. United States invalidated AAA. The Hoosac Mills Corporation had refused to pay the AAA's processor's tax, and the government had brought suit against Butler *et al.*, receivers of the company. The Court held six to three that agricultural production was not interstate commerce and that the processing tax was a device for unconstitutional regulation of agricultural production. In Ashton v. Cameron Co. Water District the justices by a five to four vote struck down the Municipal Bankruptcy Act of 1934 as an invasion of state sovereignty. In Carter v. Carter Coal Company a majority of five invalidated the Guffey-Snyder Coal Conservation Act, which Congress enacted after the Court had defeated NIRA in an effort to rewrite NRA benefits for the coal industry. The majority opinion in the Carter case, written by Justice Sutherland, had such a narrow view of the commerce clause of the constitution that FDR's "horse-and-buggy" comment fitted it well. Then came the Tipaldo case, in which by another five to four division the Court nullified a New York state law regulating the hours and wages of women workers. The decision, written by Justice Butler, reasserted the old doctrine that such state laws ran counter to the freedom of contract provisions of the Fourteenth Amendment, previously stated in the 1909 Lochner case and Adkins v. Children's Hospital (1923).

These decisions against New Deal measures, which evoked such headlines as "AAA Plowed Under," brought a considerable demand that something be done to change the situation. From Capitol Hill came a flurry of proposals to curb the Court's powers. The newspaper columnists Drew Pearson and Robert Allen in 1936 published *Nine Old Men*, a very popular attack upon the Court conservatives. Yet throughout 1936 Roosevelt made no overt move, although he and millions of others were concerned about what the Court might do when the Wagner Act and the Social Security Act came before it for review.

FDR's effect was electric when he proposed his Federal Judiciary Reorganization bill in February, 1937. The proposal was both ingenious and naive —ingenious in the way that FDR seemed to obscure the proposal's real intention and naive in the assumption that the public would not see through the ingenuity. Roosevelt proposed that Congress empower him to appoint a new federal judge, at any level in the system, whenever any incumbent judge should fail to retire within six months after becoming seventy years old. No more than fifty additional judges might be appointed, and no more than six of these might be to the Supreme Court. In making his proposal, FDR put his emphasis upon supposedly crowded court dockets, the alleged result of aged and infirm jurists. No special perspicacity was necessary to see that behind the reform was a desire to appoint enough new justices to override the four Supreme Court standpatters.

There was a great deal of hogwash as well as some good sense in the national debate that followed. Many of the President's supporters saw nothing wrong about altering the traditional division of powers among the government's three branches and failed to see that in some circumstances a Supreme Court could resist an executive and a Congress in such a way that those who call themselves liberals would applaud. Many of the President's opponents used a constitutional shield to obscure their opposition to the New Deal and exploited the rather popular conception of the Constitution that confused that document with Holy Writ and saw the Supreme Court as a collection of reincarnated Biblical prophets.

What happened in the struggle over the "court-packing" bill is fairly clear; how to interpret what happened is something else. Immediately the nation's press came out in overwhelming opposition to FDR. Then a group of Senate Democrats, most of them conservatives, met at the home of Senator Millard Tydings of Maryland and planned their strategy. Among the Senators at the meeting were Walter George of Georgia, Frederick Van Nuys of Indiana, Harry F. Byrd of Virginia, and Burton K. Wheeler of Montana, who was then regarded as an extreme liberal and had been LaFollette's running mate in 1924. Wheeler's position was a strange one. His opposition to FDR's proposal was strong, but he had sponsored an even more radical proposal: an amendment to the Constitution which would have empowered Congress to override with a two-thirds vote any Supreme Court decision which had declared a law of Congress unconstitutional. Wheeler assumed leadership in the Senate fight against the bill. These Democrats met for lunch with a group of Republicans a few days later, and the Republicans agreed as a matter of tactics to stay in the background.

The Senate Committee on the Judiciary opened hearings on the bill on March 10, and a parade of witnesses provided good headlines. Later in the month, Chief Justice Hughes addressed a public letter to Wheeler in which he stated, "The Supreme Court is fully abreast of its work. . . . There is no congestion of cases upon our calendar." Then on March 29 the Court announced its decision in West Coast Hotel v. Parrish in which by a five to four vote it upheld the state of Washington's minimum wage law and reversed itself on the Tipaldo case. At the time most people interpreted the change in the Court's opinion, made possible by the change in Justice Roberts' view of the matter, as a strategic retreat in the fight. Actually, Roberts had decided to uphold the Washington law shortly before Christmas, 1936, almost two months before FDR let fly with his Court bomb. Hughes had postponed the decision until the return of Justice Stone who had been ill. On April 12, the

Court upheld the Wagner Act with three decisions: National Labor Relations Board *v.* Jones and Laughlin Steel Co. (the most important), NLRB *v.* Fruehauf Trailer Co., and NLRB *v.* Friedman-Harry Marks Clothing Co. With these developments, widely interpreted as a capitulation by the Court, the strength of the President's forces waned, although he insisted on a showdown. In late May, the Court upheld the validity of the Social Security Act in two cases.

On May 18, the Senate Judiciary Committee voted to reject FDR's court plan, although its report, signed by seven Democrats and three Republicans against eight Democratic dissenting committee members, did not appear until the next month. The report stigmatized FDR's proposal as "a needless, futile, and utterly dangerous abandonment of constitutional principle." Also on May 18 Justice Van Devanter informed the President of his desire to retire the following month.

Both Van Devanter and Sutherland had wanted to retire before the whole struggle began but had been deterred from doing so because of the failure of Congress to keep its pledge to retired Justice Oliver Wendell Holmes. When Holmes stepped down from the Court in 1932, Congress had agreed to continue the salaries of judges who retired after reaching seventy years of age if they had served for ten years. But Congress had later reduced the pay. After FDR made his proposal, opponents of his plan rushed through another retirement bill in the hope of heading off a more drastic measure. Senator Borah then prevailed upon his friend Van Devanter to retire.

Van Devanter's retirement filled FDR with consternation despite the opportunity it afforded him to make his first Court appointment. Before the Court fight began, FDR had promised the first appointment to Senator Joseph T. Robinson, the Senate Democratic majority leader who was then fighting a strenuous but losing battle for the Roosevelt proposal. But Robinson was sixty-five years old, hardly a specimen of the "younger blood" Roosevelt said the Court needed, and, furthermore, Robinson was clearly an old-style Arkansas conservative. As Senate majority leader, Robinson continued the fight on into the hot Washington summer. Roosevelt refused a compromise, and he and Farley used their patronage powers to try to force Senators into line.

Then, on July 13, Senator Robinson died of a heart attack. His death got Roosevelt off the hook of his Court appointment, but Robinson's friends in the Senate—and they were many among the conservative Democrats—regarded his death as the result of overwork for a cause they did not even like. On the train coming back from the Robinson funeral in Arkansas, the southern conservative Democrats mapped their strategy. Upon their return to Washington, Vice-President Garner, who opposed the Court measure, and the new Senate majority leader, Alben W. Barkley of Kentucky, told the President that he did not have the votes for his Court plan and that he had better compromise. Roosevelt relented. The result was the Judicial Procedure Reform Act of August 27, 1937, which expedited the movement through the federal court structure of cases involving the constitutionality of federal laws and which inhibited the power of federal judges to stay the execution of federal laws with injunctions.

These were the main facts of the Court fight. How to interpret them? Many have argued that Roosevelt lost the battle but won the war, pointing out that after March, 1937, the Supreme Court's decisions were compatible with New Deal intentions. Certainly, it is true that thereafter the Court was in harmony with Congress and the executive. But if Roosevelt won the war he lost his army in the process. Roosevelt lost his magic with the big Democratic congressional majorities after his defeat in the Court battle. The co-operation of White House and Capitol Hill that had characterized the reform wave of 1935–1936 was gone, never again to be revived behind a reform program.

The Elections of 1938

The battle over Roosevelt's Court proposal was not the only matter to disrupt the Democratic coalition which had been so successful at the polls in 1936. Foreign affairs began to intrude increasingly upon domestic policies, and the natural alliances of domestic issues did not necessarily transfer to questions of foreign policy.

One foreign matter that tended to disrupt the Democratic party was the Spanish revolution. In 1931, a democratic movement had overthrown the Spanish monarchy. In July, 1936, General Francisco Franco led a revolt against the Spanish republic supported by the army, the Roman Catholic church, the large landholders, and most of the businessmen. In some respects the Franco movement was similar to German and Italian fascism, yet it was in other respects more like preindustrial reaction. The German and Italian fascists supported Franco and used the Spanish battlefields as testing grounds for their troops and their new military equipment and techniques. The republican government—generally called the "Loyalists"—moved increasingly to the left and accepted the support of the Comintern. The civil war became a conflict between fascist and communist. Many were the views in America as to what course the federal government should pursue in the Spanish conflict, but in general the "liberals" who had worked for Roosevelt and the New Deal sympathized with the Loyalists and American Roman Catholics supported the pro-Franco position of the Spanish church. Roman Catholics constituted a considerable part of the leadership and the rank-and-file in the big urban political machines in the Democratic party. The tensions between the liberals and the city machines seldom came out into the open over the Spanish question, but the Franco revolution added still another factor to the precarious balance of forces which is the Democratic party.

The threat of general European war and anxiety over American neutrality in the event of war similarly created problems for the political coalition that the mid-nineteenth century politicians had called the Democracy. In October, 1937, Roosevelt delivered a speech at Chicago in which he advocated a "quarantine" of aggressor nations. The speech was definitely unpopular. In December, 1937, Democrats in the House became sharply divided over an amendment to the Constitution offered by Representative Louis Ludlow, Democrat of Indiana. An idea greatly like one the Socialists had advocated in 1916 and that Bryan and LaFollette had come to favor in early 1917, the Ludlow amendment would have required a majority vote in a national referendum before a declaration of war could be made, except in the case of an invasion of the United States or its territories. Roosevelt strongly urged the resolution's defeat, and it was defeated but only by a margin of twenty-one votes. A majority of House Democrats from the Midwest and the West voted for the Ludlow amendment; a majority of Democrats from the East and the South voted against it. Three-fourths of the Republican votes were in favor of the measure.

The Wagner-Van Nuys antilynching bill pointed up the North-South division among the Democrats. The bill proposed to make lynching a federal crime and to allow the families of lynching victims to sue the county in which the crime had occurred. The bill had strong support in the North, but southern Senators defeated it by threatening a filibuster. Roosevelt, to the dismay of northern liberals, said nothing in support of the measure.

Roosevelt himself further disrupted the party with his so-called purge attempts in the Democratic primaries of 1938. On June 24, 1938, he declared in one of his radio "fireside chats" that he would use his influence to defeat some Democratic conservatives in the primaries. "Never before," he said, "have we had so many Copperheads." The results of the "purge" were disastrous from FDR's point of view. In the contests in which the President publicly expressed his preference, only two of his choices won: James H. Fay beat John O'Conner for a House seat in New York City and Barkley, the incumbent, defeated A. B. "Happy" Chandler for the Senatorial nomination in Kentucky. But Senator Tydings won over FDR's opposition in Maryland; Roosevelt's choice came in third in Georgia where Walter F. George, whom the President had marked for defeat, won re-election; in South Carolina it was probably only FDR's opposition to Ellison D. "Cotton Ed" Smith that enabled that ancient reactionary to win. Roosevelt's favorite in South Carolina, Governor Olin D. Johnston, hardly met most people's standards of what constituted a liberal. When one considers that Claude Pepper in Florida and Lister Hill in Alabama, both considered southern liberals, had already won their primaries before Roosevelt announced his "purge" plan, it is clear that FDR did not do southern liberals any favor.

With the Democratic party at war with itself, it was no surprise when the Republicans regained a great deal of lost ground in the general elections in November. In the new Congress the GOP had eighty more House seats than it had in the Congress elected in 1936, and it picked up eight seats in the Senate. The Republicans also regained power in a number of state governments in what before the depression had been heavily Republican territory. Ever since the 1938 elections, Congress has been governed by a tacit alliance of Democratic and Republican conservatives. Ironically, Roosevelt contributed to the making of that alliance.

The "Recession" of 1937–1938

The downswing in the business cycle that came in the fall of 1937 considerably embarrassed the Roosevelt administration, which tried to reduce the sting of the depression within a depression by calling it only a "recession." Until September, 1937, the New Deal had brought about a fairly steady improvement of the nation's economic condition, as Table 7 indicates.

TABLE 7

(100 is 1935–1939 average)

	Physical Volume of Industrial Production	Factory Employment	Payrolls	Wholesale Prices
1929	110	108.3	127.5	118.2
1932	58	67.8	54.0	80.4
1933	69	74.9	57.9	81.8
1934	75	87.6	74.5	93.0
1935	87	93.2	85.6	99.3
1936	103	101.0	99.1	100.3
1937	113	110.9	118.3	107.1

That the New Deal had by no means ended the Great Depression, despite the fact that some of these statistics show a return to 1929 levels, was seen in the persistent problem of unemployment. The volume of unemployment had declined—from roughly 12,500,000 in 1933 to 7,250,000 in 1937—but no economy with roughly 14 per cent of its civilian labor force without jobs could be called healthy.

Nevertheless, some people feared that the recovery trend might become a runaway inflationary boom. Early in 1937, the Federal Reserve Board raised its reserve requirements by 50 per cent and began to buy government bonds on a large scale. Roosevelt, in his budget message of January 5, 1937, heeded the loud cry against deficit financing and the growing national debt and announced that it was time for a cutback in federal spending. Secretary Morgenthau called for a reduction in expenditures for agriculture, public works, and relief. The new budget, consequently, was significantly lower. The federal deficit for the fiscal year 1936 (July 1, 1935, to June 30, 1936) had been $4.3 billion, for fiscal 1937 the deficit was reduced to $2.7 billion and for fiscal 1938 down to only $740 million. The reduction in deficit had been accomplished by cutting back sharply on WPA, reducing farm subsidies, and stopping future commitments for RFC and PWA.

The restriction of credit, the reduction in federal spending, and other factors, such as the decrease in purchasing power brought by the new social security taxes, had a quick effect. But the effect was not what holders of orthodox economic views had predicted if only "that man" would give business a "breathing spell" and balance the budget. There was instead the "recession." Unemployment in 1938, according to Bureau of Labor Statistics estimates, was 2,637,000 greater than in 1937. Every other important economic indicator showed trouble. Farm prices, for example, fell from 15 to 20 per cent.

During the winter of 1937–1938, there were sharp struggles within the administration about what course to pursue to combat the economic decline. Morgenthau argued for continued economy. Others argued that business had declared a "strike of capital" and that an antimonopoly program should be undertaken. The few Keynesian economists in the administration called for a vast injection of federal financial plasma into the ailing body economic. Roosevelt remained undecided until April, 1938, when he announced an easing of credit restrictions, asked Congress for increased appropriations for relief and agriculture, and embarked upon an antitrust policy that was the reverse of the NRA.

Congress responded. WPA expenditures for the last six months of 1938 were roughly 50 per cent greater than they had been in the last six months of 1937. Agricultural subsidies increased almost fourfold. Military and naval spending increased sharply, although the amounts spent were small in comparison with what they would be in just a few years. These actions succeeded in reversing the direction of the economy. The economic indicators for 1939 were almost as high as they had been for 1937. Average unemployment in 1939 was better than one million less than in 1938.

The antitrust drive was doubleheaded. Congress provided the Antitrust Division of the Department of Justice an increased appropriation, and Roosevelt appointed the vigorous Thurman Arnold of the Yale Law School to be head of the Division. Arnold began nearly a hundred new antitrust suits, although by the time the cases could reach their climax defense and war considerations had changed the administration's antitrust policy once more. The other part of the antitrust program was the Temporary National Economic Committee, created by Congress in June, 1938. The TNEC conducted hearings for several months and launched many special research projects to study how concentrated economic power was in America and how that concentration had been achieved. Never before nor since has there been such a thorough study of American monopoly and its methods, and the TNEC hearings and research monographs, which run several feet on the library shelves, constitute a goldmine of information about the operation of the American economy in the late 1930's. The TNEC's final recommendation in the spring of 1941 contained nothing startling; by then defense and foreign policy matters had long before supplanted the reform impulse.

The Death of the New Deal

To say precisely when the New Deal died is impossible, for it did so without announcement and without drama. Reform did not die of a heart attack; it died of a slow smothering. Certainly, when Roosevelt said after the United States entered the war, referring to himself, that "Dr. Win-the-War" had replaced "Dr. New Deal" he only recognized a change that had occurred long before. Perhaps recognition of the death of the New Deal came in FDR's message to Congress of January 4, 1939, when he said, "We have now passed the period of internal conflict in the launching of our program of social reform. Our full energies may now be released to invigorate the processes of recovery in order to preserve our reforms." Perhaps its death could be dated even earlier.

Indeed, after the 1936 elections the Fair Labor Standards Act of 1938 was the only important reform measure enacted, the only new departure that directly benefited large numbers of ordinary people. The idea of this measure was by no means altogether new, since in 1936 the Walsh-Healy Government Contracts Act had become law. The Walsh-Healy law required all employers who had contracts with the federal government of $10,000 or more to pay at least the prevailing wages of their locality, to provide an eight-hour day and a forty-hour week, and not to hire boys under sixteen and girls under eighteen years of age. Thereafter, the movement to spread "a floor under wages and a ceiling over hours" bogged down. In 1937, an FDR-sponsored wage-hours bill passed the Senate but failed to get through the House. Southern communities regarded low wages as their best lure in persuading northern businesses to move south, some northern businessmen wanted to continue paying low wages to at least some of their employees, and farmers everywhere who employed much labor opposed any increase in their business costs. The wage-hours bill finally got through Congress in the spring of 1938, but only after exempting sailors, domestic employees, and agricultural workers from its provisions. The new law applied to employees engaged in interstate commerce or in production of goods destined for such interstate movement. The minimum wage under the law was twenty-five cents an hour, to be increased gradually until reaching forty cents in 1945. Maximum hours were forty-four, to be reduced by 1940 to forty hours. Employees were to be paid time-and-a-half for all work over the maximum hours. The Act also forbade employment of children under sixteen years of age and under eighteen in certain dangerous industries. These minimums were modest enough; a worker might still receive only $10 for forty hours' work. But when the law went into effect its outcome was to increase wages for roughly 350,000 employees and to reduce the workweek of about one million people.

Two other laws of the first half of Roosevelt's second term deserve mention: the new AAA and the Wagner-Steagall National Housing Act of 1937. Neither of these measures in any significant way began programs that had not already been pursued earlier in the New Deal. When the Supreme Court invalidated the first AAA in January, 1936, Congress responded the following month with the Soil Conservation and Domestic Allotment Act. This law made soil conservation rather than crop restriction its ostensible purpose and circumvented the Court's objection to the AAA processing tax by paying benefits to farmers from regular federal revenues. In February, 1938, a new, permanent Agricultural Adjustment Act became law.

The new AAA retained the soil-conservation and benefit-payment aspects of the earlier programs. If the growers of five basic crops—cotton, tobacco, rice, wheat, and corn—so voted by a two-thirds majority in a referendum, marketing quotas would be enforced. Farmers who sold more than their established quota of these crops were subject to heavy fines. The Act also authorized the Commodity Credit Corporation to make storage loans of up to 75 per cent of the parity price—later increased to 85 per cent. In other words, if the market price of one of the five basic commodities should fall below 75 per cent of parity, the farmer had the option of storing his crop and receiving a loan from the government. Agriculture Secretary Wallace called this feature of the Act the "ever-normal granary," the idea being that a surplus in abundant years would be stored for lean years. The trouble in practice was that, for most crops in most years, there was only surplus. The new AAA also provided federal crop insurance for wheat-growers, the premiums and the benefits to be paid either in wheat or its cash equivalent.

Most of the Act was only a new device for subsidies to commercial farmers who took the option of participating in the program. But there was one new feature which worked for the direct benefit of urban families. The Act empowered the Surplus Marketing Administration to purchase food surpluses and distribute them to families on relief or on WPA and to school lunch programs. Under this arrangement a food stamp plan developed. Relief families received food stamps entitling them to a half-dollar's worth of surplus food for every dollar they spent for food in the usual way. The return of prosperity, which came only when defense and war contracts stimulated industry, ended the food stamp plan.

The National Housing Act of 1937 provided for the continuation and expansion of urban slum clearance and public housing that had begun under PWA. Under this Act the United States Housing Authority could lend local housing authorities up to 100 per cent of the cost of new public-housing apartments which were reserved for families with low incomes. Private real estate interests prevented an expansion of USHA activities in 1939. New housing under the law was only a beginning of a solution to the enormous slum and housing problem that confronted, and still confronts, the nation's poor, but it was a necessary step toward a vital goal.

But despite such laws, after 1937 the New Deal was on the wane and on the defensive. In 1939 and 1940, the conservative congressional alliance of southern Democrats and northern Republicans attempted to pass crippling amendments to the nation's labor law which were defeated only by all-out efforts in labor's camp. The tax laws of the period reveal the drift of politics: the nerve that runs from the wallet to the brain is an exceedingly sensitive one. The Revenue Act of 1938 lowered the undistributed profits tax and lowered the tax bill of corporations in general. The tax bill of the next year eliminated the undistributed profits tax altogether. Business received other benefits during these years. The Miller-Tydings Act of 1937 amended the antitrust laws to make manufacturers' price maintenance agreements legal. Under such agreements, euphemistically known as "fair trade," manufacturers determined the prices retailers must charge for their products.

What can one say of the New Deal to summarize it? This much seems clear: it relieved economic distress, although it by no means eliminated poverty; it improved the nation's economic condition, although it was the war rather than the New Deal that brought a return of prosperity (there still were 7,600,000 unemployed in January, 1941); it brought vitally needed social-economic reforms that brought to fruition some of the demands of progressives of the previous half-century. What were the motives of Roosevelt and the other New Dealers? The motives of human beings are complex, but most people would agree that the New Dealers wanted to provide relief and bring about recovery, that they were ever sensitive to political advantage, and that most of what they did was tempered by humanitarian considerations. Did the New Deal "save capitalism" from failure as many historians have written and as Roosevelt himself so confidently assumed? To know really the answer to the question, one must know what would have happened if there had been no

New Deal. In a sense, capitalism had failed before Roosevelt took office. The question was: Would it be rebuilt or would it be scrapped for some other economic arrangement? It was in fact rebuilt. The capitalism that emerged from the New Deal years was not a duplicate of the predepression model. The federal government had assumed a larger role in the operation of the economy and had acquired new powers to regulate it, and organized labor and organized agriculture were stronger than they had been before 1933. But the new model was unmistakably still capitalism; production for profit rather than production for use was still the economic order of things.

CHAPTER EIGHTEEN

Economic Change in a Time of Trouble

IMPORTANT FOR THE ECONOMY AS THE POLITICAL EVENTS IN WASH-ington in the 1930's were, one cannot grasp all the important economic changes of the period by focussing on Washington alone. In areas of activity not related to the nation's capital, or only indirectly related to it, there were many economic developments which affected the way Americans lived. Perhaps the most significant of these were the growth in the strength of the labor movement, the social and economic experiment of the Tennessee Valley Authority, the continuing technological revolution, basic changes in the economics of agriculture, and a continuing tendency toward industrial and financial monopoly.

Organized Labor, 1929–1935

The year of the Wall Street crash found organized labor in the United States weaker than it had been during World War I. In 1929, the AFL had only 2,769,700 members. Its poor condition was due partly to concerted opposition of employers and the cooperation employers received from government at all levels, but part of the responsibility for labor's decline fell upon its leadership which was, for the most part, lacking in militance, ambition, and imagination.

The early depression worked hardship even on the craft unions. Unemployment and partial employment made it difficult or impossible for members to pay their dues. Some employers took advantage of growing unemployment and resulting competition for jobs to weaken the unions. Others who had no quarrel with the unions in their shops were in difficulty when their business competitors broke unions and lowered their labor costs. By 1933, AFL membership had declined to 2,317,500. Unaffiliated unions had about 650,000 members. One can only speculate about such a subject, but the possibilities of what might have happened after 1929 if the labor movement had been as strong then as it is today are interesting indeed.

Section 7a of NIRA, which declared "employees shall have the right to organize and bargain collectively through representatives of their own choosing," stimulated labor organization. Using such slogans as "The President wants you to join the Union," trade unions increased their membership to 3,600,000 in 1934 and to 3,890,000 in 1935. But labor was soon to find that Section 7a was not the boon that labor leaders at first thought it would be.

A few employers, such as Henry Ford, chose to stay outside of NRA altogether rather than to give an inch toward unionism. More employers circumvented the spirit but not the letter of the law by resorting to "company unions." A company union is not a bona fide labor organization; it is by definition dominated by and dependent on the employer. By 1935, there were 593 company unions, of which almost two-thirds had been founded after passage of NRA. These "phony unions" had 2,500,000 members.

The administration of Section 7a also vitiated the law. The National Labor Board, of which Senator Wagner was chairman, set up under the law, tried to give the NRA labor provision real substance, but the NLB had little actual power, and NRA administrators and the President himself on important occasions made administrative decisions contrary to NLB's wishes. When Roosevelt abolished NLB in July, 1934, and established a new National Labor Relations Board, the new board was only slightly more effective.

The auto industry illustrated the frustrations that labor organizations found under NRA. This relatively new industry was traditionally "open shop." Craft unions had made a few efforts to organize skilled workers in the industry and there had been sporadic attempts to organize the mass of the unskilled, but company opposition and employee disinterest had prevented any real results. In March, 1934, however, two thousand workers at Fisher Body voted for a strike to achieve union recognition, a 20 per cent wage increase, and a thirty-hour week. Labor unrest was considerable, and a strike threatened to spread and tie up the industry. Since auto production was a vital part of the economy, the administration in Washington was eager to prevent an interruption of production. The day before the strike was to begin FDR got a postponement and persuaded management and labor to accept a "compromise" which fell far short of granting the union what it wanted. Instead of majority representation by a union within a company, Roosevelt forced through a plan that called for proportional representation and circumvented the NLB by creating a special Automobile Labor Board. Proportional representation made real unionism impossible. Under this arrangement any number of unions, including company unions and all kinds of splinter organizations, could represent its members in collective bargaining, and management, confronted with divided opposition, could play off one group against another. Before the Supreme Court killed NRA in May, 1935, Roosevelt had created special labor boards for textiles and steel as well as auto.

The Wagner Act of July, 1935, eliminated most of the legal roadblocks to a vigorous labor movement. The year 1935 also saw startling developments within the labor movement itself. The combination of the Wagner Act and the new CIO brought a vastly altered labor-management situation. Until the New Deal, Big Business had stood almost alone in the industrial sector of the American economy. Early in the Roosevelt first term, Big Government had come into being. After 1936–1937 Big Business was to be confronted by Big Labor.

Labor's Civil War

For several years there had been conflict within the AFL between the leaders of a handful of industrial unions and the main body of the leadership. In 1935, the conflict came to a head and resulted in a division in the camp of labor into CIO and AFL.

Advocates of industrial unionism argued that only with industrial unions —that is, "vertical" unions embracing all of the workers of an industry no matter what their craft or degree of skill—could the mass production and basic industries such as steel and auto be organized. Craft unionists were not interested in unionizing the unskilled workers in such industries. Furthermore, they identified industrial unionism with economic radicalism and pointed with alarm to the old IWW, despite the fact that the AFL had long contained the industrially organized United Mine Workers whose president, John L. Lewis, was usually a Republican. But the industrial *versus* craft union argument was only part of the conflict which led to the founding of the CIO, although it was a central part. In general, the leaders of the industrial unions in the AFL were more interested in political action than the more conservative leaders who dominated the AFL executive board. Further, the industrial unionists were far more militant. The record of craft and industrial unions under NRA demonstrated that. From June, 1933, to May, 1935, craft union membership grew by 13 per cent; the few industrial unions then in existence increased their membership by 132 per cent. Lewis' UMW grew from about sixty thousand to about five hundred thousand; it organized not only coal miners but incorporated into its grab-bag District 50 almost any kind of employee group interested in organizing. The International Ladies' Garment Workers Union (ILGWU) increased fourfold, and the United Textile Workers trebled its membership.

The progressive yeast that was working in the minds of millions of Americans and the upturn of business that came in 1933 and 1934 led thousands of workers in basic industries to try to organize themselves. They received "federal charters" from the AFL. They were not component national or international unions, such as the printers or the painters; they were only local unions affiliated loosely with the AFL. Membership in such "federal locals" increased from 10,396 in 1933 to 111,489 in 1935. The conservative craft unionists who controlled the AFL proposed to divide these members up among the various craft unions; the industrial unionists proposed to make the "federal locals" the nuclei of industrial organizations in each basic industry.

At the San Francisco convention of the AFL in 1934, Lewis, with great parliamentary skill, guided through a resolution which called for an organizing campaign in steel and the granting of provisional charters to industrial unions in auto, cement, and aluminum. But during the next year the AFL hierarchy did practically nothing to put the resolution into action. John L. Lewis was furious, and a furious John L. Lewis was something dramatic to behold.

Built like a bear with the mane and head of a lion, John Llewellyn Lewis had been born of Welsh parents in Iowa in 1880. The father had been a victim of coal operators' blacklists; the son began to work in the mines at the age of twelve. Young Lewis married a schoolteacher, who gave him the education he had been denied in his coal-mining community. At the age of thirty-nine, in 1919, he became president of the miners. He had a roaring voice and a tongue spiced with Elizabethan rhetoric (he was a passionate admirer of Shakespeare).

At the 1935 AFL convention at Atlantic City, Lewis told the delegates, "At San Francisco they [the AFL old guard leadership] seduced me with fair words. Now, of course, having learned that I was seduced, I am enraged and ready to rend my seducers limb from limb." He introduced a resolution condemning the AFL leadership and denying craft unions the power to organize basic industry. His resolution was defeated by a two to one vote, but during the roll call there was an incident which revealed how deeply and passionately labor felt about the matter. William L. Hutcheson, politically conservative president of the carpenters' union who was a member of the Liberty League, called Lewis an unprintable name. Lewis replied with a fist to Hutcheson's face, and the two men brawled briefly.

Three weeks later, November 10, 1935, Lewis and leaders of seven other AFL unions met again at Atlantic City and formed the Committee for Industrial Organization. Green charged them with dual unionism and urged them to disband, but instead in January they again demanded charters for industrial unions from the AFL executive board. The board ordered the CIO to dissolve, and when it refused to do so suspended the CIO unions from the AFL. The 1937 AFL convention expelled them altogether. The ten expelled CIO unions were: the UMW; Sidney Hillman's Amalgamated Clothing Wokers; the Oil Field, Gas Well, and Refinery Workers; Mine, Mill, and Smelter Workers; United Textile Workers; United Auto Workers; United Rubber Workers; the glass workers; Amalgamated Iron and Steel Workers; and David Dubinsky's ILGWU. After their final expulsion from the AFL, the CIO unions reorganized as the Congress of Industrial Organizations.

The CIO's Victories

The CIO was particularly eager to organize the steel industry. Lewis, the CIO president, wanted organized allies in steel since that industry was so closely related to coal. In early 1936, the CIO reached an agreement with the weak and ineffective Amalgamated Iron and Steel Workers and established the Steel Workers Organizing Committee (SWOC). CIO put $500,000, mostly from the UMW, and many of its best organizers into the campaign to unionize steel workers. SWOC worked largely within the company unions where there was considerable dissatisfaction.

The plan was to postpone organization of other industries until the CIO succeeded in steel, but the auto workers would not wait. In the fall of 1936, the UAW had only thirty thousand members and no contracts; a year later, it had about four hundred thousand members and contracts with 381 companies. The sit-down strike was the weapon that got such dramatic results. In December, 1936, employees of the Fisher Body plant in Cleveland sat down at their jobs, declared themselves on strike, refused to leave the plant, and presented their demands to management. Their idea spread quickly. In January, 1937, when General Motors officials refused to bargain, UAW began a sit-down against that firm, the largest of the industry. There was little that management could do to break a sit-down strike. Any effort to bring in strike-breakers or to clear out the strikers with police or company guards would result in a pitched battle that would endanger the company's machinery. GM made one effort to dislodge the strikers from a Chevrolet plant in Michigan, but the Chevrolet local president, a young man named Walter Reuther, proved an able battle tactician and the company police gave up the fight. GM, unable to defeat the UAW and eager for the profits that the optimistic economic outlook promised—the "recession" did not begin until the fall of 1937—had no alternative but to surrender. The UAW got almost all it asked. A strike against Chrysler brought quick results; Chrysler signed a contract with the UAW in April.

Of the important auto firms only the Ford Motor Company was able to resist the UAW. Henry Ford, the founder of the business, still directed it, and the Ford family controlled almost all of its stock. The company was one of the few giant family firms left in America. Ford had an effective antiunion organization in what it called the Ford Service Organization, headed by an ex-boxer named Harry Bennett. Using labor spies and violence when he thought necessary, Ford was able to hold off the UAW until 1941, when, after a strike, he too capitulated.

The wave of sit-down strikes in auto in the winter of 1936–1937 presents some interesting insights into the social psychology of American workers during the depression. The auto workers were militant. They would not take no for an answer, and they were ready to fight. Morale was superb among the strikers. But—and this attitude confounded Marxist revolutionaries—the sit-down strikers were not the least interested in social revolution. They did not present demands for a labor owned and controlled industry, and they were careful not to damage industrial property during the sit-downs. Their demands were only for a union contract. If ever in America's recent history there was what Marxists call a "revolutionary moment" it was in Detroit in early 1937—even young girls working at soda fountains, excited by the UAW's success, took keys by force from their drug store managers, locked the doors, and declared a sit-down—but the goals of this wave of labor excitement were the traditional ones of the labor movement.

Unionism's successes in auto put a new light upon the SWOC campaign. In March, 1937, the month after GM signed with UAW, officials of the Carnegie-Illinois Steel Company, the largest of the firms in the huge United States Steel holding company, agreed to a contract with SWOC without a strike. The contract gave union recognition, a forty-hour week, a 10 per cent wage increase, seniority rights, and paid vacations. Other United States Steel subsidiaries and many independent firms quickly followed suit. Here, indeed, was a turning point in American industrial history. Within two months, two of the nation's largest aggregations of capital, General Motors and United States Steel, long vigorous opponents of unionism, had surrendered to the CIO.

The four companies of "Little Steel"—Republic, Inland, Bethlehem, and Youngstown Sheet and Tube—led by Tom Girdler of Republic, fought on against the CIO in the old-fashioned manner. SWOC began a conventional strike in May, 1937. Inland agreed to unionize, but the others resisted. On Memorial Day at the Republic plant in South Chicago, police killed ten pickets and wounded many others. The strike was lost. Eventually, in 1941, when again a bright economic future made management want industrial peace and uninterrupted production, "Little Steel" bowed to the law as interpreted by the Wagner Act's National Labor Relations Board and signed contracts with SWOC.

The CIO went on to organize most of the nation's other basic industries. By the time the United States entered World War II in December, 1941, the CIO had about five million members. But the growth of the CIO had not weakened the AFL. Significantly, when it was presented with competition, the AFL began to expand as it had not done since World War I. By the end of 1941, about 4,500,000 workers belonged to AFL unions. About another million were in independent unions. Trade union membership had grown roughly three and one-half times since 1933.

The trade unions had achieved their new status only through their own efforts. The Wagner Act had been a tremendous boon, but it had not been the gift of the Roosevelt administration. And employers had fought the unions tooth and nail until they came to the conclusion that further resistance would cost them more in profits than it was worth. Eventually, most big employers not only learned to live with the unions but to welcome the production stability they usually offered. But at first they almost universally regarded unions as dangerous intruders into what they considered their exclusive right to determine all corporate policy, including labor policy. A special investigation by the Subcommittee on Civil Liberties of the Senate Education Committee in the late 1930's, headed by Robert M. LaFollette, Jr., revealed the lengths to which many employers went to defeat unions. Many of the important and respected firms of the nation employed the services of so-called industrial detective agencies for antiunion espionage. Labor spies sought the position of recording secretary of locals in order to get lists of names and other union records; spies also acted as *agents provocateurs*, and the amount of union violence and crime that was actually employer-inspired will never be accurately known. An NLRB member estimated that, in the 1930's, employers spent $80 million a year for labor spy services. A few employers also spent large amounts of money for fire arms, ammunition, and tear gas.

One of the most effective weapons against unions was the ancient charge that unionism was economic radicalism and that trade union leaders were foreign-inspired subversives whose purpose was to destroy the republic. This charge in various forms was common, especially against the CIO. Until the late 1940's, there were just enough Communists in the leadership of certain CIO unions to give sting to the accusation. In the great wave of unionization, workers in basic industry had clamored for organization to such an extent that the existing supply of organizers was inadequate. Into the vacuum rushed Communist functionaries. Established CIO leaders were usually able to keep them out of fields in which they were directly interested. A few Communists managed even to infiltrate national CIO headquarters, although they were never strong enough there to determine policy.

The Tennessee Valley Authority

In the late seventeenth century, thousands of so-called Scotch-Irish began to come to Pennsylvania, one of the few colonies that welcomed these wild and independent people who had long been the victims and opponents of powerful government and privilege. As they filled up the better lands of western Pennsylvania, they moved south through the Great Valley of the Appalachians and then toward the West. By the early nineteenth century, they had settled

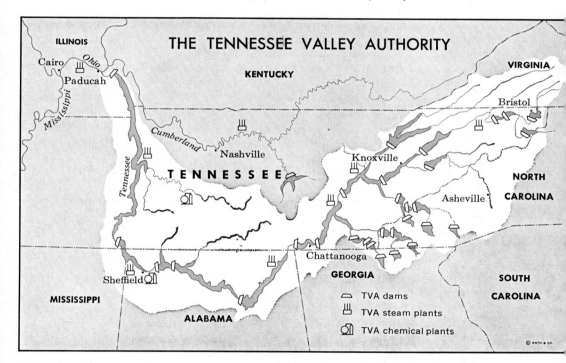

THE TENNESSEE VALLEY AUTHORITY

△ TVA dams
TVA steam plants
TVA chemical plants

the region today embraced by the Tennessee Valley Authority (TVA). Planters later brought Negro slaves into part of the area. It was a rich area when they came to it; by the end of the nineteenth century its natural heritage had been despoiled. Much of its forest lands had been denuded. Farmers had plowed the sides of hills and mountains to eke out a miserable living, and heavy rainfall had carried away much of the vital topsoil. Little industry had come in to fill the economic gap as it had in western Pennsylvania. By the 1920's, it was an area of poor land and poor people.

Harnessing the Tennessee River had been a political issue long before TVA came into being. The National Defense Act of 1916, among other things, authorized the President to construct a plant for the manufacture of nitrates by the use of water power and thereby relieve American dependence on Germany and Chile for nitrates. In late 1917, President Wilson designated Muscle Shoals on the Tennessee River in extreme northern Alabama as the site. The war ended before the plants there could become productive, but in the early 1920's work on Wilson Dam was completed. In the first month of the Harding administration in 1921, the Secretary of War invited proposals from private business for acquisition of the facilities. Henry Ford submitted a complicated plan that would have cost him millions of dollars but would also have profited him enormously. The Harding and Coolidge administrations were enthusiastic about Ford's plan, as were southern agricultural interests which wanted the fertilizer the plants could produce. The House of Representatives accepted the Ford scheme in March, 1924, but George W. Norris of Nebraska, chairman of the Agriculture and Forestry Committee, blocked the bill in the Senate. Norris had conceived the idea that was the kernel of TVA: a vast hydroelectric and water control system operated by the federal government. Norris' idea was at first unpopular, and it was only by unusual parliamentary maneuvering and threatening to filibuster that Norris succeeded in 1925 in preventing Wilson Dam from being turned over to private interests. In 1928, however, Norris got a bill through Congress which called for the government's operation of the dam and nitrate plants and the building of a new dam upstream to insure a steady supply of adequate water for Wilson Dam. Coolidge killed the bill with a pocket veto. Norris got another Muscle Shoals bill through Congress in February, 1931. Hoover vetoed the bill on the conventional private enterprise grounds.

Between his election and first inauguration, Franklin D. Roosevelt visited the Tennessee Valley with Senator Norris. FDR agreed with Norris and even expanded on the Senator's vision. On April 10, 1933, FDR asked Congress to create the TVA.

> It is clear that the Muscle Shoals development is but a small part of the potential public usefulness of the entire Tennessee River. Such use . . . transcends mere power development: it enters the wide fields of flood control, soil erosion, afforestation, elimination from agricultural use of marginal lands, and distribution and diversification of industry. In short, this power development of war days leads logically to national planning for a complete river watershed. . . .

He signed the TVA bill into law on May 18. In 1935, Congress amended the TVA act to clarify and expand its powers to generate and market electric energy.

In the next twenty years, TVA became one of the biggest engineering projects and social experiments in the history of the world. Its activities extend over forty thousand square miles—about the area of England and Scotland—and over parts or all of seven states: Virginia, North Carolina, Georgia, Alabama, Mississippi, Tennessee, and Kentucky. It built twenty new dams and improved five others. It built locks and provided a navigable channel for over six hundred miles. It produced thousands of tons of fertilizer and taught the farmers of the region how to use it and to farm more wisely in general. It produced billions of kilowatt hours of electrical energy which were used not only for the convenience of the inhabitants of the valley, but for the powering of the aluminum industry and the manufacture of the atom bomb during World War II. Its reservoirs provided excellent recreation facilities. It saved untold millions of dollars in flood control; it well protected the valley itself from flood, and by holding back flood waters until the worst was over along the Ohio and the Mississippi, it helped to limit floods for hundreds of miles downstream.

TVA made its achievements despite both internal and external conflicts. Although its difficulties with private power companies were the more hampering, it was for the first few years beset with serious disharmony within its three-man board of directors. The first chairman of TVA was Arthur E. Morgan, an engineer and president of Antioch College of Yellow Springs, Ohio. The other board members were Harcourt A. Morgan, an agricultural scientist and president of the University of Tennessee and David E. Lilienthal, a young lawyer specializing in utility regulation who at the time of his TVA appointment was a member of the Wisconsin Public Service Commission. Personality conflicts and differences over policy soon divided Chairman A. E. Morgan from the other board members, and by the fall of 1937, the Chairman was publicly impugning the sincerity and honesty of his colleagues. The private utility company opponents of TVA were quick to attempt to take advantage of the situation. Finally, in March, 1938, President Roosevelt removed Chairman Morgan from office.

Opposition to TVA from private power companies and their representatives was far more of a block to TVA than its own divided leadership. The statutes provided that TVA's primary function was water control but that it could sell its "surplus" electric power, giving preference to publicly owned power-distribution systems and electric cooperatives. It also could transmit its own power and retail it to farms and villages that could not buy power privately at reasonable rates. Very important, TVA could also regulate the retail rates for the electricity it generated and sold wholesale.

TVA early announced that it had no intention of duplicating already existing privately owned transmission systems and began to attempt to purchase some facilities from private companies in the area. In 1934, it made two contracts to purchase parts of the holdings of Commonwealth and Southern Corporation, a utility holding company, and of National Power & Light Company, another holding company which in turn was a subsidiary of Electric Bond and Share. TVA and these companies also agreed to grant one another special territorial guarantees. TVA would stay out of the private companies' areas; the private firms would stay out of TVA's territory. The agreement on spheres of influence was to expire in five years or when the power house at the new Norris Dam was completed, whichever was earlier. At this point, a small minority of stockholders of Alabama Power Company, a Commonwealth and Southern subsidiary, sued to prevent the company from carrying out the contract for sale of part of its property. They argued that it was unconstitutional for TVA to sell power generated at Wilson Dam. A judge of the federal district court in Birmingham agreed and voided the contract. The Supreme Court in this case, Ashwander v. TVA, upheld the constitutionality of the contract in February, 1936, but the case pertained only to power generated at Wilson Dam, and the Court's opinion did not clearly indicate the constitutional boundaries of TVA's power activities. Nineteen power companies, led by Wendell L. Willkie, president of Commonwealth and Southern, thereupon sued to block the sale of power from other dams. In January, 1939, the Supreme Court again upheld TVA. Without a legal leg left to stand on, Willkie was ready to sell the Commonwealth and Southern holdings in the TVA area. In August, 1939, he sold the entire Tennessee Electric Power Company to TVA. He was able to get his asking price of $78.6 million which came more nearly representing the value of the firm as a going concern than the value of its depreciated physical plant.

Another bone of contention between TVA and private power companies was the so-called yardstick concept of electricity rates. The "yardstick" idea—FDR himself coined the term—was that federally operated electric operations furnished a guide by which to compare the rates charged by private firms. The charges, countercharges, and general confusion over the term were rather fantastic. Actually, to compare TVA's rates with those of private companies was extremely difficult or even impossible because TVA was a multipurpose organization. Arbitrary accounting was involved in determining what should be considered as a cost of electricity generation and transmission and what should be a cost of water control. The privately owned utilities wildly charged that since TVA paid no taxes and they did, it was unfair to compare their rates with TVA's. They conducted a broad-scale advertising campaign to sell this idea to the public, the cost of which they included in determining their costs, an accounting procedure not designed to save the consumer's money. The Constitution and interpretations of it by John Marshall and subsequent justices being what they are, TVA of course paid no taxes to state and local governments. But authorities did recognize that the existence of large amounts of tax-free property in a local district would create important revenue and social problems, and it paid millions of dollars to local governments in lieu of taxes. The private firms, nevertheless, asserted that TVA's consumers were subsidized by American taxpayers in general. Whatever the merits of the whole complicated argument, the entire nation's average electric rate dropped 23 per cent in the seven years after TVA's establishment whereas they had dropped only 2 per cent in the previous seven years—and the privately owned utilities still made profits.

TVA has a significance in political and social theory completely apart from its relationship with capitalist enterprise. Wise men have long been concerned about a conflict between efficiency and democracy. Centralized power, often necessary to accomplish a huge and complicated task efficiently, runs the danger of becoming autocratic or bureaucratic, whether the centralized power be in a government, a business, a union, a university administration, or anything else. Defenders of TVA have asserted that TVA represents a solution to the dilemma in that it divorces the central authority (the federal government at Washington) from the administrators of the job of generating and distributing electric energy (TVA officials, cooperatives, municipalities, and the private electric companies that buy TVA electricity wholesale). If there has been a great deal of mystic vapor written about "grass roots democracy," it is still true that there is a serious problem in centralization and that TVA has avoided at least some of the bureaucratic bogs that characterize centralized power.

In 1937, Roosevelt asked Congress to consider the establishment of other "valley authorities." Congress failed to do anything important on the subject, and the President did not insist. There have been no further TVA's. The federal government's hydroelectric activities, however, already begun at Boulder Canyon on the Colorado River near Las Vegas, Nevada, continued without the unified regional concept that characterized TVA. The Boulder Canyon project, with its canal to the arid Imperial Valley of California, was completed in 1936. The federal government also built Bonneville and Grand Coulee dams on the Columbia and the earthen Fort Peck Dam, primarily for flood control, on the Missouri.

Technological Change, 1929–1940

The Great Depression did not appreciably slow down the long-term trend toward greater technological efficiency in industry. Indeed, increased productivity of labor through technological innovations complicated the problem of unemployment. By the end of the decade, fewer workers could manufacture more products than they could in 1929. In 1939, there were almost one million fewer employees in nonagricultural establishments than there had been in 1929, but the physical volume of what they produced was almost as high as it had been the year of the great crash.

New industrial products in the 1930's wrought changes in the national economy. Engineers during the decade developed a new process of electric welding that made possible the fabrication of steel alloys that had theretofore been impossible or too expensive for most purposes. There was also a great increase in the use of aluminum, of which the Aluminum Corporation of America, Alcoa, had a monopoly until World War II. At first used mostly for kitchen utensils, aluminum came to be used as the basic metal in a great many products in which its lightness was a distinct advantage. The first all-aluminum railroad car was built in 1931, and many truck trailers were made of aluminum. Aircraft of aluminum almost entirely displaced the older wood and fabric craft of the 1920's. By the mid-1930's, the DuPont Corporation had developed nylon, a new synthetic fiber far superior for most purposes to the older synthetic rayon, but problems of modifying knitting equipment and of dying the new material delayed its introduction on the market until the fall of 1939. The first nylon product to be used extensively by consumers was women's hosiery; the new nylon stockings were less expensive, longer wearing, and quicker drying than those made of silk.

Technological change in agriculture, stimulated by the AAA's acreage restrictions and the money it paid farmers to keep some of their land out of production, amounted almost to a farming revolution. Horses and mules still provided the power on most American farms at the beginning of the depression. Only relatively few farmers who had many acres found that purchase of the heavy and expensive tractors, which had steel-rimmed wheels with lugs or cleats for traction, was economically feasible. About 1930, farm implement manufacturers replaced the steel rims with low-pressure pneumatic tires which increased the efficiency of the tractor about 25 per cent and, by reducing the size of the engine, made it possible significantly to reduce a tractor's cost. By 1940, the tractor had practically eliminated the horse and mule from the farms that produced most of the nation's food and fiber. Tractors with their power take-offs and the development of smaller combines also made the harvesting of wheat and other grains far more efficient. By 1938, half of the nation's wheat was cut and threshed by combines.

Agricultural scientists, many of them in the state universities and the state agricultural experiment stations, developed new plant strains that increased yields per acre and resistance to disease. Thatcher wheat largely displaced other hard red spring wheat varieties in the late 1930's and increased the national production by millions of bushels. Even more dramatic were the results of hybrid corn culture. In 1933, only 40,000 acres were planted with hybrid corn; by 1939, hybrid corn grew on 24,000,000 acres, about one-fourth of the national corn acreage. The great corn producing states of the Middle West used hybrid seed to a greater extent than the national average.

Communications and transportation underwent important changes during the 1930's. Scientists and engineers in the communication industry made advances in the 1930's which made possible a communications revolution during and after World War II. The Radio Corporation of America, for example, in 1935 built a television transmitter atop New York's Empire State Building and announced the inauguration of a vast television research program. On April 30, 1939, RCA and the National Broadcasting Company made the first television broadcast to the public from the New York World's Fair. President Roosevelt was on camera during the broadcast. Only a few hundred people in New York City had television receivers, however, and television did not become a major communications medium until the late 1940's. Another electronic development of the 1930's that was to affect the television viewing public years later was the coaxial cable. In 1936, engineers of the American Telegraph and Telephone Company installed the first coaxial cable from New York to Philadelphia, thereby making it possible for the long-distance telephone wires to transmit hundreds of messages simultaneously. E. F. W. Alexanderson perfected frequency modulation radio, FM, which eliminated the static inherent in regular amplitude modulation, or AM, radio broadcasting in 1933. The major radio broadcasting networks, however, were uninterested in the new system because it required special radio receivers, which the public was not likely to buy during the depression, and because the broadcasting range of an FM transmitter was limited by the earth's curvature. FM radio broadcasting did not become significant until after World War II.

Some of the most startling technological innovations in the 1930's were in transportation. Commercial aviation at the beginning of the decade was in its infancy, inefficient and irregular despite the handsome subsidies commercial airlines received from the federal government through fat air mail contracts. Although air service was available between most major cities, travelers shunned flying because of the danger and the risk of being grounded by poor weather. Commercial aviation could not be successful until it had better, more dependable aircraft, adequate airfields, and improved night- and blind-flying electronic equipment. During the decade, a vast network of beacons and radio directional signals made bad visibility flying relatively safe, the federal government undertook airfield construction and modernization as part of its public works program, and, in 1936, the Douglas Aircraft Company began to sell the famous DC-3. The DC-3, a single-wing, aluminum, twin-engined craft with a distinctive bump on its nose, became to aviation what the Model T Ford had been to automobiles. It carried a payload of nine thousand pounds, had accommodations for twenty-one passengers, and cruised at 180 miles per hour. As the C-47, it was the workhorse of the armed forces during World War II, and even twenty-five years after its introduction it was still the most economical plane to use for short-haul commercial flying. By 1940, plane travel was no longer the novelty it had been only a few years earlier. But flying was still more expensive than rail travel, and most people associated air travel with glamour and opulence. The air lines did little to counteract this impression; they even employed attractive waitresses, dressed them in chic uniforms, and called them hostesses. Not until after the war with the introduction of "air coach" or economy flights, did the airplane become a civilian mass transportation device.

Cars and trucks became more reliable, faster, and cheaper during the thirties. As sales of new cars fell off because of the economic pinch, auto dealers stepped up their used car promotion. For as little as $50 one could buy an automobile which, while no beauty, provided transportation. The speed capabilities of the new cars with increased horsepower were greater than most of the highways warranted. The first four lane, no intersection, "super highway" of important length was not opened for traffic until October, 1940, when the Pennsylvania Turnpike, a toll road which then connected a point east of Pittsburgh to the Harrisburg vicinity, went into operation. The Turnpike set new standards of highway construction; it had no grades of over three and no curves of over six degrees. Better engines, including the new Diesel engine, enabled trucks to haul economically a larger proportion of the nation's freight. Trucks had a ready business in the areas not served frequently by railroads and required relatively little capital investment. In 1940, the states issued licenses for over four million trucks.

Motor and air transport inevitably had a serious impact upon the older means of public transportation. In city after city during the depression, streetcar companies changed to buses, and the urban bus lines in turn limited their service as the privately-owned automobile decreased passenger demand. Railroads were also caught in a technological and economic bind. Already hard hit in their operations because of the general decline of the economy, they faced stiff competition from the trucking industry for the nation's freight carrying. As natural gas and fuel oil, carried to the consumer by pipeline, increasingly displaced coal for space heating, the railroads lost one of their most important cargoes. Competition from automobiles, intercity buses, and, to a lesser extent, commercial airlines ate into railroad revenues from passenger traffic. Some of the railroads, particularly the western systems, tried to compete with their new passenger competition by special excursion fares and by introducing faster and more comfortable trains. Some of the new and fast express trains, notably the Burlington's Zephyr, captured the public imagination for a while in the mid-1930's, but in general railroad management displayed little initiative in its passenger operations. Some railroad officials appeared to abandon hope for profitable passsenger traffic and actually to discourage rail travel. Their primary answer to declining revenues was to petition the Interstate Commerce Commission and the state regulatory bodies for permission to increase fares and cut operations. Wartime stimulation of passenger traffic only postponed the process of the railroads' pricing themselves out of the market.

Agriculture

A discussion of the AAA programs, important as they were, omits some vital developments on the nation's farms in the 1930's. Perhaps the most important fact about agriculture during the Roosevelt era was the continuing trend toward bigness, bigness both in acreage and in capitalization, a drift toward concentration that was due to several factors and that had been in process for decades.

The drop in farm prices that came in the early 1920's quickened the agricultural concentration movement and the tragic further decline of prices after 1929 moved it even faster. When farm prices were low, inefficient farm units could not meet their costs of production, and, generally, big farms were more efficient than small ones. Big or small, the technologically improved and scientifically farmed agricultural unit was the more efficient one, and it took capital to make innovations. The reasons for lower farm prices were many, including nonagricultural technological advance. Synthetic fibers, for example, such as rayon and nylon, reduced the market for cotton and depressed its price. The only way out for the cotton farmer, then, was to increase his efficiency of production, which he did with the tractor and, beginning in the late 1930's, the mechanical cotton picker. The cotton farmer who could not raise the capital for such equipment inevitably fell by the wayside.

Even the weather during the depression decade hastened concentration. Beginning in 1931, western farmers were plagued with a series of droughts. Then came the grasshoppers which left a path of ruin in their wake. They even ate the paint off houses. Successive droughts and the steady winds that are characteristic on the Great Plains resulted in dust storms. The first serious dust storms began in 1933. A particularly hard-hit area in western Kansas, Oklahoma, and Texas, and eastern New Mexico and Colorado came to be called the "Dust Bowl," but wind erosion was a serious problem as far north as North Dakota. One of the worst dust storms came in May, 1934. The vital top soil of hundreds of farms was literally gone with the wind. Huge clouds of dust obscured the sun as far east as the Appalachians; nearer to the Great Plains the flying grit made breathing difficult, worked its way into automobile engines and other machinery, and was the despair of house-cleaning wives. (Pare Lorentz in 1936 made a great documentary film of this storm entitled "The Plow That Broke the Plains" and followed it a year later with another on water erosion entitled "The River.") Farmers with low capital and credit were wiped out for good, as were even some who had big investments. One economic effect of the dust storms was to reduce the number of farm units and give greater advantage to the well capitalized and efficient farmer outside the dust center.

372

Farm owners who were unable to compete frequently became tenants, and those who were tenants found their chances of becoming owner-operators diminishing. Throughout the 1930's, there was an increase in the proportion of the national agricultural product that came from tenant-operated farms and from big farms that hired large numbers of wage laborers. Actually, according to a survey by the President's Committee on Farm Tenancy, appointed in late 1936, farm ownership rose very slightly from 1930 to 1935, but that fact was hardly heartening because the figure reflected only the number of un-employed industrial laborers, many of whom were originally farm boys who moved to submarginal farms early in the depression. The main fact was that the economic importance of farm tenancy was increasing. In 1935, over two-fifths of all the farms in the United States were tenant operated; 47 per cent of all the national farm acreage was tended by tenants or wage laborers. The Committee concluded that the old American concept of the "agricultural lad-der," in which the farm laborer became a tenant and eventually an owner, no longer reflected reality. Indeed, the Committee reported that its study "indi-cated that in recent years movement from rung to rung has been predomi-nantly in the direction of descent rather than ascent. It has also indicated an increasing tendency for the rungs of the ladder to become bars—forcing im-prisonment in a fixed social status which it is increasingly difficult to escape."

"Imprisonment" was the proper term for farm tenancy, especially in the South. In 1934, the average net income of sharecroppers in seven cotton states, including their "sow belly" and molasses "furnish," was only $312, or $71 per capita. In the lower Mississippi delta, where the land was richest, the tenants were poorest. They averaged only $38 a year per capita. Their living condi-tions were indicated by the average value of their shacks. North Carolina's tenant shacks were the best in the seven cotton states surveyed, and their aver-age value was only $417. In Alabama the figure was $194. At the other end of the agricultural scale were the well-capitalized Associated Farmers of Cali-fornia, about one-fifteenth of that state's farmers, whose holdings were so vast that they employed most of the 350,000 farm migrants who trekked to the Golden State.

The weight of the evidence indicated that, for agriculture in general and excepting only a few special crop raisers, the family-sized and family-operated and owned farm was doomed. Farming had become a business, subject to the same tendencies toward concentration that affected industry. But ideas die hard, and the farmer himself, the public in general, and the federal govern-ment continued to think of agriculture as a family enterprise.

Business and Concentrated Economic Power in the Depression

According to classical economic theory, when there is a downswing in the business cycle in a capitalist economy and the demand for goods and services decreases, competition among those who sell goods and services causes them to lower prices until supply and demand are again in balance. The theory did not describe the facts during the Great Depression. Lack of competition, the power of businessmen in monopolistic or oligopolistic industries to maintain prices, prevented the smooth functioning of the theoretical economic model. Instead of reducing prices, most industries reduced production thereby causing unemployment which further depreciated demand. Indeed, there was a strong correlation between the degree of concentration in an industry and its degree of price maintenance. In industries where there was a great deal of competition prices fell during the depression, but in only a few of the industries where monopoly or near-monopoly conditions prevailed was there an important lowering of prices. For example, agriculture, which was in general characterized by a multitude of producers without power over the market, saw its prices fall 86 per cent from 1929 to 1933 while its production declined only 6 per cent. On the other hand, the prices for twenty leading agricultural implements, which are made by an oligopolistic industry, declined only 6 per cent between 1929 and 1934 while production and employment fell 80 per cent.

But officers of companies in oligopolistic industries were not averse to increasing prices when it appeared to them that the market would accept a rise in prices. The economy improved in the first Roosevelt term of office, and in the spring of 1937 industrial production was nearly as high as it had been in 1929, although, because of increased productivity per man-hour and growth of the labor force, unemployment remained serious. Industry increased its prices to such an extent that economists warned that there would be serious consequences unless wages and mass purchasing power kept pace. Leon Henderson, then an economist for the WPA, even predicted that, because of too rapidly rising prices, there would be a major business recession within six months. He proved to be right. The recession of 1937–1938 began in October.

The degree of concentration of economic power into the hands of a relatively few businessmen increased during the New Deal years despite the supposed antibusiness attitude of the federal administration. Part of the increased power came from the continuing growth of the large companies within an industry. For example, between 1928 and 1938, the control of the twenty biggest oil companies over crude oil production increased from 46 to 53 per cent, over refining capacity from 66 to 76 per cent, and over gasoline production from 71 to 84 per cent. The percentage of the nation's total copper production controlled by the sixteen largest copper companies increased from 81.4 in 1929 to 87.5 in 1937. But perhaps more important than the trend toward bigness in business firms during the 1930's was a great increase in the number and power of trade associations, organizations formed by businessmen within the same industry, and the National Recovery Administration played a major role in the stimulation of these groups. NRA gave the activities of these associations legality and power. The code authority in steel was the board of directors of the Iron and Steel Institute, and the officers of the Distilled Spirits Institute became the regulators of the NRA code for their industry. Existing trade associations were the dominant power in the writing of the NRA codes or their administration, or both; in industries without a trade association the NRA frequently called one into being. The Supreme Court's opinion in the Schechter case in May, 1935, killed the NRA, but it did not kill the trade associations, which continued to function as always. After the death of NRA, industries accused in antitrust actions frequently made the defense that they were only following practices that had been sanctioned or even required under their NRA code.

Government, both state and federal, also helped to eliminate price competition with so-called fair trade laws. In a 1922 case, the Supreme Court found agreements between a manufacturer and a retailer in which the retailer agreed to charge consumers a price fixed by the manufacturer illegal under the antitrust laws. Such agreements were called "resale price maintenance" agreements. In 1931, California passed the first of the state "fair trade" laws to permit such agreements. Only a few other states followed suit until after the end of NRA, when business pressure groups lobbied such laws through state legislatures at a feverish rate. By 1939, only six states remained without "fair trade" laws. In most of the states the bills went through the legislature without much public debate and without becoming an issue before the public. Only three legislatures of the first thirty-two to pass such laws conducted public hearings at all, and in one of these the hearings came only after the bill was passed. Evidence that these state laws were the result of a concerted lobby is seen in the fact that one of the original bill drafts contained a stenographic error that made nonsense of an important provision. The stenographic error went through the legislature of that state and ten others before it was caught and corrected.

The Supreme Court in a case involving the Illinois law ruled that a state could constitutionally sanction resale price maintenance contracts when the products were specifically designated. Then in 1937, Congress passed a federal "fair trade" law, the Miller-Tydings Act. The Act, which was passed as a rider to a District of Columbia appropriations bill so that Roosevelt would be in no position to veto it, amended Section 1 of the Sherman Antitrust Act to exempt from prosecution parties to a resale maintenance agreement in states where such arrangements were sanctioned by "fair trade" laws. In other words, in most states manufacturers could control the prices of their products even after they had yielded control of them to jobbers, wholesalers, and retailers. Should a retailer violate the agreement and sell below the established price, he ran the risk of having the manufacturer shut off his source of supply. The Temporary National Economic Committee recommended that the Miller-Tydings measure be repealed and the Antitrust Division of the Department of Justice supported repeal, arguing that "fair trade" laws were a cloak for many conspiracies in restraint of trade. Congress did not act. The law remains on the books, although suits brought by "discount houses" after World War II and the dissatisfaction of some manufacturers with the price maintenance system greatly diminished "fair trading."

Akin to the "fair trade" laws was the effort by some states and municipalities to hamper the operation of chain grocery stores with special "chain store taxes." Food and other items purchased in grocery stores took a large part of the consumer's take-home pay, and prices were usually less in the chain stores than in the "independents" because the chains had the economic advantage of volume. During the depression, however, local merchants struck a responsive chord when they argued that chain stores, with their absentee ownership, took profits out of the community. When the chain grocery gradually shifted to "self-service" or "supermarket" methods during the decade, they were able to lower their costs even more and to prove irresistible. In all but the most densely populated cities, in which there were serious traffic and parking problems, the chain groceries overcame the special taxes upon them. The "independents'" practice of extending consumer credit probably helped them more in their struggle with the chains than discriminatory taxes.

By the late 1930's, it appeared to many observers of the economy that power had become centralized or, to use a popular term of the decade, "collectivized." No single economic institution—government, business, labor, or agriculture—controlled the whole economy, and no single branch or agency of government, no individual corporation, no union, no farm organization controlled all its sector of the economy. But, nevertheless, centripetal forces operated to build clusters of economic might with powerful leverage. This was no new trend. It had existed for a long time, particularly in financial and industrial ownership and management, and it probably was inherent in an industrial society. In the 1930's, the trend was only accentuated with the further development of industrial and financial concentration of power, with the extension of the federal government's economic role, and with the growth of labor unions.

The industrial employee most likely worked for a giant corporation. One per cent of the nation's employers accounted for 48 per cent of all employment, and 5 per cent of the employers had 70 per cent of the workers on their payrolls. The "blue collar" worker, especially in basic industry, was likely to be a member of a large labor union. The "white collar" worker and the business executive more often than not were cogs in a vast corporation's intricate personnel system. The small businessman was sensitive to the policies and activities of the corporate mammoths. Even the farmer, the supposedly independent "sturdy yeoman," was likely to receive benefit checks from the AAA and belong to a powerful farm organization such as the American Farm Bureau. He might even be a wage employee of one of the agricultural corporations that operated "factories in the fields." And no matter how the individual made his living he, as a consumer, bought the products of the huge industrial combinations. Individuals, economically at least, were atoms of the mass.

CHAPTER NINETEEN

Society and the Great Depression

THE APOSTLE LUKE WROTE THAT MAN DOES NOT LIVE BY BREAD ALONE. Few would question, however, the fact that the availability of bread and the way man earns it have tremendous implications for his society. In the 1930's, the availability of bread was very much on men's minds, and economic distress colored American society in many of its noneconomic aspects, both obviously and subtly. The fundamental assumptions Americans made about their society, the manner in which they educated their young, what they did in their leisure time, even how many they were and where they were were all fundamentally affected by the overriding, omnipresent, dismal economic situation.

Population, Health, and the Family

Three factors determine a nation's population: the birth rate, the death rate, and the immigration-emigration rate. During the Great Depression, only a declining death rate operated to increase the American population. During the 1920's, the population had increased 16.1 per cent, but between 1930 and 1940 it increased only 7.2 per cent. With hard times came an important decline in the birth rate which had been falling gradually for some years. In 1933, there were only 6.5 births per thousand population, and for the decade as a whole the figure was about 18. In 1915, the rate had been 25 per thousand.

A declining death rate and increased longevity coming at the same time as a declining birth rate had important implications for the composition of society. The average age increased; there was an increasing number of old people—5.4 per cent of the population was over sixty-five in 1930 and 6.9 per cent in 1940—and a decreasing number of young ones. Since people over forty had great difficulty in finding remunerative employment—to a greater degree than ever before or since—it appeared that the time would come when a relatively small, economically productive group of young people would support the rest of the population. And if the population became stable, as demographers then predicted it would, there would be troubling implications for the economic market.

The declining death rate was due primarily to advances in medical treatment. Nutritionists' discovery of the importance of vitamins to health led to an improvement of the diet, and the biochemists' ability to synthesize vitamins led to their sale across drug store counters. The discovery that nicotinic acid was a cure for pellagra was a boon to poor southerners. In the mid-1930's, doctors began to use sulfa drugs extensively, and these worked miracles in pneumonia, erysipelas, and meningitis. Research on the sulfa drugs had been started in Germany and perfected and applied to more uses by physicians at The Johns Hopkins University.

The advantages of good medical care, however, did not extend to all parts of the population. The poor spent far less for medication than the economically comfortable. President Hoover's Committee on the Costs of Medical Care reported in 1932 that the total medical bill of the nation amounted to $30 per person per year. Those with incomes of between $1,200 and $2,000 spent only $13 and those who received less than $1,000 only $9. Even in 1929 about half of the population had incomes under $2,000 a year. A 1936 survey by the Federal Public Health Service indicated that the duration of illness among low-income families was longer than among the rest of the population. Nor was hospital service readily available to all. Eighteen million people lived in counties where there were no hospital facilities. The problem was not a shortage of doctor services; in 1932, the average doctor was idle at least one-third of his time.

Americans traditionally had moved about over their nation far more than Europeans, and their quest for economic betterment during the depression did not stop their wandering. Six states lost population between 1930 and 1940: Vermont, North Dakota, South Dakota, Nebraska, Kansas, and Oklahoma. The Pacific Coast states, Arizona, and Florida had the highest rates of population increase, and California led all the states in absolute growth. The movement toward the city continued, although the suburban movement muddied the statistical picture. Many cities grew only slightly or actually decreased, but when one included the suburban population as part of the urban group the census figures showed no reversal of the long-term urban trend.

In the first years of the depression many unemployed industrial workers, particularly unemployed coal miners in the West Virginia-Pennsylvania-Kentucky fields, departed for subsistence farming on marginal lands in the Appalachian South, but this movement proved temporary. Over the decade far more people moved from the rural Appalachians and other parts of the rural South than moved into the area. The industrial cities of the North and West received thousands of uprooted southerners, both Negro and white. The influx created social tensions among many groups, although the Negro-white conflicts were the more publicized. In many of the industrial cities of the Great

Lakes Basin, animosity became serious between the older inhabitants and the newly arrived Appalachian whites—Wasps (white Anglo-Saxon Protestants) the social workers called them. In Akron, a tire manufacturing center, calling a recently migrated worker from West Virginia a "snake" started many an ugly incident.

All this migration and economic distress in general undoubtedly had profound effects upon the family, but observers during the Great Depression and since have not agreed upon just what the effects were. Those of an optimistic turn of mind concluded that the depression had revitalized American family life, that families through economic necessity had become more cohesive than they had been in the 1920's, that they now sought their pleasures together in inexpensive pastimes such as listening to the radio, playing games, and growing their own food in family gardens. Optimists also cited the decline in the divorce rate, which fell sharply during the early depression. In 1929, there were 1.66 divorces per thousand population; in 1932 and 1933, the figures were 1.28 and 1.31. As times improved the incidence of divorce quickened; in 1940, there were 2.0 divorces per thousand population, a new record.

Others, however, could see no compensation in family life for the economic calamity. They pointed out that the alarming number of child tramps who roamed the nation by freight car during the early depression hardly indicated a trend toward closely knit families and answered the divorce statistics by calling attention to the increase in desertion, the "poor man's divorce." Further, having a wife and children improved one's chances of receiving relief, although it was estimated that about 1,550,000 young people postponed marriage because of lack of income. Realists deplored the widespread consolidation of clans under one roof. In order to save rent, many families "doubled up" with those of brothers, sisters, or parents, frequently creating crowded conditions prejudicial to family harmony. A clue to how families in distress regarded their situation is seen in what they did when prosperity returned during and after the war: the "doubled up" families sought houses or apartments of their own, adopted more expensive leisure activities, divorced more frequently, and married younger.

"Melting Pot" or "A Nation of Nations?"

European immigration during the 1930's shrank to numerically insignificant proportions. The restrictive immigration laws had an effect, but most countries did not exhaust their immigration quotas. In the 1920's, 2,477,564 European immigrants had come to the United States (more than in the 1870's), but during the 1930's the number declined to 348,289 (fewer than in any decade since the 1820's). The limited economic opportunities of depression America did not attract immigrants. Further, some of the European nations were less hard hit by the depression than the United States, and some, Sweden for example, had welfare-state features that offered the ordinary worker far more security than he could then obtain in the New World. Indeed, from 1931 to 1936, the number of people abandoning American life for the Old World was greater than the number of immigrants.

Although they were relatively few in numbers compared to the mass immigration of the years before World War I, refugees from Nazism and fascism, both Jewish and Gentile, were culturally important. A remarkable number of the refugees were intellectuals and artists, and their cultural contribution to America was rich beyond all measurement. Among the physicists were Albert Einstein and Enrico Fermi whose fame among laymen became great when they helped to develop the atom bomb during World War II, but who were deservedly respected by scientists long before the war. Other refugee figures of prominence were the novelist Thomas Mann; the composers Kurt Weill, Arnold Schoenberg, and Paul Hindemith; the painters Piet Mondrian, George Grosz, and Hans Hoffman; the architects Walter Gropius and Ludwig Mies van der Rohe; and the conductor Arturo Toscanini. Many American universities improved themselves with the appointment of refugee professors, and Alvin Johnson, president of New York City's New School for Social Research, even created The University in Exile, composed of 178 European professors which later became the New School's graduate faculty. At least part of the reason for America's rise to cultural eminence in the mid-twentieth century was central and southern Europe's social insanity.

The reduced size of the immigration stream and the change in its nature from poorly educated peasant or proletarian to intellectually sophisticated cosmopolite helped to bring about a partial change in the attitude of Americans toward immigrants. For decades—even centuries—most Americans of all shades of political opinion had either been skeptical of the wholesomeness of mass immigration or believed that the new immigrant should become assimilated as soon as possible or both. The goal was for the immigrant to lose all trace of his "foreignness," to adjust to his new nation by becoming indistinguishable from his fellow citizens. Early in the twentieth century, a few liberal intellectuals had begun to doubt the desirability of this "melting pot" goal and to argue the virtues of "cultural pluralism." They saw much that was valuable in the culture of immigrants and believed it should be preserved. They also denied the validity of the stereotyped impressions of immigrants held even by many who were progressives politically and economically. During the 1920's, probably partly in reaction to the excesses of the Ku Klux Klan, "cultural pluralism" as a socially desirable attribute gained considerable ground, and toleration of minority groups and their ways of living came to be one of the commonest tenets of the liberal creed. By the end of the 1930's in the overwhelming majority of educated circles, to express a hostile sentiment toward a minority group, especially an anti-Semitic or anti-Negro slur, was to place oneself beyond the pale of respectability. Anglo-Saxonism, once almost universal except among minority groups themselves, was a weak force except among people of little education.

But there were many people of little education. In earlier periods of national stress, such as the late 1880's and 1890's, there had been an upsurge of nativism; it was not surprising in the depression decade that that particular kind of prejudice would again appear. The organized nativist movements of the 1930's had fascist overtones—some were outright fascist—and were primarily opposed to Jews and Negroes. The Ku Klux Klan revived to a small extent, and the Silver Shirts of America, founded in North Carolina in 1933 by William Dudley Pelley, were similar in their prejudices. Gerald L. K. Smith,

Gerald Winrod of Kansas, and Father Coughlin had a following of anti-Semites in the Middle West and the South as well as eastern industrial cities; an anti-Semitic rabble rouser in New York City, one Joe McWilliams, had some success in selling a blackjack he termed "the Kike Killer." The frankly Nazi German-American Bund, led by Fritz Kuhn, had a small following among German immigrants. In general, however, organized nativists were not powerful, however distasteful and potentially dangerous. White minority groups suffered far more from personal and social discrimination, sometimes subtle and disguised and sometimes not, than they did from the organized hate groups. Identification of the "shirt organizations" with European fascism, which became unpopular after it began to threaten world peace, hampered their growth in the United States.

The once scorned "new immigrants" increasingly expressed themselves in politics during the 1930's in the urban areas where they were most numerous, just as earlier immigrant groups, such as the Irish and Germans, had become politically mature. A perusal of the Congressional Directory revealed a sprinkling of Italian and Slavic names among the members of the House of Representatives. In New York State, where minorities were a majority, nationality bloc politics became more complicated. Both major parties there endeavored to present a "balanced ticket" to appeal to Anglo-Saxon, Irish, Jewish, and Italian voters. No small part of the phenomenal political success of Fiorello LaGuardia, the vigorous and efficient reformer who became mayor of New York City in 1934, was the fact that he had an Italian father and a Jewish mother and could speak many of the languages used in America's greatest city.

The Depression and the Negro

The depression's economic effects upon the Negro were disastrous. Even during periods of prosperity Negroes had by no means fully shared the benefits of good times; with hard times came more than their fair share of economic want. An old Negro saying that they "were the first to be fired and the last to be hired" accurately described the situation. In both the South and North, jobs that had once been reserved mostly for Negroes, menial, dirty, backbreaking jobs, came to be filled by whites as the whites' chances of finding better employment diminished.

Lessened economic opportunity in industry slowed down the southern Negro's migration to the North. The net migration of Negroes out of the South during the 1930's was an estimated 317,000, about half of the figure for the 1920's. The southern Negro knew that his chances of finding a decent job in the North were remote, but he figured that he would not be any worse off economically, that he stood a better chance of getting relief, and that his children's education was likely to be better. Therefore, undoubtedly, more southern Negroes would have left Dixie if they had had the money for train or bus tickets. One migration statistic foreshadowed a development that was to become major in the next decade: between 1930 and 1940 the Negro population of California increased 53 per cent.

The economic impact of New Deal legislation on the Negro was complicated. On the one hand, some New Deal legislation actually decreased Negroes' earnings. The NRA codes in the steel, tobacco, and laundry industries provided for lower minimum wages for Negroes than for whites, and in industries where there was no discrimination in the minimum wage employers frequently fired Negroes and hired Caucasians rather than pay the black man what the employer considered "white man's wages." The AAA's acreage restrictions program created a crisis for sharecroppers, as has already been described on page 335, and since a large proportion of sharecroppers were Negro, the burden fell largely on that race. Incidentally, some white and Negro sharecroppers, seeing no discrimination in their common calamity, organized the biracial Southern Tenant Farmers Union which stirred large southern landowners to a frenzy of reaction. On the other hand, in the administration of federal relief, New Deal Washington consistently avoided discrimination, although at local levels, particularly in the South, officials sometimes undermined Washington's policy. NYA did not discriminate in selection, nor did CCC, although it segregated Negro boys in its camps. About one-third of the public housing apartments built with federal funds housed Negroes, although the number of such apartments was too small to raise significantly Negro housing standards which even a generation later were considered a scandal by European travelers. PWA built many structures for Negro colleges, and WPA, although it discriminated against Negroes in some communities, had over a million Negroes on its rolls in 1939.

But if the economic balance sheet is not clear, the New Deal's political impact on Negroes is: the New Deal successfully shifted the bulk of the Negro vote from the Republicans to the Democrats. Negro political leaders began to desert their historic affiliation with the party of Lincoln in 1928, when the GOP, in its attempt to get the votes of southern whites, ignored its southern Negro leaders to concentrate on their Republican "lily-white" rivals. During his administration, Hoover lost the support of many Negroes, just as he lost the support of whites, because his depression policies were inadequate to halt its course or to ameliorate the hardship of its victims. Roosevelt attracted the support of colored people, both as Negroes and as economic beings. He greatly increased the number of Negroes among his advisers, and he and his wife treated Negroes socially without discrimination. In the congressional elections of 1934, the shift in the Negro vote became apparent. In 1928, Oscar De Priest, a Republican alderman in Chicago and a political crony of the incredible Mayor William Hale "Big Bill" Thompson, became the first Negro to be elected to Congress since Reconstruction and the first ever from a northern state. In 1934, the voters in his district, the heavily Negro South Side, replaced him with a Negro Democrat, Arthur W. Mitchell, who as late as 1930 had been a registered Republican. In 1936 and since, the overwhelming proportion of the Negro vote—as well as it can be identified—has gone to Democratic presidential candidates. In some northern states, the Negro vote became so important as to be almost a balance of power between the two parties, and the growth of Negro power within the Democratic party served to further complicate that party's intricate relationship between North and South, agriculture and industry, liberalism and conservatism.

Many militant Negroes, however, were not altogether happy about the Democratic party or even about Roosevelt himself; they considered the Democrats only the better alternative. As late as 1940, only three southern states—North Carolina, Florida, and Louisiana—had repealed their poll tax laws, and it was Democratic politicians and economic interests within their party that blocked repeal efforts. FDR never asked Congress for a federal law against lynching and did not use his position to further the Wagner-Van Nuys antilynching bill. The ambivalence, frustration, and occasional exasperation Negro militants felt toward Roosevelt was best dramatized in the "March on Washington" movement.

As defense contracts in 1940 began to improve employment and wages, Negroes noted with bitterness that employers were pursuing a rather consistent policy of hiring and wage discrimination against them. In January, 1941, A. Philip Randolph, militant president of the Brotherhood of Sleeping Car Porters, proposed the idea of fifty thousand to one hundred thousand Negroes going to Washington to demand from their government that it do something to prevent color discrimination in defense industries. After all, less than a month before Randolph announced his idea the President, in urging aid for Nazi-beleaguered England, had referred to the United States as an "arsenal of democracy"; Randolph was only urging that Negroes be democratically allowed to enter the arsenal. The "March on Washington" idea became popular; by June, Negroes all over the nation by the thousands were getting ready to go to the nation's capital as Coxey's Army and the Bonus Marchers had gone before. Official Washington was in a panic. "What will they think in Berlin?" was a common question, and what would they think in Dixie if he capitulated must have been another question in Roosevelt's mind. Mrs. Roosevelt and Mayor LaGuardia met with Randolph and argued that his March would do no good and might cause adverse reaction. Randolph refused to call off the March. The President called Randolph to several meetings at the White House, but Randolph would not relent. On June 25, FDR capitulated and issued Executive Order 8802 in which he said "there shall be no discrimination in the employment of workers in defense industries or Government because of race, creed, color, or national origin. . . . And it is the duty of employers and of labor organizations . . . to provide for the full and equitable participation of all workers in defense industries, without discrimination. . . ." The order also created a Committee on Fair Employment Practices to police against discrimination.

Randolph was wise in insisting that labor organizations be included in the President's order. Most labor unions discriminated against Negroes until the mid-1930's. With a few exceptions, unions until then were only for skilled workers, and not very many Negroes were in that category. When they did have skills, the unions frequently refused to admit them to membership, which meant that in the few closed shop industries employment was impossible. On the other hand, union men argued that all too often employers used Negroes as strike breakers. Racial discrimination in the CIO's industrial unions, however, would be economically disadvantageous, and most of the CIO leaders were vigorous opponents of discrimination. Many Negro workers were at first skeptical of the CIO; they found it hard to believe that a union could, first, be effective in unskilled industries and, second, would not invoke some kind of Jim Crow. When the CIO's practices reassured Negro employees, they rallied to it strongly. Most of the AFL unions, by one device or another, continued discrimination.

Perhaps the most important development concerning Negroes in the 1930's was an important growth in the numbers of Americans, both Negro and white, who refused to accept the *status quo* in racial relations. There had, of course, long been militants in both races; they only became more numerous and more vocal during a decade that saw widespread criticism and reaffirmation of democracy. Time and again during the 1930's there were incidents, some major and some not, that outraged many people's sense of fairness and decency, which in an earlier time might have passed almost without notice. For example, at the 1936 Olympic Games in Berlin, Nazi track officials grossly handicapped the great Negro sprinter from The Ohio State University, Jesse Owens, and after Owens won despite unfair officiating Hitler refused personally to give him his award, as he did with "Aryan" athletes. The whole affair was in the newspapers for several days. To show their disapproval, some of the other winning American athletes refused to accept their trophies from the Nazi chief. In 1939, the Daughters of the American Revolution refused to rent their Washington auditorium, called Constitution Hall, for a concert by Marian Anderson, the world renowned contralto, because she was a Negro. The outcry was loud, and Interior Secretary Ickes, once president of the Chicago chapter of the National Association for the Advancement of Colored People, arranged for Miss Anderson to give her famous concert from the steps of the Lincoln Memorial. The heightened militancy of Negroes and the sharper pangs of conscience among whites about Negro matters helped to prepare the way for the advances in the Negro's march toward equality that came after the war.

The Erosion of Social Assumptions

It is extremely difficult to say with any certainty how popularly believed assumptions about society and widespread social values changed during the Great Depression. The vast bulk of people seldom reflect deeply upon what makes a society operate or fail to operate properly and are largely inarticulate about what they do believe. Articulate intellectuals often fail to examine and make explicit their social assumptions, and even when they do the historian can never be sure to what degree intellectuals reflect or affect popular thought. The whole field of popular social thought, even after the refinement of polling techniques, remains a sticky one that requires caution. Nevertheless, observers of different shades of political opinion agreed during the 1930's that some widely held ideas were becoming increasingly doubted.

An old and optimistic assumption, so prevalent and commonplace in America that it went almost unnoticed, was that the world in general and the United States in particular was ever progressing. Only a few die-hard reactionaries such as Federalists like Harrison Gray Otis and out-of-the-way intellectuals such as Brooks Adams had dissented from the almost universally held view that progress was inevitable. There might be a temporary halt in

America's forward march people thought, but only a temporary one, and the direction was certainly forward.

Most people never abandoned their faith in progress despite the mess in which the nation and the world found themselves. President Roosevelt called a volume of his speeches *Looking Forward*, and the official name of the 1933 World Fair at Chicago was The Century of Progress. The Chicago fair well symbolized the confusion many Americans had about progress. Its technological and scientific exhibits indicated a splendid improvement in man's ability to control and employ natural forces. Yet the fair, held on the shorefront of America's second city, only emphasized the slums, the poverty, and the general social sickness of Chicago. At least some visitors to the fair wondered if progress in medical knowledge compensated for widespread hunger and if efficiently harnessed mechanical horsepower offset the gray grimness that permeated the society whose economic inefficiency was so obvious. Certainly, few people rejected hope for progress, although many lost their confidence about it. That the catchwords of the day were the skeptical questions, "Oh, yeah?" and "So what?" was not surprising.

Another widespread social assumption that suffered retreat during the depression was what might be called Horatio Algerism. It had long been a fundamental belief of Americans that the degree of "success" that a person enjoyed was a fairly fine index of his ability and character. Both Calvinism and Darwinism had left most Americans with the assumption that the most successful people had achieved their status because of superior qualities and determination and that "failures" were the result of personal inadequacy, with the various levels between the extremes being the result of degrees of competence and virtue. In such a view of society, if taken to its logical conclusion, there was no such thing as social injustice; there was only personal strength or weakness. This was the social assumption implicit in the 119 novels written by the immensely popular Horatio Alger (1834–1899) which boys continued to read avidly at least through the 1920's.

But the contracting economy of the 1930's was not conducive to continuation of the belief. Many a highly able person of exemplary character found that the assumptions of Alger no longer rang true. Perhaps you could keep a good man down after all. At least it so appeared to many a good man who saw himself and others like him suffer defeat after defeat in efforts to build themselves a decent life. Again, a popular expression was revealing: "You've got to have pull." Horatio Alger's faith in "push" did not entirely disappear, but "pull" appeared to many to be a necessary ingredient of "success."

How Red Was the Red Decade?

This question was one that was not of much interest to most people during the 1930's themselves. Rather than concern about the growth of Socialist and Communist organizations and influence, such basic questions as a decent living standard for all, the elimination of special privilege and discrimination, and the threat of fascism and war in Europe were the source of far more worry about society's future. After World War II, however, the question of how red was the Red Decade (to use the title of a famous article by Granville Hicks in a postwar issue of *Harper's*) became an issue of politics, and it warrants consideration.

As the depression began, both the main radical parties, the Socialist party and the Communist party, were quite weak. The Socialists had never recovered from the loss of their left wing when the Communists split off from them in 1919, and in the late 1920's the Communists were rent by internal struggle between the disciples of Josef Stalin, who won the battle, and those of Leon Trotsky. As it became plain to see that capitalism was not functioning properly, it was natural that socialism of some kind or another would attract greater attention. The democratic socialism advocated by the Socialist party and its most prominent leader, Norman Thomas, gained in influence among well-educated people during the early depression years but not very much in the working class. Thomas, an excellent speaker with a sharp analytic mind who had once been a Presbyterian minister, continued to appeal to idealistic college students long after his party went into further decline, as it did when the New Deal shifted left in 1935.

The Communists gained strength and influence after 1935. Before that time, while the party's leader was William Z. Foster, the Communists had dismissed Roosevelt as a worse than average bourgeois politician and opposed even such basic legislation as the Wagner Act. In 1935, however, Earl Browder came to power in the party and the Seventh World Congress of the Communist International, or Comintern, changed the Communist line. Frightened by the rise of fascism, the Comintern called upon Communists to make common cause with all antifascists in a so-called Popular Front. The new world line of communism was immediately advantageous to American Communists, and the party soon flourished as it never had before. The new Communist position was epitomized in its slogan, "Communism is Twentieth Century Americanism." At the same time that they asserted they were in the American revolutionary tradition dating from 1776 and before, the Communists denied that their intention was to achieve power by violence. Their purpose, they said, was to unite all democratic forces into a coalition to halt the spread of fascism, further democracy, and stimulate social justice. By organizing new "Communist fronts" and infiltrating established non-Communist organizations, the Communists were able to extend their influence far beyond their own membership, which never exceeded one hundred thousand. But it was more than their line and their techniques that advanced the Communists during the 1930's and again during World War II; their identification with the Soviet Union actually helped their movement then. Despite the purging of the "old Bolsheviks" in Russia during the mid-thirties, which was not well reported in the American press, many loyal Americans looked with interest and sympathy upon the Russian revolution, which had in 1917 overthrown one of the world's most reactionary governments, which had expressed, although not fulfilled, noble sentiments about the rights of workers, which had increased the nation's industrial production, and which had opposed fascism more consistently than other powers, although its opposition had not been perfect. Perhaps most important, the Soviet Union had not been affected by the world depression; its economy continued to grow during the 1930's, despite the fact that the standard of living there was miserably low compared to the average American's even during the depression. Still another reason for the growth of Communist influence in America was the ineffectiveness of anti-Communist propaganda. Before World War II, most anti-Communist spokesmen were either economic reactionaries or extreme nationalists, or both, who made wild charges that did their cause no good. Representative Martin Dies of Texas, chairman of the first Committee on Un-American Activities and a transparent publicity seeker, and professional anti-Communists such as Mrs. Elizabeth Dilling, author of the fantastic *Red Network*, discredited anti-Communism with unbelievable accusations. Many of these crusaders against Communism were the "red baiters" the Communists said they were.

Communists never succeeded in persuading more than a tiny fraction of American workers to their point of view, but they were able through hard work and duplicity to capture the leadership of from one-fourth to one-third of the unions in the CIO and to control some locals in other unions, both AFL and CIO. Two officials in CIO national headquarters, General Counsel Lee Pressman and *CIO News* editor Len De Caux, were either party members or cooperating closely with the party. The most important Communist-led unions were the United Electrical Workers, the International Longshoremen's and Warehousemen's Union of Harry Bridges on the West Coast and Hawaii, and the Mine, Mill, and Smelter Workers Union. There was a strong Communist faction in the United Auto Workers. Despite their strength in CIO, the Communists were never able to determine its national policy. The main value of their CIO influence, apparently, was to provide the Communists with a sounding board and an opportunity to spread their propaganda among union members.

Communists were active in New York's American Labor Party, founded in 1936 by the unions, anti-Tammany supporters of Roosevelt, some dissident Socialists, and the most liberal wing of the Republican party, headed by Mayor LaGuardia. During the war (which the Communists vigorously supported) the Communists increased their influence in the ALP with the tacit consent of Sidney Hillman, president of the Amalgamated Clothing Workers and the CIO's chief political worker. Rather than be in the same organization with an active Communist faction, David Dubinsky, president of the International Ladies Garment Workers Union, Alex Rose, president of the Hat and Cap Makers Union, and Professor George S. Counts of Teachers College, Columbia University, bolted the ALP and organized the new Liberal party. Both parties nominated the Democratic national ticket.

The extent of Communist influence among the nation's intellectuals is difficult to assess. Only very few prominent writers and artists were actually members of the party, although many of them were willing to cooperate with Communists in a "front" if they thought the purposes of the organization warranted their support. The largest of these "fronts," significantly, was the American League against War and Fascism, later called the American League for Peace and Democracy, which claimed seven million members, although that figure probably was inflated beyond the true facts. Many American writers adopted the Popular Front mystique and participated in the Communist-minority controlled American Writers' Congresses. Among these authors were John Dos Passos, James T. Farrell, and, briefly, Ernest Hemingway. Richard Wright was a party member for a few years. Most college and university campuses had a few Communist students, particularly the tax-supported, low-cost institutions in large cities. Very few professors were party members, although some were in one or more "fronts." Certainly, however, although more intellectuals were Communist than ever before or since and although there was widespread toleration of Communists, neither Communists nor Marxists of any kind were able to set the tone of the nation's thought. The literary product of the depression generation of writers was clearly more to the left than it had been before, but it was seldom Communist-inspired. Indeed, most intellectuals, including those of a leftist bent, deplored the rigid controls over thought and art that characterized the discipline of the Communist party.

After the war, the question of the extent of Communist espionage within the federal government became a political football, and the political charges and countercharges fairly well obscured the real story. This much seems clear: the Soviet government successfully established at least one espionage ring among Washington officials. The head of it was Harold Ware, a son of the American Communist matriarch "Mother" Bloor, who went to work in the Department of Agriculture during the Hoover administration. Julian Wadleigh confessed to espionage; a federal jury found Alger Hiss guilty of perjury for denying he had engaged in espionage. None of these men was in a position to determine national policy; their service to the Soviet Union consisted of adding to that nation's store of information about the government and its operations by carrying from their offices documents to be photographed and relayed to Moscow.

Communist prestige suffered a hard blow in August, 1939, when the Soviet Union signed a nonaggression pact with Hitler's Germany. A large part of the Communists' attraction had been their opposition to fascism, but now they changed their line to one of apology for Germany and opposition to France and Great Britain in their war with the Nazis, and they cried for peace at all costs. When Germany broke the pact and invaded Russia in June, 1941, the American Communists switched again. Realistic observers did not need better evidence that the American Communists arrived at their positions through consideration of Soviet foreign policy rather than the needs of American workers or the interests of the United States. The Nazi-Soviet pact shattered the American Communists' reputation among intellectuals.

How red, then, was the Red Decade? One cannot give an answer with mathematical precision. Clearly, it was redder than the previous decade or the postwar period. Equally clearly, no more than a small minority of the American people were attracted to communism even during the worst of the depression. The nation did not abandon either democracy or capitalism as an ideal. The malaise that plagued America during this dreary period did not lead more than a relative handful of citizens to reject the essence of American political and economic traditions. Considering the seriousness and duration of the depression and the failure of the New Deal to solve the unemployment problem in eight years of peace, the wonder is not that there was as much Communist sentiment as there was but that Marxism did not grow stronger than it did.

Education

One of the most deplorable aspects of the Great Depression was its effect upon the education of children and young people. The first two school years after the crash were not seriously different from the norm, but by the fall of 1931 the restricted financial situation of local government began to affect education. Even in some of the larger cities, school boards cut teacher's salaries, shortened the school year, and ceased instruction in art, music, and physical education. The 1932–1933 school year was the worst. By the end of March, 1933, so many schools had run out of money and closed their doors that about 335,000 children were out of school. The poorer states were the hardest hit. In Alabama four-fifths of all of the rural schools for white children were closed, as were 1,318 schools in Georgia. In Arkansas over 300 schools were open for only sixty days or less for the whole academic year. Even in relatively rich Ohio almost every public school system in the state had to shorten its term by a month.

Many municipal governments, in effect, placed the burden on the teachers. Salaries fell to rock bottom. In Iowa the minimum salary, which in many towns actually was the maximum compensation, was $40 a month. Oklahoma established maximum salaries; a school board in that state could not legally pay an experienced elementary teacher with a bachelor's degree more than $85 a month, or $680 a year, even if it had the money and wanted to. Several cities opened the school year in the fall, spent the available funds until they were exhausted, and then told the teachers they either could leave or finish the year without pay. The most widely publicized school disgrace was in Chicago where in May, 1931, the city began to pay its teachers in "tax-anticipation warrants." When the city had money again, the teachers could redeem the warrants for cash. But meanwhile they and their families had to eat. Banks accepted the warrants at from 12 to 20 per cent discount until the spring of 1932, when the financial plight of Chicago was so desperate that banks would not accept the warrants at all. Teachers, with understandable bitterness, pointed out that the coal dealers who supplied the schools with fuel were paid in cash. It was not until World War II that all the back pay was given the teachers in the nation's second city.

The cutbacks in school programs came in the face of growing enrollments, particularly in the high schools. Young people were aware that if a job should become open it probably would go to a person with a high school diploma, and over the country thousands of boys and girls who in the 1920's would have left school at the earliest permissible age stayed on until graduation. There was little else for them to do. By the end of the decade in most parts of the United States twelve years of schooling for all children was the accepted norm. Most Americans came to regard a more or less automatic high school diploma as part of their birthright. The trend toward universal high school education had been underway for three or four decades; the depression merely brought it to culmination.

With thousands of young people in high school whose limited intellectual capacities would have excluded them in an earlier day, the schools were forced to operate somewhat differently. At one time the function of the high school was to prepare young people for the college and university. The term "prep school" survived. But in the 1930's the high schools were filled with students who had no thought of higher education. The educational needs of these young people were somewhat different from those who would go on to the campus. The high schools had two alternatives: they could keep the old college preparatory curriculum and water it down to a point consistent with the capacities of the students or they could segregate the students who planned to quit after graduation and endeavor to prepare them for their careers and adult life. Actually, most high schools chose combinations of the two alternatives.

During the 1930's, educational philosophers continued to adjust their ideas of what the schools should be as the environment around them changed. One important group, claiming John Dewey as their intellectual godfather (although often the relationship was dubious), asserted that "progressive education" consisted of preparing the child to adjust to life and that little learning was possible unless the child felt the need for the knowledge to be learned. Soon "life adjustment" and "felt needs" came to be educational catchwords. A quite distinct group, of whom Professor Counts was the most prominent, argued for quite a different program for the schools. American society, they maintained, was becoming increasingly collective. The "progressive schools" were "child-centered," putting their emphasis on the student as an individual without taking into account that the student was a social being in a society that was steadily becoming less individualistic. Critical of the tendency of schools to develop in children the values of an individualistic and capitalistic society, this group urged that the schools should emphasize the interdependence of American life and strengthen the students' desire and ability to make collective society democratic. One must, however, beware of the supposition that the ideas of educational philosophers of whatever kind were reflected in the nation's classrooms. New educational thought is very slow to affect the way children are actually taught, and only a few schools in the 1930's actually put these educational theories into practice. Resistance was particularly strong against the ideas of Professor Counts. When Professor Harold Rugg wrote a series of textbooks in the social studies from the new point of view, the American Legion charged that he was a Communist and in many cities successfully kept the series from being adopted.

The colleges and universities also felt the strains and pressures of the Great Depression. In the depression's early years enrollments declined as students and their families found themselves unable to finance higher education. National enrollments for the 1933–1934 year were 8 per cent lower than they had been in 1930–1931. But the next year enrollments began to increase, and they climbed steadily for the rest of the decade. In 1940–1941, almost 1,500,000 students were on the nation's campuses, between one-seventh and one-sixth of the college-age population. This, incidentally, was a new record.

Students decided to go to college or stay in college for many of the same reasons that their juniors elected to stay in high school. If one had to be economically idle because of business stagnation, he might as well spend his time in a worthy manner. Students with inadequate funds usually chose to go to tax-supported institutions, which supplemented FERA and NYA funds with student loans to the best of their financial ability. College people found new devices for cutting expenses to the minimum. A few farm boys took cows and chickens to college with them, and cooperative eating and housing groups became common. Some students had ingenious ways of earning a little money —being a professional blood donor was a favorite device because it took little time—and college part-time employment offices were busy places.

Because so many students were sacrificing pleasure, comfort, and even health to stay in college, there were larger numbers of serious students on the campuses than there had been in the 1920's. Rah-rah and antics by no means disappeared, but a new mood prevailed in most colleges during the depression decade. Certainly, students of the 1930's had a greater interest in social, economic, and political problems than their older brothers and sisters had displayed. Political clubs and discussion groups, many of them leftist in nature, were more active than they had ever been previously. An increased number of students chose to study history and the social sciences, a reflection of heightened concern for such matters that was stimulated by the depression.

Here and there in American colleges and universities faculties and administrators pursued educational experiments. Unconventional Bennington and Sarah Lawrence, which opened in 1932 and 1928 respectively, attracted considerable attention, and two of Columbia University's administrative units, Teachers College and Columbia College, began new experiments. Teachers College's innovation was New College which continued until 1939; the other was Bard College. The higher educational experiment which evoked the most publicity and controversy was the one President Robert M. Hutchins inaugurated at the University of Chicago. Hutchins, who became president of Chicago in 1929 when he was only thirty years old, tried to end the campus lock-step by allowing students to take examinations as quickly as they could. This permitted bright and ambitious students to finish their undergraduate work in less than four years. Chicago also admitted able students who had not yet finished high school. Hutchins was disturbed by the commercial character of intercollegiate athletics, particularly football, and proposed to eliminate that evil by taking money away from it and charging spectators only ten cents a seat. He retreated, however, and abolished football at Chicago altogether.

These changes, startling as they were, were minor compared to Chicago's inauguration of the "great books" curriculum. Relying heavily upon the thought of the thirteenth-century theologian, St. Thomas Aquinas, Hutchins and his associates tried at Chicago, through concentrating on the great literature of the world, to imbue students with "the eternal intellectual verities." It was their belief that materialism, shoddy thinking, false democracy, pragmatism, and the departure from the unity of thought that characterized medieval west-European society were the root difficulties of the world. Hutchins' ideas, of course, by no means went unchallenged. Pragmatists denied the whole validity of the concept, and some critics saw even fascist implications in its assumption of an intellectual elite. Critics at a less profound level wisecracked that Chicago's experience proved a lack of wisdom in appointing such a young president and commented that the University, founded by the Baptist John D. Rockefeller, had become an institution "where Jewish professors taught Catholic philosophy to Protestant students." But Hutchins had his supporters, too. A small band of Chicago professors inaugurated the new—or the old—curriculum at St. John's College in Annapolis, Maryland, and the Hutchins idea was a factor in the decision at many universities to put a greater emphasis in the first two years of college on the western world's cultural heritage.

The Press

Newspapers and magazines, one of the most important agencies affecting the education of adults, had their own troubles and developments during the 1930's. Newspaper circulation did not decline significantly during the early depression—the 1933 total was only 12 per cent below 1930—and by 1937 sales topped the figure for the 1920's. Revenues from advertising fell off sharply because advertisers had a tighter budget and because radio commercials took a larger part of the advertiser's dollar. A few newspapers went under altogether, the most famous collapse being Pulitzer's New York *World* which folded in 1931. Mergers with less straitened newspapers became common. About 48 per cent of the independently published newspapers in business in 1930 were gone by 1941. By that time only about 120 American cities had more than one newspaper management, although frequently the merged management continued to publish the former papers, usually one morning and one evening and sometimes even one Republican and the other ostensibly Democratic. By 1940, newspapers owned about one-third of the nation's radio stations. In some communities a single firm had a monopoly on all the local news outlets. The rural weekly newspapers, with less capital than the urban dailies, had similar problems. By the end of the decade most small-town weeklies attempted to do no more than report the strictly local news—high school basketball scores and the less than abandoned social affairs of the church ladies—and many of them ran "canned" editorials that were prepared by publishers' associations and economic pressure groups which often provided editors with "mats" that required no further composition of type.

With such consolidation, a tendency toward uniformity of editorial opinion was no surprise. And the opinion was usually conservative. In 1932, 60 per cent of the nation's dailies supported Hoover's re-election; in 1936, the number supporting the Republican candidate rose to 63 per cent and in 1940 to 75 per cent. Since Roosevelt won all three of these elections handily, there was considerable talk about the "failing power of the press." Politics is an inexact science and we do not know precisely how much influence a newspaper wields in determining the citizen's vote, but it appears likely that newspapers, as they had always done, continued to condition their readers' political positions. It is interesting to note, therefore, that, on the whole, Roosevelt and his more liberal advisers received a poor press from about 1934 until the war. Editors frequently selected unflattering photographs of FDR for publication, although they carefully avoided photographs that revealed how crippled he was. Most people on seeing Roosevelt for the first time were surprised by his extreme handicap.

Another development that tended toward uniformity of opinion was the increased syndication of columnists. Walter Lippmann, whose home base was the New York *Herald-Tribune* after the *World* closed shop, was syndicated to an estimated ten million readers. Some of the other widely read columnists of public affairs were Dorothy Thompson, Eleanor Roosevelt, who began her "My Day" in 1935, the conservative David Lawrence, and the sensational Drew Pearson and Robert S. Allen. Easily the most violent of the prominent columnists was former sports writer Westbrook Pegler, who was given to apoplectic anger at the mere mention of Roosevelt. Many a commuter turned first to his column to see what "Old Peg" was exploding about currently.

The tabloid newspapers, begun right after World War I, grew tremendously in number and circulation during the 1930's. Although they cleaned themselves up considerably after the collapse of Bernarr Macfadden's New York *Daily Graphic* in 1932—this tabloid was so smutty that it was generally called the Daily Pornographic—most tabloids were sensational in nature and characterized by many photographs, a twelve-year-old vocabulary, and a conservative to reactionary editorial policy. There were a few exceptions. One of them was the relatively dignified Chicago *Times*, an evening paper that supported Roosevelt. Another exception was the experimental *PM*, founded by Marshall Field III in New York in 1940. *PM* did not accept advertising, was never a financial success, and was consistently left Democratic in its policies. The sensation of the tabloids influenced most regular newspapers which also gave considerable space to stories of superficial importance but of morbid public interest. Two of the biggest such stories of the 1930's were the kidnapping of Charles A. Lindbergh's son and the subsequent apprehension and trial of the kidnapper and the birth in 1934 of quintuplets to a French-Canadian family named Dionne. Newspapers devoted miles of newsprint to the five little Dionnes. The tremendous change in American journalism was to be seen by comparing the treatment of the Dionne sisters to newspaper coverage of the live birth of quintuplets to a Schenectady woman in 1833. The New York press in 1833 had seen fit to devote only ten lines to the multiple birth, despite the additional juicy fact that the children were born out of wedlock.

The tabloids had a parallel development in magazine publishing when the picture magazines got off to a blazing start with Henry Luce's launching of *Life* in 1936. *Look* and several other imitations soon were on the newsstands, but *Life* continued to lead the field. From the first its formula was to have a scattering of almost everything so as to appeal to as broad a market as possible—a kind of magazine smorgasbord with a little politics, art, science, sex, and sport, all larded with human interest and simplified and accompanied by good photographs. Almost everyone from the highbrow to the illiterate could find in it something of interest. In some ways Luce's older venture, *Time*, was a magazine tabloid. A newsmagazine begun in the 1920's that became a giant in the 1930's, *Time* featured a highly unusual writing style, many photographs with snappy captions, and concise simplifications. It, too, had imitators, notably *Newsweek* begun in 1933.

The pocket-sized monthly *Reader's Digest* was the publishing sensation of the decade. At the start of the depression it had about 250,000 circulation; by the war it approached 7,000,000 copies, counting foreign language and Braille editions, and was the most widely circulated magazine in history. It condensed all kinds of articles from other magazines, but its emphasis was on the folksy and the optimistic. When it undertook a crusade against evil, the object of its concern was always something about which there would be little disagreement such as automobile accidents and microbes. Late in the 1930's it began to affect the content of other periodicals by "planting" articles in them for later condensation in its own pages.

America continued to produce a vast variety of magazines of all levels of quality, most of them with small circulations, despite economic conditions. The specialist, the esthete, and the intellectual could find plenty to whet his interest. Yet the huge commercial success of the tabloids, picture magazines, and digests, all of which appealed to the lowest common intellectual denominator, indicated a development that was to become a cultural crisis after the war.

Leisure in the Depression

By 1929 much of American entertainment had become commercialized. People had learned to prefer the pleasures that cost them money. But in the 1930's most people had less money to spend for their leisure, and some had no money at all for such purposes. Of course, the more expensive ways to pursue pleasure, such as luxury travel, nightclubbing, and some outdoor sports like golf and yachting, did not disappear, for not everyone was broke. As conditions improved, more and more people resumed the costlier pleasures of a happier era. But for most people cost was an important factor throughout the period and seriously limited the possible range of entertainment.

The least expensive way to spend one's leisure time was by reading—if one could get books for nothing. The sale of books dropped precipitously, but library circulation took a sharp turn upward. The American Library Association estimated that the public libraries of the country acquired about four million new borrowers from 1929 to 1933, and the circulation of their books increased by almost 40 per cent. Libraries, however, suffered from the same financial problems as the public schools. Most cities cut their library budgets. Some bought no new books at all; the Chicago public library had no budget for book purchases for three consecutive years. Public libraries were crowded places throughout the depression as many Americans learned what some of the more intellectual bums had long known: the public library was a warm place to idle away many pleasant hours. The number of people in the United States who acquired fairly good, although usually quite uneven, educations in public libraries is incalculable but probably large.

Another almost free leisure activity was radio listening. In 1929 a radio cost about $100; 12,000,000 families owned one. During the 1930's, manufacturers put out small wood or plastic table models that sold for about $10, and by $1940, 28,000,000 homes had one or more radios, 86 per cent of the population. One 1937 survey indicated that the nation's radios were turned on an average four and one-half hours a day.

While radio was quite inexpensive to the consumer, it was by no means uncommercial. In its commercialism lay most of its problems. Radio stations and networks were in the business of selling their services for profit, and advertisers bought their services to increase their own sales. The entertainment and edification of the radio listener were secondary to monetary gain. The listener was important, to be sure, but as a potential customer. These being the ground rules of the business, the widest possible audience for a program was the producer's aim, for that meant the largest possible number of potential purchasers of the advertiser's product. Thus radio programs, like tabloid newspapers, tended to appeal to the lowest common intellectual denominator.

Some of the radio programs, particularly during the daylight hours when "soap operas" dominated the air, were downright bad; the great majority were fairly pleasant (to most people) pieces of fluff, not very memorable one way or another; only a few programs merited critical praise. Music was on the air more than one-half of a station's time. The enormous radio demand for popular music was far more than composers could meet with a consistently creditable product. Although some of the "hit tunes" of the 1930's were of sufficient quality to be deservedly revived time and again since then, most of them lie fortunately forgotten. In the later evening hours when there was little or no commercial demand for radio time, many stations, particularly in the big cities, ran broadcasts from dances, and, through these broadcasts, a new interest in jazz grew. Theretofore, jazz was relatively little known among most white Americans. During the 1930's, it increasingly influenced popular music, and by the end years of the decade dance bands found that young people especially preferred jazz to the popular sentimental ballad.

The major networks, Columbia Broadcasting System and the National Broadcasting Company, made one experiment in musical education during the 1930's that indicated something of radio's powers. In 1930, CBS began Sunday afternoon broadcasts of the New York Philharmonic. NBC in 1931 began broadcasts of the Metropolitan Opera Company's Saturday matinées, and in 1937 it organized its own symphony orchestra with Arturo Toscanini as conductor. These ventures were at first financial losses, but the networks persisted and the audiences grew steadily. A poll in 1939 indicated that ten million people listened to serious music broadcasts and that a majority of people, except those on the farm and in the lowest economic brackets, enjoyed such broadcasts and were happy that radio music was not exclusively popular. It is impossible to know how many of these people merely thought they should like serious music and how many actually did, but sales of tickets to concerts and of "classical" recordings improved.

Hollywood enjoyed a boom despite the depression. Movie tickets were not very expensive—usually fifteen cents at the theaters that showed "second runs"—and the theater operators provided a lot of escape for the money, frequently with two feature films, a newsreel, and a short subject. Many theaters attracted customers with such inducements as "bank night" at which the lucky winner of a drawing would receive cash if he were present, bingo, and free cheap dishes. An evening at the movies was by far the most popular away-from-home entertainment.

Movies had a cultural problem similar to radio's. Maximum profits demanded mass audiences, and tailoring a film for a mass audience limited its intellectual and artistic quality. As one prominent Hollywood producer put it, "The picture industry is no different from the underwear business, for example. It is completely governed by the law of supply and demand." Moviegoers who had seen scores of mediocre pictures understood the comment well enough. As in radio, the production volume was too great to be consistent with quality. Each year the major studios turned out hundreds and hundreds of quickly conceived and executed screen plays on a mass production basis, films so full of clichés they were entirely predictable. When a film maker did employ a new artistic device he was usually imitated so widely, if the new idea were commercially successful, that the innovation soon became hackneyed. The volume of films was greater than was warranted. Exhibitors were driven to the double feature by Hollywood's insistence upon block booking. The film companies insisted that exhibiters accept their film rentals in blocks of fifty titles; if they refused they would be denied the titles they wanted. The only way exhibiters could use such a volume was to show double features and change their programs frequently, usually twice a week. In 1940, a group of exhibiters went to the courts to stop block booking, and with the help of the Department of Justice arranged a compromise that cut the block size to five.

The press for mass audiences seriously hampered the artistic expressions of Hollywood. An experiment might be financially disastrous if the public did not like it, and producers were careful to avoid themes and ideas that might alienate any substantial part of the potential audience. For example, the more expensive productions had to have a large foreign sale to make a profit, and criticisms of totalitarianism were few until the late 1930's because such films were not permitted in Germany and Italy. The rulings of the Hays office (an agency instituted by the film makers to police the morality of screen plays, headed by President Harding's postmaster-general, Will Hays) were so mechanical that they ridiculously hampered valid artistic expression while frequently falling short of their original purpose. It is not surprising, given this economic framework, that Hollywood's contributions in the 1930's were for the most part limited to techniques of production.

American movie producers, of course, came forth with some movies of quality despite themselves and their system. Charlie Chaplin's "City Lights" (1931), "Modern Times" (1936), and "The Great Dictator" (1940) were memorable, as were "I Am a Fugitive from a Chain Gang" (1932), "The Informer" (1935), "Dodsworth" (1936), and "Citizen Kane" (1941). These films, however, were not notable commercial successes on their first release. The big money-makers were musical comedies, which were turned out by formula, or Hollywood versions of popular novels, which had a built-in market and which usually disappointed viewers who had read the book.

CHAPTER TWENTY

The Culture of the Great Depression

IN THE 1920's, MOST INTELLECTUALS AND ARTISTS HAD FELT APART from the mainstream of American culture, aliens in their own land. Indeed, hundreds of them found both material and spiritual life more compatible in France. The Great Depression changed this situation quickly. It was not just that the crash dried up the expatriates' flow of checks from home, for those who stayed in America during the Coolidge era found, as much as the expatriates, that after the depression they were no longer alienated from society. It was not that intellectuals, or anyone else, found the United States more attractive during depression than during prosperity; it was only that some of the things to which intellectuals had objected during prosperity, such as Rotarian optimism, blatant materialism, and glorification of dollar success, were now subdued if not gone.

One cannot summarize the cultural developments of a people as diverse and dynamic as Americans in a few words or even a few thousand words. Nevertheless, (as one examines literature, the arts, and scholarship during the depression decade, he is struck by two main threads: social protest and a kind of cultural nationalism with a strong element of regionalism.) Two songs illustrate well these threads. In the mid-1930's, the International Ladies Garment Workers Union sponsored a musical show written and produced by needle trade workers called *Pins and Needles* that did well on Broadway and went on national tour. Its hit song was "Sing Me a Song of Social Significance." Then at the end of the period Hollywood filmed John Steinbeck's *The Grapes of Wrath*. The score relied heavily on "Red River Valley," haunting, sad, and distinctively Great Plains and American folk music.

397

Fiction, Drama, and Poetry

Most of the big names among the disillusioned authors of the 1920's "Lost Generation" seemed unable to come to terms with depression society. Sinclair Lewis' ridicule of small-town Philistines seemed irrelevant to most readers in the 1930's. Babbitts still existed by the score and Main Street shallowness and pettiness had not disappeared, but somehow Lewis struck readers as old hat. The horses that Lewis had flayed so excellently were not dead, but they were pretty sick. America's most famous author in 1930 when he became the first United States citizen to win a Nobel prize for literature, he was a tragic misfit by the end of the decade when he appeared as an actor in a road company that played an embarrassingly poor farce of his called *Angela Is Twenty-Two*. His antifascist novel, *It Can't Happen Here* (1935), which sought to prove that it could happen here, enjoyed a vogue when the WPA Theater Project dramatized it and produced it simultaneously in several cities, but it did not by any means match the impact of his earlier novels. Although Scott Fitzgerald improved as a literary craftsman during the 1930's despite alcoholism and hack work in Hollywood, his *Tender Is the Night* (1934) and *The Last Tycoon* (1941) were not fully appreciated until several years after his death in 1940. Eugene O'Neill, America's most famous dramatist, produced nothing important in the decade after *Mourning Becomes Electra* in 1931, although he too won the Nobel award in 1936. His *Ah, Wilderness* (1933) was popular but shallow, quite unlike typical O'Neill fare. Once popular bohemian radicals such as Floyd Dell were unread and forgotten.

The most exciting new novelist of the 1920's, Ernest Hemingway, was only a partial exception to the intellectual irrelevance of the lost generation. Of his books during the depression only *For Whom the Bell Tolls* (1940), in which the hero was an American fighting with the Spanish Loyalists, smacked much of the mood of the thirties. *Death in the Afternoon* (1932), a paean to bull fighting, seemed, when it appeared, to be something left over from a long-ago day. Except for the *Bell*, it was Hemingway's literary virtuosity rather than his themes or his thought that kept him in the front ranks of American fiction during the decade.

John Dos Passos, whose postwar novels had marked him as one to be watched, started the decade's theme of social criticism with a roar in 1930 with the first volume of his *U.S.A.* trilogy, *The 42nd Parallel*. *Nineteen Nineteen* appeared in 1932 and *The Big Money* four years later. The trilogy amounted to an impressionistic and left-wing history of America from the beginning of the century into the early depression. Its mood of anger toward economic privilege and political phoniness well matched the feeling of its readers and was an enormous success. Dos Passos was a major innovator in technique as well with his profiles of actual figures inserted into the novel and his placement of characters into historical context with what he called "The Camera Eye."

Another important trilogy was James T. Farrell's series about an Irish working class family in Chicago and the degeneration of the main character,

Studs Lonigan. *Young Lonigan* appeared in 1932, *The Young Manhood of Studs Lonigan* in 1934, and *Judgment Day* the following year. Farrell was prolific; he had two other novels of urban Irish during the decade, *Gas-House McGinty* and *A World I Never Made*, and his *A Note on Literary Criticism* was one of the most able discussions of literature from a Marxist point of view ever undertaken. Farrell was like his mentor, Theodore Dreiser, in several ways: he wrote with remarkable force but little grace, was an angry left-winger, and was too independent to accept the discipline of Marxist organizations.

Perhaps the greatest novelist of the 1930's—some would say of the twentieth century—was California's John Steinbeck whose *The Grapes of Wrath* (1939) came as close to being "*the* great American novel" as any. His novels during the depression were full of social criticism, his characters were the dispossessed, and his sympathies were clearly with the down-and-out against their exploiters. Yet compassion rather than anger or rebellion was the dominant emotion that ran through his pages, and he was almost sentimental in *Of Mice and Men* (1937). That he was not a politically naive primitive, as some people thought until his masterpiece appeared in 1939, was indicated by his novel about a strike of California agricultural workers, *In Dubious Battle* (1936). Most of all, Steinbeck was not doctrinaire. His characters were believably real people, not caricatures and not merely sociological specimens. For this ability to portray human situations in certain segments of American life, he was awarded the Nobel Prize for Literature in 1962.

Social criticism on Broadway became commonplace during the thirties. In the year of the crash, Elmer Rice partly foreshadowed the direction of the theater for the next several years with his *Street Scene*, and he became more frankly political with *Judgment Day* and *Between Two Worlds*. Maxwell Anderson, collaborator on the best antiwar play of the 1920's, was another notable playwright critic of society. His *Both Your Houses* (1933) dealt with the conflict between practical politics and idealism, and *Winterset* (1935), a dramatic comment on the Sacco-Vanzetti case, became probably the best known "depression play" after it was made into a successful motion picture. Robert Sherwood, one of the least critical of the prominent dramatists, wrote an incisive social commentary on war in *Idiot's Delight* (1936). Lillian Hellman's *The Little Foxes* in 1939 was later than most of the bitter dramatic attacks on capitalism. The outstanding theatrical production of the decade that voted the other way was George M. Cohan's musical satire of the New Deal in 1937, *I'd Rather Be Right*.

Poetry, once the special form for sentimentality and later for obscure experiment, expressed much of the 1930's social discontent and criticism of the *status quo*. Archibald MacLeish, an unusual poet who was then an associate editor of *Fortune* and later Librarian of Congress, in 1937 had an anti-fascist poem, *The Fall of the City*, dramatized on radio, and the following year he put out a combined picture book and long poem entitled *Land of the Free* in which he made clear his dissatisfaction of much in that land. Edna St. Vincent Millay, once the darling of flaming youth, began to burn her candle at both ends over social questions and in 1937 published *Conversations at Midnight*. In this volume symbols of different economic interests and political points of view argued their cases, and the conservatives lost the argument.

399

Carl Sandburg turned from the Whitman tradition toward social realism with *The People, Yes* (1936) with the well-known lines:

> Stocks are property, yes.
> Bonds are property, yes.
> Machines, land, buildings are property, yes.
> A job is property,
> no, nix, nah, nah.

Readers of a later generation who come across this critical literature sometimes make the error of dismissing it as Communist propaganda. It was not. Writers, almost by definition, are sensitive people who articulate more widely-held views, and in the depression dissatisfaction with the *status quo* was a majority sentiment. There were Communist propagandists, of course, and some of the writers mentioned here flirted with Communism as a possible solution for America's problems, usually only to reject it either as no answer at all or as substituting one set of evils for another. The Negro novelist Richard Wright is a case in point. For a while in the 1930's, before he became a writer of reputation with his *Native Son* in 1940, Wright was an active member of the party. In an autobiographical piece about his Communist experience in a postwar volume edited by R. H. S. Crossman called *The God That Failed*, Wright described why he became a Communist and why he quit. Interestingly, his motives were constant; he joined the party because he thought that by so doing he could advance a little the cause of human freedom, and he left it for the same reason.

With few exceptions, the Communist literature of the 1930's was not great, essentially because it subordinated people to broad abstractions and made propaganda its main purpose rather than artistic validity. Most of the so-called proletarian novels by such as Leane Zugsmith, Albert Helper, Grace Lumpkin, and Albert Maltz basically were the old Horatio Alger tales stood on their head—stories in which a revolutionary achievement instead of financial success were the climax. In fact, the personalities of the heroes in Alger and the proletarian novels were remarkably similar. Their impact has been much exaggerated; they had little, mostly because of their poor quality as novels. Occasionally, a Communist produced an effective piece. Perhaps the best example was the strike play by Clifford Odets, a party member at the time, entitled *Waiting for Lefty* (1935).

Another strong current in American letters after the crash was the Whitmanesque "We Sing America" theme. The current ran alongside social protest in that its emphasis was upon democracy and ordinary people—being for "the little people" and against their being "pushed around" were the clichés of the time—and had in it a strong element of regionalism. Frequently this kind of literature, and the school of painting that was its parallel, was exuberant. Sometimes, in its emphasis upon ordinary people and upon what was distinctively American, it had about it a vaguely mystic primitivism.

The sprawling but intense novels by the sprawling but intense Thomas Wolfe, an uprooted North Carolinian, were of the "We Sing America" current. In *Look Homeward, Angel* (1929), *Of Time and the River* (1935), *The Web and the Rock* (1939), *You Can't Go Home Again* (1940), in which the central character was sometimes named Eugene Gant and sometimes George

Weber but was always actually Wolfe himself, ran a persistent concern with one's family and regional roots and a disquieting uncertainty when wrenched from them. Wolfe had a tremendous talent and might have gone on to other themes had he not died in 1938 when still under forty. An unfinished manuscript, published posthumously as *The Hills Beyond* (1941), however, was even more explicitly regional although it was written in a somewhat different style. Quite different was the short story writer William Saroyan, who was nevertheless an American Singer. A second-generation Armenian from rural and small-town California, Saroyan's passionate exuberance burst upon the scene with his collection, *The Daring Young Man on the Flying Trapeze* (1934). He was prolific, inventive, democratic, and frequently primitive. Robert Sherwood worked in the same current when he went back to the humble youth of Lincoln for his play *Abe Lincoln in Illinois* (1938), and in that state Edgar Lee Masters continued to write his poems about its people.

Some of the major writing of the 1930's does not fit into these classifications of social criticism and a regional kind of cultural nationalism. William Faulkner sometimes seemed to work in either or both categories, but usually he plowed his own furrow. Two of America's celebrated expatriate poets, T. S. Eliot and Ezra Pound, were quite at odds with majority thought during the depression, Eliot removing himself from the present with Anglo-Catholic fascination for the Middle Ages and Pound obscurely translating classical Japanese poetry and praising Italian fascism.

Many, perhaps most, of the novels published even during the depression's tense years were intended as popular entertainment. The trials of the depression may even have heightened popular demand for escape literature. Easily the most successful novel commercially was Margaret Mitchell's *Gone with the Wind* (1936), which sold millions of copies and, two years after publication, matched the Bible in sales. It was a good yarn, ably told and romantic, nothing more and not intended to be. Long historic novels like Miss Mitchell's were a rage. Some were well done and some were not. Among the better popular ones were Hervey Allen's *Anthony Adverse* (1933), Walter D. Edmonds' *Drums Along the Mohawk* (1936), and Kenneth Roberts' Tory voting *Oliver Wiswell* (1940). The adventure books and westerns of Zane Gray and others flowed by floods from the press and found an audience, and there was the usual seriously intentioned but banal and shallow "soap opera" novel from such as Temple Bailey and Lloyd C. Douglas. The "how to" book came into its own as a big seller during the thirties, the most popular being Dale Carnegie's *How To Win Friends and Influence People*. A kind of Horatio Alger handbook for a corporate age, Carnegie's book in effect advised readers to delude themselves into being sincerely interested in other people until they really were interested or until delusion became habit. Of detective stories there was an abundance. James M. Cain's *The Postman Always Rings Twice* (1934) started the hard-boiled, violent school of detective fiction that came to full flower, if that is the term, after World War II. Poetry had its entertainers and homely "philosophers"—Edgar Guest was America's most widely known versifier—and the theater continued to produce some quickly and properly forgotten plays.

Some changes in the economics of writing and publishing were significant. Since money was tight, most publishers issued fewer titles than they had before and concentrated on those likely to have a wide sale. The book clubs, which became large enough to influence the trade, furthered this trend. The Book-of-the-Month Club mixed a few serious novels into its middlebrow offerings and by membership bonuses and clever advertising became a vast enterprise. In its wake were several book clubs for specialized interests. Book clubs were a natural depression growth. They offered bargain prices and by briefing the membership on its choices narrowed the likelihood of the reader's buying a book that would not interest him. Probably the clubs broadened the base of the book-buying public.

A more important extension of book buying came at the end of the depression years with the paperback. Inexpensive paperbound books had long been prevalent in Europe, and in America, besides the "dime novel," there had been *Blue Ribbon Books* which sold for a dollar. In 1939, Robert F. de Graff began *Pocket Books*, attractively covered paperbacks held together with a new glue instead of stitching or staples. The books sold for twenty-five and thirty-five cents at drug stores and news stands and attracted buyers who seldom bought books in hard covers. Historical romances and mystery stories, with provocative pictures of hypermammary young women on the cover to attract the potential customer's eye, were the stock in trade of paperback publishers who soon became numerous, but they also issued reprints of fictional and nonfictional classics. In 1941, Americans bought ten million paperback books, and the boom was only beginning.

Some observers detected an economic influence on writing emanating from Hollywood. The cinema companies frequently paid very high prices for the screen rights to a book, and some novelists wrote with Hollywood rather than the reader in mind. Scores of novelists went to the movie capital, sometimes more or less permanently, to write scenarios at a higher salary than most of them would earn from royalties. Rising income taxes, which bore heavily on a writer who worked several years on a novel only to receive most of its royalties and tax-bills within a year or two, may have increased the numbers of literary travelers to Hollywood. In any case, few people in the literary world thought that motion pictures had a beneficial effect on serious professional writers.

Art and Architecture

The depression's mood of hard-headed immediacy brought realistic art back to popular favor, and the modernists, who dominated the art scene in the 1920's, faded into the background until happier times when painters and viewers again felt they could forget society. Modernism by no means disappeared, but social painting and "We Sing America," both with a realistic approach, dominated American painting during the Great Depression. Hard and fast distinctions between the social protest painters and those who concentrated on the American scene are difficult, for the angry protest artists usually painted American subjects and there was at least some social criticism implied in many of the works of those who clearly were America Singers.

William Gropper, Joseph Hirsch, Jack Levine, and Adolph Dehn, of whom Gropper was the best known, perhaps boiled over with social rebellion more consistently than other artists. Gropper's painting "Legislative Paunch," with its arm-waving politicos with skull-like heads and obscene bellies, packed a great blow among people who were disgusted with political action. Hirsch and Levine frequently painted lawyers and policemen in the same bitter fashion, and Dehn pictured wealthy matrons as grotesque and cruel. These artists frequently did cartoons for left-wing magazines (Gropper was at his best in black and white) and some of their paintings were exceptionally high-grade cartoons in color.

Ben Shahn and Philip Evergood were perhaps the most artistically gifted of the angry social painters. Shahn first came to major attention in 1932, when he had a show of over twenty paintings on the Sacco-Vanzetti case. His "Miners' Wives," done in the late 1930's, was a masterpiece. Evergood's "My Forebearers were Pioneers," with its bitter, frustrated, and ruined old-fashioned New England lady, was a painting of major importance.

Equally angry but quite different in his style was Peter Blume, who was what might be described as a social protest surrealist. His most famous painting of the period, "The Eternal City," was a dreamlike composite of life under Mussolini so biting that the Corcoran Gallery in Washington refused to hang it in 1939, perhaps fearing a diplomatic incident. That the ugly, livid-green head in the painting was the Italian dictator was unmistakable.

The 14th Street School of painters in New York (Raphael and Moses Soyer, Edward Laning, Isabel Bishop, and Morris Kantor) painted that seamy district and its people in a general mood of protest but usually without bitterness. The Soyer brothers were more in the tradition of the Ash Can School of before the war, and Moses had studied with Henri. Their training was with different teachers, rather catch-as-catch-can in the settlement houses of the Lower East Side where they had grown up, but they were remarkably alike in their mood of sympathy and tolerance. Moses caught fatigue in the faces of the ballet dancers he so frequently painted, and Raphael's "Waiting Room," with its hunched, tired women and men in T-shirts and three-day beards, compassionately caught the depression's mood of despair. Both of them were masters of catching their subjects at unguarded moments, similar to the candid camera's "slice of life." One of the most remarkable pictures of the school was Kantor's "Farewell to Union Square," done just before he left for New England. He gently painted huge roses the size of six buses across the square's traffic lanes.

The America Singers painted the great cities, the small towns, and the country, although frequently they were thought of as only small town and rural. Edward Hopper painted in all three locales, although he was at his best with his big-city canvases. A contemporary of Bellows but slow to hit his stride and find a public, Hopper first came to prominence in the 1930's. He was trained in the humanistic tradition of Henri but worked out his own feeling for cold light that gave his paintings an uncompromising harshness. Hopper's painting of an all-night cheap restaurant in a big city, "Nighthawks," now at the Chicago Art Institute, caught the kind of loneliness that only a walker in a large American city can feel. The canvas was a major American masterpiece. Reginald Marsh was somewhat similar to Hopper in his subject matter but quite different in his style and mood. Marsh was greatly impressed with the vitality of the urban masses, and he squeezed into his paintings crowds of shoppers in Union Square, Bowery bums, and seekers of diversion at Coney Island. Marsh's statement that "well bred people are not fun to paint" was one that many America Singers could endorse.

The best known painter of small-town life was Charles Burchfield of Salem, Ohio, and later western New York State. Burchfield's work wavered between the realistic and the romantic, but during the 1930's he usually worked in a realist vein. One of the best known painters of the mid-twentieth century, Burchfield sometimes seemed to revel in small-town life and sometimes to point up its bleak ugliness, yet certainly he was no Sinclair Lewis with a brush.

The so-called regionalists of the 1930's received tremendous acclaim, perhaps more than they deserved although they were far above the ordinary in quality. The big names among the regionalists were Thomas Hart Benton, grandson of the great pre-Civil War Missouri senator, Grant Wood, and John Steuart Curry. They were all from the western Midwest, and they all glorified that region and regarded the East, particularly the eastern cities, as stifling, degenerate, and effete. The critic Thomas Craven who publicized the regionalists and proclaimed them the nation's greatest artists, sometimes seemed pathologically hostile in his denunciations of modernism and French art and could be ridiculously chauvinistic. The fact that artists of the Middle Border should react strongly to the sometimes supercilious attitude of eastern art collectors and gallery proprietors toward painters who were not from Paris or New York was understandable, but sometimes their reaction was extreme. Yet the characterization of some later art historians from the East to dismiss the regionalists as simple-minded artist examples of *Chicago Tribune* "isolationism" only reveals how little these writers understood life west of the Hudson.

Benton was at his best as a muralist, and he invented a technique of ingeniously overlapping his mural panels that was widely imitated. With the completion of his murals for the New School for Social Research in 1930, for the Whitney Museum of American Art in 1932, and for the Indiana State Building at the Chicago World's Fair of 1933 (now at Indiana University), Benton deservedly became the nation's best known muralist.

Grant Wood grew up in Cedar Rapids, Iowa, as an indigenous bohemian, and although small-city Iowa did not produce many bohemians, they were proud of Wood. He made several trips to Paris, and on returning from one of them was commissioned by a Cedar Rapids American Legion post to do a stained glass memorial window. With a fine disregard for the amenities, Wood went to Munich to do the work; but with its war memories still fresh, the post refused to accept a work done in Germany. Wood retaliated with his "Daughters of the American Revolution," a biting artistic satire. His best work was "American Gothic," a portrait of his sister and a friend in the yard of an Iowa farm in the style of the fifteenth-century German primitives.

Curry was born and grew up on a Kansas farm and as a young man studied at the Chicago Art Institute. He worked as an illustrator for pulp magazines before making the usual artist's trek to Paris and New York, but he did not feel at ease with the expatriates and the would-be expatriates of New York and returned to the region he knew and liked best. Curry painted such typical but dramatic midwestern rural events as baptisms, tornadoes, and

404

fighting boars. The violence in his subject matter frequently lent his work a power it would not have merited on strictly artistic values. He ended his career as artist in residence at the University of Wisconsin where he died in 1946.

Among the lesser known but able regional artists elsewhere were Paul Sample and Luigi Lucioni in New England and Peter Hurd, Maynard Dixon, and Alexandre Hogue in the Southwest. Southern regional painters could be either sentimentalists like Hobson Pittman or critical of the color line like Robert Gwathmey.

Primitivism in painting had a considerable vogue in the 1930's, perhaps because here modernists and America Singers had a common enthusiasm. The early German and French modernists had been interested in primitivism, and the America Singers believed that the work of the untrained painter most truly reflected the thought of the people. Primitivism also received an impetus from the WPA Federal Arts Project's Index of American Design, twenty thousand plates made by hundreds of artists to preserve earlier American designs in all kinds of materials and all subjects, from elaborately carved circus wagons to weather vanes. The search for genuine living primitives turned up a seventy-year-old former Pittsburgh housepainter and coal miner named John Kane, who had amused himself over the years by painting landscapes and pictures of picnics. Now the old man found himself the rage of the art world. Horace Pippin, a Negro from Philadelphia who had been wounded in the war and had turned to a crude kind of painting, originally on paper doilies, for something to do in his enforced leisure, became another idol. But Grandma Moses of Eagle Bridge, New York, became the all-time favorite primitive when she was discovered late in the period. She had a store of literally thousands of rural landscapes and genre scenes which were snapped up by New York City people with the same kind of adoring attitude toward rural primitives that had characterized the eighteenth-century French court when it dressed as simple peasant milkmaids and plowboys.

Several artists of major stature stood outside these two streams of protest and America Singers. One curious exception to the dominant art of the period was the haunted Ivan Le Lorraine Albright of Chicago, who painted what might be called psychological horror pictures. His "Room 203" featured a fat man with threadbare underwear and grotesquely rotten flesh undressing in a sordid hotel room. His "That Which I Should Have Done I Did Not Do," which took Albright ten years to finish, depicted a clearer-than-life rotting door with a funeral wreath. The son of a Chicago painter of sentimental portraits of children, Albright had been assigned during the war to paint pictures of soldiers' wounds because color photography was still in its infancy. The war experience left him with the belief that life is senseless and tragically frustrating.

Many of the modernists of the 1920's continued with their earlier experiments. Stuart Davis tried to make his painting evoke the same sensation as hot jazz. Georgia O'Keeffe did many cold and precise landscapes of the Southwest that prominently featured bleached cattle skulls and horns. Marsden Hartley reached his greatest powers in his Maine landscapes of the 1930's, and Max Weber gained greater intensity with his jewel-like encrusted colors. Several younger artists who became well known in the 1940's were already experimenting in abstraction. Worth special mention are Irene Rice Pereira and

Balcom Greene. Mark Tobey, who settled permanently in Seattle, Washington, in the late 1930's and who thereafter had a great influence on the young artists of the Northwest, had traveled in the Orient. The Far East affected his "white line" style, which was a kind of brush calligraphy.

Art photography, which became highly respected and popular in the 1930's, had counterparts of the modernist, social protest, and America Singer schools of painting. Ansel Adams and Edward Weston, who featured the rocks of the California coast and desert sands, turned their cameras upon interesting wind and water erosions that were close to abstractions. Paul Strand, an America Singer with a Leica, set a whole generation to scouring the country for weathered wood after he published his famous picture of a boarded up window in Red River, New Mexico. Margaret Bourke-White and the Farm Security Administration photographers, with their tragic portraits of share-croppers, were akin to the social protest painters.

Modernism in sculpture was generally more popular than it was in painting. Indeed, most of the exciting work of the period was modern. David Smith worked in sharp enameled steel. Hugo Robus and Isamu Noguchi created rounded and beautifully contoured abstractions in the Brancusi manner, and Alexander Calder started a craze with his light, free-swinging, metal "mobiles." Another sharp break with convention were Emma Lu Davis' "handies," small sculptures meant to give pleasure to the sense of touch rather than sight. Later, some sculptors would argue that a work must feel good to the hands when the eyes are closed to be good design. Carl Milles, who came from Stockholm in 1931 and remained for most of the decade, used conventional materials and was not abstract, but his stylized, elongated figures represented a departure from the idealized realism that dominated monumental sculpture.

Artists of all kinds were hard hit economically during the Great Depression, yet during the decade American society felt it had an economic responsibility to support artistic expression. The most vivid manifestation of this sense of responsibility was the WPA's Art Project. But the artists often shocked and outraged the rather conventional people who held the strings to the money bags, and Congress, after a philistine discussion that did its members no credit, all but killed off the WPA cultural activities in June, 1939. Time and again economic and cultural conservatives objected to the work of a WPA muralist in the local post office or high school. Murals, which were popular during the 1930's, perhaps aroused the great reaction since they were painted in places where they attracted the attention of people who would never go to a gallery or a museum. The Mexican muralists, left-wingers politically and innovators artistically, came in for the lion's share of abuse. When José Orozco did a mural at Dartmouth College, the alumni protested vigorously, and when Diego Rivera was commissioned to do murals for the Detroit Institute of Arts, local patriots of the type Wood had lampooned protested that the Institute had "sold out to an outside, half-breed Mexican Bolshevist." Perhaps the most famous incident occurred when Rivera was fired from his commission at Rockefeller Center. When someone discovered that he had put a head of Lenin into his "Man at the Crossroads of Life," the owners of the real estate pulled the artist down from his scaffold, paid him his fee, and covered the offending head with canvas. They later had the mural destroyed.

The audience for art surely became broader because of the muralists and their controversies and because of the many WPA art classes. The audience also was enlarged by two new and important New York museums. The Museum of Modern Art, established by seven wealthy art collectors, opened in 1929. Perhaps no other institution in the nation has been so influential in shaping American taste in painting as the Modern, both by its exhibitions and its extensive reprint and publication programs. In 1930, the Whitney Museum of American Art became the first major museum to feature art of the United States exclusively.

Functionalism and modernism in architecture came strongly to the fore during the 1930's, particularly in large public buildings but to a lesser extent in homes of moderate size and expense. Wright did his magnificent Johnson Wax Company building at Racine, Wisconsin, during the decade. Perhaps no other building ever brought its designer and its owner greater publicity. The Bauhaus gave up on Hitler's Germany in 1934 and closed its doors. Walter Gropius and Marcel Breurer moved to Massachusetts, and Richard J. Neutra settled in California. A few venturesome families built homes in the "international style" for themselves, clean lined and rather austere boxes that had already found favor here and there in Germany and Scandinavia. Scandinavian architects and city planners had quite an influence in the United States. The "Greenbelt" communities of the Farm Security Administration were a modification of the new small Swedish factory towns, and Williamsburg Houses, an island in the Brooklyn slums, were similar to new Scandinavian apartment buildings in their emphasis on light and air.

Music

Perhaps only because music is a medium which does not permit as precise an expression of ideas as the written word or even painting, musicians in the 1930's did not put into their art the degree of social unrest and criticism that marked literature and the plastic arts. Musical theater did sometimes, as in *Pins and Needles* and Marc Blitzstein's 1937 opera *The Cradle Will Rock* which was about the labor movement. The outstanding current in American music during the depression years, however, was the kind of cultural nationalism that characterized the writers and artists who have in this chapter been called the America Singers. Musical independence from Europe—although not necessarily hostility toward the European tradition—and effort to stimulate a native musical tradition were the keynotes. Emphasis upon things American was by no means entirely new in the 1930's; the emphasis was only greater and broader than it had previously been.

The composer Roy Harris, himself from an Oklahoma farm, summarized well the thinking of many American men of music:

Music reflects the humanistic climate out of which it arises. Music communicates the spirit of generations, nations, centuries, always migrating to the social fermentation in which it thrives. . . . Native music is no more a dead art today than we ourselves are dead people. And American music is in a provident spot. We have been developing in the historical cycle development in which all national cultures matured. We have passed through the initial period of musical culture: that of importing our musicians and our music. We have fulfilled the second period: that of developing our own musicians, who are able in interpreting the music of other nations. We have already entered the third period, wherein the quantity and quality of our musicians and our audiences are ready for a new native music, conceived in the mood and tempo of our time.[1]

Harris may have been over-optimistic, especially about the quality of the audiences, but certainly the activities of many composers indicated that he was not entirely wrong. Harris himself during the thirties wrote four symphonies, and for *Song for Occupations* (1934) he worked the rich mine of folk tunes. Howard Hanson of the Eastman School of Music turned to seventeenth-century New England for his inspiration in *Merry Mount*, produced by the Metropolitan Opera Company in 1934. Another opera drawing on the American past was *The Devil and Daniel Webster,* the result of the collaboration of composer Douglas Moore and poet Stephen Vincent Benét in 1939. Aaron Copland, soon to become the country's best-known composer, came as close to social criticism as is possible with instrumental music when he contributed the score to the documentary film *The City* (1938), a striking plea for city planning and architectural vision written by Lewis Mumford.

Easily the best-known native opera of the thirties was George Gershwin's operatic version of Du Bose Heyward's play about Negroes of Charleston's Catfish Row, *Porgy and Bess.* It was an instant hit when it appeared in 1935, two years before the composer's death, and its simple and strong melodies, capable of being hummed, soon were frequently heard on the radio. "Summertime," especially, came to be well known as dance orchestras added it to their books. Some who regarded themselves as serious music listeners were perplexed by *Porgy and Bess* and its reception. An American music, they said, should come from the people and Americans generally should participate in it. Gershwin's opera met those criteria. But Gershwin was a graduate of Tin Pan Alley, although an unusual one, and he wrote in the idiom of American popular music. Was he just a talented but pretentious routine songwriter, or was he an important harbinger of the new American music? Older conceptions of what constituted highbrow, middlebrow, and lowbrow confused matters.

One of the major aspects of the emphasis on musical nationalism was an unusual interest in folk music. Folk music can be divided into two categories: rural folk songs—mountain ballads, cowboy songs, slave work chants, and so forth—and urban folk music, which is primarily jazz. The interest paralleled the movement in primitive art, although much jazz was anything but primitive. Alan Lomax published volumes of the rural folk songs he had gathered on expeditions to backwaters of formal culture. Carl Sandburg, newspaperman, poet, and biographer, displayed his versatility by editing *The American Songbag* and singing for audiences some of the folk songs to his own guitar accompaniment. The WPA's Federal Music Project, begun in 1935 to provide help for 15,000 depression-struck musicians, collected and

---

[1] Personal communication from Dr. Roy E. Harris to author, February, 1963.

phonographically recorded folk music in all parts of the nation. The more dedicated jazz fans, professional and amateur, scoured through second-hand stores in search of early jazz records, and a few jazz historians took recording equipment into remote places to get facsimiles of the music of old and obscure jazz musicians before they died. The sales statistics of jazz records attested to its growing popularity, and the presence of bands like Benny Goodman's in Carnegie Hall indicated its growing respectability.

The number of people in the United States who had a rather active interest in music, either folk music of some kind or more formal music, apparently grew during the 1930's. As pointed out in the previous chapter, radio audiences for symphonies and opera became steadily larger. The technical quality of phonograph recording improved considerably over what it had been in the 1920's, and electrically powered players with automatic record changers made listening to records less of an up-and-down nuisance than it had been. Sales of records grew as the economy slowly climbed. Early in the depression, music education was one of the first "frills" to be cut from the curriculum of many schools, but when it revived it did so with force. High school bands may not have been paragons of musical virtue, but they did teach young people a little about music and widened interest in it. Music teachers in the schools increasingly tried to teach "music appreciation," frequently with the aid of special educational radio programs. How much permanent effect, if any, the Federal Music Project had is difficult to say, but it did make a serious effort to bring live music to the people. More than one hundred million people attended its programs, which featured music by American composers far more than did regular music groups. If millions of Americans still lived in a musical void except for the simplest rhythms and melodies from their radios, the 1930's laid the foundation for the great upsurge of interest in music that came after the war.

Science and Scholarship

Although universities were forced to restrict their budgets and philanthropic foundations had less money for subsidies, researchers in the 1930's made some important basic discoveries in the pure sciences. Perhaps the work that had the greatest implications for the future was in the new field of nuclear physics. The new discoveries were based on the earlier work of, among others, Albert Einstein, who during the decade joined the new Institute for Advanced Study at Princeton, New Jersey. Very few laymen had better than a hazy idea of what nuclear physics was all about, largely because nothing in the Newtonian physics they had studied in school prepared them for it. They slowly came to realize from popularized accounts of the researches of Harold C. Urey and Enrico Fermi of Columbia University, Ernest O. Lawrence of the University of California, and Carl D. Anderson of California Institute of Technology that by "smashing" the atom a force of undreamed of power could be released. When people thought of harnessing the energy in atoms they usually thought of its peaceful applications and the social implications the widespread use of such energy would have. In 1939, word came from militarist and expansionist Germany that scientists there had successfully split the uranium nucleus, and Professor Einstein advised the President of the possible military uses of nuclear energy if a chain reaction could be achieved. Roosevelt appointed a committee of scientists to study the matter. Then, in the summer of 1940, government offiicials imposed strict censorship over information about nuclear fission, and only a relatively few scientists and a few readers of science fiction thought further about the subject until the summer of 1945.

Nuclear physics, with its assumption of probabilities rather than absolutes and its, to most people, mysterious transmutation of one radioactive element into another, created an attitude of uncertainty about the workings of nature and the universe. So did some of the new discoveries in astronomy. Edwin P. Hubble of the Mount Wilson Observatory made observations which indicated that the universe was much larger than previously had been supposed. He photographed galaxies outside the Milky Way (of which the earth was an infinitesimal part), galaxies which he estimated were five million light-years away. Man and his world seemed less important than ever in the total order of things. Astronomers also questioned whether the universe was a static and finite entity, as had always been assumed. It might be, they said, that the universe was constantly expanding. Laymen were bewildered and troubled by the metaphysical implications of the new discoveries in the microcosm and the macrocosm, of dynamic atoms and a possibly expanding universe. Was nothing absolute? Was nothing immutably true? The questions deeply disturbed most people who thought about them. If any group of philosophers could find solace in the new science, or, to use the phrase of the humanist philosopher Max Otto, found "man's hunger for cosmic support" comforting in the new circumstances, it was the relativists. In actuality, the relativist point of view gained favor, especially in the social sciences.

Biological scientists made discoveries about life that were almost as disturbing to the layman as the new work in physics and astronomy. Geneticists announced experiments and theories quite at odds with the established principles of the textbooks. Richard B. Goldschmidt, another refugee gift to American culture from Nazi totalitarianism, concluded that biological mutations might be greater than had been thought earlier, that under certain circumtances there might be a transition from one species to another very quickly. Hermann J. Muller's experiments in exposing fruit flies to radiation indicated that radiation hastened mutation frequency 150 times, thereby causing drastic changes of traits within a few generations. On the borderland between physiology and psychology, researchers learned there was a relationship between the brain's electric waves and some mental illness, that the introduction of malaria into the bloodstream improved the balance of some victims of mental disease, and that insulin and other shock treatment brought improvement and sometimes cure to the unfortunate who had dementia praecox.

The humanities and the social sciences were much affected by the relativism that flowed from the new science and also reflected the twin cultural depression currents of social realism and renewed interest in America. One of the intellectual vogues of the thirties was the new field of semantics, which influenced writers in many of the humanities and social sciences and was in turn under the influence of scientific relativism. The basic idea in semantics

—that words are symbols without absolute, unvarying meaning and that the perception of these symbols is relative to their context and other associations—was not an entirely new one by any means. But to many people who read such popularizations of semantics as Stuart Chase's *The Tyranny of Words* and the writings of S. I. Hayakawa the concept was new, exciting, and useful. Soon writers in several fields used a semantic concept in one way or another. Historians to a greater extent, for example, pointed out that the religious framework of much of the writing of seventeenth-century New England took on a new and important meaning when it was understood in its political context. Thurman Arnold applied semantics to government and economics with interesting and sometimes amusing results in *The Symbols of Government* and *The Folklore of Capitalism*. Related to semantics was a considerable interest in propaganda analysis.

Philosophers, generally considered the most cloistered of academicians perhaps because most of them had long maintained their discipline was above the clash of ordinary passions and events, came out of their library cells and entered debates on the issues of the day as they had never before done. The instrumentalist John Dewey, the nation's most eminent philosopher, was particularly active. He was the prime mover of the social democratic League for Independent Political Action, a staunch champion of civil liberty, and a leader in an investigation of Stalin's purges and trials in the mid-1930's that roundly condemned the Communists.

An increased academic concern with American literature reflected both a trace of America Singing and, in the commonest approach to American literature, a degree of social criticism. Professor Parrington's monumental work had appeared in the 1920's, and in the next decade his approach to the study of the nation's literature dominated the profession. The emphasis was upon the context of literature, upon regarding literary works as documents of social history rather than the traditional emphasis on esthetics. Being now interested in an author's social values, literary scholars perhaps inevitably revealed their own, and in most cases they were critical of the *status quo* and traditionalism. The elitist New Humanism of Paul Elmer More and Irving Babbitt had little appeal for the depression generation of literary scholars.

The charge against social scientists of being in an ivory tower, never fully valid, had a hollow ring during the depression years. The New Deal called many such specialists from the campus to Washington, some for important assignments, some for relatively slight duties. Many were active in political parties, wrote for political magazines, and selected subjects for their professional research that had relevance to the social issues of the day. The effects of the professors on politics were not easily discerned, although the Roosevelt haters heaped abuse upon them as "braintrusters" and "visionaries who never met a payroll." Some undoubtedly were naive in practical politics, and some undoubtedly were more than necessarily sordid in an effort to appear practical men, but the same might be applied to other politicos as well. Certainly, the special technical competence of the social scientists improved the information available to policy makers when they made decisions.

Economics was a particularly fertile field during the decade. A Rip Van Winkle economist who went to sleep in the summer of 1929 would hardly have recognized his specialty had he awakened in 1941. Economists enjoyed a special prestige if they were not one of the unfortunate few who had made notoriously bad public predictions about prosperity. Some laymen, of course, thought that economics was a special division of astrology and agreed with Edward Bellamy, himself a kind of economist, who called them "soothsayers learned in dark sayings" and tools of capitalists. But most people recognized that economic troubles were the main problem facing America, and the writings of economists gained an unprecedented audience.

Economists would surely disagree about what were the major tendencies and accomplishments of their discipline during the depression, but a few landmarks were obvious. The historical school of economics produced some major works, for example the completion of *History of Labour in the United States* by John R. Commons and his colleagues at the University of Wisconsin and Joseph Dorfman's biography of Thorstein Veblen. A major contribution to macroeconomics was the three volumes by the Brookings Institution of Washington: *America's Capacity to Produce*, which indicated that even in 1929 the nation's productive facilities operated at only about four-fifths of capacity; *America's Capacity to Consume*, which showed that inequitable distribution of income rather than saturation of needs was the reason the productive plant did not operate to capacity; and *The Formation of Capital*, which concluded that the major share of savings in the late 1920's had not gone into new productive facilities but into the bull market. Perhaps the biggest new development in economics was the interest shown in the "compensatory economics" of John Maynard Keynes.

Political scientists turned away from the formal structure of government and political parties to consider increasingly what might be called the economics of politics. They concentrated upon economic pressure groups which "lobbied" legislative and executive officers to achieve their economic ends, and in their studies of constitutional history put a new emphasis upon economic forces. A title by Harold D. Lasswell of the University of Chicago well illustrated a primary concern of scholars of government: *Politics, Who Gets What, When, How* (1936). Both political scientists and sociologists moved into the field of measuring public opinion and by better sampling techniques, more careful phrasing of questions, and statistical inference considerably refined the opinion poll compared to such statistical crudities as that operated by *The Literary Digest*.

Sociologists specialized during the decade as they had never before, and broke down their field into several distinct categories. They also tended to put their emphasis upon discovering and reporting sociological facts and shunned interpretation. Some of the most interesting studies were dissections of community societies, and the most widely known of these was done by Columbia's Robert and Helen Lynd, a sequel to their earlier analysis of Muncie, Indiana, entitled *Middletown in Transition*. Perhaps the most ambitious sociological research project of the period was an extensive study of the Negro in the United States, financed by the Carnegie Corporation, undertaken in 1938 by a whole phalanx of sociologists and anthropologists under the direction of the eminent Swedish sociologist and economist Gunnar Myrdal. The main report of the study appeared in two volumes in 1944 under the title *An American Dilemma*. Among the best-known studies by anthropologists were the researches into race conducted by Professor Franz Boas and his colleagues at Columbia University, which indicated that cultural differences among races were not so great as commonly thought and were definitely not biological in origin. If these research conclusions had little impact on the racial attitudes of ordinary laymen, they became generally known among intellectuals and began to spread out from them to Americans of less education.

Historians, standing between the humanities and the social sciences and embracing both of them, reflected the decade's main intellectual currents. The numbers of historians who considered themselves relativists increased. Most relativist historians by no means abandoned their purpose to write history objectively; they only held they must recognize that their environments conditioned the way they saw the past. "Each generation rewrites history." Related to relativism was the historians' tendency to study those aspects of the past that had a special relevance for the present, to search in the past for policy guidelines for their own era. Thus, for example, the frontier thesis of Frederick Jackson Turner, especially its "safety valve" aspect because of its relevance to the depression's labor upheaval, was subjected to scrutiny and revision, and the South, the nation's poorest region, increasingly became the object of historical research. The degree of objectivity in the works of historians who considered themselves relativists varied considerably, as it did in the writings of those who believed it humanly possible to write history "as it actually had been," the goal of the "scientific" historians of nineteenth-century Germany.

Some historians had long held that all aspects of man's past, not only his political and economic activities, were proper subjects for their study; in the 1930's this view of the scope of history, both for those who specialized in the American past and for those whose interest was in other parts of the world, gained wide favor although not quite universal approval. Before the 1930's history textbooks rarely considered subjects such as those treated in this chapter. What was commonly termed social-intellectual history became increasingly general, and although some of it was made of rather flimsy stuff part of it was substantial indeed. Most of the volumes in the *History of American Life* series, edited by Professor Arthur M. Schlesinger of Harvard and Dixon Ryan Fox, president of Union College, appeared between the crash and the war. The first of the volumes by Professor Carl Bridenbaugh, now of Brown University, on the cultural history of the American colonies appeared in the 1930's, and 1940 saw the publication of Yale Professor Ralph Gabriel's *The Course of American Democratic Thought*. In 1943 Professor Merle Curti published his *The Growth of American Thought*, which won the Pulitzer prize for history of that year and was the first modern comprehensive account of the subject.

CHAPTER TWENTY-ONE

Depression Diplomacy, 1929-1938

THE GREAT DEPRESSION ULTIMATELY HAD TO AFFECT AMERICA'S relations with other countries. The central fact of the depression was in either the foreground or the background of developments in American foreign policy from 1930 until Pearl Harbor.

Economic conditions forced both Hoover and Roosevelt to make modifications in the nation's foreign economic policies, although neither departed seriously from traditional objectives. Hoover faced a direct effect of the depression in the crisis over European reparations and war-debt payments. The depression indirectly was a factor in the Japanese Manchurian crisis confronting Hoover since Japan had decided to take a militarist course partly because of economic disruption. Roosevelt faced the problem during his first months in office of whether to combat the depression through international cooperation or through national policies at odds with the desires of other nations. His reciprocal trade program was a frontal attack upon the depression, his recognition of the Soviet Union had economic motives, and his headaches over German and Italian militarism and expansion were due, ultimately, to the depression's effects in Europe.

America's Foreign Economic Policies

During the 1920's there had evolved an irrational but, in the short run, workable scheme of loans, reparations, and war debts. American investors, through Wall Street bankers, lent money to Germany which enabled that country to pay its reparations to the Allies and which in turn enabled the Allies to keep up payments on their war debts to the United States Treasury (see pp. 241–245). The Wall Street crash brought the circular financial complex to an abrupt halt. As the flow of American loans to Germany dried up, the stoppage of reparations and war debt payments was only a matter of time. If the American tariff wall had been lowered, thereby stimulating European imports and building up dollar exchange funds in Europe, payment of war debts might have continued. However, Congress raised the tariff with the Hawley-Smoot Act in June, 1930.

The international financial crisis came to a head in the spring of 1931. In March, Germany and Austria announced their intention to form a customs union. France denounced the proposal as the first step toward union of the two countries which the peace treaties forbade, and eventually the World Court ruled against such a customs arrangement. French bankers recalled millions in short-term loans to German and Austrian banks which were thereby placed on the brink of ruin. In May, the largest bank of Austria, the Kreditanstalt, announced its imminent failure, and it was saved only by the actions of the Austrian government. A large bank of North Germany did go under due to the strain. Far more was involved than the failure or saving of just a bank. If a major financial institution such as the Kreditanstalt closed its doors, foreign holders of assets in Kreditanstalt would have to compensate for their loss by calling back other funds, thereby jeopardizing the whole economic and political stability of Central Europe.

President Hoover made a startling proposal on June 20. Congress was not then in session, but after consulting with congressional leaders from both parties, Hoover proposed a one-year moratorium, or postponement, in the payment of international obligations. Subject to the approval of Congress, Hoover announced that the United States would not demand payments on war debts for a year beginning July 1, 1931, if other governments would do the same. Hoover's hope was that in a year free of reparations commitments Germany and Austria could overcome the financial crisis. The European nations agreed, although France resisted for three weeks and thereby worsened the German situation.

When Congress convened late in 1931, Hoover submitted the moratorium for approval and urged the re-establishment of the World War Foreign Debt Commission with authority to negotiate further on foreign debts. Congress approved the moratorium but balked at any step that might further reduce the war debts. So far as Congress was concerned, the United States would expect to receive full payment on the next due date after the end of the moratorium, December, 1932.

Hoping for a long-term settlement, Germany and her creditors met at Lausanne, Switzerland, in June and July, 1932, and reached an agreement by which about 90 per cent of the remaining German reparations bill would be cancelled if the former Allies could get corresponding relief from their creditors. In other words, since the United States was the creditor at the ultimate end of the line, ratification of the Lausanne agreement was contingent upon American cooperation. But Congress was in no mood to change its position. After the 1932 election, Hoover vainly pleaded with Roosevelt to use his influence with Congress. When he got no results, Hoover sent the debtor nations notices of payments due December 15, 1932. Most of the debtors met this payment, but except for some subsequent token payments these were the last payments on the war debt. (Finland was a special exception. She had an export surplus to the United States and was able to continue paying her small obligation.) In April, 1934, Congress passed a law sponsored by Senator Hiram Johnson of California designed to punish debtor governments in default. The Johnson Act made it illegal to sell within the United States the bonds or other securities of foreign governments, or their subdivisions, which were in default on debts owed to the American federal government. The measure did not stimulate any further payments from depressed Europe. The Attorney-General later ruled that token payments did not prevent a country's being considered in default under the terms of the Johnson Act; thereafter, even token payments stopped.

Despite Roosevelt's failure to act on Hoover's urging to persuade Congress to accept war debt reductions—motivated probably by political considerations—and despite his "bombshell message" to the World Economic Conference at London in June, 1933 (see pp. 327–328), Roosevelt clearly, at least from late 1933, considered the revival of foreign trade as a direct assault on the depression. In seeking to stimulate American exports and to find foreign markets for American goods as a means of getting the domestic economy on its feet again, Roosevelt was operating within a tradition at least as old as the depression of the 1890's. In 1895, a group of industrialists had organized the National Association of Manufacturers, and the original purpose of the NAM had been to stimulate exports and thereby ease the economic difficulties within the nation that came from the panic of 1893. The search for foreign markets and investments had played a major role in the American decision to embark upon a colonial imperialist role later in the decade. Exports of munitions to the Allies after the outbreak of war in Europe had lifted another depression, and the Webb-Pomerene Act had been designed to give American industrialists a competitive position in foreign markets by exempting their overseas operations from the antitrust laws. Oddly enough, one of the Roosevelt administration's first efforts to stimulate exports involved recognition of the Soviet Union, since 1917 a prize exhibit in American conservatives' chamber of horrors.

It was a painful fact in the early depression that the Soviet economy continued to grow while the western economy sagged. In the fall of 1932, about one hundred thousand Americans applied for jobs in Russia through Amtorg, the Russian foreign trading organization. Hoover was fully committed to continue the nonrecognition policy toward Russia, but he did yield a little when the Reconstruction Finance Corporation underwrote some cotton exports to the USSR. Roosevelt had not committed himself to nonrecognition, and businessmen from both parties put considerable pressure on the State Department to recognize the Soviet Union so that exports to that country would be facilitated. There were other considerations in Roosevelt's mind besides a foreign market (the logic of recognizing a government of sixteen years' standing, for example, and a hope that recognition might hamper Japan in Manchuria), and he began a correspondence with Soviet leaders looking toward formal recognition. The Soviet government agreed to refrain from spreading propaganda designed to overthrow the United States government, to grant religious freedom and protection in its courts to American nationals living in Russia, and to negotiate the question of unpaid prerevolutionary debts and claims. The United States recognized Russia on November 16, 1933; the Soviet Union's first ambassador to Washington was Maxim Litvinov, hardly a typical Russian leader of the 1930's in that he was Jewish and well acquainted with the western world. The negotiations on debts and claims came to nothing. Nor did Russian-inspired Communist propaganda cease, although technically the Russians could truthfully say that the American Communist party had its affiliation with the Third International, or Comintern, rather than directly with the Soviet government. Actually, the distinction was not real: the Comintern was a willing tool of the Russian government. Nor did the fond hopes of American businessmen to send large orders to the Soviet materialize in any significant way.

The Export-Import Bank, a government agency that later played an important role in American foreign economic policy, developed directly from the hope to sell to the newly recognized Soviet government. American business firms hoping to export or make investments abroad sometimes found that private bankers considered the risks too great to undertake the financing. Such was the case with many proposed deals with the Russians. Roosevelt established the first Export-Import Bank under National Industrial Recovery Act authority early in 1934 to finance exports to the USSR. Its original funds came from the Reconstruction Finance Corporation. When the negotiations with the Russians over the debt fell through, the first Export-Import Bank became inactive. Early in 1935, Congress set up "Ex-Im" on a two-year basis, renewing its life each biennium until it made the Bank a permanent independent agency in 1945. By 1938 the Bank began to make development loans to underdeveloped nations. A $5 million loan to Haiti in that year went for improved roads, agricultural experiment stations, and drainage facilities. A $25 million loan to China for the Burma Road, from Chungking to Burma, strategically important in World War II, strengthened China's position against the Japanese. Besides the obvious benefits to the countries involved—helping them to create the capital prerequisite for a more advanced economy—these loans helped to create new foreign markets for American products. Thus "Ex-Im" gradually changed from underwriting of exports to already existing markets to active creation of foreign markets in economically backward areas.

Secretary of State Cordell Hull's reciprocal trade agreement program was another facet of the New Deal's assault on the depression by stimulating foreign trade. Indeed, the purpose of the June, 1934, law as stated in its preamble was "expanding foreign markets for the products of the United States (as a means of assisting in the present emergency . . .)." The idea of reciprocity was an old one, and Hull, a traditional low-tariff southerner, pushed the idea vigorously when he took the State Department's direction. He had hoped that reciprocal trade agreements would come from the fruitless London Economic Conference in 1933. Hull saw reciprocity as a precondition to world peace. Commercial rivalry, as he viewed it, jeopardized peaceful international relations, and reciprocity would reduce commercial rivalry.

The Reciprocal Trade Agreements Act of 1934 empowered the executive branch for a period of three years to negotiate agreements with other countries to change by as much as one-half the existing American duties on imports in exchange for reciprocal concessions by the other nation on its duties on

417

American products. Such agreements did not need Senate ratification to become effective. The law further directed that such agreements contain a "most favored nation" clause. That is to say, if an agreement with Venezuela reduced United States duties on certain imports, the United States would be obligated to reduce its duties on those same commodities imported from any other country that did not discriminate against American trade. Venezuela would have the same obligation. Thus, for the commodities included in reciprocal trade agreements, there developed a wide tendency toward lower tariffs. Congress has extended executive authority to conclude such agreements by two- and three-year periods since 1934.

By the spring of 1939, the State Department had negotiated twenty-one reciprocal trade agreements, not only with Latin American nations and Canada, but with the more important non-Fascist West European nations as well. The precise effect of these agreements on trade and the business cycle was impossible to determine since there were several other variables affecting international trade, but it was clear that until the recession of late 1937 and 1938 American exports increased more rapidly than the total exports of all nations. The United States increased its relative share in world markets. This was because every trade agreement concluded affected America's important exports while few agreements affected the important exports of other countries. The share of American imports from agreement countries increased more rapidly than those from nonagreement countries, and the Latin American economies became more closely tied with the United States.

"Yanquis" as "Good Neighbors"

Roosevelt in his first inaugural address said, "In the field of world policy I would dedicate this Nation to the policy of the good neighbor—the neighbor who resolutely respects himself and, because he does so, respects the rights of others." From this vague, even meaningless, statement about foreign relations in general came the label used to describe the New Deal's extension of the better manners in Latin American matters instituted during the 1920's.

The Seventh International Conference of American States was to meet at Montevideo, Uruguay, in December, 1933. Latin American nations were eager to get through the conference a resolution condemning intervention by one country into the affairs of another, a proposal aimed particularly against the United States. In 1930, the State Department had published the Clark memorandum which denied that the Monroe Doctrine could be used as justification for American intervention, but at the last conference, in 1928, Charles Evans Hughes as head of the United States delegation had refused to allow a nonintervention resolution even to be discussed. The United States had by no means renounced intervention as a Latin American policy.

Secretary Hull, head of the American delegation to the Montevideo conference, surprised the Latin American delegations and fully accepted the nonintervention position. The conference went on to write a Convention on the Rights and Duties of States that included the statement, "No state has the right to intervene in the internal or external affairs of another." The United

States signed the convention. Two days later, the President in a speech at home said, ". . . the definite policy of the United States from now on is one opposed to armed intervention." In December, 1936, at a special Latin American conference at Buenos Aires, Argentina (a meeting initiated in Washington which the President himself attended), Hull signed a protocol which forbade intervention "directly or indirectly, and for whatever reason." The Senate approved the protocol without reservation and without even a record vote. Nonintervention was the essence of the Good Neighbor policy, but another aspect of it was increased trade between the northern Colossus and the Latin nations. Hull at Montevideo helped to prepare the way for the yet-to-be-authorized reciprocal trade agreements by getting a resolution through the convention calling for lower trade barriers.

Simultaneously with its renunciations of intervention, the administration moved to make the Monroe Doctrine multilateral. Enunciated by President James Monroe in 1823, the Doctrine had declared the United States opposed further European colonization in the New World and further European "interposition" into the affairs of American nations. The United States had invoked the Monroe Doctrine upon several occasions. But it had been a unilateral policy of Washington alone. Now, after 1935, when Mussolini's Italy and Hitler's Germany threatened the peace of the world, the United States sought to commit all of Latin America to the Monroe Doctrine's principles.

It was in pursuit of this intention that the administration initiated in 1935 the calling of the Buenos Aires conference. No conference was scheduled until 1938. At the conference the delegates signed documents that called upon Latin American nations to consult one another in situations that formerly would have brought the United States to invoke the Monroe Doctrine unilaterally. Consultation in the face of any threat from outside America to the peace and independence of an American state did not necessarily mean that action would follow, but the step was clearly in the direction of "continentalizing" the old Doctrine.

The Buenos Aires documents did not stipulate just how consultation should be done. At the next regularly scheduled international Conference of American States at Lima, Peru, in December, 1938, the delegates agreed that the foreign ministers of any of the twenty-one American states could call a meeting to consider methods of meeting any outside threat. The American states did in fact meet under this plan: at Panama just after the outbreak of war in Europe in the fall of 1939; at Havana, Cuba, in the summer of 1940 after the fall of France; and at Rio de Janeiro, Brazil, in January, 1942, after Pearl Harbor. All of the Latin American powers followed the United States into World War II, although some followed late and reluctantly. The Good Neighbor policy, in effect, paid off in a time of crisis.

The United States, with but one partial exception in the case of Cuba, observed well the nonintervention policy it had adopted. Most of the Cuban partial exception occurred before the Montevideo conference. Cuba's president, Gerardo Machado, led a tyrannical government over that politically unhappy island when Roosevelt took office. Machado had suppressed a rebellion in 1931 and was still using dictatorial powers in a futile effort to stamp out his opposition. Roosevelt's intervention was diplomatic rather than military, although parts of the fleet did go to Cuba for the announced purpose of being ready to evacuate United States citizens if necessary. The proximity of naval power unquestionably lent weight to the statements of Sumner Welles, the Foreign Service officer who had recently been appointed ambassador to Cuba and whose ostensible mission was to mediate between Machado and his opponents. Welles's real mission was to get Machado to resign. This Welles accomplished in the summer of 1933 with the support of some Cuban army officers. For the rest of the year, the United States helped select the next Cuban president by withholding recognition from those of whom it did not approve. In January, 1934, Carlos Mendieta became president of Cuba with the blessing of the United States, and thereafter intervention ceased. Four months later the United States and Cuba negotiated a new treaty which abrogated the Platt Amendment of 1903. In other words, the United States renounced its treaty right to intervene in Cuban affairs and to supervise Cuban finances. The Senate ratified the treaty without a dissenting vote only two days after it was signed. The American naval base at Guantanamo Bay was to remain until the right to maintain it was withdrawn by mutual action.

The United States pulled back elsewhere in the Caribbean during the Roosevelt years. FDR inherited a problem in Haiti from the Hoover administration. Hoover had sent an investigating commission to Haiti in 1930 when internal difficulties flared up there. The commission recommended new elections, and Haiti held its first elections since World War I. Americans relinquished control of Haitian public works to the islanders. A treaty in the fall of 1932 provided for withdrawing American marines and relinquishing control of the Haitian constabulary but for continuation of United States control of Haiti's finances until its American-held bonds were paid off. The Haitian legislature rejected the treaty, objecting to United States financial control. Roosevelt in the summer of 1933 reached an executive agreement with Haiti. The constabulary was to be controlled entirely by Haitians after October 1, 1934, and the marines were to be withdrawn within a month thereafter. Through an American-appointed "fiscal representative," United States control over the customs was to remain, although less obviously, until the bonds were satisfied. Roosevelt in fact withdrew the marines in the summer of 1934, the first time in decades that American marines were not stationed somewhere within the boundaries of a nominally sovereign Caribbean state. In 1941, the United States government withdrew the "fiscal representative." In 1940, a treaty with the Dominican Republic, at the other end of Santo Domingo, relinquished American control of Dominican customs but imposed a lien on the little state's general revenues until its bonds were discharged. An American remained as collector of the customs in Nicaragua until its American loans were repaid in 1944.

It was Mexico far more than any other Latin American nation that put the Good Neighbor policy to the test. More dollars were involved in the Mexican crisis than elsewhere in the Caribbean. The Mexican revolution progressed in a series of waves, each of them demanding foreign withdrawal from Mexican oil fields and other resources and then subsiding. A wave had subsided in 1927 and 1928 when the clever Dwight Morrow had been the American ambassador. Another wave began to build in 1934 with the election of Lázaro Cárdenas to the Mexican presidency. It came to a crest in early 1938.

Cárdenas accelerated the expropriation (taking national possession with compensation) of foreign-owned agricultural lands and led in the organization of a single large union of Mexican oil company employees. The oil workers' union presented the companies, both American and British, with extensive demands that infringed conventional management prerogatives. The oil companies rejected them. A Mexican arbitration board found the demands just and ordered the oil companies to accept them. Again the companies refused. On March 18, 1938, Cárdenas expropriated the property of foreign oil companies within Mexico. Simultaneously, the anticlericalism of the Mexican revolution aroused intense opposition to the Cárdenas government among Roman Catholics north of the border.

The British broke diplomatic relations with Mexico and did not reach a settlement on compensation of their oil companies' claims until after World War II. The United States, despite the touchy political situation created by American Catholic opposition, lived up to its good-neighbor declarations. Roosevelt's smooth politicking (he even arranged to have his letters in reply to outraged Catholic leaders written for him by a priest); the folksy shrewdness of the American ambassador in Mexico City, Roosevelt's old boss in the Navy Department, Josephus Daniels; and the administration's firmness with the American oil companies saved the Good Neighbor policy.

The American oil companies conducted their own negotiations with the Mexican government. They claimed $260 million in compensation. This the Mexican government rejected, although it did come to terms with the Sinclair Oil Company. The oil companies hoped that the next Mexican president, to be elected in 1940, would be less demanding and were disappointed with the election of Manuel Avila Camacho. Both Cárdenas and Camacho were vigorously anti-Nazi and eager to make some arrangement with the United States before the Western Hemisphere might become embroiled in war with Hitler, but neither would back down on expropriation.

Mexico and the United States signed an agreement on November 19, 1941. The United States agreed to continue purchasing Mexican silver at the world price, to extend Mexico credits through the Export-Import Bank, and to negotiate a reciprocal trade agreement. Mexico agreed to pay $40 million for all American claims exclusive of oil claims. The oil claims were referred to two commissioners, one from each country. The commissioners set the total of the claims at $24 million, payable over several years. Mexico completed the payments in 1949. The United States oil companies protested that they should receive more, but the administration refused to support them further.

Latin Americans had a special interest in United States treatment of its Spanish populations in its colonial empire, Puerto Rico and the Philippines. Under the New Deal, the Washington-appointed governors of Puerto Rico made an effort to diversify the economy, to make it less dependent upon sugar. Public works with Washington's financial support both relieved hardship on the island and provided some of the prerequisites for the development of industry. Illiteracy (over 77 per cent in 1898) also handicapped economic growth, and Puerto Ricans put a special emphasis upon elementary education. Their results were gratifying but less than fully satisfactory: illiteracy in 1940 was still 31.5 per cent. The governorship of Rexford Tugwell from 1941 to 1946 brought the island's difficulties to the attention of citizens of the mainland even more. In 1948, Puerto Rico for the first time was permitted to elect its own governor.

The progress of the Philippine Islands toward independence was a confusing one, complicated by Filipino hesitation to be outside American tariff barriers and by United States naval strategic considerations in the western Pacific. In 1932, Congress passed the Hawes-Cutting Act granting the Philippines independence in 1945 with a transitional period until then. Hoover vetoed the measure, and Congress overrode the veto. Manuel Quezon, leader of the Filipino Nationalists, opposed the law because it left American naval bases in the islands and put Filipino products outside the American tariff system. The Philippine legislature rejected the law. There matters stood when FDR became president. In 1934, Congress passed and Roosevelt signed the Tydings-McDuffie Independence Act, which provided for independence on July 4, 1946, and commonwealth status meanwhile. The Filipinos accepted the arrangement in a plebiscite and installed Quezon as their president.

Difficulties with Japan, 1931–1938

In 1931, Japanese militarists embarked upon an expansionist policy on the Asian mainland that eventually led to war with the United States and defeat in 1945. The late 1920's saw shifts in the relative strength of Asian national power and an increase in international tension. In 1924, Dr. Sun Yat-sen, leader of the Chinese revolutionary nationalists, accepted aid from the Russian Communist government and strengthened the Chinese nationalist movement. Upon his death in 1925, his successor as head of the Kuomintang party, Chiang Kai-shek, continued collaboration with the Russians. The central Chinese government extended its authority in the north and hoped to bring reunification with Manchuria. Two years after assuming leadership, Chiang broke with the Russians, and in 1929 and 1930 Sino-Russian relations were severely strained; there was even undeclared warfare before China backed down in the face of superior Soviet strength. But Chinese power in North China was growing. In the winter of 1929–1930, the warlord of Manchuria acknowledged Chinese suzerainty. Simultaneously, the Chinese organized a boycott of Japanese goods and began to skirt treaty obligations they had been forced to yield to the Japanese under duress. Japanese militarists, fearful of growing Chinese strength, were eager for action before China became too strong for them to handle.

Without the consent of the Premier or the Foreign Office, Japanese troops on the night of September 18–19, 1931, seized the Chinese garrison at Mukden, Manchuria, and several key points along the South Manchurian Railway. Their pretext was an explosion on the railroad, which was minor in any case and may have been altogether fictitious. The Kuomintang government of China protested Japan's action to the United States and to the League of Nations. Japan's action was inconsistent with her membership in the League, with the Kellogg-Briand Pact, and the Nine-Power Treaty of 1922, but the League's first action, after the Japanese government promised to withdraw as soon as practicable, was only to request China and Japan to do nothing to irritate the situation. Secretary of State Henry L. Stimson at first was cautious in the hope that American forbearance would strengthen the moderates in the Japanese civil government against the militarists and the army.

When the Japanese army continued its aggressions in Manchuria, President Hoover instructed Prentiss Gilbert, an official in the American consulate at Geneva, to sit with the League Council in discussions of Manchurian matters. Although the decision to cooperate this closely with the League raised eyebrows in the United States, the cooperation had little practical effect. The Japanese ignored the League's resolution calling for withdrawal of all Japanese troops to the area that they had occupied before the Mukden incident.

Stimson and Hoover did not see eye-to-eye on the proper course to be followed. After he recognized that moderation was having no effect, Stimson was for a policy of nonrecognition of Japanese conquests and was prepared to impose economic sanctions against Japan. Secretary of War Patrick Hurley wanted even to threaten military force, but Hoover was unwilling to go beyond nonrecognition and moral sanctions. Events moved swiftly at the turn of the year. On December 11, 1931, the Japanese cabinet resigned; the new one was more militaristic. On the following January 3, Japanese forces practically completed their conquest of Manchuria. On January 7, Stimson addressed identical notes to Japan and China setting forth what at the time was known as the Stimson Doctrine, since then more generally called the Hoover-Stimson Doctrine because it went no further than the nonrecognition policy upon which the two men agreed and did not threaten economic sanctions such as Stimson favored. The notes declared that the United States would not "admit the legality of any situation de facto nor . . . recognize any treaty or agreement . . . which may impair the treaty rights of the United States or its citizens in China . . . or the international policy relative to China, commonly known as the open-door policy. . . ." The Hoover-Stimson Doctrine was unilateral; Stimson had asked Britain and France to join in his declaration, but each declined.

Then the Japanese attacked the Shanghai area in an attempt to get the Chinese to repeal their boycott, and the British were moved to action for the first time. British naval units joined American ships in going to Shanghai to protect each nation's citizens. Both the United States and Britain stimulated negotiations between China and Japan which in time led to the end of hostilities in the Shanghai area. By the end of May, 1932, Japanese troops in the international city had been reduced to their normal number. But the Japanese did not retreat in Manchuria. Their method of fastening control over the area was to create a puppet state, called Manchukuo, which declared its independence from China on February 18, 1932.

The creation of Manchukuo was a direct challenge to the Hoover-Stimson Doctrine. Five days later Stimson released a public letter to William Borah, chairman of the Senate Foreign Relations Committee, that was intended for the eyes of the Japanese, the Chinese, the League, the British, and the American public more than it was for Senator Borah. Stimson had based his previous condemnations of Japanese aggression upon the Kellogg-Briand Pact. In the letter to Borah he urged that other nations join the United States in nonrecognition and shifted his basis for judging the Japanese to the Washington naval treaties of 1922. The Nine-Power and the Five-Power treaties,

Stimson pointed out, released all signatory nations from the treaty provisions if any one of the signatories violated the pacts. In other words, if Japan violated the integrity of China (one of the provisions of the Nine-Power Treaty) America would no longer be obligated to limit the size of her navy. The United States moved its fleet to the Pacific in 1932, but it did not build its navy beyond treaty strength limitations. In fact, until Roosevelt became president there was no effort to keep the navy up to the strength authorized by the Washington treaties.

If the Borah letter had no visible effect upon Japanese policy, it did bring the League around to nonrecognition. In March, 1932, the League Assembly declared League members should not recognize any situation achieved by means contrary to the League Covenant or to the Kellogg-Briand Pact. The League later received the report of its special commission to investigate the Manchurian problem headed by a British subject, the Earl of Lytton. The Lytton report was moderate, urging Chinese sovereignty in Manchuria but protection of Japanese economic interests. The Japanese were not content with its recommendations and on September 15, 1932, recognized Manchukuo as an independent power. When the League advised its members against recognition of Manchukuo, Japan served the necessary two-year notice of its withdrawal from the League.

Roosevelt assured Stimson between the election of 1932 and the inauguration that his administration would continue the Hoover-Stimson policies in East Asia. Roosevelt kept the fleet in the Pacific and announced that it would be built up to treaty strength, but during his first few years in office tensions with Japan became less serious. When the Japanese began expanding from Manchuria they encountered stiffer Chinese military resistance, and in late May, 1933, the Chinese and Japanese signed a truce. The truce was not altogether effective, but until 1937 there was no more large-scale military action in East Asia.

During these years, however, there were other matters of Japanese-American relations that form part of the background to war in 1941. The two main issues were Japanese efforts to close the open door in China and naval armaments. Over intermittent protests from the State Department, Japan used her control of the Manchukuo puppet government to slam the open door shut in that part of the Chinese mainland. Manchuria became a private preserve for Japanese trade and capital, and Japan consistently denied she had anything to do with Manchukuo policies that kept trade from other nations out of the area. Japan even proposed to Secretary Hull in 1934 that the United States, in effect, withdraw from the Far East, a "Japanese Monroe Doctrine" for Asia. Although America was at the time making preparations for ultimate withdrawal from territorial control of the Philippines, there was no intention of withdrawing from open-door imperialist policies in East Asia. Hull rejected the Japanese proposal. Continued American determination to retain the East Asian *status quo* and Japanese determination to make the area a special reservation for her commercial and military interests made an increase in international conflict inevitable. East Asia was an arena of conflict between empires: between American and British, on the one hand, primarily economic or informal in nature rather than colonial, and the Japanese, on the other hand, militaristic and colonial as well as economic.

The Japanese announcement in December, 1934, that they would not renew the naval limitations agreed upon at Washington and London when those agreements expired at the end of 1936 indicated that they meant business. Japan did send delegates to a naval conference at London in 1935–1936, but the delegates withdrew when the American and British delegations would admit no change in the traditional ratios. The American, British, and French delegations reached an agreement on the size of vessels but not on their number, and early in 1938 these three nations abandoned limitation of any kind by mutual consent. The naval race had begun. In January, 1938, while the economy was suffering from a serious recession, Roosevelt in a special message to Congress asked for the largest naval authorization in the nation's history. The measure passed a few months later.

The 1933 truce between China and Japan ended dramatically in a skirmish at the Marco Polo bridge near Peiping on July 7, 1937. (This city was known as Peking until 1928 when the Kuomintang moved the capital from there and renamed the city Peiping. The Japanese called the city by its old name, as have the Chinese Communists since 1949.) The incident at the bridge seems not to have been a staged one as the one at Mukden had been in 1931, but the Japanese army used it as an excuse to launch a full-scale offensive in the northern China provinces. The Kuomintang and the Chinese Communists under Mao Tse-tung had recently concluded a truce in their civil war and made a common front against Japan. Japan decided to move before China could become stronger.

Japan enjoyed quick military success. Her method was to bomb major cities and follow the raids with land expeditions. Japan had bombed civilians at Chinchow, Manchuria, in 1931, Italy had bombed defenseless Ethiopians in 1935, and Germany and Italy had used airplane bombardment against civilians in Spain in their aid to Franco, but most of the world was still repelled by the airplane's bringing war to noncombatants. A photograph widely published in America showed a terrorized Chinese infant crying amidst bomb rubble. Japanese troops took Nanking in December, 1937, and the Chinese moved their capital to Hankow, which fell in October, 1938, along with Canton. The Chinese retreated to the interior and set up their capital at Chunking. Japan controlled the coastal cities and the principal railroad lines by the end of 1938. But the Chinese armies had not been destroyed and they would not quit. As the Japanese learned, to defeat China in battle to gain control of the strategic positions was one thing, to win a war with all China and to control the whole country, with its vast distances and its enormous population accustomed to a low living standard, were something else.

Though disgusted by Japanese bombing of civilians, the American public was not ready to pursue policies with Japan that might lead to war. At an international conference at Brussels in November, 1937, convened to consider what Japan called the Chinese incident or the Chinese affair but never the Chinese war, the American delegation was instructed not to press for economic sanctions because the administration knew the position was more advanced than public opinion would support. On December 12, 1937, Japanese aircraft bombed and sank a United States navy gunboat, the *Panay*, in the Yangtze River although the American flag was painted on its decks and it was obviously an American ship. Japan apologized profusely and quickly made financial restitution for the loss of property and the lives of two crewmen. In 1898, the sinking of the *Maine* had brought a sharp demand for war with Spain. The *Panay* sinking provoked only fear of war. What business, many people asked, did a naval vessel have in convoying Standard Oil Company tankers in the Yangtze? The memory of the horrors of 1917–1918 were too strong for most Americans to consider risking war on the other side of the world. Within two weeks after the *Panay* sinking, the whole affair was a closed matter. The most that was done against the Japanese until the outbreak of war in Europe was to aid China (for example, the Export-Import Bank's credit to China for the Burma Road) and to request American airplane manufacturers in July, 1938, not to supply planes to Japan.

Yet the United States government did not retreat from its historic Far Eastern policies. Japan in November, 1938, announced a "new order" in East Asia based on "a tripartite relationship of mutual aid and coordination between Japan, Manchukuo and [Japanese-controlled] China." The State Department protested that such a "new order" could not legitimately annul previous treaty rights, meaning mostly the open-door safeguards in the 1922 Nine-Power Treaty. The United States never abandoned its open-door policy in East Asia; Japan would not abandon its position as the paramount power in the "new order." By the winter of 1938–1939, Japan and the United States were completely at loggerheads, but American public opinion was far more concerned with the situation in Europe than it was with Asian tensions.

Fascism in Europe: Hitler and Mussolini

When Benito Mussolini came to power in Italy in late 1922 and instituted his fascist order, majority opinion about him in the United States was not adverse. Many Americans commended Mussolini for driving beggars from the streets and praised him for "making the trains run on time."

Majority public opinion, however, was opposed to Adolf Hitler's National Socialist or Nazi rule in Germany almost from the time the Nazis came to power early in 1933, although Italian Fascism and German Nazism were only national variations of the same totalitarian idea. Hitler's blatant anti-Semitism alarmed many Americans, and millions, remembering the war, feared the resurgence of German militarism. When both Italy and Germany endangered the peace of the world with their expansionist policies, only a small proportion of the American population favored the two nations.

To summarize fascism (both Italian Fascism and German Nazism were generally known as fascism) in a few sentences is not simple. Fascist nations were vigorously anti-Communist. Both Hitler and Mussolini rode to power on middle-class fear of communism, and both their regimes essentially maintained the class systems that had existed earlier. To a degree, then, fascism was "capitalism by violence." But it was not conventional capitalism. The corporate state intervened extensively in the nation's economic life and regulated it. Industrial and landed capitalists accepted fascist regulation in preference to some form of Marxist control. Ironically, fascism had one major similarity to Stalinism: totalitarianism or the subordination of the individual and all social institutions to the needs of the national state. Hitler's Nazis, for example, urged children to inform on their parents to the authorities. Fascist nations were also extremely militaristic. They glorified the military life and praised war as a means of bringing out the best in a people. Fascists had nothing but contempt for democracy, either in the sense of shared decisions by a wide electorate or in the Bill of Rights' sense of protection of the individual from the state. In sum, fascism was antidemocratic nationalism run riot.

Fascism in Germany was extremely racist, although it was not in Italy and in some lesser fascist states. The Nazis exploited the latent anti-Semitism of the German people in their rise to power and used the Jews as a scapegoat to explain away all of the country's difficulties. At the same time, Nazis exalted the mythical racial purity, "Aryanism," of non-Jewish Germans. Beginning with mob action against Jews, the requirement that they wear identifying clothes, and boycotts of their businesses, German anti-Semitism ended with what the Nazis euphemistically called "the final solution of the Jewish question": killing all Jews and eradicating Jewish culture in all areas under German control. By the time Nazi Germany collapsed in 1945, the Nazis had killed six million Jews, most of them in efficient slaughterhouses, where their corpses were rendered into fats for soap manufacture and other uses.

For the first few months after Hitler came to power in Germany (January 30, 1933), he displayed an attitude toward other nations which, while not cooperative, would seem remarkably moderate in retrospect. Perhaps he was only waiting for consolidation of his power within Germany. In March, 1933, he was voted dictatorial powers for four years, and after Paul von Hindenburg's death in 1934 he combined the offices of the German presidency and chancellorship. He was, however, always known as Der Führer (the leader) rather than as president or chancellor. Hitler at first was even willing to talk about disarmament. A General Disarmament Conference had met first at Geneva in February, 1932. It met again in the spring of 1933. Hitler announced that he was willing to go along with disarmament and to postpone for five years his insistent demands for German arms equality, but he refused to sign any agreements or to consent to abide by majority votes of the Conference members. In October, 1933, Germany withdrew from both the Conference and the League of Nations. A few months later the Conference broke up altogether.

In March, 1935, Hitler declared the Treaty of Versailles limitations upon German armed strength no longer valid, instituted compulsory military service, and began to build the German army toward an announced five hundred thousand men. At the same time he said Germany would continue to respect the rest of the treaty, including keeping the Rhineland as a demilitarized zone. With such promises he managed to prevent France and Britain from presenting a solid front of opposition. Britain three months later even signed a treaty with Germany which allowed the Reich a navy 35 per cent as large as Britain's. In March, 1936, Hitler again took advantage of French-British discord, this time over what to do about Italy's undeclared war against Ethiopia, and he denounced the whole of the Treaty of Versailles, as well as the Locarno Treaty of 1925, and marched two hundred thousand soldiers into the Rhineland. The League of Nations failed to take any action.

Germany's and Italy's increased belligerence and disregard of international agreements caused grave concern in the United States, but the reaction was not so great as it would have been if the citizenry could have known what the end of German-Italian policies would be. In the mid-1930's the American population was far more concerned with domestic problems than with foreign affairs in either Europe or Asia and was undergoing a deep reaction against its involvement in the war of 1914–1918.

Neutrality and Anxiety, 1933–1938

In discussions of foreign policy with respect to expansionist Germany, Italy, and Japan in the 1930's, politicians and publicists used terms of opprobrium for their opponents that did little to clarify the actual situation. All too often, historians since that decade have trapped themselves by accepting these political catchwords without efforts to use them with precision. The most common loosely used term in the lexicon of commentators about foreign policy is *isolationist*, which has described those who opposed colonial imperialism in 1898 and after, who opposed American participation in World War I, who fought ratification of the Treaty of Versailles, who resisted entrance into World War II, and, in recent years, who criticized the United Nations and foreign aid programs. Actually, the term means one who advocates a policy of nonparticipation in international affairs, and very few Americans indeed have advocated such a position. In the context of the 1930's, "isolationism" embraced a wide range of positions. All they had in common was a fear of engagement in another world war. An insignificant number were partisans of fascism (for example, members of the German-American Bund) who, seeing that the United States would not become an ally of Germany or Italy, wanted the nation to stay clear of associations with antifascist governments. Another small group was composed of pacifists, many of them religiously motivated, who believed that violence and war were un-Christian and subversive of all decent values. Most "isolationists" were antifascist but fearful that vigorous opposition to expansionist foreign nations would involve the United States in an unwanted war. Some would have taken a few risks of war to hamper fascism; some would not. Some were for a strong military defense; some were not. To lump all of these positions into any single term is not precise, but some kind of general term is valid on occasion if one remembers that it is loose and general. The term *isolationist* will not be used here because it has become emotionally loaded. *Noninterventionist* is no more precise, but it avoids political passion.

    Interventionist also is a loose term, but it is one that has somehow not acquired strong emotional overtones. Almost no one was an open, outright interventionist demanding a quick declaration of war against fascist nations until war began in Europe in September, 1939, and they were few even then. However, especially after the beginning of the European war, an increasing number of people advocated strong aid to the antifascist European nations and actions "short of war" that might result in armed conflict. As with the noninterventionists, the interventionists represented a considerable range of positions, from the quite bellicose to those who genuinely believed that only

428

through cooperation with the western democracies could American belligerency be prevented.

Foreign policy cut across conventional political lines, whether party, regional, ethnic, or ideological. Both major parties, all regions of the nation, and all major nationality and racial groups divided on foreign policy issues. Frequently, debates between interventionists and noninterventionists made bedfellows of political leaders who vigorously opposed one another on domestic matters. Thus, on the interventionist side, the Roosevelt administration worked in harness with conservative eastern and southern congressional leaders of both parties, and the other side displayed the unusual spectacle of Colonel Robert R. McCormick, publisher of the extremely conservative *Chicago Daily Tribune*, agreeing with the leader of the Socialist party, Norman Thomas.

Clearly, in the early and middle 1930's American public opinion was overwhelmingly and vigorously antiwar. Given the depression-induced popular hostility to bankers and manufacturers and what was known about loans to the Allies from 1914 to 1917 and of profits in munitions, it was perhaps inevitable that antiwar sentiment would focus upon the role of business in American entrance into the war in 1917, widely felt to have been a disastrous mistake. In the spring of 1934, the Senate created a special committee, headed by Senator Gerald P. Nye, Republican of North Dakota, to conduct an inquiry into the adequacy of legislation on government control of munitions. For nearly three years the Nye Committee provided headlines and newspaper stories full of sordid details of greed and chicanery in the American munitions business during the war. It was easy for people to conclude that "merchants of death," a favorite phrase of the time, had been solely responsible for America's going to the aid of the Allies. Operating upon the assumption that legislation that presumably would have prevented participation in the war of 1914–1918 would prevent entrance into a future war, Congress moved to write a series of neutrality measures into the statutes.

At the end of his administration, Hoover, with a view to cooperation with the League in economic sanctions, requested Congress to pass a bill authorizing the chief executive to deny the export of arms from the United States to whatever countries the president might designate. The House passed such a bill, but the Senate amended it to make an arms embargo applicable to all parties in a war. Roosevelt succeeded Hoover before the Senate and House reached agreement, and the bill died.

In the summer of 1935, it seemed likely that Mussolini would soon begin a war to expand his colonial empire in North Africa. Roosevelt and Hull had a bill introduced which would have authorized the president to impose an arms embargo upon the nation he considered the aggressor. The bill was much like the one Hoover had desired in January, 1933. Instead, Congress passed the First Neutrality Act, which Roosevelt signed with misgivings on August 31, 1935. This law required the president to impose an embargo on arms to both nations engaged in conflict, created a government board whose special permission was necessary before munitions could be exported to any country, whether at war or not, and prohibited American ships from carrying munitions to or for a belligerent. The president's only discretionary power under the Act was whether or not to warn citizens that they traveled on ships of belligerent nations at their own risk.

429

Then, on October 3, 1935, well-equipped Italian troops invaded Ethiopia, whose soldiers were armed with the most primitive of weapons. Two days later FDR declared that a state of war existed and thereby invoked the Neutrality Act of 1935. Italy at no time made an official war declaration. In this case the prohibition of arms shipment to both sides probably did not harm Ethiopia, which had no seaport and probably would not have been able to get American arms anyway, although many people at the time thought it did. But, on the other hand, the arms embargo did not hurt Italy to any appreciable extent, particularly in a war against a foe as defenseless as Ethiopia. The Neutrality Act made no provision for an embargo on oil, and it was petroleum products that Italy needed most desperately for her motorized legions and air force. Hull applied a "moral embargo" on oil to Italy, requesting American oil companies to keep their shipments to Italy at normal levels. Hull thought the "moral embargo" was "reasonably successful," but how much American gasoline the Italians diverted from peaceful uses to tanks and army trucks is not known. Mussolini completed his conquest of Ethiopia in May, 1936.

Most of the provisions of the First Neutrality Act were due to expire at the end of February, 1936. Congress passed the Second Neutrality Act on the last day of February. The new measure extended the previous legislation until May 1, 1937, and added some new features. Under the old legislation, the president had been authorized but not directed to impose an arms embargo against any third power that might become involved in war with a nation already embargoed. The new legislation made such an embargo of a third nation mandatory. The new law also exempted from embargo any American nation that became a belligerent against any non-American nation and forbade loans by any person living in the United States to belligerent governments. This last provision was designed to prevent the repetition of such loans as the House of Morgan began to handle for the Allies in 1915.

None of this neutrality legislation mentioned civil wars and thus did not apply when the Spanish Civil War began in July, 1936. In 1931 the Spanish had overthrown their monarchy and established a republic; five years later General Francisco Franco led a revolt against the republican government. Franco and his followers were unmistakably Fascist, although not cut precisely from the German pattern. Franco's revolt was ostensibly directed against communists in the Spanish government, who at the beginning of the Civil War did not control the Spanish state. Fearful that the Spanish war would lead to a general European war, France persuaded other European governments to agree to a nonintervention policy. However, Germany and Italy soon violated the agreement, sent military units to aid Franco, and made Spain a testing ground for their new military techniques. Russia also violated the nonintervention agreement with direct aid to the Spanish government, or Loyalist cause, although her intervention was less extensive than was that of the Fascist powers.

When the European nations decided upon nonintervention, Roosevelt and Hull complied and declared another "moral embargo" upon shipments to either side of the Spanish conflict. No further action was possible under existing law. When Congress convened in January, 1937, Roosevelt asked Congress to extend the neutrality laws to civil as well as international wars. According to Hugh Thomas, a British author who has written the best single book on the Spanish Civil War, Ambassador to Great Britain Joseph P. Kennedy, a prominent Catholic layman, was influential in bringing about the administration's refusal to aid the Loyalists. Congress complied hastily. The decision to take a hands-off policy toward the Spanish war—in effect, to aid Franco because denying the Spanish government help made German and Italian intervention decisive—sharply divided the American population. The American Catholic hierarchy approved of the arms embargo to Spain because of the Spanish government's anticlericalism and the support the Spanish hierarchy gave Franco. The American political left, both Communist and non-Communist, vigorously condemned the embargo. The Communists organized the Abraham Lincoln Brigade, and almost three thousand young Americans, all of them anti-Fascist but not all of them Communist, enlisted in this military organization to fight Spanish fascism. Hundreds of thousands of others donated funds to Spanish war relief organizations.

The Third Neutrality Act of May 1, 1937, the date of the expiration of the second measure, extended the main provisions of earlier neutrality laws without a definite time limit. The Third Act also made two minor and one major change in the basic legislation. The new law gave the president discretionary power in invoking an embargo in the case of a foreign civil war and forbade United States citizens to travel on the ships of nations at war. An embargo against both sides of a civil war had been mandatory since January, 1937, and existing legislation had only authorized the president to warn citizens that they traveled on belligerent ships at their own risk. Potentially more important was the "cash and carry" provision of the Third Neutrality Act, which gave the president considerable discretionary power to wage economic war. As in earlier legislation, whenever the president declared that a state of war existed between two or more foreign powers an arms embargo would become mandatory. But the "cash and carry" provision empowered the president also, for a period of two years, to extend the embargo, if he so wished, to commodities that were not arms or munitions if the commodities were carried in American ships or title to them had not yet been transferred to a foreign buyer. No such situation arose during the two years this provision was in effect. (After war began in Europe in September, 1939, Congress enacted another "cash and carry" provision but one that was quite different in nature.) Interestingly, Roosevelt did not invoke the Third Neutrality Act until war broke out in Europe. He declined to take official recognition that a state of war existed between Japan and China after July, 1937. Apparently, Roosevelt concluded that to "find" the Asian war and thereby make neutrality legislation applicable would have the practical effect of strengthening Japan's hand. Instead, he relied upon appeals to other nations to reaffirm their treaty obligations and to pleas for international morality. Since American public opinion would not support strong measures, the American delegation to the Brussels Conference on the Asian situation was powerless to provide strong leadership.

Indeed, it became increasingly apparent in 1937 and 1938 that noninterventionist public opinion was a thorn in the President's side and that noninterventionists meant to keep the thorn sharp. This antagonism between the public and the President over foreign policy was illustrated by the reaction to Roosevelt's speech at Chicago, October 5, 1937, at the dedication of a new bridge on the Outer Drive. In this address, commonly called the "Quarantine the Aggressors Speech," Roosevelt said, "It seems to be unfortunately true that the epidemic of world lawlessness is spreading. And mark this well! When an epidemic of physical disease starts to spread, the community approves and joins in a quarantine of the patients in order to protect the health of the community against the spread of the disease." Such a medical methaphor was not precise language, and no one could say just what Roosevelt had in mind. But whatever he had in mind, the public did not approve of it. Press reaction to the speech was unfavorable. Later in the month a public opinion poll put this question to a supposedly scientifically calculated cross section of the population: "Which plan for keeping out of war do you have more faith in— having Congress pass stricter neutrality laws, or leaving the job up to the President?" Only 31 per cent preferred the latter alternative. The strength behind the Ludlow amendment to the Constitution was another indication of noninterventionist power and distrust of the President's foreign policies. An idea that went back at least as far as the period of American neutrality during World War I, the Ludlow amendment, named for Representative Louis Ludlow, Democrat of Indiana, proposed that a national referendum would be necessary to declare war except in the case of armed invasion of the United States or its territories. Roosevelt had to use great pressure to defeat the amendment in the House where it failed by only twenty-one votes in January, 1938.

Also in January, 1938, the State Department perceived that Hitler's next move would be to absorb Austria under German rule. With public opinion being what it was, Hull only impressed upon the German ambassador in Washington that the United States would not look favorably upon any such aggression. This did not deter Germany whose troops marched into Austria with the aid of Austrian Nazis in March.

In the summer of 1938 Hitler began a war of nerves over the question of the Sudetenland of Czechoslovakia, an area populated largely by German-speaking people. Hitler demanded the area, and the Czechs were willing to fight to keep it since it was vital to the defense of the rest of the country. But Britain, France, and the United States were by no means prepared to go to war to defend Czechoslovakia. Indeed, many British and French leaders regarded Hitler as less of a menace than the Russians. Prime Minister Neville Chamberlain and Premier Édouard Daladier were prepared to go to great lengths at Czechoslovakia's expense to prevent the outbreak of war. Matters came to a crisis in late September. Millions of Americans kept close to their radios to hear the frequent news bulletins. After European heads of state and foreign ministers had conferred both personally and by cable for days without a final settlement, Roosevelt, on September 26, sent messages to Hitler, Chamberlain, Daladier, and President Eduard Beneš of Czechoslovakia in which he asserted that war would only wreck every country involved and urged continued negotiations. Hitler's reply only repeated his previous demands for the Sudetenland. Three days later the State Department urged all other countries to support the American appeal for further negotiations, and Roosevelt personally appealed to Mussolini to use his influence with Hitler. At the last minute, Hitler issued invitations to Mussolini, Chamberlain, and Daladier for a conference at Munich. When Roosevelt heard that Chamberlain had accepted the invitation, he dispatched a cabled instruction to his ambassador at

London, Joseph P. Kennedy, to give Chamberlain this oral message: "Good man." On September 30, Chamberlain and Daladier signed a Four-Power Pact at Munich which gave the Sudetenland to Germany in exchange for only a promise from Hitler, who had already broken several promises, to refrain from further demands for European territory. When the gray Chamberlain returned to London, carrying the umbrella which came to be considered a symbol of appeasement, he announced, "I believe it is peace for our time." The same day the State Department in a press release announced that the Munich agreement had brought "a universal sense of relief," but it declared that the United States would not "pass upon the merits of the differences to which the Four-Power Pact . . . related."

War in Europe had been averted—for about eleven months.

Part IV

WAR AND BOOM AGAIN
1941–1963

CHAPTER TWENTY-TWO

And the War Came

IF PRESIDENT ROOSEVELT AT ANY TIME THOUGHT THE MUNICH PACT would avert war in Europe, he was disillusioned within a week after the crisis. The ambassador to France, William C. Bullitt, reported to him that French premier Édouard Daladier did not for a minute believe Hitler's assurances. Daladier's skepticism was well founded. Almost immediately after Munich, Hitler called for an increase in German armaments upon the pretext that Britain would not keep the peace if a man like Winston Churchill, who opposed the Munich settlement, should come to political power. At this point, Roosevelt announced a $300 million increase in the American arms program. While public-opinion polls continued to show overwhelming American opposition to war, the President enjoyed some support for rearmament because he couched his statements in national defense terms and because the Nazis, in November, 1938, intensified their oppression of the Jews. Nevertheless, Roosevelt could not move very far very fast. He was at the moment at about his weakest point in domestic political strength, and he remembered the difficulties President Wilson had when he allowed his political fences to rot while he concerned himself with foreign affairs.

On March 14, 1939, Germany gained control over the balance of Czechoslovakia. In early April, Mussolini's troops took Albania. A week after Italy's invasion of her neighbor across the Adriatic, Roosevelt, without consulting Paris or London, proposed in a message to Hitler and Mussolini that they should assure thirty-one European and Near Eastern countries that for at least ten years they would commit no aggression. In return, the United States would participate in disarmament discussions and in easing the way of all nations to obtain necessary raw materials. Mussolini in a speech of April 20 called the idea "absurd." In a speech to the Reichstag, Hitler said he had surveyed the governments Roosevelt had asked assurances for and found none of them felt any need for assurance. The whole idea collapsed on this cynical note.

As early as his annual message to Congress in January, 1939, Roosevelt had urged revision of neutrality legislation to give him a stronger hand to aid an invaded nation if war should begin. After Hitler began to press Poland in April, 1939, to grant Germany access across the Polish corridor between the main part of Germany and East Prussia and for consent to annex the free city of Danzig, Roosevelt renewed his efforts to get amendment of the neutrality laws. The "cash and carry" provisions of the Third Neutrality Act (1937) expired on May 1; after that date, if war came, Britain and France would be forbidden to buy arms in America even if they carried them in their own ships. Despite great pressure from the administration, neither house would budge to amend the law. Senator Borah even, upon being informed by Secretary Hull that State Department cables indicated European war was imminent, said, "I have my own sources of information . . . and on several occasions I've found them more reliable than the State Department." Congress adjourned without yielding to the President.

In Europe tension mounted but events dragged from April, 1939, when Hitler began to torment Poland, until August. During those months, Russia, Britain, and France conferred, at Stalin's invitation, about forming a defensive alliance against Germany. The difficulty lay in the status of the small countries between Germany and Russia. Fearing Russian power almost as much as German, sometimes more, the Baltic countries (Lithuania, Latvia, and Estonia), Poland, and Rumania felt that acceptance of Russian protection would mean Russian occupation. Britain and France refused to enter an alliance with Russia against these countries' wishes, and the negotiations dragged on uselessly.

In May, Vyacheslav Molotov replaced Maxim Litvinov as the Russian foreign minister. Molotov soon began secret negotiations with Germany but made no commitments until he became convinced no agreement could be reached with the English and French. On August 20, 1939, Germany and Russia announced that they had signed a trade agreement. Three days later the two countries shocked the world by signing a nonaggression pact that assured Germany of Russian neutrality should the Nazis invade Poland. A secret part of the agreement split Poland between the two countries and arranged spheres of influence in the Baltic states.

On September 1, after a week of fruitless last-minute efforts by the United States, Britain, France, and Poland for a settlement, German troops crossed the Polish frontier. Two days later, acting on previous commitments, Britain and France declared war on Germany. World War II had begun, less than twenty-one years after the end of the first tragedy.

The "Phony War"

The winter of 1939–1940 saw no real war in western Europe. After Germany overran Poland with a Blitzkrieg, or lightning war, so quickly that Britain and France could not endanger the Third Reich from the west, the western front settled down to a Sitzkrieg, or sitting war. The main area of hostilities that winter was Finland, which Russia invaded November 30, 1939. American opinion strongly supported the Finns—"brave little Finland" that paid its war debts —and Herbert Hoover headed a Finnish war relief organization that collected $2 million in the United States. But neither Congress nor the administration would go beyond an effective "moral embargo" on war shipments to Russia, partly because of political caution, partly for fear of strengthening the unexpected German-Russian alliance with outside pressure. In March, 1940, the "Winter War" ended with Russia settling for its minimum demands. (By the end of the war, Finland had a peculiar record. When Germany invaded Russia in June, 1941, Finland cooperated and invaded Russia from the northwest. In the fall of 1944, after a successful Russian campaign, the Finns capitulated, but the German troops in North Finland refused to leave, and Finland fought a bitter campaign against her former comrades at arms.)

The night Britain and France declared war, September 3, 1939, Roosevelt spoke to the nation by radio.

> This nation will remain a neutral nation, but I cannot ask that every American remain neutral in thought as well. . . . Even a neutral cannot be asked to close his mind or his conscience. . . . I hope the United States will keep out of this war. I believe that it will. And I give you assurance and reassurance that every effort of your Government will be directed toward that end.

Two days later, the President invoked the existing neutrality law, thereby prohibiting exports of war material to the belligerents. But at the same time, the President continued his campaign to have the law amended.

After calling a special session of Congress, Roosevelt on September 21 addressed the assembled Senators and Representatives, telling them "that by the repeal of the embargo the United States will more probably remain at peace than if the law remains as it stands today." He urged new legislation to keep American ships and citizens out of combat areas and to prohibit credits by individual citizens to the belligerents, but to permit belligerents to take title to American products in American ports on a "cash and carry" basis. After sharp debates, Congress passed the Fourth Neutrality Act, or the Neutrality Act of 1939, by 243 to 172 in the House and 55 to 24 in the Senate. Roosevelt signed the bill November 4, 1939, and put it into effect immediately. The "cash and carry" provisions of the law applied to all commodities, arms or not. Roosevelt's executive order prohibited American ships to sail to belligerent ports or in the Baltic Sea, the North Sea, and the waters around Great Britain, including the English Channel.

A conference of the twenty-one American republics at Panama City— called by Panama as provided for by the conference at Lima in 1938—met only days after the war began and unanimously made the Americas neutral territory. The Panama conference created a neutral zone three hundred miles wide around the Americas (with the exception of belligerent Canada), in which the American states would admit no war action. In December, 1939, when British cruisers damaged the German battleship *Graf Spee* and it limped into port at Montevideo, the government of Uruguay ordered the German captain to leave the neutral zone within seventy-two hours. Rather than face the British again, the crew scuttled the ship and subsequently were interned in Uruguay.

The period of "phony war" afforded Americans an opportunity to clarify their thinking about neutrality, but they reached no consensus. The population was torn between a strong desire to remain apart from the horrors of war and sympathy for the Allies. Despite imperfections of British and French democracy and these nations' colonial imperialism, most people in the United States preferred an Allied victory to military success for the positively antidemocratic, militaristic, and expansionist German and Italian governments. For the United States to go to war, most citizens thought, would be a disaster; for Germany to win, practically all agreed, would also be a disaster. Which was the worse eventuality? In the absence of real war in the West, Americans hoped the dilemma would not come to a showdown, but they arrived at no firm conclusions about what to do if a choice had to be made. The American people never made a clear-cut decision through their regular representative processes, but they moved ever closer to full-scale belligerency. The war came eventually from outside, but by then the United States was practically a belligerent in everything but name.

Roosevelt's views about the war were of particularly great importance because he was the most effective individual molder of public opinion in the nation and because, as leader of the majority political party and as chief executive, he could create conditions which reduced the range of practical choice of the citizens and their elected representatives. But to describe his personal views on the war is difficult because he did not reveal his thoughts candidly to the people, and if he recorded them privately the record has not become available. We must infer his personal views from a less than perfect record.

Clearly, from the beginning of the war in September, 1939, Roosevelt's sympathies were strongly with the Allies. To Roosevelt, defeat of the Axis powers was paramount. (Germany and Italy were generally known as the Axis powers; Japan joined the Axis with the Berlin Pact of September 27, 1940, which created a German-Italian-Japanese military alliance.) His desire for Axis defeat became stronger after the German victories of the spring of 1940. Just as clearly, at least early in the European conflict, Roosevelt genuinely wanted the United States to stay out of the war as a full-scale belligerent. The question was which was the lesser evil, Axis victory or American participation? Gradually, Roosevelt came to believe that an Axis victory was more to be deplored, over the long run, than his nation's entrance into war, and at some time in mid-1941 he apparently became convinced that American participation was necessary to bring Axis defeat. He meanwhile led the nation away from neutrality to what came to be known as *nonbelligerence*—not at war but actively supporting one belligerent side through loans, armament aid, and, to a limited degree, military and naval cooperation. That Roosevelt was not candid with the public and that his executive actions brought the nation ever closer to active war participation are obvious. Also, his policies and actions raised serious constitutional questions about the power of the president in a democratic country. This is not to say that Roosevelt "tricked us" or "lied us" into World War II, as the more extreme "revisionist" critics of Roosevelt have written; it is to say that the President, without taking the people fully into his confidence, moved the United States into what amounted to undeclared war in such a manner that causes serious concern to those who believe that the electorate, through its representatives in Congress, should make the basic and ultimate decisions about war and peace.

Majority public opinion lagged behind the President's position until Pearl Harbor, but it moved in the President's direction. According to public opinion polls, only a minority believed in September, 1939, that the declaration of war in 1917 had been a proper decision, but a majority came to that opinion during the fall. Until the collapse of France and the subsequent Battle of Britain in the skies over England, a minority thought aid to England more important than keeping the United States out of the war; thereafter, a majority would have risked war to help the British. In the early spring of 1941, for the first time, a majority came to think it wise to risk war with Japan rather than allow her to continue her expansion.

Although public opinion slowly came toward Roosevelt's position with each major change in the war in Europe, the heat of the arguments between interventionists and noninterventionists increased. Diametrically opposed to one another were two important nonpartisan propaganda groups, the interventionist Committee to Defend America by Aiding the Allies and the noninterventionist America First Committee. Just after war began in Europe, William Allen White, progressive Republican editor of the Emporia, Kansas, *Gazette* and a journalist of national reputation, organized the Non-Partisan Committee for Peace through Revision of the Neutrality Law. The Committee faded after the passage of the Fourth Neutrality Act, but came to life in May, 1940, after the Nazi invasion of France, under its new name. White again was its chairman, and it was widely known as the White Committee. By August, 1940, the White Committee had six hundred local chapters and sufficient money for national advertising and radio network time. It had considerable influence with the national leaders of both political parties. Among the prominent newspapers editorially supporting the Committee to Defend America were the New York *Times* and the New York *Herald-Tribune*, whose columnists were syndicated nationally.

The America First Committee organized in the summer of 1940. The prime mover in its establishment was R. Douglas Stuart of Chicago, then a student in the Yale Law School; its national chairman was General Robert E. Wood, who was Acting Quartermaster General in World War I and was then chairman of the board of Sears, Roebuck and Company. Like the White Committee, it tried to influence public opinion through print and radio. The most important papers supporting it were the *Chicago Daily Tribune* and the Hearst chain.

In each camp there was considerable diversity of opinion on domestic affairs. Within the White Committee the range was at least as far as from Lewis Douglas on the right to Paul H. Douglas and Reinhold Niebuhr on the left. The national committee of America First contained such diverse types as Hanford MacNider, Iowa manufacturer and former national commander of the American Legion, Oswald Garrison Villard, former editor of *The Nation*, and Chester Bowles. Both sides had military men: in the White group, Clark M. Eichelberger; in the America First, besides General Wood himself, Colonel Charles A. Lindbergh and "Eddie" Rickenbacker, the most celebrated American pilot of World War I. Nor was either camp unanimous in its foreign policy positions. Although the official position of America First was for strong continental defenses, many traditional pacifists and antimilitarists belonged to the organization. Differences within the White Committee became so intense that White himself resigned as chairman in January, 1941, and growled about a nucleus of "warmongers" in the organization.

From the Fall of France through the Elections

On April 9, 1940, Hitler unleashed his powerful war machine on Denmark and Norway. Militarily weak compared to the Germans and without natural geographic barriers, the Danes offered no more than token resistance. They were more than usually bitter, considering that only a year before, at Hitler's suggestion, they had signed a nonaggression pact with Germany and that some of the Nazi troopers who invaded their country had as children during World War I been taken in by Danish farmers so that they could get enough to eat. The Norwegians put up greater resistance and received some help from the British. But they were no match for the Nazis, and they were betrayed by native Nazis, "fifth columnists," led by Vidkun Quisling.

On May 10, the Nazis invaded the Netherlands, Belgium, and Luxembourg and the following day entered France. Although the Dutch declared Rotterdam an open city, the Luftwaffe bombed and utterly destroyed forty blocks in Rotterdam's central district to demonstrate its power to the world. The Nazi motorized battalions swept toward Paris and pinned the British army against the English Channel. In late May and early June, a motley collection of British boats managed to evacuate their army from Dunkirk in an heroic and miraculous operation. The Germans occupied Paris on June 14, and on June 22, 1940, Hitler received the French surrender in the same railroad car in the same Compiègne forest in which the Germans had agreed to armistice in November, 1918. On June 10, Mussolini's Fascist legions had attacked France from the southeast. In six weeks Hitler and Mussolini had conquered more than had the Central Powers in all of World War I.

The new turn in the war had a great impact upon American opinion and actions. An overwhelming majority of Americans, including those who were ardent noninterventionists, sympathized with France. The new British prime minister, Winston Churchill, who replaced Neville Chamberlain the day the Nazis began their sweep through the Low Countries and who installed a national government including Labor party leaders, captured the imagination of America with his pledge to fight on and on in his "blood, sweat, and tears" speech. Roosevelt's speech at the University of Virginia on the day Italy invaded France was well received. The President described his efforts to keep Mussolini out of the war and declared, "The hand that held the dagger has struck it into the back of its neighbor." With anxious interest, the nation followed the progress of the air battles between the Luftwaffe and the Royal Air Force for control of the skies and, after the Germans switched from the strategy of destroying RAF bases to a punishing bombardment of London, the "blitz" of the fall and winter of 1940–1941.

Even before the German conquest of France was complete, the United

States indirectly began sending some of its arms to Britain. The navy sent some of its planes back to the manufacturer on a "trade in" for new models to be delivered much later. The manufacturer then sent the planes on to belligerent Canada. The United States also permitted the Royal Canadian Air Force to send its personnel to Florida air fields for training. This kind of hemispheric cooperation for the Allies and against the Axis extended to Latin America. In July, 1940, the foreign ministers of the American nations met at Havana. Besides arranging for the United States, through the Export-Import Bank, to engage in economic warfare with Germany in the Latin American market, the Havana Conference created a system for American states to take over as trustees the American territory of European countries conquered by the Nazis. Eventually, the United States became the trustee for Greenland which had been Danish.

The Republican party met in national convention at Philadelphia on June 24, just two days after Hitler received France's surrender. Until soon before the convention the main contenders for the GOP presidential nomination were all noninterventionists: Senators Robert A. Taft of Ohio and Arthur H. Vandenberg of Michigan and Thomas E. Dewey, the thirty-eight year old district attorney of New York's Manhattan who had gained national attention as a "racket buster." Late in the preconvention campaign a group of eastern interventionist Republicans advanced the name of Wendell L. Willkie, president of the Commonwealth and Southern Corporation that had led the fight of the privately owned public utilities against TVA. Willkie, originally of Elwood, Indiana, a big rumpled man who had been a Democrat, even a delegate to the 1924 convention, and who had registered as a Republican for the first time earlier in the year, moved up fast. His initial support was from the eastern elements in the GOP, but he soon picked up popular backing in the Midwest. Willkie managers packed the convention galleries, and his claque there kept up the chant "We want Willkie." Dewey led on the first ballot, with Taft second and Willkie third, but Willkie gained thereafter and won a majority on the sixth ballot. Charles McNary of Oregon, Republican leader in the Senate and co-sponsor of the McNary-Haugen bills, received the vice-presidential nomination.

The Republican convention, sensing the general popularity of the New Deal, did not offer the electorate a platform sharply different from what was expected from the forthcoming Democratic convention. Its criticisms of the New Deal were restricted to its administration rather than its general outline. It promised retention and even extension of the Social Security Act. It demanded a constitutional amendment to restrict the president to two terms. On foreign policy, the platform straddled in the historic fashion of the major parties, which have to satisfy the major wings of their coalitions. The Republicans stated that they were unalterably opposed to American involvement in a foreign war but supported aid to countries under attack or the threat of attack. On the whole, the Republican convention produced another "Me Too" candidate and platform but had come up with the first candidate with flair and potential wide personal support since Theodore Roosevelt.

The President said nothing about a third term despite frantic efforts to get him to commit himself. He allowed his name to be entered in state primaries, and in each case he won handily. But several other Democratic politicians, notably Postmaster General Farley, Vice-President Garner, and former Governor of Indiana Paul V. McNutt, yearned for the nomination. They were at a considerable disadvantage. Roosevelt had a well-organized machine working at the Chicago convention—its leader Harry Hopkins had a direct telephone to the White House installed in his hotel bathroom, the only place he could be assured of privacy—but few in the machine knew the President's intentions for sure. Finally, Senator Alben Barkley in a rip-roaring convention speech declared that Roosevelt wished "in all earnestness and sincerity to make it clear that all the delegates . . . are free to vote for any candidate." This ambiguous statement started a huge Roosevelt demonstration. After all, Roosevelt too was "any candidate." Delegates placed other names in nomination—Farley, Garner, Senator Millard Tydings of Maryland, and Secretary of State Hull—but Roosevelt ran away with the nomination on the first ballot. He received 946 votes; all the others combined received only 147. The real fight at the convention was over the choice of FDR's running mate. The President wanted Secretary of Agriculture Henry Wallace, who was never popular with the professional party leaders. At the White House, Roosevelt threatened not to accept the nomination unless Wallace were nominated, but his threat was not known to the Chicago delegates. In a hard struggle, Wallace beat out McNutt and Speaker of the House William B. Bankhead of Alabama. The Democratic platform emphasized the New Deal accomplishments and straddled opposition to foreign war and aid to the allies on foreign matters.

Willkie began his campaign in a big way in mid-August before a huge crowd in his hometown, but Roosevelt restricted himself to well-publicized inspections of defense industries and avoided campaign speeches until almost time for balloting. Nevertheless, during the summer FDR took two actions relevant to the war-peace issue that were risky immediately preceding an election; he urged the passage of and signed the nation's first peacetime military conscription act and by administrative action alone negotiated the Destroyer-Bases Deal with Great Britain.

Although both sides had resorted to a draft during the Civil War and conscription had proved necessary to build an effective army during World War I, Americans had never liked the idea of military conscription. Conscription, especially during peacetime, evoked visions of European autocracy. However, in June, 1940, Senator Edward Burke, a Democratic conservative from Nebraska, and James W. Wadsworth, Jr., a conservative Republican Congressman from New York, jointly introduced a conscription bill. Roosevelt supported it. He urged the draft in his acceptance speech to the Chicago nominating convention. Congress passed the bill by almost two-to-one votes in each house, and on September 16, Roosevelt signed the Burke-Wadsworth or Selective Service Act of 1940. The measure called for the registration of all men between the ages of twenty-one and thirty-six. Those called to service by a lottery system, a maximum of nine hundred thousand in any year, were subject to a year's military training at a base pay of $21 a month. Draftees were not to be sent outside of the western hemisphere. In addition, in another measure, the president received authority to call National Guard units into federal service. The first Selective Service Administrator was Clarence Dykstra, former city manager of Cincinnati and then president of the University of Wisconsin. Potential draftees registered under the Act on October 16. On October

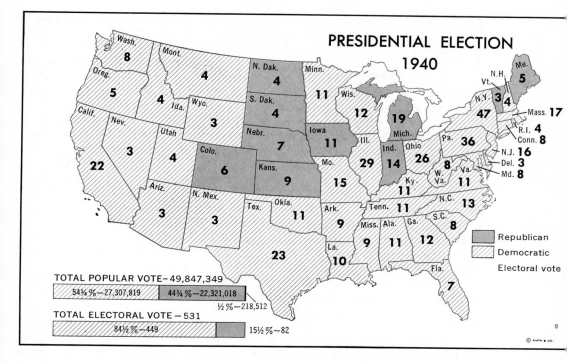

PRESIDENTIAL ELECTION
1940

TOTAL POPULAR VOTE – 49,847,349

54¾% – 27,307,819	44¾% – 22,321,018

½% – 218,512

TOTAL ELECTORAL VOTE – 531

84½% – 449	15½% – 82

Republican
Democratic
Electoral vote

29, just a week before election day, Department of War officials held the ceremony of drawing the draft lottery numbers. The first draftees began their training in November.

The Destroyer-Bases Deal arose from British need for more protection against submarines in the North Atlantic and from an anticipated German invasion of their island in the late summer. Attorney General Robert Jackson found a legal route through a maze of possibly prohibiting laws for the United States to turn fifty destroyers over to the British. These vessels constituted about two-sevenths of a reconditioned fleet from World War I storage. To turn over the destroyers, Jackson found, did not violate the neutrality laws because they had not been built specifically to be granted to a belligerent power. An amendment to a naval appropriations act in June, 1940, had forbidden transfer of such equipment to a foreign nation unless the Chief of Naval Operations and the Army Chief of Staff certified that the equipment was not necessary to the nation's defense. General George C. Marshall and Admiral Harold R. ("Dolly") Stark approved the transfer to Great Britain, calculating that bolstering English defenses strengthened American security. But there was no precedent for the Destroyer-Bases Deal and no express constitutional authority; FDR clearly altered the conventional, constitutional role of the president's power to conduct foreign affairs. Representatives of Great Britain and the United States signed an agreement at Washington, September 2, 1940. In return for the fifty reconditioned destroyers, Britain granted America ninety-nine year leases for naval and air bases in Jamaica, the Bahamas, St. Lucia, Antigua, Trinidad, and British Guiana. America received leases for bases on Newfoundland and Bermuda in addition as gifts, although it is doubtful if the gifts would have been forthcoming if the destroyers had not been. The British also guaranteed that the destroyers would never be surrendered.

When Roosevelt announced the agreement to Congress on the following day, there was a storm of protest from some newspapers and politicians. The Destroyer-Bases Deal was clearly a major move away from neutrality. Churchill later wrote in his memoirs that by earlier standards of neutrality Hitler would have been justified in declaring war upon the United States. The ablest defenders of Roosevelt's prewar foreign policies have written, "After the Destroyer Deal American neutrality was hardly more than a technicality. . . ."[1] But Willkie had already gone on record as an advocate of a strong British fleet and confined his criticism to FDR's failure to consult Congress about the deal before he consummated it. Noninterventionists were partially disarmed by the bases given to the United States; they were for strong hemispheric defense, which would be improved with the new bases. In the absence of the Republican candidate's strong opposition, the Destroyer-Bases Deal passed by without most people being fully aware of the implications of the arrangement. Analyses of public opinion showed that a bare majority of the population favored the Roosevelt-Churchill agreement.

For most of the campaign Willkie was inhibited by his basic agreement with the Roosevelt policies. He confined his criticisms to the failure of the New Deal to solve unemployment and to charges that national defense was inadequate. He also hammered away at the idea of a third term, but none of these themes produced any marked response. Then in late September, taking the advice of Republican professionals, Willkie let go on the war-peace issue and charged that Roosevelt was a warmonger. "If his promise to keep our boys out of foreign wars is no better than his promise to balance the budget, they're already almost on the transports." The Republican campaign caught fire. Roosevelt saw that he would have to campaign. October public opinion polls showed Willkie gaining. Roosevelt announced in mid-October that he would make a series of five political addresses. In these addresses he not only proudly enumerated the New Deal reforms and stated that his Republican opponents had resisted them all, he reassured the nation about war. At Philadelphia: "There is no secret treaty, no secret obligation, no secret commitment, no secret understanding in any shape or form, direct or indirect, with any other Government, or any other nation in any part of the world, to involve this nation in any war or for any other purpose." At Boston: "I have said this before, but I shall say it again and again and again: Your boys are not going to be sent into any foreign wars."

Roosevelt's popular vote on November 5 was 27,243,466; Willkie's was 22,304,755. The popular plurality, while significant, was less than any since 1916. But Roosevelt had a huge majority in the electoral college, 449 to 82. Besides Maine and Vermont, Willkie carried Indiana, Michigan, and Iowa and five Great Plains states. Roosevelt carried the big cities. The Democrats gained six seats in the House and lost three in the Senate.

With little change in the congressional party line-up, the legislative branch remained under the control of the Republican-Dixie coalition. But by

---

[1] William L. Langer and S. Everett Gleason, *The Undeclared War, 1940–1941* (New York: Harper and Brothers, 1953), p. 2.

1940, the administration itself was something of a conservative coalition. In May, 1940, when Roosevelt created the Defense Advisory Commission, he appointed William S. Knudsen, a General Motors official who had been a heavy contributor to the Liberty League. Just before the Republican convention in June he had startled the nation by appointing two prominent Republicans to the cabinet: Henry L. Stimson, who had been Secretary of War under Taft and Secretary of State under Hoover, became Secretary of War again; Frank Knox, who had been Landon's running mate less than four years before, became Secretary of the Navy.

Moving toward "Shooting Nonbelligerence"

In early December, 1940, Roosevelt embarked on a vacation cruise on the U.S.S. *Tuscaloosa*. While on the cruise he received a long communication from Prime Minister Churchill. Great Britain was in a desperate situation, wrote Churchill, even if it had been able to prevent the Nazis from delivering a knockout blow. To prevent defeat in 1941 and to lay the groundwork for eventual victory over Germany, assistance from the United States would be vital. To hold out, Britain needed American goods transported on American merchant ships and protected by American naval vessels. For eventual victory, Britain needed all kinds of war supplies, including seven thousand combat planes by the spring of 1942 and a like number of training aircraft. Churchill wrote not as a suppliant but as a fellow opponent of fascism:

> If, as I believe, you are convinced, Mr. President, that the defeat of the Nazi and Fascist tyranny is a matter of high consequence to the people of the United States . . . you will regard this letter not as an appeal for aid, but as a statement of the minimum action necessary to the achievement of our common purpose.[2]

Roosevelt quickly went to work on the problem of how best to aid the British. The difficulty, as FDR saw it, was how to provide the material of war Britain needed without creating a festering sore of bad will through a war loan. Allied loans during World War I had created collection problems that plagued the 1920's and 1930's. Roosevelt's solution was to lend goods rather than money to be repaid after the war in goods and services. This idea became the essence of the Lend-Lease Act. In a press conference on December 17, 1940, FDR used the analogy of lending a neighbor one's garden hose to put out a fire in the neighbor's house. Roosevelt said that one would not say, "Neighbor, my garden hose cost me $15; you have to pay me $15 for it." One would just connect the hose and get it back after the fire was out. In a radio "fireside chat" on December 29, he took his argument for massive aid to the British directly to the people. "We must," he said, "be the great arsenal of democracy." His argument was that such a policy would lessen the chances of American belligerence: ". . . there is far less chance of the United States

---

[2] Winston S. Churchill, *Their Finest Hour* (Boston: Houghton Mifflin Company, 1949), p. 567.

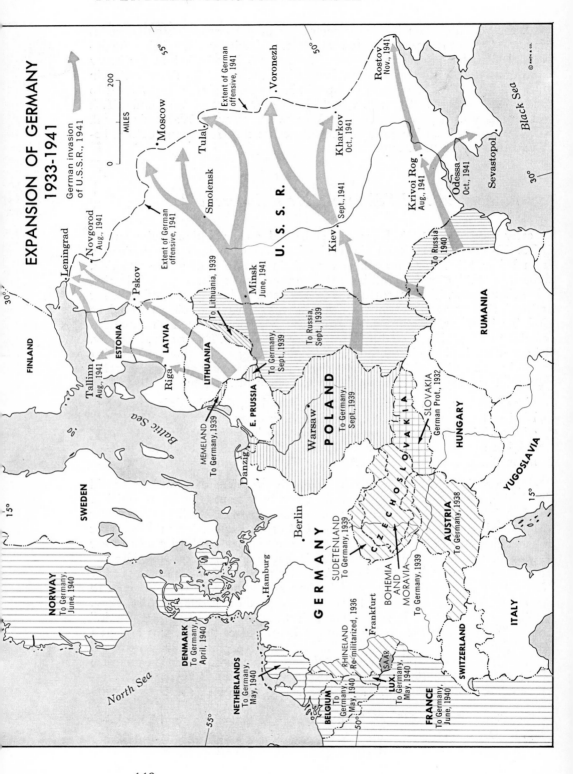

EXPANSION OF GERMANY
1933-1941

German invasion
of U.S.S.R., 1941

200

MILES

0

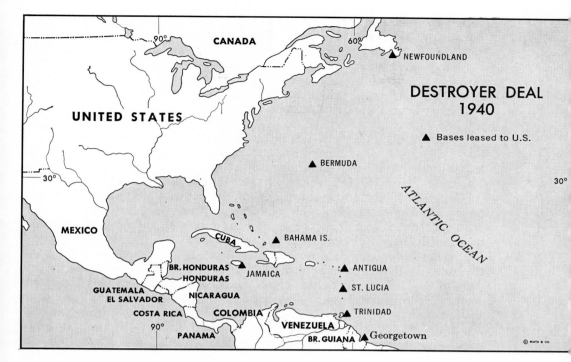

getting into the war, if we do all we can now to support the nations defending themselves against attack by the Axis than if we acquiesce in their defeat, submit tamely to an Axis victory, and wait our turn to be the object of attack in another war later on." Public response to the radio talk, somewhat to FDR's surprise, was heavily favorable.

Treasury Department officials drafted the Lend-Lease bill in the first week of January, 1941. On January 6, FDR helped prepare Congress and the people for the measure in his State of the Union message. In the speech he called upon America to pledge itself to give the victims of Axis aggression "the strength to regain and maintain a free world." The United States should send "in ever-increasing numbers, ships, planes, tanks, guns." He looked forward, he said, to a world "founded upon four essential human freedoms": freedom of speech and expression, freedom to worship as one chooses, freedom from want, and freedom from fear. He optimistically added, "That is no vision of a distant millennium. It is a definite basis for a kind of world attainable in our own time and generation."

The Lend-Lease bill, H.R. 1776, was introduced in the House on January 10. Despite hearings in each house of Congress and prolonged debate by the bill's opponents, the measure went through fairly quickly. Secretary Hull guided the administration witnesses in the congressional hearings. Its opponents were a mixed lot. Among those appearing against the bill were Colonel Charles A. Lindbergh, Colonel Robert R. McCormick of the *Chicago Daily Tribune*, General Robert E. Wood of the America First Committee, the constitutional lawyer John Bassett Moore, historian Charles A. Beard, and the editor of the *Christian Century*, Charles Clayton Morrison. Wendell Willkie publicly supported the bill. The House passed H.R. 1776 on February 8. The vote was 260 to 165; 236 Democrats and 24 Republicans voted for the bill; 25 Democrats, 135 Republicans, and one American Labor party member (Vito Marcantonio) voted against it. The bill passed the Senate on March 8 by a margin of 60 to 31; voting against it were 13 Democrats, 17 Republicans, and one Progressive (Robert M. LaFollette, Jr.). Roosevelt signed the bill into law three days later. Soon thereafter Congress appropriated $7 billion to put the measure into effect.

Clearly, the passage of Lend-Lease indicated that the United States was by no means a traditionally neutral power. Even before Lend-Lease, America had at times moved beyond the conventional bounds of neutrality to aid Great Britain. In March, 1941, the United States abandoned all pretense of neutrality and became a nonbelligerent, neither at war nor neutral. Before many months passed, the United States would even draw up with Great Britain a statement of general war aims and engage in naval warfare with the Axis, all the while without becoming a declared belligerent.

Lend-Lease pledged America's enormous economic power and resources to defeat the Axis. Now the problem was to produce the goods and deliver them to England. Production was under the general planning and coordination of the Office of Production Management created in December, 1940, with William S. Knudsen as director and labor leader Sidney Hillman as associate director. Production problems were many and intricate, but the economy's basic capacity to produce was never seriously in question. Economic indices climbed with the stimulation of enormous spending for defense and Lend-Lease. Delivery, however, was a serious problem. In the spring of 1941, German submarines stepped up their operations in the North Atlantic. On March 25, Germany extended the war zone westward to include all of Iceland and the strait between Iceland and Greenland. That month German action destroyed over five hundred thousand tons of merchant shipping, and bettered that mark in the succeeding two months.

In the spring and summer of 1941, Roosevelt took many actions calculated to increase the number of ships engaged in delivery to Britain and to protect them from German attack. At the end of March, he permitted a British battleship to be repaired in an American port; thereafter, British naval vessels frequently used United States repair facilities. At about the same time, the Coast Guard seized thirty Axis ships and thirty-five Danish ships that had been interned in American ports and soon thereafter FDR obtained from Congress authority to put the ships to general use. Roosevelt transferred ten Coast Guard cutters to the British navy for antisubmarine operations. Then on April 10, Roosevelt proclaimed that the neutral zone set by the Panama Conference in 1939 should be extended eastward to the twenty-fifth meridian. This was a line running roughly halfway between the Brazilian bulge of South America and the westernmost bulge of Africa north to the northeastern coast of Greenland. West of that line American ships and planes would patrol convoys, notifying them of the presence of enemy force. Also on April 10, Roosevelt removed the Red Sea region from the areas banned to American shipping since the British needed supplies for the defense of Egypt and the Middle East.

In another "fireside chat" on May 27 Roosevelt declared "an unlimited national emergency exists and requires the strengthening of our defense to the extreme limit of our national power and authority." Historians have sometimes cited the German sinking of the *Robin Moor*, an American merchant ship, on May 21 about seven hundred miles off the Brazilian coast as the stimulus to this emergency proclamation, but that could not have been the case because the sinking was not known in Washington until the crew was rescued from its lifeboats nearly three weeks after the sinking. Probably the reason was that Hitler was at the moment enjoying great successes in North Africa, the Mediterranean, and the Balkans.

In July, the United States navy began regular convoy escort duty as far east as Iceland. Iceland, then a Danish possession, had been occupied by British and Canadian troops after the fall of Denmark in April, 1940. On July 7, 1941, American marines replaced them. With American troops to support on Iceland, the navy began convoy escort service. Admiral Ernest J. King's order of July 19 directed a naval unit to "escort United States and Iceland flag shipping, including shipping of any nationality which may join such . . . convoys, between United States ports and bases, and Iceland." The British navy escorted the convoys on to British ports. So far as the western Atlantic was concerned, only one order remained to be made before undeclared naval war was a fact: an order to shoot the enemy on sight. Until then, American naval vessels could only track submarines, direct convoys in evasive action, and notify British destroyers of the location of the enemy.

The nature and scope of the war changed dramatically on Sunday, June 22, 1941, when the Nazis invaded the Soviet Union. Hitler betrayed Stalin, and, as Nikita Khrushchev revealed in his "secret" speech of February, 1956, Stalin was so stunned and unprepared for attack that at first he refused to believe it or take effective counter measures. The Nazi panzer divisions struck quick and deep blows, often being welcomed by subject Soviet peoples such as the Ukrainians. (The Nazis so mistreated these people that in time they turned against their new masters.) American military experts predicted that Germany would conquer Russia in three weeks. Now, American Communists, for the first time since the Nazi-Soviet pact, came out strongly for the defense effort and war. They suddenly ended a strike they had fomented in the aircraft industry in California. In mid-July Harry Hopkins, Lend-Lease administrator and by then FDR's closest adviser, went to London to arrange for a meeting between Roosevelt and Churchill. Churchill suggested he go on to Moscow and discuss affairs with Stalin. Stalin and his lieutenants told Hopkins that they would be able to stop the Nazi advance and launch a counterattack in the winter, which proved to be true. He also said Russia wanted Lend-Lease supplies and hoped the United States would enter the war. He offered to allow American military units to fight under their own command on the Russian front. In October, Britain and the United States promised to give Russia $1 billion worth of aid by mid-1942; Congress also increased Lend-Lease appropriations by another $6 billion and defeated an amendment to deny the Soviets Lend-Lease equipment. In early November, FDR officially declared Russia eligible to receive Lend-Lease. The Soviets eventually received over $11 billion worth of aid.

The meeting between Churchill and Roosevelt that Hopkins arranged for in London took place aboard the American battleship *Augusta*, Admiral

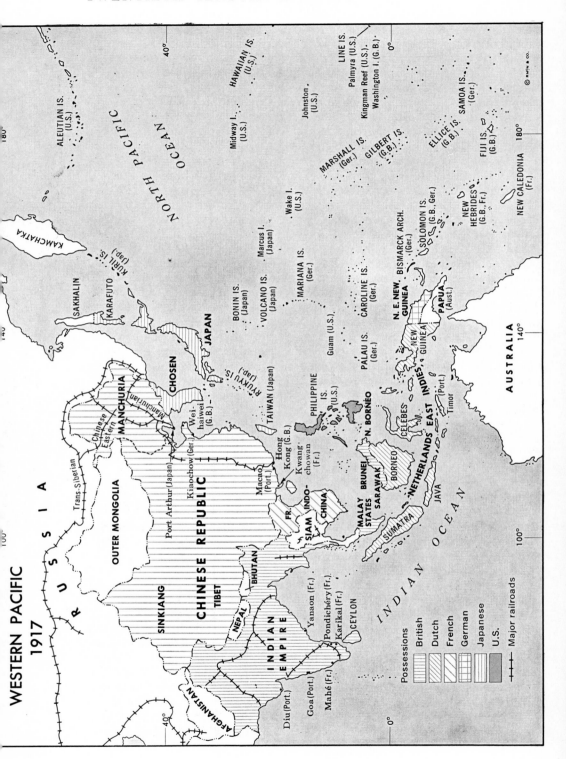

WESTERN PACIFIC
1917

Possessions
British
Dutch
French
German
Japanese
U.S.
Major railroads

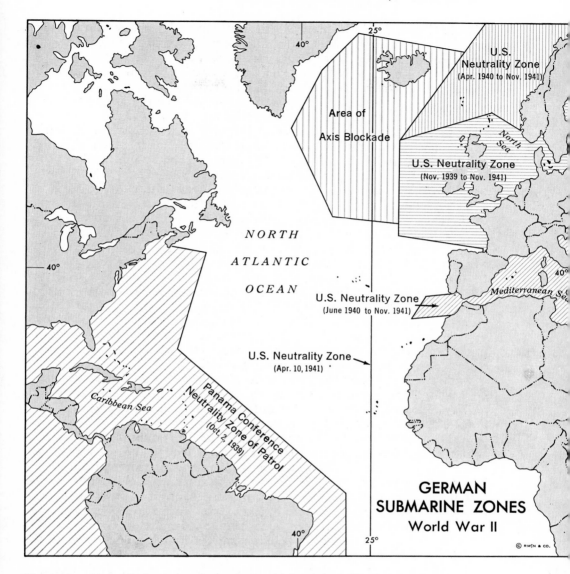

King's flagship, off the coast from Argentia, Newfoundland, August 9 to 12, 1941. Never before had an American president during a time of official peace had such a conference with a prime minister of a belligerent power. Roosevelt and Churchill discussed technical matters such as long-range purchasing policies, general strategy, and postwar aims. Churchill tried but failed to get a commitment from Roosevelt that the United States would come to Britain's aid if the Japanese attacked British possessions or dominions in the Pacific. Roosevelt agreed only to warn Japan against such a course and did not accept the British draft of the warning. The most publicized result of the meeting was the Atlantic Charter, which was released to the world's press on August 14, the first public announcement of the Argentia Conference. The President

453

and the Prime Minister "deem it right to make known certain common principles in the national policies of their respective countries on which they base their hopes for a better future for the world." There followed a set of eight points similar to Wilson's Fourteen Points of World War I: no aggrandizement of any nation of any kind; no territorial changes not in accord with the expressed wishes of the people concerned; the right of all people to choose the form of government under which they live and self-government restored to those people forcibly deprived of it; equal access for all nations to world trade and raw materials; economic collaboration of all nations to improve the material status of all; freedom from fear and want; freedom of the seas; and disarmament after the war. The American noninterventionist press replied to the announcement of the Atlantic Charter with outraged editorials, but the high-sounding principles enunciated in the document had an appeal to the electorate. Public opinion polls indicated no great change of opinion about war and peace one way or another.

The public was more loath to accept the new amendment to the Selective Service Act of 1940 than to accept the Argentia Conference. In June, 1941, the administration began a campaign to extend the terms of service of the draftees who had been inducted. Roosevelt originally wanted the term of service extended to the end of the emergency and wanted to lift the ban on sending draftees overseas. Congressional leaders informed the White House that this would not pass. Many argued that to extend the term of service beyond the original twelve months amounted to a breach of faith with the soldier. Roosevelt dropped the request for lifting the overseas ban and had to settle for an eighteen-month extension. The Senate passed the amendment on August 7; on August 12, the House passed the bill by one vote, 203 to 202. The House Democrats divided in favor of the bill, 182 to 65; the Republicans lined up against it, 133 to 21.

The German-proclaimed war zone and the American-proclaimed neutral zone overlapped in the waters west and south of Iceland. With both German U-boats and American naval vessels engaged in convoy escort in these waters, it was only a matter of time before a serious incident occurred. On September 4, a British patrol plane notified the American destroyer *Greer*, on its way to Iceland with passengers and mail, that a German submarine was submerged about ten miles ahead of it. The *Greer* then located the submarine and trailed it for several hours, meanwhile broadcasting the submarine's position to the British. Finally, the submarine fired two torpedoes at the *Greer*. Both of them missed the target. The *Greer* answered with depth charges. Their effect, if any, was not known.

The *Greer* affair provided the President the kind of incident he wanted. In a worldwide radio broadcast on September 11 he declared, ". . . our patrolling vessels and planes will protect all merchant ships—not only American ships but ships of any flag—engaged in commerce in our defensive waters." His speech ended, "From now on, if German or Italian vessels of war enter the waters the protection of which is necessary for American defense, they do so at their own peril." Two days later official naval orders implemented the new policy: the fleet in the Atlantic was to provide "protection against hostile attack of United States and foreign flag shipping (other than German and Italian shipping) by escorting, convoying and patrolling as circumstances may require, or by destroying German and Italian naval, land, and air forces encountered." Without a declaration of war, a shooting war in the North Atlantic had begun.

The undeclared Atlantic war proceeded. In mid-October a Nazi torpedo hit the destroyer *Kearny*, and eleven of the crew were killed. On October 31, a German submarine sank another destroyer, the *Reuben James,* with the loss of 115 lives.

With shooting war and Lend-Lease, the neutrality law still in effect became an anachronism. On October 9, 1941, Roosevelt asked Congress to repeal the critical parts of the Neutrality Act of 1939. He asked specifically for repeal of Section VI, which forbade the arming of merchant ships, but expressed the additional hope that Congress would repeal the sections preventing American ships from traveling in combat zones the President designated and from visiting belligerent ports. Since naval vessels were already authorized to shoot on sight, there seemed little point in denying merchant ships authority to arm themselves. The House passed a bill repealing Section VI of the Neutrality Act on October 17 by a vote of 259 to 138. With such a wide margin, the President was emboldened to ask the Senate to include his other repeal requests. The Senate complied on November 7, but the vote, fifty to thirty-seven, was the narrowest administration victory in the Senate on any foreign policy issue since the beginning of the war in Europe. Back went the bill to the House, as the Senate had repealed more of the Neutrality Act than had the House in its October vote. Again, Roosevelt's proposal had a narrow majority, 212 to 194. Democrats supported the measure, 189 to 53; Republicans opposed it, 137 to 22. Representatives from the South generally supported the repeal, those from the Midwest generally opposed, and those from the Far West and the large industrial states of the East divided about evenly.

By November 13, 1941, when the Neutrality Act was finally repealed and armed American ships were free to go even to British ports and when American naval convoy escorts had standing orders to shoot German and Italian craft on sight and had exchanged blows with Axis vessels, it may fairly be said that the United States through its elected constitutional officers had decided to accept war with Germany and Italy. Still, such was the strength of the belief that the United States should not declare war without extreme provocation that, as late as December 6, it is almost certain that Congress would not have passed a war resolution if Roosevelt had asked. A public opinion poll in November indicated that less than 35 per cent of the people would have voted for war if a national referendum had been held. "All aid short of war" remained the motto of the majority until the war came. And it came not at the focus of primary attention in the Atlantic, but in the Pacific.

The Long Negotiations with Japan

In February, 1939, the Japanese seized the Chinese island of Hainan in the South China Sea. While actually fighting only China, Japan was moving south

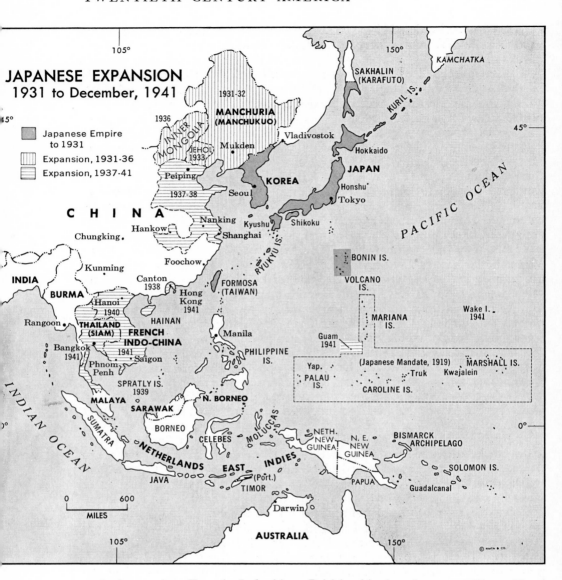

JAPANESE EXPANSION
1931 to December, 1941

Japanese Empire to 1931
Expansion, 1931-36
Expansion, 1937-41

and threatening French Indochina, British shipping between Hong Kong and Singapore, and even the Philippines. The United States replied with a threat of economic warfare. On July 26, 1939, the United States gave Japan the six months' notice necessary to abrogate the Japanese-American commercial treaty of 1911. After late January, 1940, no treaty obligation prevented the United States from withholding such strategic materials as oil and scrap iron from Japan. Deficient in many natural resources, Japan had relied upon America to fulfill over half the raw materials for its military and naval needs.

The "phony war" in Europe, September, 1939, to April, 1940, brought no change in Japanese ambitions. In January, 1940, a moderate government headed by Mitsumasa Yonai came to power. But Hitler's spectacular successes in the spring of 1940 encouraged Japanese militarists to press for a more aggressive policy. The defeat of France and Holland left French Indochina and the Dutch East Indies ripe for Japanese plucking, and hard-pressed Great Britain was hardly in a position to resist strongly. Japanese militarists' dream of a Greater East Asia Co-Prosperity Sphere seemed impelled toward realization by European events. The militarists successfully applied pressure on the Yonai government to begin negotiations for a military alliance with Germany, and on July 16 the army high command succeeded in toppling the regime altogether. The new government, headed by the moderate Prince Fumimaro Konoye, had at least two ardently expansionist and militaristic officials in key positions: the Minister for Foreign Affairs, Yosuke Matsuoka, and the Minister of War, General Hideki Tojo. The new government lost no time in pressing expansionist policies and forming an alliance with Germany and Italy.

The Konoye government sought from the Vichy government, the accommodating French government in the south of France that Germany allowed to exist after the conquest, the right to station Japanese troops in northern Indochina. It sought from the Churchill government in London an order closing the Burma road, one of the main lifelines to the Nationalist Chinese capital at Chungking. Neither was in a strong position to resist, and both granted Japanese demands quickly. The British reopened the road in October, 1940. The Dutch stalled the Japanese and managed to prevent them from getting all the East Indian oil they wanted until war began and the Japanese took the islands by force.

Then, on September 27, 1940, the Japanese concluded the Tripartite, or Berlin, Pact with Germany and Italy. Japan recognized German and Italian leadership in a new European order, and the European powers reciprocated. The critical clause was Article Three, in which the three powers agreed "to assist one another with all political, economic and military means when one of the three contracting powers is attacked by a power at present not involved in the European war or in the Chinese-Japanese conflict." Since another part of the agreement specifically excluded Russia, the treaty obviously was aimed at the United States. The alliance was defensive in its wording. There was no guarantee, for example, that Germany would or would not declare war on the United States if Japan should attack America. Japan completed its treaty arrangements with European powers on April 13, 1941, when it made a neutrality agreement with Russia. The Japanese and the Soviets agreed to remain neutral if either were attacked by another power or powers. This left Japan free to develop her plans for Asia, but it also allowed Russia to put its main attention upon Europe. The agreement proved much to Russia's advantage when Germany attacked in June.

Washington responded to these Japanese developments with a policy of economic pressure and diplomatic warnings. When the Japanese made their demands upon the French and British, Roosevelt replied with an order requiring a federal license for permission to export petroleum or its products and high-grade scrap metal. Soon thereafter, he completely embargoed shipments of aviation gasoline out of the Western Hemisphere. When it became apparent that the Tripartite Pact was in the offing, he also embargoed all scrap iron and steel, making an exception only for Great Britain. At the same time he announced an additional Export-Import Bank loan to China of $25 million. The diplomatic notes were equally strong. In February, 1941, the State Department notified Japan that threats to its sources of "essential primary commodities" in Southeast Asia—oil, rubber, and tin—"would not be tolerated." These actions, as well as publicized discussions of American naval officers with their counterparts from Britain, the Netherlands, and Australia, induced Japan to adopt a more conciliatory position at least temporarily. Roosevelt thus was able to forestall an all-out Japanese drive while the anti-fascist powers of Europe suffered their heaviest reverses in 1940 and most of 1941.

Important Japanese political groups and figures were sharply divided about how adventurous Japan should be in its expansionist ambitions. Some moderates, including important naval officers, were fearful of a war with the United States; others, particularly the army high command, itched for war. Few Japanese moderates, however, were willing to concede Washington's intractable position on China: that Japan should withdraw and grant Chinese political integrity. Failure to reach any agreement on the central Chinese question strengthened Japanese extremists and increased the likelihood of war, perhaps making it inevitable.

Division in Japanese political circles was apparent from the tangled story of negotiations, official and unofficial, between Tokyo and Washington in the first half of 1941. Two American Roman Catholic clergymen, Bishop James E. Walsh and Father James M. Drought, in Japan on business for their order, discussed Japanese-American problems unofficially with moderate Japanese officials. Eventually, the two were asked to carry some generous proposals to President Roosevelt that they understood came from Prince Konoye himself. The proposals they carried conceded a great deal on China; in return, Japan wanted the United States to let up on its anti-Japanese economic policies. Secretary Hull, dubious that any Japanese government could actually and officially deliver on such generous offers in the face of Japanese militarist strength, suggested that nothing be done until the arrival in Washington of the new Japanese ambassador, Admiral Kichisaburo Nomura, who had attended the United States Naval Academy as a youth. Discussions with Admiral Nomura proceeded promisingly but inconclusively until Foreign Minister Matsuoka returned to Tokyo from Moscow, where he had been negotiating the Russo-Japanese neutrality agreement. Angry about the discussions in Washington conducted during his absence from Tokyo, Matsuoka insisted upon very hard terms. The discussions thereupon deadlocked with no results.

In late July, 1941, after Germany had moved deeply into Russia and thereby changed the Asian picture despite the Russo-Japanese neutrality agreement, Japan completed its military domination of French Indochina. In the summer of 1940, Japan had moved troops into northern Indochina; now it moved them into the South as well, all with the consent of the Vichy government. The suspicion that the real purpose of this maneuver was to put the Japanese in position to attack the Dutch East Indies and British Malaya was confirmed by "Magic," the United States Navy Intelligence code-breaking operation, which had recently succeeded in solving one of the important Japanese codes. Roosevelt retaliated on July 25 by freezing Japanese funds in the United States, thus seriously crippling Japan's power either to buy or sell in America. The Netherlands government in exile and Great Britain soon followed suit. Roosevelt also closed the Panama Canal to Japanese shipping and called the Philippine militia to active duty. American public opinion seemed more strongly behind FDR's Japanese policy, at least in the summer of 1941, than it was behind his European policies. When FDR left for the Atlantic Conference with Churchill in early August, Japanese-American relations were more strained than they had ever been.

At the Argentia meeting, Churchill urged Roosevelt to take an even stronger position with Japan. Roosevelt agreed that upon his return to Washington he would inform Ambassador Nomura that "any further encroachment by Japan in the Southwestern Pacific would produce a situation in which the United States Government would be compelled to take countermeasures even though these might lead to war between the United States and Japan." The very day FDR returned to the White House, August 17, he and Hull had a conference with Nomura. Nomura, however, had come to the conference with a conciliatory proposal about which he had already informed Hull. Hull, fearful that the strong statement agreed to at the Atlantic Conference might even cause the Konoye cabinet to fall and be replaced by a less moderate one, persuaded FDR to water down the American warning.

Nomura's proposal was no less than a suggestion that Roosevelt meet with Konoye in a Pacific conference to attempt to resolve the difficulties between their nations. Konoye had decided that in the face of the economic stranglehold America had on his country only two alternatives remained: either some kind of Japanese-American agreement or war. Afraid that war would bring Japanese defeat, probably quickly, Konoye decided to make a major effort to bring about an agreement despite the considerable pressure for war that came from the military. If an agreement were possible, Konoye calculated, only he and Roosevelt could do it. If an agreement still proved impossible, the world at least would know that the greatest efforts had been expended to prevent war. Joseph C. Grew, the United States ambassador in Tokyo, was optimistic about such a Pacific conference and strongly supported it.

Roosevelt at first was inclined to view a meeting with Konoye favorably. He especially was impressed with Japanese notes in late August and early September that indicated that Japan was "prepared to withdraw its troops from Indo-China as soon as the China Incident is settled or a just peace is established in East Asia" and that it could be induced to loosen its ties with the Axis. But Hull urged caution. Before Roosevelt agreed to a meeting, Hull argued, the Japanese must be specific about what they would concede, and unless they were prepared to make concessions about China there should be no bargain. Roosevelt took Hull's advice. Konoye made no more specific concessions in writing, perhaps because politics within Japan dictated that he should avoid a stance that looked like appeasement. On October 16, the Konoye government had to resign when it could not produce anything solid as the fruit of its moderation. Two days later, General Tojo himself became premier.

Because Roosevelt declined to "go to the summit" with Konoye, to use a journalistic phrase not coined until years later, and because war did come between Japan and the United States, Roosevelt has been severely criticized. No one, of course, knows what would have happened if there had been a Pacific conference. Both Roosevelt's critics who say that a conference with Konoye could have prevented war or postponed it until after Germany and Italy were defeated and his defenders who say that a conference would have been useless argue from assumption rather than evidence.

Pearl Harbor

Even the elevation of General Tojo to the premiership did not mean an immediate Japanese decision for war. Emperor Hirohito himself, with the support of the navy, urged restraint upon the militarists. At a conference of Japanese leaders with the emperor on November 5, the various factions made an agreement. The Japanese government would make one major effort for peace with the United States. The conference spelled out what Japan would concede under certain conditions and sent a second ambassador, Saburo Kurusu, to Washington to help Nomura. But, it was agreed, if some kind of agreement were not made with the United States by late November, Japan would go to war. The Japanese negotiators at Washington knew, therefore, that time was running out, that peace depended upon the success of the negotiations.

The Roosevelt administration also realized the crucial importance of the November negotiations because "Magic" had picked up and decoded important messages to the Japanese embassy in Washington. American negotiators knew that Japan had two plans, the second to be presented if the United States rejected the first. The second plan made more concessions than the first but was to be only a temporary arrangement, not so much a permanent agreement as a stopgap truce to allow still more time for negotiations. Japan conceded nothing on China in either plan. Then on November 22 "Magic" intercepted a message from Tokyo to the Japanese embassy which extended the deadline for negotiations from November 25 to November 29 but which stated if there were no results by then "things are automatically going to happen." Precisely what things and where were unknown, but the implication of war was clear.

Ambassadors Nomura and Kurusu presented the second Japanese plan on November 20. Between then and November 26, when Hull replied, activity within the Roosevelt administration was feverish; yet the activity brought relatively few results. After receipt of the "things are automatically going to happen" message, Washington warned military and naval commanders in the Pacific that surprise attacks on Guam and the Philippines were possible. Rather quickly the administration decided to reject the second Japanese plan and to concentrate on preparing a counterproposal. Discussion centered upon the provisions of a *modus vivendi* of three months to be proposed to the Japanese. During a three-month truce, Japan and the United States would continue to search for a solution to peace and the United States would build up its force of B-17 bombers in the Philippines. Secretary of War Stimson believed that a strong bomber force there could prevent a Japanese movement to the south. Since a comparable build-up of fighter support for these B-17's was out of the question, such faith in unprotected bombers was naive. Again, the Chinese question proved to be the stumbling block. One draft of the *modus vivendi* had a vague statement to the effect that the United States "would not look with disfavor" upon conversations between China and Japan looking toward a peaceful settlement of their differences. When the State Department showed this draft to the Chinese, British, and Dutch embassies, the Chinese protested and the Dutch and British expressed no enthusiasm. In any case, it is dubious that Japan would have been attracted by the proposal about China, vague as it was.

By November 26, the administration was so pessimistic about any real solution that it proposed no *modus vivendi* at all but rather put forward a ten-point program for a long-range settlement that encompassed all the American demands. The statement Hull read to Nomura and Kurusu on November 26, demanding as it did complete Japanese withdrawal from China and Indochina and abandonment of the puppet Japanese government in China, was obviously unacceptable to Tokyo. Hull knew that the Japanese would not accept the United States demand. On the day after he replied to the Japanese ambassadors, he told Stimson that the situation was in the hands of the military rather than the diplomats. Actually, both sides had by late November taken a "take it or leave it" attitude and accepted the probability of war, even though reluctantly.

In the discussions within the American government, November 20 to 26, one of the main subjects was what the United States would do if the Japanese launched a major attack in Southeast Asia. A large Japanese convoy was moving south along the China coast. The United States anticipated an attack, possibly a surprise attack, on Malaya, Thailand, the Dutch East Indies, or the Philippines, maybe against all of them. The focus clearly was on the western Pacific and the perimeter of Asia rather than the middle Pacific and Hawaii. The administration believed that if Japan attacked toward the south then the United States should enter the conflict. To the administration, the main question was how to persuade the American people that a Japanese attack upon a non-American territory was sufficient grounds for war. Roosevelt's speech writers worked on a message to Congress designed to persuade Congress and the public that Japanese advance southward jeopardized the United States and constituted justifiable cause for a war declaration. At a meeting of the so-called war cabinet—Roosevelt, Hull, Stimson, Secretary of the Navy Knox, Chief of Staff George C. Marshall, and Chief of Naval Operations Harold R. Stark—on November 25, according to Stimson's diary, the group discussed "the question of how we should maneuver them into the position of firing the first shot without allowing too much danger to ourselves." After World War II, this selection from Stimson's diary was a major arrow in the quiver of Roosevelt critics who charged that FDR tricked the American people into the war by maneuvering the Japanese into attack. FDR's purpose, according to these critics, was to get into a war with Hitler that the public would accept. The soundest interpretation of the "maneuver" sentence is that "we" meant the Americans, British, and Dutch and that the first shot was expected in the western Pacific or Southeast Asia, not that the quotation indicates a Roosevelt scheme to bait Japan with Pearl Harbor in order to get into

461

war with Europe.[3] In fact, it is not certain, despite Roosevelt's predilection and the advice of his cabinet and military subordinates, that the United States would have gone to war over a Japanese movement south. Indeed, when on December 6 Washington received word that Japanese troops were moving on Malaya, Roosevelt dispatched a final desperate plea for peace to Emperor Hirohito. The message did not arrive before the shooting actually began.

On November 25, a Japanese naval force set out from the Kurile Islands north of Japan proper with orders to attack the American naval base at Pearl Harbor and airfields elsewhere in Hawaii at dawn on Sunday, December 7. The task force was prepared to turn back without attacking upon word from Tokyo. No word ever came. At 7:55 A.M. on December 7, planes from Japanese carriers attacked Hawaiian airfields and the American fleet at Pearl Harbor. The attack was an utter surprise. A second wave of planes attacked fifty minutes later. So thorough and devastating was the first attack that only a few American planes from a base the Japanese had negligently overlooked were able to get into the air for the second attack. Only a few antiaircraft batteries were able to respond. Some destroyers went into action against attacking Japanese submarines. The Japanese attack, on the whole, was one of the best planned and executed major raids in the history of warfare. In less than two hours the American military and naval establishment in Hawaii, one of the biggest in the world, was reduced to impotence. Japanese losses consisted of six submarines and twenty-nine planes. Over half of the American planes in Hawaii were destroyed or disabled, five battleships were sunk or seriously damaged, and over three thousand soldiers, sailors, and marines were killed or missing. So serious were American losses that the government refrained from making their extent public for fear of damage to national morale. The Japanese launched almost simultaneous attacks upon Thailand, Malaya, and the Philippines.

Japan timed its reply to the American counterproposal of November 26 to be delivered in Washington early on Sunday afternoon, December 7, a few minutes before the first bombs were to fall on Hawaii. In one of the few hitches in the whole Japanese operation, the Japanese embassy had difficulty deciphering the message and delayed its delivery until just after the American government received word of the Pearl Harbor attack. When Nomura and Kurusu saw Hull, all three parties knew their meeting was a diplomatic mockery.

Who was responsible for the American debacle? This has been a major question of partisan politics and historical bickering ever since the war's end. Obviously, someone was negligent. Was it the commanders in Hawaii, General Walter C. Short and Admiral Husband E. Kimmel, their military and civilian superior officers in Washington, or both? Despite the reams that have been written and the weeks of congressional investigations, the whole story is not yet clear. No major American figure was blameless, nor was any solely responsible. A bigger and more important question is why had American foreign relations deteriorated to such an extent that a surprise attack was

---

[3] For the best account and interpretation of the Stimson diary entry see, Richard Nelson Current, "How Stimson Meant to 'Meaneuver' the Japanese," *Mississippi Valley Historical Review*, XL (June, 1953), 67–74, and the same author's *Secretary Stimson: A Study in Statecraft* (New Brunswick, 1954).

possible. There is no simple answer. Quite obviously, the answer will not be reached by debates, professional or political, between those who, on the one hand, want to prove Roosevelt a devilish conspirator who tricked the nation into war by the back door or those who, on the other hand, argue that FDR was entirely blameless and candid.

Japan officially declared war upon the United States about two hours after the Pearl Harbor attack. On December 8, Congress voted a declaration of war against Japan, unanimously in the Senate and with one dissenting vote in the House. The lone dissenter was Jeannette Rankin, Republican of Montana. A former suffragette, the first woman to sit in Congress, and a congressional opponent of war in 1917, she tearfully explained that Christian principles dictated that at least one vote should be cast against war and that it was appropriate that a woman should cast it. Great Britain had declared war upon Japan only hours before the American declaration. The day of the American declaration, Japan asked Germany to declare war upon America. On November 29, Germany had notified Japan she would join her if Japan went to war with America. On December 11, Germany and Italy declared war upon the United States. The same day the United States declared war upon the Axis, this time without a dissenting vote.

Such unanimity for a declaration of war would have been an impossibility before the Japanese attack at Pearl Harbor. Indeed, never before had the United States ever entered a war with such unanimity. In the long run, the Japanese attack was a psychological mistake because it unified America without knocking it out of contention. Grimly, almost fatalistically, with little of the evangelical spirit that characterized America in 1917 and 1918, the American people as a nation set about finishing up the distasteful and ugly business they felt had been forced upon them.

CHAPTER TWENTY-THREE

Mobilizing for Victory

TOTAL WARS ARE FOUGHT AT HOME AS MUCH AS THEY ARE AT THE front. Modern war is a contest between competing industrial complexes as well as combat between military units. As great as the achievements of America's fighting men were in World War II, the United States and its allies could not have won the ultimate victory without the efforts of those who stayed home.

The magnitude of America's wartime economic problem was perhaps as great as its depression problem, although it was considerably different. The task for all productive and distributive facilities and workers was to get sufficient numbers of trained fighting men wherever they were needed in the world and to supply them and allied forces with more and better arms and other material than the enemy's. This meant the economy had to function at forced draft and at well-oiled efficiency. To get the job done, it was necessary, intelligently and forcefully, to allocate and coordinate manpower resources, raw materials, fuel and other energy sources, industrial and agricultural products, and transportation facilities. It followed that the volume of the economy had to be increased and many more goods and services had to be made available and distributed systematically. To insure the ultimate success of these efforts required central planning and direction of the whole complex operation—some kind of national economic planning.

America did the job, but did not do it perfectly; poor decisions, injustices, raids of organized greed, big and small inefficiencies there were in plenty, but still America did the job. The farmer, the worker, the manager, the bureaucrat, and the investor succeeded in enlarging the relative trickle of war production of 1941 to a huge and steady flow by 1945. Indeed, protected as it was from enemy action, America's power to produce grew mightily during the war. No other major nation emerged from the war industrially stronger than it had entered it.

Politics, Almost as Usual

A supposed advantage of a totalitarian state over a demoracy is that it eliminates the indecision, disunity, and distraction of democratic politics. Yet, if World War II was fought to protect democracy in an increasingly totalitarian world, it was necessary to preserve conventional democratic politics. Although there were some who strongly urged the creation of a national economic czar and many who voiced a hope that partisanship would be submerged in national unity, few were ready to give up political advantage or hope for advantage. Political conflict among organized groups, Democrats and Republicans, labor and capital and agriculture, inevitably continued; for the most part, it continued within the traditional democratic ground rules.

The trend was toward increasing power of the political and economic conservatives. Ever since the congressional elections of 1938, the Congress had in fact been governed by a cautious, orthodox coalition of Democratic and Republican conservatives who controlled the chairmanships, through the seniority principle, of most of the important committees. The White House, eager to have the cooperation of Congress, compromised in its requests and found usually that Congress compromised them further. Although many Democrats and a few unusual Republicans hoped the war could be used to extend the social welfare principles of the second New Deal, the President explicitly said that "Dr. Win-the-War" had been substituted for "Dr. New Deal." The President's opponents succeeded in keeping "Dr. New Deal" permanently on the sidelines.

The voters seemed to endorse this rightward drift in the 1942 congressional elections. The party out of the White House usually gains in congressional elections in nonpresidential years, but the Republicans in 1942 went beyond the usual by gaining forty-seven seats in the House of Representatives and ten in the Senate. Senate Democrats lost still another vote on most issues when Nebraska Republicans in their primary elected Kenneth Wherry, who bowed to no man in his conservatism, to replace George Norris, the man who had curbed the power of Speaker Cannon in 1910 and become known as "the father of TVA." Probably part of the anti-Democratic vote reflected concern over the poor way the war was going (the landing in North Africa came just after the election) and with the quite obvious confusion in Washington over industrial mobilization.

Heartened by the off-year elections and strife between the President and conservative congressional Democrats, especially in the Senate and in particular over tax matters, Republicans dared to hope for victory in 1944. The main contenders for the GOP presidential nomination were Wendell Willkie, Governor John W. Bricker of Ohio, and Governor Thomas E. Dewey of New York. Willkie did not stand high with most Republican leaders because of his defeat in 1940 and because of his rather close identification with FDR's policies after the election. Bricker did not have a great deal to command national attention, but, being the chief executive of an important mid-western state, he had good support in that part of the nation. Dewey, who had received national headlines as a "racket-busting" district attorney in New York City before he became governor, was not only attractive and vigorous but had the support of the financially strong eastern wing of the GOP. Willkie withdrew from consideration after his defeat in the Wisconsin presidential primary. (He died before the end of the year.)

The Republican convention in Chicago in late June nominated Dewey on the first ballot and went on to name Bricker as his running mate. Perhaps the most interesting aspect of the convention was the platform it advocated. First, it adopted a strongly internationalist declaration that party leaders had written the previous year at a special conference at Mackinac Island, Michigan. Second, although it was critical of the way Democrats had administered the laws, it endorsed such New Deal measures as social security and aid to farmers. One could fairly conclude that, no matter what political groups actually thought, it was good politics in 1944 to appear to be for the measures that had gained Roosevelt such electoral success.

Roosevelt, as in 1940, played coy and cool. Not until eight days before the Democratic convention did he publicly announce that he was available. The real Democratic battle was over the nomination for the vice-presidency. The incumbent, Henry A. Wallace, was anathema to conservatives in the party as well as to others for a variety of reasons of which the most important probably was that he was the darling of the farthest left elements in the party. However, if one considered what Wallace had done rather than what he had said or what his critics said of him, the intensity of the conservative opposition was puzzling. At any rate, most of the party leaders were bent upon unseating the Iowan. Since FDR did not appear to be in good health—he had lost weight upon doctor's recommendations after a bout of bronchitis—interest in the vice-presidency had a special urgency. The main opposition to Wallace came from former Supreme Court Justice and then "Assistant President" for war mobilization, James F. Byrnes of South Carolina. FDR publicly supported Wallace but said the nomination was the convention's responsibility. Just before the convention Byrnes thought he had FDR's nod. But others in the party vigorously opposed Byrnes. Edward Flynn of the Bronx, as a Roman Catholic, informed Roosevelt that Catholics were uneasy about Byrnes because he had left the church; Sidney Hillman, the main spokesman for labor in the Democratic fold, flatly and firmly told Roosevelt that Byrnes would not do because labor and Negroes would not support the conservative South Carolinian. Roosevelt thereupon informed Party Chairman Robert E. Hannegan that Senator Harry S. Truman of Missouri or Justice William O. Douglas were acceptable to him but that in any case he should "clear it with Sidney." Sidney, of course, would not clear Byrnes.

The convention, as was to be expected, nominated Roosevelt on its first ballot. His opponents mustered eighty-nine votes for Senator Harry F. Byrd of Virginia, and one die-hard delegate cast a vote for former Postmaster General Jim Farley. The convention went through the motions of a contest for the second spot, but Truman's nomination was foreordained. Wallace led on the first two ballots but Truman, who had only recently come to national

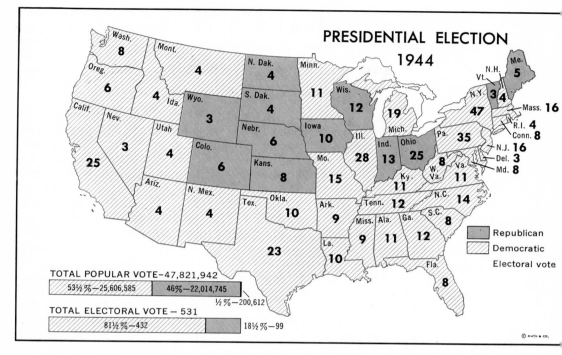

PRESIDENTIAL ELECTION
1944

Wash. 8
Oreg. 6
Calif. 25
Nev. 3
Ida. 4
Mont. 4
Utah 4
Ariz. 4
Wyo. 3
Colo. 6
N. Mex. 4
N. Dak. 4
S. Dak. 4
Nebr. 6
Kans. 8
Okla. 10
Tex. 23
Minn. 11
Iowa 10
Mo. 15
Ark. 9
La. 10
Wis. 12
Ill. 28
Mich. 19
Ind. 13
Ky. 11
Tenn. 12
Miss. 9
Ala. 11
Ga. 12
Ohio 25
W. Va. 8
Va. 11
N.C. 14
S.C. 8
Fla. 8
Pa. 35
N.Y. 47
Vt. 3
N.H. 4
Me. 5
Mass. 16
R.I. 4
Conn. 8
N.J. 16
Del. 3
Md. 8

Republican
Democratic
Electoral vote

TOTAL POPULAR VOTE—47,821,942
53½%—25,606,585   46%—22,014,745
½%—200,612

TOTAL ELECTORAL VOTE — 531
81½%—432   18½%—99

© RAND & CO.

notice as chairman of a special Senate committee investigating mismanagement in war industries, won on the third. For a platform, the Democratic party cited its record.

The newly formed Political Action Committee of the CIO, generally called the CIO-PAC, provided about all that was novel in the campaign. The PAC spent a lot of money for the Democratic cause, conducted many a mass rally, and bought radio time. When Republicans attacked hard on the "clear it with Sidney" theme, first reported by an admirer of Byrnes, Arthur Krock of the New York *Times*, they apparently only consolidated the big city vote behind FDR. Roosevelt, extremely busy with the duties of commander in chief, restricted his campaign to well-publicized visits of war installations until late in the race when it appeared that Dewey was gaining rapidly. In a speech aboard a ship at Bremerton, Washington, FDR had appeared overtired, uncertain, and old. Rumors circulated that the President had suffered a stroke. Then the old campaigner went to work. He demonstrated his champion deft touch in a speech to the Teamsters' Union convention in Washington on September 23 that lives as a masterpiece of light but effective campaign oratory. His later campaigning in eastern cities, including a day-long drive in an open car in a hard rain at New York, seemed to dispel fears about his health.

The voters again overwhelmingly elected FDR. He received 25,602,505 popular votes and 432 in the electoral college to Dewey's 22,006,278 and 99. Roosevelt lost only Maine, Vermont, Ohio, Indiana, Wisconsin, Iowa, Kansas, Colorado, Nebraska, Wyoming, and North and South Dakota. The new Sen-

467

ate had the same balance as the old: 57 Democrats, 38 Republicans, and 1 independent. Democrats gained 20 House seats, to give them 242 to the Republicans' 190 and 2 independents.

Mobilizing Manpower

The nation's first task after Pearl Harbor was to expand its armed services enormously. Accordingly, Congress quickly amended the Selective Service Act of 1940 so as to extend the service of men already in the armed forces to the duration of the war plus six months and to require draft registration of all men between the ages of twenty and forty-four for possible military service and of all men over military age up to sixty-five for possible labor service. None were ever drafted for labor service, however. In November, 1942, another amendment lowered the draft age to eighteen. Only a few men past thirty-eight were ever drafted, and in 1944 the services began to release enlisted men in noncritical positions who were over forty-one.

The key administrative unit in Selective Service, which was under the general administration of General Lewis B. Hershey, was the local draft board, of which there were almost 6,500 over the country. Congress and Hershey set general policy, and the draft boards administered it. The citizens who served as draft board members, without pay, had a thankless, time-consuming, and heart-breaking task. The plan was to draft unmarried men without dependents first, then married men without children, and fathers last of all. Some boards, however, exhausted their registration of men without dependents and began to induct fathers while other boards still had a supply of young unattached men.

About 31,000,000 men registered for selective service, of whom 9,867,707 were inducted. Still others volunteered. A total of over 15,000,000 men and women were in uniform at one time or another, although the services never had that many at any one time. The army, which then included the air corps, gave the oath to almost 10,500,000, the navy to about 4,500,000 including almost 600,000 marines, and the coast guard to about 250,000. About 200,000 women volunteered for the various women's branches: the Women's Army Corps (WAC), the largest with about 100,000 of whom one-sixth served overseas; the navy's Women Accepted for Volunteer Emergency Service (WAVES), who numbered about 85,000; the marine corps' Women's Reserve; and the coast guard SPARs.

Industry's immense task required a startling growth of the civilian labor force, which increased from 46,500,000 in 1940 to over 53,000,000 at the same time as the armed forces took millions off the labor market. About 7,000,000 came from the unemployed. Almost 4,000,000 came from young people growing into the labor force, including altogether too many youngsters who quit high school to take jobs. About 1,000,000 elderly people left retirement to go back to work. The rest of the difference came from women, hundreds of thousands of whom took jobs that had once been considered only for men. The lure of the dollar was probably a greater incentive for women working than the image of Rosie the Riveter, the propaganda symbol of the wartime woman industrial worker who managed in the ads to look glamorously attractive even in coveralls, but Rosie undoubtedly stimulated social acceptance of women workers.

In the hope of getting the right skilled worker at the right job at the right time and of minimizing "job hopping," Roosevelt in April, 1942, established the War Manpower Commission with Paul V. McNutt, former governor of Indiana, as its head. At first practically without real powers, the WMC later made it mandatory for defense workers who wanted to change jobs to get permission from the United States Employment Service. Actual enforcement, however, was next to impossible when both the employee and his prospective employer wanted a change. To meet this situation, the suggestion came of a total national service system to mobilize all labor power more effectively, such as Great Britain had adopted. Objections were vigorous. Opponents of the scheme argued that national labor service was at least not yet necessary and that it would be too easily misadministered at the worker's expense. Trade unions feared such a plan would become an antilabor device. Roosevelt delayed taking action for concern about the possible political consequences, but in his annual message to Congress in January, 1944, he requested such legislation. For nearly a year Congress let the proposal lie fallow. In December, in the wave of near hysteria over the Nazi counteroffensive in the "Battle of the Bulge," the House passed a labor draft bill. The Senate delayed, and as American forces soon began once again to force the Germans back, pressure for the measure decreased. The Senate never acted.

Mobilizing Industry

Government direction of the extremely difficult task of coordinating and stimulating production got off to a bad start long before Pearl Harbor, went through a painful and involved series of reorganizations, and eventually became adequate for the task in the winter of 1942–1943. In August, 1939, the War Resources Board under the War and Navy Departments, composed mostly of executives from big corporations, came into being to advise upon industrial mobilization. The Board, in effect, made political recommendations when it urged that businessmen should administer mobilization through agencies apart from the regular executive offices and that labor laws should be shunted aside for the duration of the defense emergency. The Board further recommended that in the event of war an economic czar should direct the whole operation, a suggestion that would have taken power from regular constitutional officers. Roosevelt dissolved the Board. Bernard Baruch, who had been chairman of Wilson's War Industries Board, suggested another plan, which FDR sat on promptly. Finally, after the fall of France in the spring of 1940, FDR, drawing upon a World War I congressional authorization, appointed an Advisory Commission of the Council of National Defense. The Advisory Commission represented a broader cross-section of economic interests, and it was clearly under Roosevelt's authority. The Commission, however, abdicated authority to allocate supplies and raw materials to the military, and Roosevelt quite properly objected because American civilian and allied military interests also were involved.

In January, 1941, FDR established the Office of Production Management with William S. Knudsen, formerly of General Motors, and Sidney Hillman in command. OPM began to direct a gradual transformation to a war economy but got bogged down on the central and critical issue of allocating supplies, such as steel, building materials, and aluminum, which were too few for industrial demands even before the United States was officially at war. In August, FDR made still another but on the whole inadequate reshuffle when he created a special Supplies Priorities and Allocation Board with Sears, Roebuck executive Donald M. Nelson as its head. Allocation improved, but still confusion and working at cross purposes were prevalent. When one considers that almost until Pearl Harbor the task was essentially one of putting depression-idle men and machinery to work, the prewar defense mobilization must be termed a failure.

Still, confused and inefficient though it was, American production in December, 1941, was greater than that of any other nation, including Germany. Further, the building of an expanded industrial plant was well under way. Some of the expansion had come directly from government, through the Reconstruction Finance Corporation, which in June, 1940, had been authorized to finance construction of new facilities or expansion of old ones and lease them to private enterprises. In many cases, the task of persuading corporations to expand their productive capacity was difficult. Continuing to think in terms of the restricted markets of the depression and of an economy of scarcity, many corporation officials were dubious about expanding their potential for a relatively short term and ending up with excess productive capacity. One way out of this was for government to go far toward underwriting expansion's cost and toward practically guaranteeing profits. Congress, in the Revenue Act of October, 1940, allowed fast tax write-offs for capital put into expanded defense capacity. Instead of the usual 5 per cent a year depreciation, businesses were allowed to take a 20 per cent annual depreciation on the cost of new defense plants. Generous ordinary contracts or "cost plus" arrangements, under which the contracting corporation received the cost of production plus an agreed upon percentage of profit, sweetened the pot and attracted industry to defense production. The trouble with "cost plus" was that it was an invitation to squander on production costs. Senator Truman's committee, acting as a watchdog on defense and war contracts, inhibited corporate raids on government funds.

Roosevelt juggled industrial mobilization machinery again soon after the declaration of war when he created the War Production Board under Nelson. WPB was given the powers that Baruch had urged be granted such an organization in his report in 1940. Nelson, however, fell short of success. Under his administration the military continued to dictate supply priorities, and he let expansion develop unevenly. For example, facilities for ship construction, an industry that had grown very quickly, got far ahead of steel and engine production and had to be cut back. Nelson also was under a great deal of fire, much of it from the Truman Committee, for allowing a disproportionate share of defense contracts to go to the biggest industrial corporations. In October, 1942, FDR appointed Justice Byrnes to a new agency set up above WPB, the Office of Economic Stabilization. Byrnes got results, but the job became too big for any one man to administer. In May, 1943, Roosevelt made the last reorganization. He created still another agency, the Office of War Mobilization, with Byrnes in charge. Many of the details continued to be handled by OES, headed then by a former Congressman from Kentucky, Judge Fred M. Vinson. Thereafter, government's direction of war production went reasonably smoothly.

Indeed, production and transportation performed what to depression-conditioned eyes seemed an industrial miracle. The war economy was, in one way of looking at it, an economy of abundance. Total production nearly doubled between 1939 and 1945. By early 1944, American industry was producing twice as much each month as all of the Axis powers combined. Whole industrial centers came into being where nothing had been before the war, and small centers evolved under pressure into vast industrial complexes. Aluminum production, necessary for aircraft, almost tripled. The totals in some categories were astronomically impressive: nearly 300,000 airplanes, almost 12,000 ships (both merchant and naval), 64,000 landing craft, 86,000 tanks, and millions of machine guns, rifles, carbines, and side arms. These items were not useful to a society in normal times, but they nevertheless represented economic abundance of a sort. In 1944, the government was able to relax production restrictions on some civilian articles so successful had war production become.

The new economy of abundance had come primarily through a special kind of government economic pump priming. Federal spending during the depression, undertaken to revive the economy, was minor compared to what it became during the war. A glance at the statistics reveals the point. In 1939 the GNP (gross national product) stood at about $88.6 billion, of which federal expenditures contributed about 9 per cent. In 1944, the peak wartime year, GNP was $199.2 billion, of which federal spending contributed about 45 per cent. Incidentally, government controls of the economy of all kinds increased tremendously along with its increased spending. Much of the grousing about "Dr. New Deal's" governmental "meddling" would be more accurate if attributed to "Dr. Win-the-War."

Yet, in another sense, the wartime economy was quite the reverse of an economy of abundance because many of the goods and services which Americans considered necessary to a good life were in exceedingly short supply. Japanese conquest of Southeast Asia cut America off from its main source of rubber, and the government stockpile was insufficient to last a year of normal demand. Roosevelt delegated Baruch to make a study of the problem in mid-1942. FDR took his suggestions and ordered construction of synthetic rubber plants, stepped up production of rubber in other parts of the world, and instituted a national speed limit of thirty-five miles per hour to save tires. The government imposed gasoline rationing to save rubber as well as petroleum. Before the end of the war, the synthetic rubber industry was producing well over the normal peacetime rubber demand. The government found it necessary also to ration shoes when leather ran short and shoe manufacturers were occupied with making footwear for the armed forces. Housewives had to have rationing stamps to buy meat, fats, coffee, and sugar. Government control of these items was partly to combat inflation, partly to assure more equitable distribution of scarce items. Although never rationed, cigarettes became difficult to purchase in the winter of 1944–1945. Soldiers in the European theater were short of smokes, and at home long lines appeared at drug stores fortunate enough to have a supply. Nylon stockings, which had come onto the market only soon before the war, became almost impossible to purchase. Some services became difficult to obtain. As the armed forces inducted more and more physicians and dentists, their colleagues at home, at least in some communities, were unable to treat adequately all patients.

Mobilizing Money

War is expensive. For the five years, 1941 through 1945, the federal government spent $320,189,941,396, most of it on military purposes. This sum was about twice as large as the government had spent in its entire history since 1789. How to raise and spend such a vast figure without wrecking the economy by wild inflation was the primary fiscal problem of World War II. Roughly two-fifths of the funds came from taxes. The balance came from borrowing (the sale of government bonds and other securities) which increased the national debt from $49 billion in 1941 to $259 billion in 1945.

The first part of 1942, during which American armed forces were suffering reverses, saw a considerable debate over taxation and fiscal policy concerned, essentially, with who should pay for the war. The business community, speaking through the National Association of Manufacturers and the United States Chamber of Commerce, was concerned about the growth of the national debt and wanted the war to be paid by taxation to as great a degree as possible, but by a national sales tax and an excess profits tax. The President at one time talked about limiting incomes so as to prevent anyone from receiving over $25,000 net income a year, but he did not pursue the suggestion. The Revenue Act of 1942, not passed until October, which FDR called "the greatest tax bill in American history," increased tax revenues by more than $7 billion. It set the ordinary corporate tax at a maximum of 40 per cent and excess profits taxes at a flat 90 per cent, 10 per cent of which could be rebated to corporations for reconversion to peacetime activity after the war. It also set rather steep excise taxes on communication, transportation, amusements, and luxuries, most of which were not repealed after the war. But most important for the immediate interests of many people was an increase in revenue to be collected through personal income taxes. The new tax rate went up to as high as a maximum of 94 per cent, but most of the new revenues came from lowering personal exemptions, thereby increasing the number of people under the tax net. In 1939, only about 4,000,000 Americans paid any income tax whatsoever. This number increased to about 12,000,000 in 1941, and the 1942 Revenue Act brought enough new taxpayers into being to make the total over 50,000,-000. Since most people were inexperienced at filling out income tax reports, the filing system had to be simplified. Most people were also inexperienced at putting money aside to pay their income tax in one lump sum. Congress in 1943 began a withholding system ("pay as you go" it was popularly called) which considerably improved the collection of taxes from people with relatively low incomes.

Roosevelt, in his budget message of January, 1943, asked for a tax in-

TABLE 8

PUBLIC DEBT OF THE FEDERAL GOVERNMENT, 1940-1946.

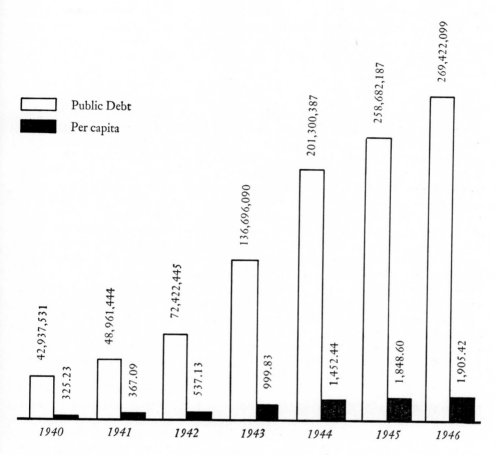

crease of $16 billion. Response was overwhelmingly negative. The executive branch trimmed its requests to $10.5 billion, but Congress still refused to go along. Not until February, 1944, did Congress pass a new revenue measure at all, and it increased tax yields by only an estimated $2.2 billion. Roosevelt vetoed the new revenue act with a message so sharp that it brought a congressional rebellion. Senate Majority Leader Alben W. Barkley of Kentucky, normally the manager of the President's measures, resigned his office rather than support the veto. The Democratic caucus in the Senate quickly reappointed Barkley by unanimous vote and went on to override Roosevelt's veto, as did the House.

So far as taxes were concerned, the answer to the debated question about who should pay for the war was that practically everyone paid for it. The bulk of tax revenues came from the personal income taxes of people with modest incomes, yet, due to improved wartime earnings, most of these people

473

were economically better off during the war than they had been before it. The wealthiest recipients of income did not suffer despite the increased tax rates. It is true that the share of disposable income received by the top 1 per cent declined from 11.5 per cent in 1940 to 6.7 per cent in 1944, but this was a relative decline, not an absolute one. The disposable income of lesser income groups and the total disposable income increased sufficiently to reduce the share, but not the amount, of the richest. To the degree that there was income leveling during World War II, the leveling was upward rather than downward.

Roughly three-fifths of the war's expenses came from funds gained by the sale of Series "E" bonds, the type purchased by individuals. This kind of bond buying was anti-inflationary since it took money that probably otherwise would have gone to purchase scarce consumer articles. The government, therefore, pushed series "E" sales vigorously through a payroll deduction scheme, but it refrained from the coercive techniques used in World War I. Nonbanking institutions took $60 billion in bonds of other series, and banks bought $87 billion worth. Bank bond purchases were inflationary since they increased bank credits and, thereby, the amount of money in circulation.

Series "E" bonds and taxes helped to combat inflation, but the most publicized agency to keep prices at a reasonable level was the Office of Price Administration, created by executive order in April, 1941. Without effective power, its first head, the New Deal economist Leon Henderson, was unable to prevent a steady price rise during the defense period that reached 2 per cent a month by the end of 1941. Roosevelt demanded greater power for OPA, and in January, 1942, Congress responded with the Emergency Price Control Act. In April, an OPA directive froze prices of consumer goods and rents in defense areas at their March level. However, the law prevented fixing prices of farm products until they reached 110 per cent of parity, a legislative work of the farm bloc. Consequently, the cost of living continued to rise. FDR notified Congress that unless it rectified this situation that he would act himself, basing his action on presidential war powers. Congress in October passed the Anti-Inflation Act. Immediately, Roosevelt froze prices, including agricultural prices, wages, salaries, and rents throughout the country. People, thwarted by this order, took it out on Henderson, who in December, 1942, resigned his job. Former Senator Prentiss S. Brown of Michigan held the job for a half-year and was succeeded by a former advertising firm official, Chester Bowles of Connecticut. The farm bloc twice got bills through Congress designed to permit a rise in farm prices, but FDR vetoed them. In May, 1943, Roosevelt even ordered a 10 per cent reduction in the retail prices of coffee, meat, and butter.

People complained about rationing, there was a black market in some items, and families that moved frequently were often the victims of devious ways to avoid rent control. Still, the government managed to win the battle against a runaway cost of living. Living costs increased less than 2 per cent in the last two years of the war. The cost of living increased only 29 per cent from 1939 to the end of the war, most of it in 1941 and the first three quarters of 1942. Considering that living costs increased by almost two-thirds from 1914 to the end of World War I, the record in World War II was good indeed.

Workers, Farmers, and Living Standards

Soon after Pearl Harbor, both the AFL and the CIO adopted a no-strike pledge for the duration of the war. With a few exceptions, organized labor honored the pledge. But the exceptions were well publicized, antilabor sentiment increased, and, although trade union membership and general strength grew, organized labor faced a more hostile public opinion at the end of the war than it had in 1941.

During the whole war, labor went out on strike 14,371 times, resulting in the loss of an estimated 36,301,000 man-days. Most of the strikes were short, and most of them were "wildcat," called by locals against the policy of the national organization. Although the strike statistics seem big, actual time lost due to strikes was only an estimated one-ninth of 1 per cent of total working time.

Labor's two main problems during the war were to maintain its position in industry and to keep workers' incomes in line with rising living costs. The first problem was solved by the adoption by the War Labor Board, composed of management, labor, and public representatives and established in January, 1942, for the purpose of being responsible for the settlement of labor disputes which the Secretary of Labor deemed dangerous to the war effort, of the compromise called "maintenance of membership." Some managements hoped to break the power of unions with the flood of new industrial employees; unions wanted to require all new employees to join in shops that were already organized. The "membership of maintenance" compromise provided that workers who were union members and those who might join would remain members during the life of the labor contract and that failure of a worker to maintain his membership would make him liable to discharge from his job. The union would remain as the bargaining agent. On the other hand, new employees were under no obligation to join. The solution prevented management from using the no-strike pledge to destroy unionism; it did not allow unions to use their power automatically to improve their position. Total union membership grew during the war from about 10,500,000 to about 14,000,000; about 3,000,000 workers chose not to join a union under the "maintenance of membership" scheme.

The problem of keeping wages in line with living costs proved far more difficult. The fairly sharp rise in prices in early 1942 brought the first crisis. Labor in Little Steel demanded a raise of a dollar a day to offset higher prices. The WLB recognized a hardship existed, granted a pay increase of forty-four cents a day, and made this Little Steel formula of a 15 per cent increase the pattern for industry generally. Prices were said to have increased a similar amount. The Little Steel formula of July, 1942, became the norm. Thereafter, the administration made it the basis of both wage and price stabilization. In 1944, however, labor began to complain that the Little Steel pattern was preventing it from participating in wartime prosperity to the degree that other economic groups did. The WLB that year yielded "fringe benefits," such as health insurance, pay for vacations and holidays, and bonuses for night work, but it retained the 1942 formula.

475

The history of labor in the war's last two years can largely be told by an account of John L. Lewis of the United Mine Workers, still labor's best-known leader and certainly its stormiest and most controversial major figure. Lewis, who had resigned as CIO president over its support of Roosevelt in 1940, quarrelled with his old friend and colleague, Philip Murray, the CIO's new chief. In October, 1942, Lewis pulled the UMW out of the CIO and a year later took it into the AFL. While this little war within labor's larger civil war was in progress, Lewis in April, 1942, demanded a $2.00 a day raise for miners when the contract expired at the end of the month. The WLB reminded Lewis of his no-strike pledge, and he replied that he would not call a strike but that he doubted if the miners would want to "trespass" upon mine property when the contract expired. The miners went out on May 1. FDR quickly seized the mines and urged the miners to return under the old contract until a new settlement could be made. Lewis announced a thirty-day truce. FDR put the mines under the jurisdiction of the Department of the Interior, and for six months two of the most pugnacious public figures in the country, Secretary Ickes and Lewis, bargained with one another in an attempt to reach an arrangement the WLB would accept. During the bargaining, the miners struck briefly three more times. The ultimate agreement was complicated. It provided for an hourly wage increase within the Little Steel formula, but it gave the UMW additional benefits, vacation pay, and payment for all times spent underground—"portal to portal" pay.

Lewis' actions were largely responsible for a considerable growth of antilabor sentiment which resulted in restrictive labor legislation. Five states prohibited the closed shop. Congressional hoppers received many antilabor proposals. One of these, sponsored by Representative Howard Smith of Virginia and Senator Tom Connally of Texas, passed through Congress with large majorities only to run into a veto. However, Congress overrode the veto and the War Labor Disputes Act, more often called the Smith-Connally Act, became law in June, 1943. The new law forbade union contributions to political campaigns, provided for government seizure of strike-bound plants engaged in war production, permitted strikes only after an election during a thirty-day "cooling off" period, and sanctioned criminal prosecution of persons who instigated strikes.

World War II brought the agricultural sector of the economy to a degree of health such as it had not enjoyed since the last war. Yet the major benefits went to the most efficient farms, usually the large ones, and hundreds of thousands of submarginal farms went out of production altogether. Although farmers were frequently plagued with labor shortages and found new equipment difficult to obtain, they expanded their production from an index of 108 to 123. The increase in food production alone was even greater. Favorable weather and heavier use of hybrid seed and fertilizer brought about these increases despite a 17 per cent decline in the farm population. When one considers that farm prices more than doubled and net cash incomes climbed fourfold, the prosperity of the more favorably situated farmers becomes apparent.

Indeed, it was the war, far more than federal depression agricultural policies, that brought prosperity back to the farm. Farmers not only cut their mortgages by a national total of $2 billion, they saved an estimated $11 billion. At the same time, the war hastened the process of "factoryizing" most farm production, of specialized production by big, efficient, and at least partly scientific farm units. The small, family farm with diversified production faded into limbo faster than ever.

In fact, during the war years most Americans lived better than they had for years. In 1943, ten million families received less than $1,675, the figure then deemed a minimum to provide a decent standard of living, but the others, while by no means rolling in luxury, were better off than they had been since at least the 1920's. Better family incomes came not so much from higher wage rates as from working wives, steadier employment, and more overtime pay. Over considerable management protest, the administration stuck to the time-and-one-half for over forty hours standard, and labor gave up double time for Sundays and holidays. In 1941, the average work week was 40.6 hours; in 1944 it was 45.2. The average of gross weekly wages increased from $25.20 in 1940 to $43.39 in 1945, a greater increase than there was in the cost of living. No small factor in prosperity was the serviceman's family allotment. In 1942, Congress amended pay legislation to provide a $50 allotment to the wives of servicemen in return for a deduction of $22 in the man's pay. The soldier's first child brought an additional allotment of $12, and each additional child brought $10. These figures were later changed to $30 and $20. One family complained bitterly in December, 1945, when its husband and father was discharged; this family of thirteen children had to give up an allotment of $320 monthly.

Two aspects of wartime prosperity were to have postwar significance. First, only in the United States did the people live better than they had before the war, a fact that had worldwide repercussions. Second, unable to spend their incomes on new houses, new household appliances, or new cars (none were produced after a few in 1942), and urged to put their excess income into war bonds, more Americans saved more money than ever before. This fact contributed to postwar prosperity brought about by a buying spree and to postwar inflation.

Mobilizing Science and Technology

With the fall of France in the spring of 1940, Roosevelt appointed the National Defense Research Committee with Vannevar Bush, head of the Carnegie Institution, as its head. A year later the President reorganized the governmental research program by establishing the Office of Scientific Research and Development, again under Bush's direction. OSRD proved a highly effective organization, and the work of its scientists and technicians shortened the war.

The most spectacular scientific achievement, of course, was the development of the atom bomb. In 1939, Albert Einstein and Enrico Fermi, each of them refugees from fascism, informed the President indirectly that German scientists had accomplished atomic fission in uranium. Physicists realized the destructive possibilities of this achievement, although to most laymen the whole concept was a mystery, and urged the administration to support a huge research program. Research groups at Columbia University, the University of Chicago, and the University of California at Berkeley advanced the solution, and in December, 1942, physicists brought about the first controlled chain reaction in an atomic pile constructed under the stands of Stagg Field at the University of Chicago. Huge problems remained: how to produce fissionable material in usable quantities and how to build a nuclear bomb.

The Army Engineer Corps created a special project, the Manhattan District, under the command of General Leslie R. Groves, to work on plutonium production. The government secretly spent nearly $2 billion in the huge Manhattan District installations at Oak Ridge, Tennessee, and Hanford, Washington, and in the scientists' bomb-building project, headed by J. Robert Oppenheimer, at Los Alamos, New Mexico. The security problem of such a huge undertaking was extremely complicated, and, as it turned out, security was not perfect. Finally, on July 16, 1945, near Alamogordo, New Mexico, the scientists hopefully and yet apprehensively detonated the world's first nuclear fission bomb. An eerie mushroom cloud, to become the midcentury symbol of nightmarish destruction, floated up from the detonation site. The atomic age was born.

Not so dramatic but important nevertheless were such scientific and technological achievements as proximity fuses, radar, and rockets. The proximity fuse, developed by ORSD alone, was a tiny radio set in the head of an artillery shell which detonated the shell as it neared its target. Near misses thereby became hits. At first used only above oceans and against German rockets aimed at English cities to prevent an unexploded shell from falling into enemy hands and being copied, the proximity fuse proved a potent destroyer when first used by ground forces late in the war against Germany. Radar, first developed crudely by the navy in the 1920's, was developed into an effective device in Great Britain. Radar detection of German aircraft in the Battle of Britain provided Britain's narrow margin of victory, and it was an invaluable aid in navigation and detection of submarines. Rocket research was not as advanced as Germany's, but small rockets on airplanes and the bazooka, an infantry weapon with which two men could launch a small rocket capable of knocking out a tank, were highly effective.

Fortunately for the modern conscience, not all research was directed toward destructive devices and some of the principles discovered in working for destructive ends had wholesome and peaceful possible applications. Medical researchers developed penicillin and other antibiotics until they were available for mass treatment of disease. DDT provided a better weapon for man's war with the insect world than he had ever had. Routine DDT dusting of wartime refugees and prisoners of war prevented the outbreak of any serious epidemics which had previously been a grisly companion of major wars. Blood plasma, a kind of "instant blood," had enormous advantages over the old direct blood transfusion and saved an untold number of lives both during the war and later. Regardless of all the positive wartime scientific achievements, however, the development of nuclear fission with its fantastic power presented mankind with a problem it never before had had to face so clearly.

Civil Liberties and Minorities in Wartime

Americans in World War II were far less hysterical about disloyalty than they had been in 1917-1918, probably because after Pearl Harbor opposition to the war was only negligible. The United States won its greatest war while maintaining a toleration at home of which, with one glaring exception, it could well be proud.

Censorship worked fewer injustices than it had in World War I. The Office of Censorship, established in December, 1941, under Byron Price, an Associated Press executive, was at times overcautious in what it allowed newspapers to publish, but the war was still the best reported one the nation had ever fought. A large staff of censors cut information that might be useful to the enemy from mail destined for overseas delivery, but civilian censors abused their power much less than officers in the armed forces overseas who sometimes went beyond the limits of reason when they censored letters written by their enlisted men. The Office of War Information, headed by Elmer Davis, drew the ire of many Republicans who accused the OWI of pro-Roosevelt domestic propaganda, but it certainly never approached the earlier Creel Committee's irresponsibility. The OWI all but ceased aiming at American minds after 1943 and concentrated on shaping opinion abroad. Religiously motivated conscientious objectors, if they would register for the draft, fared far better than their World War I counterparts. They went to Civilian Public Service camps rather than to prison; many entered the military medical services.

Pacifists were rarely seriously harmed, and enemy sympathizers, mostly ideological pro-Fascists, suffered far less than war opponents in the Wilson administration. The Supreme Court in 1944 ruled that in cases under the Espionage Act the prosecution had to prove the accused had specifically intended to hamper the war effort, and intent is extremely difficult to prove in law. The biggest wartime dissent trial was a Smith Act case against twenty-eight defendants, of whom one was Mrs. Elizabeth Dilling, author of The Red Network, indicted for attempting to establish a Nazi system in the United States and for inciting disloyalty in the armed forces. A wild mass trial in 1944 went on for several months, only to end in mistrial when the presiding judge died. A second indictment in 1945 ended with an appellate court's dismissal.

The government recognized that the presence of thousands of aliens who were citizens of enemy countries constituted a potential menace. Enemy aliens were required to register with the government, denied access to defense areas, and required to deposit with the government their cameras, firearms, and short wave radios. Federal Bureau of Investigation agents rounded up 1,700 enemy aliens suspected as potential saboteurs within a week after Pearl Harbor, thereby successfully preventing German sabotage plans. Germany later landed saboteurs by submarine on the beaches of Long Island and Florida, but the FBI apprehended them quickly. There was no known act of sabotage committed in the United States during the war.

Of popular hostility to Italian-Americans there was practically none, and German-Americans were the objects of only a little overt discrimination. But Japanese-Americans suffered badly. Their treatment was by far the blackest mark on the World War II record. The government and the army surrendered to regional prejudice. The West Coast, where most Japanese-Americans lived, became highly panicky in the weeks following the Japanese attack. Although the roundup of potentially dangerous enemy aliens had included Japanese, many people on the coast demanded that something be done about the Japanese-Americans, who had long been victims of discrimination there. Roosevelt caved in. On February 19, 1942, he authorized military commanders to remove "any or all persons" from any area the Secretary of War or other military commanders might designate. Soon thereafter the commanding general of the Pacific Coast army district, John L. De Witt, ordered the removal of all Japanese-Americans from the western parts of Washington, Oregon, and California, even though he did not declare martial law. About 112,000 people were forced into barbed wire stockades and then moved out to ten permanent camps in the interior, euphemistically called "relocation centers." Two-thirds of those removed were American citizens. All but about eighteen thousand Japanese-Americans were released in time. Only a few returned to the coast when the evacuation order was rescinded. Forced sales and abandonment of property cost the removed people heavily. The whole affair was the result of panic and prejudice; this was indicated by the contrast of the Japanese-Americans in Hawaii, where much less prejudice existed. There these people lived as they had for years without serious incident.

The Supreme Court in Hirabayashi v. United States (1943) and Korematsu v. United States (1944) upheld the removal order on grounds of national security in a time of crisis. It did not reverse itself when in the Endo case it granted a writ of habeus corpus to a loyal Japanese-American; it only ruled that a person against whom no charge had been made and whose loyalty was not questioned could not be interned after being removed from an excluded zone. Constitutional scholars agree upon the seriousness of the whole Japanese removal episode. One of them, E. S. Corwin, has called the affair "the most drastic invasion of the rights of citizens . . . by their own government that has thus far occurred in the history of our nation."

The Jehovah's Witnesses flag salute cases, however, illustrated that the federal government could maintain traditions of civil liberty during wartime. In mid-1940, the Supreme Court in the Gobitus case had held that public school children could be compelled, upon pain of expulsion, to salute the flag in school ceremonies even though such action violated the students' religious principles. After the outbreak of war, the Witnesses were frequent victims of persecution. Nine states had requirements that school children salute the flag. In mid-1942 the Department of Justice began to intervene to prevent flagrant persecution, and a West Virginia Witness family went to court rather than obey the flag salute requirement of the state board of education. In June, 1943, the Supreme Court in the Barnette case held in a six-to-three decision that no civilian could constitutionally be required to salute the flag or to take part in a pledge of allegiance.

Despite a great deal of prejudice directed against them, Negroes in general improved their position in American society during the war years. Although the army never permitted any more than token integration during the war, and that only at the front in the German war when manpower of any color was badly needed; although the Red Cross yielded to demands that Negro blood plasma be segregated; although Detroit in June, 1943, indulged itself in a race riot; and although many southern whites so resented the loss of cheap Negro labor to better paying war jobs that some southern communities became tension-ridden tinder-boxes, the Negro in general was better off by V-J Day than he had been at Pearl Harbor.

The main improvement in Negro relations was economic. A. Philip Randolph's wresting the FEPC order in 1941 made discrimination in war industries illegal, and a handful of state fair employment practice laws forbade employment discrimination in all kinds of work. But it was mainly the availability of cash-paying jobs of any description that put Negroes on the move. From the farms they moved into southern towns and cities, and from there they moved on to northern and western industrial centers. Negro migration in the first war was minor compared to the 1941–1945 conflict, and Negroes jammed into New York City, Philadelphia, Cleveland, Chicago, Los Angeles, and other major cities.

The long-term effects of migration and relative prosperity were many. For one thing, the Negro in the North and the West could vote, and he increasingly constituted a voting bloc with which candidates had to deal. For another, his newly achieved degree of economic independence stimulated militant demands for the exercise of equal rights. For still another, millions of Negro youngsters gained access to schools far better than their parents had attended. Negroes' postwar surge forward thus derived largely from wartime experiences.

CHAPTER TWENTY-FOUR

Fighting for Victory

UNTIL DECEMBER, 1941, THE WAR THAT HAD BEGUN IN SEPTEMBER, 1939, had been almost altogether a European war. With Pearl Harbor the conflict became a truly global war, the first one in the world's history. Asia, Europe, Africa, and the seas and oceans, including those around the Americas, were the scene of warfare between Axis powers and the United Nations.

The role of Americans in this global war was more important than they ever before had performed. Although they had participated in other "world wars"—the three colonial wars, the War of 1812, and World War I—Americans had never before played so decisive or central a part in the final outcome. From 1941 to 1945, Americans produced the war supplies, delivered them, planned the strategy, and did the actual fighting as full senior partners.

In 1917–1918, the United States had insisted that it was no more than an "associated power" and refused to be considered as one of the Allies. In World War II, the United States took the lead in uniting into a loose alliance the various nations at war with one or more of the Axis powers. On January 1, 1942, at the White House, Roosevelt, Churchill, Ambassador Litvinov from Russia, and representatives of twenty-three other nations signed the Declaration by United Nations. Subsequently, twenty other countries signed the document which restated the "four freedoms" enunciated in the Atlantic Charter and pledged each signatory nation to "employ its full resources" in the war effort, to cooperate with other signatory powers, and not to make a separate armistice or peace.

More important in the actual conduct of the war, however, was the close cooperation that developed between Great Britain and the United States and, to a lesser extent, between them and Russia, China, and, later, France. The Grand Alliance, as it came to be called, had actually begun before the

482

United States declared war when Roosevelt and Churchill met and corresponded freely. Churchill arrived in Washington for a series of conferences only two weeks after the United States war declaration. From then until the end of the war, the Prime Minister and the President were in almost daily communication. At this first wartime conference, Roosevelt and Churchill agreed to war production goals for the next two years, to the establishment of a Combined Chiefs of Staff in the American capital, to the creation of a joint Munitions Assignment Board, to a joint command in the Pacific which included the Dutch, and to some future military strategy, notably an invasion of North Africa sometime in 1942.

The most basic decision at the Washington conference in December, 1941, was to put a higher priority for the immediate future on the European war than on the Asian theater. The strategy was to fight a holding action in the Pacific and concentrate on the defeat of Germany and Italy. Then, when victory seemed assured in Europe, the allies would concentrate their efforts against Japan. Actually, the United States began to carry the war against the Japanese long before Hitler's downfall was assured, but the military emphasis remained in Europe. To make this decision in the first weeks of the war involved a degree of risk since Japan's first thrusts were devastating. Japan's strategy was to make a series of lightning blows at the beginning of the war and stake everything upon them. Japan's high tide came before the middle of 1942. But in the war's first half-year it looked as if the flag of the rising sun were really rising.

The Japanese blow at Pearl Harbor had been only a relatively minor part of a general Japanese attack. As the United States government had expected, the Japanese moved south. The list of Japanese victories was impressive. Japanese armies had no difficulty landing in Thailand and quickly controlling it. They moved on into the Malay peninsula, routed the British, and moved south to capture the big British naval base at Singapore on February 15, 1942. During the campaign, incidentally, Japanese planes sank two British battleships off the Malayan coast, the *Prince of Wales* and *Repulse*, the first time unassisted airplanes had sunk modern battleships equipped for combat. The British had lost their base at Hong Kong on Christmas Day, 1941. Allied defeat in the Battle of the Java Sea, February 27 and 28, 1942 (a defeat so disastrous that only four American destroyers escaped) sealed the fate of the Dutch East Indies. The Dutch surrendered to the Japanese on March 9. The Japanese also took control of the Celebes, Borneo, New Britain, the Solomons, and part of New Guinea. These Japanese acquisitions were of tremendous strategic importance; they afforded Japan a major source of oil and denied their opponents the world's major source of rubber.

Less important in terms of resources but of major importance to American pride were the losses of two small islands, Guam on December 10, 1941, and Wake on December 23. The marines' defense at Wake Island was heroic but hopeless; for sixteen days they held off a numerically superior foe. More important strategically was the loss of the Philippines. General Douglas MacArthur, the former chief of staff, commanded about one-hundred twenty thousand men, not counting army air corps personnel. The Japanese quickly gained control of the air after their initial landings on December 10 and soon had the Philippine and American forces in retreat. Overwhelming numbers of

Japanese pushed MacArthur's forces toward the Bataan Peninsula, one of the arms of land forming Manila Bay. In March, 1942, Roosevelt ordered Mac-Arthur to leave in order to save his military talents for a happier day; the thankless task of fighting the hopeless fight fell upon Lieutenant General Jonathan M. Wainwright. After being on half rations or less for three months, the last forces on Bataan surrendered April 9; those holed up on the small island fortress of Corregidor succumbed on May 6. Isolated from help and supplies, doomed almost from the start, the defenders of the Philippines, American and Filipino alike, fought gallantly and delayed the inevitable far longer than the Japanese had reasonably expected.

The War Against Germany and Italy: First Phase

No two allied nations in the history of warfare ever better coordinated their efforts than did the United States and Great Britain in World War II. Their leaders also, with but few exceptions, saw eye to eye on general objectives. Coordination with the other major Allied military power, the Soviet Union, was another matter. Russian, American, and British leaders meshed their supply and shipping schedules with one another, and late in the war the Russians and Americans even brought about a degree of tactical cooperation with the flight of a few B-17 American bombers from their English bases, over the German targets, and on to Russian air bases. Yet, on the whole, Russian-Western tactical coordination was infrequent. Their troops fought mostly in different theaters. Neither was there consistent agreement on strategy between Russia on the one hand and Britain and America on the other, because strategy inevitably involved postwar international politics. Although Roosevelt's more ardent defenders would dispute the generalization, Churchill and Stalin were usually more acute than FDR in preceiving the postwar implications of wartime decisions.

Churchill and Roosevelt had their first difficulty with Stalin soon after Pearl Harbor. Stalin asked British Foreign Minister Anthony Eden in December, 1941, for an Anglo-Russian treaty of alliance in which Britain would agree to Russia's extending her boundaries to include the Baltic countries (Latvia, Lithuania, and Estonia) and parts of Finland and Poland. Russian foreign minister Vyacheslav Molotov repeated the proposal to Churchill in London the following May. But Churchill refused, and Russia and Britain agreed to a twenty-year treaty of alliance that ignored the question of Russia's postwar boundaries. That Russian leaders dared to present such a request when the German armies had the Russians deep in their own territory and still on the defensive indicated a strong appetite for territory.

Molotov went on to Washington where he strongly urged Roosevelt to open a second front in western Europe, presumably in an amphibious operation across the English Channel so as to take Nazi pressure off the Russians. He wanted the invasion of the European continent as soon as possible, certainly no later than the end of 1942. He said it was possible, unless diverted from the west, that Hitler's Wehrmacht might be able to knock out Russia, thus leaving Britain and America to face Germany alone. Roosevelt told

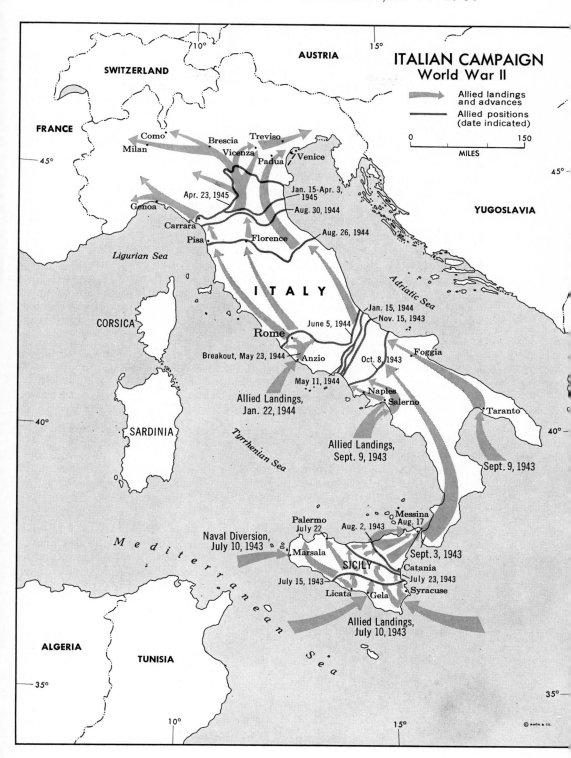

ITALIAN CAMPAIGN
World War II

Allied landings
and advances
Allied positions
(date indicated)

0   150
MILES

SWITZERLAND

AUSTRIA

FRANCE

Como
Milan
Brescia
Vicenza
Treviso
Padua
Venice

YUGOSLAVIA

Apr. 23, 1945

Jan. 15-Apr. 3,
1945
Aug. 30, 1944

Genoa

Carrara

Pisa   Florence   Aug. 26, 1944

Ligurian Sea

ITALY

Adriatic Sea

CORSICA

Rome   June 5, 1944   Jan. 15, 1944
Nov. 15, 1943

Breakout, May 23, 1944   Anzio
Oct. 8, 1943   Foggia

May 11, 1944

Naples
Salerno

Allied Landings,
Jan. 22, 1944

Taranto

SARDINIA

Tyrrhenian Sea

Allied Landings,
Sept. 9, 1943

Sept. 9, 1943

Palermo
July 22   Aug. 2, 1943   Messina
Aug. 17

Naval Diversion,
July 10, 1943   Marsala   Sept. 3, 1943

SICILY   Catania

July 15, 1943   July 23, 1943
Licata   Gela   Syracuse

ALGERIA

TUNISIA

Mediterranean Sea

Allied Landings,
July 10, 1943

485

Molotov he would do whatever possible to start a continental invasion in the next few months.

Soon after Molotov's departure from Washington, Churchill arrived for his second face-to-face meeting with Roosevelt within six months. Churchill and his military advisers vigorously opposed a cross-Channel operation in the immediate future, arguing that Allied strength did not yet permit such an invasion and that they should use what power they had to drive the Germans and Italians from North Africa. The breakthrough at about that moment of German General Erwin Rommel's Afrika Korps, forcing the British Eighth Army back into Egypt and thereby threatening the Suez Canal, helped to decide the issue. After the chief of staff General George C. Marshall and his commander in the European theater, General Dwight D. Eisenhower, had failed to bring the British around to agreement on an invasion of Europe, Roosevelt agreed in July to a North Africa campaign provided it be launched by the end of October.

The Allied operation in North Africa was a giant pincers movement. On October 24, the British Eighth Army, under the command of General Sir Bernard L. Montgomery, opened an attack from the east. On November 8, three American task forces, to which were attached some British units, landed by sea at Casablanca, Oran, and Algiers. The three-pronged attack was a surprise to the enemy, an amazing lapse of German intelligence. General Eisenhower commanded this operation. Then Eisenhower's force drove to meet Montgomery's advancing army, trapping the Axis forces in Tunisia. General Rommel fought shrewdly, taking advantage of every opportunity, and succeeded in inflicting a serious but not fatal defeat at the Battle of Kasserine Pass in February, 1943. By the middle of May, German resistance had ended in Africa. Germany's loss of fifteen divisions and over two thousand airplanes hurt her seriously, but perhaps equally important was the fact that Britain and America had turned the tide against the Nazis. They had begun to "tighten the ring."

A political-diplomatic tangle relating to the American operations in North Africa will be debated for a long time. The proud but weak and hopelessly divided-against-themselves French created a sticky problem in that their pro-Nazi Vichy government had at least nominal control of the area where the United States planned its landings. The Vichy French in Africa resisted the American landings. On November 11, 1942, three days after the North African landings, Germany took over the unoccupied part of France, until then controlled by the Vichy government, whereupon the Vichy commander in Africa, Admiral Jean Darlan, reached an armistice with General Eisenhower. Darlan agreed to a cease-fire; Eisenhower agreed to recognize Darlan's control of the French forces in Africa. The outcry at home against cooperating with a Vichy officer was considerable. Darlan was assassinated on December 24. Then the question for the United States was whether to recognize the vigorously anti-Vichy General Charles De Gaulle, with whom the British were working, or General Henri Giraud, who had escaped from the Germans but whose supporters had served the Vichy government. In January, 1943, Roosevelt personally got De Gaulle and Giraud to meet and ostensibly compromise their differences. De Gaulle soon eased Giraud aside, and in time Roosevelt recognized De Gaulle as the French leader.

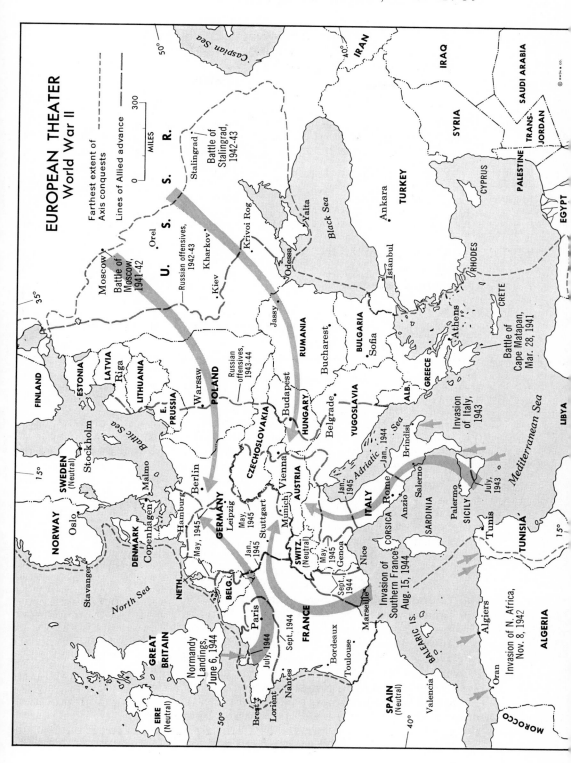

EUROPEAN THEATER
World War II

- - - - Farthest extent of
Axis conquests
━━━━ Lines of Allied advance

300
MILES

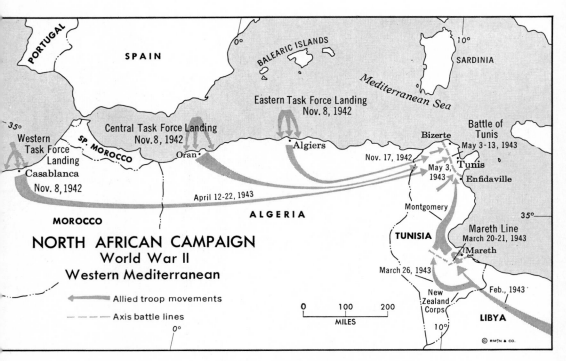

NORTH AFRICAN CAMPAIGN
World War II
Western Mediterranean

Allied troop movements
Axis battle lines

0   100   200
MILES

The Churchill-Roosevelt conference at Casablanca, January 14 to 24, 1943, during which Roosevelt brought about the surface solution of the De Gaulle-Giraud impasse, was notable for two decisions: to demand "unconditional surrender" of the Axis powers and to invade Sicily and Italy. The unconditional surrender demand, like the Vichy episode, will long be a subject for debate. Roosevelt's critics have argued—with the advantage of hindsight—that unconditional surrender caused Germany to fight on until destroyed, thereby prolonging the war and creating a power vacuum in central Europe which the Russians filled. The other side of the argument is that Roosevelt explicitly said that unconditional surrender did not mean the destruction of the German population but the end of fascism and that a compromise with Nazism would have been immoral. But, clearly, the unconditional surrender policy did stiffen Axis resistance and narrowed America's range of alternatives in its dealings with its allies.

The fighting for North Africa was by no means over when Roosevelt and Churchill ordered Eisenhower to invade Sicily in July. Landing craft and paratroopers hit Sicily on July 10. With bold tank tactics by General George S. Patton's troops, American forces were able to complete the whole Sicilian operation in only thirty-eight days. The loss of Sicily brought about Mussolini's downfall. The Italian people, including the soldiers, had long shown a lack of enthusiasm for the war and for the Germans. On July 25, 1943, a group of Mussolini's opponents got the consent of King Victor Emmanuel III to form a new government under Marshal Pietro Badoglio, who ordered Mussolini's arrest and began secret negotiations to surrender. (Early the next month a daring operation by German paratroopers rescued Mussolini

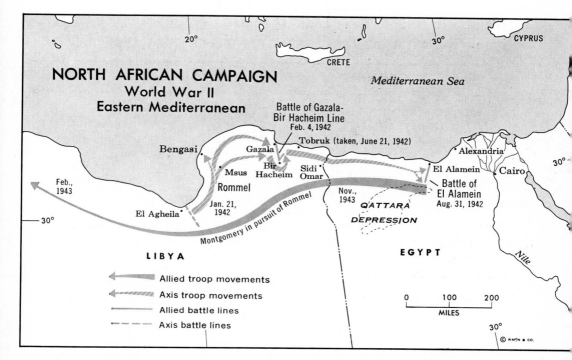

NORTH AFRICAN CAMPAIGN
World War II
Eastern Mediterranean

Battle of Gazala-
Bir Hacheim Line
Feb. 4, 1942

Mediterranean Sea

CYPRUS

CRETE

20°   30°

Bengasi   Gazala   Tobruk (taken, June 21, 1942)   Alexandria

Msus   Bir   Sidi   El Alamein   Cairo
Hacheim   Omar

Rommel   Battle of
El Alamein
Aug. 31, 1942

Feb.,
1943   Nov.,
1943   QATTARA
DEPRESSION   Battle of
El Alamein

El Agheila   Jan. 21,
1942   Montgomery in pursuit of Rommel

LIBYA   EGYPT   Nile

30°   30°

— Allied troop movements
← Axis troop movements
— Allied battle lines
--- Axis battle lines

0   100   200
MILES

© RMCN & CO.

and took him to the north of Italy.) The Germans suspected the Italians and moved additional troops into Italy in an attempt, if possible, to prevent Italian surrender and in any case to secure the territory against the Allies. Badoglio surrendered unconditionally on September 3. By that time, German forces in Italy were strong enough that the surrender made little actual military difference.

The Allies began their invasion of Italy the very day of Badoglio's surrender. At the Roosevelt-Churchill meeting in Washington in May, 1943, known by the code name TRIDENT, it had been agreed the Allies would move on into Italy as soon as possible. General Montgomery's forces landed at Reggio Calabria, at the toe of the Italian boot, on September 3. On September 10, the American Fifth Army under General Mark Clark landed near Salerno, down the coast from Naples. The Allies advanced well at first, and by early October had taken Naples on the west coast and Foggia near the Adriatic and moved on north. However, the Germans dug in on a line south of Cassino in November. Taking advantage of the geography, the Germans held out all winter. A daring amphibious "end run" in January, 1944, established an American beachhead behind the German lines at Anzio, south of Rome, but the Germans soon nailed the attack down there. Not until spring did the Allies begin to roll again, taking Rome on June 4, 1944, and grinding on toward the Alps.

During the year 1943 the Grand Alliance began to function with more harmony and clearly turned the tide against Germany. Russia began to push back the Nazis during the winter of 1942–1943. The turning point came at Stalingrad, where on February 2, 1943, the Nazis surrendered about ninety

TABLE 9

INTERNATIONAL CONFERENCES OF WORLD WAR II

Place	Name	Date	Participants
Argentia, Newfoundland		August, 1941	Roosevelt, Churchill
Washington	ARCADIA	December, 1941-January, 1942	Roosevelt, Churchill
London		April, 1942	Churchill, Eden, Hull
Washington		June, 1942	Roosevelt, Churchill
Casablanca		January, 1943	Roosevelt, Churchill, De Gaulle
Washington	TRIDENT	May, 1943	Roosevelt, Churchill
Quebec	QUADRANT	August, 1943	Roosevelt, Churchill
Moscow		October, 1943	Hull, Eden, Molotov
Cairo-Teheran	SEXTANT EUREKA	November-December, 1943	Roosevelt, Churchill, Chiang Kai-shek, Stalin
Washington	DUMBARTON OAKS	August-September, 1944	Stettinius, Cadogan, Gromyko
Quebec	OCTAGON	September, 1944	Roosevelt, Churchill
Moscow		October, 1944	Churchill, Stalin
Yalta	ARGONAUT	February, 1945	Roosevelt, Churchill, Stalin
San Francisco		April-June, 1945	Representatives of all UN members
Potsdam	TERMINAL	July-August, 1945	Truman, Stalin, Churchill, Atlee

thousand men. German losses in the Stalingrad campaign were so terrible that never again was Hitler able to unleash a major, sustained offensive operation. By the end of the year, with great loss of life on each side, the Russians had steadily moved the Germans back until they had lost control of much of the Ukraine. The British and Americans had cleared Africa of the Nazis, Italy had given up, and the Allies controlled Sicily and the foot and ankle of the Italian peninsula. The war in the Atlantic had turned in the Allies' favor. The foremost historian of American naval operations in World War II, Samuel Eliot Morison, who was both an admiral and a Harvard professor, placed the turning point in the Battle of the North Atlantic in the spring of 1943. Germany lost 41 submarines to enemy action in May, 1943, alone and 237 for the year.

In 1943, the question of the shape of the postwar world came increasingly into public consideration, but even in the face of this potentially explosive matter, relations between Anglo-America and Russia improved. One matter, clearly, was the Roosevelt-Churchill decision at the TRIDENT conference in May, 1943, to launch a cross-Channel invasion of France, called OVER-LORD, by May 1, 1944. They reaffirmed this decision at the Quebec Conference in August, 1943, and they also heartened Russia at that conference by their acceptance of the Morgenthau plan. Secretary of the Treasury Henry Morgenthau, Jr., had proposed that defeated Germany be entirely stripped of its industrial power and reduced to a permanently agricultural economy. Churchill never really liked the idea and FDR quietly abandoned it before the end of the year, but Nazi propagandists skillfully got full mileage out of the Morgenthau plan in their efforts to stiffen German resistance.

Roosevelt determined in 1943 to create a postwar international organization designed to mediate conflicts between national states and to keep the peace. In the fall of 1943, Congress, at the administration's urgings, passed the Connally and Fulbright Resolutions, which declared the nation "through its constitutional processes" should participate in a postwar international body. At a meeting of the Big Three foreign ministers in Moscow in October, Russia, Britain, and the United States committed themselves to a postwar substitute for the old League of Nations. At this conference and at the Roosevelt-Churchill-Stalin conference at Teheran in November (to which the American and British leaders had flown after conferring with Chiang Kai-shek in Cairo), Roosevelt and Churchill reassured Stalin about the second front, and Stalin agreed to go to war with Japan once Germany was defeated. The three leaders at Teheran and their foreign ministers at Moscow had been unable to come to important explicit agreements about postwar boundaries or about which rival Polish government should be recognized, but they agreed in principle on a harsh postwar policy toward Germany, an anti-Fascist Italy, and an independent Austria. From these Roosevelt-Churchill-Stalin conferences would come a whole bagful of problems to be faced when the war finally ended, but at the time all seemed harmonious and optimistic. The Grand Alliance was ready to deal Nazism its death blow.

Triumph in Europe

The Allies had carried the war directly to the German homeland through air bombardment since early in the conflict. When the German Luftwaffe in the fall of 1940 shifted its objective from destroying the Royal Air Force to punishment of London and other English cities, it permitted the survival of an Allied weapon that would in time seriously hurt Germany and soften it for invasion. The RAF conducted occasional attacks upon German-held Europe even in late 1940 and 1941, but not until 1942 did Allied bombing of Germany begin to be significant. On August 17 of that year, B-17's of the American Eighth Air Force in England first dropped their bomb loads on Germany. By the end of 1943, planes from the Ninth Air Force, transferred to England from the Mediterranean theater, and the Fifteenth Air Force in Italy were likewise hitting German targets.

The usual pattern was for the R.A.F. bombers to fly their missions at night and for the more heavily armed American bombers to operate during daylight. Although danger was greater during daylight, the accuracy of the bombing was much better when the bombardier could actually sight his target. Radar bombsights were not available at all for most of the war and were never fully satisfactory. After suffering heavy losses in B-17 missions deep into Germany—particularly during a disastrous raid against ball bearing plants at Schweinfurt in October, 1943—American officers decided to postpone further missions deep into Germany until long-range fighters capable of escorting bombers all the way to the target were available. Such a fighter plane, the P-51, became available in sufficient numbers early in 1944. In February, 1944, the Luftwaffe's fighters made one last desperate attempt to eliminate Allied daytime bombing. So many German planes went down in the week-long engagement that Germany never again was able to offer effective fighter opposition to bombers or to control the air over her ground forces. Jet fighters, the Germans' best hope, became operational late in 1944 but only in small numbers, due largely to lack of fuel. The German jets more than matched any Allied aircraft; had they been more numerous the final months of the war would undoubtedly have been quite different. With almost the only opposition being antiaircraft batteries, which frequently were quite effective, Allied bombers stepped up their work. From April through June, 1944, the Allies dropped over 50 per cent more tons of bombs on Europe than they had in all of 1943. A United States Strategic Bombing Survey conducted just after the war indicated that bombardment had shattered civilian morale, had destroyed or seriously disrupted German war production, and had almost ended efficient functioning of transportation throughout Germany and German-controlled west Europe. Others maintained, however, that strategic bombing had not been nearly as effective as its proponents claimed. But, clearly, Allied bombing harassed the enemy and helped prepare the way for the cross-Channel invasion.

OVERLORD, the code name of the Allied invasion of Normandy, was the biggest and most carefully planned major military offensive ever launched. General Eisenhower had directly under his command 2,876,000 officers and men in the American, British, and French land, sea, and air units. Orginally promised by May 1, 1944, D-Day had to be postponed until June 5 because of a shortage of landing craft. Then the giant operation had to be postponed another twenty-four hours because of bad weather. Three divisions of paratroopers dropped behind German lines soon after midnight on June 6. At 6:30 A.M., after both aerial and naval bombardment, the first troops hit the beaches. To disguise or hide an operation as large as D-Day was impossible, but nevertheless the plan contained an element of deception. Eisenhower and his advisers chose to make the landing on the Cotentin, or Cherbourg, peninsula, roughly one hundred miles from England, rather than in the Calais area, only about twenty-five miles from England, where the Germans expected the assault. The Germans were so convinced that the Normandy landings were a feint that six weeks later they still had nineteen divisions in reserve waiting for the main blow near Calais.

The second phase of the invasion, after securing the beachhead, was to capture the port at Cherbourg and build up forces and supplies for a breakthrough out of Normandy. Cherbourg fell after bitter fighting on June 27. The breakthrough began on July 25. General Patton's Third Army encircled the Germans, who were caught in a pocket near Falaise. The Germans then decided to retreat to the Westwall, or Siegfried Line. French troops led the march into Paris on August 25. By mid-September, Allied forces controlled Dieppe, Brest, Le Havre, Antwerp, and Brussels. Meanwhile, another invasion of France, this one from the south, had begun on August 15, and American forces were moving up the Rhone valley.

On July 20, just before the Normandy breakthrough, a loose alliance of German officers, Social Democrats, churchmen, and intellectuals unsuccessfully attempted to assassinate Hitler. A time bomb in a brief case left under Hitler's chair unaccountably only injured the German dictator while killing four of his companions. About five thousand people died in the resulting purge, and thereafter Hitler's control of the armed forces was absolute.

Western military operations in the fall and winter of 1944–1945 were concentrated in northwestern France, Luxembourg, western Belgium, Holland, and adjacent parts of Germany. The most dramatic military event of the winter was Germany's desperate counterattack in an effort to split the Allied forces and regain the port at Antwerp. This Ardennes campaign, often called the Battle of the Bulge, began December 16 when Field Marshal Gerd von Rundstedt attacked with twenty-four divisions, of which ten were armored. Heavy fog helped the surprise. After the German breakthrough, capture of the American-held Belgian towns of St. Vith and Bastogne was necessary to make the whole operation a success. St. Vith held out long enough to upset the Nazi schedule; Bastogne never capitulated. The first ten days of the battle settled its eventual outcome, but not until the end of January was the bulge the Germans had made in the American lines completely eliminated. The temporary setback caused widespread alarm in Britain and the United States, but the German counteroffensive's eventual failure so seriously depleted Nazi strength that Germany was never able again even briefly to reverse the tide. She had gambled her last crack troops in the Ardennes and lost them.

Germany's high hopes for her terror weapons, the V-bombs, proved unfounded. A week after D-Day, the Germans sent the first V-1 "buzz bombs" against England. In the next three months the Germans aimed about eight thousand of these low-flying, jet-propelled, pilotless flying bombs at London; about 2,400 got through the defenses. Then the Nazis switched to the V-2, a rocket against which there was no defense at the time. About five hundred of these hit London. Altogether the V-bombs caused about 35,000 casualties, a serious matter indeed but not sufficient to reverse the direction of the war.

The Russians had extraordinary military success in 1944. They decisively defeated the Germans on the central part of their front, and by July 1 were on the Vistula River, within sight of Warsaw. Rather than push on through Poland toward Germany, however, Russia concentrated upon conquering the Balkan peninsula and the Danube basin from the Nazis. The move had the effect of bringing the area into the Russian zone of influence after the war. While the Russians were stopped at the Vistula, the Poles fought the Warsaw Uprising. Russian troops stayed on the other side of the river, refused Polish pleas for help, let the Germans put down the rebellion and eliminate the most nationalistic elements of Poland, and then, after the whole affair was over, took Warsaw without difficulty in mid-January, 1945. On their northern sector, the Russians knocked Finland out of the war in September.

The last meeting between Roosevelt, Churchill, and Stalin, at Yalta in the Russian Crimea, February 3–11, 1945, was the subject of much political

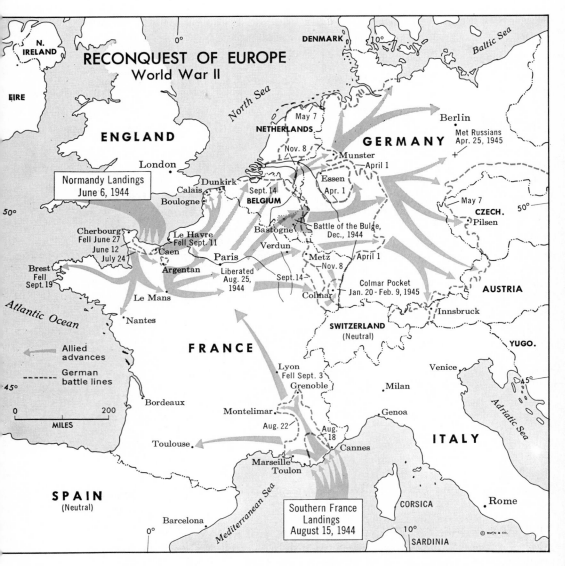

RECONQUEST OF EUROPE
World War II

Normandy Landings
June 6, 1944

Allied advances

German battle lines

0   200
MILES

Southern France
Landings
August 15, 1944

heat in the years after the war. Matters between East and West left standing
from the Teheran conference remained to be settled as well as new problems.
It was obvious that this would be the last Big Three conference before
Germany was defeated, and settlement of differences within the Grand
Alliance was imperative. Churchill and Eden met Roosevelt and his new Secretary of State, Edward R. Stettinius, Jr., former chairman of the board of
United States Steel Company, for a preliminary meeting at Malta in order to
decide upon certain matters before seeing Stalin and Molotov. (Cordell Hull
had resigned in November, 1944, because of poor health.)

Four main subjects occupied the Yalta meeting: details of the proposed
United Nations, postwar Germany, government of East Europe, and terms

of Russia's entry into the war against Japan. Russia conceded practically all its positions on the UN. At the Dumbarton Oaks conference in Washington the previous September, Russia had been balky about a UN veto power and had demanded sixteen seats in the UN General Assembly, one for each of her constituent republics. At Yalta, Stalin agreed to three General Assembly seats and agreed not to oppose an American demand for three seats. The United States never asked. The veto question was met by a complicated formula, the essence of which was that any permanent member of the UN Security Council could veto sanctions against itself although it could not veto consideration of a dispute in which it was a party. The veto has since been severely criticized, but it is clear that in 1945 the Senate of the United States would not have ratified any UN charter that did not provide an American veto. Russia agreed to make France a permanent member of the Security Council and consented to allow any nation at war with Germany by March 1 to become a UN member. Apparently, Stalin saw that the UN, at least in its early years, was to be dominated by the Anglo-American bloc and resigned himself to that situation after he was guaranteed Soviet veto power on matters that directly affected Russia.

The conference hedged considerably on Germany's future but it did take some actions. The three leaders agreed that their governments were to be the "supreme authority" in Germany, although the French might be brought into the occupation. These governments could disarm, demilitarize, and dismember Germany as they thought necessary to bring about "future peace and security." Roosevelt and Churchill came to no final reparations settlement with Stalin, but they agreed to the establishment of a reparations commission at Moscow, they accepted the Russian figure of reparations of $20 billion (one-half of which was to go to the U.S.S.R.) as "a basis for discussion," and they went along with Stalin in declaring that reparations should be paid in kind from German capital goods, from the product of current German production, and from German labor. The three foreign secretaries were to decide among themselves the question of punishment of German war criminals.

The East European questions, particularly the thorny Polish problem, had special relevance for American politics and its ethnic voting blocs. Churchill and Roosevelt agreed to the Russian-Polish border being drawn roughly along the old Curzon Line. Because this border was somewhat to the west of the 1939 Polish-Russian border, Stalin proposed that the Polish-German border also be moved west to the Oder-Neisse Line, but the English and American leaders would do no more than consent to Poland's receiving "substantial accessions of territory in the north and west." East and West came to loggerheads over the Polish government question and finally reached only a surface and unenforceable compromise. Russia insisted upon a Polish government friendly to Russia and demanded western approval of the Russian-sponsored government at Lublin. Roosevelt and Churchill refused and argued for the Polish government in exile at London. The settlement was for the Lublin government to bring into it "democratic leaders from Poland itself and from Poles abroad" and for the Lublin government to pledge itself "to the holding of free and unfettered elections as soon as possible on the basis of universal suffrage and secret ballot." Such elections were never held. Poland's government remained Communist and, until 1956, altogether under Russian domination. For elsewhere in East Europe the three powers promised governments chosen in free elections.

Although Stalin had earlier agreed to enter the war against Japan once Germany was defeated, he began to get tough on that issue as European victory came into view. In December, 1944, Stalin demanded a *quid pro quo* from the American ambassador, Averell Harriman. At Yalta he received what he demanded. In exchange for war against Japan "in two or three months" after Germany's defeat, Russia received: (1) assurance of the continuation of Russian dominance in Outer Mongolia, which China claimed; (2) transfer of the Kurile Islands from Japan; (3) restoration to Russia of what Japan had won from her in the war of 1904–1905, which was (a) the south half of Sakhalin, (b) the lease of Port Arthur for a naval base, (c) the internationalization of the port of Dairen, and (d) joint control with China of the Chinese Eastern and Southern Manchurian railroads. Stalin also agreed to recognize Chinese sovereignty in Manchuria and to sign an alliance with the Chinese Nationalists. Neither Chiang Kai-shek nor anyone else knew of the Yalta decisions on Asia until later, but when Chiang heard of the agreements he was satisfied because he thought it meant Russian support of his government against the Chinese Communists.

These, in brief, were the Yalta agreements about which there has been much debate. There is much to be said both in defense and criticism. The outstanding fact to be remembered about the East European settlement is that the Red armies in February, 1945, already controlled that part of the world completely or had it within their ready grasp. The West had little bargaining power there. As for Germany as well as East Europe, no one could really foresee Russian postwar intransigence and aggressiveness in February, 1945. The mood at the moment was almost universally one of toughness with Germany, which was Russia's and America's common enemy, not toughness with Russia. The least defensible parts of the agreements had to do with the Far East. Roosevelt and his military advisers wanted Russian help against Japan badly. Such help was considered necessary to save hundreds of thousands of American servicemen's lives. The atom bomb, it should be remembered, was not yet developed. On the other hand, intelligence reports which for some inexplicable reason had not reached the White House or the Joint Chiefs of Staff indicated that Japan was much weaker, as a result of conventional warfare than generally assumed. Further, it was naive to assume that Russia had to be baited to be active in East Asia. Her desire to be an Asian power was obvious, and it was unlikely that she would have passively watched America defeat Japan and become the area's sole major power. The Yalta agreement's inadequacies, however, were the result of honest error, of human frailty, of inability to penetrate the future. There is no evidence for the charge of subversion at Yalta despite the presence there in a relatively minor capacity of Alger Hiss, who later was convicted of perjury for denying complicity in Soviet espionage. Nor is there foundation for the belief that Roosevelt was so sick and feeble he was unfit properly to perform his duties. Stettinius in his memoirs described FDR at Yalta as "mentally alert" and in better health than he had been.

In late March, the Anglo-American armies crossed the Rhine in force, and events began to move with bewildering speed. An American offensive in northern Italy, begun April 2, ended in German surrender on April 29. On April 28, Italian anti-Fascists captured Mussolini for the second time, killed him, and left his decaying body hanging by its feet. On April 11, American troops reached the Elbe, about fifty miles west of Berlin, and soon thereafter turned south to prevent the Germans from carrying out their threat of holing up in a supposed National Redoubt in the southern mountains for a bitter and bloody Wagnerian fight to the death. The National Redoubt proved to be a myth. On April 12, Roosevelt died at Warm Springs, Georgia, from a cerebral hemorrhage, and Vice-President Harry S. Truman succeeded to the chief executive responsibilities. On April 25, American and Russian troops met at the Elbe near Torgau, south and slightly west of Berlin. By late April, the Russians had surrounded Berlin and were pounding the suburbs. On April 29, deep in his air-raid bunker under the Reichschancellery, Hitler turned over the reins of government to Admiral Karl Donitz. The next day Hitler committed suicide. On May 2, the German troops in Berlin surrendered to the Russians, and the armies in northwest Germany, Denmark, and Holland capitulated two days later. Very early in the morning of May 7, at Eisenhower's headquarters at Rheims, the Germans unconditionally surrendered all their forces that remained. V-E Day—victory in Europe—saw vigorous celebration of the end of the war that had been going on for almost six years. Only the war with Japan remained.

In later years there was considerable criticism of the American failure to accept Churchill's advice and press on for the capture of Berlin and Prague before the Russians could get there. Churchill argued that the West should get as much of a foothold in Central and Eastern Europe as possible in order to be able to require the Russians to live up to their Yalta promises about that part of the world. In his memoirs Churchill even professed to have had an "aching heart" on V-E Day because of the Russian situation. Most people today would agree that, in the long run, it was a political mistake to turn south and not proceed east when the Elbe was reached. Although at the time of the Yalta Conference the Russians were much closer to Berlin and Prague than were the western armies, by early April the West had the better chance of reaching those cities first. The decision to turn south was prompted by military rather than political considerations, although perhaps the real weakness was the general American failure to see clearly the relationship between the two.

The War in the Pacific Theater

During the first several months of war in the Pacific, the Allies were steadily forced back, unable to make more than occasional counterblows to show the enemy they still had fight. The most spectacular counterpunch was the raid by sixteen B-25 bombers, led by then Colonel James Doolittle, against Tokyo itself on April 18, 1942. The planes took off from the carrier *Hornet*, completely surprised the Japanese, and created considerable confusion. The daring operation, however, had no real strategic importance other than helping American morale.

The American forces first stopped a Japanese offensive in the naval Battle of the Coral Sea, May 7–8, 1942. General MacArthur had decided to reinforce Port Moresby in southern New Guinea and build a major air base there. The Japanese determined to take the area. Fortunately, the American command knew about the Japanese decision through intercepted and decoded messages. An invasion force led by two carriers and eleven cruisers met the American force, likewise led by two carriers, the *Lexington* and *Yorktown*. Carrier-based planes decided the whole issue; surface craft did not exchange a single shot. Each force heavily damaged the other. The battle itself could be called a draw, but the Japanese were compelled to withdraw and thereby suffered a strategic loss. The engagement made less likely Japanese conquest of Australia.

The Japanese decided next to extend their operations to the east and north, toward Hawaii and the Aleutians, by a small diversionary attack in the Aleutians to be followed by a major one on Midway Island, roughly 1,300 statute miles from Hawaii. Again, American commanders learned of the plan through broken radio messages. Both sides moved naval units to the Midway area from hundreds, even thousands, of miles away. The Japanese force had four carriers with 250 planes; the United States had three carriers, *Enterprise*, *Yorktown*, and *Hornet*, with 225 operating aircraft and additional land-based air power. In the Battle of Midway, June 3–6, 1942, again planes rather than surface craft were decisive. The Japanese lost all four carriers; the Americans lost only the *Yorktown*. Having lost air superiority, the Japanese withdrew in their first major defeat of the war. The Coral Sea and Midway engagements reversed the direction of the war in the Pacific. The Japanese attack on the Aleutian chain, stretching from Alaska to Siberia, won them Attu and Kiska islands, where they established bases. Americans the next year, however, reseized each island.

At this point the Japanese shifted their operations back to the south. This was done with a land operation on Port Moresby from Gona, across the Owen Stanley Mountains on the other side of the island, and the beginning of construction of a large air base on Guadalcanal in the Solomon Islands that would afford them air superiority in the Southwest Pacific.

The Guadalcanal campaign developed into one of the bloodiest of the war after initial spectacular success. Within two days after the assault on August 7, 1942, the marines captured the partly completed air base. But then the Japanese counterattacked from other island strongholds. They sent in replacement troops regularly from Rabaul in New Britain via an efficient troop transport system that American forces nicknamed "the Tokyo Express." The First Marine Division, reinforced by one army regiment, held out gallantly while the navy went to work to gain control of the surrounding waters. A whole series of naval encounters, culminating in the fierce naval Battle of Guadalcanal, November 13–14, 1942, finally afforded the United States control of the approaches to Guadalcanal. It took until the following February, however, to eliminate the Japanese on the island.

Meanwhile, MacArthur was handling the Japanese attack back at New

Guinea. Australian and American units drove the Japanese back to the other side of the mountains, but then they became literally bogged down in the incredibly slimy mud and fell victim to fever. The Australians took Gona on December 9. The Americans took Buna Mission, the last Japanese stronghold in the area, on January 2, 1943. The whole campaign was over by the end of the month. Having defeated the Japanese offensive in the Solomons and New Guinea decisively—it turned out to be the last major offensive the Japanese would take—MacArthur was now in position to begin the huge counteroffensive "island-hopping" operation that slowly tightened the noose around Japan.

The strategy followed by MacArthur and Admiral Chester Nimitz was to attack in two areas in 1943–1944. In the Southwest Pacific MacArthur's forces proceeded with their task of clearing New Guinea of Japanese forces, a huge action not completed until February, 1944. Marine and army units pushed north from the Solomons to isolate the Japanese base at Rabaul, which was accomplished with the taking of the Admiralty Islands in the spring of 1944. Simultaneous with this huge mopping-up operation in the southwest, naval and amphibious forces under Nimitz cracked into Japanese defenses in the Central Pacific, first in the Gilbert Islands.

In November, 1943, marines landed on Tarawa and Makin Islands in the Gilberts. Makin fell easily, but Tarawa, while it fell in three days, was a much tougher problem of a kind American troops were to face time and again in Pacific islands. The Japanese on Tarawa holed up in strongly fortified and protected pill boxes that heavy bombardment before the landing had hardly affected. Then when the marines hit the beach the Japanese opened up with a deadly fire. The only way to clear out such defenses was to subject them to unusually heavy bombardment and to follow up with hand-to-hand combat. Moving north from the Gilberts, marines took control of the Marshall Islands with the successful conquest of Kwajalein and Eniwetok Atolls in February, 1944, and then moved on to Saipan and Guam in the summer. Both were under American control by August, although fighting continued in parts of Saipan for months afterward. This series of island hops into the center of the Japanese circle of armed strength, besides encircling Japanese centers of power such as Truk in the Carolines, afforded American forces a shot at the Philippines reconquest and gave them a base from which to conduct air raids against the Japanese home islands themselves. The bomber used for these raids against Japan, the first of which was executed on November 24, 1944, was the B-29, the biggest bomber yet developed.

The great American naval victory in the Battle of the Philippine Sea, June 19–20, 1944, also helped in the reconquest of the Philippines. Since her naval defeat in the Solomons, Japan had been rebuilding her carrier and naval air strength. This new strength disappeared in the Battle of the Philippine Sea in which Japan had one carrier sunk and four severely damaged.

Upon the suggestion of Admiral William F. Halsey, the high command moved forward the date for the invasion of Leyte, one of the Philippine Islands, from December to October 20, 1944. The Japanese spotted the huge invasion armada and decided to risk roughly half their total naval strength in an attack. A successful American invasion of the Philippines would cut the communications between Japan and Southeast Asia, which Japanese armies

U. S. S. R.

MONGOLIA

MANCHUKUO
(MANCHURIA)

KAMCHATKA

SAKHALIN

Soviet Forces
Invade Manchukuo,
Aug. 9, 1945

100°

140°

INNER MONGOLIA

40°

CHINA

CHOSEN
(KOREA)
(Jap.)

Targets of
U.S. A-bombs,
Aug. 6-9, 1945

Hiroshima

Japanese Surrender,
Sept. 2, 1945

JAPAN

Tokyo

Tokyo to Pearl H

Nagasaki

BHUTAN

NEPAL

Burma Campaigns,
Dec. 1944-Aug., 1945

Pre-invasion
Operations,
July-Aug., 1945

INDIA
(Br.)

BURMA
(Br.)

Hong Kong

Okinawa

Okinawa
Operations,
Apr.-June, 1945

Iwo Jima

Iwo Jima Operations,
Feb.-Mar., 1945

TAIWAN
(Jap.)

Tokyo to Manila
1,866 miles

FR. INDO-CHINA

HAINAN

Rangoon

SIAM
(THAILAND)

Japanese Attack
Philippine Is.,
Dec. 8, 1941

Manila

Lingayen Gulf Landings,
Jan., 1945

MARIANA
IS.

Mariana Is.
Operations,
June-Aug., 1944

PHILIPPINES
(U.S.)

Leyte Landings,
Oct., 1944

MALAY
STATES
(Br.)

Singapore

Western Caroline
Operations,
Sept., 1944

Pona

CAROLINE   ISLAND

SUMATRA

BORNEO

CELEBES

Hollandia
Operations,
Apr., 1944

Battle of the
Bismarck Sea,
Mar. 2-4, 1943

Solomon Is. Camp
Aug., 1942-June

SOLOMON IS

NETHERLANDS   INDIES

Hollandia

BISMARCK
ARCH.

NEW
GUINEA

Battle of
the Java Sea,
Feb. 28, 1942

JAVA

INDIAN   OCEAN

0°

Borneo Operations,
May-July, 1945

Port Moresby

Battle of
the Coral Sea,
May 7-8, 1942

AUSTRALIA

100°

140°

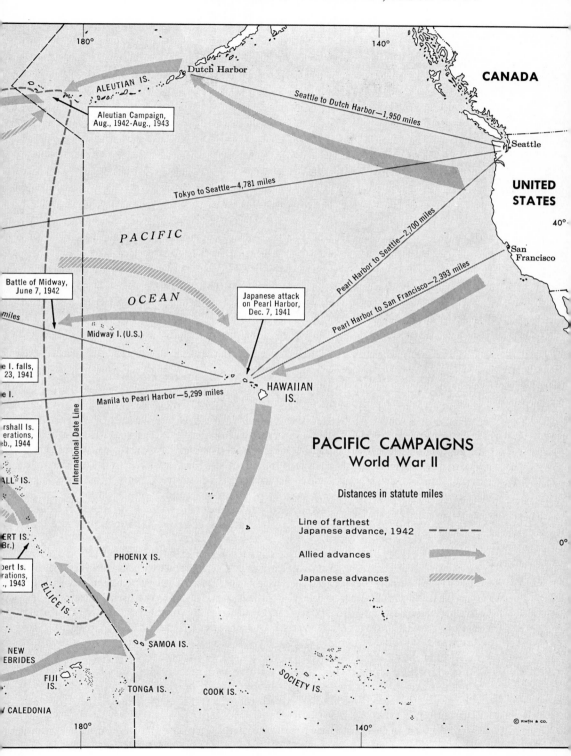

CANADA

Dutch Harbor

ALEUTIAN IS.

Seattle to Dutch Harbor—1,950 miles

Aleutian Campaign,
Aug., 1942-Aug., 1943

180°

140°

Seattle

UNITED
STATES

40°

PACIFIC

Tokyo to Seattle—4,781 miles

San
Francisco

Battle of Midway,
June 7, 1942

OCEAN

Midway I. (U.S.)

Japanese attack
on Pearl Harbor,
Dec. 7, 1941

Pearl Harbor to Seattle—2,700 miles

Pearl Harbor to San Francisco—2,393 miles

miles

e I. falls,
23, 1941

e I.

Manila to Pearl Harbor—5,299 miles

HAWAIIAN
IS.

rshall Is.
erations,
b., 1944

International Date Line

PACIFIC CAMPAIGNS
World War II

ALL IS.

Distances in statute miles

ERT IS.
Br.)

Line of farthest
Japanese advance, 1942 — — — —

ert Is.
rations,
, 1943

PHOENIX IS.

Allied advances

Japanese advances

ELLICE IS.

NEW
EBRIDES

SAMOA IS.

FIJI
IS.

SOCIETY IS.

TONGA IS.

COOK IS.

W CALEDONIA

180°

140°

© RM¢N & CO.

501

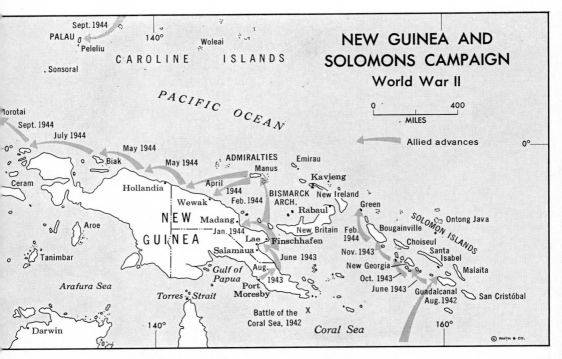

NEW GUINEA AND
SOLOMONS CAMPAIGN
World War II

for the most part still controlled, and the Nipponese commanders were prepared to take great risks to keep the islands. The troops went ashore as scheduled. On October 24–25, the Japanese and American fleets engaged one another in a series of battles known collectively as the Battle of Leyte Gulf although parts of the battle occurred miles away. The greatest navy battle in history, it left the Japanese without the naval power to resist seriously. Japan lost all four of the carriers it had in the battle, three of its nine battleships, nine cruisers, and nine destroyers; the United States lost one light carrier and two escort carriers, two destroyers, and one destroyer escort. Both sides had extensive repairs to make, but the American navy was in a better position to make them. At the battle's end the Japanese first used the kamikaze or suicide bomber.

In the 1941–1942 Philippines campaign the Americans had the disadvantages of air inferiority and isolation from replacements and supplies. But in 1944–1945, Japan had these disadvantages, plus the opposition of Filipino guerillas. In December, while the fighting for Leyte was still intense, MacArthur was able to land forces on Mindoro, the southernmost big Philippine island, and in January he invaded Luzon, the largest of the islands and the one upon which Manila is located. By March, American ships were unloading in Manila Bay. By June, the Japanese had been defeated in the Philippines. Some Japanese soldiers hid in the remote and inaccessible highlands, there to remain until Japan's final defeat. Indeed, some of these troops, isolated from the news, remained in hiding until months and even years after the war had ended.

American forces invaded more island stepping stones on the difficult

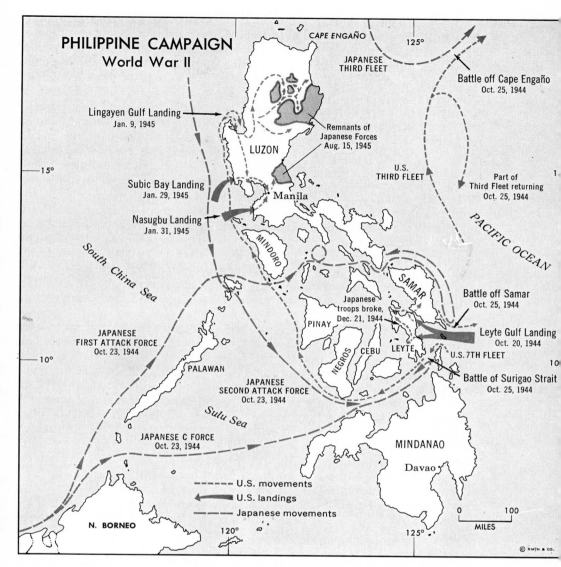

PHILIPPINE CAMPAIGN
World War II

Battle off Cape Engaño
Oct. 25, 1944

Lingayen Gulf Landing
Jan. 9, 1945

Remnants of
Japanese Forces
Aug. 15, 1945

LUZON

U.S.
THIRD FLEET

Part of
Third Fleet returning
Oct. 25, 1944

Subic Bay Landing
Jan. 29, 1945

Manila

Nasugbu Landing
Jan. 31, 1945

MINDORO

PACIFIC OCEAN

South China Sea

SAMAR

Battle off Samar
Oct. 25, 1944

Japanese
troops broke,
Dec. 21, 1944

Leyte Gulf Landing
Oct. 20, 1944

PINAY

JAPANESE
FIRST ATTACK FORCE
Oct. 23, 1944

NEGROS

CEBU

LEYTE

U.S. 7TH FLEET

PALAWAN

JAPANESE
SECOND ATTACK FORCE
Oct. 23, 1944

Battle of Surigao Strait
Oct. 25, 1944

Sulu Sea

MINDANAO

JAPANESE C FORCE
Oct. 23, 1944

Davao

CAPE ENGAÑO

JAPANESE
THIRD FLEET

N. BORNEO

- - - - - U.S. movements
⟶ U.S. landings
- - - - Japanese movements

0   100
MILES

© RMcN & CO.

road to Tokyo before the completion of the Philippines campaign. Marines invaded Iwo Jima on February 19, 1945, and had the eight-square-mile island under control within a month, but the action was one of the most difficult of the Pacific war. The Japanese had fortified Iwo Jima so cleverly that its camouflaged guns could cover every yard of the island and so deeply that seventy-two consecutive days of aerial bombing and three days of intense fire from naval vessels did little damage. The tiny volcanic island, only 775 miles from the main Japanese island of Honshu, was important as an air base. If the Japanese held it, they endangered the American air base at Saipan; if the Americans held it, they could use it as a base for fighters to escort the big B-29's on their Japanese attacks.

503

The successful American invasion and conquest of Okinawa, April 1 to June 20, were notable for several reasons. The largest amphibious operation of the whole Pacific war, the Japanese offered the landing almost no opposition. Their plan was to knock out the supporting naval force with an all-out attack by air and naval forces. About seven hundred planes, half of them kamikazes, struck incessantly on April 6 and 7. American guns destroyed about half of the attackers, but the Japanese aircraft, particularly the kamikazes, sank or put out of action thirty-six American ships. Never before had the American fleet suffered such losses so quickly. The next day, American carrier planes spotted a fleet of nine Japanese ships moving in for a hit-and-run attack, among them Japan's last superbattleship, *Yamato*. A concentrated attack sank five of the nine, including *Yamato*, and Japanese surface naval strength was all but wiped out. A wicked typhoon at this point seriously endangered the American fleet. Actually part of the same archipelago as Japan and only 350 miles from the southernmost Japanese island of Kyushu, Okinawa fitted into American plans as a base of operations for the invasion of Japan. The Okinawa campaign was the first one in the Pacific theater in an area fairly heavily populated by hostile people. Also, in this campaign Japanese soldiers surrendered in mass numbers for the first time. Some Japanese soldiers, at least, had become aware that the war was in its last stages and that Japan's cause was almost hopeless.

In the spring and summer of 1945, American naval and air forces brought the war home to Japan with a vengeance. Land-based bombers and fighters and carrier-based planes hit Japanese industrial centers with such overwhelming power that the nation's war potential was devastated. Raids on Japanese cities were terrible in their effects. Napalm incendiary bombs caused more havoc and death in flimsily built Japanese cities in a few months than did the far heavier bombing of Germany. Roughly 330,000 Japanese civilians died from American bombings; another 500,000 were injured. A single fire raid against Tokyo in March, 1945, destroyed sixteen square miles of the city. Planes and submarines destroyed what was left of the Japanese navy and systematically cut off shipping. With her industry strangled for lack of raw materials and many of her interisland railroad ferries destroyed, Japan was well softened up for the American invasion. The plan was to invade Kyushu in November, 1945, and Honshu the following March. American casualties were expected to run to about one million. The atom bomb, however, hastened the end of the war and made the invasion of Japan unnecessary.

The decision to drop the atom bomb on Japan was not taken lightly, although perhaps not with the recognition of the ramifications that hindsight would indicate as proper. The idea of warning Japan of the existence of the new weapon and urging Japan to surrender before the weapon was used was rejected as unworkable. The plan of demonstrating to Japan the power of the new weapon over some uninhabited island and then demanding surrender was rejected on grounds that the bomb might not detonate, and indeed there was no assurance that it would. Desire to finish off Japan with as little help from Russia as possible, so as to keep Russian influence in Asia to a minimum, was another consideration. Japanese reaction to the Potsdam Declaration also figured in the decision to drop the bomb. Some background to this declaration and its reception is necessary.

Japan's military successes in 1941 and 1942 submerged the political moderates' opposition to the most rabidly militaristic and imperialistic army leadership. But as Japan's military fortunes turned, the moderates again began to exert themselves, and in July, 1944, a group of navy moderates brought about the downfall of the Tojo government. The new government headed by General Kuniaki Koiso had moderates within it who were eager to bring the war to an end, saving whatever of Japan's territorial conquests her enemies would allow. In February, 1945, Emperor Hirohito gave his support to the moderates. In early April, he appointed still another premier, Admiral Kantaro Suzuki, and delegated him to sue for peace. Suzuki opened secret discussions with the Russians, whom he wanted to serve as mediators between Japan and America and Great Britain, but Suzuki's powers were severely restricted since he had no control over the army. The Japanese army leadership threatened revolt and assassination, its old weapons, if the government made peace. Just before the Potsdam Conference, Hirohito directed the Japanese ambassador in Moscow to urge the Russians to bring about peace.

One of the difficulties within the Japanese government was what was meant by "unconditional surrender." If that meant abandonment of the imperial monarchy, surely surrender would have more opponents within Japan than it would have if the Japanese could keep their traditional government. President Truman in a statement on V-E Day said nothing explicit about the government of Japan when he again called for Japanese unconditional surrender. He only pointed out that "unconditional surrender does not mean the extermination or enslavement of the Japanese people," which seemed rather obvious. The participants in the last wartime conference at Potsdam, July 17 to August 2, 1945, were preoccupied with European problems and were new as representatives in the Grand Alliance. Truman and his new Secretary of State, James F. Byrnes, spoke for the United States. Churchill and Eden opened the conference as the British delegates, but the British people had already voted in a new Labor party government and on July 28, Clement Atlee, the new prime minister, and Ernest Bevin, the new foreign minister, took over from their more conservative fellow countrymen. Stalin and Molotov, of course, had no voters to threaten their tenure.

The Potsdam Declaration of July 26 called upon Japan to surrender unconditionally or suffer "the utter devastation of the Japanese homeland." The Declaration said nothing to indicate such devastation would be by other than conventional weapons. With surrender, the Declaration went on, Allied forces would occupy Japan until militarism was utterly eliminated, war criminals punished, peace and security established, and a government installed that was consistent with the wishes of the Japanese people. Although much of this Declaration was vague to the point that different Japanese leaders could interpret it quite differently, Japanese moderates at least could take heart from it. The Suzuki government had still to mollify the army diehards and was still hopeful of negotiating peace through the Russians. A government statement on July 28, intended for home consumption, called the Declaration "unworthy of public notice." The top American leaders at Potsdam, now aware that a test of the atom bomb in New Mexico had been successful, understood this statement to be the Japanese reply, considered it inadequate, and ordered the dropping of the bomb on any of four Japanese industrial cities any time after August 3.

Early in the morning of August 6, 1945, a B-29 dropped an atom bomb on Hiroshima equal in power to twenty thousand tons of TNT. The bomb killed an estimated eighty thousand people and maimed thousands more. The blast and subsequent fire utterly destroyed the city. The Japanese army still balked at surrender. On August 8, Russia entered the war as agreed, charging quickly into Manchuria and Korea. On August 9, an American plane dropped a more powerful atom bomb on Nagasaki. The next day, Emperor Hirohito overruled the army and notified the United States that Japan accepted the terms of the Potsdam Declaration if the status of the Emperor were not altered. America replied that during the occupation the Emperor's authority would be secondary to that of the Supreme Commander of the Allied Powers and that the ultimate government of Japan would be decided by the Japanese people. Despite the disasters of Hiroshima and Nagasaki, the army still wanted to refuse these terms. Hirohito again overruled the army. On August 14, the Suzuki government accepted the Potsdam terms and President Truman announced Japan's surrender. On September 2, the Japanese formally surrendered aboard the American battleship *Missouri* in Tokyo Bay.

The destruction and death was over at last. The total costs could never accurately be assessed. Of American peak strength of 12,300,000 men in the armed forces, 291,557 were killed by enemy action. American monetary costs were about $330 billion, if we can say that the costs ended when the fighting stopped. Great Britain had fewer men killed in action, 244,723, but this was a higher proportion of her men under arms. China lost an estimated 2,200,000 men. Russia lost far more men than any other country in the war on either side: an estimated 7,500,000 killed by enemy action. Russia lost a similar number of civilians. The Axis powers lost heavily, too. Germany, which at one time had 10,200,000 men under arms, suffered 3,500,000 battle deaths; Japan had 1,219,000 battle deaths out of a little over 6,000,000 servicemen.

CHAPTER TWENTY-FIVE

The Truman Era: Foreign and Domestic Cold War

FEW AMERICANS DURING THE WAR HAD THE WISDOM TO SEE THAT Axis defeat would not solve most of the nation's problems. The hardships and horrors of war were such that their end, it seemed to most people in their innocent optimism, would mean automatically an era of peace and internal harmony. The most widespread anxiety about postwar America was that cessation of war spending would bring about the depression's return.

Fear of depression proved unfounded. The United States after World War II enjoyed the greatest and most sustained period of economic prosperity in its history. But optimistic expectation of a "brave new world" proved equally unfounded. On the domestic scene the nation faced inflation and shortages, labor unrest, irresponsible political battling, and deep, frustrating social problems arising from a rapidly increasing population and a general heightening of individual and family social aspirations. Nor was the world situation reassuring. On the world scene the nation faced a sharp and continual conflict between its desires and those of the communist parts of the world, upheaval and imbalances that arose with the revolt of dark-skinned peoples against colonial imperialism, and the constant dreadful knowledge that man's new weapons could, if used to their capacity in an all-out war, destroy civilization and perhaps life itself. Perhaps most confusing and frustrating was the increasing realization that the nation's problems, both foreign and domestic, were wondrously complex and subtle. Even relatively unsophisticated minds perceived that America's foreign, political, economic, social, and cultural problems had no simple solution, that to see them in sharp black and white or good and evil terms was naive, and that all alternatives for their solution contained the seeds of new predicaments.

A nation must have wise and efficient leadership to cope with situations of such nature. It must be said that America had no leadership adequate to the task. No party, no organized group, no individual was up to the mark. Perhaps the mark was too high for mortal men to reach.

Truman's Ordeal

Harry S. Truman took the oath of office as president the evening of April 12, 1945, a few hours after Roosevelt's death. The next day he told reporters, "I don't know whether you fellows ever had a load of hay or a bull fall on you. But last night the moon, the stars and all the planets fell on me." Truman had been born in May, 1884, in Jackson County, Missouri, and had spent nearly all of his life in that vicinity. He graduated from high school in Independence in the spring of 1901, just before Theodore Roosevelt became president. Denied admission to West Point because of poor eyesight, he became a bank clerk and then a farmer. He was an officer in a state guard artillery unit, and when his regiment went into federal service during the war he served overseas. After the Armistice, Captain Truman and his sergeant opened a retail men's clothing store in Kansas City; the business failed in 1922 in the postwar depression. Thirty-eight years old and broke, Truman accepted the offer of the Tom Pendergast Democratic machine of Kansas City to be nominated a county commissioner, called a judge in Missouri. Except for the election of 1924, when he opposed the Ku Klux Klan and went down to defeat, he kept getting re-elected and served efficiently and honestly despite the corruption of the machine that supported him. With Pendergast's help he won election to the United States Senate in 1934. There he had a consistent New Deal voting record, was too quiet and colorless to make a national reputation, and fitted in well in the Senate's clubby atmosphere. He won re-election in 1940 despite FDR's lack of support and Pendergast's 1939 conviction for income tax fraud. From a border state, a loyal party man, unidentified strongly with any ideology, Truman was an ideal compromise vice-presidential nominee in 1944. On the whole, his career had not educated him well for the presidency, and FDR had almost ignored him while he waited in the wings as a standby performer. At least the superficial contrast with Roosevelt was striking: the one urbane, tactful, articulate, confident; the other provincial, blunt, not clever with words, unprepossessing.

Truman never became a Roosevelt, but he grew in the White House as few other presidents had. Although his administration never solved the basic problems confronting the country (at best they attained only short-term satisfactory arrangements while waiting for a happier and more propitious time), Truman by the time he left the White House had shown his enemies he was a far stronger man than they had estimated and demonstrated to his friends that their misgivings had been exaggerated. He displayed courage, toughness, and a willingness to make hard decisions.

Within a week after Japan's surrender, Truman submitted to Congress a long domestic program, reminiscent of the political mood of the mid-1930's, that he in time came to call the Fair Deal. Truman wanted Congress to raise the minimum wage from forty to sixty-five cents an hour; to extend social security; to establish a permanent Fair Employment Practices Commission; and to enact a full employment program, an extensive slum clearance and public housing plan, and a series of regional flood control and hydro-electric projects. Before the end of the year, he asked Congress for legislation to provide nationalization of atomic energy, the St. Lawrence seaway, national health insurance, and federal aid to education. Some of these requests eventually became law, most of them were compromised, some were defeated.

It is easy to overlook some of the Truman administration's positive accomplishments in the era's political furor. Some of Truman's requests became law even early in his administration. "Full employment" after the war had been a Democratic pledge in 1944; Henry Wallace had written confidently of a postwar economy with "sixty million jobs" and been attacked as a wild visionary. (Employment reached sixty million in August, 1946.) The administration's Full Employment bill stated it was the federal government's responsibility to maintain the nation's economic health and contained a plan for compensatory deficit spending during economic slumps. The law that emerged from the congressional compromise mill was called the Maximum Employment Act. Becoming law in early 1946, it established a three-man Council of Economic Advisers and required the president to make an annual report on the nation's economy. It contained no guarantee of government action against recession, although in fact both Democratic and Republican administrations have since used federal power to compensate for and correct downswings in the business cycle. The Atomic Energy Act of 1946 vested all policy decisions about nuclear power in the hands of the civilian-controlled Atomic Energy Commission, as the manager of the legislation in Congress, Democratic Senator Brian McMahon of Connecticut wished, and over the opposition of Senator Arthur H. Vandenberg, Republican of Michigan. The Act provided for a Military Liaison Committee to work with the AEC, but the Committee had no statutory policy power and only the commander in chief was authorized to order the use of nuclear weapons.

Another measure affecting the military establishment was the National Security Act of July 26, 1947, adopted after nearly two years of backbiting and wrangling between the army and navy. Nearly everyone accepted in principle the idea of unification of the armed forces, but the admirals were fearful that their service would be subordinated to land-based air power, and marine officers, then under the Navy Department, were apprehensive that the corps might be abolished. The new law created a separate air force and maintained the marines, thereby creating four branches rather than three (five branches if one counts the coast guard which remained under the Department of the Treasury), but the old Departments of War and Navy disappeared to be replaced by the Department of Defense. Under the Secretary of Defense (the first was James V. Forrestal) were secretaries of army, navy, and air force with subcabinet rank. A Joint Chiefs of Staff with a rotating chairman was supposed to provide further coordination among the services, and three other new agencies, the National Security Council, the National Security Resource Board, and the Central Intelligence Agency, had the task of advising Congress and the president on national security. The new law by no means ended interservice rivalry, which extended to public propaganda and lobbying in Congress. Indeed, the fight over long-range bombers versus super aircraft carriers, which went on for years while attention to missiles lagged, was if anything more intense than interservice bickering before unification.

The vast and complicated civilian side of the executive branch also was the subject of reorganization. In 1947, Truman asked Congress to create a study group to study how best to straighten out the maze of bureaus and agencies. Congress consented, and Truman appointed former President Hoover to head the investigation. The Hoover Commission reported in 1949, suggesting the merger of sixty-five units into twenty-three and the creation of a new federal department to handle education, public health, and welfare. The Reorganization Act of June, 1949, authorized Truman to submit reorganization plans to Congress which would become effective unless Congress disapproved. Of Truman's many reorganization plans, Congress disapproved of only his proposed Department of Welfare.

The most spectacular aspect of the Truman era's political history, however, was the fierce, fluid, shifting partisan brawling, both between the parties and within them. Despite the Missourian's Fair Deal requests, he frequently appeared to be far removed from any New Deal sympathies. Those who had been enthusiastic FDR supporters found Truman extremely disappointing in his first two to three years. At the same time, division within the old New Deal coalition over foreign policy questions further reduced Truman's political base. The flight of Roosevelt aides from the new administration revealed disillusion in high places. After he had been in office only a few months, Truman nominated Edwin W. Pauley as Undersecretary of the Navy. Interior Secretary Ickes charged publicly that the nomination had a smell of oil about it reminiscent of Teapot Dome. Ickes said that Pauley had asserted when he was treasurer of the Democratic national committee that he could raise $300,000 for the party from oil interests if the administration would drop its test suit claiming title to California's offshore oil fields. In February, 1946, Ickes resigned in a well-publicized huff. Truman continued to support Pauley, but in August he vetoed a bill that would have yielded control of tidelands oil to the states. In September, 1946, Truman asked Secretary of Commerce Henry A. Wallace for his resignation after Wallace had given a speech in New York which appeared at the time to have had Truman's prior approval and in which Wallace had attacked the "get-tough-with-Russia" policy being conducted by Secretary of State James F. Byrnes. Byrnes had replaced Stettinius in that office in mid-1945.

Other Truman policies in 1945, 1946, and early 1947 contributed to conflict within the coalition Roosevelt had so skillfully put together. Needless to say, the Republicans, hungry for office after failing to win every congressional election since 1930 and every presidential election since 1932, were delighted with the fissures in the Democratic camp and pressed their attacks on Truman with uncommon vigor. The liberal-labor bloc in the Democratic fold became positively alarmed by Truman's vacillation over high prices and his labor policy.

Pressures building under prices were tremendous, more than the administration showed itself able to handle. Wartime controls disappeared quickly after V-J Day; OPA stopped rationing but was able to hold the cost of living index to only a 3 per cent increase between the war's end and mid-1946. Some goods were in genuine short supply, but businessmen and farmers held some commodities back from market in the expectation of higher prices and, they hoped, the elimination of price controls altogether. Clothes, cars, soaps and other fat products, and beef were the scarcest items. At the same time, consumers had billions to spend from their more or less enforced wartime savings. Black market operations and devious methods of circumventing price regulation became far more common than they had been during the war. Organized labor went on strike for higher wage rates to maintain at forty hours a week the incomes workers had received for overtime, aggravated by their long pent-up frustrations that grew under the no-strike pledge and anxiety about an antiunion drive such as followed World War I. Higher labor costs further built pressure for higher prices.

Yet millions of people saw clearly that significantly higher prices would seriously lower their standards of living. Retired people on relatively fixed incomes were exceedingly vulnerable, as were teachers and others who received their livelihood from public funds since government payrolls usually catch up with increased prices more slowly than private ones. Veterans of the armed forces living on the "GI Bill of Rights" were in no position to pay higher prices for basic necessities. (Congress in 1944 had passed the Servicemen's Readjustment Act which granted unemployment compensation of $20 a week for up to fifty-two weeks to unemployed veterans and provided free tuition and books and a subsistence cash allowance for veterans who went to school, either trade school or college.) The political pressures of consumers and the counterpressures of business put congressmen in an unenviable position.

Congress debated long and hard throughout the spring of 1946 about the extension of price controls due to expire under existing legislation at the end of June. Truman, on the one hand, urged Congress to extend price controls and on the other told a press conference that peacetime government controls were "police state methods." Three days before the deadline, Congress passed a weak bill that extended OPA for a year but eliminated most of its power and ordered it to cease price controls as soon as possible. To most people's surprise, Truman vetoed the bill thus ending controls altogether.

On July 1, the first "free-market" day, beef prices at the Chicago stockyards went up 22 per cent. Farmers flooded the livestock markets, yet prices continued to rise. Faced with vigorous protests, Congress quickly went to work on another price control bill. It produced a bill only slightly more effective than the one Truman had vetoed. This time, on July 25, Truman signed the measure but apologized for doing so. In August, OPA moved meat prices down again, and again livestock raisers kept their animals off the market. The administration slowly yielded. In October Truman announced the end of controls on meat. The butcher shops quickly had meat aplenty, but at prices that angered housewives. In November, Truman announced the lifting of all controls except for rent, rice, and sugar. Truman's popularity was low indeed. He had resisted inflation just enough to anger those who wanted higher prices for their products and had yielded enough to alienate large sections of the Democratic coalition that wanted strict controls.

Nor did Truman's labor policy in 1946 endear him to a big bloc in his party. His reputation grew not a bit in the wave of strikes of late 1945 and early 1946. The administration, which still had wartime powers and agencies, brought about compromises which granted labor slightly more than two-thirds

TABLE 10

BUREAU OF LABOR STATISTICS CONSUMER PRICE INDEX, 1926-1960.

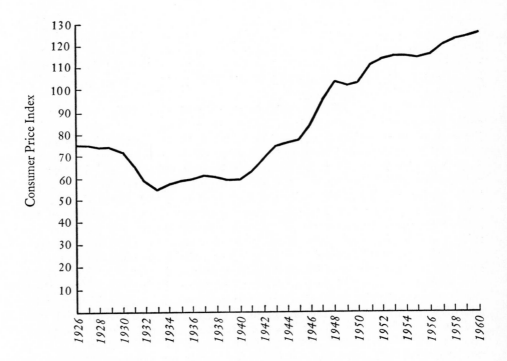

of the pay increases it demanded and granted employers price increases to compensate for the additional production costs. Many asserted, with considerable justification, that the price increases more than compensated for the higher wages. But the President's conduct in the May, 1946, railroad strike thoroughly displeased labor. The railroad brotherhoods and railroad management had negotiated for months over wages and working rules but had come to no agreement. When the brotherhoods threatened to strike, Truman on May 17 invoked the Smith-Connally Act and seized the railroads. He worked out a compromise which all the brotherhoods but the Engineers and the Trainmen accepted. They walked out on May 23, and rail transportation stopped utterly. Truman prepared an appeal to Congress to grant him extreme powers to deal with strikes that imperiled the public. Although he received a note informing him that the Engineers and Trainmen had surrendered just as he began his address to Congress, he went ahead and presented his request: power to draft strikers into the armed services in government-seized industries, loss of strikers' seniority benefits, and stiff fines for union leaders who continued strike activities. The House passed his measure; the Senate did not act.

Not since Wilson in 1918 or Hoover in 1930 had a president been so unpopular as he prepared to lead his party in congressional elections. Scenting victory, the Republicans capitalized on the administration's ineptitude with the slogan "Had Enough? Vote Republican." But perhaps more important, Democrats of most varieties were thoroughly disgusted with the administration. Southern Democrats disliked Truman's plea for a permanent FEPC and had defeated it. Northern and western urban Democrats, still divided among themselves over Truman's Russian policies, were mostly in agreement in condemnation of his price control and labor record. On November 5, the GOP won its first national victory since 1928. And it was a sweeping Republican electoral triumph. Elected to the House were 246 Republicans to the Democrats' 188; in the Senate there were 51 on the Republican side and 45 on the Democrats' aisle. Outside the South, Republicans elected governors in 25 states. The only direction Truman's popularity could go was up after this election.

The manner in which Truman restored his personal popularity and his party's strength in 1947 and 1948 was one of the most dramatic political comebacks in American history. His own foreign policies and developments of Soviet policy brought about a substantial healing of the divisions within the Democratic party on foreign affairs. The Truman Doctrine, enunciated in March, 1947, did not evoke popular response at first, but the Marshall Plan later that year proved a very popular proposal (see pp. 523–525). At the same time, the Soviets pursued a "get-tough" policy that dissolved most of the Democratic criticism of the kind Wallace had made in his September, 1946, speech.

The greatest percentage decline in Democratic votes in 1946 had been in the cities. For Truman, then, the task was to pursue domestic policies that would attract that part of the voting population in which labor and minority groups were important. In May, 1947, speaking from his hometown where he had gone to visit his sick and aged mother, he urged Congress to pass a long-range public health program, including provisions for worker disability insurance. He made a series of appointments that were popular with the liberal-labor bloc: Gordon Clapp to the TVA, David Lilienthal to the AEC. In 1948, he systematically began a program to eliminate segregation of and discrimination against Negroes in both the armed forces and civil federal employment that attracted large groups of voters in northern and western cities. His prompt recognition of Israel as an independent nation on May 14, 1948, within only minutes after the British mandate in Palestine ended also appealed to this voting group.

The Republicans seemed determined to help Truman in his effort to drape himself in Roosevelt's domestic mantle. Senate Republicans consistently challenged Truman's more liberal appointments, frequently impugning the loyalty of the nominees. Farmers, who had expected an agricultural depression momentarily since the end of the war, began to rally behind Truman when he beat down Republican demands for "flexible" price supports to maintain farm prices at from 65 to 90 per cent of parity. In June, 1948, Congress enacted a measure to continue supports at 90 per cent of parity for another year and a half. Republican Congressmen opposed Truman on rent controls and other anti-inflationary proposals, and prices continued to rise. And when Truman objected to tax reduction on grounds of inflationary pressures, he at least partly undermined whatever political advantage lower taxes gave the GOP. In both 1947 and 1948, Congress enacted tax bills over the President's veto.

But it was the Taft-Hartley Act of July, 1947, the first major overhaul of federal labor legislation since 1935, that provided the most political dynamite (see p. 581). Proposals to curb the power of organized labor had been gaining strength during the postwar strike wave, particularly when John L. Lewis and the UMW defied the government and public opinion. In 1946, Truman had successfully vetoed the quite restrictive Case bill. In the spring of 1947, Congress passed a labor bill sponsored by Senator Robert A. Taft of Ohio and Representative Fred Hartley of New Jersey, both Republicans. Organized labor called the measure a "slave labor act" and roundly condemned the Republicans for passing it, although it had actually been passed with a combination of Republican and conservative Democratic, mostly southern, votes. On June 20, 1947, Truman vetoed the measure with a strong message. Congress quickly overrode the veto, again with near unanimity on the Republican side.

Truman had allowed the old Roosevelt coalition to begin to fall apart before he began to rebuild it after the 1946 elections. Ironically, the Republican party, by playing the role of conservative bogey-man, helped Truman to paste the coalition back together.

Truman's Triumph—and Further Troubles

Yet in mid-summer of 1948, the old coalition appeared to be a long way from rehabilitation. At the end of December, 1947, Henry A. Wallace had announced his independent presidential candidacy on a program of negotiation with Russia and a kind of domestic reform he called "progressive capitalism." Hardly any important Democrats threw in their lot with Wallace, but a great many normally Democratic voters were sympathetic to him at first. In early 1948, in a special House of Representatives election in the Bronx, New York City, the Wallace-backed candidate won in a three-cornered race. Although much of Wallace's organization came from the Communists and those who cooperated with the Communists—Wallace, clearly, was not a Communist—early in the year political observers were granting Wallace from five to ten million votes in November, enough probably to insure Truman's defeat. Democratic Senator Glen Taylor of Idaho, a singing cowboy entertainer, became Wallace's running mate at the July, 1948, Progressive party convention.

In and around Americans for Democratic Action (ADA), an anti-Communist and anti-Wallace but left of center group founded in early 1947 by Democratic intellectuals, labor leaders, and urban political professionals, were many Democrats who wanted to dump Truman. They looked around desperately for another presidential candidate. When Justice William O. Douglas declined consideration, some of them wanted General Dwight D. Eisenhower, who had recently become president of Columbia University. Some Democratic city bosses—Jacob Arvey of Chicago, Frank Hague of Jersey City, and Edward Flynn of New York—joined them in this venture, which was to prove ironic in just a few years. Eisenhower was not interested.

With such apparent division in Democratic ranks, Republican hopefuls were more than usually eager for the nomination. The main contenders were Governor Dewey, former Governor of Minnesota Harold E. Stassen, and

Senator Taft. General Douglas MacArthur had some support. After the primaries, the fight settled down to Dewey versus Taft. Although perhaps even a majority of the Republican convention delegates—at Philadelphia in June— respected and loved Taft more than Dewey, they thought that Taft "could not win." Taft had remarkable talents and commanded wide respect, but he lacked the personal traits that denoted political magnetism. Further, as a professed conservative, although a flexible one, many GOP professionals feared that he could not attract the independent vote. On the third ballot the nomination went to Dewey; Governor Earl Warren of California received the vice-presidential nomination. The GOP platform was even more of a "me too" document than its 1944 declaration. Apparently, Republican party leaders were not confident that a conservative statement would attract enough votes to win. Republicans promised to do everything Democrats had done or promised to do but to do them more efficiently.

Frustrated because they really had no choice but to nominate Truman, the ADA faction at the Democratic national convention, also at Philadelphia, fought through a progressive platform over the southern delegations' opposition. When Senator Hubert Humphrey of Minnesota insisted upon and got a strong civil rights plank that called for a permanent FEPC, a federal antilynching law, and a law to eliminate poll taxes, many of the Alabama and Mississippi delegates walked out of the convention. With Wallace going off in one direction and the strong possibility of Dixie delegations going off in the other, the convention was indeed dismal in spirit. It nominated Truman and Senator Alben W. Barkley of Kentucky, president pro tempore of the upper house.

Within a week after the Democratic convention adjourned the Democratic bolters and other southerners met at Birmingham to form the States' Rights Democratic party and to nominate Governor J. Strom Thurmond of South Carolina and Governor Fielding Wright of Mississippi for the national executive positions. These so-called Dixiecrats controlled what had been the Democratic parties in South Carolina, Alabama, Mississippi, and Louisiana.

About the only person who thought Truman would win was Truman himself. He began a fighting campaign with his acceptance speech in which he announced that he was calling Congress into special session on July 26 so that the Republican majority could enact the "anything-you-can-do-I-can-do-better" platform the GOP had adopted at its convention. Congress met for almost two weeks and, as Truman expected, did practically nothing. Truman shrewdly aimed his campaign against the Republican Congress—the "do-nothing" Congress and "that awful Eightieth Congress" he called it—rather than against Dewey. The President undertook personal speaking tours that took him more than the distance around the world, speaking at "whistle stops" and wherever he could get a crowd. He seldom spoke from a prepared text; his extemporaneous stump speeches were much more effective. Truman had told his running mate, "I'm going to give them hell"; before long, people in the crowds gathered at the rear of the campaign train began to shout, "Give 'em hell, Harry," and Truman poured it on. As the campaign wore on, Truman's crowds became bigger and increasingly enthusiastic. Political commentators said that the voters liked Truman because he was the underdog and a battler but that they would not vote for him.

Since the polls and the experts declared that Dewey's victory was all

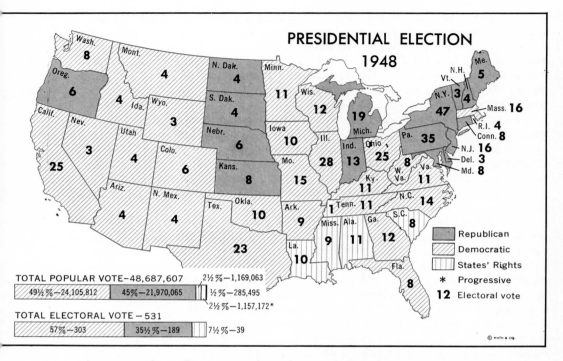

PRESIDENTIAL ELECTION 1948

TOTAL POPULAR VOTE–48,687,607
| 49½%–24,105,812 | 45%–21,970,065 |
2½%–1,169,063
½%–285,495
2½%–1,157,172*

TOTAL ELECTORAL VOTE–531
| 57%–303 | 35½%–189 | 7½%–39 |

Republican
Democratic
States' Rights
* Progressive
12 Electoral vote

but a certainty, Dewey conducted a campaign calculated to alienate no one, similar to Roosevelt's in 1932 when his election was as predictable as the tide. Dewey, of course, had no way of knowing that his basic premise was unfounded. Republicans other than Dewey frequently spoke as if they were still running against FDR, which played well into Truman's hands because he was doing his utmost to persuade the voters that he was Roosevelt incarnate.

So certain were the pollsters of Republican victory that they ceased their operations well before election day. So certain were editors and radio commentators of Truman's defeat that even when the early returns showed Truman leading they refused to believe the evidence and said to wait until the rural precincts reported. The *Chicago Daily Tribune* carried a banner headline proclaiming Dewey's victory. But Truman defeated Dewey by a rather large margin. Truman received 24,105,695 popular votes to earn him 304 votes in the electoral college to Dewey's 21,969,170 and 189. Democratic candidates also won a majority of congressional seats. The new Congress would have Democratic margins of ninety-three in the House and twelve in the Senate. Wallace received only 1,157,172 popular votes and none in the electoral college; the Dixiecrat candidate received 1,169,021 popular and 39 electoral votes. Dewey won in sixteen states: Oregon, Kansas north to Canada, Indiana, Michigan, and Maryland and Delaware north to the border with the exceptions of Massachusetts and Rhode Island. Thurmond carried the four states where the Dixiecrats pulled out of the Democratic party and picked up one additional electoral vote when a Tennessee elector refused to honor the Truman popular vote. In three of the states Truman lost, New York, Maryland, and Michigan, he would have won if all the Wallace vote had gone Democratic.

Why did Truman win? Politicians debated the subject strenuously. Conservative Republicans whose heart belonged to Taft argued that Dewey had lost the election rather than that Truman had won it. However, the record showed that Dewey did not fail to get any significant number of normally Republican votes. The hard fact for the Republican party was that the Roosevelt political revolution had tipped the scales until those who considered themselves Democrats outnumbered those who considered themselves Republicans, although "independents" or "swing voters" were numerous enough to throw a presidential election either way. The Wallace and Thurmond candidacies probably worked to Truman's benefit. Because Communist support of Wallace was so obvious—even to the stupid tactic of selling the *Daily Worker* at Wallace rallies in Texas—the red issue was largely irrelevant in the Truman-Dewey struggle. Thurmond's white supremacy movement only gained for Truman votes in the North and West, not only among Negroes but among ethnic groups that fearfully identified the Dixiecrats with the spirit of the Ku Klux Klan. Truman capitalized on this reaction outside of the South and stumped hard for civil rights carrying his campaign into Harlem, the first presidential candidate ever to do so. A final factor: Truman cut into the expected Republican farm vote with his strong support for continued high agricultural subsidies at a time when farm prices were falling and Republicans were talking about "flexible," meaning lower, federal price supports.

Election day of 1948 was the high tide of Truman's strength. His Fair Deal got only slightly off the ground, due mostly to the conservative Democrat-Republican coalition in Congress, partly to Truman's less than wholehearted support of proposed new departures, and partly to the press of foreign affairs and their consequences for domestic politics. On the whole, the Fair Deal only extended social welfare legislation a bit farther down already well-marked roads. It failed to enact laws that blazed new domestic trails.

Among the extensions of old programs by the Eighty-first Congress was a 1949 amendment to the Fair Labor Standards Act of 1938 that increased the hourly minimum wage to seventy-five cents an hour but added to the exemption list; a 1950 change in the Social Security Act of 1935 that brought an additional ten million people under the coverage of the Old Age and Survivors' Insurance plan and increased retirement benefits by slightly more than 75 per cent; and the National Housing Act of 1949, which provided for the building of eight hundred and ten thousand new housing units over the next six years, subsidies to builders of low-rent apartment buildings, and grants to aid in the clearance of slums, both urban and rural. Senator Taft, incidentally, supported federally financed public housing. Public housing administrators and builders rarely used great imagination, and many of the public housing apartment buildings erected on the sites of razed tenement slums actually housed more people per acre than the old housing. Despite its great wealth, the United States still had slums in all its major cities that shocked visitors from some less affluent nations.

Organized labor supported such legislation, but repeal of the Taft-Hartley Act was its primary goal. Truman, at trade union urging, argued in 1949 for full repeal and got nothing; probably Congress would have passed amendments altering some of the law's features—Taft was willing to make some concessions—but the administration refused a compromise. Indeed, at one point the House came close to making the law even more restrictive. A 1951 amendment, however, permitted union-shop clauses in labor contracts without a special vote of affected employees.

The northward migration of Negroes in the 1940's intensified the Democratic party's regional differences. Negro populations—voting populations, it should be noted—nearly doubled in northern industrial cities. In 1947, Truman's special Committee on Civil Rights, composed of distinguished people of both races from both the North and South, had recommended substantially what became the 1948 Democratic civil rights plank plus prohibition of segregation on public interstate transportation. But practically the entire Dixie delegation in Congress was dead set against any federal legislation to advance the Negro's status. Southern Congressmen who personally viewed changed racial relations in the South as inevitable knew that it was almost sure political suicide to vote for the Truman program. Southern Democrats had an almost foolproof defense against civil rights legislation in the Senate rule that granted unlimited debate. A two-thirds majority was necessary to invoke the cloture rule and shut off a filibuster. Civil rights advocates, therefore, concentrated on changing the Senate rule. A civil rights bipartisan group in March, 1949, sought to make it easier to stop a filibuster by changing the two-thirds rule to two-thirds of the Senators present and voting rather than two-thirds of the whole body. The Senate defeated the change sixty-three to twenty-three, twenty-nine Democrats voting for the amended procedure and fifteen against, eight Republicans for and thirty-four against. In other words, more Republicans voted to retain the stricter rule than did Democrats, despite the Republican 1948 civil rights plank. In May and July, 1950, Senate civil rights advocates brought motions to invoke cloture to a vote under the old rule; they failed by twelve votes on the first test and by nine votes on the second. FEPC was dead.

Unable to gain any civil rights legislation, Truman concentrated on executive actions. By the end of his term, segregation in the army and air force had practically disappeared; some southern white recruits took drill from Negro sergeants. He also appointed Negroes to higher positions than they had held heretofore and strengthened the Civil Rights Section of the Department of Justice.

Truman was more successful with Congress in getting it to admit displaced persons from Europe, those who had been set on the march by Nazi or Communist oppression or made homeless by the war. The Eightieth Congress had, near the end of its tenure, passed a measure admitting 205,000 "DP's" as they were commonly called. Truman signed the bill but criticized it on the grounds that it discriminated against Jews and Roman Catholics. Truman asked the next Congress for further DP legislation, and in June, 1950, Congress voted to admit a total of 415,000 without discrimination. But even the second act was filled with such qualifications for admission to the United States that thousands of aspiring refugees were unable to take advantage of the enlarged quota.

Two of Truman's proposals ran into such opposition that Congress never even brought them up for vote. Truman in 1949 proposed a national health insurance plan for prepaid medical, dental, and hospital care to be financed with employee and employer contributions through a payroll tax and government subsidy. The American Medical Association, which had opposed almost every public health proposal ever considered in Congress, vigorously opposed the scheme, both in Capitol lobbies and in mass communication media. It raised a $3 million fund to fight what it called "socialized medicine" by a special assessment on each AMA member. AMA propaganda easily carried the day. Congress would do no more than vote increased appropriations for medical research and education and for hospitals. The administration presented a plan also for federal aid to public education. This proposal triggered a Protestant-Catholic conflict over whether federal aid should go also to parochial schools. The Democratic party was particularly vulnerable to this kind of religious division, and the bill died in Congress without action.

Perhaps the most original administration proposal was a new plan for agricultural subsidies put forward by Secretary of Agriculture Charles F. Brannan. Brannan argued that the consumer paid twice for agricultural subsidies, once in taxes and once in high food prices at the store. The Brannan Plan, announced in April, 1949, would have kept the existing system of purchasing imperishable farm commodities and storing them but revised it somewhat: the main innovation was an arrangement whereby prices of perishable products would seek their natural levels, presumably lower, and the farmer would be reimbursed sufficiently to give him an estimated fair price. For each farmer, government subsidy would be granted only for enough production to bring a payment not to exceed $20,000 at 1949 prices. It was probably this feature that brought the Brannan Plan the opposition of the American Farm Bureau Federation and the Grange, but the public argument of these organizations was that Congress would be less likely to maintain direct subsidies to farmers than it would through the existing commodity surplus purchase scheme. The Brannan Plan excited considerable interest among consumers, but it got nowhere at all in Congress, many of whose members were sensitive to the wishes of the major farm organizations. Instead, Congress in 1949 passed a law that provided for 90 per cent of parity prices through 1950 on imperishables, at least 80 per cent through 1951, and 75 per cent to 90 per cent thereafter. Producers of perishable products, primarily milk and eggs, would be subsidized by "flexible" supports. How the adopted plan furthered "free enterprise" more than the Brannan Plan, as the Farm Bureau asserted, was a mystery to amateur agricultural economists.

The Cold War to 1950

Antagonism between the Communist parts of the world, especially the Soviet Union and later China, and the nations of the West has been a fundamental condition of the postwar world that has affected in greater or lesser degree almost all aspects of public life, foreign and domestic. Some things about the conflict need to be understood at the outset to see this aspect of recent history clearly and dispassionately. First, the issue has not been purely between democracy and totalitarianism, for some of the governments within the western camp—Spain and South Korea, for example—have not been democratic by a reasonable definition. Nor has the issue been purely between capitalism and opposition to it, for some of the anticommunist nations have been socialist or semisocialist—Great Britain and Norway, for example. Both camps have had within them both underdeveloped and industrial nations, both Christian and non-Christian peoples, both Caucasians and non-Caucasians. Each side has committed acts which fall short of international moral conduct when measured by their own standards: Great Britain and France in the Suez affair, the United States in Guatemala, the Soviet Union in Hungary, to cite some examples, although it is not fair to equate the Central Intelligence Agency's 1954 ousting of the Guatemalan regime with the Russian armed suppression of the Budapest rebellion. The mutual distrust and suspicion has been complicated, deep-rooted in history, and pervasive as well as nearly universal in its effects.

We have already considered deteriorating relations between the Russians on the one hand and the United States and Great Britain on the other in the last months of the war. Their relations disintegrated even further in 1946 over Germany, the Middle East, and atomic energy. Our consideration of the German question will await treatment of the Berlin crisis of 1948.

Late in 1941, British and Russian troops invaded Iran to establish a supply route from the West to Russia, and in early 1942 Russia and Britain signed a treaty with Iran guaranteeing withdrawal of their troops at the end of the war. The British and few American troops there withdrew soon after the war. Russia not only left her troops but sent in more and applied pressure on the Iranian government through a Communist-controlled party. In early March, 1946, Washington and London sent notes to Moscow that only thinly veiled a threat to use force to defend Iran if that became necessary. Russia agreed to withdraw later in the month. In August, 1946, Russia demanded from Turkey leases for naval bases in the Dardanelles and notified London and Washington of its intention of "joint defense" of the area with Turkey. The United States sent a naval task force to the Mediterranean and rejected the whole idea of Turkish-Russian "joint defense."

At the time of these Russian-Iranian-Turkish developments American public opinion was by no means unified in belief that an era of Russian-American discord lay ahead. Only few Americans ever really approved of the Bolshevik regime (although many, perhaps most, considered that peculiarly Russia's affair), but during the war two sentiments had grown in the United States that delayed acceptance of cold war: the notion of "One World," the title of a best-selling wartime book by Wendell Willkie, so firmly and widely held that the "two worlds" actually developing were slow to be recognized; and respect and admiration for the Soviets' truly great and extremely sacrificing war against the Nazis. Furthermore, Americans were war-weary. Servicemen wanted to go home, and their families wanted them to. In early 1946, most Americans were far more interested in healing the wounds of the last war than in pursuing policies that might lead to another. Popular reception of Winston Churchill's "Iron Curtain" speech at Westminster College, Fulton, Missouri, in March, 1946, was indicative. Truman had arranged for Churchill to speak, and the President sat on the platform. Churchill, a master of language, said that although he did not think the Russians wanted war they wanted the fruits of war and that only military strength against them would prevent their getting the fruits of war. Americans adopted his "iron curtain" metaphor, which, incidentally, was somewhat of an exaggeration, but they only slowly came to agree with Churchill's general position.

The Russian leaders revealed a measure of their distrust of the United States in their reaction to the Baruch atom plan of 1946. The United States had a world monopoly of atom bombs from 1945 until September, 1949, when the Russians detonated their first one. Instead of using the terrible weapon against Russia, as a few "preventive war" proponents advocated, the United States offered, under certain conditions, to lay the weapon aside. In June, 1946, before the first meeting of the Atomic Energy Commission, Bernard Baruch presented a plan that State Department officials had formulated. Baruch called for an International Atomic Development Authority to own and operate all installations pertaining to atomic power and to conduct research. The atom bomb would be outlawed, and the international authority would have the power, without veto, to punish any violator of the agreement and to inspect throughout the world with an eye cocked for violations. The United States proposed the plan in the United Nations and promised, when the plan was accepted and the international authority was functioning, to tell the world what American scientists already knew of atomic energy, to stop manufacturing atom bombs, and to destroy its A-bomb stockpile. The Russians said "nyet." At first they rejected the idea of the international authority and inspection, demanding instead that the United States unilaterally divest itself of the atomic weapon. (The Soviets, of course, continued to work on their own atom bomb.) Later they yielded to the principle of inspection by an international authority but insisted that violators could be punished only by the United Nations Security Council where, of course, the Soviet Union had a veto. Russian leaders apparently decided that it was better for them to gamble on the success of their own development of an atomic bomb than to enter an international authority which of course would be dominated by the United States and powers friendly to it without a veto power. The United States rejected the Soviet atomic recommendations, and international nuclear disarmament became practically a dead issue until the mid-1950's.

Until 1947, the Truman administration, although it had been at loggerheads with Russia on several points and although it had practiced a "tough" policy, had no long-term policy toward the Soviet Union. In that year it adopted the "containment" policy, and its first application was with the Truman Doctrine in the Greek crisis. George F. Kennan, then of the State Department's policy-planning staff, prepared the classic statement of containment in an anonymous article (X was the only identity of the author when it first appeared) in the semi-scholarly, semi-official journal *Foreign Affairs* in July, 1947, months after the policy had been adopted. The article warrants examination.

Kennan concluded, " . . . United States policy toward the Soviet Union must be that of a long-term, patient but firm and vigilant containment of Russian expansive tendencies." Washington should not indulge in "threats or blustering or superfluous gestures of outward 'toughness' " and should at all times keep its wits and put forward its demands on the Soviets "in such a manner as to leave the way open for a compliance not too detrimental to Russian prestige." But containment would protect the West if applied intelligently, "by the adroit and vigilant application of counter-force at a series of constantly shifting geographical and political points. . . ." Although primarily defensive, offense was involved too: "It would be an exaggeration to say that American behavior unassisted and alone could exercise a power of life and death over the Communist movement and bring about the early fall of Soviet power in Russia. But the United States has it in its power to increase enormously the strains under which Soviet policy must operate, to force . . . a far greater degree of moderation and circumspection . . . and in this way to promote tendencies which must eventually find their outlet in either the break-up or the gradual mellowing of Soviet power. . . ."

The administration first applied the containment policy in Greece in March, 1947. At the end of the war Greece had been badly divided between left and right. Great Britain backed the royalist right, and in the March, 1946, elections, which the left boycotted, the right won. Thereafter, Communist guerillas in Greece, who had the support of Communist governments at the borders, became embroiled in a civil war with the government. Britain backed the Greek government as best she could, as well as the Turks against the Russians. But Britain was in poor economic condition as a result of the war, and in February, 1947, London notified Truman that it could no longer afford its Greek and Turkish aid. On March 12, 1947, Truman went to Congress and asked for an appropriation of $400 million for support of Greece and Turkey and for authority to send a team of military advisers. Truman declared, "I believe that it must be the policy of the United States to support free peoples who are resisting attempted subjugation by armed minorities or by outside pressures." This was the Truman Doctrine. In May, Congress granted the President the power he asked and appropriated the money. By 1950, the United States had spent $659 million for Greek aid, and a lesser amount in the less troublesome Turkish situation.

Stabilizing Greece proved no easy matter. Communist guerillas continued to achieve success until Tito's Jugoslavia broke with Stalin in mid-1948 and closed the border to the guerillas. Even then Greek unrest was widespread because the government was reactionary, inefficient, and adamant against any proposal to better the economic and social conditions against which Greeks revolted. Reluctant to intervene politically into domestic politics between non-Communist groups, the United States seemed to the Greeks actually to support the government a majority of them disliked. Finally, the Greek parliament, in the face of what it thought was American disapproval, voted no confidence in the government, which then resigned. The new regime, far more efficient, finished up the guerilla war in six months.

There were significant things to be noted in the Greek affair. First, for the United States to undertake the Greek commitment and for the President to declare himself for similar actions in other areas was a radical departure from traditional American foreign policy. Never had the United States done anything comparable in peacetime, although aid to Britain, 1939–1941, had some similarities. Second, in its support of an unpopular Greek government, the United States appeared to be a pillar of reaction. The American assumption that all anti-Communists were equally deserving of help was frequently embarrassing. Third, the United States learned that when it became involved in another country's internal affairs it was difficult, if not impossible, to get only its feet wet. Intervention of one kind led to intervention of another, because aid to the government that ruled a nation implied approval of that government.

Although the Greek-Turkish aid bill passed Congress with safe margins, the Truman Doctrine was not nearly as popular with the public at large as the Marshall Plan, first enunciated clearly by Secretary of State George C. Marshall at the Harvard University commencement in June, 1947. Going beyond a speech Undersecretary Dean Acheson had given at Cleveland, Mississippi, the previous month, Marshall proposed that the nation undertake a vast reconstruction of the still weak European economies. Healthy economies would produce a more stable political and social order less vulnerable to Communism; the Marshall Plan was containment plus humanitarianism. Secretary Marshall made it clear that he did not exempt Communist East European governments or even Russia itself, although he must have been confident that the Russians would reject the idea and refuse to allow other Communist regimes to participate and thereby put the blame for exclusion upon themselves rather than upon the United States.

Before the end of June, European foreign ministers met at Paris to consider the proposal. Ernest Bevin, Labor foreign minister of Britain, and Georges Bidault of France were enthusiastic; Molotov not only disapproved but tried unsuccessfully to disrupt the conference. During the summer, representatives of Britain, France, Italy, Turkey, and other non-Communist European nations planned how aid best could be used and asked the United States for a total of $22.4 billion in aid. The political situation in France and Italy was tense; Communists, who were numerous in each nation, made an all-out effort both in parliament and in street riots to block the Marshall Plan.

Opposition to the Marshall Plan in the United States was remarkably small. The major pressure groups in labor, industry, and agriculture supported it. One reason for popular support, other than the humanitarian and anti-Communist aspects, was that Marshall Plan aid would have a beneficial effect upon the American economy as well as the European. The United States did not give the European nations dollars with which they could go elsewhere in the world to purchase machine tools, generators, and tractors; it granted the European nations credits to be spent primarily in the United States. Thus, Marshall Plan government spending stimulated the domestic economy in much the same way government spending had during the war. Furthermore, some special interest groups within the United States assured themselves of a share of the spending; shipping companies and the National Maritime Union, for example, got Congress to require that half of Marshall Plan equipment be shipped in American ships. The proposal went through Congress without major difficulty or serious amendment. Truman signed it on April 3, 1948.

Inevitably, a confusing set of initial agencies conducted the program, which became known as the European Recovery Program (ERP). The American agency, the Economic Cooperation Administration (ECA), worked with the Committee of European Economic Cooperation (CEEC). Over the next three years, ECA spent $12 billion, and the scheme accomplished what it had been planned to do. Industrial production in the Marshall Plan countries of Europe increased 64 per cent. Their gross national products increased by about one-fourth. In many respects, by 1951 the European economy was stronger

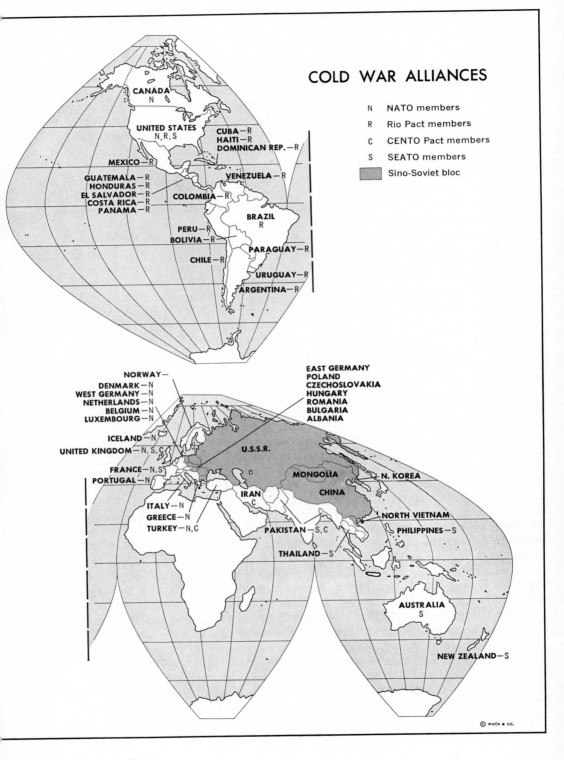

COLD WAR ALLIANCES

N   NATO members
R   Rio Pact members
C   CENTO Pact members
S   SEATO members
    Sino-Soviet bloc

CANADA
N

UNITED STATES
N, R, S

CUBA — R
HAITI — R
DOMINICAN REP. — R

MEXICO — R

GUATEMALA — R
HONDURAS — R
EL SALVADOR — R
COSTA RICA — R
PANAMA — R

VENEZUELA — R

COLOMBIA — R

BRAZIL
R

PERU — R
BOLIVIA — R

PARAGUAY — R

CHILE — R

URUGUAY — R

ARGENTINA — R

NORWAY —
DENMARK — N
WEST GERMANY — N
NETHERLANDS — N
BELGIUM — N
LUXEMBOURG — N

ICELAND — N
UNITED KINGDOM — N, S, C

FRANCE — N, S
PORTUGAL — N

ITALY — N
GREECE — N
TURKEY — N, C

EAST GERMANY
POLAND
CZECHOSLOVAKIA
HUNGARY
ROMANIA
BULGARIA
ALBANIA

U.S.S.R.

MONGOLIA   N. KOREA

IRAN   CHINA
C

NORTH VIETNAM

PAKISTAN — S, C   PHILIPPINES — S

THAILAND — S

AUSTRALIA
S

NEW ZEALAND — S

© RMꞐN & CO.

524

than it had been in 1939. Furthermore, while the Communist parties of western Europe did not disappear, their strength declined significantly and the likelihood of these countries becoming Communist through internal pressures became small.

The German question, unsuccessfully solved since V-E Day, brought about a crisis in 1948. In early 1946, Russia declined to join the United States in an alliance to prevent resurgence of German military might. In September, 1946, Russia blocked an American proposal for the political and economic unification of the various military occupation zones in Germany. At that time, the Soviet Union was busy dismantling factories within its occupation zone and sending the equipment home and making its eastern zone a Communist satellite similar to the others. Through 1947, western policy continued to be neutralization and unification of Germany, but the Russian leaders demanded terms that would have given them influence in Germany's industrial western area. Although the western powers at no time explicitly embraced the idea of two Germanies, they began to move in that direction when in February, 1948, they consolidated the British, French, and American zones and created a German government with limited powers. In June, they adopted currency reforms in the consolidated zone and brought western Germany into the Marshall Plan. In October, the Germans in the western zone organized state governments, adopted a federal constitution the following spring, and formally launched the German Federal Republic in September, 1949. The western powers made West Germany a constitutional entity only slightly before the Russians transformed East Germany into the German Democratic Republic, another constitutional entity. The two Germanies had come into being. The sticky problem was Berlin, occupied jointly and deep within the Russian zone of East Germany.

On April 1, 1948, the Russians began to interrupt traffic from the western zone entering the Russian zone destined for West Berlin. On June 23, they stopped all traffic to West Berlin from the western zone. Their purpose was to get the West either to abandon its Berlin position or to back down on its program for western Germany. West Berlin, unable to feed itself, became an international pawn.

Rejecting the idea of sending armed convoys across the line of the Russian zone in an effort to shoot their way to West Berlin for fear of bringing on war, Truman decided to supply the city by a vast airlift and to impose a counterblockade. If the Russians began a war by shooting down the planes, the onus would be on them. The American and British air forces did an enormous job. Between late June, 1948, and May 12, 1949, when the Russians lifted the blockade, planes delivered to West Berlin almost 2,500,000 tons of supplies, largely food and coal. Within three months after starting the airlift, the RAF and the USAF were flying four thousand tons a day. The airlift, of course, could not have been a long-term solution, but it solved the immediate crisis.

Not only did Germany become two Germanies, but Europe became two Europes. The Soviets directed the essential political and economic integration of East Europe, and the West European nations increasingly cooperated with one another. In January, 1948, Bevin announced Britain's willingness to join some kind of West European organization. A year later, all the countries of

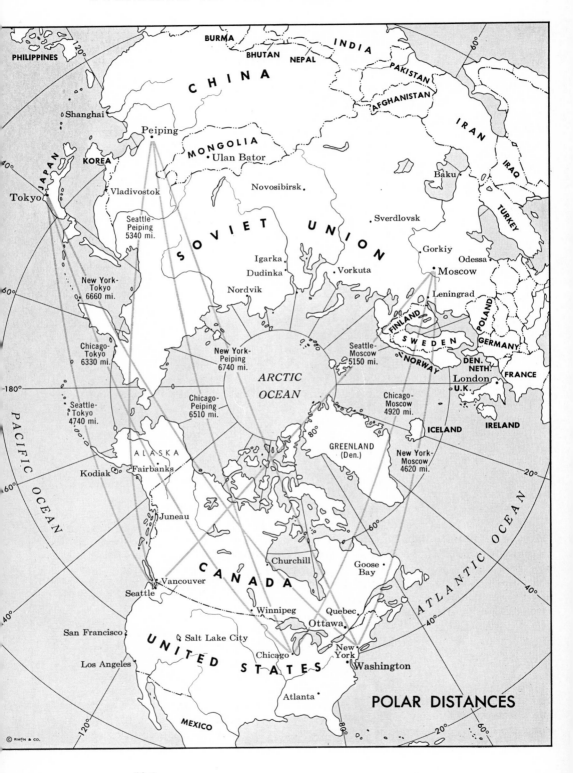

POLAR DISTANCES

West Europe, including West Germany but not Spain and Portugal, instituted the Council of Europe. More importantly, France and West Germany began negotiations for coal-steel integration which developed in 1951 into the Schuman Plan (named for French foreign minister Robert Schuman). Belgium, the Netherlands, and Luxembourg (the Benelux powers) and Italy joined with France and West Germany to erect an international authority, the European Coal and Steel Community, to govern and coordinate the production and distribution of those commodities. ECCS so interwove French and German heavy industry that these two historic enemies, within a decade after their biggest war, were economically dependent upon one another.

In June, 1948, the Senate passed the Vandenberg Resolution promising cooperation with a West European Alliance, and the next month the West European powers and the United States began discussions in Washington which resulted in the North Atlantic Treaty Alliance (NATO). On April 4, 1949, representatives of the United States, Canada, Iceland, France, Great Britain, Italy, Portugal, the Netherlands, Belgium, Luxembourg, Denmark, and Norway signed the treaty, which the Senate ratified by overwhelming vote in July. Greece and Turkey subsequently joined NATO. The treaty declared that an attack upon any of the signatory nations would be considered an attack on them all and provided for the creation of a joint NATO military force. General Eisenhower became the commander of SHAPE (Supreme Headquarters, Allied Powers in Europe) when it set itself up near Paris in early 1951. Much of its financial support came from the United States; Congress had passed the Mutual Defense Assistance Act in September, 1949, to appropriate a billion dollars for NATO armies. A West European–North American military alliance, inconceivable in 1939, was reality by 1949. Although NATO did not have as many divisions in Europe as the Russians had, it had enough to make a fight of it if it should come to that; more importantly, the Russians knew that any military adventures toward the west would result in a fight.

American Troubles in Asia

As America and Britain slowly proceeded toward alliance with their former common enemy, Germany, against their former ally, the Soviet Union, so did Japan and the United States slowly come together against China. The world's experience since 1940 should give pause to those who try to predict the future.

Japan's occupation, demilitarization, and eventual rebuilding was almost altogether America's project. Stalin demanded Russian occupation of half of the northern main Japanese island, but Truman rejected the idea firmly. General Douglas MacArthur, Supreme Commander of the Allied Powers (SCAP) in the Japanese occupation, encountered little resistance from the Japanese. The United States tried and executed some Japanese war criminals, but soon the occupation lost whatever punitive aspects it had and concentrated on reforming the former enemy. The occupation insisted upon and got considerable democracy in Japanese society, drastic reform of the land system, a

527

restriction on the power of the monopolistic industrial class, a great growth of labor unions, woman suffrage, and vast expansion and reform of the educational system. In 1947, the administration began economic policies designed to rebuild the Japanese economy. In 1950, Truman appointed John Foster Dulles, a Republican Wall Street lawyer, prominent Presbyterian layman, and student of foreign relations, to begin negotiations with Japan for a peace treaty and an alliance. The clear fact was that Japan was becoming America's friend as Chinese-American relationships changed from amity to hostility.

During the war, when the Russians said they would not aid the Chinese Communists, American policy was to urge the Chinese Nationalists, or Kuomintang, headed by Chiang Kai-shek, to form a coalition with the Chinese Communists. Chiang consistently refused. At the end of the war, the United States quickly transported Nationalist troops to formerly Japanese occupied areas so as to prevent their occupation by Chinese Communists or Russians, and the Kuomintang controlled the major ports and cities outside Manchuria. But the Communist armies, headed by Mao Tse-tung, controlled much of the countryside. Full-scale civil war seemed imminent when Truman dispatched General Marshall to China in December, 1945. The United States did not want a Communist China—later charges that important people in the administration regarded the Communists only as agrarian reformers were gross exaggerations —and quite correctly perceived that the Kuomintang government was inept, corrupt, and somewhat unpopular. But it quite strongly wanted to avoid becoming involved in a civil war on the other side of the earth. Marshall, therefore, tried to prevent the outbreak of such a conflict. He succeeded in bringing about a cease-fire, but months of work at finding some basis for agreement between the Communists and the Kuomintang came to nothing. Their differences were irreconcilable. In early 1947, Marshall abandoned the effort with a parting shot that damned both sides.

The civil war resumed. Chiang's troops were more numerous and had good equipment, both captured Japanese and American arms. But Mao's troops won most of the battles. Truman sent General Albert C. Wedemeyer, who had served with Chiang during the war, to investigate and suggest policy. Wedemeyer reported that indeed the Kuomintang was all its critics said it was but that the Communist alternative was worse. Further, if the United States intervened in a major way in behalf of the Nationalists, it might be able to bring about necessary reform. The general urged Truman to seek United Nations support for a five-nation UN trusteeship of Manchuria to prevent that province from becoming a Soviet-Communist Chinese satellite and to send ten thousand American military officers and other advisers to bring about reform and efficiency. Massive material assistance would be necessary, Wedemeyer added.

Truman neither accepted nor made the Wedemeyer recommendations public, for which he later suffered severe castigation including charges of disloyalty. Chiang's cause was not popular with the American people if it involved American intervention, and Truman held that the defense of western Europe was more important. In addition it was by no means guaranteed that the adoption of Wedemeyer's report would save the Nationalists from Communist defeat. Truman did request Congress to appropriate $570 million for aid to China; Congress cut the appropriation to $400 million, the same amount as the original Greek-Turkish grant of which just $125 million was for military supplies.

In October, 1948, Chinese Communist troops took Mukden, Manchuria. Thereafter, the Nationalists faded fast, more from poor morale and continued inefficiency than from lack of arms. Some Kuomintang units defected to the Communists en masse. The Communists took the important cities and ports of central and south China during 1949. In October, Chiang retreated to Chungking, his capital during the war with Japan, roughly a thousand miles into the interior. In December, he moved what was left of his government and army by air to Formosa, called Taiwan by the Chinese. Nationalists continued to hold, besides Formosa, some tiny offshore islands in the Formosa Strait.

The United States refused to recognize the new Communist regime in China, officially the People's Republic of China, although some of its European allies did. Nor would America countenance Red China's admission into the United Nations. To the United States government, the country of China was officially the Chiang government on Formosa and the offshore islands. On the mainland, the Communists quickly stamped out American influence. American citizens of all kinds (missionaries, government officials, businessmen) fled. Far harder, more anti-American, and less flexible than their Russian comrades, the Chinese Communists made their territory the headquarters for a campaign to eliminate American influence in Asia. On the whole, the Chinese Communist anti-American efforts failed. Japan moved ever closer to the United States. The two other major powers of Asia, India, which became independent from Great Britain in 1947, and Pakistan, which divided from India at the time of independence, likewise moved closer to the United States, in no small part because of their giant and aggressive Communist neighbor to the north. South Korea, too, remained in the American camp, but thereby hangs a tragic and painful tale.

The Korean War

Russian forces invaded Korea from the north on August 10, 1945. Nearly a month later and after V-J Day, American troops occupied the southern part of the peninsula. Russia and the United States agreed to divide their zones at the thirty-eighth parallel. Korea, which Japan had occupied for a generation, soon became two Koreas. The Russians introduced their system of government and economy in North Korea and raised and equipped an army. The United Nations Temporary Commission on Korea, created by the General Assembly upon American instigation, in early 1948 visited Seoul, the old capital, was denied permission to go north of the dividing line, and conducted elections for a national assembly in southern Korea. In July, 1948, the assembly adopted a constitution, calling the country the Republic of Korea (ROK), and elected Syngman Rhee, who had spent much of his life as an exile in the United States, as president. Rhee would have been pleased to have the whole peninsula under his government's jurisdiction, and the North Koreans were just as eager to have the South in their realm. Fearful of what Rhee might do and not wanting to get involved in a conflict over territory it did not deem militarily significant, the United States did not provide the South Korean government sufficient arms to engage in northern adventures. It did, however, furnish it considerable economic assistance, a factor of importance since the thirty-eighth parallel dividing line badly disrupted the Korean economy. By mid-1949, both Russian and American occupation troops had left. The United States maintained a five-hundred-man military advisory group to train the ROK army; the Russians furnished military advisers to the North Korean government. Few people in the United States, in fact few people in the western world, were more than dimly aware that Korea existed. Remote, economically unimportant, far from the main focus of existing international tensions, Korea seemed the last place in the world that anyone would fight over.

With the Chinese mainland under the Communists, the administration re-examined its policy for that part of the world in the winter of 1949–1950. Hoping that eventually Russia and China would become engaged in conflict as Russia and Jugoslavia had—"Mao Tse-tito" was the wisecrack—and thinking only in terms of total war rather than a limited war, the State Department, headed since January, 1949, by Dean Acheson, for all practical purposes wrote off the Chinese Nationalists on Formosa as an instrument of containment because they had been ineffective. In January, 1950, Acheson made public what the United States regarded as its "defense perimeter," a line that ran through the Aleutians, Japan, the Ryukyus (Okinawa the main island), and the Philippines. Formosa and Korea were not within the perimeter. When the implication became clear that the administration did not plan to defend Formosa if the Chinese Communists attacked, a group of Republican Senators, notably Taft, Wherry, and William Knowland of California, attacked Truman and Acheson mercilessly. Actually, a more propitious time for great pressure on the administration would have been before Chiang was run off the mainland. By early 1950, only massive American participation could have re-established the Nationalists, and that probably would have meant full-scale war.

After months of small skirmishes between the North and South Koreans, the North Koreans launched an all-out invasion across the thirty-eighth parallel at 4:00 A.M., Sunday, June 25, 1950, Korean time. Who made the decision for invasion (North Koreans, Chinese, or Russians) and why has never become known in the West. Neither is it known whether or not the invaders expected resistance from any country except the Republic of Korea, although they may well have interpreted Acheson's "defense perimeter" statement to mean the United States would not defend South Korea. Acheson's statement had hedged; if areas outside the perimeter were attacked, he had said, the invaded people would have to count upon their own power to resist "and then upon the commitments of the entire civilized world." One thing only is certain: North Korean troops invaded South Korea. Communists the world over asserted that the South Koreans had attacked first and that the North Koreans had only counterattacked, but no military operation of the magnitude of the invasion could have been begun without long and extensive preparation. The decision to invade had obviously been made long before the invasion.

News of the invasion reached Washington when it was still Saturday night there. Truman was visiting his home in Missouri. Acheson summoned his aides in the State Department. At about midnight Acheson telephoned Truman who agreed that the invasion should come before the Security Council of the United Nations immediately. For several months the Russians had been boycotting Security Council meetings because the other council members had refused a seat to the Communist Chinese. At a Sunday afternoon emergency session, the Security Council voted nine to zero to accept a resolution calling upon North Korea to withdraw north of the thirty-eighth parallel. The absent Russian delegate missed his opportunity to veto. Two days later, the Council by a vote of seven to one (Jugoslavia opposing, India and Egypt abstaining) called upon UN member nations to send a UN force to repel the attack. On June 29 and 30, after having returned to Washington and conferred with the Joint Chiefs of staff and congressional leaders of both parties, Truman ordered two divisions of MacArthur's ground troops in Japan to Korea and ordered the air force to bomb North Korean targets. At the time all concerned assumed that this American force would be sufficient to drive the North Koreans back. Simultaneously, Truman ordered the United States Seventh Fleet to neutralize Formosa. Fearing the conflict might spread to full-scale war, Truman wanted neither the Red Chinese to invade Formosa nor the Nationalists to try a mainland invasion. His Formosan order received more Republican criticism than the decisions on Korea.

At first the war went very badly for the UN forces. In the whole war, never more technically than "a police action by the United Nations," American troops fought under UN auspices; when UN forces were at their greatest strength, 48 per cent of them were from America, 43 per cent from South Korea, and the remaining 9 per cent from seventeen other nations, mainly Britain, the Philippines, Australia, and Turkey. By early September, 1950, the North Koreans had pushed UN forces south until they held only the port of Pusan in extreme southeastern Korea and a little area around it. Upon receiving reinforcements, MacArthur, the chief UN commander, first pushed back from Pusan and then executed a daring and brilliant end run with a landing at Inchon on the west coast not far from Seoul and the thirty-eighth parallel. His troops took Seoul on September 27. The North Korean units fled north of the border.

Now the war entered a new political phase: whether or not UN troops should cross the thirty-eighth parallel. As early as October 1, some ROK units crossed the border, but MacArthur held back to await a clear mandate. On October 1, Communist China announced that she would be displeased if the war crossed the border; soon thereafter she informed India, which relayed the message to the UN, that she would send troops to North Korea if UN troops crossed the boundary. But on October 7 the UN Assembly approved forty-seven to five, with eight nations abstaining, a resolution recommending that "all appropriate steps be taken to ensure conditions of stability throughout Korea." On October 23, MacArthur's troops moved across the border in force. In a special conference at Wake Island on October 14, Truman had questioned MacArthur about the possibility of Russian or Chinese intervention and MacArthur had replied that the chance was, "Very little." MacArthur estimated that the Chinese would not be able to get more than fifty or sixty thousand men across the Yalu River, the northern boundary between Manchuria and North Korea, and that these men would be slaughtered.

These Korean events shared the front pages with news of the congressional election campaigns. On November 7, the voters handed the Democrats a defeat. Each house of Congress remained in Democratic hands but by such a narrow margin as to strengthen the bipartisan conservative coalition. The most significant aspect of the campaign was the extent that accusations of Communism and of being "soft on Communism" were part of Republican activity. Senator Joseph R. McCarthy, Republican of Wisconsin, was out to get rid of Senator Millard Tydings of Maryland whom he called an "appeaser" and smeared with a fake photograph that purported to show the Maryland Senator in a friendly pose with a Communist official. Representative Richard Nixon made Communism the main issue in his defeat of Helen Gahagan Douglas for a California Senate seat.

Back in Korea, the Chinese Communists were playing havoc with MacArthur's predictions. Late in October, UN troops captured a few Chinese "volunteers"; soon thereafter the air force reported encountering Russian-made MIG fighter planes. The UN invited China to explain its actions, which the Chinese Communists declined to do; but they did send a delegation to UN headquarters where they charged that the United States had been guilty of aggression against Formosa. On November 24, 1950, the day the Red Chinese delegation arrived at the UN, MacArthur launched a full-scale offensive, announcing that the drive would go to the Yalu. He intimated American troops might be home by Christmas.

Perhaps military intelligence was never faultier. MacArthur marched his men into an enormous trap. Red Chinese units counterattacked on November 26 and split the center of the UN line. The United States Eighth Army under General Matthew B. Ridgway retreated on the eastern part of the line back toward and then beyond the thirty-eighth parallel. The First Marine Division, two army infantry divisions, and ROK units fought desperately in bitter cold to get to the port of Hungnam, far north on the east coast, where the navy evacuated them and returned them to the main UN force in South Korea. Chinese troops crossed south to the thirty-eighth parallel, and now India cautioned the Chinese to stop. In January, 1951, the UN forces began to hold; in March they counterattacked and took Seoul for the second time. Soon thereafter they moved across the thirty-eighth parallel for the second and last time. The conflict stabilized along a line slightly north of that famous mark on the globe.

Partisan politics over military policy came to a head when, on April 11, 1951, President Truman relieved General MacArthur of his command. The news stunned the nation. The General, who had not come home after World War II, returned to an enthusiastic reception. Congress invited him to address a joint session on April 19, and millions watched the scene on their television sets. It was a dramatic speech whether one supported Truman or MacArthur. The General defended his position and ended by quoting from an old barracks song: "Old soldiers never die; they just fade away."

The Truman-MacArthur controversy involved more than a personal conflict. Throughout the Korean War, MacArthur had, upon several occasions, gone beyond his stated orders from Washington and had publicly disagreed with civilian superior officers. In July, 1950, without authority from Washington, he had gone to Formosa to confer with Chiang Kai-shek. The next month he had sent a message to the national convention of the Veterans of Foreign Wars that was extremely critical of the administration's Formosa policy. Truman heard of the message before the convention and ordered MacArthur to withdraw it. MacArthur did so, but the message became public knowledge. In it MacArthur described Truman's position as "the threadbare argument by those who advocate appeasement and defeatism in the Pacific." At the Wake Island conference in October, the President informed his general that he must make no further provocative public statements. After the Red Chinese intervention in November, MacArthur publicly and frequently criticized Washington for refusing him authority to bomb supply bases in Chinese territory north of the Yalu. Wanting the war to remain limited, fearing that a full-scale war in Asia would make western Europe vulnerable to Soviet attack, Truman refused to allow action north of the Yalu other than that of fighter planes in "hot pursuit" of the enemy. On December 6, Truman forbade all civil and military officers to make public statements on foreign policy without prior clearance with the State Department. MacArthur continued to recommend to the Joint Chiefs of Staff that the United States blockade China, use the navy and air force to bombard China, and support a Kuomintang invasion of the mainland. The Joint Chiefs of Staff rejected the suggestions. On March 20, 1951, the Joint Chiefs of Staff informed MacArthur that a new statement on Korean policy would soon be forthcoming. Instead of waiting for it, MacArthur issued one of his own in which he said he was willing to meet with the Chinese commander and try to arrange a truce, but that if proper terms could not be arranged there should be raids on the Chinese coast and bombings of interior Chinese bases. Truman at that point was looking for a way to bring about a truce and negotiate a Korean settlement, the front having by then been stabilized. Truman also again warned MacArthur about making public policy statements without clearing them with Washington.

MacArthur's reply to this warning was to send a letter to Joseph W. Martin, Jr., of Massachusetts, Republican minority leader in the House of Representatives, in which he strongly disagreed with the administration's limited war policy: ". . . we must win. There is no substitute for victory." It was this point precisely that caused so much of the frustration of the Korean War. The American people were not accustomed to fighting for less than total victory, but total victory against North Korea and China was likely to erupt in World War III, and hardly anyone wanted that. After Representative Martin read MacArthur's letter in the House on April 5, Truman went to the Joint Chiefs of Staff and received their endorsement of his proposal to dismiss MacArthur. The die was cast.

Perhaps Truman wished at first that he had not started such action against MacArthur for Americans were initially strongly for MacArthur. Public opinion polls showed it; the General's reception showed it. Senator McCarthy's hammering at the Truman administration had helped to build support for MacArthur's point of view. But during the congressional hearings from May 3 to June 25, public opinion began to shift. More and more people came to agree with the statement of General Omar Bradley, chairman of the Joint

Chiefs of Staff, that the kinds of policies MacArthur recommended would lead to a war which would be "the wrong war at the wrong place, at the wrong time and with the wrong enemy." Many did not accept the implication that war with Russia in Europe was right, but they agreed that a war with China in Asia was undesirable. More and more people, too, saw that the Truman-MacArthur controversy involved the traditional authority of the civil government over the military establishment. The crowds at "total victory" rallies began to dwindle. The old soldier, probably to his distress, did fade away. When he gave the keynote address at the 1952 Republican convention he seemed a figure from the remote past.

On June 22, 1951, the Russians suggested an armistice. On July 10, General Ridgway, who had replaced MacArthur, began armistice negotiations with Chinese and North Korean officers at Kaesong. The negotiations later moved to Panmunjom, an unlikely name that was in the news for two years while the negotiations went on fruitlessly. Thereafter, the fighting in Korea was only sporadic, and the battle line remained relatively stationary slightly north of the thirty-eighth parallel.

During the Panmunjom armistice negotiations, the Truman administration concluded treaties with European powers to strengthen the United States position in Asia. On September 8, 1951, the United States and Japan signed the peace treaty that Dulles had negotiated. The treaty took Okinawa away from Japan, but otherwise it was generous; no reparations plus recognition of Japan's right to rearm. Since then Japan has shown no enthusiasm for rearmament. At the same time, the United States and Japan signed a Security Treaty that gave the United States the right to maintain bases in Japan. On August 30, 1951, the United States and the Republic of the Philippines signed a mutual defense treaty. On September 1, New Zealand, Australia, and the United States formed the "Anzus" mutual defense pact.

Disloyalty and Politics

American society has periodically indulged itself in waves of intolerance. In the 1840's and 1850's and again in the 1880's, large numbers of people were irrationally anti-Catholic. Alarm about anarchists became hysterical after McKinley's assassination in 1901. During World War I, anxiety about pro-Germans led many to attitudes and actions that went beyond ordinary reason, as did fear of Bolshevism in the years immediately after the war. From the late 1940's to the mid-1950's, the United States went on another such binge, this time over the question of national loyalty. Irrational intolerance has never completely disappeared; but it has risen to periodic high tides. The post-World War II Red scare was one of the highest tides.

Anti-Communism was by no means altogether irrational. Many anti-Communists maintained their sense of perspective and balance. Although by far the greatest danger to the United States from Communism came from outside the country, there was a basis for concern about it internally. Early in the postwar period some "liberals" were inclined to be sympathetic to the Soviet Union, to regard the Soviet Union as a great and noble experiment, a fulfillment of workers' aspirations the world over, perhaps not be copied in the United States because America had special advantages for the common man but not to be the object of hostility. This attitude waned to insignificance. As early as 1947, when the anti-Communist ADA came into existence, the Soviets were quickly losing American sympathizers by their foreign policy. Just after the war, almost one-third of the votes on the executive board of the CIO could be counted upon to support the position of the Communist party. Revolts by the membership against Communist leadership and a housecleaning by the CIO itself in 1949 and 1950 ended that situation. The Communist party had roughly eighty thousand dues-paying members in 1946. It shrank steadily; by 1953, according to FBI Director J. Edgar Hoover, its membership was a little under twenty-five thousand. It continued to shrink thereafter. But espionage cases probably did more than anything else to arouse public opinion.

Early in 1945, the FBI apprehended two of the editors of *Amerasia*, a Communist-connected magazine, collecting classified documents from government offices. In 1946, a Canadian royal commission revealed that at least twenty-three Canadians in "positions of trust" were involved in espionage for the Soviets and had sent classified information, some of it about atomic fission, to Russia. In early 1950, Klaus Fuchs, a British scientist of German origin who had worked on the atomic bomb project, confessed in London that he had been part of an espionage ring. His confession implicated four American citizens, Julius Rosenberg and his wife Ethel, David Greenglass, and Morton Sobell. A jury convicted them, and after several appeals, which went as high as the Supreme Court, the Rosenbergs died in the electric chair in mid-1953. Greenglass and Sobell went to prison.

But by far the most celebrated case was that of Alger Hiss. In 1948, a former Communist named Whittaker Chambers testified before the House Committee on Un-American Activities that Hiss, head of the Carnegie Endowment for International Peace and a former official in the State Department, had passed him classified documents in 1937 and 1938. Hiss denied the charge before the Committee. When Hiss sued Chambers for slander, Chambers produced microfilm from a pumpkin on his Maryland farm that he said proved his charge. The statute of limitations prevented an indictment for espionage, but Hiss stood trial for perjury. He asked some prominent people to serve as character witnesses, among them Justice Felix Frankfurter and Illinois Governor Adlai E. Stevenson, who said that to the best of their knowledge Hiss was a man of good character. The trial ended with a hung jury. A second trial ended in January, 1950, with Hiss's conviction. Hiss continued to profess innocence, served his prison sentence, and emerged to go into obscurity. But the superficial facts of the case reveal little of its political implications. In the popular mind, Hiss was the personification of the bright, young New Deal administrator. If Hiss was guilty, who else might be a disguised Communist? Were Roosevelt's braintrusters a pack of disloyal spies, as some of FDR's more violent critics had charged?

It was fears such as these that Senator Joseph R. McCarthy, Republican from Wisconsin, exploited for his and his party's—or a wing of his party's—political advantage. In a speech at Wheeling, West Virginia, on February 9, 1950, McCarthy charged that he had "here in my hand" a list of 205 (some said McCarthy claimed only 57) names of Communists and fellow-travelers then employed by the State Department. A Senate Foreign Relations Committee unit investigated the charge and found not one, but McCarthy's allegation had created the kind of sensation the freshman Senator wanted and needed. Although McCarthy never turned up a single proved Communist in government employ, he went on with sensational charge after sensational charge so quickly that, by the time the accused could deny, the front pages were already spread with a new accusation.

McCarthy was neither the first political figure to be concerned with Communism within the United States nor the first to use the issue for political advantage. President Truman had shown his concern when, in 1947, he instituted a "loyalty check" on government employees. In 1950, he authorized the firing of those whose present loyalty was not at issue but who were found to be "bad security risks." The investigation was remarkably thorough. It found and fired some who were suspicious indeed, but as Truman later admitted, it fired some people on flimsy evidence. Truman's Republican successors were unsuccessful in their attempts to find disloyal government employees who had slipped through the Truman administration comb. The Truman administration brought indictment after indictment of Communist party leaders under the Smith Act, and nearly all indicted were convicted and imprisoned. In the Republican party, the respected Senator Taft as early as January, 1946, had found it difficult to avoid the temptation to use the Red issue against a political opponent; he called Truman's legislative program in part "communist" and "left-wing." But no political leader developed anti-Communism as an instrument for political advantage to the degree that Senator McCarthy did. The fact that "McCarthyism" became the accepted term for politically motivated exploitation of fear about domestic Communism was recognition of his mastery of the technique.

With the outbreak of the Korean War, McCarthyism became so powerful that even many politicians who deplored what they considered its un-American means to protect America knuckled under its pressure. Various anti-Communist bills had been introduced in Congress since the war, and in 1950 Congress lumped many of these proposals together into the McCarran Internal Security bill, named for Democratic Senator Pat McCarran of Nevada. The bill provided for the establishment of a bipartisan Subversive Activities Control Board which, after hearing evidence, could declare an organization subversive and require it to register and submit membership lists and financial reports. The bill expressly stated that to be a member or even an officer of a Communist organization did not of itself constitute a criminal act, but made it illegal to perform "any act" that would "substantially" contribute to totalitarian overthrow of the government. It also banned Communists from defense industries, provided for the arrest of Communists in the event of war, required that printed matter distributed by organizations found by the SACB to be Communist must be labelled Communist propaganda, made Communists ineligible to receive passports, and forbade the entry into the country of any person who had ever been a member of a totalitarian organization. Truman, upon the advice of the Department of Defense and the Central Intelligence Agency, vetoed the bill. Among other things, Truman said that its registration feature was "about as practical as requiring thieves to register with the sheriff." Congress passed it over his veto. In 1952, Congress passed, again over Truman's veto, the McCarran-Walter Immigration and Nationality Bill which eased the deportation of aliens found to be subversive and provided for denaturalization in some cases. The measure did broaden immigration and naturalization in one respect: Asians went under the quota system for the first time (two thousand a year), and they became eligible for citizenship.

McCarthyism certainly was not restricted to either party, but it reacted far more to the Republicans' electoral advantage than to the Democrats'. How many voters who otherwise would have voted Democratic decided to vote Republican in 1950 and 1952 because of the fog of distrust of New Deal Democrats created by McCarthy and the McCarthyites can never be known—there were other issues, of course—but undoubtedly McCarthy substantially aided the Republican cause. However, Republicans were soon to learn that McCarthyism could divide and disrupt their own party as well as their opponents.

CHAPTER TWENTY-SIX

The Eisenhower Era: Moderation and Brinkmanship

EVEN WITH ONLY THE LITTLE TIME PERSPECTIVE AVAILABLE TO US, we can see that fundamentally there were no important or basic differences between the policies of the Truman and Eisenhower administrations. Political partisanship on both sides tended to magnify actual differences. Truman's administrations were more different from Roosevelt's, and Eisenhower's were more different from Harding's, Coolidge's, and Hoover's than they were different from one another. Their greatest difference was in their political rhetoric. Truman's style was that of an orator at a labor convention, and he endeavored mightily to appear to wear Roosevelt's cloak. Eisenhower strived above all to give the impression of moderation—"the middle of the road." He once even described his policies as "liberal conservatism." Although a strong wing of Truman's party wanted to extend the New Deal, his administration and Congress extended it only slightly; although a strong wing of Eisenhower's party wanted to repeal the New Deal, his administration and Congress not only did not rescind it but even extended it slightly. Truman and Eisenhower certainly were no Tweedledee and Tweedledum, but in actual results—new laws and new policies—there was little to distinguish them on domestic affairs.

There were other similarities. Both used the power of the federal government to even out fluctuations in the business cycle. Both were anti-Communist and both were plagued by "radical right" anti-Communists. Both resisted Communism abroad and both avoided World War III. In the fifteen years after World War II, both major parties controlled the White House, but the era had no real political watersheds. Under both parties the domestic political mood was one of moderation, prosperous complacency, and notable lack of enthusiasm for new departures.

538

The Election of 1952

Confident that it would defeat the Democratic ticket in 1952, the Republican party indulged itself in one of its sharpest internal battles for the nomination. The early front runner was Senator Robert A. Taft of Ohio, who had three times been passed over for a nominee that large parts of the GOP considered not quite such a "true blue." Announcing his candidacy in October, 1951, Taft had the support of a majority on the party's national committee.

GOP leaders in the East, notably Governor Dewey, Senator Henry Cabot Lodge, Jr., of Massachusetts, and Senator James H. Duff of Pennsylvania, vigorously opposed Taft's nomination. They thought he would be unable to attract independent voters and distrusted his tendency to put American interests in Asia ahead of concern for Europe. Their problem was to find a candidate. Dewey, as a two-time loser, was unacceptable. They wanted General Dwight David Eisenhower, then on leave as president of Columbia University while serving as the head of NATO. Well known because of his military leadership, Eisenhower seemed to millions of Americans the kind of man they conceived of as typical of their nationality: guileless, frank, friendly, quick to smile, able to get discordant subordinates to work together harmoniously. The trouble was that in 1951 no one knew for sure whether Eisenhower was a Republican. It was an open secret that Truman wanted him to be his party's champion in 1952. In January, 1952, Eisenhower, upon the urging of Senator Lodge, announced he would accept the Republican nomination, but that he would not battle for it. He won the Republican presidential primary in New Hampshire, and Minnesota Republicans advanced his nomination by a huge write-in vote in their primary. But the Taft forces, controlling most of the party machinery, continued to get convention delegates into their camp. Eisenhower could not win the nomination without working for it. Rallies that chanted "I like Ike" could not go on forever unless their hero seemed determined to win. Eisenhower resigned his command and returned from France on June 1. His first halting, undistinguished speeches did little to attract delegates, but the fact that he had decided actively to seek the nomination was enough to stimulate his wing of the party.

Many political commentators noted the similarity between the 1952 Republican convention at Chicago in early July and the 1912 convention which had nominated Taft's father and passed over Theodore Roosevelt. Both Tafts had the more numerous delegates and control of the national committee but both Roosevelt and Eisenhower had broad popular support and rank-and-file following. Senator Taft went to Chicago with 469 pledged delegates; only 392 had pledged themselves firmly to Eisenhower. The 1912 and 1952 similarity continued when the national committee granted seats temporarily to the Taft-pledged delegations from Georgia, Louisiana, and Texas, each of which faced opposition from an Eisenhower delegation claiming that it was the duly elected representative. But the similarity ended when the convention, by a narrow vote, changed its rules. Under the new rule, temporarily seated delegations could not vote on the seating of other contested delegations if the contestants had the support of one-sixth or more of the national committee. Seating the Georgia delegation provided the test. With the Taft-pledged delegates from Texas and Louisiana unable to vote under the new rule, the convention voted by another narrow margin to seat the Eisenhower-pledged delegation from Georgia. Seating of the other contested Eisenhower delegations followed.

On the first ballot the General received 595 votes to Taft's 500. Enough delegations switched their votes to Eisenhower after the roll call of the states to make a second ballot unnecessary. The nominee selected Senator Richard M. Nixon as his running mate, a move calculated to allay the bitterness of Taft supporters. The Republican platform was vague enough to prevent any wing of the party from rebelling. In a bid for southern votes, the GOP diluted its 1948 civil rights demands and promised to transfer control of tidelands oil from the federal government to the states.

The Democratic nomination was nearly as confusing. Although the Twenty-second Amendment to the Constitution (submitted to the states in March, 1947, and ratified February, 1951, forbidding a president more than two terms or, in the case of a president's coming to the office by his predecessor's death, more than ten years' tenure) specifically exempted Truman, he announced late in March, 1952, that he would not be a candidate. Governor Adlai E. Stevenson of Illinois, who had run well ahead of his ticket in 1948, declined to seek delegates but left the impression he would consent to a party draft. The hardest running contender was Senator Estes Kefauver of Tennessee, who had achieved a national reputation as chairman of a televised Senate investigation of organized crime. Vice-President Barkley's hat was in the ring, but his chances disappeared when the CIO announced that the popular "Veep," as he liked to be called, was too old—they meant too conservative—for their approval. Senator Richard B. Russell of Georgia was the favorite of the South, and Averell Harriman of New York and Senator Robert Kerr of Oklahoma had some support.

Kefauver, never popular with his party's leaders, led on the first ballot, but on the third the Stevenson draft blew hard. Stevenson came within two and one-half votes of a majority. Then Senator Kefauver moved that Stevenson be nominated unanimously, and the contest ended. In an effort—unsuccessful as it turned out—to keep southern Democrats happy, the party nominated one of the more liberal southern Senators, John Sparkman of Alabama, for the vice-presidency. The civil rights plank was not as strong as it had been in 1948, and northern and western Democrats were unsuccessful in their attempt to extract a "loyalty pledge" from the southern delegates and thereby head off another Dixiecrat revolt. There was no independent Dixiecrat ticket in 1952, but James F. Byrnes, then governor of South Carolina, came out for Eisenhower, as did Democratic Governor Allan F. Shivers of Texas when Stevenson refused to support state control of tidelands oil and Eisenhower consented to. In other southern states there were "Eisenhower Democrat" slates.

The urban and highly literate Stevenson aroused great enthusiasm among those who thought of themselves as liberal intellectuals, but his campaign to "talk sense to the American people," as he put it, fell far short in popular appeal to the more platitudinous Eisenhower speeches. (The New York *Times*

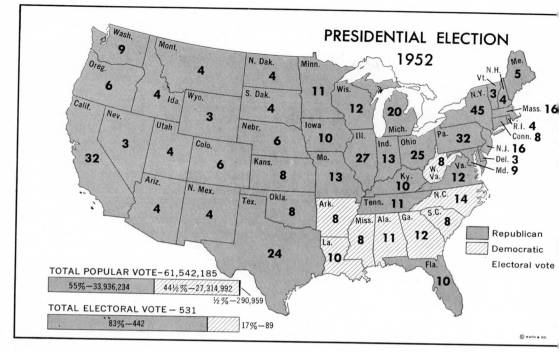

PRESIDENTIAL ELECTION
1952

Wash. 9
Mont.
Oreg. 6
Ida. 4
Wyo.
Calif. 32
Nev. 3
Utah 4
Ariz. 4
N. Mex. 4
Colo. 6
N. Dak. 4
S. Dak. 4
Nebr. 6
Kans. 8
Okla. 8
Tex. 24
Minn. 11
Iowa 10
Mo. 13
Ark. 8
La. 10
Wis. 12
Ill. 27
Miss. 8
Ala. 11
Ga. 12
Fla. 10
Mich. 20
Ind. 13
Ohio 25
Ky. 10
Tenn. 11
N.C. 14
S.C. 8
W. Va. 8
Va. 12
Pa. 32
N.Y. 45
Vt. 3
N.H. 4
Me. 5
Mass. 16
R.I. 4
Conn. 8
N.J. 16
Del. 3
Md. 9

Republican
Democratic
Electoral vote

TOTAL POPULAR VOTE—61,542,185
55%—33,936,234   44½%—27,314,992
½%—290,959
TOTAL ELECTORAL VOTE—531
83%—442   17%—89

© RAND & CO.

reported the story of a journalist on the Eisenhower campaign train who awakened from a nap while Eisenhower was giving a speech from the rear of the train. He asked, "Where are we?" "Crossing the 38th platitude," another reporter told him.) First, Eisenhower healed the wounds his nomination had caused by effecting a compromise with Senator Taft. In a well-publicized conference, the General promised the Senator to make "creeping socialism" the main issue of his campaign and to grant some patronage to the Taft camp. Actually, the Republican battle cry was "Korea, Communism, and Corruption," a slogan that requires further explanation.

At the time of the political coventions the truce talks in Korea had been dragging on for a year, the main dividing issue being whether or not North Korean and Chinese prisoners who did not want to be repatriated should be forced to return. When Communist prisoners of war rioted, American leaders became convinced the enemy was using the truce talks only for propaganda purposes. In October, 1952, the armistice talks ended temporarily, and the UN forces started a limited offensive. Later in the month, Eisenhower promised to bring the war to an end, and his promise struck a responsive chord with the frustrated American people. Just before election day, Eisenhower's further promise to go to Korea—for precisely what purpose he did not make clear—undoubtedly attracted more votes for him.

The "Communism" part of the slogan was a sop to the McCarthyite wing of the Republican party. Highly effective as an anti-Democratic device in 1950, labeling the Democrats "soft on Communism" did not become part of Eisenhower's personal campaign but he did not disavow Republicans, including Senator McCarthy himself, who used the red brush. Indeed, by elimi-

541

nating a favorable comment about General Marshall, a long-time friend of Eisenhower's but an object of one of McCarthy's attacks, from a speech in Milwaukee, Eisenhower seemed to accede to the McCarthyites.

The "corruption" part of the slogan hit the Democrats where they were vulnerable. Republicans had uncovered clear cases of corruption in the administration, and Truman's reactions had been inept. It was clear that Bureau of Internal Revenue officials had been bribed to sidetrack investigations of tax evaders, as it was that Reconstruction Finance Corporation officials had yielded to the blandishments of "five percenters," who arranged RFC loans for clients for a 5 per cent commission. Republicans tried to make it appear that honest Democrats were as scarce as Venezuelan snowballs, and mink coats and deep freeze units, used in two highly publicized bribes, became symbols of corruption. Truman reorganized the Internal Revenue Service by putting district collectorships under civil service, and he appointed Newbold Morris, an independent Republican from New York, to investigate the whole tax collection administration. But Attorney General J. Howard McGrath obstructed Morris. In the end, Truman fired both McGrath and Morris. Republican talk of "the mess in Washington" had such strong voter response that Stevenson quite obviously tried to disassociate himself from the Truman administration.

The most dramatic moment in the campaign, however, came with the disclosure that Nixon had received $18,000 while in the Senate from southern California businessmen to help him cover his Washington expenses. Eisenhower, who had announced that his administration would be "clean as a hound's tooth," was on a spot. Many powerful Republicans urged him to dump Nixon, and he briefly considered doing so. But the vice-presidential nominee staged a sentimental defense of his actions on a national television program, and Eisenhower accepted him once again. Republican efforts to pin a similar scandal on Stevenson by pointing out that the Illinois governor had used surplus Democratic campaign funds to supplement the salaries of some of his appointees who suffered income loses when they went into state service did not create the furors of the Nixon disclosure.

Two aspects of the campaign that aroused comment and concern were the tremendous costs to the parties that television entailed and the increased role of professional advertisers and public relations counselors in shaping the candidates' appeals. Candidates could be sold like detergents, according to Madison Avenue opinion-molders who specialized in creating an "image" of their political clients. Just before election day the Republicans' advertising agency ran dozens of television spot commercials in which professional actors, taking the roles of taxi drivers, nurses, and other ordinary people, delivered Eisenhower testimonials. These spot commercials were thought to be effective. Whether a Lincoln could ever have been elected in an era of calculated and synthetic "image" manipulation was a question that troubled serious citizens.

Eisenhower won by an overwhelming victory on election day. He received 33,824,351 popular votes and 442 electoral votes; Stevenson finished with 27,314,987 popular and 89 electoral votes. Stevenson carried only West Virginia, Kentucky, and seven former Confederate states even though he polled more popular votes than had any previous Democratic presidential candidate with the exception of Roosevelt in 1936. Eisenhower made inroads into the South, carrying Texas, Oklahoma, Virginia, Tennessee, and Florida. Yet the Republicans had only an eight-seat majority in the House of Representatives and a tie in the Senate. (Vice-President Nixon's vote enabled the GOP to organize the new Senate.) Quite obviously, despite "Korea, Communism, and Corruption," Eisenhower was far more popular than his party.

"Modern Republicanism"

The new President's background and experience determined the nature of his administration. Born in Denison, Texas, in 1890, "Ike" Eisenhower, as he was called all of his adult life, grew up in Abilene, Kansas. Despite his mother's membership in a pacifist Protestant sect, he accepted an appointment to West Point and graduated in 1915. During World War I, the new second lieutenant served as an instructor in the tank corps. Between the wars he gradually worked up in rank and responsibility. During the Hoover administration he was an assistant executive in the War Department. After he made an unusually good record in the 1941 Louisiana army maneuvers, he rose quickly, becoming first the army's chief of operations and then, in June, 1942, commander of American forces in the European theater.

Given the nature of modern warfare and the huge bureaucracy of recent military organization, no commander in World War II could be a Napoleon or Alexander or Washington. Strategy came from committees in the Pentagon, not from commanders in the field. Eisenhower's greatness as a military leader during the war had its roots in his personality; he had the patience, amiability, and flexibility to get generals from different nations and branches of service, some of whom were notorious prima donnas, to work together harmoniously. As a general, Eisenhower was primarily an administrator—and an excellent one. His simplicity and forthrightness helped to give him a highly favorable press.

As President, Eisenhower again was primarily an administrator, the head of a team or staff. He relied heavily on his cabinet and other assistants and avoided routine matters. He wanted reports to him condensed to no more than one typewritten page. He depended on staff briefings for information; indeed, normally he did not read newspapers except on Sunday. Just as he did not play the role of a strong president within the executive department, he did not attempt vigorously to lead Congress. After twenty years of Roosevelt and Truman, Eisenhower's administrative and leadership methods were a distinct change of style.

In this kind of administration, cabinet members played more important roles than they traditionally had. In Eisenhower's first term the most important members of the administration were Sherman Adams, former governor of New Hampshire, a close-mouthed Yankee who served as the President's principal assistant; Secretary of State John Foster Dulles; Secretary of the Treasury George Humphrey of Ohio, who had been head of the coal and steel firm named for Mark Hanna; and Secretary of Defense Charles E. Wilson, former president of General Motors. The new Attorney General, Herbert Brownell, had been closely associated with Thomas E. Dewey. Sinclair Weeks, a successful New England manufacturer, became Secretary of Commerce, and two automobile dealers, Arthur Summerfield and Douglas McKay, became the heads of the Postoffice and Interior Departments. Mrs. Oveta Culp Hobby became the head of the new Department of Health, Education, and Welfare when that department came into being in April, 1953. Mrs. Hobby, commander of the WAC's during the war, was the wife of a wealthy Houston newspaper publisher. Ezra Taft Benson, a remarkably conservative elder of the Mormon church, became Secretary of Agriculture. The most out-of-place member of the assemblage was the Secretary of Labor, Martin Durkin, president of the plumbers' union, who had supported Stevenson in the campaign. Durkin resigned before a year was completed. The snide remark that the Eisenhower cabinet was composed of "eight millionaires and a plumber" was not far from accurate, but more important was the fact that in the cabinet there were few politicians and many businessmen. They provided a businessman's administration.

Immediately, many people announced their misgivings about these men with a business background in the nation's highest offices. Among those who were dubious was Senator Taft. Secretary Wilson, who was to suffer an acute case of "foot in mouth" disease during his whole tenure, alarmed many with a statement before the Senate committee conducting hearings on his appointment. In a discussion of whether or not he should be required to sell his General Motors stock before his Senate confirmation, Wilson told the committee that he had always assumed that "what was good for our country was good for General Motors, and vice versa." If one substituted the term "business community" for General Motors in Secretary Wilson's famous quotation, one would have an expression of the whole Eisenhower administration's view.

Soon after taking office the new administration adopted fiscal policies similar to what business had been advocating for years. Although the Korean conflict was not yet at an end, the new administration dropped almost all wartime controls. In their place as anti-inflation devices, the government changed Federal Reserve Board policies and reduced government spending. The Federal Reserve Board stopped its practice of pegging the price of government bonds, and bond prices fell. One effect of this was to increase the government's debt-management charges; another was to increase private banker demand for Federal Reserve Bank loans. Rather than sell their government bonds in a falling market, bankers naturally preferred to borrow to meet their customers' loan requirements. The Federal Reserve then raised its discount rate—the interest rate it charged member banks—and thereby drove up the interest rates on loans by member banks. Credit became tighter and more expensive. Democrats claimed this tight money policy brought on the recession of 1953–1954, and it probably was a factor; but lessened military spending after the end of the Korean War was probably more important.

The Eisenhower administration began by promising a balanced budget and reduced federal spending. The administration soon came to realize, however, that most items in the budget just could not be cut very much for either national security or political reasons. The administration let about one hundred thousand government jobs remain unfilled when their occupants resigned, but the money saved was relatively insignificant. Military spending could not be cut back much. Particularly before the Korean armistice, the State Department would not countenance a cut in foreign aid to nations it feared would go Communist, and fixed obligations such as veterans' pensions could not be importantly reduced. When Secretary Benson proposed that the administration reduce agricultural price supports where the law permitted, Congressmen in both parties quickly brought overwhelming pressure to bear.

The downswing in the business cycle which began in the fall of 1953 changed the problem from one of combatting inflation to trying to prevent severe deflation. The administration, understandably reluctant to admit that a recession was a real possibility, referred to the downswing as a "rolling readjustment" and condemned Democratic Senator Paul Douglas of Illinois, a former professor of economics, as a "prophet of gloom and doom" when he asserted that unless the government soon adopted antirecession measures the results would be unhappy. Nevertheless, the administration did quietly and mildly pursue the kind of policies that Douglas and other Keynesian economists held were proper under the circumstances. It relaxed its tight money policy, reduced taxes by $3 billion, and incurred a federal deficit. The last quarter of 1954 saw a sharp rise in the business cycle, and 1955 became the nation's most prosperous year.

The tax bill of 1954 was one that Andrew Mellon, whose portrait Secretary Humphrey kept in his office, would have approved. Beating down demands by a group of Democrats for an across-the-board increase in personal exemptions, which would have increased mass purchasing power, the Congress granted significant tax favors for low-income groups only by a reduction on the income taxes of retired workers. The new tax law lowered the wartime excises on transportation and luxuries such as jewelry, perfume, and furs. It excluded from income taxation the first $70 that a taxpayer received from stock dividends, a provision that proved a boon to few workingmen. And, perhaps most important, it granted faster depreciation allowances to businesses.

The oil and electric power industries received special treatment from the Republican administration. True to his campaign pledge, Eisenhower secured the passage of the Submerged Lands Act of 1953. This measure passed control of tidelands oil to the states, which then received royalties from the companies it allowed to work the off-shore fields and which were more generous with the companies than the federal government. Congress decided that the states could control up to three leagues into the sea (10.3 land miles) if the states had such boundaries at the time the states entered the Union. From this confusing provision there arose a curious series of court cases which the Supreme Court did not decide until June, 1960. The Court ruled that Louisiana, Alabama, and Mississippi had never claimed more than three nautical miles (3.45 land miles) off shore and were, therefore, entitled to jurisdiction only to that point. Texas and Florida, on the other hand, had made bolder claims, and their boundaries, therefore, extended three leagues seaward.

Democrats gleefully hoped the Eisenhower policies on electric policy would provide them with a hot election issue. The Dixon-Yates affair and the Hell's Canyon dispute probably did help the Democratic cause, but the results were nothing spectacular. The Dixon-Yates fracas grew from the Atomic Energy Commission's unusual demands for electric power. TVA had supplied most of the AEC's needs, and it proposed to meet the increased demands by constructing a steam generating plant. A syndicate headed by two southern utility executives, Edgar H. Dixon and Eugene A. Yates, proposed instead to organize a private company to supply the city of Memphis with power and make TVA expansion for AEC needs unnecessary. Eisenhower, who in 1953 had referred to TVA as an example of "creeping socialism," supported Dixon and Yates. In mid-1954, he ordered the AEC to sign the agreement. Public power supporters, notably Republican maverick Senator William L. Langer of North Dakota, declared war with an investigation. The Dixon-Yates proposal fell through when, in July, 1955, the city of Memphis, calculating it could produce its own power cheaper than it could buy it from Dixon-Yates, announced it would build its own generator. The President thereupon cancelled the Dixon-Yates contract. But there was still more to come. The congressional committee revealed that Adolphe Wenzell, a vice-president of the First Boston Corporation, had been employed by the Bureau of the Budget to help negotiate the Dixon-Yates contract and that his corporation had later become Dixon-Yates's financial agent. The AEC held that Wenzell had been involved in a clear conflict of interest and refused to pay the Dixon-Yates group for its expenses while the contract had been in force.

Hell's Canyon is a deep chasm along the Snake River between Oregon and Idaho. The Truman administration had proposed building a high dam there, one of the last good sites for a multipurpose dam in the nation still unexploited. The Idaho Power Company had submitted a scheme for three smaller dams. The issue was unresolved when Eisenhower took office. The new administration came forth with what it called its "partnership" principle on such matters, and the Federal Power Commission gave permission to private utilities to build the three small dams. The fight became hot indeed in the West. When public power advocates concentrated their fight in Congress with a measure to substitute the federal high dam, the White House rallied its strength on Capitol Hill and defeated them. Then the high dam supporters took their case to the courts.

The Federal Power Commission was the focus of another battle royal in the 1956 proposal to exempt natural gas in interstate pipelines from FPC regulation. Oil Democrats and southern states-righters joined most Republicans in support of the measure which would have become law but for the sensational revelation of Republican Senator Francis P. Case of South Dakota. Case said that an oil company had donated $2,500 to his campaign fund without his asking for it and that the company expected him to vote for the natural gas exemption. Case sent the money back and voted against his would-be briber's wishes, but the measure passed Congress anyway. The uproar, however, was too much for an administration that had come to office partly because of its promise to "clean up the mess in Washington." Eisenhower vetoed it. He said he favored the purpose of the bill but that the oil company methods left him no alternative but to reject the measure.

The Republican party was a bit embarrassed by its inability to solve the problem of agricultural surpluses. They had criticized the Democrats for their failure with the problem, but internal pressures and indecision worked as much against Republican as against Democratic success. Republicans were further embarrassed by their large government spending for surplus commodities, a policy that was inconsistent with the ideology of many party members.

During the campaign of 1952, Eisenhower had spoken of "full parity," but Secretary Benson appeared to regard government price supports as at best a temporarily necessary evil. The Agricultural Act of 1949 had established a plan for changing from rigid to flexible—that is, lower—supports, but throughout the rest of the Truman administration and for the first two years of Eisenhower's term, farm pressure had actually been sufficient to keep supports at a 90 per cent parity level. Stocks of government-owned commodities became mountainous; the government spent billions each year in purchasing cotton, wheat, corn, tobacco, and peanuts that no one would buy at a price sufficiently high to keep farm prices in line with other costs. Benson insisted upon lower supports, and Eisenhower backed him. Although the congressional fight was hot, the administration got through the Agricultural Act of 1954, which authorized the Secretary of Agriculture to cut supports on basic commodities to 82.5 per cent in 1955 and 75 per cent in 1956, authorized him to sell government-owned surpluses abroad at low prices, and arranged for part of the surplus to be used in school lunch programs.

Farm prices fell, and Secretary Benson was a highly unpopular man in many agricultural communities. Hoping to benefit from this criticism and with an eye cocked on the 1956 elections, congressional Democrats in early 1956 put through a bill restoring mandatory 90 per cent of parity supports. Eisenhower vetoed it. But he adopted one feature of the Democratic measure, the so-called soil bank idea, and Congress in May appropriated funds for this scheme of taking acres out of farm production. Actually, however, efforts to restrict production by restricting acreage in production were less than successful. The newly developed nitrogen fertilizers made it possible for a wheat farmer, for example, to get, within limits, about any yield per acre he desired. The farmer, then, took his check for his soil bank acreage and grew as much as ever on fewer acres.

The administration supported some extensions of general welfare principles commonly associated with the New Deal. A 1954 law extended Social Security Act coverage to self-employed people. Two years later a Democratic Congress (the Democrats after the 1954 elections had a forty-nine to forty-seven margin in the Senate and a 232 to 203 advantage in the House, less than the usual off-year comeback of the "out" party) further amended the Social Security Act to allow women to retire and receive pensions at age sixty-two and disabled workers to do so at age fifty. In 1956, Eisenhower also asked Congress to raise the minimum wage from seventy-five to ninty cents an hour; Congress raised it to $1.00 an hour.

Government spending for general welfare did not get far under the Eisenhower administration when the proposed spending was in areas which were conventionally in the private sector of the economy. The Housing Act of 1955 provided for only 45,000 new public housing units a year for four years. Eisenhower's proposal for a $25 million program to provide government support to private health insurance schemes so as to enable them to give broader and less expensive coverage received censure from two sides, from some who said the proposal was woefully timid and inadequate and from the American Medical Association who said that it was too close to "socialized medicine." Congress dropped the proposal. Federal aid to states for education similarly came to nothing. Many Republicans opposed the idea on principle, and southern Democrats prevented its passage after Democratic Representative Adam Clayton Powell, Jr., a Negro from New York City, attached a proviso that federal aid could not go to school districts that segregated children by race.

In areas that were traditionally in the public sector of the economy, the administration and the Congress further extended federal spending. For a generation the St. Lawrence Seaway had sporadically become an issue, with the Midwest supporting the idea and the railroads and the eastern states opposing it. When it became clear that Canada would go ahead and construct the Seaway on her own, the United States at last acted. In May, 1954, the President signed a bill that provided for joint Canadian-American construction. Spending for highways was also safe politically. In 1956, Congress and the White House got together on a vast superhighway construction program, the federal government to assume 90 per cent of the costs and the states to do the actual building from federal minimum specifications. Under the law, states were allowed to charge the traveler for use of the roads, and most of them did so.

By far the most spectacular political story of the first Eisenhower term was the further rise and then the rapid fall of Senator Joseph R. McCarthy. In the 1952 campaign, many anti-McCarthy Republicans argued that only with a Republican president could the obstreperous Wisconsinite be calmed down and satisfied. But, if anything, McCarthy's charges became more sensational after Eisenhower's inauguration. McCarthy became the chairman of the Senate Government Operations Committee and its Permanent Subcommittee on Investigations. He used the post to establish himself as his party's official anti-Communist, despite the President's obvious anti-Communism revealed by his administration's further prosecution of Communist party leaders under the Smith Act and by his order imposing a "blank wall" between J. Robert Oppenheimer and government nuclear secrets. (Oppenheimer had been the director of the Los Alamos operation during the war, and many scientists were incensed by the decision.) Although the President made occasional public statements that could be interpreted as critical of McCarthy, he refrained from outright public opposition.

Matters came to a head soon after McCarthy began to attack the army. McCarthy discovered a New York dentist, called to army duty in 1952, who had been a Communist. The army found the dentist's Communist connection and took the easy way out by releasing him with an honorable discharge. McCarthy charged that someone in the army was either a Communist or "soft on Communism" for taking such action. He called General Ralph Zwicker before his subcommittee, but Zwicker was under orders not to reveal who in the service had been responsible for the handling of the dentist's discharge. McCarthy called the general "a disgrace to the uniform." The army soon counterattacked. It charged that McCarthy and his assistant Roy Cohn had sought to get preferential treatment in the army for Private G. David Schine, a former McCarthy committee staff member and a friend of Cohn's. The upshot was a nationally televised hearing by McCarthy's own committee with Senator Karl Mundt of South Dakota presiding.

The televised hearings were intensely dramatic. For their first few days, no television drama was their equal for theatrical thrill. Before long, the public began strongly to turn against McCarthy, whose manners in front of the camera were crude and who, before the whole nation's eyes, revealed the methods that had brought him to national prominence. Soon comedians began to imitate the Senator's rasping refrain, "Point of order, Mr. Chairman, point of order," and other obstructing tactics he frequently used.

Republican Senator Ralph Flanders of Vermont, Democratic Senator William Fulbright of Arkansas, and independent Senator Wayne Morse of Oregon introduced resolutions of censure against McCarthy, and the Senate appointed a committee of three Democratic and three Republican members, headed by former federal judge Arthur Watkins, Republican from Utah, to conduct hearings on the charges. The Watkins committee maintained an especially judicious air. It finally recommended to the Senate that Senator McCarthy be condemned on two counts: for refusing to give the committee information about his finances that the committee held to be relevant to his fitness as a Senator and for contempt of the Senate for his remarks about his colleagues. In December, 1954, the Senate by a sixty-seven to twenty-two vote condemned the junior Senator from Wisconsin. Eisenhower publicly complimented Senator Watkins. McCarthy faded fast, perhaps more because of adverse public opinion after the army-McCarthy hearings than because of the Senate's action. When he died in May, 1957, he was a bitter and largely forgotten man.

McCarthyism subsided almost as rapidly as McCarthy. Undoubtedly, the Korean armistice in July, 1953 (see p. 555) relaxed tensions and set the stage for McCarthy's personal downfall. The nation's attitude became no less opposed to either foreign or domestic Communism. Indeed, in 1954, congressional Democrats, in an effort to defend themselves against Republican charges of softness, instigated the Communist Control Act which for all practical purposes made the Communist party illegal. The Justice Department has not used the law. But irrational suspicion on the whole declined, and political candidates far less frequently tried to demonstrate their fitness for office by appearing to be more intensely anti-Communist than their opponents. In 1956 and 1957, the Supreme Court inhibited the power of congressional committees to demand answers from witnesses to questions not directly relevant and provided better guarantees of constitutional rights to those charged with having Communist sympathies. What little was left of the Communist party engaged in a fierce internal controversy prompted by Premier Nikita Khrushchev's revelations of Stalin's repressions which resulted in many resignations.

We Like Ike, Part II

On September 24, 1955, while on a vacation in Denver, President Eisenhower suffered a heart attack. At first it appeared that a second Eisenhower candidacy was out of the question, but slowly the President resumed his executive activities. In early 1956, when the President's press secretary staged a conference between a group of Eisenhower's physicians and reporters in which the doctors reported that their patient's heart had healed, it became obvious that Eisenhower again would run. His subsequent announcement was

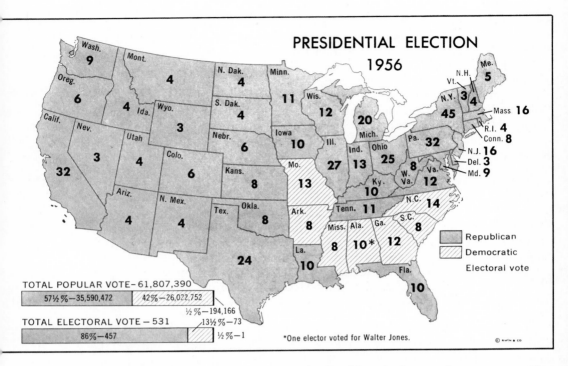

PRESIDENTIAL ELECTION
1956

Republican
Democratic
Electoral vote

TOTAL POPULAR VOTE—61,807,390
57½%—35,590,472   42%—26,022,752
½%—194,166
TOTAL ELECTORAL VOTE—531
86%—457   13½%—73
½%—1   *One elector voted for Walter Jones.

an anticlimax. Then in June, 1956, the President had to undergo an operation for ileitis. Partisan Republicans read the newspaper medical reports with more than detached interest.

Contrary to custom, the Democrats held their convention first. The main contenders in the preconvention struggle for the nomination were Stevenson, Governor Averell Harriman of New York, and Senator Kefauver of Tennessee. Kefauver withdrew from consideration just before the convention. Although former President Truman supported Harriman, the convention nominated Stevenson on the first ballot. The real excitement came with the vice-presidential nomination. Stevenson declined to express a preference for a running mate, and the delegates at Chicago settled down to a dogfight such as Democratic conventions seem to enjoy. The battle was between Kefauver and Senator John F. Kennedy of Massachusetts. Although Kefauver was from the South and Kennedy was a Roman Catholic, most southern delegates voted for Kennedy. Kefauver won by a hair. The party platform criticized the Republican agricultural record, called for 90 per cent of parity supports, and condemned their opponents for their electric power policies. Fear of southern disaffection prompted the convention to adopt a weasling plank on civil rights.

Eisenhower's nomination at the San Francisco convention in August was a foregone conclusion despite his health. Political parties are seldom favored with such popular figures. The only stir about the ticket came from an undercurrent of dissatisfaction with Vice-President Nixon. Harold Stassen, who had moved from the presidency of the University of Pennsylvania to become Eisenhower's adviser on disarmament, announced that Governor Christian Herter of Massachusetts would give the ticket better drawing power than would Nixon. But before the convention opened he backed down and consented to give one of Nixon's seconding speeches. At the convention an independent-minded Nebraska delegate created a sensation when he got the floor and nominated a mythical "Joe Smith" for the second place on the ticket. Chairman Joseph Martin silenced the audacious Nebraskan. Both Eisenhower and Nixon received their nominations by acclamation. The platform was an expression of "modern Republicanism"; it put the GOP on record as opposed to racial segregation in the schools.

The campaign was dull. Stevenson failed to show the sparkle of 1952, and the Republicans lacked a Truman scapegoat. One campaign development was interesting for the future. Stevenson urged an international agreement banning the testing of nuclear weapons on the grounds that radioactive fall-out was dangerous to the health and safety of the entire world. Eisenhower declared that the proposal was dangerous unless an international agency had the power to inspect anywhere in the world to see if any nation infringed the agreement. Before Eisenhower left the White House in 1961, he agreed to the kind of proposal Stevenson had made.

A tense international situation developed just before election day. In October, Hungarian nationalists revolted against the Russians only to be ruthlessly suppressed. Then, in the week before the polling, Israel invaded Egyptian territory. France and Great Britain joined with Israel, and full war was a real possibility. These international tensions probably helped Eisenhower because he was experienced in the White House and had military knowledge.

Eisenhower's margin of victory was even greater than in 1952. He received 35,585,316 popular votes to 26,031,322 for Stevenson. In the electoral college Eisenhower's victory was 457 to 73. One Alabama elector cast his vote for an obscure state judge rather than for Stevenson. Stevenson carried only southern states plus Missouri, and Eisenhower won such traditionally Democratic strongholds as Texas, Louisiana, Florida, Tennessee, and Virginia. The congressional elections again showed that Eisenhower was far more popular than his party. Democrats held their previous margin of two seats in the Senate and won 235 of the House positions. Once again different parties controlled Capitol Hill and the White House.

Two Texas moderate Democrats, Speaker of the House Sam Rayburn and Senate Majority Leader Lyndon Johnson, cooperated with Eisenhower. Indeed, Eisenhower had to rely upon their congressional leadership. In general, they supported the President's position with only the modification necessary to mollify dissident sections of their own party. Inevitably, such bipartisan moderation produced no important new departures. Perhaps as great an event with a long-run impact as the Eisenhower-moderate Democratic leadership provided was the admission of Alaska and Hawaii to statehood, the former in January, 1959, and the latter in August of the same year.

At the very beginning of his second term Eisenhower encountered more difficulty with his own party, even his own cabinet, than he did with the Democrats. In January, 1957, he presented Congress with a budget totalling $71.8 billion, the largest any president had ever offered in peacetime. Very quickly, Secretary of the Treasury Humphrey at a press conference, when a reporter asked if there was any hope that the defense budget could be cut, replied: "I think there is, yes, I do. I would certainly deplore the day that we thought we couldn't ever reduce expenditures of this terrific amount, the terrific tax take we are taking out of this country. If we don't, over a long period of time, I will predict that you will have a depression that will curl your hair." When he resigned about a year later Eisenhower replaced him with Robert B. Anderson of Texas, who went on record for deficit financing during a depression although he never actually supported such fiscal policies when a minor recession came. Congress was slow to act, but finally, despite Secretary Humphrey, it cut the budget only about $4 billion.

Congress did not cut taxes and no hair-curling depression developed, but in the last quarter of 1957 and through 1958 the economy did undergo one of its major postwar recessions. Instead of arising from government spending, it probably resulted from a shift in government spending. Less of the budget went for military aircraft, and the recession apparently started when aircraft workers in southern California found themselves on reduced hours or no work at all. The 1957–1958 recession was an odd one. Gross national product continued to grow—from $419.2 billion in 1956 to $442.8 billion in 1957 to $444.2 billion in 1958—but not as fast as the population growth would warrant. Unemployment increased significantly. In July, 1957, just over three million workers were unemployed. The figure rose to about 4,500,000 in January, 1958, and to almost 5,300,000 in July. To carry the story of the national economy on to the end of the Eisenhower administration, recovery in the last half of 1958 and the first half of 1959 was strong. Increased government spending, mostly on defense matters in response to the Soviet Union's successful launching of Sputnik I, the first man-made satellite, in October, 1957, was a factor in the recovery. In the second half of 1959 a long steel strike slowed the economy again. Expectations in early 1960 were high, but in the second quarter of the year the economy's rate of growth slowed again. Unemployment statistics fluctuated but stayed close to four million throughout this period. Another oddity of the economy in Eisenhower's second term was that the cost-of-living index continued to rise gradually despite other economic fluctuation. In summary, one might say that after the 1957–1958 recession the country enjoyed prosperity but not as much economic growth as desirable and that the chronically unemployed in the chronically depressed "sick-industry" areas found small comfort from the happier national picture.

Democrats in 1958 looked forward eagerly to the fall elections because of the recession and because they saw a chance to pin the corruption label on the Republicans that their opponents had pinned on them in 1952. Several GOP officials had resigned under charges of improperly using their office to further their personal finances, including a chairman of the Republican national committee, a Secretary of the Air Force, an Assistant Secretary of Defense, and an Eisenhower-appointed Democrat on the Federal Communications Commission. Then in the spring of 1952 a House subcommittee hit political pay dirt. It alleged that Sherman Adams, Eisenhower's "Assistant President," had interceded with federal agencies in behalf of a friend, Bernard Goldfine, a New England textile manufacturer. Adams, the House group charged, had in return received lavish Christmas presents. The industrialist had given Adams a topcoat made of vicuña, a wool taken from South American goats, and Republican vicuña coats became almost as notorious as Democratic mink ones. President Eisenhower, when warned that keeping Adams as his assistant might be political dynamite, replied, "I need him." Nevertheless, in the late summer of 1958 enough prominent Republicans put pressure on the White House for Adams to leave office; the accused resigned on September 22.

It would be a mistake to ascribe the recession and the Adams case as the only reasons for Democratic victory in November, 1958. As in all elections, local and state issues were important. In 1958, "right-to-work" laws were an issue in several states. ("Right-to-work" laws were a euphemism for prohibitions of the union shop.) When some employers persuaded a few candidates, mostly Republicans, to support such legislation, labor only became more determined to help the Democrats win. The labor vote, plus a division within the Republican organization, was clearly influential in the defeat of Senate Republican leader William F. Knowland for governor of California. Democrats ended up with larger majorities in each house of Congress than they had enjoyed since the Congress elected in 1936: 64 Democrats in the Senate and 283 in the House. Furthermore, Democrats elected governors in usually Republican states such as Iowa, Wisconsin, and Ohio. In both parties, the more progressive candidates fared better than the more conservative members of the same party. In New York, the Republican gubernatorial candidate, Nelson Rockefeller, who seemed as progressive as his Democratic opponent, Averell Harriman, won by an overwhelming majority, while conservative John Bricker lost in Ohio.

It would not have been unreasonable in the winter of 1958–1959 to predict that the new Congress would pass a series of progressive bills. But such was not to be the case. The moderation of the congressional Democratic leadership and the constant threat of a veto prevented the Eighty-sixth Congress from being substantially different from its predecessor. It failed to enact any increased public housing program. Debates over including a medical care program for the aged under the Social Security Act of 1935 were long and well publicized, but Congress made no real change. One generous aged medical care plan passed the House, but the Senate, where presidential aspirant John F. Kennedy supported it, voted it down fifty-one to forty-four. Only one Republican Senator voted for the measure; thirty-two Republicans and nineteen Democrats voted against it. In April, 1960, when the approaching elections were very much on congressional minds, Congress passed a new Civil Rights Act to be described in Chapter 28. Although southern Congressmen opposed the law, they were able to water it down so much that Negro leaders said it made little difference.

Labor unions received much attention from Congress. In 1957, a Senate committee headed by Senator John L. McClellan of Arkansas and assisted by its counsel, Robert Kennedy, Senator Kennedy's brother, began investigating racketeering in labor unions. McClellan and Kennedy concentrated on the Teamsters Union, perhaps the nation's least democratic major union. The Committee alleged that Teamster president David Beck of Seattle had used union funds for his own use. Beck subsequently was indicted and convicted for income tax evasion. When he declined to run for re-election, the Teamster convention elected James Hoffa of Detroit, whose reputation was less savory even than Beck's. While holding no brief for Beck and Hoffa, many friends of labor argued that the Senate committee actually was spotlighting the worst characters in the labor movement so as to discredit all unions, honest and democratic as well as crooked and high-handed. Public opinion polls showed a growing disapproval of the whole labor movement. The investigation resulted in the Labor Reform Act of 1959. This law guaranteed union members secret elections of officers and provided for government supervision of union funds, including welfare funds, which had grown tremendously since the end of the war. It also expanded the Taft-Hartley Act's inhibitions on boycotts and restricted union activities in jurisdictional disputes.

Asia and Brinkmanship

The Republican party divided sharply over Asian policy. A considerable group in the party, usually quite conservative in domestic policies, were commonly called "Asia firsters." That is, they valued American supremacy in Asia and defeat of the Chinese and other Asian Communists more highly than Communist containment in Europe. Eisenhower clearly was not in sympathy with the views of this wing of his party, but he had to yield to it occasionally.

Eisenhower began his administration by seeming to throw support behind the "Asia first," "total victory" in Korea point of view. Followers of the MacArthur line had long been critical of Truman's ordering the Seventh Fleet to neutralize Formosa, charging that the fleet was "shielding" Communist China. Eisenhower announced he would "unleash Chiang Kai-shek." The unleashed Chiang, however, remained quietly on Formosa, undertaking no more than an occasional minor raid of the Chinese mainland which he had been doing even before he was "unleashed."

The Korean truce talks at Panmunjom had been stalled for months over the issue of the return of prisoners. The talks had been suspended altogether since September, 1952. Whether or not Stalin's death on March 5, 1953, was a factor in the resumption of truce negotiations was not known, but at any rate before the end of the month North Korean and Chinese army commanders accepted an American proposal for the exchange of invalid prisoners of war that they had earlier rejected and suggested resumption of negotiations.

Negotiations began again in April. The problem of what to do with the prisoners who did not want to return to their homes remained the main obstacle. In June, both sides agreed to a plan, to be administered by a commission of neutral nations, under which each side would have three months to explain to its prisoner compatriots why they should return. Then Syngman Rhee, president of South Korea, all but wrecked everything by secretly ordering the immediate release of all the North Korean and Chinese prisoners who did not want to return. He also threatened to resume the war unless his terms were met—reunification of all Korea under the South Korean government. Hard pressure from Washington persuaded Rhee to back down, but he won the promise of American military assistance if North Korea should attack again. The United States and South Korea signed a mutual defense treaty in August. Obviously, the major obligation fell upon the United States.

When Rhee released the prisoners, the Communists at first demanded that all twenty-seven thousand of them be rounded up, which would have been extremely difficult if not impossible, but they seemed determined to bring the conflict to an end and on July 27, 1953, signed an armistice. The truce line ran from about thirty miles north of the thirty-eighth parallel at its east end to a little south of the line at its west end. A demilitarized area four kilometers wide ran the length of the line. Repatriation of prisoners was complete by September. Although nearly one-fourth of the North Korean and Chinese prisoners declined to go home, American attention focused on the twenty-two Americans who elected to stay with the Communists.

The war that had never officially been more than a "police action" was over at last. Americans killed in action totalled 33,237, along with an estimated 50,000 South Koreans and 3,124 other UN troops. Estimates of Communist losses ranged from 1,500,000 to 2,000,000.

The end of the Korean war by no means ended America's problems with Asian Communism. The year 1954 saw crises in Southeast Asia and in the Formosan Straits. In Southeast Asia, French Indo-China to be specific, the United States came perilously close to war. Secretary of State John Foster Dulles, upon whom the President leaned heavily, himself gave the term which characterized American policy: *brinkmanship*. *Life* magazine in early 1956 quoted Dulles from an interview:

> The ability to get to the verge without getting into war is the necessary art. If you cannot master it, you inevitably get into war. If you try to run away from it, if you are scared to go to the brink, you are lost. We've had to look it square in the face—on the question of enlarging the Korean War, on the question of getting into the Indochina war, on the question of Formosa. We walked to the brink and we looked it in the face. We took strong action.[1]

Many people were alarmed for fear that in going to the brink the nation might get shoved over it by accident or fail to realize where the precise edge was because of the fast movement of events. Although the entire story is not yet known, it appears that congressional caution and the opposition of Great Britain had more to do with keeping on the peace side of the brink in Indo-China than did State Department calculation.

Since the end of the war, the French had been on the defensive in Indo-China. They declined to make any firm commitments about independence and maintained a reactionary puppet, Bao Dai, over the country. Their position in the guerilla warfare against the Communists, led by Ho Chi Minh, steadily deteriorated, and despite the aid they received from the United States for the Indo-Chinese war (which amounted to about 70 per cent of their costs), French domestic sentiment opposed the financial drain. The French secretly notified Washington in March, 1954, that, unless the United States intervened, Indo-China was lost. French forces were under siege at Dienbienphu, and the situation was hopeless without a great deal of additional force.

On April 7, President Eisenhower told a press conference that if Indo-China fell to the Communists the situation would be analogous to pushing over the first in a row of dominoes. The rest of Southeast Asia, perhaps more, would quickly be led into Communist hands. Although a general conference

---

[1] James Shepley, "How Dulles Averted War," *Life* (January 16, 1956), 78.

KACHIN STATES

Kunming ·

100°

106°

CHINA

Yuan (Red)

0   100   200
MILES

SHAN STATES

Mandalay ·

BURMA

Irrawaddy

TONKIN

N. VIETNAM

Dienbienphu ·

Hanoi ·

Haiphong ·

20°

LAOS

Luang Prabang ·

Gulf of Tonkin

HAINAN

KARENNI STATE

Salween

Vientiane ·

Mekong

Hué ·

ANNAM

South China Sea

Rangoon ·

Moulmein ·

THAILAND

Menam

Nakhon Ratchasima ·

S. VIETNAM

Andaman Sea

Bangkok ·

CAMBODIA

Phnom Penh ·

Saigon ·

Cholon ·

10°

ISTHMUS OF KRA

Gulf of Siam

COCHIN CHINA

SUMATRA

Strait of Malacca

Penang ·

MALAYA

Kuala Lumpur ·

Johore Bahru

Singapore ·

100°

106°

BORNEO

© RMcN & CO.

SOUTHEAST ASIA

—·—·— Present international boundaries

——— Division between North and South Vietnam near 17th parallel

- - - - Borders of Burmese states

·········· Borders of old divisions of Vietnam

Areas annexed by Thailand during World War II

Provinces in Laos occupied by Communist forces

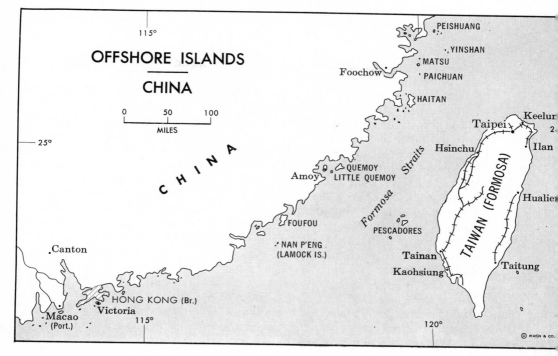

OFFSHORE ISLANDS
—
CHINA

for discussion of Indo-Chinese matters had already been scheduled to be held in Geneva, Dulles and the chairman of the joint chiefs of staff, Admiral Arthur W. Radford, proposed that the United States send carriers and planes to Indo-China to relieve the French. Congressional leaders warned Dulles that such action would very probably mean full war and urged him to line up support from America's allies. The British government, then under the Conservative party, flatly refused to support the idea. The United States stepped back from the brink. On April 26, the day the Geneva conference opened, President Eisenhower announced that what was sought was a *modus vivendi* with the Chinese Communists. Dienbienphu fell on May 7, 1954. In July, the Geneva conference ended with an armistice and the partition of Indo-China. The states of Cambodia and Laos were to be independent. Vietnam was to be divided, as was Korea, along the seventeenth parallel, Communist to the north and anti-Communist to the south. The United States gave military and economic aid to the anti-Communists; Communist China aided the Indo-Chinese Communists. Continuing Communist penetrations of Loas and South Vietnam created constant tensions.

After the Geneva conference of 1954, Dulles brought about the formation of a Southeast Asian counterpart of NATO, the Southeast Asia Treaty Organization (SEATO). Signers of the treaty in September, 1954, were the United States, France, Great Britain, Australia, New Zealand, the Philippines, Thailand, and Pakistan. The treaty declared that an attack upon any of the signatory powers—and a separate agreement included an attack on Laos, Cambodia, and South Vietnam—would be regarded as a threat to all of them. It did not precisely commit the signatory nations to war; it required each nation

557

"to act to meet the common danger in accordance with its constitutional processes." Actually, SEATO, in comparison to NATO, has been little more than a paper organization.

The United States did not go as close to the brink in the conflict between the Nationalist and Communist Chinese over the islands in the Formosan Strait. When the Nationalists were forced to flee the mainland and go to Formosa, they had left garrisons on several tiny islands in the Formosan Strait and just north of it: Quemoy and Matsu just off the coast; the Tachen Islands near the coast and to the north; and the Pescadore Islands off the coast of Formosa. In September, 1954, the Chinese Communists began artillery bombardment of Quemoy, only five miles off the coast. An invasion of the island appeared likely. That the United States would help defend Formosa from attack was clear, but what would it do if the offshore islands, which had little or no strategic importance, should be attacked? Admiral Radford advocated aerial bombardment of mainland Communist bases. Other military leaders objected, arguing that the risk of general war over islands whose only importance was psychological was useless. The President refused to support Radford's position. There was no invasion.

The mutual defense treaty signed on December 1, 1954, between Nationalist China and the United States did not entirely clarify just what the United States would help defend. The United States made clear it would regard an attack on Formosa or the Pescadores as a provocation of war, but the treaty said nothing about the islands just off the mainland coast. At the time of the treaty's signing, the State Department received a promise from Chiang Kai-shek that he would not attack the mainland without clearing the action with Washington. He was thus "leashed" again. Congress passed the buck back to the President in its resolution of January 28, 1955, which authorized the President to order American forces to the defense of Formosa and the Pescadores but left the status of the "related positions" up in the air.

Two subsequent developments failed to clarify the American position. In January, 1955, the Communists began to move into the Tachen Islands. Eisenhower's party leader in the Senate, William S. Knowland, demanded full support for Chiang, but in the end Eisenhower agreed only to help Chiang retreat from the Tachens. Again in 1958 the offshore islands were in the news when the Communists began heavy shelling of Quemoy. Secretary Dulles at first implied that the United States would defend the island but later indicated that, if the bombardment stopped, Chiang might demilitarize it and perhaps abandon it. The Chinese Communists let up on the shelling, but Chiang kept his troops on Quemoy.

At this point the Chinese Communists inadvertently strengthened the American position in India by blundering in Tibet. After suppressing a Tibetian revolt, Chinese armed forces moved across a vague boundary into territory claimed by India. That vast country had since its independence studiously maintained a neutralist or "third camp" position in the cold war, and it had been anxious about American military aid to its hostile neighbor, Pakistan. Chinese occupation of Indian territory by no means made India bellicose, but her neutralism became considerably less rigid as she moved closer to the West.

Eisenhower and Khrushchev

The Eisenhower administration's view of the proper nature of the American military establishment was at least partly the result of traditional Republican opposition to massive government spending. A military establishment capable of coping successfully with any situation that might develop would be terribly expensive, more expensive than Republican budgeters wanted. The administration compromised by keeping conventional armed forces down as much as it dared and concentrated on nuclear weapons and the instruments for delivering them. As Secretary Dulles put it in a January, 1954, speech, Communist armies were too powerful to match and the United States must rely on the "deterrent of massive retaliatory power." In other words, Communist fear of being exterminated by nuclear weapons would deter them from aggressions.

President Truman had given the green light to the development of the hydrogen fusion bomb, and the United States first successfully tested the new weapon in November, 1952. In August, 1953, Russia tested her first H-bomb. The arms race continued. Each side increased its arsenal of this most devastating weapon and improved its means of sending the weapon to its target. In 1957, the Communists seemed to be at least temporarily ahead in the matter of delivery when they successfully tested intercontinental ballistic missiles and demonstrated by putting Sputnik I into orbit that they had rockets of enormous thrust.

West Europeans were torn between desire to increase their armed strength through NATO and fear of recreating a powerful and possibly dangerous German armed force. The French government, which until 1958 underwent constantly recurring constitutional crises, put forward the idea of the European Defense Community (EDC). EDC would be an international army, composed of troops from West Germany, France, Britain, and the Benelux countries. The United States vigorously encouraged the proposal, and in May, 1952, the European nations signed the EDC treaty. But the French then drew back out of fear of Germany's military potential under the scheme. Dulles' statement that French failure to ratify the EDC treaty would cause the United States to undertake an "agonizing reappraisal" of its policies —an implied threat to cut off military aid to France—did not prevent the French from rejecting the treaty. But the idea was not dead. The British allayed French fears by promising to keep four divisions and an air force in Europe to be used against any aggressor, and Washington said it would also keep troops in Europe, at least for the moment. In the fall of 1954, West Germany, Italy, France, and the Benelux countries formed the Western European Union (WEU). In this arrangement Germany would furnish up to twelve divisions but forbore having nuclear, chemical, or biological weapons. France consented. However, in 1957, West German Chancellor Konrad Adenauer asked for tactical atomic weapons, and the United States granted them. West Germany, however, did not obtain independent control of the weapons.

For a time in the middle years of the Eisenhower era it appeared that some kind of more or less permanent relaxation of cold war tensions might be effected. Stalin's death quite obviously changed the situation within the Soviet Union, although one cannot say yet what the end of the changes will be. Georgi Malenkov succeeded Stalin. In February, 1955, he resigned under pressure to be succeeded by Nikolai Bulganin. However, the new secretary of the Soviet Communist party, Nikita Khrushchev, was the actual force. In March, 1958, Khrushchev himself became the premier, holding the government office as well as the party office, as had Stalin. Whatever Khrushchev was, however (and there was little agreement in the West about this bustling figure), it was clear that he was not a carbon copy of Stalin. He was more flexible, both in internal and external policies, perhaps more of a realist and less doctrinaire, although, clearly, firmly committed to the Communist viewpoint.

Encouraged by Soviet developments and alarmed by the United States and Russia having hydrogen weapons capable of hideous destruction, the people of western Europe yearned for some kind of *rapprochement* between East and West. The aged prime minister of Britain, Winston Churchill, who retired in the spring of 1955, urged a conference of world leaders "at the summit." In the 1955 British elections the Conservatives promised to seek a summit meeting, and the idea was popular in internally torn France. Such a meeting was the hope of probably a majority of Americans. At first scornful of a summit conference, President Eisenhower was impressed by the force of opinion and by Russian willingness to negotiate about an Austrian peace treaty. (On May 15, 1955, the World War II allies signed a peace treaty with Austria which in effect made that country a neutral zone in the cold war.) Just five days before the Austrian treaty's signing, Great Britain, France, and the United States invited Russia to a meeting of the four chiefs of state. Russia accepted.

Eisenhower, Bulganin, the current French premier, Edgar Faure, and the new British prime minister, Sir Anthony Eden, met at Geneva in July. No meeting of heads of state ever received greater publicity. But, even though the meeting was to be only exploratory and was to be followed by subsequent meetings of the foreign ministers, it actually came to no important agreement. At this first meeting of Big Four chief executives since Potsdam ten years earlier, the Russians refused to consider German reunification on the basis of popular elections until they had first, in effect, an American commitment to withdraw from Europe. Eisenhower made his "open skies" proposal: the two sides to exchange maps of their military establishments and to allow one another aerial inspection so as to prevent secret arms concentration. The Russians insisted upon a prior ban on nuclear weapons before they would consider any kind of inspection, a position they clung to tenaciously.

Neither the 1955 summit conference nor the Big Four foreign ministers' meeting made any advance on the critical German and disarmament questions, but there were some less important improvements. In September, 1955, Russia announced it was ready to withdraw from Finland's Porkkala peninsula where it had a naval base, and in 1956 actually did so. East and West began a cultural interchange program that obviously enriched at least the musical experience of both camps. Russia began to admit tourists from the United

States and other NATO countries. The Soviets and the Americans initiated a student exchange program on a small scale.

At the Twentieth Congress of the Soviet Communist party in February, 1956, Khrushchev made statements that were startling indeed. First, he indicated a new Russian position when he said that ultimate war between Communist and capitalist nations was not inevitable. He maintained that the people of the world would sooner or later come to believe that Communism offered them more than capitalism, that Communists would inevitably win the struggle but that the struggle would be peaceful. "Peaceful co-existence" was Khrushchev's phrase. He recognized that really neither side could win a full war in the traditional sense of victory: ". . . there are only two ways: either peaceful co-existence or the most devastating war in history. There is no third alternative."

Then in a "secret" speech before the Congress Khrushchev was highly critical of Stalin. He reported that Stalin had been insanely suspicious, cruel, and unnecessarily dictatorial. He confirmed almost everything that western critics for years had said of the dead Soviet dictator. Needless to say, this kind of speech from the world's number one Communist about the man who had stood in his place only three years earlier shook the Communist movement throughout the world to its very foundations. One result was to stimulate revolts among the more nationalistic satellites.

The Poles, long fierce nationalists, elected Wladyslaw Gomulka, only recently released from a Soviet prison, to their party secretaryship. Gomulka refused to join the government unless a Russian general were dismissed as defense minister. Khrushchev objected, but the Poles dismissed the Russian general, installed Gomulka, and, to the world's surprise, got away with it. The Poles were hardly in a position to break entirely from the Russian orbit, but they did achieve a measure of independence and used it to allow a freer internal atmosphere. Although the Polish government was still undeniably Communist, the United States offered Poland limited economic aid to encourage its "Titoist" policies.

Encouraged by the Polish example, the Hungarians also rebelled against Russia, but their rebellion was against Communism as well as against Russian control of their Communist state. "Titoism" the Russians had demonstrated they would tolerate, even if they did not like it; but anti-Communism they would not tolerate. In early November, 1956, the Russians unleashed a strong military offensive against the Hungarian revolution. Tanks rolled through Budapest. The Hungarians fought back, but they were no match. Nearly two hundred thousand Hungarians fled to the West over the Austrian border.

Neither the United States nor any other power offered to come to the military aid of the Hungarian revolutionists. To have done so almost certainly would have meant full war with the Soviet Union. Secretary Dulles had been critical of the containment policy, arguing that liberation rather than containment was the proper goal. But his argument was apparently intended for domestic political advantage. When the chips were down in the fall of 1956, he and the Eisenhower administration refrained from any more than containment.

The anticolonial peoples of Asia, the Middle East, and Africa, naturally horrified by the Russian suppression of Hungarian self-determination, could

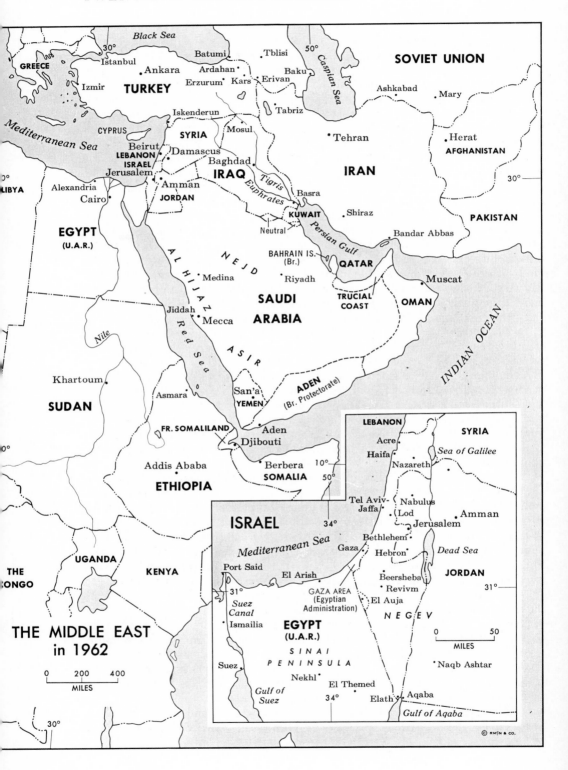

**THE MIDDLE EAST
in 1962**

0   200   400
MILES

562

have been drawn closer to the western camp but for the almost simultaneous Suez fiasco. Some background is necessary.

In 1952, a nationalist military group in Egypt, led by Colonel Abdel Gamel Nasser, overthrew King Farouk. Nasser became premier of Egypt in 1954. He proposed not only to improve the internal conditions of his country but to unite the various Arab countries into one nation. Secretary Dulles was hopeful of making Nasser an anti-Communist friend and was ever mindful of the vast American investment in Middle Eastern petroleum which had become of much greater importance in the previous fifteen years. But he was not consistent. On the one hand, he encouraged the formation in 1955 of the so-called Baghdad Pact or Middle East Treaty Organization, a defensive alliance among Great Britain, Pakistan, Iraq, Iran, and Turkey, which Nasser vigorously opposed. Nasser's opposition to the Baghdad Pact prompted the Communist camp to try to get Middle Eastern allies. Egypt and Czechoslovakia got together on a cotton-weapons exchange. On the other hand, Dulles cut off arms aid to Nasser's Israeli enemies, hastened British withdrawal of troops from Suez, and in December, 1955, together with Great Britain, offered Egypt $70 million for the construction of the Aswan Dam, a proposed hydroelectric installation on the Nile. A World Bank loan for the dam was contingent upon British and American help.

But Nasser increased his economic ties with the Soviet camp, much to Dulles' disappointment, and on July 19, 1956, Dulles withdrew the offer of help for the Aswan Dam. Nasser replied quickly. Seven days later he nationalized the Suez Canal. Revenues from canal operation would go for the dam's construction. Western European nations, dependent upon the canal and the Middle East for its oil products, were anxious lest Nasser cut off their use of the canal. With Dulles' help, they made several proposals for international control of the canal, all of which Nasser rejected. Then the real trouble erupted.

On October 19, 1956, Israel launched a full-scale invasion of Egypt. The United States supported a UN Security Council resolution calling upon Israel to withdraw and upon all other nations to refrain from using force. Britain and France vetoed the resolution, and the next day, October 31, they began bombing Egypt. On November 5, the day after Russian tanks entered Budapest in force, British and French troops invaded Nasser's territory.

The British and French had not consulted Washington before their invasion. Eisenhower, the press reported, indulged in "barracks room language." The United States and the Soviet Union independently of one another introduced resolutions in the Security Council condemning the Anglo-French-Israeli invasion; Britain and France vetoed. But the UN Assembly, where there is no veto, passed an American-sponsored resolution calling for a cease-fire and withdrawal of armies. The invaders of Egypt first ignored the UN resolution, but the Egyptians blocked the canal by sinking ships and dumping bridges and thereby made the invasion fruitless. On November 6, the British and French agreed to the cease-fire. A UN force supervised the truce between Egypt and Israel. By the end of 1956 British and French troops had withdrawn from Egypt.

The Suez fiasco had a sequel. With France and Britain no longer a major influence and with the Soviets eager to cement their relations with

Nasser and other Middle Eastern leaders, Eisenhower, in a message to Congress on January 5, 1957, asked for authority to grant military and economic aid to any Middle Eastern country that asked for it to preserve those nations' territorial integrity from the Communists. Many Congressmen believed that this Eisenhower Doctrine, as it came to be called, was a kind of buck passing to Capitol Hill. Congress passed the buck back to the White House. It authorized the President to use American forces in the Middle East but left it to him to say when and where they were required. It also appropriated $200 million for military and economic aid.

The administration invoked the Eisenhower Doctrine in July, 1958, in Lebanon. Early in 1958 Nasser had taken a big step toward Arab unification by getting Syria to agree to come into a newly created United Arab Republic with Nasser as its president. Fearful of the potential power of the UAR and distrusting its dealings with the Russians, the administration was sympathetic to Lebanon's request for help in quelling a UAR uprising. Eisenhower dispatched marines to the little country at the east end of the Mediterranean; they withdrew in the fall. The real trouble at the time was in Iraq, where a rebellion in July, 1958, overthrew the pro-Western government. The new government withdrew from the Baghdad Pact but failed to join the UAR, as it was expected to do. The United States was the prime mover in 1959 in remodeling the Baghdad Pact into the Central Treaty Organization (CENTO), composed of the former Baghdad Pact members, excepting Iraq and including the United States.

The Eisenhower administration was unable to do more than maintain the American foothold in the Middle East and failed to resolve the basic conflicts, but perhaps the situation was too complex to permit a more permanent solution to the problems. The Israeli-Arab conflict, the ambitions of the Soviet Union and the Egyptian nationalists, the economic interests of American and other western oil companies, semifeudal governments and land systems, and some of the world's worst mass poverty still combine to make the Middle East a powder keg. A further difficulty was sharply divided opinion within the United States about Israel and the Arab nations. American oil companies with Middle Eastern investments wanted to maintain harmony with the Arabs; American Zionists, concentrated in states with big electoral college votes, strongly resented pro-Arab policies.

During Eisenhower's second term, Russian-American relations continued to stumble along from crisis to crisis, neither side retreating significantly from any of its positions but neither side willing to take a major risk that might set off a mutually destructive war. A "balance of terror" kept the peace, or at least the absence of war, but nothing changed fundamentally.

Clearly, the United States gained a new measure of respect for Soviet technology after the Russians put Sputnik I into the skies. The complacent assumption that American science and technology was and always would be the best in the world all but disappeared; indeed, many Americans became frantic in their talk of "crash programs" for science education. As a practical and immediate countermeasure to Soviet intercontinental rockets, Eisenhower persuaded the heads of the NATO powers at the December, 1957, meeting in Paris to agree to an arrangement whereby the United States would give intermediate range missiles to any NATO country that asked for them. (Eisenhower had suffered a mild stroke on November 25, 1957, but recovered sufficiently to attend the Paris meeting the next month.) At the same time, however, America's allies urged continued negotiation with the Russians to prevent the arms race from going on indefinitely.

Also in December, 1957, Bulganin and Eisenhower began an exchange of letters in which the Russian urged a nonaggression pact between East and West, a prohibition of nuclear testing, an agreement not to use nuclear weapons, and the establishment of a zone in central Europe in which nuclear weapons would be banned. But neither side would give an inch, and the correspondence ended with no result. Independently, however, both sides ended nuclear testing, which had produced enough radioactive fallout in the world to cause justifiable anxiety about health and genetic mutation. Khrushchev announced in the spring of 1958, after Russian scientists had apparently decided that further testing was at least for the moment of no great advantage, that his nation was stopping further bomb tests. Eisenhower announced that American tests would end for a year on October 31. Thereafter, Eisenhower extended the test ban annually. Meanwhile, Russian and American negotiators met in Switzerland for years of fruitless efforts to arrive at a mutually agreeable treaty to prohibit nuclear testing.

Khrushchev dropped a bomb shell at a press conference in Moscow in November, 1958, when he announced that the status of Berlin was out of date. He soon thereafter announced a six-month deadline, after which West Berlin would become a "free city." He would negotiate a separate peace treaty with East Germany and turn over to the East Germans control of East Berlin and access to West Berlin. This threat had the effect of more tightly uniting the West rather than dividing it, as Khrushchev had hoped, and Khrushchev became more conciliatory. He began to urge another summit meeting. Eisenhower consented at first only to a meeting of foreign ministers at Geneva. Secretary of State Christian Herter, who succeeded Dulles when the older man resigned in April, 1959, because he was fatally ill, was unable to achieve anything concrete at the Geneva meetings, but still pressure for a summit meeting grew.

Soviet Deputy Premier Anastas Mikoyan visited the United States in January, 1959; Vice-President Richard Nixon reciprocated with a visit to the Soviet Union in July. While conducting Khrushchev through the American industrial exhibit at Moscow, Nixon engaged the premier in a hot debate over the merits of communism or capitalism. In August, Eisenhower and Khrushchev announced plans for an exchange of visits, Khrushchev to visit America the following month and Eisenhower to visit Russia in 1960.

Khrushchev's thirteen-day American visit was a mixture of earnest but unsuccessful personal diplomacy, incredible press coverage, and low comedy. The visit ended with Khrushchev's staying for two days with Eisenhower at the President's retreat near Washington, Camp David. They discussed disarmament and Berlin but came to no agreements. Khrushchev dismissed any deadline for a Berlin settlement but asserted that the problem could not be left as it was indefinitely.

The face-to-face meeting of the President and the premier eased the way to another summit meeting which Prime Minister Harold Macmillan of Great Britain had long been urging. (Macmillan had succeeded Eden who retired in disgrace soon after the Suez affair.) President De Gaulle of France resisted a summit conference, but after many preliminary talks among the Western powers, the diplomats arranged for a conference at Paris in mid-May, 1960. Meanwhile, both Eisenhower and Khrushchev tried to advance their nations' interests in Asia by personal visits. Khrushchev visited India and Indonesia. Eisenhower had tremendous receptions in the Middle East and India.

Although both Khrushchev and Eisenhower went to Paris, the summit meeting never actually took place. On May 1, 1960, the Russians downed an American reconnaisance plane, the U-2, about a thousand miles within the Soviet border and captured the pilot alive. The resulting confusion would have been humorous if it had not been so dangerous. Khrushchev made the first announcement on May 5 and offered no details. Washington announced that a weather plane was missing and that it might have strayed over the Soviet border. Two days later Khrushchev told more: the pilot, Francis Gary Powers, was alive, had confessed to espionage, and had related that he began his flight in Pakistan and planned to end it in Norway. The State Department, seeing that its first story's falsity was transparent, announced that American planes had been flying over Russia but that Washington had not authorized this particular flight. Western capitals wanted to know what kind of government the United States had if the President was not aware of such a flight only days before a scheduled summit conference. Washington changed its story again. Now it reported to the press that Eisenhower had known of the Powers flight. Such fumbling did not reassure America's allies, and the flight itself was poor preparation for an international conference intended to relax cold war tensions.

At the opening meeting of the conference on May 16, Khrushchev ranted against the United States and the U-2 flight, demanded that the American government punish those responsible for the flight, rescinded the invitation for Eisenhower to visit his country, and demanded that Eisenhower apologize for the "deliberate violation of the Soviet Union." Eisenhower refused to apologize. Khrushchev refused to attend further conference meetings. The conference broke up without achieving anything but bad feelings. On his way home, Khrushchev in an East German speech seemed to retreat when he said that he believed Eisenhower still wanted peace. Perhaps Khrushchev belatedly recognized that he had overplayed his hand at Paris. When the conference began, Eisenhower had been the object of European criticism because of the U-2 flight; when it ended, the Russian premier's bumptious rudeness had turned sentiment against him.

A few weeks later the Soviets tried and convicted Pilot Powers of espionage. He served almost two years in a Russian prison. In February, 1962, to the world's surprise, Moscow and Washington traded spy prisoners, the Russians returning Powers and the Americans returning Colonel Rudolf Abel, who had been convicted of conventional espionage in New York in 1957.

After the Paris fiasco Eisenhower resumed his world travels. He visited the Philippines and South Korea, where Syngman Rhee had recently been overthrown. His visit to Japan, however, had to be canceled because of intense anti-American demonstrations instigated by Communists against the new Japanese-American security treaty to replace the one signed in 1951.

While Americans were warming up to another presidential election in the fall of 1960, the United Nations was the scene of a sort of informal summit meeting. The heads of state of many of the world's powers attended the opening of the Fifteenth General Assembly. Again Khrushchev's exuberant bad manners served to strengthen the United States, at least among its allies. He heckled other speakers and at one point even took off a shoe and used it to pound on his desk. His attacks on UN Secretary General Dag Hammarskjold attracted no new supporters. Quite obviously, whatever his vagaries, Khrushchev realized that the United States had in effect a lame duck administration and that he must await the new administration before beginning a new tack in the cold war.

CHAPTER TWENTY-SEVEN

Troubled Affluence

IF A PROPHET IN THE GRIMMEST YEARS OF THE GREAT DEPRESSION HAD predicted that within a generation the United States would be enjoying the greatest prosperity it had ever known and still be concerned about its economy, he would have been called mad. However, since the war the United States has basked in its greatest and most sustained period of prosperity; yet all has not been perfect in the economy. Economic problems since the war have been different from prewar economic problems, but they have been no less real.

The New Prosperity: How Affluent, How Stable?

In 1940, the population of the United States was about 136,500,000 and the gross national product, measured in 1959 dollars, was about $229 billion; in 1960, the population was about 180,000,000 and the gross national product, measured by the same standard, was about $500 billion. The increase in the GNP was considerably greater than the population increases. In other words, many more goods and services were available to the mythical average person in 1960 than there were in 1940. The pie had more than doubled in size while the number of people to share it had increased by only a little less than one-third. Further, as Table 11 indicates, the growth of the GNP had been fairly stable; when there was a downswing a good surge upward followed.

Statistics can become puzzling, but they are necessary in any discussion of economic matters. The statistics of prosperity were impressive. In 1940, the United States produced just under 67,000,000 tons of steel; in 1959, the figure was 93,446,000. During the same period, primary aluminum production grew

TABLE 11

	GNP in Billions of 1959 Dollars	Output per Man-Hour 1947=100
1940	229	82
1944	353	101
1945	349	105
1946	314	100
1947	314	100
1948	326	103
1949	325	108
1950	353	116
1951	380	119
1952	393	121
1953	410	126
1954	403	129
1955	436	134
1956	447	134
1957	453	138
1958	437	141
1959	480	146
1960	500	150

from 206,280 to 1,953,017 tons. Oil production almost doubled. Passenger car production in 1940 had been 3,700,000; it was 5,900,000 in 1959. In the peak auto year of 1955 it had been 7,920,186. In 1956, there were 315 passenger cars in the United States for every thousand people. Literally, the whole nation could get into its cars at one time, and in some traffic jams a reasonable man might be persuaded that it had. By the end of the 1950's, roughly one-fifth of all American families owned more than one car; at the beginning of the decade about one-tenth had. People spent more for housing and house furnishings. In 1940, they spent $51 billion and in 1959, $83.8 billion (both figures are in 1959 dollars).

Prosperity was the subjective impression as well. Foreign visitors remarked that the United States seemed more prosperous each time they came to its shores. They saw more cars on the road, people better dressed, and families better housed. Most families could look back upon the immediate pre-war or immediate postwar years and feel that they had improved themselves materially. And they had. Most of them had money in their pockets and a full stomach. Indeed, overweight was a common problem. It is valid to generalize that never before had such a large part of a national society been blessed with such an abundance of material things.

However, prosperity had not created a heaven on earth or in the United States—not even an economic one. Two basic problems persisted: distribution of income and stability of the economy. Some distribution figures illustrate what is meant. In 1935–1936 the average income of the bottom one-fifth of the families was only $607, measured in 1950 dollars. By 1950 the average family income of this group had risen to $1,080, an increase of 78 per cent. The next-to-bottom one-fifth had bettered themselves by 81 per cent, from $1,349 to $2,444. This was an obvious and most welcome improvement. Yet anyone who tried to maintain a family in 1950 on $1,080 or even $2,444 knew that it was extremely difficult to do. The Bureau of Labor Statistics in 1950 calculated that a family income of $3,717 was necessary to maintain a family of four on a "modest but adequate" budget.

In 1935–1936, this poorest one-fifth of the families had received just 4.1 per cent of the total family income, and the richest one-fifth had received 51.7 per cent. In 1950, the percentages stood at 4.8 and 45.7 respectively, and by 1958 they were 4.7 and 45.5. The distribution of personal income had actually changed very little. In other words, the improvement in the living standard of the poorest one-fifth came about because total income increased tremendously rather than because they got a significantly larger share of this total.

If figures were available to show the distribution of wages and salaries, they would show a more equitable distribution than do personal income figures. This is because stock and bond ownership was concentrated in the upper income group. A survey by the National Bureau of Economic Research, based upon an examination of estate tax returns, showed that the richest 1.6 per cent of the nation's population which held 30 per cent of the personal wealth, "owned at least 80 per cent of the corporate stock held in the personal sector, virtually all of the state and local government bonds and between 10 and 35 per cent of each other type of property."

Furthermore, personal income was not regionally well distributed. In 1959, the per capita personal income of the entire United States (total of personal income divided by population) was $2,166. In other words, the mythical average American family received that amount for each family member. State figures showed a great diversity: Connecticut, $2,817; California, $2,661; New York, $2,736; South Dakota, $1,476; Mississippi, $1,162. Examination of a time series of these statistics shows that, although the South was behind the rest of the country, its rate of growth was faster than elsewhere. But then the South had farther to go.

A breakdown of per capita personal income by counties would show considerably greater divergence than the state figures. Poor rural areas were a persistent problem. In 1960, more than 60 per cent of the rural families in the Mississippi clay hills received less than $2,000. The situation was also bad in northeast Texas, the Missouri Ozarks, and north central New Mexico. Certain industrial areas were plagued with persistent depression, all the more frustrating with the industrial prosperity so much in evidence elsewhere. The coal industry was even more depressed after 1945 than it had been in the period between the wars, and since so much coal production was in one-commodity communities unemployed miners had little opportunity at home to find work. Coal communities in Pennsylvania and West Virginia were on every dreary list of depressed areas. Towns heavily dependent upon railroading were similarly in a bad way as airplanes, cars, and trucks increasingly took business away from the once high and mighty rail companies. New England textile communities suffered as the long-term movement of the industry to the South continued.

Even when the economy as a whole boomed it seemed unable to provide full employment. In July, 1961, a time when the economy was booming and expanding, 5,140,000 American workers were unemployed. They constituted 6.9 per cent of the labor force, a staggering percentage for a prospering economy. In 1929 the unemployed had constituted only 3.1 per cent of the working force. The nature of unemployment was particularly disturbing. Labor shortages existed in many skilled occupations. The unemployed were, for the most part, the unskilled and untrained. Unskilled workers constituted only 6 per cent of the labor force, but they accounted for one-fifth of the 1,026,000 workers who had been out of work for six or more months in July, 1961. Nonwhites constituted 11 per cent of the total number of workers, but they were 25 per cent of the long-term unemployed. One-fifth of those out of work for six or more months were under twenty-five years old—mostly people who had dropped out of school and were unprepared for any kind of skilled labor. The future for these young people was not encouraging.

Yet, despite persistent unemployment, the postwar years saw a change in the composition of the American poor. Families headed by a person sixty-five years old or older in 1954 accounted for 64 per cent of all the families with incomes of less than $2,000. Most of the aged had low incomes: in 1960, 67.8 per cent of the individuals over sixty-five had incomes of less than $1,000 and 94.3 per cent of them received less than $3,000. Since the number of aged was expected to increase, there was a cause for concern. True, the aged usually had smaller family units, had double personal income tax exemptions, and frequently had savings in the form of paid-for housing and furnishings. But they also had relatively inflexible incomes in the face of steadily increasing living costs, and they generally had higher medical bills than younger adults.

Nor was the economy as stable as one would wish. There was no postwar depression approaching anything like the magnitude of the ones in 1893, 1907, or 1929 and after, but there were three disturbing recessions: 1948–1949, 1953–1954, and 1957–1958. Furthermore, the economic cycles were becoming shorter but no less severe. Although economic growth over periods as long as a decade was heartening, still individuals made most economic decisions in the short run.

Thinking people of all ideological persuasions were also concerned by the degree to which prosperity depended upon government spending or the nature of that spending. Since the war, the federal, state, and local governments have purchased roughly one-fifth of the gross national product each year. Roughly one-tenth of the national product has been armament. What if real peace and disarmament should come? In the highly unlikely event that the federal government would cut back its defense spending to zero within a year, the effect upon the economy would be cataclysmic, just as it would be if any other one-tenth of total spending should suddenly cease. Of course, if the federal government compensated for a reduction of payments for armament by an increase in spending for other purposes there would be only a temporary readjustment. But the political possibilities of spending $55 million more a year for roads, hospitals, schools, and other conventional areas of public spending is a moot point. Furthermore, schools do not become obsolete as quickly as rockets.

Despite sticky economic problems, the national mood was optimistic. Professional economists in general shared the optimism, although they protected themselves with guarded statements. Their argument was that economists and politicians had learned enough about how a capitalist economy functions to take effective compensatory counter action to prevent violent fluctuations of the business cycle. They also emphasized the "built-in stabilizers," such as unemployment compensation. Indeed, unemployment compensation plus privately negotiated arrangements between employers and unions had made a considerable difference.

President Walter Reuther of the United Auto Workers in the early 1950's began to demand a "guaranteed annual wage" from the auto companies. They did not consent, but the 1955 contract between the UAW and the Ford Motor Company broke new ground with supplementary unemployment benefits (SUB). The company agreed to put five cents an hour into a trust fund for each worker to be used to supplement state unemployment benefits during layoffs. Several other labor contracts adopted the Ford-UAW scheme. The 1957–1958 recession first put the SUB scheme to work on a significant scale. Donora, Pennsylvania, an industrial town of a little over twelve thousand population, had a zinc plant operated by the United States Steel Company that closed during the recession throwing 460 wage employees completely out of work. Others were on short hours. Such a percentage of idle workers normally would badly depress a town's economy, but Donora bankers reported that mortgage payments continued to be met and merchants disclosed that installment purchase loans were paid. SUB provided the unemployed from $15 to $25 a week on top of the state unemployment compensation checks which averaged $30 a week. The unemployed worker's income was nothing spectacular, but it was enough to keep him going temporarily and to keep the town's whole economy from the danger of collapse. SUB and state unemployment compensation had put a significant brake on the downward spiral that characterized the early years of the Great Depression.

Whether there were enough such stabilizers and whether government action would be compensatory enough in a severe recession was uncertain. All that was certain in the 1950's was that people did not want to think of the possibility of a depression. When Senator Homer Capehart, conservative Republican of Indiana, proposed to give the president "stand-by" controls to combat recessions, he aroused little enthusiasm in Congress, particularly in his own party. If the economists were right, a severe depression *could* be prevented; the question remained whether one *would* be.

The Supercorporations

Consternation was the general reaction when J. P. Morgan founded the United States Steel Company in 1901, the first American corporation with a capitalization of as much as $1 billion. In the 1950's, billion-dollar corporations became commonplace. The number of corporations with assets of $1 billion or more increased from twelve to twenty-seven during the decade. To become one of the hundred largest American corporations in 1949, a company had to have assets of $141 million. By 1960 such assets would place a firm only among secondary big businesses: the hundredth largest had assets of $378 million. Indeed, in 1955, the General Motors Corporation made a profit of over $1 billion on sales amounting to about $12.5 billion. The early United States Steel Company was a dwarf by comparison. In 1959, the American Telephone and Telegraph Company joined the select circle of firms who made more than $1 billion in a single year.

In the 1950's, huge corporate giants dominated almost every area of business. There were 325,000 manufacturing companies in the United States in 1955, but the fifty largest ones accounted for 27 per cent of all manufacturers' sales. The fifty biggest corporations in all fields that year had sales of $86 billion, more than one-fourth of the gross national product. General Motors alone had sales equal to 3 per cent of the GNP. The fifty largest insurance companies had 90 per cent of the assets of all insurance companies. The "Money Trust" exposed by the Pujo Committee was poverty stricken compared to some banks in the late 1950's. In 1956, there were about 14,000 banks in the country, but the real banking power lay with the 24 banks that had assets of more than $1 billion. The Bank of America in California had resources of over $9 billion and was becoming bigger all the time.

Concentration was the general rule and it was increasing. The Federal Trade Commission reported 617 mergers in 1954, 846 in 1955, and 905 in 1956. In 1958, 812 companies absorbed 1,116 other business units, and the next year 985 firms acquired 1,480 other business entities. In New York and California bank mergers were spectacular. In 1950, California had 149 separate banking firms (as compared with over 600 in economically less important Kansas), but by the end of 1955 mergers and consolidations had removed all but 63 of them. More than 60 per cent of the California banks lost their identity. It became almost routine for big companies to buy up smaller ones. In 1959 alone, 42 per cent of all American corporations in the $100 million class absorbed at least one other corporation.

Holding company pyramids came back into style. They were not as top heavy as the Insull and Van Sweringen empires of the 1920's, but they were wider in their diversity of interests. For example, a former investment banker named Gurdon W. Wattles was the key figure in building a holding company pyramid that skipped across industries. His top firms, Century Investors and Webster Investors, originally in the aircraft and cigar business respectively, controlled American Manufacturing Co., Inc., which in turn controlled the Mergenthaler Linotype Company by owning 25.5 per cent of its stock, which in turn controlled the Electric Auto-Lite Company by owning 11.2 per cent of its stock, which in turn controlled a plumbing supplies firm, the Crane Company, by owning 9.5 per cent of its stock. Every dollar invested in the two top holding companies controlled $26 to $53 in assets in the two lowest companies of the pyramid. Another pyramid, headed by the New York Dock Company, controlled firms in the cosmetics, tobacco, engraving, and sports equipment fields. Pyramids like these hardly integrated production and distribution.

But if the public was aware of the merger trend and the increased strength of the largest corporations, it did not seem to care. News on the financial page did not create more than a ripple of interest unless it concerned a company with which the public had a first-hand acquaintance (e.g., the merger of the Packard and Studebaker automobile companies in 1954 and the decision four years later to stop producing the Packard and the proposed merger of the two largest eastern railroads, the New York Central and the Pennsylvania). Bigness as such in American business aroused practically no popular opposition.

Only when the power of large corporations or combinations of them appeared to be used brazenly against the public interest did the citizen seem concerned. And then the abuse of power had to be dramatic. Senator Estes Kefauver, chairman of the Senate Judiciary Committee's Subcommittee on Antitrust and Monopoly, brought forth hundreds of pages of testimony that pointed up the degree to which price competition was a thing of the past. Kefauver was particularly concerned about the distribution of gains from increased productivity of labor. He pointed out that in the steel industry, for example, there was an average annual increase in productivity of from 3.5 to 4 per cent. Ten years ago the amount of steel it took a hundred men to produce could now be made by only sixty-eight workers. To whom should the benefits accrue? Kefauver argued that the consumer should receive part of the advantages through lower prices, that the benefits should not be divided only between management and labor through their own private haggling. But only when the Senator brought forth evidence of fantastic profits in the drug industry, ranging to as high as 1,000 per cent on a few items, did he attract much attention.

Perhaps it was indicative of the postwar American mood that sociological criticisms of the big business community evoked much more public interest than did the economic activities of corporations. One of the best sellers of the 1950's was William H. Whyte's *The Organization Man*. Whyte, a staff man on *Fortune* magazine, was highly critical of big business bureaucracy not on economic grounds but because it smothered individuality by benevolently demanding and getting a kind of conformity of individuals that he and others found debasing. Whyte's "solution" was one for individuals: they should resist The Organization from within its own confines. His book even included an appendix entitled "How to Cheat on Personality Tests." His most radical advice was that bureaucracies should try not to act like bureaucracies, a far cry from early twentieth-century demands that huge aggregations of capital and power be shattered.

Postwar Business and Government

Despite public sentiment, the antitrust laws were still on the books, and the postwar years saw two spectacular government antitrust actions: one against the DuPont Company's link with General Motors and the other against a conspiracy in restraint of trade by a group of electrical equipment manufacturers.

In 1949, the Truman administration began a suit to force a DuPont–General Motors divorce. DuPont owned 63,000,000 shares of General Motors stock, about 23 per cent of the total. In 1957, the Supreme Court ruled that the effect of this stock ownership could be "substantially to lessen competition or to tend to create a monopoly." The stock ownership, therefore, constituted a violation of the Clayton Act. The question remained, however, of how to separate the two. DuPont lawyers argued that it would be sufficient if DuPont merely denied itself the right to vote the stock. A Chicago federal district judge ruled that the law would be satisfied if DuPont kept the stock and allowed DuPont stockholders to vote it individually. The Department of Justice objected, and in May, 1960, the Supreme Court accepted the case. A year later the Court ruled that within sixty days DuPont would have to submit a plan to get rid of its General Motors stock, that the plan must be put into operation within ninety days, and that within ten years all connection must be dissolved. The problem then was how to put about $3 billion worth of General Motors stock onto the market without depressing its price and harming other investors.

In February, 1960, the Department of Justice obtained a criminal indictment from a Philadelphia grand jury against General Electric, Westinghouse, Allis-Chalmers, and some smaller electrical companies. The indictment charged the companies with conspiring to rig secret bidding. Company executives, said the indictment, met periodically to divide the market, to determine who would bid low on a given invitation for bids, and to raise prices simultaneously. On sales to privately owned utilities and to manufacturers, the government charged the defendants with working under a formula under which the corporations took turns in submitting the low bids according to "the phase of the moon." The companies subsequently pleaded *nolo contendere* which meant that they did not admit guilt but would accept the court's punishment as if they were guilty. A few corporation executives actually served short jail sentences, and the judge levied stiff fines against the offenders. Furthermore, the companies were liable to further suits from buyers who had been the victims of bidding conspiracy.

Antitrust suits, however, were out of the ordinary. Far more common were government actions to stimulate business, even to stimulate mergers. Corporation tax laws directly encouraged financially successful corporations to acquire less fortunate firms. If Corporation A had a large bill it would look favorably upon uniting with Corporation B which had a large tax credit. Many corporations with large tax credits among their assets actually went looking for companies seeking to reduce their tax bills. What business writers called "the urge to merge" was in no small part prompted by tax considerations.

Department of Defense contracts were a mighty boon to businesses, particularly to big ones who received the lion's share of defense largesse. And the Department of Defense spent the lion's share of federal expenditures. Of a total of $77,230,000,000 for government expenditures for fiscal 1960 (ending June 30, 1960), the Department of Defense accounted for $43.7 billion. Over $14 billion of this defense expenditure went for procurement of military and naval hardware; this was a market that American corporations were eager to tap.

The Pentagon was a vast bureaucracy with complicated procedures that puzzled ordinary businessmen, but knowledge of these procedures was a great advantage in getting defense contracts. Consequently, manufacturers of products that the Pentagon was likely to want hired people with experience in the Department of Defense. Many of these people were retired generals and admirals. Negotiated contracts for orders were a target of economy-minded congressional committees. Time and again committees found that the price for some small item in a negotiated contract could have been significantly lower if it had been purchased through a system of multiple bids. A few firms were almost fully dependent upon defense contracts for their livelihood. The importance of one of these, the General Dynamics Corporation, was well illustrated in a *Fortune* magazine article appropriately entitled, "General Dynamics vs. the U.S.S.R."

During the 1950's several federal regulatory agencies displayed a most sympathetic attitude toward the companies they were established to regulate. In early 1960, the House Special Subcommittee on Legislative Oversight looked into the operations of the Federal Power Commission. In questioning the chairman of the FPC, the committee's counsel elicited the information that the FPC had granted "temporary" increases in gas rates amounting to $506 million. If after investigation the FPC found that the increase in rates was not justified, the utility was to reimburse its customers, but the utility was not required to segregate the revenues gained by the "temporary" increase. Sometimes as long as six years expired before the FPC made a permanent decision. In one case, that of the Colorado Interstate Gas Company, the FPC ruled that the utility should refund $50 million to its customers, but when the company argued that to do so would mean financial disaster, the FPC lowered the refund by $12 million. (Among the witnesses, incidentally, was a figure from the past, the New Dealer Thomas G. "Tommy the Cork" Corcoran, who was then an attorney representing utilities before the FPC.)

The Eisenhower administration seemed to support the FPC's generous policies when the President refused to reappoint William R. Connole to the commission. Connole had won the reputation as the FPC's chief defender of consumer interests; Eisenhower replaced him with a man who confessed to reporters, "I've never had anything to do with utilities outside of paying my gas bill." The President's press secretary announced that Connole's release was part of a new administration policy. It had been the practice to appoint FPC members who represented different interests. Connole had favored the consumer, and three others were considered sympathetic to the utilities. Under the new policy, appointments would be made on the basis of ability rather than on interest or sympathy. *Time* magazine, which was certainly not antagonistic to business, commented, "Presumably, to make everything fair and square, the holdovers . . . are expected to forget the grounds on which they were appointed."

One of the greatest of the federal government's services to business—and one that had enormous implications for the nation's foreign relations—was the help it gave business in overseas operations and investments. The 1950's saw the greatest growth in history in American industry's investment abroad. Industry's direct investment abroad in 1950 was about $10 billion; in 1960 it was about $30 billion. Furthermore, in the last years of the 1950's, overseas investment grew at a rate of $2 billion annually. In 1960, roughly 2,800 American firms reported to the Department of Commerce that they had direct investments abroad in more than ten thousand different enterprises. Forty-five companies, about a third of them in oil, had more than half of their assets invested abroad.

How these industrial foreign investments were distributed was of more than passing interest. The largest investments in 1960, were in Canada, amounting to $10.2 billion. Next was Latin America with $8.2 billion. Venezuela was the scene of half of all American industrial investment in Latin America, mostly in oil. European investments amounted to $5.3 billion and were fairly well diversified. Middle Eastern and Asian investments totalled $2.2 billion, again mostly in oil. African investments were relatively small, only $843 million. All other areas accounted for $3 billion.

Federal policies in many ways encouraged industry to invest abroad. Tax laws made foreign investment advantageous. Although earnings by American-owned corporations abroad were liable to taxation by the host country, they were not taxable by the United States unless and until the earnings were brought home. Some countries were virtual tax havens; many of them had lower corporate income tax rates than the United States. A corporation, furthermore, could take its earnings in one foreign nation and either use them for further expansion in that country or use them in still another foreign country. If the American parent company needed to bring the money home, it had the alternative of folding up the foreign operation and paying the lower capital gains tax rather than the corporate income tax.

Some American corporations were anxious about investing in nations with an unstable political situation for fear that their investment might be expropriated or that their assets might be frozen and thereby become unavailable to the parent firm. In 1948, the new International Cooperation Administration quietly began to allay American investors' fears by offering insurance against such possibilities. The cost to the companies was one-half of 1 per cent of the amount of protection stated in the contract. For example, in 1956, the Ford Motor Company arranged to purchase 222,269 shares of stock in a French automobile firm, Simca. It also took an insurance policy with ICA under which, if the French government refused to allow Ford to convert its Simca assets, Ford could recover from ICA up to $6,987,310. The policy also guaranteed Ford up to almost $3.5 million against expropriation. Among the holders of the biggest policies against expropriation was Edwin W. Pauley, for oil exploration in Jordan. It was Pauley's proposed appointment as Undersecretary of the Navy in 1946 that had prompted Harold Ickes' resignation from the cabinet.

The Export-Import Bank increased the sales of American products abroad by lending foreign nations funds to purchase American products. Ex-Im's lending capacity increased from its original $11 million to $7 billion by 1960. Early in the Eisenhower administration, Secretary of the Treasury George Humphrey tried to shut down Ex-Im, arguing that the government should not be in the banking business. But when he came to see that Ex-Im loans were a considerable aid to American industry and that the default rate on the loans was less than 1 per cent, Humphrey helped Ex-Im to expand its operations. In 1959 alone, Ex-Im lent $535.9 million. It became the primary United States lending institution to Latin America.

In 1959 and 1960, the federal government began to become concerned about its deteriorating position in the international balance of payments. For years and years American exports had been greater than imports, but throughout the 1950's American payments abroad exceeded foreign payments in the

United States. The United States advantage of exports over imports was more than lost by foreign aid programs, maintenance of American troops abroad, American tourists spending abroad, and corporate foreign investments. Foreign nations took part of their net gain in gold and a larger part in the form of dollar deposits in New York banks. By 1960 those dollar deposits had reached the point where they almost equalled the remaining United States gold supply.

The United States had several alternatives or combinations of alternatives. What it did was to cut back dollar spending abroad by cutting the duty-free imports that American tourists could bring into the country and reduce the number of families allowed to be with their overseas servicemen husband-fathers. Reducing the dollar gap by separating servicemen's families produced a great political outcry, and one of the first actions in the administration of President John F. Kennedy was to rescind the order. The government also made an effort to increase foreign spending in the United States by a campaign to increase the numbers of foreign tourists in this country and, more important, to widen the gap of American exports over imports.

The Departments of State and Commerce announced plans to double the number of their personnel engaged in the promotion of American exports. The State Department would increase to 225 the number of commercial attachés abroad whose function primarily was to develop the United States export business. The Commerce Department would put a greater effort on informing American firms of export possibilities. Ex-Im was authorized to grant short-term loans to exporters. When exporters went to private banks to arrange credit for a foreign sale they frequently found bankers unwilling to run the risk of possible foreign currency revaluation or nationalization. American manufacturers, therefore, urged foreign customers to arrange their own financing. West Germany and Great Britain granted purchasers of their exports better credit terms than the foreign purchaser could get from his bank where he was often forced to go to finance an American purchase. Now the Export-Import Bank would provide short-term financing in order to increase American exports and thereby help correct the international balance of payments.

Through such devices as these the government of the United States stimulated American business abroad. By the end of the 1950's, Americans who went abroad noticed that they could purchase many of the same brands they bought at home. Foreign grocery stores were stocked with American corn flakes and soap, and Coca-Cola was almost as ubiquitous abroad as it was in America. More and more American corporations that had traditionally done most of their business at home devoted a greater part of their efforts to foreign operations. In 1949, the foreign subsidiaries of the Colgate Palmolive Company had sales of $86,963,000; the parent company's home sales amounted to $203,996,000. In 1958, the sales of the foreign subsidiaries had gone up to $262,725,000; the domestic sales had increased only to $271,322,000.

The trend to international operations was nothing new; it only became greatly accelerated after World War II. Just as the period after the Civil War had been one in which American business became national in scope, in the mid-twentieth century business was becoming increasingly international—and bigger.

Unions in Postwar America

In the 1930's and early 1940's, trade unionism in the United States came into its own. It was a period of unparalleled union growth both in numbers and in economic and political strength. It was also, however, a fighting time and a lean time. Unions became strong through almost constant exercise. They won their power; it was not given to them. The life of most labor officials was a hard one. Dedicated to the vision of a labor force that would not have to wear the employer's collar, labor officials often exposed themselves to physical danger, were economically insecure, and had much the same living standard as the shop workers they organized.

A visit to AFL-CIO headquarters in Washington in the late 1950's indicated a fatter, more comfortable labor movement than there had been before the war. There was nothing about the building itself, a sleek, modern affair, to distinguish it from any other office building except the sign over the door. The building's elevators had piped-in music. Nor was there much to distinguish the offices and their inhabitants from any other business office. The personnel could as well have been selling soap or editing a magazine. If the accepted symbols of power and affluence were a valid guide, the American labor movement had fully arrived.

But there was a paradox: without shifting its goals or its methods, American unionism had both become important and begun to stagnate. It was stable and comfortable in the industries it had organized in the earlier era, but it did not expand into other fields.

Most of American union growth had come about while the AFL and the CIO were at one another's throats. By a few years after the war, the issues that had once divided the two big labor groups had largely disappeared. The birth of the CIO had ended the supine complacency that had once characterized the AFL; industrial unionism versus craft organization had become an outdated issue; most of the leadership in both camps had come around to the dominant CIO view that labor's political fortunes resided with the Democratic party. The deaths of Philip Murray and William Green in November, 1952, removed a great deal of the personality conflict that had brought about the division, and the two houses of labor began to come together.

The new head of the CIO, Walter Reuther of the United Auto Workers, and the new head of the AFL, George Meany of the plumber's union, began to work to bring about a reunion. They set up committees to work out differences. The toughest problem was raiding of one another's membership. A joint AFL and CIO committee recommended approval of a no-raiding pact which forbade attempts to sign up workers in a shop already in a union that was recognized or certified as the bargaining agent. Where disputes arose, both unions would agree to accept the decision of an impartial umpire. In the fall of 1953, the AFL and CIO conventions ratified the no-raiding agreement; it became effective in mid-1954.

Almost immediately Reuther and Meany moved on toward full reunion. In February, 1955, a joint committee agreed upon terms of a merger. At the end of the year both conventions voted for merger by overwhelming votes, and in December the American Federation of Labor–Congress of Industrial Organizations was born. The new organization had about 15,000,000 members, two-thirds of them from former AFL organizations.

Ever since World War II the ratio of union members to the total civilian labor force has remained about the same, about one to three. That is, roughly one-fourth of American workers have belonged to trade unions. In view of organized labor's unity, its bigger bank balances, and its general acceptance by employers in industries where it was well established, why did it not grow during an era of prosperity? The question involves most aspects of recent American labor history.

TABLE 12

UNION MEMBERSHIP, 1945–1958

Year	Union Membership	Civilian Labor Force	Percentage of Unionized Civilian Labor Force
1945	13,379,000	53,860,000	24.8
1946	13,648,000	57,520,000	23.7
1947	14,845,000	60,128,000	24.7
1948	14,916,000	61,442,000	24.3
1949	14,960,000	62,105,000	24.1
1950	14,751,000	63,099,000	23.4
1951	16,211,000	62,884,000	25.8
1952	16,730,000	62,966,000	26.6
1953	17,884,000	63,815,000	28.0
1954	17,757,000	64,468,000	25.7
1955	17,749,000	65,847,000	27.0
1956	18,477,000	67,530,000	27.4
1957	18,430,000	67,946,000	27.1
1958	18,081,000	68,647,000	26.3

From Irving Bernstein, "The Growth of American Unions, 1945–1960," Labor History, *II (Spring, 1961), 135.*

First, it is clear that organized labor's failure to grow significantly and relatively was not due to declining power in its established areas. Whatever employers wished (most of them were fairly well satisfied with unionized shops after they got used to them) union members were determined that their organizations would not be blasted to bits after World War II as they had been in the early 1920's. In the first four years of the Taft-Hartley Act, 1947–1951, unions won 97 per cent of the NLRB elections over the right to sign a union shop agreement. In the few cases (usually less than twenty a year and involving only small numbers of employees) over the issue of abolishing an already existing union shop, the unions won about one-third of the elections.

However, in many of the traditionally unionized industries, automation or further mechanization significantly reduced the total number of employees and thereby reduced trade union membership. Between 1940 and 1957 the percentage of the labor force in all manufacturing in the United States actually engaged in production dropped from 78.5 to 71.7. Due to increased productivity per man-hour, fewer and fewer Americans were engaged in actual production of any kind—manufacturing, mining, or agriculture. Unionism traditionally was for employees who worked with their hands, and the number of such people declined. In 1919, 61 per cent of all employees in nonagricultural employment were manual workers; in 1930 manual workers constituted 52 per cent, in 1950 the figure had fallen to 49 per cent and in 1959 to 45 per cent. In other words, blue collars were becoming increasingly scarce. The statistics in certain strongly unionized industries reveal the effects of increased productivity through technological advancement. From 1937 through 1960, steel production rose 171.7 per cent, but the number of steel workers engaged in production and maintenance declined 10 per cent. In 1937, 421,788 coal miners produced 445,000,000 tons; in 1960, 197,000 miners produced 410,000,000 tons. Daily output per miner increased from 4.69 tons in 1937 to almost 13 in 1961. Production of electrical machinery increased 21 per cent from 1953 to 1956, but the number of production workers in the industry declined from 925,000 to 836,000. The implications for trade unionism in these fields were obvious. Less obvious but no less real and prickly were the implications for full employment and a level of mass purchasing power consistent with economic health.

Political barriers were a handicap to labor's efforts to expand. Nineteen states, most of them primarily agricultural and without an important labor movement, adopted "right to work" laws barring union shops and prohibiting union membership as a requirement for employment. Other states so restricted picketing as to make successful striking difficult if the employer tried to run in strikebreakers. The Taft-Hartley Act and interpretations of it hampered union activity more than state law. The Wagner Act had prohibited employers from any kind of coercion of employees to keep them from joining a union or voting against a union in a National Labor Relations Board election, and the NLRB had interpreted the law quite strictly. The Taft-Hartley Act removed many of these restrictions, and the NLRB, particularly the members appointed by President Eisenhower, approved employer antiunion activities that would never have been sanctioned by the old board. The Eisenhower-appointed NLRB, for example, ruled that it was legal procedure for management to announce that if the union won an election the plant would be closed. Well-established unions suffered little from Taft-Hartley and NLRB decisions, but gaining a foothold in shops against the employers' wishes became extremely difficult.

Certainly a shift in public opinion about labor unions handicapped their continued growth. During the depression and the war, majority public opinion had been behind labor organization. Antiunion sentiment was based to a considerable extent on the belief that unions were too radical, too socialist or Communist. In 1949 and 1950 the CIO effectively removed Communist leadership from its unions, and ideological antiunion sentiment declined. But soon thereafter large parts of the public came to believe that labor organizations should be curbed either because they abused their power or because they were dominated by crooks or both. "Big labor" and "labor racketeers" became stereotypes with which responsible and honest unions had to contend.

Bad actors in the labor movement tarnished labor's general reputation even when the majority of labor, as represented by its national federations, condemned them. For example, in the winter of 1961–1962, the New York City unit of the International Brotherhood of Electrical Workers used its power in that city's construction industry, which was thriving, to wrest from employers a twenty-five hour week. Rather than a genuine demand for a shorter work week, the demand was only a ruse to get more overtime pay. Leaders of the AFL-CIO, powerless to overrule their constituent, publicly stated their opposition, but the newspaper editorials concentrated upon the grab rather than AFL-CIO opposition to it.

Gangsters and other crooks in a few unions gave all labor a black eye. In the early 1950's, the New York Crime Commission exposed the International Longshoremen's Association as dominated by racketeers who ruled the waterfront by terror. The AFL expelled the ILA and set up a new union for dockworkers, but in NLRB elections the workers three times rejected the new AFL unit in favor of the ILA. The International Brotherhood of Teamsters was a bigger headache. This huge union, the nation's biggest, dominated first by Dave Beck and then by Jimmy Hoffa, was atypical of the vast majority of American unions in its lack of internal democracy, its ties with disreputable figures from the underworld, and its leadership's affiliation with the Republican party. In February, 1957, the AFL-CIO adopted a code of ethical practices aimed largely at the Teamsters and in December of that year expelled them. But the public still seemed to think of all labor leaders as corrupt.

Agricultural Plenty and Farm Troubles

Bryanite agrarian orators used to make much of the argument that the cities were dependent upon agriculture for their well being, that the farmer could live without his urban cousin but the city-dweller could not live without the farmer. But by mid-century the story was different. The situation had not exactly reversed itself, but most urban food consumers were doing very well and most farmers were in trouble.

Prices in grocery stores shot up spectacularly with the end of price controls after the war, but the price curve began to level off in late 1947. After that, consumer food prices rose less than most other items in the cost-of-living index. Americans spent less of their income for food than ever before in their history. In 1959, they spent 21 per cent of their income on food, while the rest of the world spent approximately half of its income for its daily bread. And the people of the United States were eating better too— perhaps too much better judging from the number of "reducing studios" that dotted the country. In 1935, the per capita consumption of meat was 127 pounds, of poultry 16 pounds, and of dairy products 393 pounds; in 1959 the figures were 160, 35, and 428 pounds respectively. In 1959, an hour's work would buy seventeen pints of milk as compared to eight in 1929, three dozen oranges as opposed to fifteen, and a little over two pounds of round steak as compared with one pound four ounces.

But most of the farmers who kept this cornucopia filled to overflowing did not fare very well after the war. In 1959, the farm population's per capita income was only $965; nonfarm per capita income that year was $2,216. In 1945, farm mortgages totalled $4,940,915,000; the mortgage total in 1960 stood at $12,288,759,000. A special farm census in 1959 counted 3,700,000 farms in the United States. On an estimated 1,600,000 of them, gross sales were less than $10,000 a year, not enough to provide a net family income of $2,500.

With farm prices what they were, only very efficient farm units could return enough profit over the year to support a family adequately, and only big farm units were really efficient. In other words, the optimum farm unit's capital, both in land and in equipment, became steadily bigger. Barring a reversal of the long-term trend, over the long run those farmers whose production units were too far below the optimum size and capitalization to make ends meet had no alternative but to get out of agriculture. The flight from the farm, which had been going on for a long time, became almost a mass migration in the 1950's. The number of farms declined by a million from 1954 to 1959. An average of eight hundred thousand people a year left the farm in the 1950's. Total population during that decade increased by a fifth, but the farm population decreased by a fifth. In the three decades preceding 1959, more people left the farm than remained on the land. The greatest number of those leaving were young people who figured that their chances of economic comfort were better in the cities and towns than they were on the farm. The amount of capital necessary to begin farming was too great for young men who did not inherit already profitable farms. Even those who stayed on the land increasingly supplemented their farm incomes with non-farm work. In 1959, 30 per cent of all farm operators worked off the farm for one hundred days or more.

The central fact of the problem was the technological revolution on the farm. Consumers bought more food and fiber than they had only a few years previously and with a smaller fraction of their whole income, but these commodities had been produced by fewer farmers. Each farmer could feed more consumers. From 1937 to 1941, the average yield of wheat per acre was 14.5 bushels. In 1955 it was 19.8 bushels. In 1958, due mostly to the "nitrogen revolution" in fertilizing, yield per acre of wheat averaged 27 bushels nationally.

Society, as represented by the federal government, had two choices with the farm problem. In order not to subsidize inefficient production it could, at one extreme, leave agriculture to the vicissitudes of an absolutely free market and let the farm population shake itself down until only the large and efficient producers were left. The costs of the shaking-down process to those who would be omitted would be considerable. Or, if society sufficiently valued the continued existence of the family farm, it could vastly increase its agricultural subsidies and more intelligently direct them toward the family farm unit. The government's actual program involved spending billions of dollars (in 1960 about $9 billion), but is was not saving the family farm.

The government's wheat program, which took about a third of all agricultural subsidies, illustrated the problem. In 1954, the government set a maximum of 55,000,000 acres in wheat production, and wheat farmers voted to accept the government's program. But production increased because of the increased yields per acre, and the government each year bought an increased amount of wheat. Despite the Agricultural Domestic Trade and Development Assisstance Act of 1954, which provided for sales of wheat abroad in foreign currencies (many of which could not be converted to dollars) and for foreign gifts of wheat, the amount of government-owned wheat in storage grew steadily. The wheat was sealed in grain elevators and mothballed ships all over the country. In 1960, the government had 1,379,000,000 bushels of wheat in storage. The storage costs alone were about $1.5 million a day. (In 1960, one storage company, the C-F-G Grain Company, received government payments of $23,470,634.) The wheat surplus in 1960, if converted into bread, would have provided 450 one-pound loaves for every person in the nation. Yet thousands of wheat farmers were marginal and thousands of others left the farm altogether. Wheat subsidies saved many farmers from ruin, but they also helped many large and efficient producers.

Such large subsidies offered ripe opportunity for graft, and in 1962 the case of Billie Sol Estes, a west Texas agricultural plunger, focused national attention on the farm subsidy issue. Estes made his original big capital in the surplus wheat storage business and built a huge but flimsily constructed agricultural empire. His business fell to pieces when some of his creditors discovered that the liquid fertilizer tanks that he had put up as collateral for loans were mostly fictional. Investigations by a congressional committee and the Department of Agriculture revealed that Estes had bribed farmers to acquire their acreage allotments and had unethically influenced regional cotton allotment committee members for the same purpose. Estes went bankrupt and faced a series of criminal indictments. But the public, for the most part, saw the case only as an example of personal evil, rather than realizing that the nature of the whole farm subsidy system, given the usual state of mankind's morals, made such a case almost inevitable. With this general public view, the nature of the dominant farm organizations (which reflect the attitudes of the big and successful producers), and the political influence of the farm vote, a wise political solution of the farm problem seemed unlikely.

CHAPTER TWENTY-EIGHT

The American People and Their Culture

PERHAPS THE MOST SPECTACULAR ASPECT OF THE AMERICAN PEOPLE in the middle years of the century was their great and growing number. The 1940 census counted 131,669,275 people in the United States. The count in 1950 was 151,325,798, an increase of 14.5 per cent. The census of 1960 showed a population of 179,323,175, an increase of 18.5 per cent in the decade. (Many demographers, incidentally, calculate that census figures should be increased about 3 per cent.) The population increase between 1940 and 1960 was about equal to the total population of 1880.

Predictions about population often have been inaccurate, but experts predicted the population of the United States would continue to increase at a faster rate, topping two hundred million in 1970 and perhaps three hundred million by the beginning of the twenty-first century. Population prophets, who assumed continued prosperity, based their expectations upon the strong tendency of couples to marry younger than was usual before World War II, upon the trend toward more children in families in middle-income brackets, and upon a longer life expectancy.

As remarkable as the increased number of Americans was the mobility of all these people. In the late 1950's, according to some surveys, one-fifth of the population changed address each year. Quite obviously, some of the moves were long ones. Between 1950 and 1960 the population of the Pacific states increased 40.2 per cent and the Mountain states 35.1 per cent. Florida's growth was the greatest by percentage, 78.7, but California with an almost 50 per cent increase and a growth of over five million had the largest absolute population increase.

Census figures amply illustrated that the United States was an overwhelmingly urban nation. In 1960, about 111,700,000 Americans lived in areas

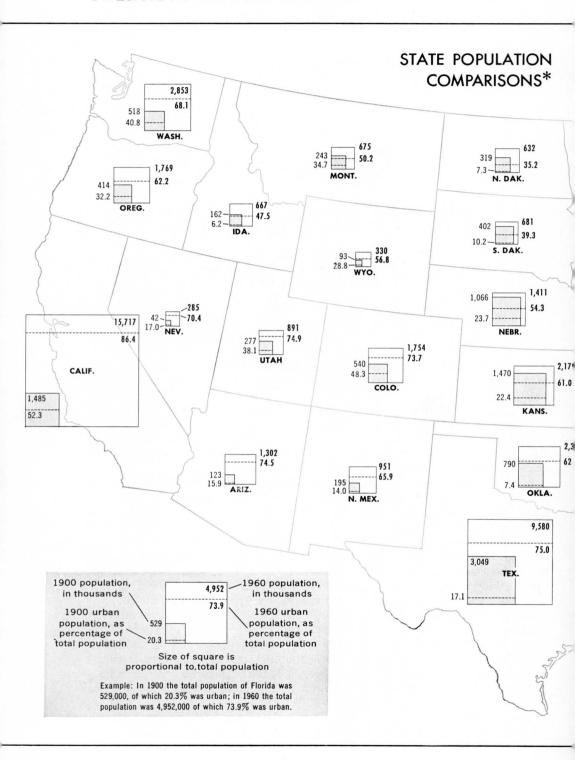

STATE POPULATION
COMPARISONS*

WASH.
2,853
68.1
518
40.8

OREG.
1,769
62.2
414
32.2

CALIF.
15,717
86.4
1,485
52.3

NEV.
285
70.4
42
17.0

IDA.
667
47.5
162
6.2

UTAH
891
74.9
277
38.1

ARIZ.
1,302
74.5
123
15.9

MONT.
675
50.2
243
34.7

WYO.
330
56.8
93
28.8

COLO.
1,754
73.7
540
48.3

N. MEX.
951
65.9
195
14.0

N. DAK.
632
35.2
319
7.3

S. DAK.
681
39.3
402
10.2

NEBR.
1,411
54.3
1,066
23.7

KANS.
2,17*
61.0
1,470
22.4

OKLA.
2,3
62
790
7.4

TEX.
9,580
75.0
3,049
17.1

1900 population,
in thousands

1960 population,
in thousands

1900 urban
population, as
percentage of
total population

1960 urban
population, as
percentage of
total population

4,952
73.9
529
20.3

Size of square is
proportional to total population

Example: In 1900 the total population of Florida was
529,000, of which 20.3% was urban; in 1960 the total
population was 4,952,000 of which 73.9% was urban.

Urban, Rural, and Totals
1900 and 1960

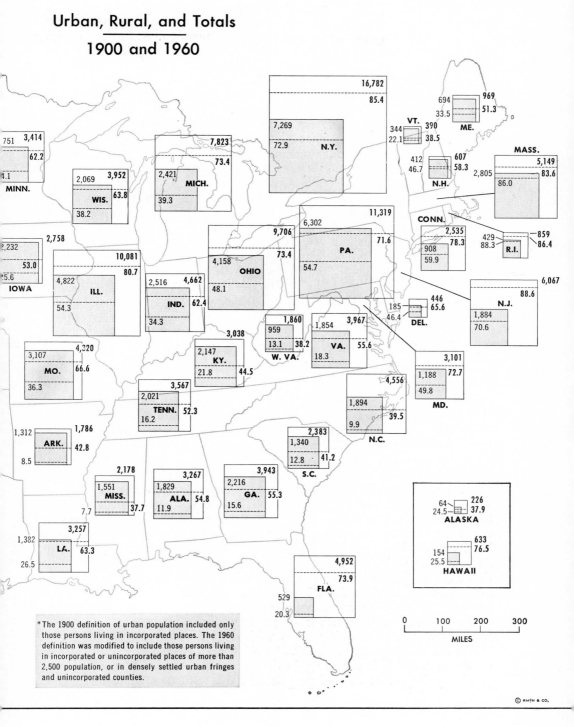

16,782
85.4
7,269
72.9
N.Y.

694
33.5
969
51.3
ME.

VT.
344 | 390
22.1 | 38.5

MASS.
5,149
83.6
2,805
86.0

751 | 3,414
62.2
4.1
MINN.

2,069 | 3,952
63.8
WIS.
38.2

7,823
73.4
2,421
MICH.
39.3

412 | 607
46.7 | 58.3
N.H.

CONN.
2,535
78.3
908
59.9

429 | 859
88.3 | 86.4
R.I.

2,232
53.0
5.6
IOWA
2,758

10,081
80.7
4,822
ILL.
54.3

9,706
73.4
4,158
OHIO
48.1

6,302
11,319
71.6
PA.
54.7

6,067
88.6
N.J.
1,884
70.6

2,516 | 4,662
62.4
IND.
34.3

185 | 446
46.4 | 65.6
DEL.

3,107 | 4,320
66.6
MO.
36.3

3,038
2,147
KY.
21.8 | 44.5

1,860
959
13.1 | 38.2
W. VA.

1,854
18.3
3,967
VA.
55.6

3,101
1,188 | 72.7
49.8
MD.

3,567
2,021
TENN. | 52.3
16.2

4,556
1,894
9.9 | 39.5
N.C.

1,312 | 1,786
ARK. | 42.8
8.5

2,383
1,340
12.8 | 41.2
S.C.

2,178
1,551 | 3,267
MISS. | 1,829
7.7 | 37.7 | ALA. | 54.8
11.9

3,943
2,216
GA. | 55.3
15.6

3,257
1,382
LA. | 63.3
26.5

ALASKA
64 | 226
24.5 | 37.9

HAWAII
633
154 | 76.5
25.5

4,952
73.9
FLA.
529
20.3

*The 1900 definition of urban population included only those persons living in incorporated places. The 1960 definition was modified to include those persons living in incorporated or unincorporated places of more than 2,500 population, or in densely settled urban fringes and unincorporated counties.

0   100   200   300
MILES

© RMPN & CO.

587

of over 50,000 people. Indeed, nearly half of the population lived in ten great population clusters. The biggest of these was one supercity that extended from the New Hampshire–Massachusetts border south to the metropolitan Washington area of Virginia. More than 31,000,000 people lived in this contiguous belt of cities and suburbs, 17.5 per cent of the national total. The nine other huge clusters were from Albany to Syracuse, New York; Pittsburgh to Youngstown, Ohio; Detroit and environs; Chicago and other cities near Lake Michigan in Indiana and Wisconsin as well as Illinois; the Miami area; Houston east to the Gulf of Mexico; the Dallas–Fort Worth district; the San Francisco Bay area; and greater Los Angeles. Add to these metropolitan clusters such relatively isolated cities as Cleveland, St. Louis, New Orleans, San Antonio, Seattle, San Diego, Buffalo, Cincinnati, Memphis, Denver, Atlanta, and Minneapolis–St. Paul and it will be seen that the average American of 1960 lived in or near a city of over five hundred thousand.

Simultaneous with the urban movement was a sharp increase in the number and population of suburbs. Some large cities—New York, Chicago, Philadelphia, and Cleveland, for example—actually lost population in the 1950's. But their suburban growth was tremendous. In the 211 American urban areas of over fifty thousand population, which had 85 per cent of the national population increase in the 1950's, the growth of the central cities was only 9 per cent between 1950 and 1960. Population growth in the suburbs within these areas was about 48 per cent.

The Negro's Battle: Against Segregation, for Equal Opportunity

About 1940 the American Negro began a militant campaign for equal rights that has not yet diminished and seems likely to continue until the battle is won. One of the most dramatic chapters of recent social history has been the Negro community's determined drive to achieve full first-class citizenship.

The advances toward equality that Negroes won during and after World War II can be attributed to many causes. Clearly, one of the most important was the improved, but by no means rosy, economic condition of the Negroes. With migration out of the South, better chances for employment whether in the South or elsewhere, and better wages, the Negro to a greater degree than ever before freed himself from the direct economic dependence on others that had long kept him from asserting himself. But there were many other factors. Although measuring prejudice is at best an elusive task, it seems highly likely that color prejudice has been in retreat ever since about World War I. As fewer and fewer Caucasians, both North and South, believed that Negroes because they were Negroes should be denied equal opportunity, the resistance to the Negro's march became weaker and his march accelerated. Undoubtedly, the cold war had something to do with the lesser resistance of the whites. If America's democracy were to be its chief social advantage over its ideological enemies, and if it were to gain the respect and cooperation of the newly politically important colored peoples of the world, then the colored people of the United States would have to share in American democracy to a greater extent than ever they had before.

Desegregation of the armed forces was one of the quickest and quietest revolutions in racial matters the United States ever experienced. As late as December 8, 1941, the War Department notified a conference of Negroes at Washington that the army would take no step to alter its racial practices. It would practice the segregation of American civilian society. "The Army is not a sociological laboratory; to be effective it must be organized and trained according to principles which will insure success. . . ." In the postwar decade, however, largely in the pursuit of effectiveness, the army in fact became a sociological laboratory.

In November, 1945, a special army board submitted a report on the Negro in the army that urged the abolition of separate Negro divisions but called for continued segregation at company and batalion levels. But the board, for the first time, also recommended that in the event of another war personnel assignments should be made only on the basis of qualification and merit and that race should be ignored. A second special committee on racial matters in the armed forces reported in the fall of 1948 that the services would be strengthened by the adoption of a "policy of equality of treatment and opportunity," and soon before the election President Truman ordered that such a policy "shall be put into effect as rapidly as possible, having due regard to the time required to effectuate any necessary changes without impairing efficiency or morale." Except for the air force, desegregation proceeded slowly. The target date for desegregation in the armed forces was June 30, 1954, but the Korean conflict hastened the process. Base commanders, confronted with the task of training thousands of draftees, decided their task would be simplified if they disregarded race, and most training camps desegregated, even in the South. In Korea, army officers began to put Negro replacements into all-white units and found that the Negro soldier fought better when he was not segregated. Behind the lines, demand for technical specialists required that the best available man be used regardless of his color. By the end of the Korean War little segregation remained in the armed forces.

Perhaps the most remarkable aspect of military desegregation was that there were very few incidents of racial conflict. Even southern rural white draftees took close order drill from Negro training sergeants without violent objection. There were apparently two reasons for the quick acceptance of military desegregation: military discipline required obedience to orders and whites who otherwise would have strongly resisted eating at the same mess table with a Negro found that, when ordered to do so, the world did not come to an end; and white soldiers accepted desegregation as part of the "army way," not dissimilar from the practice of tucking one's necktie into the shirt between the second and third buttons.

Desegregation in schools, however, was the hottest racial issue in postwar America. As early as 1938, the Supreme Court began to define equality under the 1896 Plessy v. Ferguson doctrine of "separate but equal" facilities in such a way as to pave the way for the reversal of the doctrine. In that year the Court ruled that Missouri, because it provided a state law school for whites, must provide legal education for Negroes as well. In 1950, in Sweatt v. Painter the Court gave the opinion that the law school of the University of Texas, a state institution, must admit a Negro because the state law school for Negroes that Texas provided was not substantially equal in quality. As postwar prosperity made greater public instruction expenditures easier and as it became apparent that the courts were beginning to enforce the "equal" part of the "separate but equal" doctrine, many segregated school districts tried to close the quality gap between their white and Negro schools. In 1940, the capital outlay per Negro pupil in eight southern states was only 23 per cent as much as that for whites; by 1952 the amount had increased to 82 per cent. In the wealthier southern communities with relatively small Negro populations, the quality of education in white and Negro public schools became as nearly equal as money in a brief time could make it, but in less fortunate school districts it was a cruel joke to speak of racial parity in education. A number of southern state universities abolished segregation in their graduate schools, but educational deficiencies earlier in life prevented most Negroes from having the qualifications necessary for graduate study.

In its historic decision of May 17, 1954, the Supreme Court overturned the Plessy v. Ferguson precedent. The Court considered several suits together so as to cover all constitutional aspects of school segregation; the most important of them was Brown v. Board of Education of Topeka. Earl Warren, former governor of California and Thomas E. Dewey's running mate in 1948 who had been appointed Chief Justice in 1953 when Fred M. Vinson died, spoke for the unanimous Court: "We conclude that in the field of public education the doctrine of 'separate but equal' has no place. Separate educational facilities are inherently unequal. Therefore, we hold that the plaintiffs . . . are, by reason of the segregation complained of, deprived of the equal protection of the laws guaranteed by the Fourteenth Amendment." In other words, the laws of the seventeen states that required public school segregation and of the four states that permitted local school districts to segregate were unconstitutional. On May 31, 1955, the Court, again unanimously, ruled further that federal courts "will require that the defendants make a prompt and reasonable start toward full compliance with our May 17, 1954, ruling." If local school boards thought additional time necessary before beginning desegregation, the burden of proof lay upon them; it was the responsibility of the school boards "to establish that such time is necessary in the public interest and is consistent with good faith compliance at the earliest practicable date."

Resistance to the Court's decision was considerable. Delaware and the District of Columbia integrated their schools promptly. The former border states began the gradual desegregation the Court had recommended. The former Confederate states were slower. In the 1960–1961 school year, 3,500 of the 288,900 Negro pupils in Texas were in integrated public schools; Oklahoma had 10,520 out of 40,900; Virginia had 170 out of 211,000; North Carolina had 50 out of 319,000; and Florida had 755 out of 201,100. Only four of the 287,000 Negro public school students in Louisiana were in mixed classes, and Mississippi, Alabama, Georgia, and South Carolina had not integrated at all.

Resistance to desegregation took many forms. Some state legislatures passed resolutions declaring that the Court's decision itself was unconstitutional, and, reviving the thought of John C. Calhoun, raised the constitutional theory of "interposition." What, if anything, this theory meant in practice remained to be seen. Other states authorized local school boards, if ordered by a court to desegregate, to close up shop and use public funds for segregated private schools, an action that surely would meet with constitutional disapproval. In March, 1956, a group of southern members of Congress—nineteen Senators and eighty-one Representatives—issued the "Southern Manifesto" to state their intent to reverse the Court's decision. Most of the headlines, however, went to the extralegal and illegal and sometimes violent actions of rabidly segregationist organizations and their members. White supremacists in some communities revived the Ku Klux Klan, but far more common were the White Citizens Councils. Almost each September as schools opened there was some kind of mass demonstration and violence over a school recently desegregated by court order. The most spectacular conflict was at Little Rock, Arkansas.

Some school districts in northern Arkansas had already desegregated when the trouble began in Little Rock, the state capital. In 1955, Little Rock's school board set up a desegregation schedule that called for registration of Negro students in previously all-white high schools in September, 1957. The federal court approved the plan. School administrators carefully selected a handful of Negro youngsters to be the first to attend Central High School. A group of white segregationists obtained from a state court an injunction to prevent the high school's integration, and during the court proceedings Governor Orval Faubus testified that the admittance of Negro students into mixed classes in Little Rock would bring about mob violence. The federal district court overruled the state court and issued injunctions to prevent any hampering of the already approved desegregation plan.

Apparently sensing political advantage among the white voters of Arkansas, Governor Faubus ordered national guard units to surround Central High School ostensibly to "maintain order." When the Negro pupils who were to register at the school approached the building, the national guardsmen turned them away. The school board asked the presiding judge of the federal district court for a delay, but the judge refused. When the troops continued to prevent the Negroes' entrance, the judge summoned the governor to appear before his court ten days later. Governor Faubus conferred with President Eisenhower at Newport, Rhode Island, where Eisenhower was on vacation. Just what happened at their conference was not made public, but Faubus backed down part way. He did not appear in court, but he complied with the court's injunction to remove the national guardsmen. On the first school day after the withdrawal of the state troops, Little Rock police surrounded the building. Nine Negro students were slipped into the building via a back door, and the fireworks began. An angry mob, upon hearing the news, rushed the building and were only barely turned back by police. The mob beat some Negro newspaper reporters. Photographs of the mob appeared in newspapers all over the world.

Long under fire for not taking action to ensure the edicts of the federal court, President Eisenhower at last acted after the mob scene of September 23, 1957. He issued a proclamation ordering all obstruction to the court order to stop at once, nationalized the state troopers to take them out of the Governor's control, and dispatched a thousand officers and men of an airborne division to Little Rock. On September 25, the Negro students went to school in army vehicles. A mob formed again around the school, but the paratroopers kept it under control. Slowly the hatreds and passions of Little Rock subsided, and as they cooled the soldiers were withdrawn slowly. Early in December, the last soldiers were ordered away. The nine children attended desegregated classes without further important incident. Two years later, four other senior high schools in Little Rock desegregated without trouble.

The sharpest conflict between the federal government and a state since Appomattox erupted in the fall of 1962 when James Meredith, a twenty-nine-year-old Negro air force veteran of Mississippi, endeavored to enroll at the University of Mississippi, to which he contributed in taxes as a citizen of the state. After having exhausted all legal delays, the administration of Governor Ross Barnett, which had taken over the conduct of the matter from University officials, refused Meredith entrance to the campus when he arrived with federal marshals bearing a court order for Meredith's University registration. The federal Court of Appeals at New Orleans found Barnett in contempt and granted him four days to purge himself by permitting Meredith's registration and maintaining law and order so that the new student could remain at the University. Failure to comply before the deadline would cost Barnett $10,000 a day besides arrest.

The Governor backed down part way, and early on Sunday evening, September 30, federal marshals slipped Meredith into the campus and into a dormitory room. The next morning Meredith registered; he began to attend classes following his registration. But on the critical Sunday night, while President Kennedy was addressing the nation on television, an angry mob of students and white segregationists, who had converged from all over the South, indulged themselves in an ugly riot against the federal marshals and the federalized national guard. The mob employed "Molotov cocktails," bricks, and a few conventional arms. A French journalist and a townsman who was merely observing the riot were killed. Edwin A. Walker, a former army major general and a right-wing extremist who had resigned from the army after the Pentagon reprimanded him for his troop indoctrination program and who had run badly in the Texas gubernatorial primary a few months before, was a leader of the mob. He and twenty-three others were arrested. Regular army troops dispatched by Washington soon brought an end to the violence in the once-sleepy town of Oxford that had been William Faulkner's home.

In any showdown of strength between the states and the federal judiciary and executive, the states are almost always the loser, and the kind of defiance that Faubus and then Barnett displayed can only further complicate and trouble an already complex and emotional issue. Increasing numbers of white southerners, especially after Mississippi began token integration with Meredith, hoped that the process of integration would continue to be slow but accepted it as inevitable.

No school board outside the former slave areas segregated Negroes as Negroes after the May 17, 1954, Court decision. Some of them, however, gerrymandered school attendance districts so as to segregate Negro students in actual fact. The problem was a difficult one since it was held generally desirable for students, particularly in elementary school, to attend schools near their homes and since in many northern cities Negro neighborhoods were large. New York and Chicago Negroes charged their school boards with

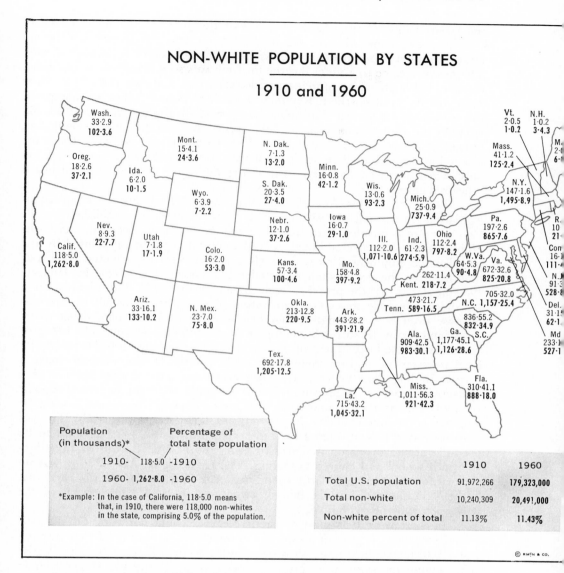

NON-WHITE POPULATION BY STATES

1910 and 1960

Wash.
33·2.9
102·3.6

Oreg.
18·2.6
37·2.1

Mont.
15·4.1
24·3.6

Ida.
6·2.0
10·1.5

N. Dak.
7·1.3
13·2.0

Minn.
16·0.8
42·1.2

Wis.
13·0.6
93·2.3

Vt.
2·0.5
1·0.2

N.H.
1·0.2
3·4.3

Mass.
41·1.2
125·2.4

S. Dak.
20·3.5
27·4.0

Wyo.
6·3.9
7·2.2

Iowa
16·0.7
29·1.0

Mich.
25·0.9
737·9.4

N.Y.
147·1.6
1,495·8.9

Nev.
8·9.3
22·7.7

Utah
7·1.8
17·1.9

Nebr.
12·1.0
37·2.6

Ill.
112·2.0
1,071·10.6

Ind.
61·2.3
274·5.9

Ohio
112·2.4
797·8.2

Pa.
197·2.6
865·7.6

R.
10
21·

Calif.
118·5.0
1,262·8.0

Colo.
16·2.0
53·3.0

Kans.
57·3.4
100·4.6

Mo.
158·4.8
397·9.2

Kent. 218·7.2

W.Va.
64·5.3
90·4.8

Va.
672·32.6
825·20.8

Con
16·
111·

N. J.
91·3
528·8

Ariz.
33·16.1
133·10.2

N. Mex.
23·7.0
75·8.0

Okla.
213·12.8
220·9.5

Ark.
443·28.2
391·21.9

262·11.4

473·21.7
Tenn. 589·16.5

N.C. 705·32.0
1,157·25.4

Del.
31·1
62·1

Tex.
692·17.8
1,205·12.5

Ala.
909·42.5
983·30.1

Ga.
1,177·45.1
1,126·28.6

S.C.
836·55.2
832·34.9

Md
233·
527·1

La.
715·43.2
1,045·32.1

Miss.
1,011·56.3
921·42.3

Fla.
310·41.1
888·18.0

Population (in thousands)*	Percentage of total state population
1910- 118·5.0 -1910	
1960- 1,262·8.0 -1960	

*Example: In the case of California, 118·5.0 means that, in 1910, there were 118,000 non-whites in the state, comprising 5.0% of the population.

	1910	1960
Total U.S. population	91,972,266	179,323,000
Total non-white	10,240,309	20,491,000
Non-white percent of total	11.13%	11.43%

© RMCN & CO.

pursuing segregationist policies, demonstrated against school actions, and took political action to amend the policies. Here was a case where Negro voting pressure influenced action.

The right of Negroes to vote, supposedly guaranteed by the Fifteenth Amendment, was the subject of much congressional maneuvering. In 1956, President Eisenhower put forward a moderate civil rights program that had been drawn by Attorney General Herbert Brownell. He called for a special commission to study civil rights, a special assistant attorney general for civil rights matters, and authority for the Attorney General to seek injunctions in the federal courts to protect citizens' right to vote. The program passed the House; the Senate bottled it up, however. In 1957, Republican leadership in the Senate managed to keep the bill out of the Judiciary Committee, whose chairman was James O. Eastland of Mississippi, and the Democratic Senate leader, Lyndon Johnson of Texas, dissuaded his colleagues from filibustering. The measure came to a vote. But the final bill was so diluted that it amounted to little, although white supremacists declared that it meant the end of their "way of life" and northern Republicans, before Negro audiences, compared themselves to the Great Emancipator. The Civil Rights Act of 1957 did establish the study commission and the special assistant attorney general, but, instead of the Department of Justice receiving the power to apply for court injunctions on any civil rights issue, it was empowered to seek an injunction only when a citizen had been denied the right to vote and had exhausted other remedies.

The Civil Rights Act of 1960 was another relatively sterile piece of legislation. In the fall of 1959, the civil rights commission established by the 1957 act recommended that wherever the presence of electoral racial discrimination had been established, special electoral registrars appointed by the president be empowered to register all qualified Negroes as voters. For four months after the commission reported the President was silent. In January, 1960, he stated that the proposal might be unconstitutional. The administration bill did not include this voter registration plan, and thus the bill was a compromise even before Congress modified it further. The Senate debated ten weeks and finally let through a complex "voter referee" scheme. The law provided that, if the Department of Justice won a suit seeking an order to require local registrars to register Negroes, it could ask the federal judge to make a further finding that Negroes had been prevented from voting because of a "pattern or practice" of discrimination. If the judge so found, he would appoint referees, who if they found that voting discrimination persisted, would be empowered to put qualified Negro citizens upon the voting rolls. The act also made it a federal offense to transport explosives across state lines to be used illegally, a provision designed to bring the Federal Bureau of Investigation into school and church bombings. The Civil Rights Act of 1960 was no victory for the Negro; Senator John Sparkman of Alabama, who boasted that he held the floor against the bill for twenty hours, said, "The effects of the legislation will be negligible. . . ."

In the fall of 1960 most southern Negroes could not vote. Of the estimated 5,900,000 Negroes of voting age in the eleven former Confederate states, just 1,500,000, slightly more than one-fourth, were registered to vote. Variations among the states were great: 52 per cent in Tennessee, 31 per cent in Texas and Arkansas, and 5 per cent in Mississippi. Still fewer, of course, actually voted.

Heartened by the May, 1954, Supreme Court decision, American Negroes began a new crusade against segregation, often at the local level and often by-passing the traditional national Negro leadership. Late in 1954, a middle-aged Negro woman of Montgomery, Alabama, the Confederacy's first capital, refused to obey a white bus driver's order to sit in the back of the bus. A local magistrate fined her $14. Montgomery Negroes, led by the Reverend Dr. Martin Luther King, a southern Negro who had earned his Ph.D. in philosophy at Boston University, organized a "stride toward freedom" movement, a boycott against public buses. Very quickly, Dr. King became nationally prominent, and his philosophy or strategy of racial relations gained wide acceptance. As a deeply religious man, he put his emphasis upon brotherly love; he added to Christian values the tactics of Indian massive but passive resistance as developed by Mahatma Ghandi in the struggle against British rule. Christian nonviolence was the watchword, and Negro ministers were the leaders. The National Association for the Advancement of Colored People, which was entirely secular and legalistic in its approach, continued to be vigorous, but the new Negro movement around Dr. King captured the imagination. For one thing, the South was less of a secular society than the urban parts of the North and West, and appeals for fairness and decency dressed in religious terminology were effective. For another, the emphasis upon nonviolence made the sporadic violence of the ultrasegregationists appear the more reprehensible.

The great wave of "sit-ins" that began early in 1960 were in the Martin Luther King tradition. Ezell Blair, Jr., a life-long resident of Greensboro, North Carolina, and three other freshmen at the Negro Agricultural and Technical College at Greensboro, late in the afternoon of February 1, went into a Woolworth store and purchased some small items. Then they sat down at the segregated lunch counter and asked for coffee. They were not served. They would not move. Policemen came in the store and watched them but took no action. The four freshmen sat quietly at the counter until the store closed. Soon Negro students all over the South began sit-ins at lunch counters, and the police retaliated with arrests. Approximately 1,500 Bible-carrying, hymn-singing Negro students were arrested before the end of the school year. White students elsewhere in the nation raised money to pay their bails and fines and picketed chain stores whose national management refused to desegregate lunch counters. What violence there was came almost altogether from the police and white mobs, frequently led by the black jacket and curled forelock type of teenager. Quietly, usually without public announcement at all, restaurants and lunch counters began to serve Negroes.

The next major wave of Negro action came in the spring of 1961 when young Negro "Freedom Riders" began a bus tour of the South to test the Interstate Commerce Commission's 1955 ruling against segregation in trains, buses, and terminals involved in interstate commerce. Most southern bus terminals continued to have segregated waiting rooms. The Freedom Riders were assaulted by mobs in Anniston and Birmingham, Alabama, and all were arrested in Jackson, Mississippi. Jackson quickly became the focus of the Freedom Riders, and throughout the college summer vacation of 1961, white and colored Freedom Riders went to Jackson to violate the local segregation laws and be put in jail.

Quite obviously, in the early 1960's, the older Negro organizations such as the NAACP and the Urban League, while still vigorous, failed to satisfy the new Negro emotionally. A cluster of new organizations took the limelight: the Southern Christian Leadership Conference, headed by Dr. King; the Congress for Racial Equality; and the Negro Labor Council, headed by the aged A. Philip Randolph and designed to eliminate Jim Crow in labor unions. Quite alarming to responsible Negro leaders was the rapid growth of racist and extremist movements among northern urban Negroes. In New York the United African Nationalist Movement, headed by a Negro public relations specialist, James Lawson, preached black supremacy, and in both New York and Chicago the Black Muslim movement gained support. Officially named the Muslim Brotherhood, U.S.A., this throwback to Garveyism of the 1920's was violently opposed to the NAACP, charging that its leaders were "Uncle Toms" selected for leadership by whites. Its two main leaders, who called themselves Elijah Muhammad and Malcolm X, even rejected their former family names as "slave-master" names. In Chicago the Muslim movement was strong enough to maintain a parochial grade school called the University of Islam.

The new Negro did not achieve the goal of his slogan "Completely free by '63," the centennial of the Emancipation Proclamation, but he moved a long way during World War II and afterward. He had momentum and determination, and he had taken matters into his own hands. That he would have further success was almost universally predicted, even by white supremacists to whom the outlook was discouraging.

Education in Crisis

From colonial times forward, Americans had great concern for public education, but perhaps never before was there such widespread interest in and worrying about the education of the young as there was after World War II. Dozens of books written for the layman about the problems of public education became big sellers, and national magazines of wide circulation carried serious educational articles. The heightened interest in education partly reflected the increase in the size of the middle class and people's higher aspirations for both themselves and their children. It reflected also the unusual, complicated, and expensive problems that American education faced.

The schools had major problems of both quantity and quality. The postwar baby boom enormously increased the number of youngsters society was obligated to educate, and the increasingly complex and technical world required that these students receive a better education than their parents had. Rather than the other-worldly and irrelevant people they had often been stereotyped as being, the nation's teachers at all levels actually stood at a most critical position in society; the future of that society appallingly depended upon the quality of the teachers' work and the support they received.

In 1940, there were 29,805,259 youngsters in the United States between the ages of five and seventeen, and total public school enrollment of this age group was 25,433,542. By 1959, the numbers had climbed to 41,728,400 and 34-758,000, respectively. Enrollments in almost every school district grew, but the real problems were in the cities of rapid growth. In the 1950's, the school boards of Greater Los Angeles had to provide the equivalent of new school facilities for two hundred additional children every Monday just to keep even. The nation needed thousands of new teachers each academic year. The best way to attract people to the profession and to attract better people to it was to increase teacher salaries. Society fell short of the goal, but it did make a tremendous effort. In 1940, the average salary of public school teachers, including principals and supervisors, was $1,441; in 1959 it was $4,940. Much of the increase came in the 1950's after inflation slowed down from its immediate postwar rate. In 1948 the nation's expenditures for all kinds of education (not including school construction) amounted to 2.4 per cent of gross national product; in 1957 it had grown to 3.1 per cent of GNP, about $14 billion. In 1950, school construction took about $2.2 billion; by the end of the decade it was taking over $3.5 billion annually and was still increasing.

TABLE 13

ELEMENTARY AND SECONDARY PUBLIC SCHOOL
ENROLLMENTS, 1940–1960

	Kindergarten through Grade 8	Grades 9–12
Fall, 1940	18,832,098	6,601,444
Fall, 1946	17,677,744	5,622,197
Fall, 1950	19,386,806	5,724,621
Fall, 1956	24,290,257	6,872,586
Fall, 1960	24,457,321[1]	11,847,783[2]

[1] Kindergarten through grade 6
[2] Grades 7–12

Society demanded that the schools provide the flood of students with a higher quality of education than they had before the war. On the whole, the schools did improve. One of the educational issues debated in America in the 1950's was over the curriculum and teaching methods. The nation's intellectuals, who had been at the forefront of the progressive education movement earlier in the century, reacted rather violently against what progressive education had come to be in thousands of schools. Curriculum specialists in the professional schools of education had in the 1940's come largely to support what they called "life adjustment education" and called upon the schools to provide instruction in whatever were the "felt needs" of the students, whether they related to geometry or improving one's appearance. Critics of "life adjustment" pointed out that the school was the only social institution equipped to provide intellectual training, that other institutions such as the family, the churches, the press, and the youth organizations existed to provide the nonintellectual parts of education, and that the school dissipated its strength at the expense of the intellect if it assumed responsibility for these other functions. These critics did not entirely carry the day, but "life adjustment" proponents, on the whole, were in retreat.

Those demanding intellectual rigor in the schools received a boost for their argument when the Russians put the first earth satellite into orbit in the fall of 1957. The post-Sputnik reaction was more than a little hysterical and some of the new educational suggestions were ridiculous, but nevertheless many schools began to put a greater emphasis upon science and foreign languages and less upon "effective living" and "adolescent problems."

597

The federal government increased its aid to education in various ways, but Congress failed to pass a general aid program. Washington continued to provide partial support for home economics and vocational instruction which it had done since the Wilson administration, and through loans for dormitories and research contracts it enormously increased its subsidies for higher education. The heterogeneity of the people handicapped a federal aid program more than did abstract attachment to locally financed schools. Representative Adam Clayton Powell, Jr., a member of the House education committee and a Negro, consistently attached a provision to federal aid bills that would withhold subsidies to segregated schools and the bills thereby lost the support of southern Congressmen. Roman Catholics worked against bills that would give financial aid to public but not to parochial schools.

Colleges and universities faced the same problems of quantity and quality. College enrollments climbed quickly after the war (due largely to veterans going to school under the GI Bill of Rights), fell off slightly during the Korean War, and then zoomed after the cease-fire. Private colleges and universities that limited their registration had no problem of quality; they were able through more rigorous student selection to improve impressively the quality of their student bodies. At the other end of the scale, many small institutions of no particular merit quickly doubled and tripled in size. They succeeded in bringing education to a larger percentage of the college-age population, but too often the standards were such as to fail to work the good students to their potential. The state colleges and universities of quality that could not restrict their enrollments became crowded places indeed. The numbers of good students attending state universities increased, but the increased numbers of poor prospects in the freshman class, from which many never emerged, taxed the universities' resources.

TABLE 14

ENROLLMENTS IN INSTITUTIONS OF HIGHER EDUCATION, 1940–1960

1940	1,494,000	1954	2,200,000
1946	1,677,000	1956	2,637,000
1948	2,616,000	1958	2,909,096
1950	2,659,000	1960	3,582,726
1952	2,302,000		

The increase in college enrollments was due both to a growth of the college-age population and a higher percentage of that population going to college. In 1920, only slightly more than 8 per cent of the population between the ages of eighteen and twenty-one was enrolled in institutions of higher education; in 1940 the percentage was about 15 and in 1960 it was about 30. By the end of the 1960's, the millions of people born in the postwar fertility binge would be college age and, presumably, the trend toward increasing percentage of college attendance would continue. The great range in the quality of American colleges and universities, which has long existed, is likely to

Herbert Hoover in early 1928

Hoover near the end of his ordeal, 1933

Unemployed men, 1930

LEWIS W. HINE FROM THE GEORGE EASTMAN HOUSE COLLECTION

A bonus army group from Cleveland, June, 1932   UNITED PRESS INTERNATIONAL

Hoover and Roosevelt on the way to the inauguration, March 4, 1933
UNITED PRESS INTERNATIONAL

Harold Ickes,
the "Old Curmudgeon"
BROWN BROTHERS

Harry Hopkins
BROWN BROTHERS

The farm holiday idea. Wisconsin farmers dumping milk, January, 1934
STATE HISTORICAL SOCIETY WISCONSIN

An example of depression painting. "*Dockworkers*," by Moses Soyer
COLLECTION OF MR. AND MRS. HERBERT A. GOLDSTONE. COURTESY ACA GALLERY, NEW YORK

A relief station distributing rough fish, February, 1935
STATE HISTORICAL SOCIETY WISCONSIN

"Okies" on the way west. U.S. Highway 70 in Arizona, 1937
CULVER PICTURES, INC.

A West Virginia coal mining town
LEWIS W. HINE FROM THE GEORGE EASTMAN HOUSE COLLECTION

Wendell Willkie campaigning in Times Square, New York City, 1940

American troops hit the beach of Wadke, Dutch New Guinea
STATE HISTORICAL SOCIETY WISCONSIN

A Normandy beachhead on D-Day plus two   U.S. ARMY PHOTOGRAPH

Harry S. Truman, November 4, 1948   WIDE WORLD PHOTO

American riflemen in the intense cold of Korea   U.S. ARMY PHOTOGRAPH

"Woman 1,"
by Willem DeKooning
(1950–1952)
COLLECTION, THE MUSEUM
OF MODERN ART, NEW YORK

The clean lines of
mid-century architecture.
Lever House, New York City
LEVER BROTHERS COMPANY

Dwight D. Eisenhower and Nikita S. Khrushchev, 1959
NEW YORK TIMES PHOTO

Rush hour in Brooklyn, 1957   WIDE WORLD PHOTO

increase. The number of properly qualified college teachers has not been increasing enough to keep up with growing undergraduate enrollments. Although undergraduate enrollments increased by approximately two million from 1940 to 1960, the number of doctoral degrees awarded increased by only about six thousand.

The Recognition of "Mass Culture"

From the time most of its people became literate and publishers began to turn out "trash" to sell in the general market, the United States, like other western nations, has suffered some of the problems of "mass culture." Almost from the beginning of mass-cultural trash, intellectuals and artists with higher standards were aware of a possible thorough debasement of the intellectual and artistic coin. The advent of television in the late 1940's and early 1950's brought the problem to general attention as it had never been before.

Television shows were expensive to produce. The hucksters who used television programs to attract an audience for their sales pitches made a heavy investment, and they wanted a maximum audience. No society anywhere at any time has had a majority of highly cultured people. Television producers and sponsors were aware of this fact of cultural life and aimed their product at the lowest common denominator which, in the opinion of the more sophisticated sections of the population, was a very low and very common denominator indeed.

Television programing dominated discussions of the problems of mass culture because it was a new phenomenon, was so widely distributed, and was such a time consumer for millions of people. In 1960, the Census Bureau reported that 88 per cent of the nation's fifty-three million households had a television set. There were more homes with television sets than there were with telephones, refrigerators, bathtubs, or indoor toilets. Estimates of the number of hours per week that the populace watched what intellectuals contemptuously called the "idiot box" varied widely, but huge numbers of people watched it for most of their leisure hours.

Early in 1960, the television industry underwent a crisis when a New York grand jury and a congressional committee turned up evidence that a popular quiz program had been rigged, that contestants whose appearance increased the program's audience rating were supplied with the answers to questions. The personality and position of one of the fraudulent contestants, Charles Van Doren, gave the revelations a special poignancy, irony, and symbolism. Van Doren, an assistant professor of English at Columbia University and a member of a distinguished intellectual family, came to symbolize both the eroding effects upon American culture of commercial enterprise and the lax morality and soft integrity that some people thought were on the increase in the nation. In early 1962, Van Doren, who had retreated from the headlines into obscurity, was found guilty of perjury before the grand jury and received a suspended sentence.

But even as the sordid details of the Van Doren disclosures came forth, there were two reasons for optimism: first, the public, especially the public with a modicum of taste, was recognizing the problems of mass culture; and, second, as the size of the well-educated population grew and increasingly clustered into a few metropolitan areas, it created a new and better than average cultural market. Books and magazine articles about the intellectual and artistic sterility of the culture aimed at the masses of people became prevalent in the 1950's and 1960's. Indeed, looking down one's nose at the effluvium coming from the television networks became so widespread that many confident intellectuals came to regard conspicuous nose holding as a pose adopted by *nouveaux intellectuels* to establish themselves as superior to the herd. But there was also genuine concern about the quality of mass culture, and concern was necessary before any action. When Newton Minow, the new chairman of the Federal Communications Commission, in a widely publicized 1961 speech characterized television programing as "a vast wasteland," he evoked a great deal of sympathetic comment. Television network executives and advertising men expressed consternation and said that Minow threatened censorship. That he had not done, but he had reminded radio and television station license holders that they used the public airways with the permission of society as expressed through the FCC and that the law did not give them automatic renewal of their franchises.

Perhaps television programing with its peculiar economics will be a long time in reaching a general level of quality tolerable to sophisticated or even middlebrow minds. But by the 1960's, there was cause for hope in other cultural media with more flexible economic foundations. In the population centers of a million or more, and to a lesser extent in smaller cities, there were enough people with taste of quality to constitute an audience or a patronage for worthwhile cultural activities. By 1961, there were 1,142 symphony orchestras in the nation, more than half of the world's total. Most of them were predominantly amateur, but that fact did not reflect upon the taste of their communities; and many of them were professional and of world-renowned quality. Many cities boasted an art museum with at least a few good works. Most newspapers did not appreciably improve, but a handful of good metropolitan papers became truly regional and the New York *Times*, as post-war improvement in air transportation made it possible, quickly moved toward becoming a national newspaper. It achieved this status in 1962 when, by the use of facsimile transmission, the paper was printed simultaneously in New York and California. The circulation of the quality magazines increased sufficiently to attract national advertisers. The American people in 1960 spent more money for concert tickets than they did for admission to baseball games and more for records and phonographic equipment than for all spectator sports. More people went to the New York Metropolitan Museum of Art than to Yankee Stadium. Paperbound books sold at the rate of a million copies a day, and, although most of these were not works calculated to raise the level of taste and culture, an increasing number of titles available in inexpensive editions were excellent. Clearly, there were more homes in 1960 with good personal libraries than there had been in 1940. (Americans, however, did not read as much as did some other peoples. A survey in 1960 indicated that only 17 per cent of the population was currently reading a book; the figure for Great Britain was 55 per cent.)

Creating a mass culture of quality was one of the most subtle and complex problems that ever faced American society. The American people organized themselves satisfactorily into a political democracy, although not without some defects, and more painfully and less thoroughly they achieved a good measure of economic democracy. Now, in the last half of the twentieth century, they had to achieve cultural democracy, both for the majority and the minorities of varying tastes. The range of cultural choice available had to be widened and enriched so that there would be something exciting and satisfying for all. The mass of cultural consumers needed to reach the point where they demanded products of such a quality as to make leisure a fulfilling part of life rather than a mere time-killing device. With the almost sure increase in leisure time that was coming with automation and further mechanization, these questions acquired a new importance and urgency.

American Literature at Midcentury

The categories of novelists this book established in Chapter 20 on the culture of the Great Depression (social novelists and "America singers") might be extended into the postwar era. Some of the giants and well-established novelists of the prewar era continued to be active. Ernest Hemingway, William Faulkner, James T. Farrell, John Dos Passos, John O'Hara, and James Gould Cozzens continued to write and be read. Indeed, some of them produced novels of major importance after World War II. Yet, as great as these writers were, one could reasonably say that their postwar work broke few new trails, that they had said substantially what they had to say before the war, and that they only sometimes improved their technique as they grew older. Other novelists, not well known before the war but active nevertheless, continued the older between-the-wars literary traditions. Conrad Richter's trilogy about Ohio's development from frontier to urban civilization was clearly in the "America singer" tradition, and much of the work of Wallace Stegner, especially *The Preacher and the Slave*, was of the social novel genre.

But a large group of younger novelists was fundamentally reshaping the American novel. The generations that came to maturity in the 1920's and 1930's found it difficult to realize that young people did not mean Wolfe, Hemingway, Faulkner, and Dos Passos when they spoke of modern novelists. A new generation of novelists had come into prominence, a generation fully as innovating and experimental as their immediate predecessors who had revolted against the Edwardian genteel tradition. The gap that separated the American novel of the 1950's from that of the 1920's and 1930's was as wide as the gulf between the interwar novel and 1910. The little attention the reading public of middle age or more devoted to these highly talented newcomers was amazing. Nor did the new wave receive as large a share of awards as its merits warranted.

The new novelists' work defied pigeon holing in conventional categories. They certainly were not "America singers," and few of them wrote explicitly social novels. They were experimental but not self-consciously so, as one senses that many of the innovators of the period after World War I were.

If any theme was consistent in their novels, it was that of the search for identity or sense of placement and relationship within the complex modern society and its values. If any mood or attitude permeated their work, it was compassion. Yet they avoided being explicit the way Sinclair Lewis was, for example. They were not naturalistic; nor were they romantic. Subtle and complex, they might be compared to impressionist painters, whereas the preceding generation could be compared to satirically realistic artists. Their styles and techniques varied widely, but many of them departed from the conventional structure of the novel. Instead of a formal sequential structure—beginning, middle, and end—they often wrote a series of incidents, perhaps chronological in order but not necessarily directly related to one another. Nor did they end their books with a note of finality. Instead of a happy ending or a tragic one, many of their novels seemed to have no ending at all.

With the short perspective we have on this generation of novelists one cannot say which ones will live. But certainly some of them will leave a mark upon American letters. Among the most popular were J. D. Salinger, especially for *Catcher in the Rye*, and Norman Mailer whose war novel, *The Naked and the Dead*, had a wide audience. Saul Bellow's *Henderson the Rain King*, the short and powerful *Dangling Man*, and *The Adventures of Augie March* received critical acclaim. A group of novelists from the South, Truman Capote, William Styron, and Carson McCullers, continued that region's remarkable literary tradition. Wright Morris' novels were among the most perceptive works written about American culture. Ralph Ellison, Herbert Gold, Bernard Malmud, Harvey Swados, and Willard Motley were other significant figures in the new wave of novelists.

The American theater, on the whole, did not have the vitality and originality of the novel. Broadway producers, faced with high costs, increasingly turned to the expense-account trade and produced machine-tooled, tried-in-the-marketplace formula shows. Musicals, of which some were charming but most were routine vehicles for popular stars, had the highest costs but yielded the greatest profits. Both the costs of Broadway tickets and the trend toward convention of the main stream of the theater encouraged what came to be known as off-Broadway theater. These small, inexpensive productions, which began in lower Manhattan and spread into other major cities, were frankly experimental. Some of the experiments were without value, but they did provide ferment and an opportunity for unknown playwrights to get their work before the public. Off-Broadway added some excitement to what seemed to be a commercially stultifying cultural institution. After a decade, however, off-Broadway was vulnerable to the criticism that it too was becoming conventional in its off-beat way—it was beginning to develop its own peculiar clichés.

Broadway and the commercial theater generally did not entirely reject serious and troubling playwrights. The commercial success of such writers as Tennessee Williams, Arthur Miller, William Inge, and Paddy Chayevsky was testimony of a survival of serious big-time theater. And the fact that all these men successfully wrote for Hollywood or television or both indicated that a significant market for serious drama truly existed.

Poetry continued to be the most respected and the least read kind of literature in America. Poets of the stature of Marianne Moore, Wallace Stevens, William Carlos Williams, and Archibald MacLeish went on receiving critical plaudits, but their readers outside of college literature courses were small indeed. The vast public, if it paid any attention to poetry at all, preferred the light verse of the clever Phyllis McGinley or the homey rhymes of Robert Frost. "Beatnik" poets such as Alan Ginsberg and Kenneth Rexroth attracted attention with their "readings" (recitations of their poetry against a modern jazz background), but they had little real impact. They were so "far out" in terms of popular taste and understanding that they were understood and appreciated only by one another. To most people they were odd curiosities and vaguely unsavory.

But for all the unevenness of American literature—indeed, of American culture generally—those who observed it from the vantage point of the Old World were impressed. There was a time when whatever cultural influence the United States had on Europe was either restricted to a few intellectuals or, at the other extreme, was mass audience and Hollywoodish. In the generation since World War II, the British and the Europeans came to regard American contemporary culture as worthwhile. American books were translated, read, and taken seriously. The libraries maintained by the United States Information Agency, although the object of attack and ridicule during the height of McCarthyism, were very popular places in European cities, particularly among young people. It is significant that in the 1950's *The Times Literary Supplement* of London, certainly no fly-by-night or capricious publication, twice devoted special editions to American writing. Its second treatment of the subject, in 1959, went so far as to conclude that "the flowering of the American imagination has been the chief event in the sphere of living art since the end of the First World War."

Postwar Art, Architecture, and Music

Perhaps the most important basic development in the arts in America after 1945 was an economic one. The steady growth of the size of the well-educated public created a potential market for the arts that was vastly larger than had ever before existed. Millions of American families wanted a well-designed home with good art and music within it, and postwar affluence enabled more of them than ever before to fulfill their desires at least partially. Architects were busy. Recordings of serious music made new sales records. The established art galleries in the nation's large cities increased their sales volume, and small galleries, even in fairly small communities if there was a university or some other intellectual center nearby, sold enough works to keep going. With more artists of all kinds better supported economically than ever before in American history, it was inevitable that the arts would be an exciting field.

American painters after the war had a greater diversity of styles and subjects. Almost all painters strived to develop a distinctive style, and the mark of a good painter was to a considerable extent the degree to which he was successful in his quest. Truly, it was an age of individualism in the arts. Super-realistic *trompe-l'oeil* (trick the eye) painters, impressionists, expressionists, surrealists, abstractionists, and various unclassifiable artists had their devoted followers.

Yet, certain trends in American painting could be discerned. One was a shift away from art with a social purpose. The word *depression* came to have a psychological rather than an economic meaning. Jacob Lawrence, who had learned to paint in a Harlem settlement house and had been on WPA art projects in the 1930's, entitled one of his 1950 paintings "Depression." It showed what appeared to be a corridor in a mental hospital. Three men in the foreground, dressed in sagging clothes and with heads hung low and faces of blank misery, shuffled about dejectedly. Indeed, psychological themes became very common after the war. In art as well as in other forms of expression, it was an age of Freud rather than of social protest. Hardly a show that represented several painters failed to have some pictures that portrayed the subconscious or projected a feeling of loneliness, personal frustration, or emotional disturbance.

About 1947, it became apparent that abstract art was the dominant form of modernism, both in the United States and in Europe. Abstract expressionist painters made no effort to portray an object realistically, and many of them were not representational at all. Those who did put a recognizable form into their works distorted the form considerably and entangled it in a mass of nonobjective blobs and slashes. Most of these abstractionists used bright and lively colors, but some turned out somber things in black, gray, and white. Some of these works were severely geometric after the manner of Piet Mondrian, some were more softly and naturally geometric, and some were strikingly amorphous. Yet, no matter what their style, abstractionists agreed that the function of the painter was to create a mood or feeling. Viewers were to look at pictures and undergo an emotional experience. Both painting and viewing, these artists believed, was intuitive rather than intellectual or even rational. Many abstractionists compared their work to music and deplored efforts to translate the natural scenes of the earth onto canvas.

Nonobjective painting in the United States was, of course, not an entirely new phenomenon. It merely came to dominate the art world after World War II. The Museum of Modern Art in New York had exhibited abstractionists throughout the 1930's, although more European work than American was on view. The Whitney Museum of American Art had a major exhibition of abstractions in 1935, a group of artists founded the Society of American Abstract Artists in 1936, and the Museum of Non-Objective Painting in New York opened in 1937. Some of the prominent abstractionists of the postwar period already had established reputations in the 1930's: Mark Tobey, of the Pacific Northwest, and Bradley Walker Tomlin, who was well known when he taught at Sarah Lawrence College from 1932 to 1941.

Certainly one of the most talented and powerful of the postwar abstractionists and probably one who will live after lesser figures have been forgotten was Willem de Kooning. Twenty-two years old when he came to the United States from his native Holland in 1926, de Kooning was best known for a series he did in the early 1950's entitled "Woman." In these only semiabstract paintings the distorted forms made a strong impression upon the viewer. Because there was a recognizable form in most of de Kooning's works, he made more of an impact on the consciousness of the average viewer than did, for example, the absolutely nonobjective Mark Rothko who was also considered a giant among the abstractionists. The viewer could admire Rothko's subtle colors, but he felt more relationship to de Kooning because as a viewer he at least thought he had a better idea of what the artist was trying to do.

Easily the best publicized and the most extreme of the prominent non-objective painters was Jackson Pollock, born in Cody, Wyoming, in 1912 and killed in an automobile accident on Long Island in 1956. Pollock was the dean of what came to be known as the "action painters," or "drip school," or *schmierkunst* practitioners. He did his huge canvases on the floor, dripping ordinary house paints on them directly from the can, splashing color everywhere, and even sloshing about on them in rubber boots. Easily burlesqued and ridiculed, Pollock, in the opinion of most art critics, really had something to offer. Despite his wildly unconventional techniques, his finished works did not seem to be accidents. On the other hand, those who asserted that Pollock and other extreme abstractionists were at best only decorative and that a society that honored an artist only because he was exuberantly innovative was a sterile one indeed had a point that could not be ignored.

Some art historians have made a category of painters of fantasies. Some of the fantasies were semiabstract, others were microscopically realistic; yet both kinds could be haunting, disturbing, illusive, and phantasmal. The sickly birds in Morris Graves's semiabstractions evoked this feeling as did the technically realistic (but quite unrealistic in content) work of Alton Pickens, a highly talented teacher of art at Indiana University. Even Andrew Wyeth, who steadfastly called himself a "realist," whose works were photographically precise, and whose technique and use of light and shadow was reminiscent of the old masters, projected this haunting quality.

Realist painting by no means stopped even if the museums often excluded it from their contemporary shows. In 1953, a group of forty-seven realistic artists, most of whom were older than the new wave of abstractionists, began a magazine called *Reality*. Its purpose was to fight for adequate exhibition in museums and to save American art from the "smothering extremes of the abstract and non-objective school." The magazine folded after a few issues, and the movement collapsed. In the early 1960's, however, the realists, still very much alive and still highly critical of abstraction, seemed to be making some headway. In April, 1960, a group of realist painters issued a manifesto which criticized the Museum of Modern Art for developing "the public image of the painter as a madly inspired child, rather than an adult human being." They even picketed the Museum briefly. Straws in the wind indicated that the great vogue of the abstractionists, at least of the absolutely nonrepresentational ones, was beginning to wane. More painters than before, even if abstract in style, began to include representational forms in their works. Art buffs who took their interest seriously, including those whose taste went beyond saccharine treatments of puppies and kittens and nostalgic, primitive snowscapes, increasingly expressed the thought that absolute abstraction was near the end of its inventiveness and that it was becoming empty and cliché ridden.

European visitors to America in the late 1950's who had not been in the country since before the war noted that the greatest change in the appearance of the nation, other than the greater number of cars on the road, was the unusual amount of building construction and of "modern" architecture. The postwar moves to the big cities and the suburbs made an unprecedented increase in new construction necessary. The growth in both size and movement of the population required new hospitals, schools, office buildings, and churches as well as residences. Architects who designed the public buildings almost universally scorned "traditional" forms and the designers of residences, inhibited by the buyers' fears about resale market, made as many "modernistic" innovations of their exteriors as they could.

Actually, "modern" architecture is too loose a term to be very useful, despite its widespread familiarity. At least two main streams were discernible. One was an evolution of the international style: clean, sweeping, geometric lines; new building materials such as stainless steel, aluminum, and vast amounts of glass; alike and anonymous in basic form even though distinctive in superficial details. The other was the continuing tradition of romantic preoccupation with experimental striving for the unique, even the eccentric, in design.

Ludwig Mies van der Rohe may fairly be said to have been the leader of the postwar international school. His Seagram Building in New York, designed with Philip Johnson, was a good example of the international style in office buildings. Another was Lever House on Fifth Avenue, designed by the firm of Skidmore, Owings, and Merrill. This style clearly predominated in the design of big public buildings. Manhattan, Pittsburgh's Golden Triangle, and Chicago's Lake Shore Drive abounded with it. Frank Lloyd Wright, was the best example of the more experimental tradition. The Solomon R. Guggenheim Museum in New York, Wright's last major completed project, indicated his emphasis upon the unique. A great, squat, white cylinder, it had a spiral ramp from top to bottom along which were hung the paintings on exhibit.

Either tradition, most critics agreed, could be good in the sense of providing livable, usable, attractive structures. Either could provide drama and interest that would not wear thin with time. But either could be bad, ill-fitted to human use, not designed with its users and inhabitants in mind, forgetful of the human scale. When one looked at some of the sleek business warrens of the international school one thought with a chill of Le Corbusier's famous comment that buildings should be "machines for living." One could sympathize with some of the artists exhibited at the Guggenheim who complained that Wright had overpowered their work and distracted the visitor. In 1960, the Guggenheim's curator, James Johnson Sweeney, left in protest against the new building.

The American public, quite obviously, was much more inclined to accept experiment and innovation in painting and architecture than in music. Relatively few music lovers followed contemporary American composers. For the most part, American composers had to look abroad for audiences, and even there they usually found them only at annual contemporary music festivals.

Americans, however, reacted with warmth and enthusiasm to the performing artist. When the versatile Leonard Bernstein, who had filmed television programs about music of various kinds, became conductor of the New York Philharmonic Orchestra, the story was front-page news. Van Cliburn became a national hero when he won a piano competition in the Soviet Union. Gossip columnists wrote about the affairs of the more celebrated opera stars as well as about Hollywood stars. Record sales reached over $500 million in 1960, and a considerable part of these were recordings of serious music.

Most people of any musical taste, no matter what their age, agreed that popular music went into a quality tailspin after the war, especially in the 1950's. The distinction between jazz and popular music widened as "rock 'n roll" and pseudofolk-music gained in popularity. Jazz remained popular on the campus, and summer jazz festivals attracted huge crowds. But it became difficult to find jazz on the radio, and television almost ignored it. The emptiness, shallowness, and puerility of most popular songs and recordings was difficult to exaggerate. The popular music industry displayed its lack of originality and musical range with gimmicks, such as recording echo chambers, and continual revival of popular songs of a generation or more in the past dressed up in the midcentury popular idiom. In 1959 and 1960, "payola," the industry's euphemism for bribery, gained public attention. Some disc jockeys accepted inducements to play certain records on the air regardless of their quality and thereby gave them an entirely spurious popularity. In the wave of resentment over "payola" there were some dismissals and even a few indictments, but the practice did not disappear.

But for better or worse—and there was some of both—American jazz and popular music had acquired a worldwide following. Students in Stockholm and Paris were avid jazz enthusiasts. One could hear Dixieland in India. King Phumiphon of Thailand played his saxophone with American jazz musicians when he visited the United States in 1960. Jazz became very popular in Poland after the 1956 upheaval, and old American records were available on the Russian black market. "Rock 'n Roll" shook British music halls and blared from juke boxes in Teheran. Some people interpreted this phenomenon as testimony to American vitality; to others it was evidence that the whole world was sick, sick, sick.

CHAPTER TWENTY-NINE

The Democrats Again

IN THE CONGRESSIONAL ELECTIONS OF 1958 AND THE PRESIDENTIAL election of 1960 the Democrats clearly demonstrated that they were the majority party. The voters again returned a Democrat, John Fitzgerald Kennedy, to the White House. The Democratic candidates for the presidency had won six of the eight elections from 1932 through 1960. In the generation after the Great Crash of 1929, the Republican party had been able to win only two congressional elections: in 1946 and in 1952. Eisenhower had a Republican majority in Congress for only his first two years.

But, despite the fears of the most orthodox Republicans, Democratic dominance had not produced fundamental alterations of the basic economic fabric. Since the elections of 1938, the nation had for all practical purposes been governed by a conservative coalition of Democrats and Republicans in Congress. And no matter what they wanted to do, which was never anything drastic in domestic affairs, the presidents of both parties were faced with Congresses that had a strong attachment to the middle of the road. American national politics was not absolutely stuck on dead center, but the moderate political center of gravity kept the balance from swinging very far either to left or right.

Many Democrats hoped and many Republicans feared that President Kennedy would bring about a revival of the spirit of the Second New Deal. But before he had been in office more than a few months, some dissident Democrats gnashed their bits and made remarks about the "third Eisenhower administration." Others, remembering the events of 1945 to 1953, replied that it was the fifth Truman administration. And others, still more historically minded, declared that, so far as domestic policies were concerned, the era had begun about 1939.

The Election of 1960

Encouraged by their success in the 1958 elections, Democrats looked hopefully toward winning the presidency in 1960. They calculated that they had an excellent chance to win the big contest since the Twenty-second Amendment to the Constitution, pushed through by Republicans still fretful about Roosevelt's four electoral successes, prevented the popular Eisenhower from running for a third term. This being the prospect, Democratic maneuvering for the nomination was more than usually intense.

The Democratic camp had a plenitude of presidential hopefuls: Adlai Stevenson, who had the backing of many Democratic intellectuals; Senator Hubert H. Humphrey of Minnesota, strong with labor; Senate Majority Leader Lyndon B. Johnson of Texas, whose efforts to project himself as a westerner rather than a southerner during the preconvention period were transparent to political observers; Senator Stuart Symington of Missouri, whose backing by ex-President Truman was not an unmixed blessing; and Senator John F. Kennedy of Massachusetts, who had the best-financed and organized personal organization.

Kennedy's main handicaps were his comparative youth (he was born May 29, 1917) and his Roman Catholicism. His youth handicap faded because Richard M. Nixon, the likely Republican candidate, was only four years older; his religious affiliation proved to be no unsuperable obstacle when he entered the primaries. In April, he defeated Humphrey in Wisconsin, and the next month he won over Humphrey again in strongly Protestant and economically depressed West Virginia where he had expected to lose. Humphrey removed himself as a candidate after the West Virginia primary. The Democrats held their national convention in Los Angeles in July, two weeks before the GOP meeting in Chicago. Kennedy won fairly easily on the first ballot. Needing 761 votes for the nomination, Kennedy received 806. His only serious opposition came from Senator Johnson who received 409 votes, most of them from southern delegations. The new nominee surprised the nation and grievously disappointed many of his northern and western supporters when he announced at a press conference that Senator Johnson was his choice for the vice-presidential nomination. Johnson accepted the place on the ticket, although he had said repeatedly that he would rather continue as Senate Majority Leader than be vice-president. Under Texas law, Johnson was permitted to run both for vice-president and for re-election to his Senate seat. Kennedy had named Johnson primarily to keep the South, which was disgruntled with the strong Democratic civil rights plank, from leaving the Democratic camp.

Republican nomination of Vice-President Richard M. Nixon was a foregone conclusion. His desire for the office was clear, as was Eisenhower's support for him. The President had given Nixon the opportunity to play a larger role than most vice-presidents, and the voters knew the forty-seven-year-old Californian well.

Nothing unexpected happened at the Republican convention in Chicago. Governor Nelson Rockefeller of New York, Nixon's only real potential opponent for the nomination, met with Nixon secretly two days before the convention opened. Nixon agreed to Rockefeller's demands for the Republican platform; Rockefeller withdrew from consideration, both for the first and second places on the ticket, and endorsed Nixon. Only one other person besides Nixon was placed in nomination, Senator Barry Goldwater, a self-pronounced conservative from Arizona. Goldwater addressed the convention, withdrew his nomination, and urged all right-wingers to work for Nixon's election. Nevertheless, ten delegates from Louisiana cast ballots for the Arizona Senator. The convention named Henry Cabot Lodge of Massachusetts as the vice-presidential candidate. Lodge, grandson of the Senator Lodge of the Theodore Roosevelt–Wilson era, had been a Senator, had been defeated for re-election in 1952 by John F. Kennedy although Eisenhower carried Massachusetts, and was currently the United States ambassador to the United Nations. The Republican platform, which also had a strong civil rights plank, was mostly a song of praise for the Eisenhower administration and an effort to identify Nixon with the popular President.

The campaign was largely a contest of personality. The substantive differences between the candidates' positions were matters of degree and emphasis. In September and October, the two candidates met in a series of four nationally televised "debates," the first time presidential candidates had tried such a device. Polls indicated that Kennedy gained strength from these television shows, especially from the first one. The main reason was that the "debates," which had an artificial format that prevented them from being very enlightening, made Kennedy nationally known; Nixon, as Vice-President for eight years, had already had a great deal of what the entertainment industry called "public exposure."

The question of Kennedy's religion could have become a nasty issue in the campaign, but the threat never materialized. The Democratic candidate was on record as a supporter of separation of church and state, and during the campaign he reiterated that if elected president he would never accept church authority when he thought that to do so would violate his presidential oath to support the Constitution. Nevertheless, some Protestants, mainly from the more fundamentalist denominations, circulated scurrilous anti-Catholic material, although not to the extent they had in 1928. Kennedy suffered a handicap late in the campaign when the three Roman Catholic bishops of Puerto Rico instructed their parishioners not to vote for Governor Luis Munoz Marin. Munoz Marin won anyway.

Kennedy eked out a narrow victory on election day. His election was indicated within a few hours after the returns began to come in, but the margin of victory was so close in some states that there was some doubt about its certainty for several days. Kennedy received 34,226,925 popular votes to Nixon's 34,108,662. The total vote was 68,412,709. The minor-party vote kept either major candidate from winning a popular majority. Kennedy had 303 electoral votes to Nixon's 219. One Nixon elector in Oklahoma, eight unpledged Democratic electors in Mississippi, and six unpledged Democrats in Alabama cast their electoral college ballots for Senator Harry F. Byrd of Virginia. Nixon carried more states than Kennedy, but Kennedy carried most of the states with the big electoral votes: New York, Illinois, Michigan, Pennsylvania, and Texas. Kennedy also came close to winning the thirty-two electoral votes of Nixon's

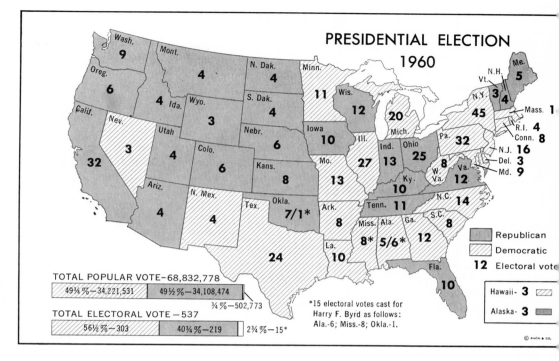

PRESIDENTIAL ELECTION 1960

TOTAL POPULAR VOTE–68,832,778

49¾ % – 34,221,531 | 49½ % – 34,108,474 | ¾ % – 502,773

TOTAL ELECTORAL VOTE – 537

56½ % – 303 | 40¾ % – 219 | 2¾ % – 15*

*15 electoral votes cast for Harry F. Byrd as follows: Ala.-6; Miss.-8; Okla.-1.

Republican
Democratic
12 Electoral vote

Hawaii - 3
Alaska - 3

home state. The Democrats retained control of Congress, about holding their own in the Senate and picking up twenty-two new House seats. They also won fifteen gubernatorial races to the Republicans' twelve.

Students of politics expended great effort in analyzing the election results. As had been the situation since 1928, Democratic strength, other than in the South, was concentrated in the big cities. Kennedy would have lost New York, Pennsylvania, Michigan, and Illinois if it had not been for his big pluralities in New York City, Philadelphia, Pittsburgh, Detroit, and Chicago. He also carried Los Angeles and San Francisco. Kennedy's religion was undoubtedly a factor in the voting. Kennedy received the votes of some normally Republican or independent Catholics, but he apparently lost a greater number of normally Democratic Protestants who would not vote for a Catholic. Some experts estimated that he had a net loss of 2 or 3 per cent of the total popular vote because of his Catholicism. The election certainly proved false the political adage, widely believed after Al Smith's defeat, that no Catholic could move into the White House; and judging from public opinion polls a few months after Kennedy's inauguration, the Catholic-Protestant issue in presidential politics had been laid to rest.

About all that Kennedy and Al Smith had in common was that they were both Democrats and Roman Catholics. Kennedy was from a wealthy background. His father, Joseph P. Kennedy, had made millions in banking, real estate, and other investments and had served under FDR as chairman of the Securities Exchange Commission and as ambassador to Great Britain. He had settled $1 million upon each of his children when they were born. The new President attended private elementary and preparatory schools and graduated *cum laude* from Harvard. He later expanded his senior honors thesis and had it published as *Why England Slept*. A naval lieutenant during the war, he was seriously injured in the Solomons when a Japanese craft rammed his torpedo boat. He entered politics soon after the war, serving three terms in the House of Representatives before winning election to the Senate in 1952. His book *Profiles in Courage* won the Pulitzer prize for biography in 1957. Vigorous, intelligent, efficient, and pragmatic, Kennedy during his campaign repeatedly talked of "moving forward" and of "New Frontiers." Large numbers of his supporters expected a new departure.

Some of Kennedy's early appointments strengthened expectations for change, and others indicated a continuation of Eisenhower and Truman policies. The appointment of Arthur J. Goldberg, general counsel of the AFL-CIO, as Secretary of Labor; of ex-Governor of Minnesota Orville Freeman as Secretary of Agriculture; and ex-Governor Abraham A. Ribicoff of Connecticut as Secretary of Health, Education, and Welfare indicated an infusion of militant liberalism into government, as did the naming of Arthur M. Schlesinger, Jr., Professor of History at Harvard University, as a presidential assistant. But the appointment of Dean Rusk as Secretary of State, who came to the cabinet from a post in one of the large philanthropic foundations; of Robert S. McNamara, a top official of the Ford Motor Company, as Secretary of Defense; and of C. Douglas Dillon, a Wall Street figure who had served under Eisenhower, as Secretary of the Treasury, reassured those who were generally satisfied with the previous administration. Stewart L. Udall, a Mormon from Arizona, became Secretary of the Interior; J. Edward Day of California became Postmaster General; and ex-Governor of North Carolina Luther H. Hodges became Secretary of Commerce. The naming of the President's younger brother and campaign manager, Robert F. Kennedy, as the Attorney General raised more than a few eyebrows. In 1962 when Justice Frankfurter retired, Kennedy appointed Goldberg to the Supreme Court. Earlier he had elevated Byron White to the Court.

Latin American Chickens Come Home To Roost

President Kennedy had little more than settled into the White House when in April, 1961, he became deeply involved in a Latin American crisis of major proportions. The unsuccessful armed attempt to overthrow the regime of Fidel Castro in Cuba requires some background knowledge of Latin American policy after World War II.

Three basic goals preoccupied most of Latin America after the war, and it was clear that the will to achieve these goals could not be deflected; Latin America was on the move. First, and basic to all else, was a demand for better economic conditions. Latin America was hit hard by the "Revolution of Rising Expectations" that swept over Asia and Africa. Second was a strong movement toward political freedom. Dictator after dictator toppled in South and Central America in the late 1950's. Third was a strong desire for independence. Free from Spain and Portugal for over a century, Latin Americans believed firmly that they had later fallen under the might of the Colossus of the North.

612

Preoccupied with the Cold War and concerned primarily with events in Europe and Asia, the United States after World War II largely ignored the developing social revolutions and rising expectations south of the border. In the first five years after the war, Latin America received only 1.8 per cent of the total of United States foreign aid. Tiny Taiwan received more than all of Latin America, as did West Germany. Above all else, the State Department wanted two things in Latin America: the prevention of Communist penetration and a favorable climate for investment by United States citizens. American investments constituted four-fifths of all the foreign capital in Latin America. More often than not, United States policy to attain these ends ran against the Latin American tide.

Continued United States participation in inter-American organizations was by no means contrary to its general goals. At the Chapultepec Conference in early 1945, the various American nations agreed that they would insist upon the preservation of their regional organizations in the writing of the United Nations Charter at San Francisco. In 1947, at the Rio Conference and the following year at Bogotá, the United States became a charter member of the Organization of American States (OAS). The treaties signed at these conferences provided for the peaceful handling of disputes among the American nations, and the OAS provided the machinery.

The United States suffered its first postwar Latin American setback in early 1946. Before and during the war, Argentina had been a center of German activity, and despite great pressure it remained neutral in the war until March, 1945, when it too declared war on the Axis. Having been neutral for most of the conflict, Argentina had a large backlog of foreign exchange which the United States ambassador, Spruille Braden, and Secretary of State James F. Byrnes hoped would be used for internal investments to stimulate the growth of the Argentine economy. In the March, 1946, Argentine elections, United States support went to the opponent of Colonel Juan D. Perón who had been a strong man in the preceding dictatorial and Axis-oriented regime of Edelmiro J. Farrell. Perón, a high-handed demagogue, had popular support because he proposed to use the backlog of foreign exchange for wage increases. Perón won the election handily. After the backlog was exhausted, the Argentine dictator pauperized his nation's agriculture to distribute benefits to his followers in the city masses. Perón was not popular elsewhere in Latin America, but neither was United States opposition to him which Latin Americans, extremely sensitive on this issue, regarded as meddling in the internal affairs of a foreign power. A revolt by the army and civilians from the interior overthrew Perón and sent him into exile in September, 1956. In the elections of March, 1960, Perónista candidates received one-fourth of the vote, and in the March, 1962, elections for the provincial governorships, Perónistas won most of the offices. After the 1962 elections, an anti-Perón military group, fearful of rising Perónista strength, overthrew the president, Arturo Frondizi, on the grounds that he would not be sufficiently anti-Perón.

The United States gained its immediate end, the prevention of Communist penetration, but lost respect and prestige in Latin America by its indirect intervention in Guatemala in June, 1954. Guatemalans had overthrown the corrupt and dictatorial regime of Jorge Ubico in 1944. The new government foundered, and in time the Communists worked their way into positions of power in the administration of President Jacabo Arbenz Guzmán. In March, 1944, at the meeting of the OAS at Caracas, Secretary of State Dulles introduced and strongly pushed a resolution that called for "a meeting of consultation to consider the adoption of appropriate action in accordance with existing treaties" should a Communist regime "constitute a threat to the sovereignty and political independence of the American states. . . ." The resolution passed seventeen to one, Guatemala opposing and Mexico and Argentina abstaining. After having set the stage for collective action through the OAS, the United States, only three months later, moved almost unilaterally to overthrow the Arbenz regime. A cargo of Czech arms arrived at a Guatemalan port, and the Central Intelligence Agency went to work quickly. The CIA armed and supported an invasion of Guatemala led by Colonel Carlos Castillo Armas, a Guatemalan anti-Communist rebel, from Nicaragua and Honduras. Together with the army within Guatemala, the Armas invading column overthrew Arbenz and installed Armas as provisional president. The Communists were stopped, but the social and economic conditions that had produced the unrest upon which the Communists could grow were not improved.

After the Guatemalan counterrevolution, Latin Americans began to talk of the Dulles Doctrine, defining it as United States assumption of the right to overthrow Latin American governments of which it disapproved. Even staunchly anti-Communist Latin Americans, who hailed the toppling of Arbenz, condemned the North American action. After the revolution of 1944, the United States had an opportunity to support a genuine social revolution and help to improve Guatemalan conditions. Instead, the United States government under Truman and Eisenhower backed up the refusal of the United Fruit Company, a North American corporation, to countenance any significant change in the *status quo*. In time, the Communists moved in, and the United States supported their removal by force. The cartoon of the British satirist David Low depicting the Statue of Liberty holding aloft a stalk of bananas was a sharp comment on the Guatemalan situation.

The United States was neglectful of Latin America except in crises such as occurred in Argentina and Guatemala, and American popularity south of the border sunk to lows unprecedented since the inauguration of the Good Neighbor policy. Mobs in Lima and Caracas dramatized the situation when they roughed up Vice-President Nixon when he visited there on a "good-will" tour in May, 1958. Thereafter, the United States tried to mend its Latin fences. It helped the coffee-producing nations to negotiate export quota agreements to stabilize the world price and viewed sympathetically the development of a Latin American common market scheme similar to the one being developed in Europe. In March, 1960, at Montevideo, Argentina, Brazil, Chile, Mexico, Peru, Uruguay, and Paraguay signed a free-trade treaty. But the legacy of implicit American support of dictators like Fulgencio Batista in Cuba and Rafael Trujillo Molina in the Dominican Republic, both of whom received their military training from United States officers when they were members of their American-sponsored constabularies, was a very serious handicap to good will.

Trujillo had been dictator of his country since 1930, although he had been forced to yield nominal control to his brothers or others periodically. In 1956, Trujillo's terror figured in the news prominently when Jesus de Galindez, a lecturer at Columbia University and a leader of exiled anti-Trujillo forces, disappeared. It was widely assumed that Trujillo agents had kidnapped and killed him, but conclusive evidence was not discovered. Trujillo was extremely unpopular in the United States, but the government continued to supply him with arms until only a few months before his downfall. In May, 1960, Trujillo followers made an attempt on the life of President Romulo Betancourt of Venezuela, and two months later the OAS met in Costa Rica, condemned the Dominican government for "acts of aggression and intervention" against Venezuela, and called upon member nations to break diplomatic relations with the Caribbean dictatorship. The United States did so. In May, 1961, Trujillo's enemies within his domain assassinated him. His son, who had recently received military training in the United States, became the head of the army in an effort to maintain the family's control, but in the fluid situation the dead dictator's brothers left the country. When they returned in November, apparently to attempt to restore the old regime fully, the United States announced its opposition. Young Trujillo resigned as armed forces chief and left for Europe on his private yacht. United States warships took positions off the coast. Strikes and riots in the capital city broke the back of Trujillo strength. The United States hoped for the emergence of political stability in the little republic under a friendly regime that was tolerant, democratic, anti-Communist, middle-class, and committed to economic growth within a capitalist framework. The United States was in a ticklish position vis-à-vis the Dominican Republic in which it was likely to be damned if it intervened and damned if it did not. But, on the whole, considering the decades it had supported Trujillo and the manner in which it had intervened unsuccessfully in Cuba in April, 1961, against a leftist revolution, its modest intervention against a right-wing regime in the Dominican Republic in the fall of 1961 was a welcome change.

United States relations with Cuba after Fidel Castro came to power on January 1, 1959, were trying to North American patience, were exasperating to most Latin Americans, and were always highly charged with emotion. Castro had begun his revolt against the Batista regime faced with great odds. After successful defense of his troops in the mountains, he rode the storm of a social revolution to power. He was extremely popular in the United States while he was fighting against Batista. Indeed, in the spring vacations of 1958 several college students went to Cuba with the romantic purpose of aiding the Castro cause. As in the case of Trujillo, the United States government did not go along with popular opinion. The government continued to supply arms to Batista, which were used against Castro, until mid-1958 and maintained a military mission with Batista until the day he resigned and fled from the island.

Castro was an unknown quantity when he came to power. He began to lose ground in United States public opinion in early 1959 after his wholesale executions of his former enemies. The United States government protested when in May, 1959, Cuba promulgated the Agrarian Reform Law, which empowered the Castro government to expropriate American-owned property. When the Fidelistas actually began to take the property, the cry went up in the United States that Castro's regime was Communist. That he had strong Communist connections and convictions was clear in 1961, but whether he had at the time that he won power is a matter of debate. It seems probable that he was an anti-American, generally Marxist but not Communist, rebel in early 1959, but that he had Communist lieutenants who had no great difficulty guiding his regime in the direction they wished when it encountered opposition from the United States and encouragement from the Soviet Union and China.

Certainly Castro encountered American opposition. Besides many vigorously worded diplomatic notes and speeches, the United States, under Eisenhower, cut the Cuban sugar import quota, severed diplomatic relations, and pressured the OAS to take a stand against the Cuban regime. The Declaration of San José, adopted by the OAS in August, 1960, condemned "intervention or the threat of intervention in the affairs of the American republics" but did not mention Cuba by name. Pro-Castro political movements had gotten underway all over Latin America. Secretary of State Herter declared that the declaration applied to Cuba and the Communist world, but not all agreed that it did. Mexico issued a special statement denying that the declaration referred specifically to Cuba, "whose aspirations for economic improvement and social justice have the strongest sympathy of the Government and people of Mexico." Mexico's position, plus the further opposition of Venezuela and Peru to the American stance, indicated that United States policy toward Cuba was hardly winning and influencing Latin Americans.

And, just as certainly, Castro received Communist encouragement. Soviet Deputy Premier Anastas I. Mikoyan visited Havana in February, 1960, and signed a trade agreement by which Russia promised to buy five million tons of Cuban sugar over a five-year period. This agreement became the model for subsequent pacts with Poland, Czechoslovakia, East Germany, and China. The Soviet Union also extended Cuba a $12 million credit, payable at 2.5 per cent interest over the next twelve years. Khrushchev obviously welcomed the break in the solidarity of the Western Hemisphere. He embraced the bearded Cuban when they attended the United Nations in New York, but, on the other hand, there was some evidence that Khrushchev basically regarded Castro as a welcome but irregular and untrustworthy thorn in the American side. Clearly, ties between Cuba and the Communist world further strained American-Cuban relations. The presence of a power friendly to China and Russia only ninety miles off the Florida coast was not reassuring, nor was Khrushchev's statement of July 9, 1960: ". . . if need be, Soviet artillerymen can support the Cuban people with their rocket fire, should the aggressive forces in the Pentagon dare to start intervention against Cuba."

The first climax of Cuban-American tension thus came in April, 1961, when an armed force of 1,400 Cuban exiles, armed and trained by the United States Central Intelligence Agency in Florida and then Guatemala, attempted to invade Cuba. The invading force made landings at Bahia de Cochino (the Bay of Pigs). The exiles expected a sympathetic uprising by the Cubans, but it never developed, and the Castro forces easily captured most of the invaders and repulsed the others. For weeks, the Cuban press had been saying that such an invasion was imminent which only lent weight to its subsequent charges against the United States.

The Cuban invasion was a disaster no matter how considered. If one takes the position that an invasion was justifiable, the invasion was vulnerable because it was thoroughly botched. The CIA did not perform its job effectively. Perhaps the greatest of its mistakes was putting the most reactionary group of the Cuban exiles in charge of the operation, which militated against the possibility of an uprising within Cuba, and preventing participation by most of the

Cuban exiles who had at first supported Castro but later disavowed him as a betrayer of the ideals of the revolution.

But many agreed with Senator J. William Fulbright, chairman of the Senate Foreign Relations Committee, who asserted that the invasion was unjustified and a grievous error. American prestige and reputation suffered badly throughout Europe, Asia, and Latin America. The invasion plan and the training of the exile force, begun under Eisenhower and continued under Kennedy, was in violation of American treaty agreements and even of United States statute. The unsuccessful invasion only strengthened the Cuban government and evoked sympathetic sentiment for it in the rest of the world. Had the invasion actually been a military success, especially given its reactionary leadership, it is quite doubtful that it would have solved the Cuban problem or enhanced the United States position in Latin America.

Yet, apparently, Kennedy's popularity increased within the United States with the Cuban fiasco. He made an impassioned and troubled defense in a televised speech before the nation's editors immediately after the invasion failed and subsequently conferred personally with Truman, Eisenhower, Nixon, MacArthur, Hoover, and Goldwater in an apparent attempt to head off criticism. As much as these conferences dismayed some of the people who had voted for him, public opinion polls indicated that the President had the support of a larger part of the population than he had before the fiasco in the Bay of Pigs.

After the invasion, American activities against Cuba took the form of economic sanctions and work against Castro within the OAS. An embargo of most items but food and medicine undoubtedly hurt Cuba as did the ban, imposed in early 1962, against Cuban imports. At an OAS meeting in Punta del Este, Paraguay, in January, 1962, the United States sought to get the other American republics to break off diplomatic relations and trade with Cuba, as well as to expel Cuba from the organization. The Latin American states refused to break diplomatic and trade relations, and the United States gained Cuban expulsion only at the cost of a split with the principal Latin nations which abstained on the expulsion vote. In the summer of 1962 Cuban-American relations again approached crisis as Moscow sent thousands of military technical specialists to Havana. Domestic political pressure on Kennedy mounted, and the administration attempted to tighten the Cuban nonintercourse policy by putting pressure on the European nations that still shipped to Castro. But yet American opinion did not support another invasion. A poll in early October showed that 63 per cent opposed an invasion at the moment.

The Cuban affair did have the effect of awakening the United States to the problems of Latin America. The Kennedy administration announced a new aid and development plan a month before the Cuban invasion. This too was begun, in a much smaller way, under the Eisenhower administration. At a meeting of the economic policy planning section of the OAS in Bogotá in September, 1960, Under Secretary of State C. Douglas Dillon (later to be Secretary of the Treasury under Kennedy) spoke of a new United States fund of $500 million to be used for social betterment in Latin America. In August, 1961, all the Latin American nations except Cuba approved the Kennedy proposal of an Alliance for Progress. The Alliance would provide over a ten-year period a minimum of $20 billion, half of which would come from the American government and the balance from international financial agencies, European governments, and private capital. To qualify for these funds, which were to be used to stimulate economic growth and improve social conditions, the Latin nations promised to cooperate in introducing necessary reforms. In the first several months of the Alliance's operation, it was not clear that the United States was adamant about the required reforms before granting the funds.

The Continuing Cold War

The United States was not so fortunate as to have an end of the Cold War, or even a relaxation of it, with the change from Republican to Democratic control of the executive branch. The Kennedy administration's foreign policy goals and methods remained substantially as they had been under Truman and Eisenhower: avoidance of war but resistance to communism, both in Asia and the West; strengthening of the armed forces and general military potential, especially in space flights and rocketry; support of the United Nations; and encouragement of American foreign trade. The foreign trade matter will be considered in the next section of this chapter. JFK, as the headlines referred to the President, sometimes showed an original flair and a slight new departure in method, but the general outlines of American policy with the rest of the world remained essentially unchanged.

The abnormal and illogical situation of Berlin remained the most dangerous point of conflict between the United States and the Soviet Union. The Berlin situation, established when America and Russia were still allies in 1945, simply did not fit the new shape of the world but neither East nor West was willing to make concessions. Much more hinged on Berlin than just the settlement of the German question. Most observers held that there could be no real disarmament agreement until the problem of Central Europe was settled and that Central Europe could not be satisfactorily stabilized until the two sides reached a workable and logical arrangement in Berlin.

Russia's objective was to force the British and Americans out of Berlin and incorporate West Berlin into East Germany. The United States and Great Britain were determined to stay in Berlin, as provided for in the 1945 agreement. West Germany was perhaps even more determined to keep West Berlin, and Chancellor Adenauer at least never lost hope for unification of the two Germanies under West German and anti-Communist control. A logical compromise would be to make West Berlin an international city, guaranteeing its freedom and ties with the West and the right of transit through East Germany from Berlin to West Germany, all under the jurisdiction of the United Nations with NATO and Warsaw Pact approval. But the Russians believed that they could not recognize that West Berlin and the corridors to it were not under the sovereignty of East Germany, and the United States believed that it could not explicitly approve the idea of two German states.

Given this impasse, which could not go on forever, the best that could be hoped was that neither side would do anything about Berlin that would bring war and that in time conditions would change sufficiently to arrange a compromise satisfactory to both sides. Apparently, Russia did not want a war over Berlin, and clearly the United States did not either, but it would not back down from conflict if Russia pressed the issue. Khrushchev periodically irritated the Berlin sore, but when the West remained adamant he stopped short of all-out attack.

During the Eisenhower administration Khrushchev had announced that if a Berlin settlement were not reached soon he would sign a separate peace treaty with East Germany and turn control of the Russian sector in East Berlin over to the East German government. Not only did the West expect the East Germans to be more difficult to deal with than the Russians, but they also refused officially to recognize the East German state at all. Khrushchev kept implicitly extending his deadline. When he renewed the threat in the spring of 1961, Kennedy met with him at Vienna for two days, and the Berlin problem simmered down momentarily.

Two of the problems from the Russian and East German governments' point of view were that West Berlin offered too easy an escape route for East Germans wanting to flee to the West and that West Berlin prosperity offered too much of a contrast with the dismal conditions of East Berlin and East Germany. Refugees from East Germany escaped to West Berlin at the rate of 25,000 a day in the summer of 1961. The East met this situation by effectively sealing the East-West border in Berlin, building a high wall at many points so as to make escape very dangerous and almost impossible. Berliners, accustomed to passing back and forth freely to visit friends and family, were furious. Tensions mounted rapidly.

The United States sent more troops to West Berlin, but the troop movement could be no more than a psychological maneuver because the western military position in the city was basically untenable in the event of major attack. Kennedy ordered some national guard divisions to active duty for a year, ostensibly to free other units for other activities but probably actually as another psychological maneuver. The federalized troops were released before the end of a year although international tensions had not significantly abated. The crisis slowly passed without more than incidents and threats back and forth across the wall. In the summer of 1962 Khrushchev again brought the Berlin problem to a boil after letting it simmer for months. The Russians in piecemeal fashion began to pass part of their military functions to the East Germans and to harass transportation from the border to isolated West Berlin. The situation was one that could easily get out of hand.

One of the sillier side effects of the 1961 Berlin crisis was the bomb shelter craze. The President in a loosely worded speech urged citizens to consider constructing family bomb shelters. Soon unscrupulous salesmen combed residential neighborhoods selling shoddily built and quite useless bomb shelters. To build or not to build effective fallout shelters—protection against direct hits was out of the question—was a complex problem. Undoubtedly, an effective system of fallout shelters would save, or at least prolong, lives in the event of full-scale nuclear war. But some people argued that they would as soon die quickly as live in a radioactive world, and many urged that the resources and energy that would go into a crash program of shelters be applied to an effort to bring about less chance of nuclear war. In late November, the President cleared the air by announcing a policy of federal aid for community shelters, although he still urged family ones. The furore subsided, and not very many families went ahead with shelter plans. Nor did the community shelters get far. Kennedy asked Congress for a $400 million program; Congress appropriated only $38 million for research and surveys.

The first two years of Kennedy's administration also saw the Cold War get a little hotter in Southeast Asia. The 1954 settlement by no means brought stability to the once-French area between the Gulf of Siam and the South China Sea. North Vietnamese and Chinese Communists, sometimes advised by Russian specialists, continued to wage guerilla warfare in South Vietnam. The United States was committed to the South Vietnam regime of President Ngo Dinh Diem, although his regime was by no means popular.

When Vice-President Johnson visited South Vietnam in the spring of 1961 and the guerilla warfare was going badly for the anti-Communists, The United States and South Vietnam reached an understanding that America would send combat troops if they were requested. General Maxwell Taylor subsequently visited the area to ascertain the possible effectiveness of greater American military aid. By 1962, about eight thousand American troops were in South Vietnam, as well as about four thousand in pro-western Thailand. These troops' function was not primarily to fight the Vietcong, or Communist guerillas, but to train, advise, and transport the South Vietnamese forces. Inevitably, however, American troops were killed even if they were technically only "advisers." The buildup of American force there did turn the tide of the warfare at least temporarily in the anti-Communists' favor. In July, 1962, a new and perhaps unworkable scheme was arranged for Laos in which both sides agreed that it would be neutral. Its neutrality was to be enforced by an International Control Commission composed of Canadian, Polish, and Indian inspectors.

Southeast Asia was another situation that, like Berlin, could easily blow up into a major conflict. If the South Vietnamese did especially well in their guerilla warfare against the Vietcong, there was a real possibility that North Vietnam and perhaps China as well might launch an all-out attack. At least in the fall of 1962, American public opinion was not ready for another Korea. On the other hand, if the United States withdrew altogether and South Vietnam and Thailand fell to the Communists, besides the loss of the rice lands that supplied much of non-Communist Asia with its staple, the status of Cambodia, Malaya, and Indonesia would at least be seriously threatened. As with Berlin, both sides seemed to be following a strategy of trying to gain advantage without precipitating a full war, hoping that in time conditions would change sufficiently to bring about a more general reapprochement. It was a frustrating strategy to live with, but a full nuclear war would be much worse.

Throughout Kennedy's first two years in office, the likelihood of a real agreement between the United States and the Soviet Union to ban permanently nuclear testing was little more than remote. The nuclear talks in Switzerland droned on, but they came to nothing. The essential difficulty was that both sides wanted to resume nuclear testing, Russia because she thought she was behind America in nuclear technique and America because she wanted to stay ahead. The Russians broke off the talks and resumed testing in the atmosphere in the fall of 1961. The administration, now more anxious than before about maintaining its nuclear lead, consented to further American tests. Many of the new American tests, but not all of them, were below the earth and did not create a fallout problem. One American shot into space created a radiation belt that might hamper future manned space flights. Given each side's understandable anxiety about relative nuclear status, it seemed likely that there would be no agreement on testing until each thought it could learn nothing more from testing in the atmosphere. But meanwhile the "nuclear club" might grow. France had already developed a crude atomic bomb. Russia did not, as far as is known, help China's effort to develop a bomb, but the prospect of China having a strong nuclear force was a frightening possibility.

The rivalry in space continued to be sharp. At the end of 1962 it appeared that Russian scientists were still ahead of the United States in this field but that Americans were doing much better than they had been only recently. In the summer of that year a Russian manned flight made eighteen orbits, which was better than their American counterparts then could accomplish. But the American astronauts were becoming more skilled and professional. The third American manned orbital flight, in early October, 1962, seemed a routine operation, and many Americans were more interested in the sensational National League pennant race. So fast had the technology of flight developed that many people who had been thrilled by Lindbergh's 1927 exploit took little notice of a man hurtling around the earth in a small satellite. But some of the space achievements of both sides were nevertheless amazing. The American Mariner spaceship, an unmanned vehicle that started its months-long journey toward Venus in the summer of 1962, was an engineering feat of major proportions.

The Kennedy administration did not restrict its military buildup to the dramatic fields of nuclear weapons and spaceships. It increased by 50 per cent the number of Strategic Air Command bombers kept on alert, increased the size and efficiency of the ground forces with a special emphasis on preparation for "brush fire" conflict rather than full nuclear war, increased the number of operational intercontinental ballistic missiles, and continued to produce and man nuclear powered submarines and other naval vessels.

The United Nations became embroiled in unusual expenses and controversy during Kennedy's first half-term, and the new President and his ambassador to the United Nations, Adlai Stevenson, vigorously supported the world organization. When Belgium withdrew from the Congo in 1960, the new central African nation was soon reduced to anarchy. So poorly had the Belgians educated the Congolese that educated native leaders were almost nonexistent. In the incredible confusion and warfare among various Congolese factions, the United Nations, by authority of its legislative bodies, stepped in to restore order. Katanga province, a mineral rich area and the only part of the Congo with appreciable industrial capacity, perhaps under the influence of the western owners of its biggest mining company, announced its secession from the rest of the new nation. Congo without Katanga would be doomed to backwardness and poverty, and the United Nations resisted the Katanga move. UN Secretary General Dag Hammarskjold called for a UN armed force to police the Congo, and soon this force was engaged in sporadic warfare with Katanganese troops, many of whom were professional mercenaries. This military venture cost more than the UN had, and it was forced to ask member nations to buy UN bonds in the amount of $200 million. President Kennedy requested Congress to authorize the purchase of up to one-half the bond issue. After some resistance from those who argued that the UN was actually intervening in the Congo's internal affairs, Congress approved the purchase but qualified it slightly by forbidding the United States to purchase more bonds than the total bought by all other UN member nations.

Hammarskjold was killed in a plane crash in September, 1961, while on a mission to the Congo to arrange a truce. Although the evidence was not conclusive, his Swedish compatriots believed he had been the victim of foul play. His death plunged the UN into a vigorous struggle in which the Soviets and their allies attempted to change the nature of the Secretariat to what they called a "troika," or three-horsed harness arrangement, composed of Communist, western, and neutralist representatives, each to have a veto. Such a scheme would have made the Secretariat powerless in matters affecting the Cold War. Early in November, the UN defeated the "troika" plan, with strong American help, and elected U Thant of Burma as Acting Secretary General.

Aside from a stronger tendency to support foreign democratic movements than with either the Eisenhower or Truman administrations—and this tendency was not consistent, as in South Vietnam, or fully realized, as in the Alliance for Progress—the main change in foreign policy under Kennedy was in better administration and some imaginative new methods. The most original and dramatic new program was the Peace Corps. The idea of sending American specialists to underdeveloped nations as teachers, agricultural specialists, medics, and engineers was not entirely new, but the emphasis on youth in the Peace Corps and the far greater number of such grass roots educational and technical ambassadors were novel. The Peace Corps captured the imagination of young people especially, although middle-aged persons were eligible to join, and thousands of college students enlisted. The Peace Corps insisted that the people it sent to underdeveloped areas, largely to Latin America and Africa, be technically competent in their specialty and able to communicate in the language of the area. The task of language training and teaching Corps members the customs, traditions, and problems of the nation concerned fell largely to American universities, which on the whole did an outstanding job. The degree of success of the Peace Corps remains to be seen and undoubtedly there will be unfortunate situations arising from the program, but if the Corps members are as good in practice as they promise to be they should improve living standards and build a reservoir of American good will.

The primary administrative change under Kennedy was strengthening the quality of many ambassadors and giving them greater control over the various missions at their posts. Two of the outstanding ambassadorial appointments were of Harvard University professors, John Kenneth Galbraith, an economist who became ambassador to India, and Edwin O. Reischauer, a Japanese specialist who became the ambassador at Tokyo. Kennedy made fewer political appointments to embassies abroad, and the percentage of Foreign Service career ambassadors appointed in 1961 was the highest in the nation's history. Nearly all of the ambassadors could speak the official language of the country to which they were assigned, an obvious prerequisite that had too often been ignored.

Clarifying the ambassador's authority and responsibility for all United States programs in his country of assignment was another obvious reform. After 1945, American missions abroad grew rapidly in size and complexity. A major foreign capital might have representatives from the Pentagon, the United States Information Service, and Departments of Labor, Commerce, and the Treasury, as well as regular State Department personnel. Sometimes the work of these representatives was uncoordinated and even at cross purposes. Putting ultimate responsibility on the ambassador made greater efficiency possible.

At a time when either the Communist or western camp could precipitate a total nuclear war with a major effort for "total victory," when political pressures in the United States against any compromise whatsoever were matched only by Communist recalcitrance, when a miscalculation or blunder by either side could trigger world destruction, to conduct foreign policy with wisdom was all the more difficult even if all the more important. To avoid full war, to prevent falling behind in the continuing struggle, and to be prepared to agree to a workable and just world arrangement were legitimate and reasonable aims of American foreign policy in the mid-twentieth century. On the successful attainment of these objectives rested the happiness of the future and perhaps even future civilization itself.

"Moving Forward"—By Short Steps

During the 1960 campaign, Kennedy spoke often of "New Frontiers" and of the need to get the nation "moving forward." With Democratic majorities of 64 to 36 in the Senate and 263 to 174 in the House and with the excitement that accompanied the new chief executive's inauguration, it was not unreasonable in early 1961 to expect an important wave of reform and progressivism. No such wave developed. Despite some executive innovations and some progressive programs and despite a quickening of liberal hopes unequalled since at least 1948 and perhaps since FDR's death, the first half of Kennedy's administration added up to only a slight shift to the left of "moderate Republicanism."

Kennedy certainly presented Congress with legislative programs that were in contrast with presidential messages of the previous eight years. He urged a major revision of the tariff structure to meet new situations and several tax changes. In the area of welfare legislation, he proposed Medicare, federal aid to education, a program to combat unemployment, and a new Department of Urban Affairs. Others, notably Senator Kefauver, urged a law to regulate the drug industry. The President also came forward with a proposed revision of agricultural subsidies. Some passed, some failed utterly, and some passed in watered down form.

Perhaps the most solid achievement of the early Kennedy administration and the Eighty-seventh Congress was the Trade Expansion Act of 1962, a measure that significantly had little to do with domestic progressive versus conservative struggles. The reciprocal trade program inaugurated in 1934 had worked reasonably well at its purpose of increasing American exports, but new conditions in the 1950's required a new policy.

In 1957, France, West Germany, Italy, and the Benelux countries signed the Treaty of Rome creating the European Common Market, often called "The Six" or "The Inner Six." The purpose of the Common Market was gradually to eliminate tariff walls between its members and thereby create a free trade market of 270,000,000 people, even larger than the American free trade market that had much to do with developing American manufacturing capacity. "The Six" also proposed to raise tariff walls around their community of nations. On many large items of American export the new tariff would be higher than the old ones of the individual nations. For example, a tariff on American automobiles and trucks of 27 per cent, effective in 1966, would replace old rates of 16 per cent in Germany, 24 per cent in the Benelux countries, 26 per cent in France, and 33 per cent in Italy. If American trade and tariff policy did not change, not only would American exporters find it more difficult to sell in the Common Market but as American exports were squeezed the French would find it easier to purchase Volkswagens and the Germans would find it easier to buy Renaults. Further, other European countries were likely either to go into the Common Market, as Great Britain was considering doing, or making more effective a parallel organization, "The Outer Seven." United States exports to Europe amounted to over $6 billion a year in the late 1950's, more than half to the Common Market nations, and the loss of this export trade would have harmful effects on the American economy.

In January, 1962, Kennedy requested legislation authorizing the executive for the next five years to negotiate trade agreements in which American duties could be reduced as much as 50 per cent on categories of goods (rather than on individual items as in the existing legislation) and to eliminate tariffs altogether on groups of products for which the United States and the Common Market together accounted for 80 per cent of world trade. For American industries and their workers who would be jeopardized by foreign competition in the domestic market, Kennedy proposed that instead of continuing protection the federal government aid the companies to modernize and diversify their production and finance the retraining of whatever workers might be displaced.

For the last several Congresses, protectionist forces had imperiled renewal of the reciprocal trade laws, and many observers predicted Kennedy's proposal would have a difficult time. A Nation-Wide Committee on Import-Export Policy organized to fight the measure. Charles P. Taft, brother of the late Senator Taft, was the head of a businessmen's organization for the proposal, which also received the support of the AFL-CIO. Within three months it became apparent that the substance of the bill would pass, and opponents concentrated thereafter on getting safeguards for particular industries. The legislation passed by large majorities in September, 1962, substantially as Kennedy requested. Negotiating favorable trade agreements would not be an easy task, but the new legislation made it possible for America to adjust its trade to changing world conditions.

The administration's greatest defeat in the Trade Expansion Act was a House amendment that denied most-favored-nation treatment to any Communist country, not only to nations in the Russian or Chinese bloc as in the previous legislation. Thus Poland and Jugoslavia, "revisionist" Communist states but Communist nevertheless, would be driven away from economic ties to the West and toward closer relations with the Soviets.

Kennedy requested tax revisions designed to stimulate the sluggish but not foundering economy and asked for other measures to give the government more tools to combat economic downswings. Congress either watered down or rejected the whole program. The tax bill the President requested would grant a 7 per cent tax credit to business firms for investment in new equipment, a proposal designed to stimulate economically beneficial new investment. To make up for the revenue loss, he suggested collecting income tax on dividends and interest by the withholding method and tightening up on expense account tax deductions for customer entertainment and similar dodges. Congress granted the tax credit for new investment, a boon to most firms, but did little on the business expense deductions and rejected withholding on dividends and interest altogether. The lobbyists against withholding resorted to deliberate distortion of the truth. Their propaganda made it appear that Kennedy's proposal was for a new tax altogether rather than a changed method of collecting an already taxable source of income. The intensity of the opposition to withholding was due primarily to the fact that tax collection on this kind of income was relatively poor because many taxpayers were dishonest in reporting income from such sources. Congress approved Kennedy's request to eliminate the 10 per cent excise on train, bus, and boat fares and to cut the excise on plane fares to 5 per cent.

Congress passed Kennedy's three-year $435 million program to get unemployed workers in sick industries off the relief rolls by retraining them for new jobs, but it almost completely rejected his three-pronged plan for fighting recessions. The President asked for authority to make personal income tax cuts for up to six months by as much as 5 percentage points. To meet the constitutional provision that only Congress can levy taxes his plan provided that any executive tax cut proposal would have to be submitted to Congress one month in advance for possible veto by joint resolution. The economic effect of a tax cut of this nature could be important in a recession because a five-point drop, from the 20 per cent most people pay to 15 per cent, would create about $5 billion in additional purchasing power. Congress, however, never seriously considered the proposal. Nor did Congress enact his request to amend the Social Security Act's unemployment insurance by bringing more employees into the coverage, enlarging the payments, and extending the number of weeks unemployed workers could collect. Congress enacted the third part of his plan, a scheme for emergency public works in areas that had shown a steady and important rise in unemployment for several months, only after cutting back the size of the program. Kennedy asked for $2 billion; Congress appropriated one-fourth that amount.

Kennedy's proposal for agriculture was relatively modest in that it contained no general solution for the intricate problem. He suggested that the size of the agricultural surplus be reduced by toughening up production controls, making most of them on a basis of actual production rather than acreage allotment. Congress disagreed. The House defeated the measure in June, 1962. Eager for some kind of a new agricultural act, the White House cut back its request considerably and pressed hard for the compromise. In September, Congress barely passed a bill that maintained the existing controls through 1963 but provided for tighter controls on wheat and feed grains beginning in 1964. Republican opposition was nearly unanimous.

Kennedy's welfare legislation proposals got the hardest beating from the Eighty-Seventh Congress. The administration measure that excited the most passion for and against was what the Department of Health, Education, and Welfare called Medicare, a modification of the Forand bill presented to the previous Congress. Medicare would have provided medical insurance under the Social Security Act for retired workers over sixty-five years old, the insurance to be financed by payroll deductions as in the case of other retirement benefits. The plan was extremely popular with the aged, of course, as well as with many younger people who contributed to the support of aged relatives. The primary opposition came from the American Medical Association, which intensified its cry of "socialized medicine," and from health insurance firms. According to the opponents, the existing Kerr-Mills law (which offered limited funds to states for medical care of the indigent aged under certain circumstances) and privately financed medical care were sufficient. They further asserted that bringing medical care for the elderly under Social Security would regiment American medical practice, although the bill in no way limited the patient's choice of medical facilities.

The administration opened all stops for Medicare's passage. The President addressed a Medicare rally of aged people at Madison Square Garden. Health, Education, and Welfare Secretary Ribicoff, who resigned in the summer of 1962 to run for the Senate in Connecticut and was replaced by Mayor Anthony J. Celebrezze of Cleveland, worked almost full time on pressuring for Medicare. But a Senate coalition of Republicans and southern Democrats defeated it fifty-two to forty-eight. When Kennedy proposed to make Medicare a major issue in the 1962 congressional elections, the American Medical Association inaugurated the AMA Political Action Committee to subsidize the campaign expenses of anti-Medicare candidates.

Medicare's defeat came after two previous rejections of White House welfare proposals. In 1961, the President had urged Congress to enact a broad program of federal aid to education in an effort to bring schooling in the poorer states closer to the national standard. Most of Kennedy's fellow Catholics in and out of Congress insisted upon including parochial and private schools under the aid provisions, contrary to the President's wishes, and the Catholic issue prevented passage. It seemed that Catholics would not support a federal aid bill that excluded parochial schools and Protestants would not support one that included them. Opponents of federal aid for ideological reasons—they maintained that local school board authority would give way to Washington control, although the experience of the Wilson administration Smith-Hughes Act and of government research contracts with universities did not seem to support their view—cleverly played off one religious group against the other. In the summer of 1962, the Senate defeated a compromise aid to education bill, one that would have subsidized only college and university building construction. Congress did, however, pass a repealer to the special non-Communist oath that students and faculty members had to take to be eligible to receive National Defense Education Act funds. Thirty-two colleges and universities had refused to participate in NDEA until the oath was repealed, and many others had participated only under protest. The other major welfare defeat was the loss of the proposed Department of Urban Affairs in February, 1962. The new cabinet level department would have incorporated all federal housing activities; after it became known that Kennedy's choice for the new cabinet post would be Federal Housing Administrator Robert A. Weaver, a Negro, the House defeated the measure.

From this account of the Eighty-seventh Congress, one might conclude that it passed nothing. Indeed, a conservative Republican Representative from Iowa called it a "goof-off Congress" and a liberal Democratic Senator from Pennsylvania agreed. But it did enact some measures. It put through a drug safety measure near the end of the second session that did not go nearly as far as the proposal of Senator Kefauver. The new law was more the result of the 1962 thalidomide scandal than Kefauver's investigation. Thalidomide, a European manufactured tranquilizer, when taken by pregnant women, had caused many babies to be badly malformed at birth. Congress also passed the Twenty-Third Amendment to the Constitution and sent it to the states for ratification after a ten-day Senate filibuster. The amendment, if ratified, would forbid states to levy poll taxes as a condition for voting.

Congress also enacted the administration's communications satellite or Telstar bill, and thereby hangs a tale that indicated the President's relations with Congress were not simply those of a progressive executive being frustrated by a conservative legislature. The development of man-made satellites made it possible to "bounce" microwaves off them and thus extend microwave communications much beyond the ground-level horizon. Two systems were possible. The American Telephone and Telegraph Company advanced a scheme of several relatively low satellites with ground stations switching to the next one coming up over the horizon as the last one disappeared over the opposite horizon. The Hughes Aircraft Corporation had another system under development. Its scheme would have three equally spaced satellites at 22,300 miles above the equator traveling at a speed synchronized with the rotation of the earth. This system would eliminate the need for ground switching.

The administration proposed that communications satellites using any system be owned by a private corporation, chartered by Congress, with two types of stock in equal amounts. One type would be available for purchase by anyone; the other could be bought only by communications companies. Given the corporate structure of the American communications industry, this meant that the giant in the new corporation would be AT&T. Senators who called themselves "liberals," led by Kefauver and Douglas of Illinois, argued that most of the research funds that had made these electronic wonders possible had come from the federal government and that the federal government should own the satellites. Kennedy firmly rejected their argument. A small group of Senators filibustered to prevent the bill's passage, but they were defeated by a cloture motion and the bill became law.

In late July, 1962, the first fragmentary transatlantic telecasts indicated the vast cultural implications of communications satellites. When Europeans and Americans routinely watch one another's television programs there will be a very strong tendency toward a common western culture. The satellites also will be used for telephonic and radio transmission.

Kennedy's ardent defenders saw him as a progressive hamstrung by a reactionary Congress. His conservative Republican opponents saw him as a wild-eyed radical restrained only by a sensible Congress. There could be little doubt that Kennedy's position on most matters was to the left of a large part of Congress. The national legislature had defeated or watered down all of his proposals that were relevant to the domestic issues that divided Americans into left, center, and right. Despite heavy Democratic majorities, Congress did this with the coalition of Republicans and southern Democrats. For example, on the Medicare vote in the Senate, defeated by four votes, only five of the thirty-six Republicans (Clifford Case of New Jersey, John Sherman Cooper of Kentucky, Jacob Javits and Kenneth Keating of New York, and Thomas Kuchel of California) voted for the bill. Forty-three Democrats voted for Medicare and twenty-one against. Of the twenty-one Democratic opponents, all but three (Robert Kerr and A. S. Mike Monroney of Oklahoma and Jennings Randolph of West Virginia) were from former Confederate states. Of the Senators from the South, only four (Kefauver and Albert Gore of Tennessee, Ralph Yarborough of Texas, and, surprisingly, Olin Johnston of South Carolina) voted for the measure.

Those who saw Kennedy as a progressive or a dangerous radical (depending upon their predilections) cited the President's actions in his April, 1962, battle with Roger Blough, board chairman of United States Steel, over a steel price increase. Since inauguration, the administration had been urging unions to be moderate in their demands so that industry would not increase prices, and only the previous month the steel workers had signed a noninflationary contract. The steel industry had argued during the labor bargaining that a significant increase in costs would jeopardize its competitive position with foreign steel. The administration opposed price increases, particularly in the basic commodities, for two reasons: the cost of living had been slowly rising despite the relatively sluggish economy, and price increases complicated the delicate international balance of payments problem by making it more difficult to sell abroad.

Late in the afternoon of April 10, Blough called at the White House and notified Kennedy that his firm had just raised its prices $6.00 a ton and that the news had been released to the press. The next day five other steel companies likewise increased their prices. Kennedy was furious. After forty-five minutes Blough left the White House visibly shaken. The administration unleashed an attack on the price rise that included Kennedy's denouncing the action at a press conference, maneuvering a break in the industry's united front by getting Kaiser and Bethlehem to decline to raise prices, threatening a Defense Department boycott of steel firms that raised prices, and announcing a grand jury investigation of the increases, which implied a possible antitrust law violation. United States Steel and the other firms that had raised prices capitulated within seventy-two hours after Blough's conference with Kennedy. With the exception of the Cuban invasion, the steel battle was the most dramatic incident of Kennedy's fifteen months in office.

Some political columnists saw the steel episode as a turning point in the Kennedy administration. The belief was widespread that Kennedy was anti-business; some hailed and others deplored this supposed stance. Soon jokes and stories about "That Man in the White House" reminiscent of the ones about FDR circulated at middle class cocktail parties. The decline of the stock market in May, 1962, was partly attributable to apprehension about a hostile administration, although the softness of the economy in general and the fall of prices on foreign stock exchanges were more important factors.

But it was probable that both those who condemned and those who praised Kennedy's supposed toughness with business were wrong in their fundamental assumption. The evidence that Kennedy was no doctrinaire opponent of the business community nor a typical progressive or liberal was voluminous.

Aware that businessmen since FDR were prone to believe any Democratic administration was hostile, Kennedy had on many occasions asserted "how really untrue" it was that "we are antibusiness." After the steel strike he again went out of his way to improve his reputation with business. He supported AT&T's position on Telstar. The Justice Department approved the merger of Standard Oil of Kentucky with Standard Oil of California. Kennedy's tax reform proposals did not include rescinding the oil industry's 27.5 per cent depletion allowance. The White House dropped Kefauver's drug control bill and supported a less inclusive one. In late July, 1962, Kennedy rejected the AFL-CIO's strong urging to bring about an immediate tax cut to stimulate the economy.

As one examines Kennedy's relations with his balky Congress, one finds other evidence that does not fit the view of the President as antibusiness or as liberal. Kennedy's method to get what he wanted from Congress was primarily to bargain with Congressmen, to entertain them, to implore them, and sometimes to pressure them with harder methods. With but a few exceptions, he refrained from taking his case to the citizens to build a public opinion fire under sluggish and conservative Capitol Hill.

It may be that the President realized that he must work with Congress, that he regarded it as impossible to bring Congress around to a more compatible point of view, and that therefore he felt that he should not antagonize an already uncooperative body. His call for the voters to elect "more Democrats" in the 1962 congressional elections, similar to Wilson's plea in 1918, may have been a compromise with a desire for a "purge" of Democratic conservatives such as FDR tried and failed to achieve in 1938. Perhaps he feared a national swing to the far right, symbolized by the strength of the extremist John Birch Society whose leader asserted that even Eisenhower was a tool of international communism. It might be that the President hoped that the reapportionment of state legislative districts, which in some states were not much different from early nineteenth-century England's "rotten boroughs" and which the Supreme Court had declared unconstitutional in Baker v. Carr in March, 1962, would weaken Democratic conservatives and thereby in time provide him with a more cooperative national party. In sum, he may only have been paying homage to the principle that "politics is the art of the possible." But in any case the practical results of the President's first two years in office had not been to move more than a few short steps away from Eisenhower's "middle of the road."

The Cuban Crisis and Elections of 1962

Kennedy's campaign to persuade the voters to send "more Democrats" to the Eighty-eighth Congress was in full swing when a Cold War crisis erupted that was to be the most serious since the Korean conflict. The manner in which the congressional elections coincided with the crisis was reminiscent of Eisenhower's re-election and the simultaneous Hungary and Suez affairs. The President was campaigning in Chicago on Saturday, October 20, when his press secretary announced that Kennedy was cancelling the balance of his trip and returning to Washington. It soon developed that Cuba was the reason for Kennedy's return. When the crisis eased soon before election day, the Republican cry that the President should "do something about Cuba" would have a hollow ring.

Early in September, Kennedy had ordered regular aerial photography flights over all of Cuba. Many of the flights were made in the U-2 type of plane that had precipitated a crisis in the spring of 1960. Hurricanes over the Caribbean interrupted the flights in early October. When the flights resumed, the cameras showed evidence that the Russians were installing about forty intermediate range missile sites in Cuba which would be capable of hitting targets as far north as northern Georgia and that Russian ships were delivering twin-engine jet bombers to Havana.

On October 18, the President met with Soviet Foreign Minister Andrei Gromyko in a session that had been scheduled long before. Kennedy did not indicate at this meeting that American intelligence services had discovered the presence of Russian offensive weapons in Cuba, and Gromyko told the President that all weapons being delivered to Cuba were purely defensive. Kennedy did not present the Russian minister with the photographic evidence because he and his administration had not yet fully decided what course of action they would pursue. There were several alternatives. At one extreme, Washington could do nothing overt and merely protest to Havana and Moscow. At the other extreme, the United States could launch another invasion of Castro's Cuba, a dangerous recourse because it might ignite a general nuclear war and because in any case it would probably be viewed unfavorably by America's allies. In between the two extremes were several possibilities: bombardment of the missile sites, commando raids at the critical places in Cuba, a blockade of offensive weapons, or a total blockade. Over the weekend, the President and his advisers decided upon a blockade of all offensive weapons destined for Cuba and a demand that the Russians and Cubans remove those weapons which had already been delivered. After alerting United States armed forces the world over, the President issued the blockade proclamation and spoke to the public on television the evening of Monday, October 22.

While the United States—indeed, the world—waited anxiously to see what would happen when an American naval vessel first intercepted a Russian freighter laden with offensive weapons, European and Latin American nations rallied to the defense of the American action. Although they had not been previously consulted, all of the NATO nations expressed their approval of the blockade, as did the Organization of American States by unanimous vote. Before there was any naval conflict, the Russians ordered twelve of their twenty-five ships then bound for Cuba to reverse direction. These ships presumably carried offensive arms. According to the press, an American invasion of Cuba remained a real possibility.

During the weekend of October 27–28 Khrushchev capitulated. Khrushchev and Kennedy had been in frequent communication, and most of the Russian premier's notes had been conciliatory. After Kennedy's refusal to abandon American bases in Turkey in exchange for Russian abandonment of its Cuban bases, Khrushchev agreed to dismantle the Cuban bases in exchange for Kennedy's pledge to lift the blockade and not to stage an invasion. The crisis eased, but the world would not have been surprised by a Russian action elsewhere where she had a military advantage, probably in Berlin. No such action came.

The next few weeks were uneasy ones. Kennedy continued to insist upon verification of the withdrawal of the offensive weapons, but Castro consistently refused United Nations inspections that the Russians were willing to grant. The Kennedy administration was firm but at the same time conciliatory, apparently not wishing to embarrass Khrushchev to the point where his position at home and in the Communist world generally might be endangered or where he might fall to a new and harder regime. (The Chinese Communists were openly critical of Khrushchev's capitulation.) Kennedy ordered the blockade lifted in mid-November after seeing photographs of Russian ships carrying missile parts away from Cuba. In early December, Russian ships were seen carrying dismantled twin-engine bombers away. It appeared that the Kennedy administration's victory had been virtually complete.

The Cuban crisis undoubtedly had an effect upon the way citizens voted on November 6, but political observers were not agreed upon just how much of the Democratic victory was attributable to Kennedy's Cuban policies. Clearly, the Cuban crisis did enhance Kennedy's stature in the eyes of most voters and did remove what many Republicans believed was their best issue. For the first time since 1934, the administration party gained seats in both Senate and House in an "off-year" election. In the new House there were 259 Democrats to 176 Republicans, as compared to 263 to 174 in the previous one. (The House had been temporarily increased to 437 seats with the admission of Hawaii and Alaska to statehood, but it reverted to the traditional 435 seats with the Eighty-eighth Congress.) The Democrats gained three seats in the Senate. Actually, they gained four, but the Republican governor of New Mexico, recently defeated for re-election, named himself to fill the unexpired term of the Democratic senator who died soon after election. Former Vice-President Nixon seemed to come to the end of his political career when he was defeated in his bid to become governor of California, but Republicans removed Democrats from governorships in Pennsylvania, Michigan, and Ohio. In general, Republican candidates with a reputation for liberalism fared better than those who avowed conservatism. The voters removed two Republican Congressmen from California who were members of the John Birch Society and rejected the candidacies of two other Birchers.

The public granted the President "more Democrats" in Congress as he had requested, but the Republican-Bourbon coalition that balked much of Kennedy's program remained strong. The new House had the same number of nonsouthern Democrats as before, 164, and southern Democrats continued to be chairmen of important committees because of the seniority rule.

SUGGESTIONS FOR
ADDITIONAL READING

This list of titles is not comprehensive. It is designed for the student and teacher in planning a program of "outside reading." For the historical researcher it is no more than a place to begin. I have tried to include titles my students have found useful over the years and upon which I relied in the preparation of this volume. For more extensive bibliographies the student should consult Oscar Handlin *et al.*, *Harvard Guide to American History* (1955) and bibliographies and footnotes in the books cited here.

When a title is available in a paperback edition it is followed by an asterisk (*). However, new paperback editions appear constantly and old ones become difficult to find.

CHAPTER 1.   A LOOK BACKWARD

Samuel P. Hays, *The Response to Industrialism, 1885–1914* (1957)* is a good basic work. Among the valuable works on the growth of industrialism and other developments of capitalism are Ida M. Tarbell, *The Nationalizing of Business, 1878–1898* (1936) and *The Standard Oil Company* (1904); the highly critical Matthew Josephson, *The Robber Barons* (1935); a reply to Josephson by Thomas C. Cochran, "The Legend of the Robber Barons," *Pennsylvania Magazine of History and Biography*, LXXIV (1950); Thomas C. Cochran and William Miller, *The Age of Enterprise* 1942)*; Adolph A. Berle, Jr. and Gardiner Means, *The Modern Corporation and Private Property* (1932); John Moody, *The Truth about the Trusts* (1904); Jeremiah W. Jenks and W. E. Clark, *The Trust Problem* (1929); Louis M. Hacker, *The Triumph of American Capitalism* (1940); N. S. B. Gras, *Business and Capitalism* (1946); Frederick Lewis Allen, *The Lords of Creation* (1935); George W. Edwards, *The Evolution of Finance Capitalism* (1938); and Ralph W. and Muriel Hidy, *Pioneering in Big Business, 1882–1911: A History of the Standard Oil Company* (1955). For the law on economic concentration, see Hans B. Thorelli, *The Federal Antitrust Policy* (1955).

Among the political histories of the late nineteenth century are Matthew Josephson, *The Politicos, 1865–1896* (1938), another product of Josephson's anti-business period; Harold U. Faulkner, *Politics, Reform, and Expansion, 1890–1900* (1959); Allan Nevins, *Grover Cleveland, A Study in Courage* (1932); Horace Samuel Merrill, *Bourbon Leader: Grover Cleveland and the Democratic Party* (1957); and John Lambert, *Arthur Pue Gorman* (1953). The agrarian revolt has attracted the attention of many historians. For a vigorous history of agriculture in the period, see Fred A. Shannon, *The Farmer's Last Frontier* (1945). Solon Buck presented a brief overview of the farmers' political upsurge in *The Agrarian Crusade* (1920); see, also, his *The Granger Movement* (1913). The standard work on the Populists is the solid John D. Hicks, *The Populist Revolt* (1931)*; but see, also, C. Vann Woodward, *Origins of the New South, 1877–1913* (1951) and *Tom Watson, Agrarian Rebel* (1938), both models of historical scholarship; Richard Hofstadter, *The Age of Reform* (1955)* depicts the Populists as cranky predecessors of the midcentury radical right. See, also, the forthcoming study of the Populists by Norman Pollock. Other valuable works are Dewey Grantham, *Hoke Smith and the Politics of the New South* (1958) and Allan G. Bogue, *Money at Interest: The Farm Mortgage on the Middle Border* (1955).

There is no fully satisfactory life of Bryan, but among the best works are Paul Glad, *The Trumpet Soundeth: William Jennings Bryan and his Democracy, 1896–1912* (1960) and M. R. Werner, *Bryan* (1929). For his protagonist Hanna, see Thomas Beer, *Hanna* (1929) and Herbert Croly, *Marcus Alonzo Hanna* (1912). For the election of 1896 see Bryan's memoir *The First Battle* (1896) and James A. Barnes, "Myths of the Bryan Campaign," *Mississippi Valley Historical Review*, XXXIV (1947).

For the pervasive effects of industrialism on social thought, see Richard Hofstadter, *Social Darwinism in American Thought* (1944)*; Irvin G. Wyllie, *The Self-Made Man in America: The Myth of Rags to Riches* (1954); Eric Goldman, *Rendezvous with Destiny: A History of Modern American Reform* (1952)*, a sprightly account that carries the story into the 1930's; Henry May, *Protestant Churches and Industrial America* (1949); Charles H. Hopkins, *The Rise of the Social Gospel in American Protestantism, 1865–1915* (1940); Sidney Fine, *Laissez Faire and the General-Welfare State: A Study of Conflict in American Thought, 1865–1901* (1956); Charles A. Barker, *Henry George* (1955); and Howard Quint, *The Forging of American Socialism: Origins of the Modern Movement* (1953).

On the Spanish-American War and colonial imperialism, see Julius W. Pratt, *Expansionists of 1898* (1936); Joseph E. Wisan, *The Cuban Crisis as Reflected in the New York Press, 1895–1898* (1934); G. W. Auxier, "Middle Western Newspapers and the Spanish-American War, 1895–1898," *Mississippi Valley Historical Review*, XXVI (1940); Ernest R. May, *Imperial Democracy: The Emergence of America as a Great Power* (1959); Walter Millis, *The Martial Spirit* (1931); Frank Freidel, *The Splendid Little War* (1948); Marcus M. Wilkerson, *Public Opinion and the Spanish-American War* (1932); Julius W. Pratt, *America's Colonial Experiment* (1950); William H. Haas, ed., *The American Empire* (1940); and the forthcoming volume by Walter La Feber.

CHAPTER 2. PROGRESSIVE REPUBLICANISM

An exceptionally good survey of the period is George E. Mowry, *The Era of Theodore Roosevelt, 1900–1912* (1958). Other treatments of the general period are Matthew Josephson, *The President Makers* (1940); Richard Hofstadter, *Age of Reform;** John Chamberlain, *Farewell to Reform* (1933); Russel B. Nye, *Midwestern Progressive Politics* (1951); Harold U. Faulkner, *The Quest for Social Justice, 1898–1914* (1931); and Benjamin P. De Witt, *The Progressive Movement* (1915). Mark Sullivan, *Our Times: The United States, 1900–1925* (6 vols., 1926–1935) is a chatty and gossippy piece of journalism which is interesting but superficial.

Biographies provide a good approach. For Theodore Roosevelt, see Henry Pringle, *Theodore Roosevelt: A Biography* (1931),* a Pulitzer prize winner critical in its treatment; George Mowry, *Theodore Roosevelt and the Progressive Movement* (1946),* indispensable for the later TR and the Bull Moose movement; John M. Blum, *The Republican Roosevelt* (1954), an intelligent interpretative essay; William H. Harbaugh, *Power and Responsibility: The Life and Times of Theodore Roosevelt* (1961); Carleton Putnam, *Theodore Roosevelt: The Formative Years, 1858–1886* (1958), laudatory and full of detail; Roosevelt's *Autobiography* (1924); and the convenient Elting Morison et al., eds., *The Letters of Theodore Roosevelt* (8 vols., 1951–1954).

Other biographical studies include Belle C. and Fola La Follette, *Robert M. La Follette* (2 vols., 1953); La Follette's *Autobiography* (1913);* Claude Bowers, *Beveridge and the Progressive Era* (1932); Henry Pringle, *William Howard Taft* (2 vols., 1939); Blair Bolles, *Tyrant from Illinois: Uncle Joe Cannon's Experiment with Personal Power* (1951) and William R. Gwinn, *Uncle Joe Cannon* (1957); Nathaniel W. Stephenson, *Nelson W. Aldrich* (1930); Merlo J. Pusey, *Charles Evans Hughes* (2 vols., 1951); John A. Garraty, *Henry Cabot Lodge* (1953); Philip C. Jessup, *Elihu Root* (2 vols., 1938) and Richard W. Leopold, *Elihu Root and the Conservative Tradition* (1954); Leland L. Sage, *William Boyd Allison* (1956); Francis Butler Simkins, *Pitchfork Ben Tillman* (1944); Martin Nelson McGeary, *Gifford Pinchot, Forester-Politician* (1960) and Martin L. Fausold, *Gifford Pinchot, Bull Moose Progressive* (1961); and W. A. Swanberg, *Citizen Hearst* (1961).

For the anthracite coal strike, see Robert J. Cornell, *The Anthracite Coal Strike of 1902* (1957) and a provocative interpretation by Robert H. Wiebe, "The Anthracite Strike of 1902: A Record of Confusion," *Mississippi Valley Historical Review,* XLVIII (1961). For conservation, see the Pinchot biographies and Samuel P. Hays, *The Gospel of Efficiency: The Progressive Conservation Movement, 1890–1920* (1959). For the Ballinger-Pinchot controversy, see Alpheus T. Mason, *Bureaucracy Convicts Itself* (1941). Studies of progressivism in the states and regions are George Mowry, *California Progressives* (1951); Robert S. Maxwell, *La Follette and the Rise of the Progressives in Wisconsin;* Ransom E. Noble, Jr., *New Jersey Progressivism before Wilson* (1946); Albert D. Kirwan, *Revolt of the Rednecks* (1951); and C. Vann Woodward, *Origins of the New South, 1877–1913.* For the congressional revolt under Taft, see Kenneth Hechler, *Insurgency* (1940).

CHAPTER 3. PROGRESSIVE DEMOCRACY

The best surveys of the period are George Mowry, *Era of TR* and Arthur S. Link, *Woodrow Wilson and the Progressive Era, 1910–1917* (1954). See, also, Mark Sullivan, *Our Times: The United States, 1900–1925* (6 vols., 1926–1935). Link's thorough and scholarly multivolume life of Wilson is a must of which *The Road to the White House* (1947) and *The New Freedom* (1956) cover this period. Other works on Wilson are Arthur C. Walworth, *Woodrow Wilson* (2 vols., 1958); H. C. F. Bell, *Woodrow Wilson and the People* (1945); John M. Blum, *Woodrow Wilson and the Politics of Morality* (1956); John A. Garraty, *Woodrow Wilson* (1956); and Alexander L. and Juliette L. George, *Woodrow Wilson and Colonel House* (1956). See, also, John M. Blum, *Joe Tumulty and the Wilson Era* (1951); Frank Freidel, *Franklin D. Roosevelt: The Apprenticeship* (1952); Josephus Daniels, *The Wilson*

Era—Years of Peace, 1910–1917 (1944); the forthcoming first volume of E. David Cronon's life of Daniels as well as his forthcoming edition of Daniels' diary; David F. Houston, *Eight Years with Wilson's Cabinet* (2 vols., 1926); Joseph Tumulty, *Woodrow Wilson As I Know Him* (1921); William Diamond, *The Economic Thought of Woodrow Wilson* (1943); and William G. McAdoo, *Crowded Years* (1931). For Wilson letters and documents, see Ray Stannard Baker, *Woodrow Wilson: Life and Letters* (8 vols., 1927–1939) and Baker and William E. Dodd, eds., *The Public Papers of Woodrow Wilson* (6 vols., 1925–1927). Arthur S. Link is engaged in editing a fuller series of the Wilson papers. See, also, Charles Seymour, ed., *The Intimate Papers of Colonel House* (4 vols., 1926–1928). Advanced students will find Richard L. Watson, Jr., "Woodrow Wilson and his Interpreters, 1947–1957," *Mississippi Valley Historical Review*, XLIV (1957) useful.

Many of the titles suggested for Chapter 2 are pertinent to this chapter, but see, also, J. Laurence Laughlin, *The Federal Reserve System* (1933); Frank Taussig, *Some Aspects of the Tariff Question* (1915); Herbert Croly, *The Promise of American Life* (1909) and *Progressive Democracy* (1914). Charles B. Forcey did a provocative study of the New Republic group in *The Crossroads of American Liberalism* (1961); David W. Noble, *The Paradox of Progressive Thought* (1958) is also a challenging interpretation.

CHAPTER 4. BUSINESS, AGRICULTURE, AND LABOR, 1900–1917

The standard economic history of the period is Harold U. Faulkner, *The Decline of Laissez Faire, 1897–1917* (1951). Parts of the following have great utility: United States Bureau of the Census, *Historical Statistics of the United States, Colonial Times to 1957* (1960); Robert F. Martin, *National Income in the United States, 1799–1938* (1939); Wesley C. Mitchell *et al.*, *Income in the United States, 1909–1919* (2 vols., 1921–1922); Paul H. Douglas, *Real Wages in the United States, 1896–1926* (1930); Solomon Fabricant, *Output of Manufacturing, 1899–1937* (1940); Victor S. Clark, *History of Manufactures in the United States*, (Vol. III, 1929); and Sidney Ratner, *American Taxation* (1942).

For banking and finance, see George W. Edwards, *The Evolution of Finance Capitalism* (1938); Lewis Corey, *The House of Morgan* (1930); Frederick Lewis Allen, *The Great Pierpont Morgan* (1949); Louis D. Brandeis, *Other People's Money* (1914), which summarizes the results of the Pujo committee investigations.

To study the concentration of economic power, see the titles under Chapter 1 and Henry R. Seager and C. A. Gulick, Jr., *Trust and Corporation Problems* (1929); William Z. Ripley, *Railroads: Rates and Regulation* (1912); G. Warren Nutter, *The Extent of Enterprise Monopoly in the United States, 1899–1939* (1951). For manufacturing, consult Harry Jerome, *Mechanization in Industry* (1934); Allan Nevins and Frank Ernest Hill, *Ford* (2 vols., 1954–1957); Keith Sward, *The Legend of Henry Ford* (1948); Allan Nevins, *Study in Power: John D. Rockefeller* (2 vols., 1953); Burton J. Hendrick, *The Life of Andrew Carnegie* (2 vols., 1932); and Kendall Birr, *Pioneering in Industrial Research: The Story of the General Electric Research Laboratory* (1957).

For the history of agriculture, see Harold Barger and H. H. Landsberg, *American Agriculture, 1899–1939* (1942); Murray R. Benedict, *Farm Policies of the*

United States (1953); Theodore Saloutos and John D. Hicks, *Agricultural Discontent in the Middle West, 1900–1939* (1951); John D. Hicks, "The Legacy of Populism in the Western Middle West," *Agricultural History*, XXIII (1949).

There is a considerable literature on the history of unionism and industrial relations. For two good surveys, see Foster Rhea Dulles, *Labor in America* (1949) and Joseph G. Rayback, *A History of American Labor* (1959). Every student of labor history should know John R. Commons *et al.*, *History of Labour in the United States* (4 vols., 1918–1935). Volume III, by Don D. Leschohier and Elizabeth Brandeis, on working conditions and labor legislation and Volume IV, by Selig Perlman and Philip Taft, on the labor movement, 1896–1932, are pertinent to this period. See, also, Philip Taft, *The A.F. of L. in the Time of Gompers* (1957); Marc Karson, *American Labor and Politics, 1900–1918* (1959); Samuel Gompers, *Seventy Years of Life and Labor: An Autobiography* (2 vols., 1925); and Leo Wolman, *Ebb and Flow in Trade Unionism* (1936).

There is also an extensive literature on left-wing unionism and radicalism. Paul F. Brissenden, *The Industrial Workers of the World* (1919) is standard. On the socialists, see David A. Shannon, *The Socialist Party of America: A History* (1955); Ira Kipnis, *The American Socialist Movement, 1897–1912* (1952); and Donald D. Egbert and Stow Persons, eds., *Socialism and American Life* (2 vols., 1952), of which the second volume is a comprehensive bibliography by T. D. S. Bassett; Ray Ginger, *The Bending Cross: A Biography of Eugene Victor Debs* (1949). For the anarchist movement, see Richard Drinnon, *Rebel in Paradise: A Biography of Emma Goldman* (1961).

CHAPTER 5. THE PEOPLE AND THE QUEST FOR SOCIAL JUSTICE

On immigration the best survey remains Carl Wittke, *We Who Built America* (1939), but see, also, George M. Stephenson, *History of American Immigration, 1820-1924* (1926). For the nativist opposition, John Higham, *Strangers in the Land* (1955) is a superb piece of scholarship. Oscar Handlin, *The Uprooted* (1951)* does an excellent job of describing immigration to America's large cities. Moses Rischin, *The Promised City: New York's Jews, 1870–1914* (1962) is perceptive. The best works on immigration law are Roy L. Garis, *Immigration Restriction* (1927) and William S. Bernard, *American Immigration Policy* (1950).

For Negro history, John Hope Franklin, *From Slavery to Freedom* (1947) is the best one-volume Negro history, but see, also, E. Franklin Frazier, *The Negro in the United States* (1949). Gunnar Myrdal, *An American Dilemma* (2 vols., 1944) is a monumental study, historical as well as sociological, economic, and psychological. Arnold M. Rose, *The Negro in America* (1948)* condenses the Myrdal study. For Booker T. Washington, see Basil J. Mathews, *Booker T. Washington* (1948) as well as Washington's many writings. Robert L. Jack, *History of the National Association for the Advancement of Colored People* (1943) is thin, and it should be supplemented with Francis L. Broderick, *W. E. B. Du Bois, Negro Leader in a Time of Crisis* (1959) and Elliott M. Rudwick, *W. E. B. Du Bois: A Study in Minority Group Leadership* (1960).

For the muckrake movement, see Cornelius C. Regier, *The Era of the Muckrakers* (1932) and Louis Filler, *Crusaders for American Liberalism* (1939), which is good for many figures of the period of all kinds. Lincoln Steffens, *Autobiography* (1931), delivers a hard impact. See, also, his, *The Shame of the Cities* (1957).* One should of course, consult the muckrake literature itself, and Arthur and Lila Weinberg, eds., *The Muckrakers, 1902–1912* (1961) is a convenient anthology, as is Harvey Swados, ed., *Years of Conscience* (1962).

For living conditions in urban slums and the settlement house movement, see Robert H. Bremner, *From the Depths: The Discovery of Poverty in the United States* (1955), the forthcoming book by Allen Davis, and the several biographies and autobiographies of settlement workers: Jane Addams, *Twenty Years at Hull-House* (1910) and *The Second Twenty Years at Hull House* (1930); Lillian D. Wald, *The House on Henry Street* (1915); Josephine C. Goldmark, *Impatient Crusader, Florence Kelley's Life Story* (1953); and J. W. Linn, *Jane Addams* (1935). Arthur Mann, *Yankee Reformers in the Urban Age* (1954) is a careful study of a variety of reformers. For small town life, see Lewis Atherton, *Main Street on the Middle Border* (1954), a classic. For the women's rights movement, Eleanor Flexner, *Century of Struggle: The Women's Rights Movement in the United States* (1959) is the best. On the prohibition movement, see Peter Odegard, *Pressure Politics, The Story of the Anti-Saloon League* (1928); Virginius Dabney, *Dry Messiah: The Life of Bishop Cannon* (1949); and Ernest H. Cherrington, *The Evolution of Prohibition in the United States* (1920). Harold U. Faulkner, *Quest for Social Justice, 1889-1914* (1931) expands upon the new leisure and its implications.

For the courts and constitutional history, good surveys will suffice for many students. Two of the best are Carl B. Swisher, *American Constitutional Development* (1943) and Alfred H. Kelly and W. A. Harbison, *The American Constitution* (1948). See, also, Louis B. Boudin, *Government by Judiciary* (2 vols., 1932) and Charles Warren, *The Supreme Court in United States History* (2 vols., 1937).

CHAPTER 6. AMERICAN CULTURE IN THE EARLY TWENTIETH CENTURY

All students should be familiar with Merle Curti, *The Growth of American Thought* (1943), a monumental work and a Pulitzer prize winner which has excellent chapters on the twentieth century. Also good is Henry Steele Commager, *The American Mind* (1950),* and the student should not miss Henry F. May, *The End of American Innocence* (1960); Ralph H. Gabriel, *The Course of American Democratic Thought* (1940); and Morton G. White, *Social Thought in America: The Revolt against Formalism* (1949).*

The best survey of the history of American education is R. Freeman Butts and Lawrence A. Cremin, *A History of Education in American Culture* (1953). Lawrence Cremin's *The Transformation of the School: Progressivism in American Education, 1876–1957* (1961) is an important book in intellectual history. Other worthwhile studies are Merle Curti, *The Social Ideas of American Educators* (1935); Isaac L. Kandel, *American Education in the Twentieth Century* (1957); Richard Hofstadter and C. DeWitt Hardy, *The Development and Scope of Higher Education in the United States* (1952); and Richard Hofstadter and Walter Metzger, *The Development of Academic Freedom in the United States* (1955).

On literature during the period, see Oscar Cargill, *Intellectual America: Ideas on the March* (1941); the third volume of Vernon L. Parrington, *Main Currents in*

638

American Thought (3 vols., 1927–1930)*; Robert E. Spiller *et al.*, *Literary History of the United States* (3 vols., 1948); Alfred Kazin, *On Native Grounds* (1942)*; Van Wyck Brooks, *The Confident Years, 1885–1915* (1952); and Fred L. Pattee, *The New American Literature, 1890–1930* (1930). Many of the novels and other works of the period are now available in paperback editions.

For art and architecture Milton W. Brown, *American Painting from the Armory Show to the Depression* (1955) is a superb work. Others are Meyer Schapiro, "Rebellion in Art," in Daniel Aaron, ed., *America in Crisis* (1952); Oliver W. Larkin, *Art and Life in America* (1949); John Baur, *Revolution and Tradition in Modern American Art* (1951); Samuel Isham and Royal Cortissoz, *History of American Painting* (1936); E. P. Richardson, *Painting in America* (1956); Lorado Taft, *The History of American Sculpture* (1924); and James Fitch, *American Building* (1948). For music, see Gilbert Chase, *America's Music* (1955); J. H. Mueller, *The American Symphony Orchestra* (1951); David Ewen, *Panorama of American Popular Music* (1957); and Rudi Blesh and J. Janis, *They All Played Rag-time* (1950).

For science and scholarship, see Bernard Jaffe, *Men of Science in America* (1944); Roger Shryock, *The Development of Modern Medicine* (1947) and *American Medical Research* (1947); Donald Fleming, *William H. Welch and the Rise of Modern Medicine* (1954); Simon and J. T. Flexner, *William Henry Welch and the Heroic Age of American Medicine* (1941); Thomas N. Bonner, *Medicine in Chicago, 1850–1950* (1958); and James Harvey Young, *The Toadstool Millionaires: A Social History of Patent Medicines in America before Federal Regulation* (1961). Merle Curti, ed., *American Scholarship in the Twentieth Century* (1958); Joseph Dorfman, *Thorstein Veblen and His America* (1934) and his monumental, *The Economic Mind in American Civilization* (5 vols., 1946–1959); Sidney Hook, *John Dewey* (1939); Ralph Barton Perry, *The Thought and Character of William James* (1935); Herbert Schneider, *A History of American Philosophy* (1946); and Howard K. Beale, ed., *Charles A. Beard* (1954).

CHAPTER 7. BEYOND THE CONTINENTAL BOUNDARIES, 1896–1916

Three provocative essays on American foreign relations in this century are William Appleman Williams, *The Tragedy of American Diplomacy* (1959), Robert E. Osgood, *Ideals and Self-Interest in America's Foreign Relations* (1953), and George F. Kennan, *American Diplomacy, 1900–1950* (1951).*

For general overviews, see Samuel F. Bemis, ed., *The American Secretaries of State and Their Diplomacy* (10 vols., 1927–1929); Foster Rhea Dulles, *America's Rise to World Power, 1898–1954* (1955); William Appleman Williams, ed., *The Shaping of American Diplomacy* (1955), a collection of documents and interpretations also available in two paperback volumes; Julius W. Pratt, *A History of United States Foreign Policy* (1955); Samuel F. Bemis, *A Diplomatic History of the United States* (1955); and Thomas A. Bailey, *A Diplomatic History of the American People* (1955). Many of the titles for Chapter 1 are relevant.

For the foreign policies of the presidents, see Howard K. Beale, *Theodore Roosevelt and the Rise of America to World Power* (1956); Henry Pringle, *William Howard Taft* (2 vols., 1939); Arthur S. Link, *Wilson the Diplomatist* (1957). For the navy, an important instrument and reflection of foreign policy, see Harold and

Margaret Sprout, *The Rise of American Naval Power* (1942); G. T. Davis, *A Navy Second to None* (1940); W. D. Puleston, *Mahan* (1939). For Latin American and Caribbean relations, see Samuel F. Bemis, *The Latin American Policy of the United States* (1945); Clarence H. Haring, *South America Looks at the United States* (1928); Dexter Perkins, *The Monroe Doctrine, 1867–1907* (1937) and *Hands Off: A History of the Monroe Doctrine* (1941); Dwight C. Miner, *The Fight for the Panama Route* (1940); Gerstle Mack, *The Land Divided: A History of the Panama Canal and Other Isthmian Canal Projects* (1944); Dexter Perkins, *The United States and the Caribbean* (1947); Wilfred H. Calcott, *The Caribbean Policy of the United States, 1890–1920* (1942); Howard C. Hill, *Roosevelt and the Caribbean* (1927); Howard F. Cline, *The United States and Mexico* (1953); Leland H. Jenks, *Our Cuban Colony; A Study in Sugar* (1928); and Russell H. Fitzgibbon, *Cuba and the United States, 1900–1935*.

For relations with Britain, the Empire, and Europe, see L. Ethan Ellis, *Reciprocity, 1911* (1939); Allan Nevins, *Henry White: Thirty Years of American Diplomacy* (1930); Richard R. Heindel, *The American Impact on Great Britain, 1898–1914* (1940); and Lionel M. Gelber, *The Rise of Anglo-American Friendship, 1898–1906* (1938).

For the Open Door policy, see William Appleman Williams, *The Tragedy of American Diplomacy* (1959); Tyler Dennett, *John Hay: From Poetry to Politics* (1933); A. L. P. Dennis, *Adventures in American Diplomacy, 1896–1906* (1928); and Charles S. Campbell, *Special Business Interests and the Open Door Policy* (1951).

On Far Eastern policy, see A. Whitney Griswold, *The Far Eastern Policy of the United States* (1938); Tyler Dennett, *Americans in Eastern Asia* (1922); Moorfield Story and Marcial Lichauco, *The Conquest of the Philippines by the United States, 1898–1925* (1926); Richard Hofstadter, "Manifest Destiny in the Philippines," in Daniel Aaron, ed., *America in Crisis* (1952); Charles Vevier, *The United States and China, 1906–1913* (1955); Herbert Croly, *Willard Straight* (1924); John K. Fairbank, *The United States and China* (1948); Tien-yi Li, *Woodrow Wilson's China Policy, 1913–1917* (1952); Paul A. Varg, *Missionaries, Chinese, and Diplomats* (1958); Fred Harvey Harrington, *God, Mammon, and the Japanese: Horace N. Allen and Korean-American Relations, 1884–1905* (1944); Outten J. Clinard, *Japan's Influence on American Naval Power, 1897–1917* (1947); Edwin O. Reischauer, *The United States and Japan* (1950); Thomas A. Bailey, *Theodore Roosevelt and the Japanese-American Crises* (1934); Tyler Dennett, *Roosevelt and the Russo-Japanese War* (1925); and Foster Rhea Dulles, *Forty Years of American-Japanese Relations* (1937).

CHAPTER 8. THE WAR COMES—
AND THE YANKS WHO WENT

On the road to war, two works by Charles Seymour, *American Diplomacy During the World War* (1934) and *American Neutrality, 1914–1917* (1935), are the standard works that in general defend the Wilson administration. See, also, Ernest R. May, *The World War and American Isolation* (1959). C. Hartley Grattan, *Why We Fought* (1929) is one of the early revisionist works; Walter Millis, *Road to War: America, 1914–1917* (1935) is the most popularly written revisionist book; and

Charles C. Tansill, *America Goes to War* (1938) is the most comprehensive. See, also, E. M. Borchard and W. P. Lage, *Neutrality for the United States* (1937); Alice M. Morrissey, *The American Defense of Neutral Rights, 1914–1917* (1939); Harley Notter, *The Origins of the Foreign Policy of Woodrow Wilson* (1937); Arthur S. Link, *Wilson the Diplomatist* (1957); Edward Buehrig, *Woodrow Wilson and the Balance of Power* (1955); and Edward Buehrig, ed., *Wilson's Foreign Policy in Perspective* (1957).

Among the special studies are: On propaganda, Horace C. Peterson, *Propaganda for War* (1939), George Sylvester Viereck, *Spreading Germs of Hate* (1930), and Armin Rappaport, *The British Press and Wilsonian Neutrality* (1950). Two studies of a vital ethnic group are Clifton J. Child, *The German-Americans in Politics, 1914–1917* (1939) and Carl Wittke, *German-Americans and the World War* (1936). Hermann Hagedorn, *The Bugle that Woke America* (1940) is an account of TR and preparedness by his most prolific and ardent admirer. On the peace movement, Merle Curti, *The American Peace Crusade* (1929), *Peace or War: The American Struggle* (1936), and *Bryan and World Peace* (1931). On the aspects of the decision for war that were popular in the 1930's, see Paul Birdsall, "Neutrality and Economic Pressures, 1914–1917," *Science and Society* (Vol. III, 1939).

Many of the participants wrote memoirs. See Robert Lansing, *War Memoirs of Robert Lansing* (1935); Josephus Daniels, *The Wilson Era—Years of War and After, 1917–1923* (1946); Burton J. Hendrick, *The Life and Letters of Walter Hines Page* (3 vols., 1924–1926); Stephen Gwynn, ed., *Letters and Friendships of Sir Cecil Spring Rice* (2 vols., 1929); James Gerard, *My Four Years in Germany* (1917); Johann H. von Bernstorff, *My Three Years in America* (1920) and *Memoirs* (1936); and Newton D. Baker, *Why We Went to War* (1936).

On the war itself, the best general account is Vol. II of Frederick Logan Paxson, *American Democracy and the World War* (3 vols., 1936–1948). See, also, John S. Bassett, *Our War with Germany: A History* (1919); Elting Morison, *Admiral Sims and the Modern American Navy* (1942); Thomas G. Frothingham, *The Naval History of the World War* (3 vols., 1925–1926); James G. Harbord, *The American Army in France, 1917–1919* (1936); David F. Trask, *The United States in the Supreme War Council: American War Aims and Inter-Allied Strategy, 1917–1918* (1961); and John F. Pershing, *My Experiences in the World War* (2 vols., 1931).

CHAPTER 9. THE HOME FRONT AND THE PEACE

For a general background, Preston Slosson, *The Great Crusade and After, 1914–1928* (1930) and William E. Leuchtenburg, *The Perils of Prosperity, 1914–1932* (1958)* give a broad overview. See John Bach McMaster, *The United States in the World War* (2 vols., 1918–1920); Frederick Palmer, *Newton D. Baker: America at War* (2 vols., 1931); and Benedict Crowell and R. F. Wilson, eds., *How America Went to War* (6 vols., 1921).

On industry during the war, see Grosvenor B. Clarkson, *Industrial America in the World War* (1923), a rich store of information; Bernard M. Baruch, *American Industry in the War* (1941); Margaret Coit, *Mr. Baruch* (1957), a readable account with some chapters on the war; and Walker D. Hines, *War History of the*

American Railroads (1928). For other aspects of war mobilization, see John M. Clark, *The Costs of the World War to the American People* (1931); Herbert Hoover, *The Ordeal of Woodrow Wilson* (1958), revealing about Hoover also; W. C. Mullendore, *History of the United States Food Administration* (1941); and Herbert Stein, *Government Price Policy During the World War* (1941). For wartime propaganda see James R. Mock and Cedric Larson, *Words That Won the War: The Story of the Committee on Public Information* (1940); George Creel, *How We Advertised America* (1920); Harold D. Lasswell, *Propaganda Technique in the World War* (1927); and James R. Mock, *Censorship, 1917* (1941). On the opponents of war and their difficulties, see Horace C. Peterson and Gilbert Fite, *Opponents of War, 1917–1918* (1957) and Zechariah Chaffee, Jr., *Free Speech in the United States* (1941), both accounts of appalling disregard for civil liberty; David A. Shannon, *The Socialist Party of America: A History* (1955); and Ray Ginger, *The Bending Cross: A Biography of Eugene Victor Debs* (1949). For the postwar hysteria, see Robert K. Murray, *Red Scare* (1955) and Richard Drinnon, *Rebel in Paradise: A Biography of Emma Goldman* (1961).

On the Versailles treaty, see Thomas Bailey, *Woodrow Wilson and the Lost Peace* (1944); Ray Stannard Baker, *Woodrow Wilson and World Settlement* (3 vols., 1922); H. W. V. Temperley *et al.*, *A History of the Peace Conference of Paris* (6 vols., 1920–1924); Ruhl J. Bartlett, *The League to Enforce Peace* (1944) on the American background to the League; John Maynard Keynes, *The Economic Consequences of the Peace* (1920), a widely read criticism of the treaty, and a critique of Keynes, Etienne Mantoux, *The Carthaginian Peace, Or the Economic Consequences of Mr. Keynes* (1946); Edward M. House and Charles Seymour, eds., *What Really Happened at Paris* (1921); Robert Lansing, *The Peace Negotiations, A Personal Narrative* (1921); Frederick Palmer, *Bliss, Peacemaker* (1934); David H. Miller, *The Drafting of the Covenant* (2 vols., 1938); Bernard M. Baruch, *The Making of the Reparations and Economic Sections of the Treaty* (1920); James T. Shotwell, *At the Paris Peace Conference* (1937); Harold Nicholson, *Peacemaking, 1919* (1939); and Paul Birdsall, *Versailles Twenty Years After* (1941). For what historians have written about the conference, see R. C. Binkley, "Ten Years of Peace Conference History," *Journal of Modern History*, I (1929) and Paul Birdsall, "The Second Decade of Peace Conference History," *Journal of Modern History*, XI (1939).

On the Senate's rejection of the treaty, see Thomas Bailey, *Woodrow Wilson and the Great Betrayal* (1945); Denna F. Fleming, *The United States and the League of Nations, 1918–1920* (1932); W. Stull Holt, *Treaties Defeated by the Senate* (1933); Selig Adler, "The Congressional Election of 1918," *South Atlantic Quarterly*, XXXVI (1937); Seward Livermore, "The Sectional Issue in the 1918 Congressional Election," *Mississippi Valley Historical Review*, XXXV 1948); Dexter Perkins, "Woodrow Wilson's Tour," in Daniel Aaron, ed., *America in Crisis* (1952); Kenneth Colegrove, *The American Senate and World Peace* (1943); Henry Cabot Lodge, *The Senate and the League of Nations* (1925); Kark Schriftgiesser, *The Gentleman from Massachusetts* (1944); and John A. Garraty, *Henry Cabot Lodge* (1953).

On other aspects of foreign policy at the time, see L. A. R. Yates, *United States and French Security, 1917–1921* (1957); William S. Graves, *America's Siberian Adventure, 1918–1920* (1941); William Appleman Williams, *American-Russian Relations, 1781–1947* (1952); Robert P. Browder, *Origins of Soviet-American Diplomacy*

(1953); and the not yet completed multivolume study by George F. Kennan, *Soviet-American Relations, 1917–1920*.

CHAPTER 10. THE POLITICS OF BUSINESS, 1919–1929

There are several general histories of the United States in the 1920's. The most comprehensive and reliable general work is John D. Hicks, *Republican Ascendancy, 1921–1933* (1960), which has an excellent bibliography. One of the most popular is Frederick Lewis Allen, *Only Yesterday: An Informal History of the Nineteen Twenties* (1931).* More perceptive but brightly written is William E. Leuchtenburg, *The Perils of Prosperity, 1914–1932* (1958). Other general histories are Harold U. Faulkner, *From Versailles to the New Deal* (1950); Karl Schriftgiesser, *This Was Normalcy: An Account of Party Politics during Twelve Republican Years* (1948), which votes vigorously Democratic; James C. Malin, *The United States after the World War* (1930); Louis M. Hacker, *American Problems of Today: A History of the United States since the World War* (1938); Vols. V and VI of Mark Sullivan, *Our Times: The United States, 1900–1925* (6 vols., 1926–1935); and Preston W. Slosson, *The Great Crusade and After, 1914–1928* (1930). For conversion to a peacetime order, see James R. Mock and Evangeline Thurber, *Report on Demobilization* (1944).

No fully satisfactory life of Harding exists, largely because there are no Harding papers. But, see Samuel Hopkins Adams, *Incredible Era: The Life and Times of Warren Gamaliel Harding* (1939), a sensational treatment; Wesley Bagby, "The 'Smoke Filled Room' and the Nomination of Warren G. Harding," *Mississippi Valley Historical Review*, XLI (1955); and Finley Peter Dunne, "A Look at Harding from the Side Lines," *Saturday Evening Post*, CCIX (1936). For the oil scandals, see J. Leonard Bates, "Josephus Daniels and the Naval Oil Reserves," *U.S. Naval Institute Proceedings*, LXXIX (1953); "The Teapot Dome Scandal and the Election of 1924," *American Historical Review*, LX (1955); and Burl Noggle, "The Origins of the Teapot Dome Investigation," *Mississippi Valley Historical Review*, XLIV (1957).

On Coolidge, see William Allen White, *A Puritan in Babylon* (1938), a masterpiece of popular biography; Claude Fuess, *Calvin Coolidge* (1940), generally sympathetic; Francis Russell, "Coolidge and the Boston Police Strike," *Antioch Review*, XVI (1956); and Gamaliel Bradford, "The Genius of the Average: Calvin Coolidge," *Atlantic Monthly*, CXLV (1930).

On Republicans of various hues during the period, see Malcolm Moos, *The Republicans* (1956); Henry Pringle, *William Howard Taft* (2 vols., 1939); William T. Hutchinson, *Lowden of Illinois* (2 vols., 1957), thorough and scholarly; George W. Norris, *Fighting Liberal* (1945); Claudius O. Johnson, *Borah of Idaho* (1936); Marian C. McKenna, *Borah* (1961); and William Allen White, *Autobiography* (1946). On the Democrats, see Arthur M. Schlesinger, Jr., *The Crisis of the Old Order, 1919–1933* (1957); Frank Freidel, *Franklin D. Roosevelt: The Ordeal* (1954), the second volume of his multivolume life of Roosevelt; and James M. Cox, *Journey through My Years* (1946).

On the La Follette movement of 1924, see Kenneth McKay, *The Progressive Movement of 1924* (1947), the standard work; David A. Shannon, *The Socialist Party of America: A History* (1955); Russel B. Nye, *Midwestern Progressive Politics*

(1951); Belle and Fola La Follette, *Robert M. La Follette* (2 vols., 1953); and James Shideler, "The Disintegration of the Progressive Party Movement of 1924," *The Historian* (1951).

On various aspects of agricultural politics, see Robert Morlan, *Political Prairie Fire: The Nonpartisan League, 1915–1922* (1955), a valuable study; Gilbert Fite, *George Peek and the Fight for Farm Parity* (1954), thorough and scholarly; Theodore Saloutos and John D. Hicks, *Agricultural Discontent in the Middle West, 1900–1939* (1951); Harold Barger and H. H. Landsberg, *American Agriculture, 1899–1939* (1951); Grant McConnell, *Decline of Agrarian Democracy* (1953); Arthur Cappter, *The Agricultural Bloc* (1922); and Alice Christensen, "Agricultural Pressure and Governmental Response, 1919–1929," *Agricultural History*, XI (1937).

On electric power struggles, see Ernest H. Gruening, *The Public Pays* (1931); Stephen Rauschenbush, *The Power Fight* (1932); Carl D. Thompson, *Confessions of the Power Trust* (1932); and Preston J. Hubbard, *Origins of the TVA: The Muscle Shoals Controversy, 1920–1932* (1961), definitive on the subject.

CHAPTER 11. THE ECONOMICS OF BUSINESS,
1917–1929

The best general economic history of the 1920's is George Soule, *Prosperity Decade* (1947). Other useful general studies are Frederick Mills, *Economic Tendencies in the United States* (1932); Joseph Schumpeter, "The American Economy in the Interwar Period: The Decade of the Twenties," *American Economic Review*, XXXVI (1946); President's Conference on Unemployment, *Recent Economic Changes in the United States* (2 vols., 1929); Eli Ginzburg, *The Illusion of Stability* (1939); and Thomas Nixon Carver, *The Present Economic Revolution in the United States* (1925), an optimistic view.

Among the special studies, many of which require some understanding of economic theory, are Harold Barger, *Outlay and Income in the United States, 1921–1938* (1942); United States National Resources Committee, *Technological Trends and National Policy* (1937); Simon Kuznets, *National Income and Its Composition, 1919–1938* (1941); Edwin Nourse *et al.*, *America's Capacity to Produce* (1934); Maurice Leven *et al.*, *America's Capacity to Consume* (1934); and Ralph Epstein, *Industrial Profits in the United States* (1934). On economic concentration, there is Arthur R. Burns, *The Decline of Competition* (1936); Adolph Berle and Gardiner Means, *The Modern Corporation and Private Property* (1932); Harry Wellington Laidler, *Concentration of Control in American Industry* (1931); George W. Edwards, *The Evolution of Finance Capitalism* (1938); Charles Chapman, *The Development of American Business and Banking Thought, 1913–1936* (1936); William Z. Ripley, *Main Street and Wall Street* (1927); James C. Bonbright and Gardiner C. Means, *The Holding Company* (1932); and Norman Buchanan, "The Origin and Development of the Public Utility Holding Company," *Journal of Political Economy*, XLIV (1936). On specific large corporations during the decade, see Sumner Slichter, "Woolworth," *Fortune*, VIII (1933), and "A & P and the Hartfords," *Fortune*, VII (1933); Allan Nevins and Frank Ernest Hill, *Ford* (Vol. II, 1957); and Keith Sward, *The Legend of Henry Ford* (1948).

On business thought and advertising, see James Prothro, *The Dollar Decade* (1954); Morrell Heald, "Business Thought in the Twenties: Social Responsibility,"

American Quarterly, XIII (1961); and Otis Pease, *The Responsibilities of American Advertising: Private Control and Public Influence, 1920–1940* (1958), a pioneering work.

For labor in the 1920's, see Irving L. Bernstein, *The Lean Years: A History of the American Worker, 1920–1933* (1960); Philip Taft, *The A.F. of L. in the Time of Gompers* (1957), and *The A.F. of L. from the Death of Gompers to the Merger* (1959); James O. Morris, *Conflict within the A.F. of L.* (1959); John S. Gambs, *The Decline of the I.W.W.* (1932); Felix Frankfurter and Nathan Greene, *The Labor Injunction* (1930); Edward Berman, *Labor and the Sherman Act* (1930); David Brodie, *Steelworkers in America: The Nonunion Era* (1960); William Z. Foster, *The Great Steel Strike and Its Lessons* (1920); Commission of Inquiry, The Interchurch World Movement, *Report on the Steel Strike of 1919* (1920); Matthew Josephson, *Sidney Hillman* (1952), a poor biography but the best existing one; Samuel Yellen, *American Labor Struggles* (1936), a useful account of several strikes, some of which were in the 1920's; J. B. S. Hardman, ed., *American Labor Dynamics* (1928); Sumner Slichter, "The Current Labor Policies of American Industries," *Quarterly Journal of Economics*, XLIII (1929); David Saposs, "The American Labor Movement since the War," *Quarterly Journal of Economics*, XLIX (1935); and Lyle Cooper, "The American Labor Movement in Prosperity and Depression," *American Economic Review*, XXII (1932).

CHAPTER 12. THE FOREIGN POLICY OF A BUSINESS GOVERNMENT

Works of a general nature are Allan Nevins, *The United States in a Chaotic World* (1950), very brief; Frank H. Simonds, *American Foreign Policy in the Post-War Years* (1935); William Appleman Williams, "The Legend of Isolationism in the 1920's," *Science and Society*, XVIII (1954) and *The Tragedy of American Diplomacy* (1959); Selig Adler, *The Isolationist Impulse* (1957)*; Denna F. Fleming, *The United States and World Organization, 1920–1933* (1938) and *The United States and the World Court* (1945).

For foreign economic policies, see James Angell, *Financial Foreign Policy of the United States* (1933); Herbert Feis, *The Diplomacy of the Dollar: First Era, 1919–1932* (1950); Harold G. Moulton and L. Pasvolsky, *World War Debt Settlements* (1926) and *War Debts and World Prosperity* (1932); the chapter on foreign affairs in Simon Kuznets, *Economic Change* (1953); M. F. Jolliffe, *The United States as a Financial Centre, 1919–1933* (1935); John Madden, *et al.*, *America's Experience as a Creditor Nation* (1957); and Benjamin Williams, *Economic Foreign Policy of the United States* (1929).

Merlo J. Pusey, *Charles Evans Hughes*, (2 vols., 1951) and Dexter Perkins, *Charles Evans Hughes and American Democratic Statesmanship* (1956) provide a good survey of foreign affairs for the first part of the 1920's. See, also, Raymond L. Buell, *The Washington Conference* (1922); Benjamin H. Williams, *The United States and Disarmament* (1931); Merze Tate, *The United States and Armaments* (1948); Robert H. Ferrell, *Peace in Their Time* (1952), on the Kellogg-Briand Pact; James T. Shotwell, *War as an Instrument of National Policy and Its Renunciation in the Pact of Paris* (1929); L. Ethan Ellis, *Frank B. Kellogg and American Foreign Relations, 1925–1929* (1961); David Bryn-Jones, *Frank B. Kellogg, A Biography*

(1937); Rodman W. Paul, *Abrogation of the Gentlemen's Agreement* (1936); and Russell M. Cooper, *American Consultation in World Affairs* (1934).

On relations with specific nations, see Graham H. Stuart, *Latin America and the United States* (1938); Isaac J. Cox, *Nicaragua and the United States* (1927); Harold Nicholson, *Dwight Morrow* (1935); Howard F. Cline, *The United States and Mexico* (1953); Robert P. Browder, *Origins of Soviet-American Diplomacy* (1953); William Appleman Williams, *American-Russian Relations, 1781–1947* (1952); and Frederick L. Schuman, *American Policy toward Russia since 1917* (1928).

CHAPTER 13. THE BUSINESS CIVILIZATION AND ITS CRITICS

For education, scholarship, and science, see the titles cited under Chapter 6.

General works are Harold Stearns, ed., *Civilization in the United States* (1922), an historically important landmark, and *America and the Young Intellectual* (1921). Robert and Helen Lynd, *Middletown* (1929) is a classic analysis of a small midwestern city; see, also, Lewis Atherton, *Main Street on the Middle Border* (1954). Many English and European travelers offered their observations: George Knoles, ed., *The Jazz Age Revisited* (1955); Andre Siegfried, *America Comes of Age* (1927); J. A. Spender, *Through English Eyes* (1928).

American literature during the decade has attracted much attention. See Frederick Hoffman, *The Twenties* (1955); John Hutchens, *The American Twenties* (1952); Arthur Mizener, "The Novel in America: 1920–1940," *Perspectives USA*, XV (1956); Joseph Wood Krutch, *The Modern Temper* (1929); Frederick John Hoffman, *The Modern Novel in America, 1900–1951* (1951); Maxwell Geismar, *Last of the Provincials* (1947); J. W. Beach, *American Fiction, 1920–1940* (1941); Alfred Kazin, *On Native Grounds* (1942)*; Malcolm Cowley, *Exile's Return* (1934)*; and Oscar Cargill, *Intellectual America: Ideas on the March* (1941). The exuberant Mr. Mencken is the subject of Edgar Kemler, *The Irreverent Mr. Mencken* (1950); William Manchester, *Disturber of the Peace* (1951)*; and Charles Angoff, *H. L. Mencken* (1956). For other aspects of literature, see William Vann O'Connor, *An Age of Criticism, 1900–1950* (1952); Alan S. Downer, *Fifty Years of American Drama, 1900–1950* (1951); and Louise Bogan, *Achievement in American Poetry, 1900–1950* (1951). For two great literary biographies, see Arthur Mizener, *The Far Side of Paradise* (1959),* on F. Scott Fitzgerald, and Mark Schorer, *Sinclair Lewis* (1961).

The "new psychology" that swept America is considered in Frederick Hoffman, *Freudianism and the Literary Mind* (1945); A. A. Brill, "The Introduction and Development of Freud's Work in the United States," *American Journal of Sociology*, XLV (1939); and Lucille Birnbaum, "Behaviourism in the 1920's," *American Quarterly*, VII (1955).

On art and architecture, see Milton W. Brown, *American Painting from the Armory Show to the Depression* (1955), and other titles listed under Chapter 6. See, also, Thomas Hart Benton, *An Artist in America* (1937); Lewis Mumford, ed., *Roots of Contemporary American Architecture* (1952); Carl W. Condit, *The Rise of the Skyscraper* (1952); and Frank Lloyd Wright, *Modern Architecture* (1932), an opinionated personal document.

For music, see titles under Chapter 6 plus Sigmund Spaeth, *A History of*

Popular Music in America (1948); Rudi Blesh, *Shining Trumpets* (1946); William C. Handy, *Father of the Blues* (1941); and Winthrop Sargeant, *Jazz* (1946).

CHAPTER 14. THE PEOPLE AND THEIR TENSIONS

For general social history of the 1920's, see Frederick Lewis Allen, *Only Yesterday: An Informal History of the Nineteen Twenties* (1931)*; Lloyd Morris, *Postscript to Yesterday* (1947) and *Not So Long Ago* (1947); Henry M. Robinson, *Fantastic Interim* (1943); Paul Sann, *The Lawless Decade* (1937); Isabel Leighton, ed., *The Aspirin Age* (1949); and James Truslow Adams, *Our Business Civilization* (1929).

On immigration, see Carl Wittke, *We Who Built America* (1939); John Higham, *Strangers in the Land* (1955); William S. Bernard, *American Immigration Policy* (1950); Kate Holladay Claghorn, *The Immigrant's Day in Court* (1923); and Joseph J. Huthmacher, *Massachusetts People and Politics, 1919–1933* (1959), which puts its emphasis on the political maturation of ethnic groups.

For Negro history, see John Hope Franklin, *From Slavery to Freedom* (1947); E. Franklin Frazier, *The Negro in the United States* (1949); Gunnar Myrdal, *An American Dilemma* (2 vols., 1944); E. David Cronon, *Black Moses: The Story of Marcus Garvey and the Universal Negro Improvement Association* (1955),* a model of scholarship.

For prohibition, see Charles Merz, *The Dry Decade* (1931) and Herbert Asbury, *The Great Illusion, An Informal History of Prohibition* (1950), which is about as informal as a history can be.

On manners and morals, see John Sirjamaki, *The American Family in the Twentieth Century* (1953) and Oliver Jensen, *The Revolt of American Women* (1952). The following sampling of contemporary titles will attest to the concern in the 1920's about changing ways: Freda Kirchwey, ed., *Our Changing Morality: A Symposium* (1924); the December, 1926, and May, 1929, issues of *The Annals of the American Academy of Political and Social Science;* John Carter, Jr., " 'These Wild Young People': By One of Them," *Atlantic Monthly,* CXXVI (1920); Viola Paradise, "Sex Simplex," *Forum,* LXXIV (1925); Mary Agnes Hamilton, "Nothing Shocks Me," *Harper's,* CLV (1927); Dorothy Dunbar Bromley, "Feminist, New Style," *Harper's,* CLV (1927); Eleanor Rowland Wembridge, "Petting and the Campus," *Survey,* LIV (1925); William Bolitho, "The New Skirt Length," *Harper's,* CLX (1930); and G. Stanley Hall, "Flapper Americana Novissima," *Atlantic Monthly,* CXXIX (1922).

For "One Hundred Percentism," see John M. Mecklin, *The Ku Klux Klan* (1924); Emerson Loucks, *The Ku Klux Klan in Pennsylvania* (1936); and Robert Moats Miller, "A Note on the Relationship between the Protestant Churches and the Revived Ku Klux Klan," *Journal of Social History,* XXII (1956). Calvin Coolidge, "Enemies of the Republic: Are the Reds Stalking Our College Women?" *The Delineator,* XCVIII (1921) is an example of one hundred percentism by the Vice-President. Bessie L. Pierce, *Public Opinion and the Teaching of History in the United States* (1926) and Howard K. Beale, *Are American Teachers Free?* (1936) discuss pressures on the schools. Ray Ginger, *Six Days or Forever?* (1958) on the Scopes trial. See, also, Walter Lippmann, *American Inquisitors* (1928). For religion's role in the period's tensions, see Norman F. Furniss, *The Fundamentalist Controversy, 1918–1931* (1954); Paul Carter, *The Decline and Revival of the Social*

Gospel (1956); and Robert Moats Miller, *American Protestantism and Social Issues, 1919–1939* (1958).

For some of the victims of intolerance, see Felix Frankfurter, *The Case of Sacco and Vanzetti* (1927); G. L. Joughin and E. M. Morgan, *The Legacy of Sacco and Vanzetti* (1948); and James Grossman, "The Sacco-Vanzetti Case Reconsidered," *Commentary*, XXXIII (1962). For Communism during the decade, see Theodore Draper, *The Roots of American Communism* (1957) and *American Communism and Soviet Russia* (1960); and Granville Hicks, *John Reed* (1936).

On the election of 1928, see Oscar Handlin, *Al Smith and His America* (1958); Henry F. Pringle, *Alfred E. Smith* (1927); Edmund Moore, *A Catholic Runs for President* (1956), a work of careful scholarship; Roy Peel and Thomas Donnelly, *The 1928 Campaign: An Analysis* (1931).

CHAPTER 15. THE GREAT CRASH AND
THE HOOVER ADMINISTRATION

For the crash and the early depression, see John Kenneth Galbraith, *The Great Crash* (1955),* by an economist who does not write like one when he does not want to; Broadus Mitchell, *Depression Decade: From New Era through New Deal, 1929–1941* (1947), a book basic to this chapter and subsequent ones; Lionel Robbins, *The Great Depression* (1934); Francis Hirst, *Wall Street and Lombard Street* (1931). For the impact of the depression on human lives, see David A. Shannon, ed., *The Great Depression* (1959)*; Gilbert Seldes, *Years of the Locust: America, 1929–1932* (1933). For the Hoover administration, see Harris G. Warren, *Herbert Hoover and the Great Depression* (1959); Arthur M. Schlesinger, Jr., *The Crisis of the Old Order, 1919–1933* (1957); John D. Hicks, *Republican Ascendancy, 1921–1933* (1960); Charles A. and Mary R. Beard, *America in Midpassage* (1939), invaluable for the decade following 1928; Herbert Hoover, *Memoirs* (3 vols., 1951–1952); W. S. Myers and W. H. Newton, *The Hoover Administration* (1936), a defense; Ray Lyman Wilbur and Arthur Hyde, *The Hoover Policies* (1937), another defense by administration officials; the relevant parts of William Appleman Williams, *The Contours of American History* (1951), an exciting and provocative interpretation; the chapter on Hoover in Richard Hofstadter, *The American Political Tradition and the Men Who Made It* (1948)*; Rexford G. Tugwell, *Mr. Hoover's Economic Policy* (1932), a contemporary indictment; Irving L. Bernstein, *Lean Years: A History of the American Worker, 1920–1933* (1960); and Mark Sullivan, "The Case for the Administration," *Fortune*, VI (1932), a contemporary defense.

CHAPTER 16. THE EARLY NEW DEAL

There is a mountain of material on FDR and the New Deal. For FDR in the years immediately preceding the presidency, see Frank Freidel, *Franklin D. Roosevelt: The Triumph* (1956); Bernard Bellush, *Apprenticeship for the Presidency: Franklin D. Roosevelt as Governor of New York* (1951), a definitive work; Arthur M. Schlesinger, Jr., *The Crisis of the Old Order, 1919–1933* (1957); Roy V. Peel and T. C. Donnelly, *The 1932 Campaign* (1935); and James M. Burns, *Roosevelt: The Lion and the Fox* (1956), the best one-volume study of FDR, a political biography.

SUGGESTIONS FOR ADDITIONAL READING

FDR's published papers include: Samuel I. Rosenman, ed., *The Public Papers and Addresses of Franklin D. Roosevelt* (13 vols., 1938–1950); Elliott Roosevelt, ed., *F.D.R.: His Personal Letters* (4 vols., 1947–1950). Arthur M. Schlesinger, Jr., *The Coming of the New Deal* (1958), Volume II of *The Age of Roosevelt*, treats the material covered in this chapter. See, also, Ernest K. Lindley, *The Roosevelt Revolution: First Phase* (1933); Charles A. Beard and George H. E. Smith, *The Future Comes: A Study of the New Deal* (1933). Among the special studies relevant to this chapter are Leverett S. Lyon *et al.*, *The National Recovery Administration* (1935); E. G. Nourse *et al.*, *Three Years of the Agricultural Adjustment Administration* (1937); Gilbert C. Fite, "Farmer Opinion and the Agricultural Adjustment Act," *Mississippi Valley Historical Review*, XLVIII (1962); G. Griffith Johnson, Jr., *Treasury and Monetary Policy, 1933–1938* (1939); Ferdinand Pecora, *Wall Street under Oath* (1939); and Leo Wolman, Rexford G. Tugwell *et al.*, *America's Recovery Program* (1934).

No fully satisfactory one-volume history of the New Deal exists at the moment, but there are several worth reading. James M. Burns, *Roosevelt: The Lion and the Fox* (1956) is excellent to about 1938; Basil Rauch, *The History of the New Deal, 1933–1938* (1944) was one of the first efforts at New Deal history and is still useful; Denis W. Brogan, *The Era of Franklin D. Roosevelt* (1950) is a clever Englishman's view, valuable mainly for an outsider's opinion, as is Mario Enaudi, *The Roosevelt Revolution* (1959); Charles A. Beard and George H. E. Smith, *The Old Deal and the New* (1940) is not as thorough as Charles A. and Mary R. Beard, *America in Midpassage* (1939); V. O. Key, Jr., *Southern Politics in State and Nation* (1949) is an important study of a relevant subject; Raymond D. Moley, *Twenty-Seven Masters of Politics* (1949) has some interesting insights.

Among the books about FDR are Harold F. Gosnell, *Champion Campaigner, Franklin D. Roosevelt* (1952); Edgar Eugene Robinson, *The Roosevelt Leadership, 1933–1945* (1955), sharply critical and containing an excellent bibliography; Rexford G. Tugwell, *The Democratic Roosevelt* (1957); John T. Flynn, *The Roosevelt Myth* (1948), a right-wing swipe; John Gunther, *Roosevelt in Retrospect* (1950)*; Robert E. Sherwood, *Roosevelt and Hopkins* (1948),* contains many letters and is especially good for the partnership of these two men during the war; Mauritz A. Hallgren, *The Gay Reformer: Profits before Plenty under Franklin D. Roosevelt* (1935), a criticism from the left; Elliott Roosevelt, *As He Saw It* (1946); Frances Perkins, *The Roosevelt I Knew* (1946); Carroll Kilpatrick, ed., *Roosevelt and Daniels, A Friendship in Politics* (1952).

Among the memoirs and biographical studies of the FDR circle are Hugh S. Johnson, *The Blue Eagle from Egg to Earth* (1935); Marriner S. Eccles, *Beckoning Frontiers* (1951), a useful document; Grace G. Tully, *F.D.R., My Boss* (1949); Raymond Moley, *After Seven Years* (1939); Harold L. Ickes, *Autobiography of a Curmudgeon* (1943) and *Secret Diary* (3 vols., 1953–1954); Edward J. Flynn, *You're the Boss* (1947); Eleanor Roosevelt, *This Is My Story* (1937) and *This I Remember* (1949); Charles Michelson, *The Ghost Talks* (1944); Samuel I. Rosenman, *Working with Roosevelt* (1952); Vice-Admiral Ross T. McIntire and George Creel, *White House Physician* (1946); Daniel C. Roper, *Fifty Years of Public Life* (1941); Lela Stiles, *The Man behind Roosevelt: The Story of Louis McHenry Howe* (1954); Nicholas Roosevelt, *A Front Row Seat* (1953); Donald R. Richberg, *My Hero* (1954) and *The Rainbow* (1936); James A. Farley, *Behind the Ballots* (1938) and *Jim Farley's Story* (1948).

CHAPTER 17. THE LATER NEW DEAL

Many of the titles listed for the previous chapter are useful for this one as well. Arthur M. Schlesinger, Jr., *The Politics of Upheaval* (1960), Vol. III of *The Age of Roosevelt*, treats in admirable detail the material of the greater part of this chapter.

On the revolt of the right, see Herbert Hoover, *The Challenge to Liberty* (1934) and *Addresses upon the American Road* (1938), as well as his *Memoirs* (3 vols., 1951–1952); Alf M. Landon, *America at the Crossroads* (1936); and George Wolfskill, *The Revolt of the Conservatives: A History of the American Liberty League, 1934–1940* (1962). For the pressure from the left and quasi-left, see Donald R. McCoy, *Angry Voices: Left-of-Center Politics in the New Deal Era* (1958); Alfred M. Bingham, *Challenge to the New Deal* (1934); Harnett T. Kane, *Louisiana Hayride* (1941), on Huey Long; and the forthcoming book on Long by T. Harry Williams.

On various aspects of later New Deal reforms, see Paul H. Douglas, *Social Security in the United States* (1939); Seymour Harris, *The Economics of Social Security* (1941); Grace Abbott, *From Relief to Social Security* (1941); Donald S. Howard, *The WPA and Federal Relief Policy* (1943); James C. Bonbright, *Public Utilities and National Power Policies* (1940); Marion L. Ramsay, *Pyramids of Power: The Story of Roosevelt, Insull and the Utility Wars* (1937); and William O. Douglas, *Democracy and Finance* (1940).

On the Supreme Court crisis and the Roosevelt court, see Merlo J. Pusey, *The Supreme Court Crisis* (1937); Joseph Alsop and Turner Catledge, *The 168 Days* (1938); Samuel Hendel, *Charles Evans Hughes and the Supreme Court* (1951); Merlo J. Pusey, *Charles Evans Hughes* (2 vols., 1951); Robert H. Jackson, *The Struggle for Judicial Supremacy* (1941); Edward S. Corwin, *Court over Constitution* (1938); Joel Paschal, *Mr. Justice Sutherland* (1951); Alpheus T. Mason, *Harland Fiske Stone: Pillar of the Law* (1956); Samuel J. Konefsky, *Chief Justice Stone and the Supreme Court* (1945); and C. Herman Pritchett, *The Roosevelt Court: A Study in Judicial Politics and Values, 1937–1947* (1948).

CHAPTER 18. ECONOMIC CHANGE
IN A TIME OF TROUBLE

General works on economic history and special studies on aspects of federal economic policies are Broadus Mitchell, *Depression Decade: From New Era through New Deal, 1929–1941* (1947); Merle Fainsod and L. Gordon, *Government and the American Economy* (1941); Clair Wilcox, *Competition and Monopoly in American Industry* (1940); David Lynch, *Concentration of Economic Power* (1946), a very useful summary of the TNEC reports and hearings; Henry H. Villard, *Deficit Spending and the National Income* (1941); John Kenneth Galbraith and G. G. Johnson, Jr., *The Economic Effects of the Federal Public Works Expenditures, 1933–1938* (1940); Arthur E. Burns and D. S. Watson, *Government Spending and Economic Expansion* (1940); Jesse Jones, *Fifty Billion Dollars: My Thirteen Years with the RFC, 1932–1945* (1951); and Harry L. Hopkins, *Spending to Save* (1936).

On labor, see Selig Perlman, *Labor in the New Deal Decade* (1945); Edwin

Young and Milton Derber, eds., *Labor and the New Deal* (1957); Irving Bernstein, *The New Deal Collective Bargaining Policy* (1950); Walter Galenson, *The CIO Challenge to the A.F. of L.* (1960); James O. Morris, *Conflict within the A.F. of L.* (1959); John B. Andrews, *Labor Laws in Action* (1938); Joseph Rosenfarb, *The National Labor Policy and How It Works* (1940); Robert R. R. Brooks, *When Labor Organizes* (1936), *Unions of their Own Choosing* (1939), and *As Steel Goes* (1940); Harold Seidman, *Labor Czars: A History of Labor Racketeering* (1938); J. Raymond Walsh, *CIO, Industrial Unionism in Action* (1937); Edward Levinson, *Labor on the March* (1938); Herbert Harris, *American Labor* (1939) and *Labor's Civil War* (1940); Carroll R. Daugherty, *Labor under the NRA* (1934); and Harry A. Millis and Emily C. Brown, *From the Wagner Act to Taft-Hartley* (1950).

For the TVA and southern problems, see C. Herman Pritchett, *The Tennessee Valley Authority: A Study in Public Administration* (1943); David E. Lilienthal, *TVA: Democracy on the March* (1953 ed.); Howard W. Odum, *Southern Regions of the United States* (1936); Rupert B. Vance, *Human Geography of the South* (1935 ed.); and National Emergency Council, *Report on Economic Conditions of the South* (1938).

Besides the works on agricultural history cited earlier, see John D. Black, *Parity, Parity, Parity* (1942); Henry Wallace, *New Frontiers* (1934); Russell Lord, *The Wallaces of Iowa* (1947); Arthur F. Raper and Ira DeA. Reid, *Sharecroppers All* (1941); Thomas J. Woofter, Jr., and E. Winston, *Seven Lean Years* (1939); M. S. Venkataramani, "Norman Thomas, Arkansas Sharecroppers, and the Roosevelt Agricultural Policies, 1933–1937," *Mississippi Valley Historical Review*, XLVII (1960); and Howard Kester, *Revolt among the Sharecroppers* (1936).

CHAPTER 19. SOCIETY AND THE
GREAT DEPRESSION

General works with a great deal of social history of the 1930's are Dixon Wecter, *The Age of the Great Depression, 1929–1941* (1948) and Frederick Lewis Allen, *Since Yesterday: The Nineteen-Thirties in America* (1940).* Robert and Helen Lynd, *Middletown in Transition* (1937) and August B. Hollingshead, *Elmtown's Youth* (1949) are valuable dissections of midwestern communities during the decade. Revealing the assumptions of a stagnant population are such demographic studies as National Resources Committee, *Problems of a Changing Population* (1939) and Walter F. Wilcox, *Studies in American Demography* (1940). For the erosion of social assumptions, see many of the titles cited in Chapter 20 and the novels of the period, particularly those of John Dos Passos, Sinclair Lewis, Thomas Wolfe, John Steinbeck, and James T. Farrell.

On the Negro during the Great Depression, see John Hope Franklin, *From Slavery to Freedom* (1947); Franklin Frazier, *The Negro Family* and his *Black Bourgeoisie* (1957); Walter White, *A Man Called White* (1948), the memoirs of the leader of the NAACP; Elbert L. Tatum, *The Changed Political Thought of the Negro, 1915–1940* (1951); Ira DeA. Reid, *The Negro Immigrant* (1939); Arthur F. Raper, *The Tragedy of Lynching* (1933); Horace R. Cayton and G. S. Mitchell, *Black Workers and the New Unions* (1939); Herbert S. Northrup, *Organized Labor and the Negro* (1944); and Bernard H. Nelson, *The Fourteenth Amendment and the Negro Since 1920* (1946).

On education, besides previously cited titles, see Malcolm W. Willey, ed., *Depression, Recovery, and Higher Education* (1937); Davis S. Hill and F. J. Kelly, *Economy in Higher Education* (1933); and Isaac L. Kandel, *The End of an Era* (1941).

On communism and the left during the period, see Irving Howe and Lewis Coser, *The American Communist Party: A Critical History (1919–1957)* (1957); Donald D. Egbert and Stow Persons, eds., *Socialism and American Life* (2 vols., 1952); Wilson Record, *The Negro and the Communist Party* (1951); Eugene Lyons, *The Red Decade: The Stalinist Penetration of America* (1941); Joseph Freeman, *An American Testament* (1936); Max Kampelman, *The Communist Party vs. the CIO* (1957); Murray Kempton, *Part of our Time* (1955); and Granville Hicks, *Where We Came Out* (1954).

CHAPTER 20. THE CULTURE OF THE GREAT DEPRESSION

General works of value are Dixon Wecter, *The Age of the Great Depression, 1929–1941* (1948); Charles A. and Mary R. Beard, *America in Midpassage* (1939), the last half of the book; Alfred Kazin, *On Native Grounds* (1942)*; Oscar Cargill, *Intellectual America: Ideas on the March* (1941); Merle Curti, *The Growth of American Thought* (1943); and Harold E. Stearns, ed., *America Now* (1938), a quite different assessment from his 1922 venture.

On literature, see the novels and other works of the writers themselves plus Granville Hicks, *The Great Tradition* (1935); John W. Aldridge, *After the Lost Generation* (1951); Maxwell Geismar, *Writers in Crisis: The American Novel, 1925–1940* (1961)*; Leo Gurko, *The Angry Decade* (1947); and Milton Crane, ed., *The Roosevelt Era* (1947).

On the arts and music, see previously listed titles, especially Milton W. Brown, *American Painting from the Armory Show to the Depression* (1955); and Homer Saint-Gaudens, *The American Artist and His Times* (1941); John T. Howard, *Our Contemporary Composers: American Music in the Twentieth Century* (1941); and David Ewen, *Music Comes to America* (1942).

CHAPTER 21. DEPRESSION DIPLOMACY, 1929–1938

For foreign affairs in the Hoover administration, particularly the Manchurian affair, see Sara Smith, *The Manchurian Crisis, 1931–1932* (1948); Reginald Bassett, *Democracy and Foreign Policy: The Sino-Japanese Dispute, 1931–1933* (1952); Robert Langer, *Seizure of Territory: The Stimson Doctrine* (1947); Henry Stimson and McGeorge Bundy, *On Active Service in Peace and War* (1948); Richard N. Current, *Secretary Stimson* (1954), critical of Stimson; Elting E. Morison, *Turmoil and Tradition: A Study of the Life and Times of Henry L. Stimson* (1960), a defense of Stimson; Robert Ferrell, *American Diplomacy in the Great Depression* (1957); Aleander De Conde, *Herbert Hoover's Latin American Policy* (1951); and W. S. Myers, *The Foreign Policies of Herbert Hoover* (1940).

On foreign economic policy under FDR, see Seymour Harris, *The Economics of Social Security* (1941); Herbert Feis, *The Changing Pattern of International*

Economic Affairs (1940); Raymond L. Buell, *The Hull Trade Program* (1938); and Jeannette P. Nichols, "Roosevelt's Monetary Diplomacy in 1933," *American Historical Review*, LVI (1951).

Allan Nevins, *The New Deal and World Affairs* (1950) provides a quick survey. Herbert Feis, *The Spanish Story: Franco and the Nations at War* (1948) and F. Jay Taylor, *The United States and the Spanish Civil War, 1936–1939* (1956); Grayson L. Kirk, *Philippine Independence* (1936) for that subject and Edward O. Guerrant, *Roosevelt's Good Neighbor Policy* (1950); Bryce Wood, *The Making of the Good Neighbor Policy* (1961); Howard F. Cline, *United States and Mexico* (1953); and E. David Cronon, *Josephus Daniels in Mexico* (1960) for New Deal Latin American policy. For the recognition of Russia, see William Appleman Williams, *American-Russian Relations, 1781–1947* (1952) and Robert P. Browder, *Origins of Soviet-American Diplomacy* (1953).

For neutrality legislation, see Edwin Borchard and William P. Lage, *Neutrality for the United States* (1937) and James M. Seavy, *Neutrality Legislation* (1939). Thomas A. Bailey, *The Man in the Street* (1948), a study of public opinion and foreign policy, treats the neutrality sentiment. See, also, Elton Atwater, *American Regulation of Arms Exports* (1941). William E. Dodd, Jr. and Martha Dodd, eds., *Ambassador Dodd's Diary, 1933–1938* (1941) is the document of the American ambassador to Berlin in the early Hitler days.

CHAPTER 22. AND THE WAR CAME

The most comprehensive general works on United States involvement in World War II are William L. Langer and S. Everett Gleason, *The Challenge to Isolation, 1937-1940* (1952) and *The Undeclared War, 1940–1941* (1953). Langer and Gleason generally support FDR'S policies but are critical at times. Other general works are Department of State, *Peace and War: United States Foreign Policy, 1931–1941* (1943); Forrest Davis and Ernest K. Lindley, *How War Came, an American White Paper: From the Fall of France to Pearl Harbor* (1942); Selig Adler, *The Isolationist Impulse* (1957)*; and Alexander De Conde, ed., *Isolation and Security: Ideas and Interests in Twentieth-Century American Foreign Policy* (1957). Wayne S. Cole, *America First, The Battle against Intervention, 1940–1941* (1951) and Walter Johnson, *The Battle against Isolation* (1944), on the Committee to Defend America by Aiding the Allies, provide good accounts of the great foreign policy debate. Hans L. Trefousse, *Germany and American Neutrality, 1939–1941* (1951) is a worthwhile special study.

For relations with Japan before the war, see P. W. Schroeder, *The Axis Alliance and Japanese-American Relations, 1941* (1958); Harold S. Quigley, *Far Eastern War, 1937–1941* (1942); Herbert Feis, *The Road to Pearl Harbor* (1950); W. C. Johnstone, *The United States and Japan's New Order* (1941); and C. A. Buss, *War and Diplomacy in Eastern Asia* (1941). For the attack on Pearl Harbor, see Walter Millis, *This Is Pearl!* (1947) and Walter Lord, *Day of Infamy* (1957),* a popular account.

There is a considerable body of historical literature critical of American entry into the war; its writers are usually called "revisionists." Basic to an understanding of some of the revisionists is Charles A. Beard, *The Open Door at Home* (1935). Beard also wrote the best of the revisionist histories, *American Foreign Policy in the Mak-*

ing, 1932–1940 (1946), and *President Roosevelt and the Coming of the War, 1941* (1948). Basil Rauch prepared a reply to Beard in *Roosevelt, from Munich to Pearl Harbor* (1950). Less judicious than Beard are these revisionist volumes: Frederick R. Sanborn, *Design for War: A Study of Secret Power Politics, 1937–1941* (1951); Charles C. Tansill, *Backdoor to War* (1952); and George E. Morgenstern, *Pearl Harbor: The Secret History of the War* (1947). Harry Elmer Barnes, ed., *Perpetual War for Perpetual Peace* (1953) contains some shrill criticisms.

Among the relevant memoirs are Cordell Hull, *Memoirs* (2 vols., 1948); Joseph E. Davies, *Mission to Moscow* (1941); Joseph C. Grew, *Ten Years in Japan* (1944) and *Turbulent Era, A Diplomatic Record of Forty Years* (2 vols., 1952).

CHAPTER 23. MOBILIZING FOR VICTORY

Historians have not made as much effort to write of events at home during World War II as of the conflict itself, and, therefore, the bibliography is not satisfactory. No single satisfactory book on World War II America exists. However, see Jack Goodman, ed., *While You Were Gone: A Report on Wartime Life in the United States* (1946), which has some good chapters, and William Kennedy, *The Crucial Years, 1940–1945* (1962),* sometimes entertaining but superficial.

On industrial mobilization, see Eliot Janeway, *The Struggle for Survival* (1951); Bruce Catton, *The War Lords of Washington* (1951), critical of the role of big business; Donald M. Nelson, *Arsenal of Democracy* (1946), the story as the WPB administrator saw it; Edward R. Stettinius, Jr., *Lend-Lease, Weapon of Victory* (1944); Civilian Production Administration, *Industrial Mobilization for War, 1940–1945* (1947); R. H. Connery, *The Navy and Industrial Mobilization in World War II* (1951); Frederic C. Lane *et al., Ships for Victory* (1951); and Henry A. Toulmin, Jr., *Diary of Democracy: The Senate War Investigating Committee* (1947). On other aspects of the wartime economy, see Seymour E. Harris, *Economics of America at War* (1943); Randolph E. Paul, *Taxation for Prosperity* (1947); W. A. Nielander, *Wartime Food Rationing in the United States* (1947); Marshall Clinard, *Black Market* (1952); John K. Galbraith, *Theory of Price Control* (1952); Harvey C. Mansfield *et al., A Short History of OPA* (1948); Seymour E. Harris, *Inflation and the American Economy* (1945); and L. V. Chandler, *Inflation in the United States* (1950).

Roland Young, *Congressional Politics in the Second World War* (1955); Jonathan Daniels, *Frontier on the Potomac* (1946); and Joseph Gaer, *First Round: The CIO Political Action Committee* (1944) are useful for wartime politics. For sociological studies, see William F. Ogburn, ed., *American Society in Wartime* (1943); Reuben Hill, *Families under Stress* (1949); and Francis E. Merrill, *Social Problems on the Home Front* (1948). For the war's effects on farmers, laborers, and scientists, see Walter W. Wilcox, *The Farmer in the Second World War* (1947); Joel Seidman, *American Labor from Defense to Reconversion* (1953); Fred Witney, *Wartime Experiences of the National Labor Relations Board* (1949); and James P. Baxter, III, *Scientists against Time* (1946).

On civil liberties during World War II, see Edward S. Corwin, *Total War and the Constitution* (1947); Carey McWilliams, *Prejudice: Japanese-Americans, Symbol of Racial Intolerance* (1944); Dorothy S. Thomas and R. S. Nichimoto, *The Spoilage* (1946) and Thomas *et al., The Salvage* (1952); Morton Grodzins, *Americans Betrayed* (1949); Jacobus ten Broek *et al., Prejudice, War and the Constitution:*

Japanese-American Evacuation and Resettlement (1958); Mulford Q. Sibley and P. E. Jacob, *Conscription of Conscience: The Conscientious Objector, 1940–1947* (1952); and David R. Manwaring, *Render unto Caesar: The Flag-Salute Controversy* (1962).

CHAPTER 24. FIGHTING FOR VICTORY

The problem for the general reader about World War II is one of selection. The reader only casually interested in military history may be satisfied with the appropriate chapters of a military history of the United States such as R. Ernest Dupuy and Trevor N. Dupuy, *Military Heritage of America* (1956). The informed citizen should be familiar with the history of military policy. Walter Millis, *Arms and Men* (1956)* is a provocative essay on the subject. Millis extends his range much wider than World War II. Roger W. Shugg and Harvey A. DeWeerd, *World War II* (1946) and Fletcher Pratt, *War for the World* (1950) are brief histories of the war, the latter popularly written. *General Marshall's Report: The Winning of the War in Europe and the Pacific* (1945) is useful. Winston S. Churchill's blend of memoir and history in his several volumes are informative and superbly written: *The Grand Alliance* (1950)*; *The Hinge of Fate* (1950)*; *Closing the Ring* (1951)*; and *Triumph and Tragedy* (1953).*

There is an abundance of more specialized works. The Office of the Chief of Military History, United States Army, has brought forth a huge list of books, of which Louis Morton, *The Fall of the Philippines* (1953), a model of military history, indicates the scale of the series' volumes. Samuel Eliot Morison has produced fourteen volumes about the *History of United States Naval Operations in World War II* (1947–1961). Wesley F. Craven and James L. Cate, eds., *The Army Air Forces in World War II* (6 vols., 1948–1955) is an official publication. Among the other worthwhile military studies are Chester Wilmot, *The Struggle for Europe* (1952); Walter Millis, ed., *The War Reports* (1947); Jeter A. Isely and Philip A. Crowl, *The U.S. Marines and Amphibious War* (1951); Hanson W. Baldwin, *Great Mistakes of the War* (1950); S. L. A. Marshall, *Bastogne: The First Eight Days* (1946); Charles A. Willoughby and John Chamberlain, *MacArthur, 1941–1951* (1954); S. McKee Rosen, *Combined Boards of the Second World War* (1951); Samuel A. Stouffer *et al.*, *The American Soldier* (2 vols., 1949), a sociological study of the fighting man; James A. Field, *The Japanese at Leyte Gulf* (1947); and Ken Hechler, *The Bridge at Remagen* (1957).*

Among the more important memoirs are Dwight D. Eisenhower, *Crusade in Europe* (1948); William F. Halsey, *Admiral Halsey's Story* (1947); George S. Patton, *War As I Knew It* (1947); Jonathan M. Wainwright, *General Wainwright's Story* (1946); Harry C. Butcher, *My Three Years with Eisenhower* (1946); Theodore H. White, ed., *The Stilwell Papers* (1948); Henry Stimson and McGeorge Bundy, *On Active Service in Peace and War* (1948); Clair L. Chennault, *Way of a Fighter* (1949); H. H. Arnold, *Global Mission* (1949); Mark W. Clark, *Calculated Risk* (1952); William D. Leahy, *I Was There* (1950); Toshikazu Kase, *Journey to the Missouri* (1950); Omar N. Bradley, *A Soldier's Story* (1951); and Robert L. Eichelberger and M. Mackaye, *Our Jungle Road to Tokyo* (1950).

On wartime diplomacy, see Robert E. Sherwood, *Roosevelt and Hopkins* (1948);* Herbert Feis, *Churchill, Roosevelt, and Stalin* (1957) and *Japan Subdued* (1961); William L. Langer, *Our Vichy Gamble* (1957); Robert J. C. Butow, *Japan's*

Decision to Surrender (1954); R. F. Fenno, Jr., ed., *The Yalta Conference* (1953); John L. Snell, ed., *The Meaning of Yalta* (1956); Felix Winner, *The Yalta Betrayal* (1953); Edward R. Stettinius, *Roosevelt and the Russians: The Yalta Conference* (1949); Sumner Welles, *Seven Decisions that Shaped History* (1951); and Carlton J. H. Hayes, *Wartime Mission to Spain, 1942–1945* (1945).

CHAPTER 25. THE TRUMAN ERA: FOREIGN AND DOMESTIC COLD WAR

Scholarly historical studies of postwar America are still relatively scarce, and the student is forced to resort to memoirs and contemporary journalistic accounts. Eric F. Goldman, *The Crucial Decade—and After: America, 1945–1960* (1960)* and Herbert Agar, *The Price of Power: America since 1945* (1957)* are two early efforts to write a general history of postwar America. Goldman's is far better than Agar's. Frederick Lewis Allen in *The Big Change: America Transforms Itself, 1900–1950* (1952) contrasts conditions at the beginning and the middle of the century.

On the Truman administration, see Truman's memoirs, *Year of Decisions* (1955) and *Years of Trial and Hope* (1956); Morris B. Schnapper, ed., *The Truman Program* (1949), a collection of the President's speeches; Louis W. Koenig, ed., *The Truman Administration* (1956); Jonathan Daniels, *The Man of Independence* (1950), not satisfactory but the best Truman biography published thus far; Walter Millis, ed., *The Forrestal Diaries* (1951); Arthur E. Vandenberg, Jr., ed., *The Private Papers of Senator Vandenberg* (1952); William S. White, *The Taft Story* (1954), a rudimentary book on the Ohio Senator who deserves better treatment; Robert S. Allen and William V. Shannon, *The Truman Merry-Go-Round* (1950), a critical journalistic treatment; and C. Herman Pritchett, *Civil Liberties and the Vinson Court* (1954), a scholarly work. Samuel Lubell, *The Future of American Politics* (1952)* is useful for postwar politics, but at many points the reader would do well to keep his critical powers sharp. See, also, Samuel Lubell, *The Revolt of the Moderates* (1956). For the 1948 election, see Lindsay Rogers, *The Pollsters* (1949), an acid comment on the subject, and for the Wallace movement, see Karl M. Schmidt, *Henry A. Wallace: Quixotic Crusade, 1948* (1960) and David A. Shannon, *The Decline of American Communism: A History of the Communist Party of the United States since 1945* (1959). On corruption and political pressure, see Paul H. Douglas, *Ethics in Government* (1952); Blair Bolles, *How To Get Rich in Washington* (1952); H. Hubert Wilson, *Congress: Corruption and Compromise* (1951); and Karl Schriftgiesser, *The Lobbyists* (1951).

Many writers have examined aspects of the postwar red scare and its relationship to civil liberties. See C. Herman Pritchett, *Civil Liberties and the Vinson Court* (1954); Robert K. Carr, *The House Committee on Un-American Activities, 1945–1950* (1952), a careful and scholarly study; Clair Wilcox, ed., *Civil Liberties under Attack* (1951); Alan Barth, *The Loyalty of Free Men* (1951); Max Lowenthal, *The Federal Bureau of Investigation* (1950), critical; Donald S. Whitehead, *The FBI Story: A Report to the People* (1956),* quite favorable; Walter Gellhorn, *Security, Loyalty, and Science* (1950) and *The States and Subversion* (1952); John W. Caughey, *In Clear and Present Danger* (1958); and James A. Wechsler, *The Age of Suspicion* (1953). On the Hiss case, see Allistair Cooke, *A Generation on Trial* (1950); William A. J. Jowitt, *The Strange Case of Alger Hiss* (1953); Whittaker Chambers, *Witness* (1952); and Alger Hiss, *In the Court of Public Opinion* (1957).

On McCarthy, see Richard H. Rovere, *Senator Joe McCarthy* (1959); Wisconsin Citizens Committee, *The McCarthy Record* (1952); Jack Anderson and R. W. May, *McCarthy, The Man and the Ism* (1952); Joseph R. McCarthy, *McCarthyism, The Fight for America* (1952); William F. Buckley, Jr., and L. Brent Bozell, *McCarthy and his Enemies* (1954); and Michael Straight, *Trial by Television* (1954).

There is no end to the writing of books about foreign policy. For a concise general history of world affairs since World War II, see Hans W. Gatzke, *The Present in Perspective: A Look at the World since 1945* (1961).* Three brief general accounts of American policy are William G. Carleton, *The Revolution in American Foreign Policy* (1957)*; John W. Spanier, *American Foreign Policy since World War II* (1960)*; and Norman A. Graebner, *Cold War Diplomacy, 1945–1960* (1962),* which contains documents. See, also, Graebner, *The New Isolationism* (1956). Denna F. Fleming, *The Cold War and Its Origins, 1917–1960* (1961) is a huge, thorough, and critical work.

Among the special studies are Leften S. Stavrianos, *Greece: American Dilemma and Opportunity* (1952); Seymour E. Harris, *The European Recovery Program* (1954); Theodore H. White, *Fire in the Ashes* (1953); Robert E. Osgood, *NATO: The Entangling Alliance* (1962); Klaus Knorr, ed., *NATO and American Security* (1959); Drew Middleton, *Defense of Western Europe* (1952); and L. V. Thomas and R. N. Frye, *The United States and Turkey and Iran* (1951).

For Far Eastern relations, see Kenneth S. Latourette, *The American Record in the Far East, 1945–1951* (1953); Department of State, *United States Relations with China* (1949); Herbert Feis, *The China Tangle* (1953); Edwin O. Reischauer, *Wanted: An Asian Policy* (1955). For the Korean conflict, see Carl Barger, *The Korean Knot, A Military-Political History* (1957); John W. Spanier, *The Truman-MacArthur Controversy and the Korean War* (1959); Richard Rovere and Arthur M. Schlesinger, Jr., *The General and the President* (1951); S. L. A. Marshall, *The River and the Gauntlet* (1953); Courtney Whitney, *MacArthur: His Rendezvous with History* (1956), highly favorable; and Department of the Army, *Korea—1950* (1952).

Raymond F. Mikesell, *United States Economic Policy and International Relations* (1952); Brian Tew, *International Monetary Cooperation, 1945–1952* (1952); and Samuel Lubell, *The Revolution in World Trade and American Economic Policy* (1955) are useful places to start on the complex problems of foreign economic policy.

CHAPTER 26.   THE EISENHOWER ERA: MODERATION AND BRINKMANSHIP

General histories of the Eisenhower administrations have yet to be written. For journalistic accounts, see Merlo J. Pusey, *Eisenhower the President* (1956), quite favorable; Robert J. Donovan, *Eisenhower: The Inside Story* (1956); Richard H. Rovere, *Affairs of State: The Eisenhower Years* (1956); and Marquis Childs, *Eisenhower: Captive Hero* (1958), quite critical. Arthur Larson in *A Republican Looks at his Party* (1956) has made the clearest statement of "modern Republicanism." Relevant memoirs are Richard Nixon, *Six Decisions* (1962); Lewis L. Strauss, *Men and Decisions* (1962); and Sherman Adams, *Firsthand Report: The Story of the Eisenhower Administration* (1961). See John Lord O'Brian, *National Security and Individual Freedom* (1955) and C. P. Curtis, *The Oppenheimer Case* (1955) for conflicting views of the Eisenhower policies on internal security. Walter F. Murphy, *Congress and the Court* (1962) and Carl B. Swisher, *The Supreme Court in Modern Role* (1958) deal with the Warren Court.

On the election of 1952, see Kevin McCann, *Man from Abilene* (1952), an Eisenhower campaign biography; Adlai Stevenson, *Major Campaign Speeches, 1952* (1953); Samuel Lubell, "Who Elected Eisenhower," *Saturday Evening Post*, CCXXV (January 10, 1953); and a compilation of voting statistics, Richard Scammon, *America Votes* (1956). Stevenson's *Call to Greatness* (1954) and *What I Think* (1956) are useful for the Democratic opposition and the 1956 campaign.

For foreign policy in the Eisenhower years, see the appropriate titles listed for the previous chapter and John R. Beal, *John Foster Dulles* (1956); the chapter on Dulles by Hans J. Morgenthau in Norman A. Graebner, ed., *An Uncertain Tradition: American Secretaries of State in the Twentieth Century* (1961); Roscoe Drummond and Gaston Coblenz, *Duel at the Brink* (1960); and David Wise and Thomas Ross, *The U-2 Affair* (1962), a journalistic account.

CHAPTER 27. TROUBLED AFFLUENCE

Among the worthwhile general books on America's postwar economy are George A. Steiner, *The Government's Role in Economic Life* (1953); Wassily W. Leontief, *Studies in the Structure of the American Economy* (1953); Alvin Hansen, *Economic Policy and Full Employment* (1947), *The American Economy* (1957), and *Economic Issues of the 1960's* (1960); John Kenneth Galbraith, *American Capitalism* (1952)* and *The Affluent Society* (1958), each of which excited a great deal of thought and comment. Robert Lampman, *The Share of Top Wealth-Holders in National Wealth, 1922–1956* (1962), an important work of economic analysis, demonstrates that wealth distribution is still far from equitable. The Editors of *Fortune* in *The Permanent Revolution* (1951),* *The Changing American Market* (1955),* and *America in the Sixties* (1960)* present an optimistic point of view.

On the concentration of economic power, see Federal Trade Commission, *The Merger Movement* (1948), *Interlocking Directorates* (1951), and *The Concentration of Productive Facilities* (1949); Corwin D. Edwards, *Maintaining Competition* (1949); and John Herling, *The Great Price Conspiracy: The Story of the Antitrust Violations in the Electrical Industry* (1962). David Lilienthal in *Big Business: A New Era* (1953) and Adolph A. Berle, Jr., in *The 20th Century Capitalist Revolution* (1954) present the midcentury revision of progressive ideas about economic power. Expressions of concern for the sociological and psychological effects of concentration, rather than economic effects, are William H. Whyte, *The Organization Man* (1956),* David Reisman *et al., The Lonely Crowd* (1950),* and C. Wright Mills, *White Collar* (1951).*

On labor in the postwar era, see Jack Barbash, *The Practice of Unionism* (1956); C. Wright Mills, *The New Men of Power* (1948); Harry A. Millis and Emily C. Brown, *From the Wagner Act to Taft-Hartley* (1950); Philip Taft, *The A.F. of L. in the Time of Gompers* (1957); and Clark Mollenhoff, *Tentacles of Terror: The Teamsters Defy the Government* (1959). On agriculture, see Murray Benedict and O. C. Stine, *The Agricultural Commodity Programs: Two Decades of Experience* (1956) and C. C. Taylor *et al., Rural Life in the United States* (1949).

CHAPTER 28. THE AMERICAN PEOPLE
AND THEIR CULTURE

There are many books about the Negro in postwar America. See Arnold M. Rose, *The Negro in Postwar America* (1950); Harry S. Ashmore, *The Negro and the Schools* (1954); Bucklin Moon, *The High Cost of Prejudice* (1947) and *Balance of Power, The Negro Vote* (1948); J. Saunders Redding, *On Being Negro in America* (1951); Carl T. Rowan, *South of Freedom* (1952); President's Committee on Civil Rights, *To Secure These Rights* (1947); Milton R. Konvitz, *The Constitution and Civil Rights* (1947); Robert K. Carr, *Federal Protection of Civil Rights* (1947); and C. Eric Lincoln, *The Black Muslims in America* (1962) and E. U. Essien-Udom, *Black Nationalism: A Search for Identity in America* (1962) on the Black Muslim movement. Thomas D. Clark, *The Emerging South* (1961) is a wise and thoughtful book on the Negro as well as the South generally. Louis E. Lomax, *The Negro Revolt* (1962) is the best survey of Negro struggles from 1955 to 1962.

On postwar education, see Lawrence A. Cremin, *The Transformation of the School: Progressivism in American Education, 1876–1957* (1961); James B. Conant, *Education in a Divided World* (1948) and *The American High School Today* (1959); Eli Ginzburg and Douglas W. Bray, *The Uneducated* (1953); Robert M. MacIver, *Academic Freedom in Our Time* (1955); Benjamin Fine, *Our Children Are Cheated: The Crisis in American Education* (1947); Ernest O. Melby, *American Education under Fire* (1951); and Arthur E. Bestor, Jr., *Educational Wastelands* (1953).

On literature, see Ihab Hassan, *Radical Innocence: The Contemporary American Novel* (1961), one of the few books on really contemporary American literature; Russel B. Nye, "The Modern Quest," *The Progressive* (October, 1960); and Lionel Trilling, *The Liberal Imagination* (1953),* perhaps the most influential postwar work of literary criticism. On religion, see Ralph L. Roy, *Apostles of Discord* (1953); Conrad H. Moehlman, *The Wall of Separation between Church and State* (1951); Paul Blanshard, *American Freedom and Catholic Power* (1949); a reply to Blanshard, James M. O'Neill, *Catholicism and American Freedom* (1952); and Will Herberg, *Protestant, Catholic, Jew: An Essay in American Religious Sociology* (1955). On art, see Sam Hunter, *Modern American Painting and Sculpture* (1959); John H. Baur, ed., *New Art in America* (1957); and John Canaday, *Embattled Critic* (1962).*

CHAPTER 29. THE DEMOCRATS AGAIN

Reliable, unbiased books on this most recent period are practically nonexistent. See James M. Burns, *John Kennedy: A Political Profile* (1960), an unusually detached biography of a contemporary political figure, and Earl Mazo, *Richard Nixon: A Political and Personal Portrait* (1959) for the major party candidates of 1960. Theodore H. White, *The Making of the President 1960* (1961)* is a reporter's popular account of the election, accurate and thorough when reporting but marred by weak historical background. Helen Fuller in *Year of Trial: Kennedy's Crucial Decisions* (1962) provides an early balanced report on the Kennedy administration.

INDEX

Abel, Rudolf, 566
Acheson, Dean, 523, 530–31
Adams, Ansel, 406
Adams, Herbert Baxter, 49
Adams, Samuel Hopkins, 96
Adams, Sherman, 543, 552–53
Adamson Act, 65, 78
Addams, Jane, 98
Adenauer, Konrad, 559
Adkins *v.* Children's Hospital, 349
Agricultural Adjustment Act (AAA), 334–35, 356–57, 382
Agricultural Domestic Trade and Development Assistance Act, 584
Agricultural Marketing Act, 307–8
Agriculture: in late nineteenth century, 10–16; 1900–1917, 73–76; and World War I, 175–77; in 1920's, 212–15; and depression, 307–8, 372–73; and New Deal, 334–35; and technological change, 369–70; and World War II, 476–77; after World War II, 513, 519, 546–47, 582–84, 625
Agriculture, Department of, 32–33, 37, 74, 213–14
Aguinaldo, Emilio, 129–30
Airplanes, 71–72, 370–71
Alaska, 17, 133, 551
Albright, Ivan Le Lorraine, 405
Aldrich, Nelson, 26–29, 32, 40–41
Aldrich-Vreeland Act, 55
Alexanderson, E. F. W., 370
Algeciras Conference, 153–55
Alger, Horatio, 385
Algonquin, 167
Allen, Hervey, 401
Allen, Robert S., 349, 393
Alliance for Progress, 617–18
Allis-Chalmers Company, 575
Allison, William B., 29
Altgeld, John Peter, 15–16

Aluminum Corporation of America, 209, 369
Amalgamated Clothing Workers of America, 78, 233, 362
Amalgamated Copper Company, 70
America First Committee, 441–42
American Academy at Rome, 121
American Anti-Boycott Association, 59, 81
American Association for Labor Legislation, 62, 97
American Association of University Professors, 112
American Bankers' Association, 55–56
American Birth Control League, 97
American Civil Liberties Union, 259
American Federation of Farm Bureaus. *See* Farm Bureau Federation
American Federation of Labor (AFL), 76; and 1908 election, 38; and Clayton Act, 59; origins and in early twentieth century, 76–83; in 1920's, 232–33; in 1930's, 359–64 *passim;* and Negro, 383–84; and CIO merger, 579–80
American Federation of Labor-Congress of Industrial Organizations (AFL-CIO), 579–80
American Labor Party, 387
American Labor Union, 84
American League against War and Fascism, 387
American Legion, 182, 205, 287, 390
American Medical Association, 519, 547, 626
American Protective League, 180
American Society of Equity, 75
American Telephone and Telegraph Company, 58, 224, 370, 573, 627
American Tobacco Company, 30, 43
American Writers' Congress, 387–88
Americans for Democratic Action (ADA), 514
Ames, A. A., 99

661